·Bartholomew·

MINI ATLAS
WORLD

· Bartholomew ·

MINI ATLAS
WORLD

Bartholomew

A Division of HarperCollins*Publishers*

Bartholomew
A Division of HarperCollins Publishers
Duncan Street, Edinburgh EH9 1TA

© Bartholomew 1994
First published by Bartholomew 1991
Revised editions 1992, 1993
Reprinted 1994, revised 1994

ISBN 0 7028 2375 9 (de luxe hardback)

Printed in Great Britain by Bartholomew, The Edinburgh Press Limited.

Details included in this atlas are subject to change without notice. Whilst every
effort is made to keep information up to date Bartholomew will not be
responsible for any loss, damage or inconvenience caused by inaccuracies in
this atlas. The publishers are always pleased to acknowledge any corrections
brought to their notice, and record their appreciation of the valuable services
rendered in the past by map users in assisting to maintain the accuracy of their
publications

GH7705

CONTENTS

viii–ix	World Physical
x–xi	World Political
xii–xiii	World Time Zones
xiv–xv	World Environment
xvi	Key to Symbols
1	Arctic Ocean
2–3	North America
4–5	Canada, West
6–7	Canada, East
8–9	USA, West
10–11	USA, East
12	USA, Alaska
13	Canada Pacific
14–15	Lower Canada, USA North-East
16	Washington – New York – Boston
17	USA, South-East
18–19	USA, South-Central
20	USA, Pacific NW
21	USA, Pacific S
22	San Francisco & Los Angeles
23	Central Mexico
24–25	Mexico & Central America
26–27	Caribbean
28	South America
29	South America, South
30	South America, Central
31	South America, NE

78	Indonesia, Central
79	Philippines
80–81	Middle East
82–83	India & West China
84–85	India, NW & Pakistan
86	India, NE & Bangladesh
87	India, South & Sri Lanka
88–89	Africa
90–91	Iran and the Gulf
92–93	Turkey, Syria & Iraq
94	Israel & Lebanon
95	Africa, North-East
96–97	Africa, West
98–99	Africa, Central
100–101	Africa, South
102–103	Atlantic Ocean
104–105	Australasia
106–107	Australia
108–109	Australia South-East
110–111	New Zealand
112	Antarctica

Index

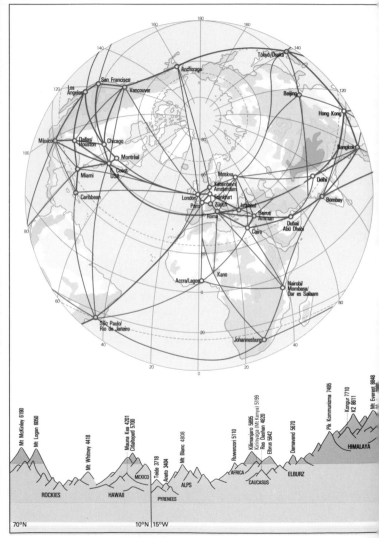

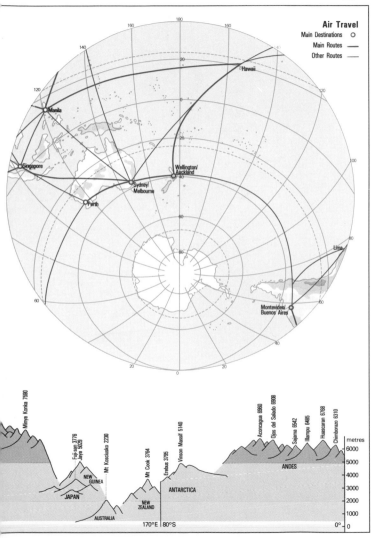

Air Travel

Main Destinations ○
Main Routes ——
Other Routes ——

• Denotes capital cities

Major Cities		Beijing *China*	10 800	**Europe**	**'000**
by Continent		Tianjin *China*	9400	Moskva *Russian Federation*	8800
	Pop.	Jakarta *Indonesia*	9300	Paris *France*	8500
Australasia	**'000**	Delhi *India*	8800	London *UK*	7400
Sydney *Australia*	3400	Manila *Philippines*	8500	Milano *Italy*	5300
Melbourne *Australia*	2800	Osaka *Japan*	8500	Madrid *Spain*	5200
Brisbane *Australia*	1200	Karachi *Pakistan*	7700	Sankt-Peterburg *Rus.Fed.*	5100
Perth *Australia*	1100	Bangkok *Thailand*	7200	Napoli *Italy*	3600
Adelaide *Australia*	1000	Tehrän *Iran*	6800	Athínai *Greece*	3400
Auckland *New Zealand*	900	Istanbul *Turkey*	6700	Barcelona *Spain*	3400
Asia	**'000**	Dhäkä *Bangladesh*	6600	Berlin *Germany*	3200
Tökyö *Japan*	18 100	Madras *India*	5700	Roma *Italy*	3100
Shanghai *China*	13 400	Hong Kong *Hong Kong*	5400	Kiyev *Ukraine*	2600
Calcutta *India*	11 800	Bangalore *India*	5000	Birmingham *UK*	2300
Bombay *India*	11 200	Shenyang *China*	4800	Manchester *UK*	2300
Söul *South Korea*	11 000	Lahore *Pakistan*	4100	Bucureşti *Romania*	2200

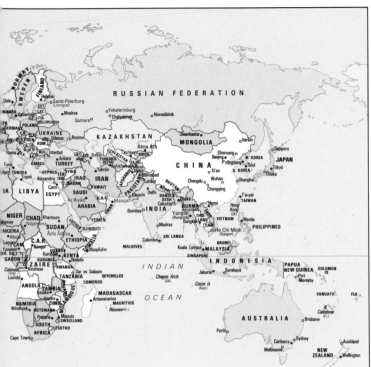

North and Central America	'000	South America	'000	Africa	'000
México *Mexico*	20 200	São Paulo *Brazil*	17 400	Cairo *Egypt*	9000
New York *USA*	16 200	Buenos Aires *Argentina*	11 500	Lagos *Nigeria*	7700
Los Angeles *USA*	11 900	Rio de Janeiro *Brazil*	10 700	Alexandria *Egypt*	3700
Chicago *USA*	7000	Lima *Peru*	6200	Kinshasa *Zaire*	3500
Philadelphia *USA*	4300	Santiago *Chile*	5000	Casablanca *Morocco*	3200
Detroit *USA*	3700	Bogotá *Colombia*	4900	Alger *Algeria*	3000
San Francisco *USA*	3700	Caracas *Venezuela*	4100	Cape Town *South Africa*	2300
Toronto *Canada*	3500	Belo Horizonte *Brazil*	3600	Abidjan *Ivory Coast*	2200
Dallas *USA*	3400	Pôrto Alegre *Brazil*	3100	Tarābulus *Libya*	2100
Guadalajara *Mexico*	3200	Recife *Brazil*	2500	Adis Abeba *Ethiopia*	1900
Houston *USA*	3000	Brasilia *Brazil*	2400	Khartoum *Sudan*	1900
Monterrey *Mexico*	3000	Salvador *Brazil*	2400	Dar es Salaam *Tanzania*	1700
Montièal *Canada*	3000	Fortaleza *Brazil*	2100	Johannesburg *South Africa*	1700
Washington *USA*	2900	Curitiba *Brazil*	2000	Luanda *Angola*	1700
Boston *USA*	2800	Guayaquil *Ecuador*	1700	Maputo *Mozambique*	1600

| 22 +10 | 23 +11 | 24 | 1 −11 | 2 −10 | 3 −9 | 4 −8 | 5 −7 | 6 −6 | 7 −5 | 8 −4 | 9 −3 | 10 −2 | 11 −1 | 1 |

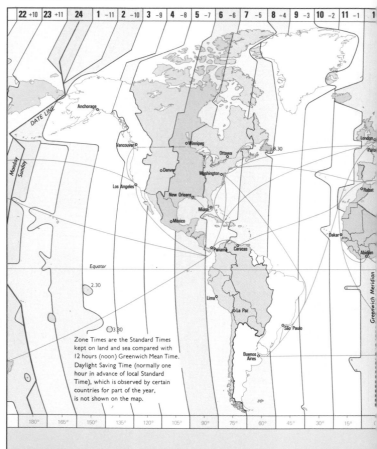

DATE LINE

Monday
Sunday

Anchorage

Vancouver

Winnipeg

Ottawa

8.30

London

Paris

Denver

Washington

Los Angeles

New Orleans

Miami

Rabat

México

Panama   Caracas

Dakar

Abidjan

Equator

2.30

Lima

3.30

La Paz

São Paulo

Zone Times are the Standard Times
kept on land and sea compared with
12 hours (noon) Greenwich Mean Time.
Daylight Saving Time (normally one
hour in advance of local Standard
Time), which is observed by certain
countries for part of the year,
is not shown on the map.

Buenos
Aires

Greenwich Meridian

| 180° | 165° | 150° | 135° | 120° | 105° | 90° | 75° | 60° | 45° | 30° | 15° | |

Journey Times

Sail (via Cape)
164 days

Steam (via Cape)
43 days

Steam (via Suez)
30 days

Supertanker
(via Cape)
28 days

Singapore ←

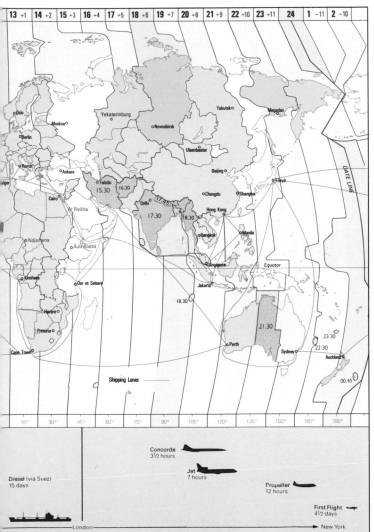

| 13 +1 | 14 +2 | 15 +3 | 16 +4 | 17 +5 | 18 +6 | 19 +7 | 20 +8 | 21 +9 | 22 +10 | 23 +11 | 24 | 1 −11 | 2 −10 |

Oslo
Moskva
Berlin
Roma
Ankara
Yekaterinburg
Novosibirsk
Yakutsk
Magadan
lger
Tehrān 15.30
16.30
Cairo
Ar Riyāḍ
Ulaanbaatar
Beijing
Delhi 17.45
Chengdu
Shanghai
Tōkyō
Ndjamena
Addis Abeba
17.30
18.30
Hong Kong
Manila
Kinshasa
Dar es Salaam
Bangkok
Singapore
Equator
Jakarta
18.30
Harare
Pretoria
21.30
Cape Town
Perth
23.30
22.30
Auckland
Sydney
00.45

DATE LINE

Shipping Lanes ————

15° 30° 45° 60° 75° 90° 105° 120° 135° 150° 165° 180°

Concorde
3½ hours

Jet
7 hours

Diesel (via Suez)
15 days

Propeller
12 hours

First Flight
4½ days

————London————
————New York→

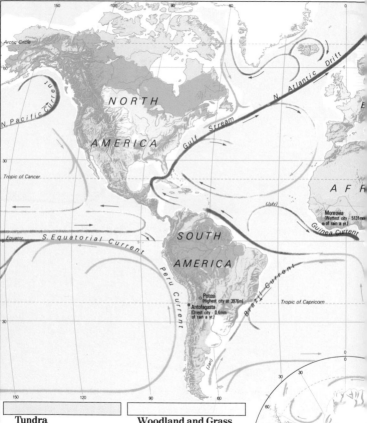

Tundra
Flat areas frozen over except during brief summers when flooding occurs. Habitat of compact, wind resistant plants; lichens and mosses: animals ; lemmings and reindeer.

Northern Forest
Extensive coniferous forest area where winters are severe, summers brief. Conifers include spruce, fir, giant redwoods. Habitat of beavers, squirrels and red deer.

Woodland and Grass
Temperate areas of richer soils, its forest characterised by deciduous trees - oak, beech, maple. Region most exploited by man for intensive farming, settlements and industry.

Grassland
Hot summers, cold winters, moderate rainfall. Vast area of grassland and 'black' soils. Ideal for growing grain crops, grazing beef cattle. Also called steppe, veld, pampas, prairie.

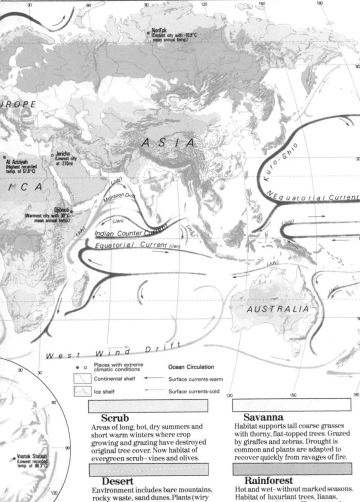

Norilsk
(Coolest city with -10.9°C
mean annual temp.)

EUROPE

ASIA

Jericho
(Lowest city
at -270m)

Al Aziziyah
(Highest recorded
temp. of 57.8°C)

AFRICA

Djibouti
(Warmest city with 30°C
mean annual temp.)

Kuro-Shio

N Equatorial Current

(July)

Monsoon Drift

(July)

(Jan)

(July)

Indian Counter Current (Jan)

Equatorial Current (Jan)

(July)

(July)

AUSTRALIA

(Jan)

West Wind Drift

Vostok Station
(Lowest recorded
temp. of -88.3°C)

• • o   Places with extreme
        climatic conditions

☐ Continental shelf

☐ Ice shelf

Ocean Circulation

→ Surface currents-warm

→ Surface currents-cold

Scrub
Areas of long, hot, dry summers and
short warm winters where crop
growing and grazing have destroyed
original tree cover. Now habitat of
evergreen scrub–vines and olives.

Savanna
Habitat supports tall coarse grasses
with thorny, flat-topped trees. Grazed
by giraffes and zebras. Drought is
common and plants are adapted to
recover quickly from ravages of fire.

Desert
Environment includes bare mountains,
rocky waste, sand dunes. Plants (wiry
grass, thorn bushes, cacti) and animals
(lizards, camels) must be well adapted
to extremes of heat and drought.

Rainforest
Hot and wet–without marked seasons.
Habitat of luxuriant trees, lianas,
monkeys and tigers. Five vegetation
layers– high trees, tree canopy, open
canopy, shrubs, ground herbs.

BOUNDARIES

International

International under Dispute

Cease Fire Line

Autonomous or State

Administrative

Maritime (National)

LETTERING STYLES

CANADA — Independent Nation

FLORIDA — State, Province or Autonomous Region

Gibraltar (U.K.) — Sovereignty of Dependent Territory

Lothian — Administrative Area

LANGUEDOC — Historic Region

Loire **Vosges** — Physical Feature or Physical Region

TOWNS AND CITIES

Square Symbols denote capital cities. Each settlement is given a symbol according to its relative importance, with type size to match.

■ ● **New York** — Major City

■ ● **Montréal** — City

□ ○ Ottawa — Small City

■ ● **Québec** — Large Town

□ ○ St John's — Town

□ ○ Yorkton — Small Town

□ ○ Jasper — Village

— Built-up-area

LAKE FEATURES

Permanent

Seasonal

OTHER FEATURES

River

Seasonal River

$=$ Pass, Gorge

Dam, Barrage

Waterfall, Rapid

Aqueduct

Reef

▲ 4231 Summit, Peak

. 217 Spot Height, Depth

ᵥ Well

Δ Oil Field

▲ Gas Field

Gas / Oil Oil / Natural Gas Pipeline

Gemsbok Nat. Pk National Park

UR Historic Site

Main Railway

Other Railway

Under Construction

Rail Tunnel

Rail Ferry

Canal

⊕ International Airport

✦ Other Airport

For pages 102-103, 104-105 only:

0	Sea Level
200m	
2000m	
4000m	
6000m	
	Depth

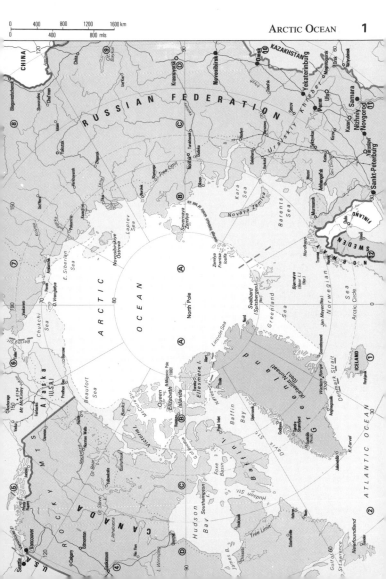

| 0 | 400 | 800 | 1200 | 1600 km |
| 0 | 400 | | 800 mls | |

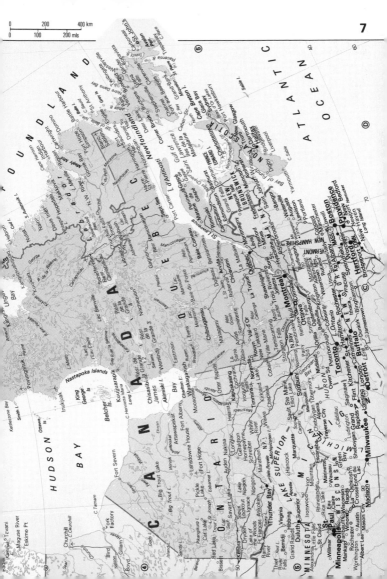

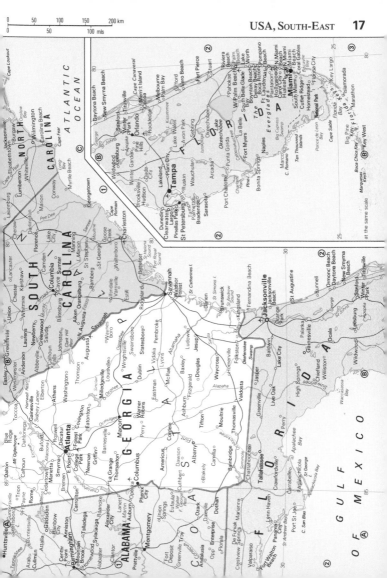

0   50   100   150   200 km
0   50   100 mls

at the same scale

ATLANTIC OCEAN

Cape Lookout
Cape Fear
Cape Romain
Cape Canaveral
Cape Sable

NORTH CAROLINA

Jacksonville
Burgaw
Wilmington
Carolina Beach
Whiteville
Elizabethtown
Lumberton
Laurinburg
Marion
Cheraw
Darlington
Florence
Lake City
Conway
Myrtle Beach
Georgetown

SOUTH CAROLINA

Lancaster
Chester
Union
Whitmire
Newberry
Camden
Sumter
Manning
St Stephen
Goose Creek
Charleston
Edisto
Easley
Westminster
Anderson
Laurens
Greenwood
Saluda
Aiken
Orangeburg
Allendale
Varnville
Estill
Ridgeland
Walterboro
Beaufort
Port Royal
St Helena Sound

GEORGIA

Toccoa
Blue Ridge
Dahlonega
Calhoun
Dalton
Tunnel Hill
Trion
Rome
Cedartown
Rockmart
Bremen
Carrollton
La Grange
Thomaston
Newnan
Griffin
Barnesville
Forsyth
Covington
Eatonton
Milledgeville
Sparta
Wrightsville
Dublin
Swainsboro
Statesboro
Louisville
Thomson
Washington
Athens
Gainesville
Buford
Roswell
Marietta
Smyrna
Atlanta
East Point
College Park
Forest Park
Decatur
Macon
Warner Robins
Perry
Americus
Cordele
Dawson
Albany
Camilla
Bainbridge
Blakely
Cuthbert
Eufaula
Fitzgerald
Ashburn
Tifton
Moultrie
Thomasville
Valdosta
Quitman
Adel
Nashville
Douglas
Waycross
Homerville
Folkston
Jesup
Ludowici
Baxley
Lyons
Vidalia
McRae
Eastman
Hazlehurst
Pembroke
Savannah
Brunswick
Kingsland
St Marys
Fernandina Beach
St Simons I.
St Catharines I.
St Andrew Sound
Blackbeard I.
Sapelo I.
Altamaha
Ohoopee
Oconee
Ogeechee
Okefenokee Swamp
Alapaha

ALABAMA

Huntsville
Scottsboro
Arab
Cullman
Gadsden
Attalla
Rainbow City
Anniston
Talladega
Sylacauga
Alexander City
Pell City
Birmingham
Bessemer
Alabaster
Centre
Centreville
Prattville
Montgomery
Tallassee
Opelika
Auburn
Phenix City
Columbus
Union Springs
Troy
Enterprise
Ozark
Dothan
Andalusia
Opp
Florala
Greenville
Fort Deposit

FLORIDA

Pensacola
Valparaiso
Fort Walton Beach
Crestview
De Funiak Springs
Marianna
Chattahoochee
Tallahassee
Quincy
Port St Joe
Apalachicola
Carrabelle
Panama City
Lynn Haven
Apalachee Bay
Perry
Live Oak
Jasper
Greenville
High Springs
Gainesville
Ocala
Leesburg
Wildwood
Williston
Chiefland
Cedar Key
Waccasassa Bay
Lake City
Baldwin
Jacksonville
Jacksonville Beach
Orange Park
Palatka
St Augustine
Bunnell
Ormond Beach
Daytona Beach
New Smyrna Beach
Sanford
Winter Park
Titusville
Gulf Hammock

GULF OF MEXICO

THE EVERGLADES

Ocala
Wildwood
Leesburg
Orlando
Winter Garden
Pine Hills
Winter Park
Rockledge
Lake Apopka
Lake Harris
Kissimmee
Lake Kissimmee
Avon Park
Sebring
Lake Wales
Haines City
Lakeland
Plant City
Tampa
Ruskin
Brooksville
Hudson
Dunedin
Clearwater
Largo
Pinellas Park
St Petersburg
Bradenton
Sarasota
Wauchula
Arcadia
Port Charlotte
Punta Gorda
Charlotte Harbour
Fort Myers
Bonita Springs
Naples
Marco
Ten Thousand Islands
C. Romano
Big Cypress Swamp
Lake Okeechobee
La Belle
Clewiston
Belle Glade
Pahokee
South Bay
Vero Beach
Sebastian
Fort Pierce
Stuart
Jupiter
Riviera Beach
W. Palm Beach
Palm Beach
Lake Worth
Boynton Beach
Delray Beach
Boca Raton
Deerfield Beach
Pompano Beach
Fort Lauderdale
Hollywood
Hallandale
N. Miami Beach
N. Miami
Miami Beach
Miami
Hialeah
Coral Gables
South Miami
Homestead
Florida City
Key Largo
Florida Bay
Tavernier
Islamorada
Marathon
Big Pine Key
Boca Chica Key
Key West
National Park
Ponce de Leon Bay
Cape Sable
Marquesas Keys

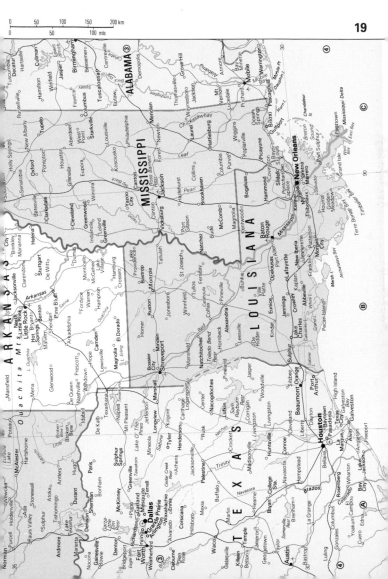

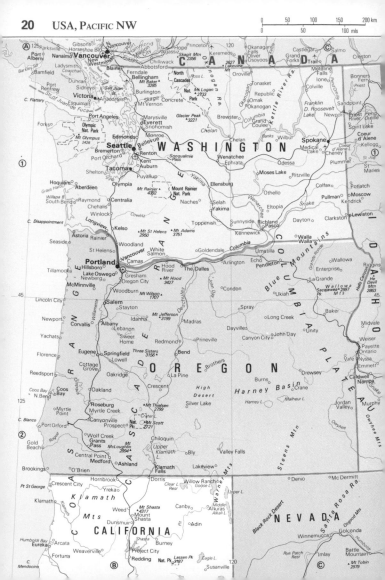

0   50   100   150   200 km
0   50   100 mils

CANADA

A [125] Parksville   Gibsons   Vancouver   Hope   Princeton   [120]   Okanagan Falls   Castlegar   Salmo   C
Port Alberni   Horseshoe Bay   Squamish   Agassiz   Keremeos   Grand Forks   Trail   Creston
Nanaimo   Vancouver   Chilliwack   Osoyoos   Oliver   Metaline Falls   Bonners Ferry
Ladysmith   New Westminster   Abbotsford   Oroville   Republic   Ione   Priest
Bamfield   Blaine   Skagit Mtn   Tonasket   Colville   Newport   River
Port   Duncan   Ferndale   North   Pass 12   Okanogan   Franklin   Sandpoint
Renfrew   Victoria   Bellingham   Cascades   Mts Logan   Brewster   D. Roosevelt   Newport   Spirit Lake
C. Flattery   Anacortes   San Juan Is   Burlington   Nat.   *2733   Chelan   Grand   Lake   Coeur
Str. of Juan de Fuca   Port Angeles   Mt Vernon   Concrete   Glacier Peak   Coulee   Banks   Spokane   d'Alene
Forks   Olympic   Sequim   Everett   *3221   Chelan   Wenatchee   Medical   Cheney   Kellogg
Nat. Park   Mt Olympus   Edmonds   Snohomish   Lake   Wilbur   Lake   Coeur
2428   Bremerton   Bellevue   Monroe   Odessa   d'Alene L.
Port Orchard   Seattle   Renton   Snoqualmie   Ephrata   Plummer   St Maries
① Hoquiam   Shelton   Tacoma   Kent   Pass   Ellensburg   Moses Lake   Ritzville   Colfax   Potlatch
Aberdeen   Olympia   Auburn   WASHINGTON   Othello   Pullman   Moscow
Grays Harb.   Puyallup   Mt Rainier   Mount Rainier   Yakima   Kendrick
Willapa B.   Raymond   Centralia   4392   Nat. Park   Naches   Selah   Dayton   Clarkston   Lewiston
South Bend   Chehalis   Yakima   Sunnyside   Richland   Walla   Snake
Winlock   Cowlitz   Toppenish   Kennewick   Pasco   Walla
C. Disappointment   Astoria   Longview   Mt St Helens   Mt Adams   Goldendale   Columbia   Umatilla   Echo   Walla
Seaside   Rainier   Kelso   2950   3751   Arlington   Pendleton   Wallowa
St Helens   Woodland   White   Columbia   Blue   Enterprise   Hells Canyon
Tillamook   Portland   Vancouver   Salmon   The Dalles   John   Ukiah   Mtns   Wallowa   *2997   Idaho
Hillsboro   Camas   Hood   Condon   La Grande   Mts   He
45   Lake Oswego   Gresham   River   Mt Hood   Day   Plateau   Devil
McMinnville   Newberg   Oregon City   *3427   Spray   Baker   2863
Lincoln City   Woodburn   Mt Wilson   Jefferson   Long Creek   Midvale
Newport   Salem   1707   Madras   Unity   Weiser
Corvallis   Stayton   Mt Jefferson   Dayville   Payette
Yachats   Albany   Idanha   *3199   Columbia   Ontario
Lebanon   Redmond   John Day   Vale   Nyssa
Florence   Eugene   Sweet Home   Prineville   Canyon City   Basin   Emmett
Springfield   Three Sisters   Bend   Plateau   Caldwell
Reedsport   Cottage Grove   Lowell   3156   Brothers   Drewsey   Nampa
Oakridge   La Pine   Burns   Crane   Jordan   Murphy
Coos Bay   Coos   Crescent   High   Harney Basin   Valley
C. Blanco   N.Bend   Oakland   Desert   Harney L.   Malheur L.   Owyhee Mts
② Port Orford   Roseburg   Mt Thielsen   Silver Lake
Myrtle Point   Myrtle Creek   2799   Crater
Canyonville   Lake   Nat. Pk   Mt Scott
Gold   Wolf Creek   Prospect   2721   Chiloquin   Valley Falls   Mc Dermitt
Beach   Grants   Mt   McLoughlin   Upper   Bly
Pass   2894   Klamath   Lakeview   Steens Mtn
Brookings   Central Point   L.   Denio   Santa
O'Brien   Medford   Ashland   Klamath   Warner   Rosa R.
Pt St George   Ashland   Falls   Willow Ranch   Goose L.   Black Rock Desert
Crescent City   Hornbrook   Dorris   Clear L.   Mts
Klamath   Yreka   Resr   Upper L.   Rye Patch
Klamath   Weed   Canby   Alturas   Resr   Mc Tobin
Humboldt Bay   Arcata   Mt Shasta   Mount   Adin   Middle Alkali L.   NEVADA   2979
Eureka   4317   Shasta   Alkali L.   Winnemucca   Golconda
Fortuna   Weaverville   Dunsmuir   Shasta L.   Project City   Battle
C.   CALIFORNIA   Burney   Pit   Imlay   Mountain
Mendocino   Redding   Lassen Pk   Eagle L.
B   Nat. Pk   3187   Susanville   C   [120]

OREGON

COLUMBIA RANGE **COAST RANGE** **CASCADE RANGE** **KLAMATH Mts** **COLUMBIA PLATEAU**

CALIFORNIA

NEVADA

[125]

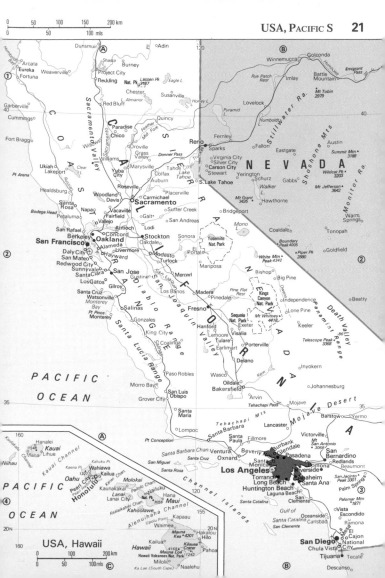

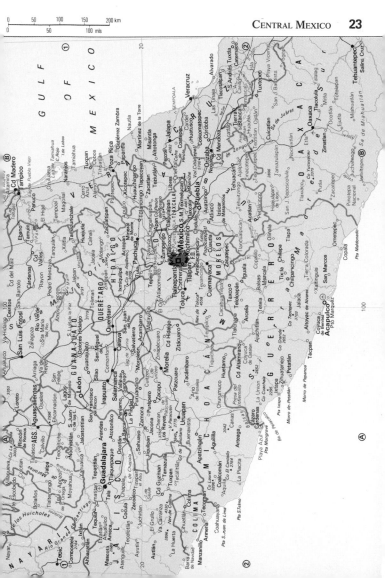

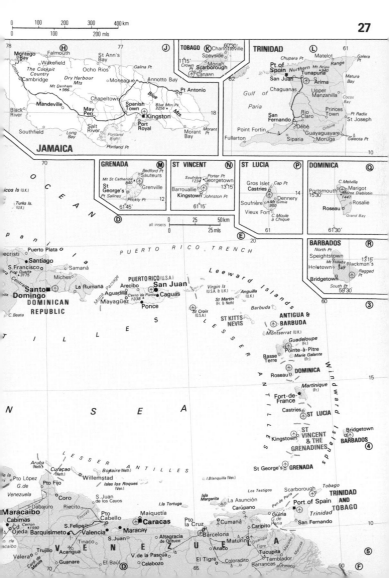

0	400	800	1200	1600 km		
0		400	800 mls			

CARIBBEAN SEA

NICARAGUA
COSTA RICA
S.José
PANAMA
Panamá
Barranquilla
Sta Marta
S.Cristóbal
Maracaibo
Caracas
Barcelona
ST LUCIA
BARBADOS
TRINIDAD & TOBAGO

VENEZUELA
Cd Bolívar
Georgetown
Paramaribo
GUYANA
SURINAM
FR. GUIANA
Cayenne

Medellín
Bogotá
COLOMBIA
Buenaventura
Cali
Popayán
S.Lorenzo
Boa Vista

ECUADOR
Quito
Guayaquil
Iquitos
Santarém
I. de Marajó
Equator

PERU
Trujillo
Pto Volho
Manaus
Belém
São Luís
I. Fernando de Noronha (Braz.)

Callao
Lima
Huancayo
Pto Maldonado
Cuzco
Teresina
Fortaleza
Natal

Arequipa
La Paz
Cochabamba
Sucre
BOLIVIA
Sta Cruz
Corumbá
B R A Z I L
Recife
Maceió

Arica
Cuiabá
Goiânia
Brasília
Salvador

SOUTH
PACIFIC
OCEAN
Antofagasta
S.Félix (Ch.)
Campo Grande
PARAGUAY
Asunción
Ribeirão Prêto
Belo Horizonte
Campos
Rio de Janeiro
São Paulo
Santos
Tropic of Capricorn

Salta
S.Miguel de Tucumán
Resistencia
Posadas
Curitiba

Córdoba
Santa Fé
Paraná
Pto Alegre
Pelotas

Valparaíso
Mendoza
Rosario
URUGUAY
Is Juan Fernández (Ch.)
Santiago
Buenos Aires
Montevideo
R. de la Plata

Concepción
Mar del Plata
SOUTH

Valdivia
Bahía Blanca
ATLANTIC

Pto Montt
A R G E N T I N A
OCEAN

Cmd. Rivadavia
G.San Jorge

Falkland Is (U.K.)
Stanley

Río Gallegos
S.Georgia (U.K.)

Punta Arenas
Tierra del Fuego

CHILE

S.Shetland Is
S.Orkney Is

0   200   400   600 km
0   100   200   300 mls

BRAZIL

Reconquista
Goya
Mercedes
Cruz Alta

Sumampa
Vera
Corrientes
Paso de los Libres
Uruguaiana
Sta Maria

La Serena
Coquimbo
Rivadavia
La Rioja
Santa
Fe
Alegrete
Cachoeira do Sul

Punitaqui
Ovalle
Jáchal
S. Agustín
La Paz
Concordia
Rivera
Artigas
Livramento
Bagé

Illapel
San Juan
La Rioja
Cruz del Eje
Córdoba
S. Francisco
Santa Fe
Paraná
Salto
Tacuarembó
Melo

Los Vilos
Va Dolores
Alta Gracia
Concepción
URUGUAY

Viña del Mar
Valparaíso
Mendoza
San
Córdoba
Villa María
Bell Ville
Rosario
San
Nicolás
Mercedes
Durazno
Treinta y Tres

S. Antonio
S. Bernardo
Santiago
S.Luis
Luis
Río Cuarto
Cda de Gómez
Pergamino
Colonia
Trinidad
Florida
Canelones

Rancagua
Pichilemu
S. Fernando
Mercedes
Rufino
Venado Tuerto
Buenos
Aires
Avellaneda
La Plata
Mercedes
Minas
Rocha

Curicó
S. Rafael
Lincoln
Chivilcoy
Chascomús
Maldonado
Punta del Este

Constitución
Talca
Grl Alvear
Buenos
Las Flores
Dolores
Montevideo

Cauquenes
Linares
Bardas Blancas
ARGENTINA
Sta Rosa
Trenque
Lauquén
Aires
Olavarría
Ayacucho
Va Gesell

Talcahuano
Concepción
Chillán
Mendoza
La Pampa
Guaminí
Carhué
Tandil
Balcarce
Mar del Plata

Tomé
Coronel
Los Angeles
Colorado
Telén
Grl Pico
Pehuajó
Tres Arroyos
Cnl
Pringles
Miramar
Necochea

Lebu
Angol
Neuquén
Bahía Blanca
Punta Alta
Claromecó

Carahue
Temuco
Toltén
Loncoche
Zapala
Grl Roca
Choele
Choel
Colorado
Bahía Blanca

Valdivia
La Unión
Río
Negro
Antonio
Oeste

Osorno
Paso Limay
Valcheta
Viedma
Carmen de Patagones

Pto Varas
Puerto Montt
S. Carlos de
Bariloche
Maquinchao
Golfo
San Matías

Ancud
Castro
Achao
El Bolsón
Pto Pirámides

Archipiélago
de las
Esquel
Chubut
Trelew
Gaimán
Pto Madryn
Rawson

Las Plumas

Chones
Pto Aisén
Coihaique
Sarmiento
Camarones
C Dos Bahías

Golfo
San Jorge
Comodoro Rivadavia

Caleta Olivia
Colonia
Las Heras
C Tres Puntas

Deseado
Pta Médanosa

Santa
Cruz
S. Julián

ATLANTIC

OCEAN

Río Natales
Río
Turbio
Río Gallegos

FALKLAND ISLANDS
(ISLAS MALVINAS)
(U.K.)

West Falkland
Stanley
East Falkland

Punta Arenas
Río Grande
Tierra del Fuego
Ushuaia

Is Wollaston
C. de Hornos
(C Horn)

at the same scale

Shag Rocks
South Georgia
(U.K.)

Grytviken

PACIFIC
OCEAN

NICARAGUA
Bluefields
S. Carlos

COSTA
RICA

PANAMA
Colón
Panamá
La Chorrera
G. de Panamá

Sta Marta
Riohacha
Pta Gallinas
Pen. de Guajira
Aruba
Curaçao
Bonaire
Is Los R...
Willemstad
Pto Fijo
Coro
Pto Cabello
Maiquetía
CARAC
Valencia
Maracay
San Juan
Cienaga
Barranquilla
Cartagena
Valledupar
Machiques
Maracaibo
Cabimas
Cd Ojeda
Barquisimeto
Acarigua
Guanare
Barinas
Mérida
Trujillo
Valera
San Cristóbal
Cúcuta
Pamplona
Bucaramanga
Málaga
Ocaña
El Banco
Sincelejo
Magangué
Montería
Caucasia
Barrancabermeja
Yarumal
Pto Berrío
Barbosa
Sogamoso
Tunja
Chocontá
Bogotá
Villavicencio
Granada
Medellín
Itagüí
Bello
Manizales
Pereira
Armenia
Cartago
Tuluá
Buga
Palmira
Cali
Santander
Popayán
Buenaventura
Quibdó

COLOMBIA

Tumaco
S. Lorenzo
El Diviso
Esmeraldas
Cojimies
Jama
Pasto
Ipiales
Tulcán
Ibarra
Otavalo
Mocoa
Pto Asis
Belén
Florencia
Pitalito
Pto Rico
Neiva

Manta
C. San Lorenzo
Quito
Chone
Cotopaxi
Coca
Tena
Lago Agrio
Leguizamo

ECUADOR

Guayaquil
La Libertad
Playas
Puná
Tumbes
Babahoyo
Ambato
Guaranda
Chimborazo
Riobamba
Milagro
Cuenca
Azogues
Gualaceo
Machala
Zaruma
Macas
Zamora
Loja

Talara
Negritos
Paita
Piura
Sullana
Catacaos
Chulucanas
Jaén
Moyobamba
Chachapoyas
Yurimaguas
Tarapoto

Lambayeque
Chiclayo
Chepén
Pacasmayo
Ferreñafe
Cajamarca
Celendín
Cajabamba

Trujillo
Huamachuco
Otusco
Pomabamba
Tingo Maria
Pucallpa

Chimbote
Huallanca
Huaraz
Huascarán
La Unión
Huánuco

Casma
Huarmey
Pat!vilca
Barranca
Huacho
Ancón
Callao
Lima

Oxapampa
Cerro de Pasco
La Merced
Tarma
La Oroya
Jauja
Acobamba
Huancayo
Huancavelica

Chincha Alta
Pisco
Ica
Andahuaylas
Ayacucho
Abancay
Cuzco
Sicuani

PERU

BOL

AM
E L
B
A

Iquitos
Tabatinga
Leticia
Caxias

Mitú
Cucuí
Icana

Apaporis
Japurá
Içá

Elvira
Solimões (Amazonas)

Cruzeiro do Sul
Feijó

ACRE
Sena Madureira
Rio Branco
Brasiléia
Cobija

Bôca do Acr...
Pto Heath
L. Rogaguado

ISLAS
GALÁPAGOS
(ARCHIPIÉLAGO
DO COLÓN) (Equ.)
Culpepper
Wenman
Pinta
Marchena
Genovesa
Fernandina
San Salvador
Santa Cruz
Baquerizo Moreno
San Cristóbal
Isabela
Santa María
Española

at the same scale

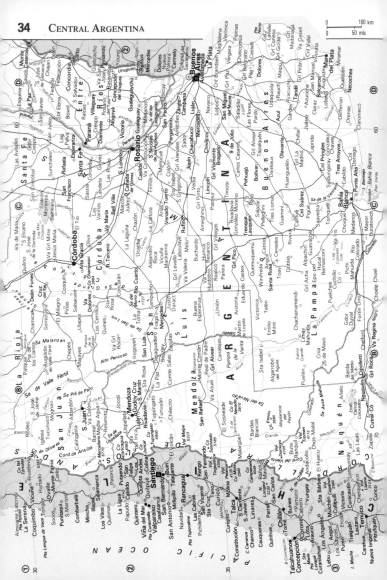

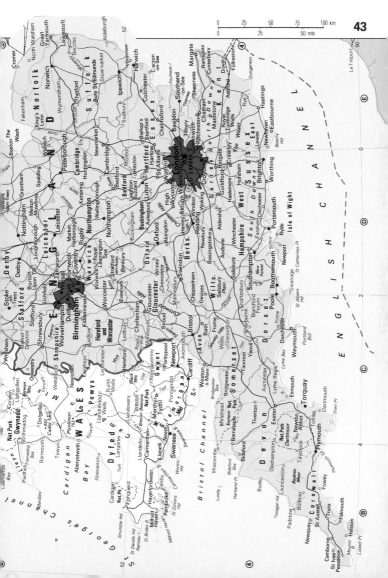

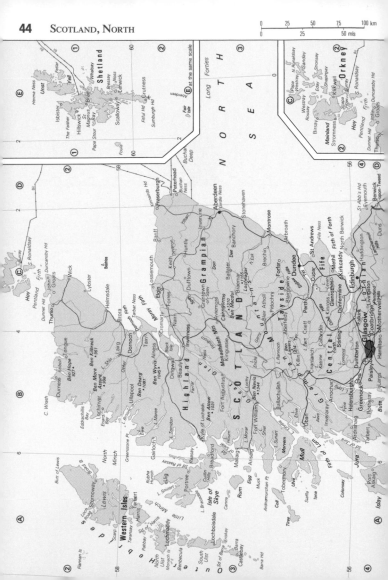

Barnstaple   Taunton   Salisbury   Guildford   Maidstone   Canterbury
Bude   Exeter   Winchester   Crawley   Folkestone   Dover
Newquay   Bournemouth   Southampton   Brighton   Hastings   Calais   St-Omer
Plymouth   Torquay   Weymouth   Portsmouth   Eastbourne   Boulogne
Truro   Dartmoor   Isle of Wight   Montreuil
Penzance   Land's End   Prawle Pt   Abbeville
Isles of Scilly   Lizard Pt   Amiens
Lizard Pt   **English Channel**   Neufchâtel   Montdidier   Beauv
Le Tréport   Dieppe

C. de la Hague   pte de Barfleur   Fécamp   Bolbec   Rouen   Cergy
Alderney   Cherbourg   Le Havre   Deauville   Seine   Pontoise
Guernsey   Sark   Valognes   Bayeux   Lisieux   Elbeuf   Mantes   Paris
Channel Is   St Helier   St-Lô   Caen   Louviers   Versailles   FRANCE
(to U.K.)   Jersey   St-Malo   Coutances   Evreux   Dreux   Rambouillet   Étampes
Golfe de St-Malo   Mont-   Argentan   Alençon   Chartres   Fontainebleau
Roscoff   St-Malo   St-Michel   Domfront   Chartres

I. d'Ouessant   Morlaix   Dinan   NORMANDIE
Brest   St-Brieuc   Fougères   Mayenne   Châteaudun
Châteaulin   Carhaix   Loudéac   Vitré   MAINE   Le Mans   Orléans
Quimper   Plouguer   Pontivy   Rennes   Laval   Vendôme   ORLÉANA
Concarneau   Quimperlé   Ploërmel   Châteaubriant   La Flèche   Tours   Romorantin
Lorient   Vannes   Redon   Nozay   Angers   Saumur   Vierzo
Quiberon   St-Nazaire   Nantes   Cholet   Thouars   Loches   Bourges
Belle-Ile   Île de   Montaigu   ANJOU   Bressuire   Châtellerault   Issoudun
Noirmoutier   Parthenay   Poitiers   Châteauroux   St Amand
I. d'Yeu   La Roche-   Fontenay-   POITOU   Argenton   La Châtre
sur-Yon   le-Comte   Niort   s.-Creuse
Les Sables-   Ruffec   Bellac   Guéret
d'Olonne   Rochefort   St Jean-   Poitiers
Île de Ré   La Rochelle   d'Angely   St-Junien   Limoges
Rochefort   Cognac   Angoulême   LIMOUSIN

BAY   OF   BISCAY   Saintes   Pons   Barbezieux   Thiviers   Uzerche   Tulle
(GOLFE DE GASCOGNE)   Royan   Blaye   Périgueux   Brive
Libourne   Mussidan   Souillac   Aurillac
Bordeaux   Bergerac   Figeac
Arcachon   Langon   Marmande   Villeneuve   Cahors   Decazeville
GUYE   Bazas   -s.-Lot   Agen   Moissac   Rode
Capbreton   Mont-de-   Castelsarrasin   Montauban
Avilés   C. de Peñas   Marsan   Auch   Albi
Gijón   Santander   C. de Ajo   Dax   Adour
Oviedo   Torrelavega   Biarritz   Bayonne   Orthez   Pau   Toulouse
Mieres   Picos de Europa   San   Oloron-   Lourdes   St-Gaudens   GASCOGNE
ASTURIAS   Baracaldo   Bilbao   Sebastián   Ste-Marie   Tarbes   Pamiers   Carcassonne
Cord.   Reinosa   (Donostia)   Eibar   (Bilbo)   Durango   Irún   Tolosa   Pyrénées
La Robla   Cantábrica   VASCONGADAS   Vignemale   RUSSILL
León   Ebro   Vitoria   Pamplona   P. de Aneto   Montgny   Andorra
Astorga   Sahagún   Miranda   NAVARRA   Jaca   Viella   La-V   Bourg-M
de Ebro   Osorno   Logroño   Tafalla   Sa de Guara   Puigcerdà
Benavente   Burgos   Calahorra   Aragón   **ANDORRA**

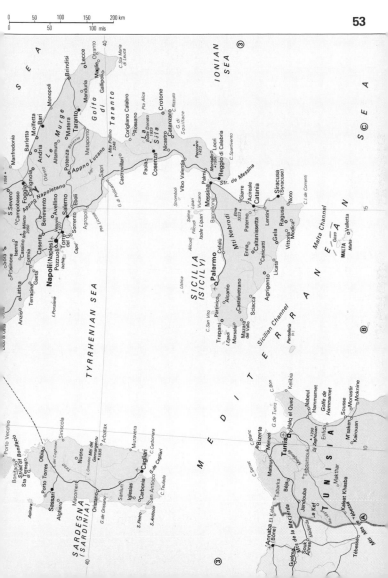

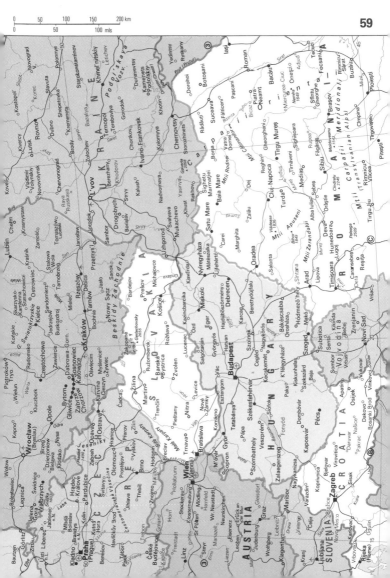

0 100 200 300 400 km
0 100 200 mls

yduga F Vel'sk Velikiy Ustyug Krasavino 45 Griva Gayny 60 Solikamsk J Serov K
Konosha Luza Pinyug Kazhim Lesnoy Kudymkar Kizel Nov K
Kharkov Brusenets Rosvatino Oparino Kudymkar Kachkanat Lyalya Sos va
Sokol Vologda Gryazovets Buy Kirov Omutninsk Nolinsk Krasnokamsk Perm Kushva Nizhniy
N F E D E R A T I O N Khaltturin Nolinsk Zuyevka Ochero Kungur Kirovgrad Tagil Reverski
Vologda Galich Manturovo Nova Glazov Igra Osa Vekaterinburg (Sverdlovsk)
oslavl Ivanovo Kostroma Kineshma Sharya Sovetsk Izhevsk Votkinsk Revda Kamensk-
Vichuga Neya Makarev Shakhun ya Yaransk Urzhum Malmyzh Mozhga Agryz Kambarka Pavlovka Kasli
Kovrov Gorodets Dzerzhinsk Nizhniy Novgorod (Gor kiy) Koz modemyansk Yoshkar-Ola Kil mez Mariyskaya Naberezhnyye Chelny Menzelinsk Birsk Chelyabinsk
Vyazniki Pavlovo Cheboksary Chuvashskaya Kazan Tatarstan Asha Kopeysk
Gus Khrustalnyy Murom Arzamas Sergach Kanash Shumerlya Chistopol Al met yevsk Ufa Bashkortostan Katav Zlatoust
Kasimov Pervomaysk Alatyr Tetyushi Nurlat Bugulma Oktyabr skiy Davlekanovo Krasnousol Magnitogorsk
Ryazan Sasovo Mordovskaya Saransk Simbirsk Dimitrovgrad Sernovodsk Abdulino Sterlitamak Salavat Yuzh. Baymak Bredy
Ryazhsk Shilovo Kovylkino Baryshr Tol yatti Kinel Belebey Meleuz Kumertau
Michurinsk Nizhniy Lomov Penza Syzran Samara (Kuybyshev) Buzuluk Gorochino Sol Orsk
Tambov Vozvyshennost Serdobsk Petrovsk Vol sk Balakovo Pugachev Ural sk Orenburg Saraktash Mednogorsk Dombarovskiy
Gryazi Rtishchevo Arkadak Balashov Saratov Yershov Aksay Sol iletsk Akbulak Novotroitsk
oronezh Borisoglebsk Povorino Krasnoarmeysk Krasnyy Kut Novo Uzensk Novoalekseyevka Aktyubinsk Alga
Pavlovsk Buturlinovka Uryupinsk Novoanninskiy Kamyshin Pallasovka Chapayev Shubar Kuduk Emba
Rossosh Kalach Mikhaylovka Frolovo Nikolayevsk Caspian Mateksay Inderborsky Uil Zharkamys
Perelazovskiy Millerovo Kalach-na-Donu Volzhskiy Saykhin Depression KAZAKHSTAN Makat
evka Shakhty Morozovsk Volgograd (Stalingrad) Akhtubinsk Ryn Peski Gur yev Balykshi Kul sary Aktumsyk
ssk Rostov-na-Donu Proletarskaya Volgodonsk Kotel nikovo Kalmytskaya R. Kharabali Sarykamys
Tikhoretsk Divnoye Elista Chernyye Zemli Krasnyy Yar Astrakhan Sor Mertvyy Kultuk Beyneu
Kropotkin Ipatovo Kuma Mumra Lagan Burynshik Ova Say-Utes Plato Ustyur
Ust Labinsk Stavropol Budennovsk M. Tyub-Karagan Poluostrov Mangyshlak
Maykop Labinsk Cherkessk Georgiyevsk Pyatigorsk Ft Shevchenko Aktau (Shevchenko) Novyy Uzen
Sochi Gagra Abkhazskaya Kislovodsk Prokhladnyy Nal chik Groznyy Makhachkala CASPIAN Fetisovo
Sukhumi Elbrus Dykh Tau Vladikavkaz Buynaksk SEA

UZBEKISTAN

Plato Ustyur

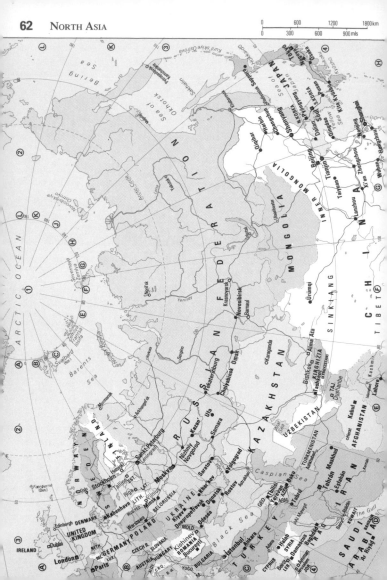

| 0 | | 600 | | 1200 | | 1800km |
| 0 | 300 | | 600 | | 900mls | |

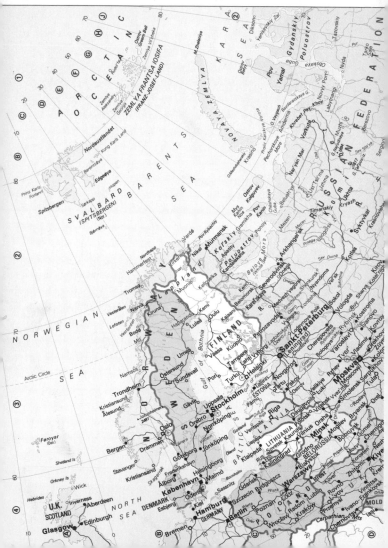

RUSSIAN FEDERATION
1 Chuvashskaya R.
2 Checheno-Ingushskaya R.
3 Severo-Osetinskaya R.
4 Kabardino-Balkarskaya R.
GEORGIA
5 Abkhazskaya R.
6 Adzharskaya R.
AZERBAIJAN
7 Nakhichevanskaya R.

Scilla
MAC. Struma
GREECE BULGARIA Burgas
Athinai Krti
Atina

Black Sea

Istanbul
Ankara
TURKEY

CYPRUS
Alexandria
Cairo
EGYPT Nile
Aswān

LIBYA

Dnepropetrovsk
Odessa UKRAINE Kharkov
Donetsk
Rostov
Saratov
Volgograd
Astrakhan

RUSSIA
Yekaterinburg
Ufa
Chelyabinsk Omsk
Samara Navosibirs
Barnau

KAZAKHSTAN

GEORGIA Tbilisi
Kars
Yerevan Baku
ARM. Tabriz

Karaganda

Aral Sea
UZBEKISTAN

Bishkek Alma Ata
Tashkent
KIRGHIZIA
KYRGYZSTAN
SI

Halab
Beirut SYRIA
Leb. Damascus
Jerusalem AMMAN
JOR.
SAUDI
ARABIA

Caspian Sea
Al Mawsil
IRAQ
Baghdad

Tehrān Mashhad
TURKMENISTAN
Ashkhabad

TAJIKISTAN
Dushanbe

Herat Kabul
AFGHANISTAN
Kandahār
Kermān

Kashmir

TI

Islāmābād
Lahore

PAKISTAN
Indus

Delhi
NEP
Kānpur Lucknow
Patna

RED SEA
SUDAN
Khartoum

Asmara
ERITREA

Makkah
Ar Riyāḍ
BAHRAIN
QATAR
Abū Dhabi
U.A.E.

KUWAIT
Eşfahān
Basra
Abādān
The Gulf

Masqaṭ
OMAN

Karachi
Hyderābād
INDIA
Ahmadābād
Nāgpur
Bombay
Godavari
Hyderabad
Krishna
Bangalore
Madurai
Madras

Jabalpur

YEMEN
Sanā
Aden
DJIBOUTI G. of Aden

Ādīs
Ābeba
ETHIOPIA

KENYA
SOMALIA
Muqdisho

Mombasa

Socotra
(Yemen)

ARABIAN
SEA

Lakshadweep
(Ind.)

SRI LANKA
Colombo Kandy

MALDIVES

Dar es Salaam
TANZANIA

Equator

INDIAN OCEAN

SEYCHELLES

Aldabra Is
(Sey.)

Chagos Arch.
(U.K.)

COMOROS
MOZAMBIQUE

MADAGASCAR
Antananarivo

Scale bars:
0 200 400 600 800 km
0 200 400 mils

SEA OF OKHOTSK

SAKHALIN

Kuril'skiye Ostrova (Kuril Islands)

HOKKAIDŌ

SEA OF JAPAN

NORTH KOREA

SOUTH KOREA

YELLOW SEA

H O N S H Ū

K Y Ū S H Ū

EAST CHINA SEA

RYŪKYŪ RETTŌ

TAIWAN (FORMOSA) (China Nat. Rep.)

P A C I F I C   O C E A N

Tropic of Cancer

MARIANAS

Northern Marianas

Ogasawara Gunto (Bonin Islands) (Jap.)

Kazan Retto (Volcano Is) (Jap.)

Major cities: Harbin, Changchun, Jilin, Shenyang, Fushun, Anshan, Dalian, Vladivostok, Khabarovsk, Blagoveshchensk, P'yŏngyang, Sŏul, Pusan, Kwangju, Fukuoka, Kita-Kyūshū, Hiroshima, Ōsaka, Kōbe, Kyōto, Nagoya, Tōkyō, Yokohama, Sendai, Sapporo, Shanghai

Ramapo Deep 10374

Vityaz Depth 10542

Fleming Deep 8651

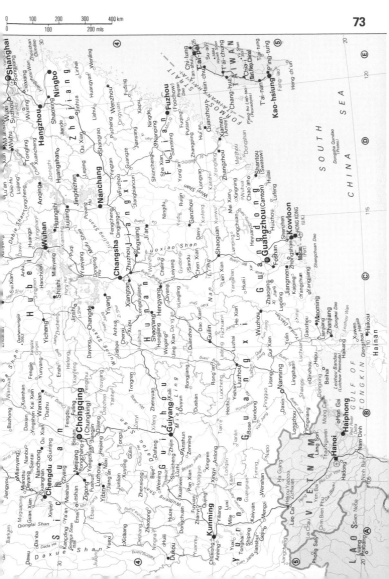

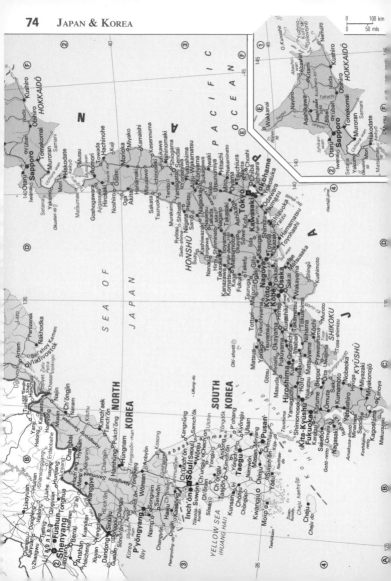

PACIFIC

OCEAN

① ①

Dongsha
Qundau

Luzon
Strait

Batan
Islands
Basco

Balintang Channel

②

Babuyan Islands

Babuyan Channel
Cape Bojeador Cape Engaño

Laoag Aparri

Bangued
Vigan Tuguegarao

Santiago
San Solano Ilagan
Fernando Bayombong
La Trinidad
Baguio
Lingayen Dagupan LUZON
San Carlos San Baler
Camiling Jose
Tarlac Cabanatuan
Angeles Gapan
San Antonio San Fernando
Olongapo Polillo
Manila Islands
Corregidor Cavite Quezon City
San Pablo Lamon
Santa Cruz Bay Jose Panganiban
Lucban Daet
Batangas Lucena Naga Catanduanes
Boac Iriga Legazpi
Calapan Marinduque Mayon Virac
MINDORO Mt Halcon Sorsogon
Sablayan Mt Baco Bulan Gubat
Sibuyan Masbate Catarman
Busuanga Burias
Calamian San Jose Romblon SAMAR
Group Sibuyan Masbate Calbayog Oras
Cuyo Sea
Linapacan Islands Kalibo Roxas Catbalogan
Pandan PANAY San Carigara
Isidro Biliran Tacloban
Cadiz Ormoc Burauen Guiuan
Iloilo Silay Bogo Danao Leyte Gulf
Bacolod Cebu Lapu-Lapu
La Carlota Binalbagan Maasin Dinagat
Puerto Sipalay Bohol Surigao Siargao
Princesa Bais Tagbilaran Sea
Aborlan Dumaguete Lazi Butuan
Siaton Camiguin
Dipolog Dapitan Gingoog Lianga
SULU SEA Manukan Oroquieta Cagayan
Liloy Mt de Oro Bislig
Ozamiz Iligan
Pagadian Marawi Malaybalay
MINDANAO
Zamboanga Illana Tagum
Pen Bay Malabang
Zamboanga Moro Cotabato Davao
Isabela Gulf Datu Digos Mati
Piang
SABAH Jolo General Cape San Agustin
Parang Santos
CELEBES

③

④

⑤

SEA

SOUTH

CHINA

SEA

PHILIPPINE SEA

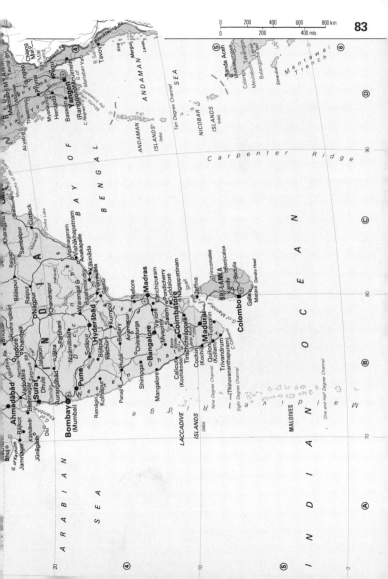

0 200 400 600 800 km
0 200 400 mils

Map labels:

CHINA

Chiang Mai
B U R M A
(MYANMAR)
Taungg Ra
Prome
Pegu
Toungoo
Henzada
Bassein
Yangon
(Rangoon)
Moulmein
Tavoy
Mergui
Akyab

ANDAMAN SEA

ANDAMAN ISLANDS
(India)

Ten Degree Channel

NICOBAR ISLANDS
(India)

Banda Aceh

Mentawai Trench

B A Y

O F

B E N G A L

Carpenter Ridge

Kharagpur
Cuttack
Sambalpur
Raigarh
Bilaspur
Raipur
Chandrapur

I N D I A

Vizianagaram
Vishakhapatnam
Anakapalle
Rajahmundry
Kakinada

Ahmadābād
Vadodara
Rajkot
Bhavnagar
Khandwa
Indore
Ujjain
Jalgaon
Dhule
Bhuj
Jamnagar
Junāgadh
Diu

Surat
Nagpur
Amravati
Nizamabad
Bhopal

Aurangābād
Pune
Sholapur
Bijapur
Bellary
Hyderābād
Warangal
Guntur
Kurnool
Nellore
Madras
Kanchipuram
Pondicherry
Cuddalore
Nagappattinam

Bombay
(Mumbai)
Ratnagiri
Kolhāpur
Panaji
Hubli
Chitradurga
Shimoga
Mangalore
Bangalore
Mysore
Salem
Coimbatore
Tiruchchirappalli
Madurai
Tuticorin

Calicut
(Kozhikode)
Cochin
(Kochi)
Quilon
(Kollam)
Trivandrum
(Thiruvananthapuram)

Jaffna
Trincomalee
Anuradhapura
Batticaloa
SRI LANKA
Kandy
Badulla
Colombo
Galle
Matara
Dondra Head

LACCADIVE ISLANDS
(India)

MALDIVES

Nine Degree Channel
Eight Degree Channel
One and Half Degree Channel

A R A B I A N
S E A

I N D I A N
O C E A N

Gulf of Mannar
Palk Strait

Deccan

Western Ghats

Eastern Ghats

0   100   200   300 km
0   50   100   150 mls

Bombay Ⓐ
(Mumbai)
Alibāg   Lonavale   Pune **MAHARASHTRA**   Ahmadnajar   Parbhani   Nānded   Nirmal   Belampalli   Sironcha   Jagdalpur Ⓒ   Kotapad

Mahād   Wai   Bārāmati   Daund   Lātūr   Udgir   Bodhan   Nizāmābād   Karimnagar   Jagtial   Mancherāl   Bijāpur   Dantewāra   Sukma

Srivardhan   Phaltan   Barsi   Solāpur   Homnābād   Bidar   Siddipet   Warangal   Yellandu   Bhadrāchalam   Kottagūdem

Chiplun   Sātāra   Pandharpur   Vite   Akkalkot   Shāhābād   Tāndūr   **Hyderābād**   Bhongir   Nalgonda   Suriāpet   Khammam   Rājahmundry   Kākināda

Ratnāgiri   Sāngli   Miraj   Bijāpur   Yādgir   Gulbarga   **A N D H R A**   Yarlam

Kolhāpur   Ichalkaranji   Jamkhandi   Shorāpur   Narāyanpet   Mahbūbnagar   Vijayawāda   Elūru   Bhimavaram

Mālvan   Belgaum   Bāgalkot   Rāichur   Wanparti   Mācherla   Narasarāopet   Guntūr   Tenāli   Machilipatnam

Vengurla   Gajendragarh   Guledagudda   Chilakalūrūpet   Bāpatla   Chirāla

Panaji   Goa, Daman   B. Diu   **K A R N A T A K A**   Koppal   Kurnool   Adoni   Nandyāl   Kani Giri   Ongole

Madgaon   Dandeli   Hubli   Gadag   Hospet   Bellary   **P R A D E S H**   Giddalūr   Kondukūr

Kārwār   Sirsi   Hāveri   Kottura   Swāmihalli   Gooty   Tādpatri   Proddutūr   Kavali

Kumta   Rānibennur   Hirihar   Rāyadurg   Anantapur   Cuddapah   Nellore

Bhatkal   Dāvangere   Kalyandurg   Dhamavaram   Kadiri   Venkatagiri   Gūdūr

Kundāpura   Shimoga   Chitradurga   Sira   Hindupur   Tirupati   Srī Kālahasti

Udupi   Bhadrāvati   Tarikere   Kadūr   Chittoor   Arakkonam   Pulicat L.

Kārkal   Chikmagalūr   Arsikere   Tiptūr   Tumkur   Chik Ballāpur   Kolār   Vellore   Kānchipuram   **Madras**

Mangalore   Hassan   **Bangalore**   Kolār Gold Fields   Amhūr

Kāsaragod   Hole Narsipur   Madikeri   Nanjangūd   Mandya   Mysore   Krishnagiri   Tiruppattūr   Jawādi Hills   Tindivanam

Cannanore   Tellicherry   Mahe   Chāmrājnagar   Dharmapuri   Tiruvannāmalai   Pondicherry

Badagara   Ootacamund   Mettūr   Salem   Villupuram   Cuddalore

Calicut   (Kozhikode)   Nilgiri Hills   Doda Betta   Erode   Vriddhāchalam   Chidambaram

Beypore   **Coimbatore**   Pālghāt   **T A M I L   N A D U**   Tiruchchirāppalli   Kumbakonam   Kāraikāl

Ponnāni   (Palakkat)   Tiruppur   Nāgapattinam

Trichūr   (Thrissur)   Anaimalai Hills   Palani   Dindigul   Thanjāvūr   Mannārgudi   Pt Calimera

Cochin   (Kochi)   Bodināyakkanūr   Pudukkottai   Kodiyakkal

Ernākulam   Kambam   Virudunagar   **Madurai**   Paramakudi   Pt Pedro

Kottayam   Alleppey   Kāyankulam   Aruppukkottai   Rāmanāthapuram   Jaffna

Puliyangudi   Rājapālaiyam   Mullaittvu

Quilon   (Kollam)   Tenkāsi   Tuticorin   Talaimannar   Mannar   Vavuniya   Trincomalee

Trivandrum   (Thiruvananthapuram)   Tirunelveli   Palayānkottai   Gulf of Mannār   Havankulam   Anurādhapura

Nāgercoil   Tiruchchendur   Puttalam   Batticaloa

Kanniyākumari   C. Comorin   **SRI LANKA**   Dambulla   **CEYLON**   Matale

Chilaw   Kurunegala   Gampola   **Kandy**   Bedula

Negombo   Nuwara-Eliya

Colombo   Adam's Pk   Ratnapura

Dehiwala-Mt Lavinia   Moratuwa   Opanake

Ambalangoda   Galle   Hambantota

Matara   Dondra Hd

Nine Degree Channel

Androth

Kalpeni

Minicoy

Eight Degree Channel

MALDIVES

Manaar Coast

Malabar Coast

Coromandel Coast

Palk Strait

Adam's Bridge

Gulf of Mannār

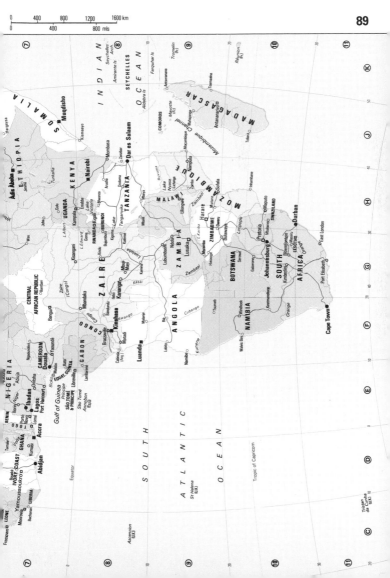

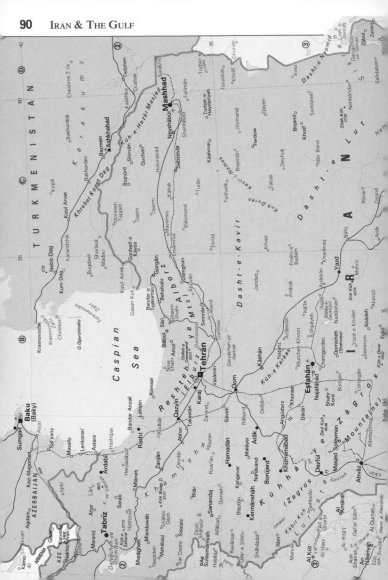

0   100   200   300 km
0   50   100   150 mls

Nosratābād°
Zāhedān°

Kūh-e Taftān
3941

Chāh
Bahār

⑤
Al Ḥadd

D

kzār-e
adad

Pashtūyeh

°Shahdād

Kermān

Rafsanjān°

°Bāghīn

Bām°

Dārzīn

Kūh-e Jebal Barez

Kūh-e
Laleh Zār
4374

Baghīn

Khāsh

Kāhnūj

Hāmūn-e
Jaz Mūrīān

Rūdān

Mīnāb

Rīgān

Kūhe-Bazmān
2821

Bazmān°

Remeshk

Bband Bonī

Chānf

Kūhistān

Nīksahr°

Tang

Qaşr-e
Qand

Khaimah

Ras al
Khaimah

Marah Masqat
Muscat

Ḡūr of Oman

Al Ḥajar ash Sharqī

Sūr

Quryyāt

Ra's al Ḥadd

Ramlat
Al Wahībah

Al Kāmil

Al Mudayrib

Al Ḥuwatsah

Umm as
Samīm

Ibrī

Adam

°Fahūd

Al Jafūrah

As Ṣanām

Al'Ubaylah

Tropic of Cancer

S   A   U   D   I   A   R   A   B   I   A

Al Hillah

Lᵃyla

Aş Şulayyil°

Al Hufūf

Al Mubarraz

Ḥaraḍ°

Wadi Sahba

Al Aḥsā

Al Hufūf

Dhahran
Al Khobar

Dammam

Manāmah

BAHRAIN

Al Muharraq

Ad Dammam

QATAR

Doha

Dukhān°

Umm
Saīd

Salwah

Khawr
ad Duwayhin

Jabal az Zannah

Ṣīr Banī
Yās

Abū
Dhabī

Tarīf

U. A. E.

Al Maḥrayqah

°Al Liwā'

'Arfadah

Al Kidan

Al Uruqal Mu'tariḍah

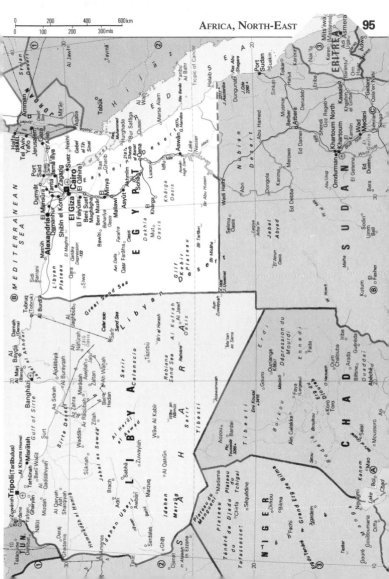

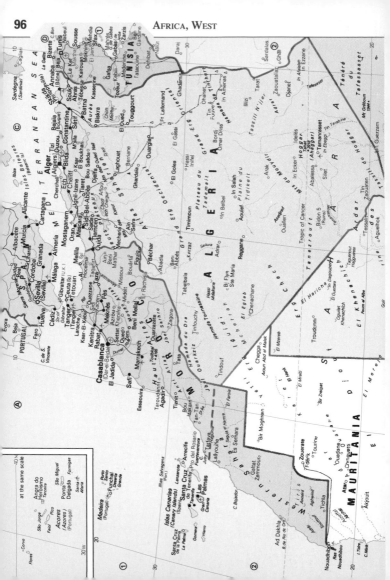

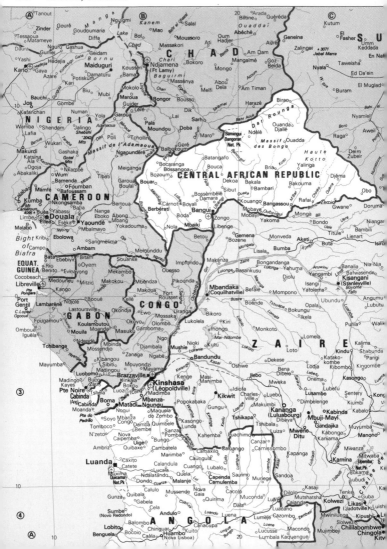

EUROPE

Black Sea

Mediterranean Sea

Nile

AFRICA

Tropic of Cancer

Niger

Guinea Basin

Bioko

N. Cape

Arctic Circle

Barents Sea

Norwegian Basin

Greenland Basin

ICELAND

Denmark Strait

North Sea

Faeroyar Is. Shetland Is.

Land's End

N.E. Atlantic Basin

Açores

Madeira

Islas Canarias

Madeira

C. Vert

Cape Verde Is.

Canary Basin

Cape Verde Basin

Equator

GREENLAND

Baffin Bay

C. Farewell

Labrador Sea

Newfoundland

Grand Banks

Newfoundland Basin

Mid-Atlantic Ridge

Guyana Basin

North American Basin

Bermuda

Puerto Rico Trench 9220

NORTH AMERICA

Hudson Bay

Mississippi

Gulf of Mexico

Cayman Trench

West Indies

Caribbean Sea

Cocos Ridge

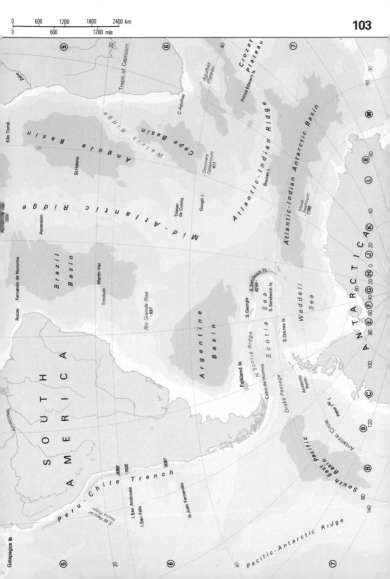

0 600 1200 1800 2400 km
0 600 1200 mls

⑤ 20 ⑥ 40 ⑦

Tropic of Capricorn

Crozet Plateau

Agulhas Plateau

C. Agulhas

Prince Edward Is

São Tomé

Zaire

Atlantic-Indian Ridge

Angola Basin

Walvis Ridge

Cape Basin

St Helena

Discovery Tablemount 411

Bouvet I.

Atlantic-Indian Antarctic Basin

Ⓜ

⑧ 60

Ⓛ

Romanche Dp 7856

Ascension

Mid-Atlantic Ridge

Tristan da Cunha

Gough I.

40

Maud Seamount 1159

Ⓚ 20 Ⓙ 0 Ⓗ 20 Ⓖ 40 Ⓕ 60 Ⓔ 80

Brazil Basin

Fernando de Noronha

Rocas

Martin Vaz

Trindade

Rio Grande Rise -637

S. Georgia

S. Sandwich Tr. 8264

S. Sandwich Is

Weddell Sea

80

A N T A R C T I C A

Ⓒ

Argentine Basin

N.Scotia Ridge

Falkland Is

Cabo de Hornos

Scotia Sea

S. Orkney Is

Antarctic Penin.

Weddell Sea

⑧ 120

Peter I. I.

S O U T H

A M E R I C A

ANTOFAGASTA

Galapagos Is

Peru - Chile Trench 8066 7635

6687

I.San Ambrosia
I.San Felix

Is Juan Fernández

Nazca Ridge
20 Peru M.S

Drake Passage

Antarctic Circle

South East Pacific Basin

Ⓑ

60

Pacific-Antarctic Ridge

⑤ 20 ⑥ ⑦ 140

① 40

② 20

A S I A

*Vityaz Depth 16(
10542*

Sea of
Japan

Huang He

Chang Jiang

Ganga

TAIWAN

J A P A N

S.Honshu Ridge

Japan Trench

③ 0

Bay
of
Bengal

Hainan

Yushu-Palau Ridge

Mariana Is.
(U.S.A.)

Guam

MICRON

Andaman Is.

PHILIPPINES

C. Johnson
Depth
10497

Philippine Trench

11022
Challenger
Depth

Mariana Trench

SRI
LANKA
(CEYLON)

Nicobar
Is.

MALDIVES

South China Sea

FEDERATED STATES

Palau
(Belau)
(USA)

Caroline Is.

OF MICRONESIA

Maldives Ridge

Celebes
Sea

6920

MELA

Chagos Arch.

Sumatera

Borneo

Sulawesi

New
Guinea

Planet Deep
9140

④

Mid-Indian Ridge

Mid
Indian
Basin

Ninety-East Ridge

I N D I A N

Jawa

Java Trench

7450

Christmas I.

Cocos Is.

West
Australian
Basin

Timor

Arafura Sea

Coral Sea
Basin

Great Barrier Reef

20

O C E A N

W. Australian Ridge

1924

Tropic of Capricorn

AUSTRALIA

⑤

2067

7102

South
Australia
Basin

Tasma

40

Crozet
Basin

I.Amsterdam
I.St Paul

Indian-Antarctic Ridge

Tasmania

Sea

⑥

Is Crozet

Is Kerguelen

Kerguelen Ridge

1922

Heard I.

Macquarie Is

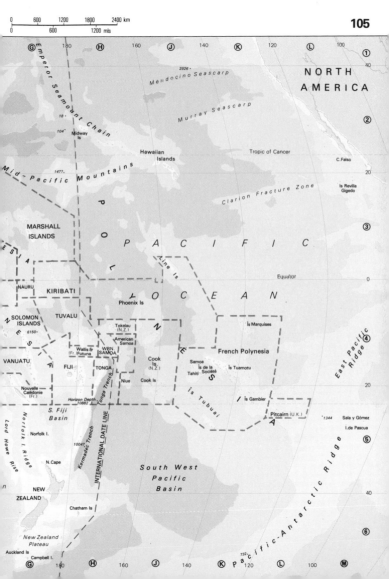

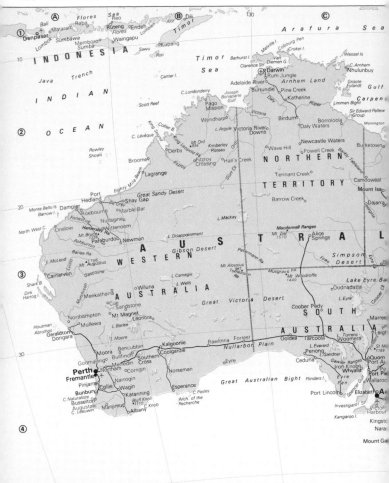

0 200 400 600 800 km
0   200   400 mis

F

140

PAPUA

Daru
Gulf of Papua   Popondetta
Port Moresby   Kokoda   D. Entrecasteaux — Woodlark
Saibai   Tobriands
NEW   Stanley Ra.   Islands
GUINEA   Kupiano   Alotau
Torres Strait C. York   Samarai   Louisiade
Pr. of Wales I. Somerset   Tagula   Arch.
                                        Rossel

New
Georgia   Santa Isabel   **SOLOMON**
ISLANDS
Florida Is.   Stewart Is   ①
Guadalcanal   Malaita   Maramasike
Hemara
San Cristobal

Weipa
Cape
York   Iron
Range
Coen
Peninsula   C. Grenville
Mitchell River
Laura   Cooktown
Princess Charlotte B.

Rennell

②

Normanton
Croydon   Gregory Ra.   Mt Bartle Frere   Cairns
Ravenshoe   Innisfail   1612
Forsayth   Ingham   Palm Is
Gilbert   Townsville   Ayr
Charters Towers   Bowen   Proserpine

Récifs
d'Entrecasteaux

Iles Belep

Coringa Is
Marion Reef
Iles
Chesterfield
(Fr.)

Cloncurry   Richmond
Hughenden   Collinsville
QUEENSLAND   Mackay
Selwyn   Winton   Northumberland
Longreach   Clermont   Is
Barcaldine   Emerald   Rockhampton
Blackall   Mount Morgan   Gladstone
Windorah   Theodore
Charleville   Roma   Bundaberg
Quilpie   Miles   Dalby   Maryborough
Cunnamulla   St George   Toowoomba   Gympie
Milparinka   Goondiwindi   Brisbane
Bourke   Walgett   Warwick   Ipswich
Wilcannia   Narrabri   Lismore
Broken Hill   Moree   Glen   Casino
Menindee   Bourke   Inglewood   Grafton
Tamworth   Round Mtn
Ivanhoe   Nyngan   Port Macquarie
NEW SOUTH   Armidale
WALES   Taree

Bellona
Reefs   Uvéa
Swan   Lifu
Reefs   Muéo
Cato   Bourail   **Nouvelle**
Calédonie   Nouméa
(Fr.)   Île des Pins
Tropic of Capricorn

PACIFIC

③

OCEAN

Norfolk I.
(Aust)

Cobar   Dubbo
Orange   Bathurst   Newcastle
Griffith   Lithgow
Leeton   Maitland
Cootamundra   Sydney
Hay   Wagga Wagga   Wollongong
Deniliquin   Albury   Goulburn
Shepparton   Canberra
Bendigo   A.C.T.
VICTORIA   Mt Kosciusko
Ararat   2230
Ballarat   Bombala
Geelong   Orbost
Melbourne   C. Howe
Morwell   Bairnsdale

Lord Howe I.
(Aust)

30

170

④

Warrnambool   Wonthaggi
King I.   Wilson's Prom.
Bass Strait
Furneaux
Group   C. Barren
Flinders

TASMAN

Burnie
C. Grim   Smithton   Devonport   Launceston
Queenstown   Mt Ossa   St Mary's
1617
Hobart   **TASMANIA**
Geeveston
South West C.   South East C.

SEA

NEW   C. Farewell
ZEALAND   Westport   Nelson
South Island   Greymouth

40

D   150   **E**   160   **F**   **G**

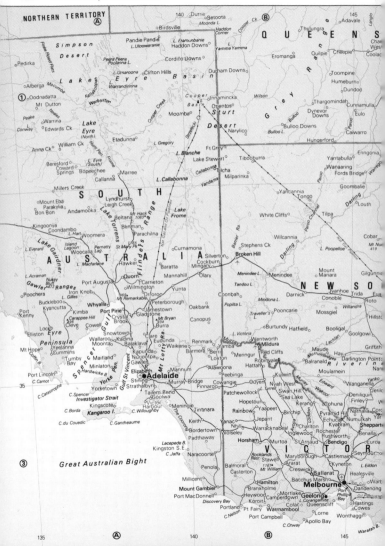

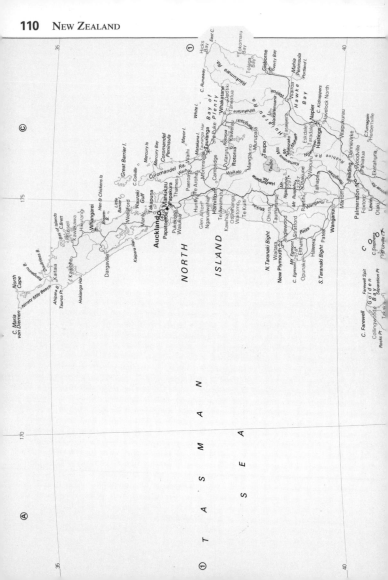

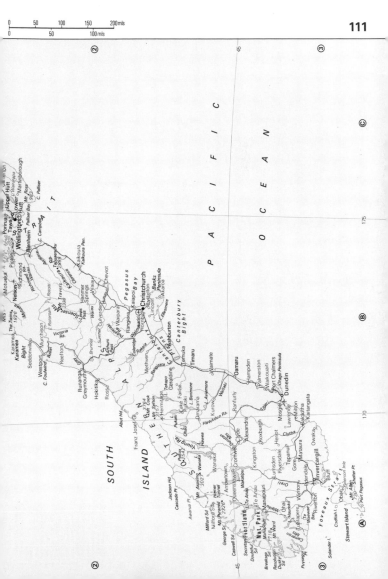

0 50 100 150 200 mls
0 50 100 mls

② ③

SOUTH

ISLAND

NEW

P A C I F I C

O C E A N

Karamea Bight
Karamea
Seddonville
Westport
C. Foulwind
Greymouth
Runanga
Hokitika
Ross
Franz Josef Gl.
Abut Hd.
Jackson Hd.
Cascade Pt.

The Twins 1978
Mt. Owen
Mtns
Murchison
Victoria Ra.
Buller
Brunner

Mokihinui
Mokau
Mt. Arthur
Motueka
Nelson
Waimea
Richmond
Riwaka
Takaka
Motupiko
Wairau
Tophouse
Lewis Pass
Arthur's Pass
Mt. Rolleston
Otira

Mt. Travers 2338
Mts
Mt. Franklin
Hanmer Springs
Culverden
Waiau
Hurunui
Waikari

Blenheim
Kaikoura
Clarence
Kaikoura Pen.

C. Campbell
Mt. Ross 903
C. Palliser
Cloudy Bay
Palliser Bay
Pigeon
Lower Hutt
Upper Hutt
Wellington
Porirua
Paraparaumu
Waikanae

S O U T H E R N

A L P S

Mt. Cook 3764
Mt. Tasman
Mt. Sefton
Hermitage
Mt. Aspiring 3027
Mt. Pembroke
Mt. Pollux 2542
Mt. Tutoko 2746
Mt. Ward

Milford Sd.
George Sd.
Caswell Sd.
Secretary Island
Doubtful Sd.
Dagg Sd.
Breaksea Sd.
Dusky Sd.
Resolution I.

Fiordland
Nat. Park
Manapouri
Te Anau
L. Te Anau
L. Manapouri
Mt. Anau
Mossburn

Waimakariri
Rakaia
Christchurch
Lincoln
Lyttelton
Banks Peninsula
Akaroa
Canterbury Bight

P e g a s u s
B a y
Rangiora
Darfield
Methven
Ashburton

L. Sumner
Waimakariri
Rangitata
Pleasant Pt.
Geraldine
Temuka
Fairlie
Timaru

L. Coleridge
L. Tekapo
L. Pukaki
L. Ohau
Twizel
L. Benmore
Omarama
Waimate

Waitaki
Kurow
Duntroon
Oamaru
Hampden
Palmerston
Waikouaiti
Port Chalmers
Dunedin
Otago Peninsula

Hawkdun Ra.
Young Ra.
Ranfurly
Naseby
Roxburgh
Clyde
Alexandra
Cromwell
Bannockburn

L. Wanaka
L. Hawea
Wanaka
Arrowtown
Queenstown
L. Wakatipu
Te Anau
Kingston

Clutha
Herbert
Middlemarch
Mosgiel
Milton
Lawrence
Tapanui
Gore
Waikaka
Balclutha
Kaitangata
Owaka

Otara
Lumsden
Riversdale
Winton
Invercargill
Bluff
Riverton
Wallacetown

Waiau
Te Waewae
Bay
Ohai
Orepuki
Tuatapere
Colac Bay
Foveaux Strait
Waipapa Pt.
Slope Pt.

Solander I.
Puysegur Pt.
Cape
Providence

Stewart Island
Oban
Paterson Inlet
Mt. Allen
Shelter Pt.
Port Pegasus

45

175

170

45

② ③ ④

Ⓐ Ⓑ Ⓒ

T I T

Antarctic Research Stations
1 Artigas (Uruguay)
2 Teniente Rodolfo Marsh Martín (Chile)
3 Bellingshausen (Rus. Fed.)
4 Chang Cheng (Great Wall) (China)
5 Comandante Ferraz (Brazil)
6 Henryk Arctowski (Poland)
7 Teniente Jubany (Arg.)
8 King Sejong (Korea)
9 Capitán Arturo Prat (Chile)
10 General Bernardo O'Higgins (Chile)
11 Esperanza (Arg.)
12 Vicecomodoro Marambio (Arg.)
13 Palmer (USA)
14 Faraday (UK)
15 Rothera (UK)
16 General San Martín (Arg.)
17 Václav Vojtěch (Czech Rep.)

Index

In the index, the first number refers to the page, and the following letter
and number to the section of the map in which the index entry
can be found. For example, 48C2 **Paris** means that Paris can
be found on page 48 where column C and row 2 meet.

Abbreviations used in the index

Afghan	Afghanistan	Hung	Hungary	Pol	Poland	Arch	Archipelago
Alb	Albania	Ind	Indonesia	Port	Portugal	B	Bay
Alg	Algeria	Irish Rep	Ireland	Rom	Romania	C	Cape
Ant	Antarctica	Leb	Lebanon	Russian Fed	Russian	Chan	Channel
Arg	Argentina	Lib	Liberia		Federation	Gl	Glacier
Aust	Australia	Liech	Liechtenstein	S Arabia	Saudi Arabia	I(s)	Island(s)
Bang	Bangladesh	Lux	Luxembourg	Scot	Scotland	Lg	Lagoon
Belg	Belgium	Madag	Madagascar	Sen	Senegal	L	Lake
Bol	Bolivia	Malay	Malaysia	S Africa	South Africa	Mt(s)	Mountain(s)
Bulg	Bulgaria	Maur	Mauritania	Switz	Switzerland	O	Ocean
Burk	Burkina	Mor	Morocco	Tanz	Tanzania	P	Pass
Camb	Cambodia	Mozam	Mozambique	Thai	Thailand	Pen	Peninsula
Can	Canada	Neth	Netherlands	Turk	Turkey	Plat	Plateau
CAR	Central African Republic	NZ	New Zealand	USA	United States	Pt	Point
Den	Denmark	Nic	Nicaragua		of America	Res	Reservoir
Dom Rep	Dominican Republic	N Ire	Northern Ireland	Urug	Uruguay	R	River
El Sal	El Salvador	Nig	Nigeria	Ven	Venezuela	S	Sea
Eng	England	Nor	Norway	Viet	Vietnam	Sd	Sound
Eq Guinea	Equatorial Guinea	Pak	Pakistan	Yugos	Yugoslavia	Str	Strait
Eth	Ethiopia	PNG	Papua New Guinea	Zim	Zimbabwe	V	Valley
Fin	Finland	Par	Paraguay				
Germ	Germany	Phil	Philippines				

A

57B2 **Aachen** Germany
46C1 **Aalst** Belg
38K6 **Äänekoski** Fin
47C1 **Aarau** Switz
47B1 **Aare** R Switz
72A3 **Aba** China
97C4 **Aba** Nig
99D2 **Aba** Zaire
91A3 **Ābādān** Iran
90B3 **Ābādeh** Iran
96B1 **Abadla** Alg
35B1 **Abaeté** Brazil
35B1 **Abaeté** R Brazil
31B2 **Abaetetuba** Brazil
72D1 **Abagnar Qi** China
97C4 **Abakaliki** Nig
63B2 **Abakan**
　Russian Fed
97B3 **Abala** Niger
96C2 **Abalessa** Alg
32C6 **Abancay** Peru
90B3 **Abarqū** Iran
74E2 **Abashiri** Japan
74E2 **Abashiri-wan** B
　Japan
71F4 **Abau** PNG
99D2 **Abaya** L Eth
99D1 **Abba** R Eth
99E1 **Abbe** L Eth
48C1 **Abbeville** France
19B4 **Abbeville** Louisiana,
　USA
17B1 **Abbeville** S Carolina,
　USA
45B2 **Abbeyfeale** Irish Rep
47C2 **Abbiategrasso** Italy
20B1 **Abbotsford** Can
84C2 **Abbottabad** Pak
61H3 **Abdulino**
　Russian Fed
98C1 **Abéché** Chad
39F7 **Åbenrå** Den
97C4 **Abeokuta** Nig
99D2 **Abera** Eth
43B3 **Aberaeron** Wales

15C3 **Aberdeen** Maryland,
　USA
100B4 **Aberdeen** S Africa
44C3 **Aberdeen** Scot
8D2 **Aberdeen** S Dakota,
　USA
8A2 **Aberdeen**
　Washington, USA
4J3 **Aberdeen** L Can
44C3 **Aberdeen** Scot
43C4 **Aberfeldy** Scot
43C4 **Abergavenny** Wales
43B3 **Aberystwyth** Wales
81C4 **Abhā** S Arabia
90A2 **Abhar** Iran
97B4 **Abidjan** Ivory Coast
18A2 **Abilene** Kansas, USA
9D3 **Abilene** Texas, USA
43D4 **Abingdon** Eng
7B4 **Abitibi** R Can
7C5 **Abitibi,L** Can
61F5 **Abkhazskaya**
　Respublika, Georgia
84C2 **Abohar** India
97C4 **Abomey** Benin
98B2 **Abong Mbang** Cam
79A4 **Aborlan** Phil
98B1 **Abou Deïa** Chad
91A4 **Abqaiq** S Arabia
50A2 **Abrantes** Port
95C2 **Abri** Sudan
106A3 **Abrolhos** Is Aust
8B2 **Absaroka Range** Mts
　USA
91B5 **Abū al Abyad** I UAE
91A4 **Abū 'Ali** I S Arabia
91B5 **Abū Dhabi** UAE
95C3 **Abu Hamed** Sudan
97C4 **Abuja** Nig
33D6 **Abunã** Brazil
33D6 **Abuna** R Bol
93D3 **Abū Kemāl** Syria
111B2 **Abut Head** C NZ
95C3 **Abu 'Urug** Well
　Sudan
99D1 **Ahiye Meda** Mt Eth
99C1 **Abu Zabad** Sudan
99D2 **Abwong** Sudan

56B1 **Åby** Den
94B3 **Aby 'Aweigila** Well
　Egypt
99C2 **Abyei** Sudan
24B2 **Acambaro** Mexico
24B2 **Acaponeta** Mexico
24B3 **Acapulco** Mexico
31D2 **Acaraú** Brazil
32D2 **Acarigua** Ven
24C3 **Acatlán** Mexico
23B2 **Acatzingo** Mexico
97B4 **Accra** Ghana
85D4 **Achalpur** India
29B4 **Achao** Chile
47D1 **Achensee** L Austria
46E2 **Achern** Germany
41A3 **Achill** I Irish Rep
63B2 **Achinsk** Russian Fed
53C3 **Acireale** Italy
26C2 **Acklins** I
　Caribbean S
32C6 **Acobamba** Peru
29B2 **Aconcagua** Mt Chile
31D3 **Acopiara** Brazil
88B4 **Açores** Is Atlantic O
　A Coruña = La Coruña
47C2 **Acqui** Italy
108A2 **Acraman,L** Aust
　Acre = 'Akko
32C5 **Acre** State, Brazil
22C3 **Acton** USA
23B1 **Actopan** Mexico
19A3 **Ada** USA
81A3 **Adaja** R Spain
91C5 **Adam** Oman
35A2 **Adamantina** Brazil
98B2 **Adamaoua** Region,
　Nig/Cam
47D1 **Adamello** Mt Italy
16C1 **Adams** USA
87B3 **Adam's Bridge** India/
　Sri Lanka
13D2 **Adams,L** USA
8A2 **Adams,Mt** USA
87C3 **Adam's Peak** Mt
　Sri Lanka
81C4 **'Adan** Yemen

92C2 **Adana** Turk
60D5 **Adapazari** Turk
112B7 **Adare,C** Ant
108B1 **Adavale** Aust
47C2 **Adda** R Italy
91A4 **Ad Dahna'** Region,
　S Arabia
96A2 **Ad Dakhla** Alg
81C4 **Ad Dāli'** Yemen
91B4 **Ad Damman**
　S Arabia
91A4 **Ad Dibdibah** Region,
　S Arabia
91A5 **Ad Dilam** S Arabia
91A5 **Ad Dir'iyah** S Arabia
93D3 **Ad Diwaniyah** Iraq
93D3 **Ad Duwayd** S Arabia
106C4 **Adelaide** Aust
4J3 **Adelaide Pen** Can
22D3 **Adelanto** USA
87C1 **Aden** = 'Adan
81C4 **Aden,G of** Yemen/
　Somalia
97C3 **Aderbissinat** Niger
94C2 **Adhra** Syria
71E4 **Adi** I Indon
52B1 **Adige** R Italy
99D1 **Adigrat** Eth
85D5 **Adilabad** India
20B2 **Adin** USA
15D2 **Adirondack Mts** USA
99D2 **Adis Abeba** Eth
95C3 **Adi Ugal** Eritrea
93C2 **Adiyaman** Turk
54C1 **Adjud** Rom
4E4 **Admiralty I** USA
6B2 **Admiralty Inlet** B
　Can
87B1 **Adoni** India
48B3 **Adour** R France
96A2 **Adrar** Region, Maur
96C2 **Adrar** Mts Alg
96A2 **Adrar Souttouf**
　Region, Mor
98C1 **Adré** Chad
95A2 **Adri** Libya
47E2 **Adria** Italy

Adrian

14E2 Adrian Michigan, USA
52B2 Adriatic S S Europe
99D1 Adwa Eth
97B4 Adzopé Ivory Coast
55B3 Aegean S Greece
80E2 Afghanistan Republic, Asia
99E2 Afgooye Somalia
97C4 Afikpo Nig
38G6 Afjord Nor
96C1 Aflou Alg
99E2 Afmadu Somalia
97A3 Afollé Region, Maur
94B2 Afula Israel
92B2 Afyon Turk
95A3 Agadem Niger
97C3 Agadez Niger
96B1 Agadir Mor
85D4 Agar India
86C2 Agartala India
20B1 Agassiz Can
97B4 Agboville Ivory Coast
93E1 Agdam Azerbaijan
75B1 Agematsu Japan
48C3 Agen France
90A3 Agha Jārī Iran
96A2 Aghwinit Well Mor
47D2 Agno R Italy
47E1 Agordo Italy
48C3 Agout R France
85D3 Agra India
93D2 Agri Turk
53C2 Agri R Italy
53B3 Agrigento Italy
55B3 Agrinion Greece
34A3 Agrio R Chile
53B2 Agropoli Italy
61H2 Agryz Russian Fed
6E3 Agto Greenland
27D3 Aguadilla Puerto Rico
24B1 Agua Prieta Mexico
24B2 Aguascalientes Mexico
23A1 Aguascalientes State, Mexico
35C1 Aguas Formosas Brazil
50A1 Agueda Port
96C3 Aguelhok Mali
50B2 Aguilas Spain
23A2 Aguililla Mexico
100B4 Agulhas,C S Africa
79C4 Agusan R Phil
93E2 Ahar Iran
110B1 Ahipara B NZ
85C4 Ahmadábád India
87A1 Ahmadnagar India
99E2 Ahmar Mts Eth
46D1 Ahr R Germany
46D1 Ahrgebirge Region, Germany
23A1 Ahuacatlán Mexico
23A1 Ahualulco Mexico
39G7 Ahus Sweden
90B2 Ahuvän Iran
90A3 Ahvaz Iran
26A4 Aiajuela Costa Rica
47B1 Aigle Switz
47B2 Aiguille d'Arves Mt France
47B2 Aiguille de la Grand Sassière Mt France
75B1 Aikawa Japan
17B1 Aiken USA
73A5 Ailao Shan Upland China
35C1 Aimorés Brazil
96B1 Ain Beni Mathar Mor
95B2 Ain Dalla Well Egypt
51C2 Aïn el Hadjel Alg
95A3 Aïn Galakka Chad
96B1 Aïn Sefra Alg
92B4 'Ain Sukhna Egypt
75A2 Aioi Japan
96B2 Aïoun Abd el Malek Well Maur
97B3 Aïoun El Atrouss Maur
30C2 Aiquile Bol
97C3 Air Desert Region Niger

13E2 Airdrie Can
46B1 Aire France
42D3 Aire R Eng
46C2 Aire R France
6C3 Airforce I Can
47C1 Airolo Switz
13E2 Aishihik Can
12G2 Aishihik L Can
46B2 Aisne Department, France
49C2 Aisne R France
71F4 Aitape PNG
58D1 Aiviekste R Latvia
72B2 Aixa Zuogi China
49D3 Aix-en-Provence France
47A2 Aix-les-Bains France
86B2 Aiyar Res India
55B3 Aíyion Greece
55B3 Aíyna I Greece
86C2 Aizawl India
100A3 Aizeb R Namibia
74E3 Aizu-Wakamatsu Japan
52A2 Ajaccio Corse
23B2 Ajalpan Mexico
95B1 Ajdábiyã Libya
74E2 Ajigasawa Japan
94B2 Ajlün Jordan
91C4 Ajman UAE
85C3 Ajmer India
9B3 Ajo USA
23A2 Ajuchitan Mexico
55C3 Ak R Turk
75B1 Akaishi-sanchi Mts Japan
87B1 Akalkot India
111B2 Akaroa NZ
75A2 Akashi Japan
61J3 Akbulak Russian Fed
93C2 Akçakale Turk
96A2 Akchar Watercourse Maur
55C3 Akdağ Mt Turk
98C2 Aketi Zaïre
93D1 Akhalkalaki Georgia
93D1 Akhalsikhe Georgia
55B3 Akharnaí Greece
12D3 Akhiok USA
92A2 Akhisar Turk
58D1 Akhiste Latvia
95C2 Akhmîm Egypt
61G4 Akhtubinsk Russian Fed
60D4 Akhtyrka Ukraine
75A2 Aki Japan
7B4 Akimiski I Can
74E3 Akita Japan
96A3 Akjoujt Maur
94B2 'Akko Israel
4E3 Aklavik Can
97B3 Aklé Aouana Desert Region Maur
99D2 Akobo Sudan
99D2 Akobo R Sudan
84B1 Akoha Afghan
85D4 Akola India
85D4 Akot India
6D3 Akpatok I Can
55B3 Akra Kafirévs C Greece
55B3 Akra Maléa C Greece
38A2 Akranes Iceland
55C3 Akra Sidheros C Greece
55B3 Akra Spátha C Greece
55B3 Akra Taínaron C Greece
10B2 Akron USA
94A1 Akrotiri B Cyprus
84D1 Aksai Chin Mts China
92B2 Aksaray Turk
61H3 Aksay Russian Fed
84D1 Aksayquin Hu L China
92B2 Aksehir Turk
92B2 Akseki Turk
63D2 Aksenovo Zilovskoye Russian Fed
68D1 Aksha Russian Fed
82C1 Aksu China
61H5 Aktau Kazakhstan

65J5 Aktogay Kazakhstan
61J4 Aktumsyk Kazakhstan
65G4 Aktyubinsk Kazakhstan
38B1 Akureyri Iceland
Akyab = Sittwe
65K5 Akzhal Kazakhstan
11B3 Alabama State, USA
11B3 Alabama R USA
17A1 Alabaster USA
92C2 Ala Dağlari Mts Turk
61F5 Alagir Russian Fed
47B2 Alagna Italy
31D3 Alagoas State, Brazil
31D4 Alagoinhas Brazil
51B1 Alagón Spain
93E4 Al Ahmadi Kuwait
25D3 Alajuela Costa Rica
12B2 Alakanuk USA
38L5 Alakurtti Russian Fed
93E3 Al Amārah Iraq
21A2 Alameda USA
23B1 Alamo Mexico
9C3 Alamogordo USA
9C3 Alamosa USA
39H6 Åland I Fin
92B2 Alanya Turk
17B1 Alapaha R USA
65H4 Alapayevsk Russian Fed
92A2 Alasehir Turk
68C3 Ala Shan Mts China
4C3 Alaska State, USA
4C4 Alaska,G of USA
12C3 Alaska Pen USA
4C3 Alaska Range Mts USA
52A2 Alassio Italy
12D1 Alatna R USA
61G3 Alatyr' Russian Fed
108B2 Alawoona Aust
91C5 Al'Ayn UAE
82B2 Alayskiy Khrebet Mts Tajikistan
49D3 Alba Italy
92C2 Al Bāb Syria
51B2 Albacete Spain
50A1 Alba de Tormes Spain
93D2 Al Badī Iraq
54B1 Alba Iulia Rom
54A2 Albania Republic, Europe
106A4 Albany Aust
17B1 Albany Georgia, USA
15D2 Albany New York, USA
8A2 Albany Oregon, USA
7B4 Albany R Can
34B2 Albardón Arg
91C5 Al Batinah Region, Oman
71F5 Albatross B Aust
95B1 Al Baydā Libya
11C3 Albemarle Sd USA
50B1 Alberche R Spain
46B1 Albert France
5G4 Alberta Province, Can
99D2 Albert,L Uganda/Zaire
10A2 Albert Lea USA
99D2 Albert Nile R Uganda
49D2 Albertville France
48C3 Albi France
18B1 Albia USA
33G2 Albina Suriname
14B2 Albion Michigan, USA
15C2 Albion New York, USA
92C4 Al Bi'r S Arabia
91A5 Al Biyadh Region, S Arabia
50B2 Alborán I Spain
39G7 Ålborg Den
93D3 Al Bū Kamāl Syria
47C1 Albula R Switz
9C3 Albuquerque USA
91C5 Al Buraymi Oman
95A1 Al Burayqah Libya

95B1 Al Burdī Libya
107D4 Albury Aust
93E3 Al Buşayyah Iraq
50B1 Alcalá de Henares Spain
53B3 Alcamo Italy
51B1 Alcaniz Spain
31C2 Alcântara Brazil
50B2 Alcaraz Spain
50B2 Alcázar de San Juan Spain
51B2 Alcira Spain
35D1 Alcobaça Brazil
50B1 Alcolea de Pinar Spain
51B2 Alcoy Spain
51C2 Alcudia Spain
89J8 Aldabra Is Indian O
63E2 Aldan Russian Fed
63E2 Aldanskoye Nagor'ye Upland Russian Fed
43E3 Aldeburgh Eng
48B2 Alderney I UK
43D4 Aldershot Eng
97A3 Aleg Maur
30E4 Alegrete Brazil
34C2 Alejandro Roca Arg
30H6 Alejandro Selkirk I Chile
63G2 Aleksandrovsk Sakhalinskiy Russian Fed
65J4 Alekseyevka Kazakhstan
60E3 Aleksin Russian Fed
58B1 Ålem Sweden
35C2 Além Paraíba Brazil
49C2 Alençon France
21C4 Alenuihaha Chan Hawaiian Is
'Aleppo = Halab
6D1 Alert Can
49C3 Alès France
52A2 Alessandria Italy
38F6 Ålesund Nor
12C3 Aleutian Range Mts USA
4E4 Alexander Arch USA
100A3 Alexander Bay S Africa
17A1 Alexander City USA
112C3 Alexander I Ant
111A3 Alexandra NZ
29G8 Alexandra,C South Georgia
6C2 Alexandra Fjord Can
95B1 Alexandria Egypt
11A3 Alexandria Louisiana, USA
10A2 Alexandria Minnesota, USA
10C3 Alexandria Virginia, USA
55C2 Alexandroúpolis Greece
13C2 Alexis Creek Can
94B2 Aley Leb
65K4 Aleysk Russian Fed
93E3 Al Fallūjah Iraq
51B1 Alfaro Spain
54C2 Alfatar Bulg
93E3 Al Fāw Iraq
35B2 Alfenas Brazil
55B3 Alfiós R Greece
47D2 Alfonsine Italy
35C2 Alfonzo Cláudio Brazil
35C2 Alfredo Chaves Brazil
61J4 Alga Kazakhstan
34D2 Algarrobo del Aguila Arg
50A2 Algeciras Spain
96C1 Alger Alg
96A2 Algeria Republic, Africa
53A2 Alghero Sardegna
96C1 Algiers = Alger
15C1 Algonquin Park Can
91C5 Al Hadd Oman
93D3 Al Hadithah Iraq
92C3 Al Hadīthah S Arabia
93D2 Al Hadr Iraq

91C5 Al Hajar al Gharbī
 Mts Oman
91C5 Al Hajar ash Sharqī
 Mts Oman
93C3 Al Hamad Desert
 Region Jordan/
 S Arabia
93E4 Al Haniyah Desert
 Region Iraq
91A5 Al Hariq S Arabia
93C3 Al Harrah Desert
 Region S Arabia
95A2 Al Harūj al Aswad
 Upland Libya
91A4 Al Hasa Region,
 S Arabia
93D2 Al Hasakah Syria
93C4 Al Hawjā' S Arabia
93E3 Al Hayy Iraq
94C2 Al Hijanah Syria
93D3 Al Hillah Iraq
91A5 Al Hillah S Arabia
96B1 Al Hoceima Mor
91A4 Al Hufūf S Arabia
91B5 Al Humrah Region,
 UAE
91C5 Al Huwatsah Oman
90A2 Alīābad Iran
91C4 Alīābad Iran
55B2 Aliákmon R Greece
93E3 Alī al Gharbī Iraq
87A1 Alībāg India
51B2 Alicante Spain
9D4 Alice USA
106C3 Alice Springs Aust
53B3 Alicudi I Italy
84D3 Aligarh India
90A3 Alīgūdarz Iran
84B2 Ali-Khel Afghan
55C3 Alimniá I Greece
14B2 Alipur Duār India
22B2 Alisal USA
93C3 Al' Īsawīyah S Arabia
100B4 Aliwal North S Africa
95B2 Al Jaghbūb Libya
93D3 Al Jalamīd S Arabia
95B2 Al Jawf Libya
93C4 Al Jawf S Arabia
93D2 Al Jazirah Desert
 Region Syria/Iraq
50A2 Aljezur Port
91A4 Al Jubayl S Arabia
91C5 Al Kāmil Oman
93D2 Al Khābir R Syria
91C5 Al Khāburah Oman
93D3 Al Khalis Iraq
91C4 Al Khasab Oman
91B4 Al Khawr Qatar
95A1 Al Khums Region,
 S Arabia
94C2 Al Kiswah Syria
56A2 Alkmaar Neth
95A2 Al Kufrah Oasis Libya
93E3 Al Kūt Iraq
92C2 Al Lādhiqīyah Syria
86A1 Allahābād India
94C2 Al Lajāh Mt Syria
12D1 Allakaket USA
76B2 Allanmyo Burma
95C2 'Allaqi Watercourse
 Egypt
17B1 Allatoona L USA
15C2 Allegheny R USA
10C3 Allegheny Mts USA
17B1 Allendale USA
111A3 Allen,Mt NZ
15C2 Allentown USA
87B3 Alleppey India
49C2 Aller R France
47D1 Allgäu Mts Germany
81C3 Al Lith S Arabia
91B5 Al Liwā Region, UAE
109D1 Allora Aust
14B2 Alma Michigan, USA
82B1 Alma Ata Kazakhstan
50A2 Almada Port
 Al Madinah = Medina
71F2 Almagan I Pacific O
91B4 Al Manāmah Bahrain
93D3 Al Ma'niyah Iraq
21A1 Almanor,L USA

51B2 Almansa Spain
13B1 Alma Peak Mt Can
91B5 Al Māriyyah UAE
95B1 Al Marj Libya
 Almaty = Alma Ata
93D2 Al Mawsil Iraq
50B1 Almazán Spain
35C1 Almenara Brazil
50B2 Almería Spain
61I3 Al'met'yevsk
 Russian Fed
56C1 Älmhult Sweden
93E3 Al Miqdādīyah Iraq
112C3 Almirante Brown
 Base Ant
34A1 Almirante Latorre
 Chile
55B3 Almirós Greece
91A4 Al Mish'āb S Arabia
50A2 Almodóvar Port
84D3 Almora India
91A4 Al Mubarraz S Arabia
92C4 Al Mudawwara
 Jordan
91C5 Al Mudaybi Oman
91B4 Al Muharraq Bahrain
81C4 Al Mukallā Yemen
81C4 Al Mukhā Yemen
93D3 Al Musayyib Iraq
44B3 Alness Scot
93E3 Al Nu'mānīyah Iraq
42D2 Alnwick Eng
71D4 Alor I Indon
77C4 Alor Setar Malay
 Alost = Aalst
107E2 Alotau PNG
106B3 Aloysius,Mt Aust
34C3 Alpachiri Arg
14B1 Alpena USA
47B2 Alpes du Valais Mts
 Switz
52B1 Alpi Dolomitiche Mts
 Italy
47B2 Alpi Graie Mts Italy
9C3 Alpine Texas, USA
47C1 Alpi Orobie Mts Italy
47B2 Alpi Pennine Mts
 Italy
47C1 Alpi Retiche Mts
 Switz
47D1 Alpi Venoste Mts
 Italy
52A1 Alps Mts Europe
95A1 Al Qaddāhīyah Libya
94C1 Al Qadmūs Syria
93D3 Al Qa'im Iraq
93C4 Al Qalibah S Arabia
93D2 Al Qāmishlī Syria
93D3 Al Qaryah Ash
 Sharqīyah Libya
92C3 Al Qaryatayn Syria
91A4 Al Qatīf S Arabia
95A2 Al Qatrūn Libya
91A4 Al Qaysāmah
 S Arabia
94C2 Al Qutayfah Syria
50A2 Alquera R Port
92C3 Al Qunaytirah Syria
81C4 Al Qunfidhah
 S Arabia
93D3 Al Qurnah Iraq
94C1 Al Quşayr Syria
92C3 Al Qutayfah Syria
56B1 Als I Den
49D2 Alsace Region,
 France
57B2 Alsfeld Germany
42C2 Alston Eng
38J5 Alta Nor
29D2 Alta Gracia Arg
27D5 Altagracia de Orituco
 Ven
68A2 Altai Mts Mongolia
17B1 Altamaha R USA
33G4 Altamira Brazil
23B1 Altamira Mexico
53C2 Altamura Italy
68C1 Altanbulag Mongolia
71F4 Altape PNG
24B2 Altata Mexico
63B3 Altay China
63B3 Altay Mongolie
63A2 Altay Mts
 Russian Fed

47C1 Altdorf Switz
46D1 Altenkirchen
 Germany
34B3 Altiplanicie del Payún
 Plat Arg
47B1 Altkirch France
101C2 Alto Molócue Mozam
10A3 Alton USA
15C2 Altoona USA
34B2 Alto Pencoso Mts
 Arg
35A1 Alto Sucuriú Brazil
23B2 Altotonga Mexico
23A2 Altoyac de Alvarez
 Mexico
82C2 Altun Shan Mts
 China
20B2 Alturas USA
9D3 Altus USA
91B5 Al'Ubaylah S Arabia
93C4 Al Urayq Desert
 Region S Arabia
91B5 Al'Uruq al Mu'taridah
 Region, S Arabia
23B2 Alva USA
23B2 Alvarado Mexico
19A3 Alvarado USA
19A4 Alvdalen Sweden
19A4 Alvin USA
38J5 Alvsbyn Sweden
80B3 Al Wajh S Arabia
85D3 Alwar India
93D3 Al Widyān Desert
 Region Iraq/S Arabia
72A2 Alxa Yougi China
93E2 Alyat Azerbaijan
39J8 Alytus Lithuania
46E2 Alzey Germany
23B2 Amacuzac R Mexico
99D2 Amadi Sudan
90D3 Amadiyah Iraq
6C3 Amadjuak L Can
74B4 Amakusa-shotō I
 Japan
39G7 Amål Sweden
63D2 Amalat R
 Russian Fed
55B3 Amaliás Greece
85D4 Amalner India
69E4 Amami I Japan
69E4 Amami gunto Arch
 Japan
100C4 Amanzimtoti
 S Africa
33G3 Amapá Brazil
33G3 Amapá State, Brazil
9C3 Amarillo USA
60E5 Amasya Turk
23A1 Amatitan Mexico
 Amazonas =
 Solimões
32D4 Amazonas State,
 Brazil
28C3 Amazonas R Brazil
84D2 Ambala India
87C3 Ambalangoda
 Sri Lanka
101D2 Ambalavao Madag
98B2 Ambam Cam
101D2 Ambanja Madag
1C7 Ambarchik
 Russian Fed
32B4 Ambato Ecuador
101D2 Ambato-Boeny
 Madag
101D2 Ambatolampy
 Madag
101D2 Ambatondrazaka
 Madag
57C3 Amberg Germany
25D3 Ambergris Cay I
 Belize
86A2 Ambikāpur India
101D2 Ambilobe Madag
101D3 Amboasary Madag
101D2 Ambodifototra
 Madag
101D3 Ambohimahasoa
 Madag
71D4 Ambon Indon
101D3 Ambositra Madag
101D3 Ambovombe Madag
98B3 Ambriz Angola
98C1 Am Dam Chad

64H3 Amderma
 Russian Fed
24B2 Ameca Mexico
23B2 Amecacameca
 Mexico
34C2 Ameghino Arg
56B2 Ameland I Neth
16C2 Amenia USA
112B10 American Highland
 Upland Ant
105H4 American Samoa Is
 Pacific O
17B1 Americus USA
101G1 Amersfoort Neth
112C10 Amery Ice Shelf Ant
55B3 Amfilokhía Greece
55B3 Amfissa Greece
63F1 Amga Russian Fed
63F1 Amga R
 Russian Fed
69F2 Amgu Russian Fed
69F1 Amgun' R
 Russian Fed
99D1 Amhara Region Eth
7D5 Amherst Can
16C1 Amherst
 Massachusetts, USA
 Amherst = Kyaikkami
78B2 Amherst India
48C2 Amiens France
75B1 Amino Japan
101D2 Amizmiz Leb
89K8 Amirante Is Indian O
86B1 Amlekhgan Nepal
92C3 Amman Jordan
38K6 Ämmänsaario Fin
56B2 Ammersfoort Neth
90B2 Amol Iran
55C3 Amorgós I Greece
7C5 Amos Can
 Amoy = Xiamen
101D3 Ampanihy Madag
35B2 Amparo Brazil
51C1 Amposta Spain
85C4 Amrāvati India
85C4 Amreli India
84C2 Amritsar India
56A2 Amsterdam Neth
*101H1 Amsterdam S Africa
15D2 Amsterdam USA
98C1 Am Timan Chad
88L3 Amu Darya R
 Uzbekistan
6A2 Amund Ringes I Can
47C2 Amundsen G Can
112B4 Amundsen S Ant
80E Amundsen-Scott
 Base Ant
78D3 Amuntai Indon
63E2 Amur R Russian Fed
33E2 Anaco Ven
8B2 Anaconda USA
20B1 Anacortes USA
55C3 Anáfi I Greece
93D3 'Anah Iraq
21B3 Anaheim USA
87B2 Anaimalai Hills India
12E1 Anakhuak P USA
101D2 Analalava Madag
92B2 Anamur Turk
75A2 Anan Japan
87B2 Anantapur India
84D2 Anantnag India
31B5 Anápolis Brazil
90C3 Anär Iran
90B3 Anärak Iran
71F2 Anatahan I Pacific O
30D4 Añatuya Arg
74B3 Anbyón N Korea
22C4 Ancapa Is USA
4D3 Anchorage USA
30C2 Ancohuma Mt Bol
32B6 Ancon Peru
52B2 Ancona Italy
16C1 Ancram USA
29B4 Ancud Chile
34A3 Andacollo Arg
108A1 Andado Aust
32C6 Andahuaylas Arg
38F6 Andalsnes Nor
50A2 Andalucia Region,
 Spain
17A1 Andalusia USA

83D4 **Andaman Is** Burma
83D4 **Andaman S** Burma
108A2 **Andamooka** Aust
38H5 **Andenes** Nor
47C1 **Andermatt** Switz
57B2 **Andernach** Germany
14A2 **Anderson** Indiana, USA
18B2 **Anderson** Missouri, USA
17B1 **Anderson** S Carolina, USA
4F3 **Anderson** R Can
87B1 **Andhra Pradesh** State, India
55B3 **Andikíthira** I Greece
65J5 **Andizhan** Uzbekistan
65H6 **Andkhui** Afghan
74B3 **Andong** S Korea
51C1 **Andorra** Principality, SW Europe
51C1 **Andorra-La-Vella** Andorra
43D4 **Andover** Eng
35A2 **Andradina** Brazil
12B2 **Andreafsky** USA
92B2 **Andreas,C** Cyprus
53C2 **Andria** Italy
11C4 **Andros** I The Bahamas
55B3 **Andros** I Greece
87A2 **Androth** I India
50B2 **Andújar** Spain
100A2 **Andulo** Angola
97C4 **Anécho** Togo
97C3 **Anéfis** Mali
34B3 **Añelo** Arg
63C2 **Angarsk** Russian Fed
38H6 **Ange** Sweden
24A2 **Angel de la Guarda** I Mexico
79B2 **Angeles** Phil
39G7 **Angelholm** Sweden
109C1 **Angellala Creek** R Aust
22B1 **Angels Camp** USA
71E4 **Angemuk** Mt Indon
48B2 **Angers** France
76C3 **Angkor** Hist Site Camb
41C3 **Anglesey** I Wales
19A4 **Angleton** USA
6G3 **Angmagssalik** Greenland
101D2 **Angoche** Mozam
29B3 **Angol** Chile
14B2 **Angola** Indiana, USA
100A2 **Angola** Republic, Africa
103H6 **Angola Basin** Atlantic O
12H3 **Angoon** USA
48C2 **Angoulême** France
96A1 **Angra do Heroismo** Açores
35A2 **Angra dos Reis** Brazil
34C3 **Anguil** Arg
27E3 **Anguilla** I Caribbean S
26B2 **Anguilla Cays** Is Caribbean S
86B2 **Angul** India
99C3 **Angumu** Zaire
56C1 **Anholt** I Den
73C4 **Anhua** China
72D3 **Anhui** Province, China
12C2 **Aniak** USA
35B1 **Anicuns** Brazil
46B2 **Anizy-le-Château** France
4C3 **Anjak** USA
48B2 **Anjou** Region, France
101D2 **Anjouan** I Comoros
101D2 **Anjozorobe** Madag
74B3 **Anju** N Korea
72B3 **Ankang** China
92B2 **Ankara** Turk
101D2 **Ankaratra** Mt Madag
101D3 **Ankazoabo** Madag
101D2 **Ankazobe** Madag
56C2 **Anklam** Germany
76D3 **An Loc** Viet

73B4 **Anlong** China
73C3 **Anlu** China
18C2 **Anna** USA
96C1 **'Annaba** Alg
92C3 **An Nabk** S Arabia
92C3 **An Nabk** Syria
108A1 **Anna Creek** Aust
80C3 **An Nafūd** Desert S Arabia
93D3 **An Najaf** Iraq
42C2 **Annan** Scot
15C3 **Annapolis** USA
86A1 **Annapurna** Mt Nepal
14B2 **Ann Arbor** USA
94C1 **An Nāsirah** Syria
93E3 **An Nāsirīyah** Iraq
47B2 **Annecy** France
47B1 **Annemasse** France
76D3 **An Nhon** Viet
73A5 **Anning** China
17A1 **Anniston** USA
89E8 **Annobón** I Eq Guinea
49C2 **Annonay** France
27J1 **Annotto Bay** Jamaica
73D3 **Anqing** China
72B2 **Ansai** China
57C3 **Ansbach** Germany
26C3 **Anse d'Hainault** Haiti
72E1 **Anshan** China
73B4 **Anshun** China
97C3 **Ansongo** Mali
14B3 **Ansted** USA
92C2 **Antakya** Turk
101E2 **Antalaha** Madag
92B2 **Antalya** Turk
92B2 **Antalya Körfezi** B Turk
101D2 **Antananarivo** Madag
112C1 **Antarctic Circle** Ant
112C3 **Antarctic Pen** Ant
50B2 **Antequera** Spain
96B2 **Anti-Atlas** Mts Mor
7D5 **Anticosti, Î. d'** Can
27E3 **Antigua** I Caribbean S
21A2 **Antioch** USA
19A3 **Antlers** USA
30B3 **Antofagasta** Chile
45C1 **Antrim** County, N Ire
45C1 **Antrim** N Ire
45C1 **Antrim Hills** N Ire
101D2 **Antseranana** Madag
30F2 **Antsirabe** Madag
101D2 **Antsohiny** Madag
76D3 **An Tuc** Viet
46C1 **Antwerpen** Belg
45C2 **An Uaimh** Irish Rep
84C3 **Anupgarh** India
87C3 **Anuradhapura** Sri Lanka
Anvers = Antwerpen
4B3 **Anvik** USA
63B3 **Anxi** China
72C2 **Anyang** China
72A3 **A'nyêmaqên Shan** Upland China
47C2 **Anza** R Italy
13E1 **Anzac** Can
65K4 **Anzhero-Sudzhensk** Russian Fed
53B2 **Anzio** Italy
74E2 **Aomori** Japan
52A1 **Aosta** Italy
97B3 **Aoukar** Region Maur
96C2 **Aoulef** Alg
95A2 **Aozou** Chad
30E3 **Apa** R Brazil/Par
31B4 **Apalachee B** USA
17B2 **Apalachicola** USA
17A2 **Apalachicola B** USA
23B2 **Apan** Mexico
64E3 **Aparity** Russian Fed
32C3 **Apaporis** R Colombia
35A2 **Aparecida do Taboado** Brazil
79B2 **Aparri** Phil
54A1 **Apatin** Croatia

64E3 **Apatity** Russian Fed
24B3 **Apatzingan** Mexico
56B2 **Apeldoorn** Neth
35B2 **Apiaí** Brazil
33F2 **Apoera** Surinam
108B3 **Apollo Bay** Aust
79C4 **Apo,Mt** Mt Phil
17B2 **Apopka,L** USA
30F2 **Apore** R Brazil
10A2 **Apostle Is** USA
10A2 **Apostle L** USA
23A1 **Apozol** Mexico
11B3 **Appalachian Mts** USA
52B2 **Appennino Abruzzese** Mts Italy
52A2 **Appennino Ligure** Mts Italy
53C2 **Appennino Lucano** Mts Italy
52B2 **Appennino Napoletano** Mts Italy
52B2 **Appennino Tosco-Emiliano** Mts Italy
52B2 **Appennino Umbro-Marchigiano** Mts Italy
47C1 **Appenzell** Switz
42C2 **Appleby** Eng
14A2 **Appleton** Wisconsin, USA
30F3 **Apucarana** Brazil
23B1 **Apulco** Mexico
32C6 **Apure** R Ven
32C6 **Apurímac** R Peru
92B4 **'Aqaba** Jordan
92B4 **'Aqaba,G of** Egypt/S Arabia
90B3 **'Aqdā** Iran
30E3 **Aquidauana** Brazil
23A2 **Aquila** Mexico
86A1 **Ara** India
17A1 **Arab** USA
81D4 **Arabian S** Asia/Arabian Pen
31D4 **Aracaju** Brazil
30E3 **Aracanguy, Mts de** Par
31D2 **Aracati** Brazil
30F3 **Araçatuba** Brazil
50A2 **Aracena** Spain
31C5 **Aracuai** Brazil
94B3 **Arad** Israel
60B4 **Arad** Rom
98C1 **Arada** Chad
91B5 **'Arādah** UAE
106C1 **Arafura S** Indon/Aust
30F2 **Aragarças** Brazil
51B1 **Aragón** Region, Spain
50B1 **Aragón** R Spain
33G6 **Araguaia** R Brazil
31B3 **Araguaína** Brazil
31B5 **Araguari** Brazil
35B1 **Araguari** R Brazil
75B1 **Arai** Japan
96C2 **Arak** Alg
90A3 **Aräk** Iran
76A2 **Arakan Yoma** Mts Burma
87B2 **Arakkonam** India
65G5 **Aral Sea** Kazakhstan/Uzbekistan
Aral'sk Kazakhstan
Aral'skoye More = Aral S
40B2 **Aran** I Irish Rep
50B1 **Aranda de Duero** Spain
23A1 **Arandas** Mexico
50B1 **Aranjuez** Spain
75A2 **Arao** Japan
97B3 **Araouane** Mali
29E2 **Arapey** R Urug
31D4 **Arapiraca** Brazil
35A2 **Araporgas** Brazil
30G4 **Araranguá** Brazil
31B6 **Araraquara** Brazil
35B2 **Araras** Brazil
107D4 **Ararat** Aust
93D2 **Ararat** Armenia
93E2 **Aras** R Azerbaijan
75C1 **Arato** Japan
32D2 **Arauca** R Ven

34A3 **Arauco** Chile
32C2 **Arauea** Colombia
85C4 **Arávalli Range** Mts India
31B5 **Araxá** Brazil
99D2 **Arba Minch** Eth
53A3 **Arbatax** Sardegna
93D2 **Arbil** Iraq
47A1 **Arbois** France
39H6 **Arbrå** Sweden
44C3 **Arbroath** Scot
47A1 **Arc** France
47B2 **Arc** R France
48B3 **Arcachon** France
17B2 **Arcadia** USA
20B2 **Arcata** USA
23A2 **Arcelia** Mexico
26B2 **Archipiélago de Camaguey** Arch Cuba
29B6 **Archipiélago de la Reina Adelaida** Arch Chile
29B4 **Archipiélago de las Chones** Arch Chile
32B2 **Archipiélago de las Perlas** Arch Panama
35B2 **Arcos** Brazil
50A2 **Arcos de la Frontera** Spain
6B2 **Arctic Bay** Can
1C1 **Arctic Circle**
4E3 **Arctic Red** Can
4E3 **Arctic Red** R Can
4D3 **Arctic Village** USA
54C2 **Arda** R Bulg
93D1 **Ardabil** Iran
93D1 **Ardahan** Turk
39F6 **Ardal** Nor
96C2 **Ardar des Iforas** Upland Alg/Mali
45C2 **Ardee** Irish Rep
90B3 **Ardekan** Iran
46C2 **Ardennes** Department, France
57A2 **Ardennes** Region, Belg
93D2 **Ardestan** Iran
92C3 **Ardh es Suwwan** Desert Region Jordan
50A2 **Ardila** R Port
109C2 **Ardlethan** Aust
9D3 **Ardmore** USA
44A3 **Ardnamurchan** Pt Scot
46A1 **Ardres** France
44B3 **Ardrishaig** Scot
42B2 **Ardrossan** Scot
27D3 **Arecibo** Puerto Rico
31D2 **Areia Branca** Brazil
21A2 **Arena,Pt** USA
39F7 **Arendal** Nor
30B2 **Arequipa** Peru
52B2 **Arezzo** Italy
52B2 **Argenta** Italy
49C2 **Argentan** France
46B2 **Argenteuil** France
28C1 **Argentina** Republic, S America
103F7 **Argentine Basin** Atlantic O
48C2 **Argenton-sur-Creuse** France
54C2 **Arges** R Rom
84B2 **Arghardab** R Afghan
55B3 **Argolikós Kólpos** G Greece
46C2 **Argonne** Region, France
55B3 **Argos** Greece
55B3 **Argostólion** Greece
22B3 **Arguello,Pt** USA
68B2 **Argun'** R Russian Fed
97C3 **Argungu** Nig
22C3 **Argus Ra** USA
100A3 **Ariamsvlei** Namibia
50B1 **Aran zón** R Spain
34C2 **Arias** Arg
97B3 **Aribinda** Burkina
30B2 **Arica** Chile
84C2 **Arifwala** Pak
Arîhâ = Jericho
27L1 **Arima** Trinidad
35B1 **Arinos** Brazil

33F6	**Arinos** *R* Brazil
23A2	**Ario de Rosales** Mexico
27L1	**Aripo,Mt** Trinidad
33E5	**Aripuana** Brazil
33E5	**Aripuaná** *R* Brazil
44B3	**Arisaig** Scot
87B2	**Ariskere** India
13B2	**Aristazabal I** Can
34B3	**Arizona** Arg
9B3	**Arizona** State, USA
39G7	**Arjäng** Sweden
61F3	**Arkadak** Russian Fed
19B3	**Arkadelphia** USA
65H4	**Arkaly** Kazakhstan
11A3	**Arkansas** State, USA
11A3	**Arkansas** *R* USA
18A2	**Arkansas City** USA
64F3	**Arkhangel'sk** Russian Fed
41B3	**Arklow** Irish Rep
47D1	**Arlberg P** Austria
49C3	**Arles** France
19A3	**Arlington** Texas, USA
15C3	**Arlington** Virginia, USA
20B1	**Arlington** Washington, USA
97C3	**Arlit** Niger
57B3	**Arlon** Belg
	Armageddon = Megiddo
45C1	**Armagh** County, N Ire
45C1	**Armagh** N Ire
61F5	**Armavir** Russian Fed
23A2	**Armena** Mexico
32B3	**Armenia** Colombia
65F5	**Armenia** Republic, Europe
107E4	**Armidale** Aust
13D2	**Armstrong** Can
7C3	**Arnaud** *R* Can
92B2	**Arnauti C** Cyprus
56R2	**Arnhem** Neth
106C2	**Arnhem,C** Aust
106C2	**Arnhem Land** Aust
22B1	**Arnold** USA
15C1	**Arnprior** Can
46E1	**Arnsberg** Germany
100A3	**Aroab** Namibia
47C2	**Arona** Italy
12B2	**Aropuk L** USA
52A1	**Arosa** Switz
97A3	**Arquipélago dos Bijagós** *Arch* Guinea-Bissau
93D3	**Ar Ramâdî** Iraq
42B2	**Arran I** Scot
93C2	**Ar Raqqah** Syria
96A2	**Ar Râqûbah** Libya
49C1	**Arras** France
96A2	**Arrecife** Canary Is
34C2	**Arrecifes** Arg
23A1	**Arriaga** Mexico
93E3	**Ar Rifā'ī** Iraq
93E3	**Ar Riḥāb** *Desert Region* Iraq
91A5	**Ar Riyād** S Arabia
44B3	**Arrochar** Scot
111A2	**Arrowtown** NZ
23B1	**Arroyo Seco** Mexico
91B4	**Ar Ru'ays** Qatar
91C5	**Ar Rustaq** Oman
93D3	**Ar Rutbah** Iraq
47D2	**Arsiero** Italy
49D2	**Arsizio** Italy
61G2	**Arsk** Russian Fed
55B3	**Arta** Greece
23A2	**Arteaga** Mexico
63B2	**Artemovsk** Russian Fed
63D2	**Artemovskiy** Russian Fed
9C3	**Artesia** USA
111B2	**Arthurs P** NZ
112C2	**Artigas** *Base* Ant
29E2	**Artigas** Urug
4H3	**Artillery L** Can
49C2	**Artois** Region, France
112C2	**Arturo Prat** *Base* Ant
93D1	**Artvin** Turk
99D2	**Aru** Zaïre
33A4	**Aruanã** Brazil
27C4	**Aruba I** Caribbean S
86B1	**Arunāchal Pradesh** Union Territory, India
87B3	**Aruppukkottai** India
99D3	**Arusha** Tanz
98C2	**Aruwimi** *R* Zaïre
68C2	**Arvayheer** Mongolia
47B2	**Arve** *R* France
7C5	**Arvida** Can
38H5	**Arvidsjaur** Sweden
39G7	**Arvika** Sweden
21B2	**Arvin** USA
94B1	**Arwad I** Syria
61F2	**Arzamas** Russian Fed
84C2	**Asadabad** Afghan
75A2	**Asahi** *R* Japan
74E2	**Asahi dake** *Mt* Japan
74E2	**Asahikawa** Japan
86B2	**Asansol** India
95A2	**Asawanwah** *Well* Libya
61K2	**Asbest** Russian Fed
15D2	**Asbury Park** USA
103H5	**Ascension I** Atlantic O
99D2	**Aschaffenburg** Germany
56C2	**Aschersleben** Germany
52B2	**Ascoli Piceno** Italy
47C1	**Ascona** Switz
99E1	**Aseb** Eritrea
96C2	**Asedjirad** *Upland* Alg
99D2	**Asela** Eth
38H6	**Åsele** Sweden
54B2	**Asenovgrad** Bulg
46C2	**Asfeld** France
61J2	**Asha** Russian Fed
17B1	**Ashburn** USA
111B2	**Ashburton** NZ
106A3	**Ashburton** *R* Aust
92B3	**Ashdod** Israel
19B3	**Ashdown** USA
11B3	**Asheville** USA
109D1	**Ashford** USA
43E4	**Ashford** Eng
	Ashgabat = Ashkhabad
74D3	**Ashikaga** Japan
75A2	**Ashizuri-misaki** *Pt* Japan
65G6	**Ashkhabad** Turkmenistan
10B3	**Ashland** Kentucky, USA
18A1	**Ashland** Nebraska, USA
14B2	**Ashland** Ohio, USA
8A2	**Ashland** Oregon, USA
109C1	**Ashley** USA
16B2	**Ashokan Res** USA
94B3	**Ashqelon** Israel
93D3	**Ash Shabakh** Iraq
91C4	**Ash Sha'm** UAE
93E3	**Ash Shatrah** Iraq
81C4	**Ash Shihr** Yemen
91A4	**Ash Shumlul** S Arabia
14B2	**Ashtabula** USA
7D4	**Ashuanipi L** Can
92C3	**'Aşī** *R* Syria
53A2	**Asinara I** Medit S
65K4	**Asino** Russian Fed
93D2	**Aşkale** Turk
39G7	**Askersund** Sweden
84C1	**Asmar** Afghan
95C3	**Asmera** Eritrea
75A2	**Aso** Japan
99D1	**Asosa** Eth
111A2	**Aspiring,Mt** NZ
93C2	**As Sabkhah** Syria
91A5	**As Salamiyah** S Arabia
92C2	**As Salamiyah** Syria
93D3	**As Salmān** Iraq
86C1	**Assam** State, India
93E3	**As Samāwah** Iraq
91B5	**As Şanām** Region, S Arabia
94C2	**As Sanamayn** Syria
56B2	**Assen** Neth
56B1	**Assens** Den
95A1	**As Sidrah** Libya
5H5	**Assiniboia** Can
5G4	**Assiniboine,Mt** Can
30F3	**Assis** Brazil
93C3	**As Sukhnah** Syria
93E2	**As Sulaymānīyah** Iraq
91A5	**As Summan** Region, S Arabia
99E3	**Assumption I** Seychelles
92C3	**As Suwaydā'** Syria
93D3	**As Suwayrah** Iraq
93E2	**Astara** Azerbaijan
52B2	**Asti** Italy
55C3	**Astipálaia I** Greece
50A1	**Astorga** Spain
8A2	**Astoria** USA
61G4	**Astrakhan'** Russian Fed
50A1	**Asturias** Region, Spain
30E4	**Asunción** Par
99D2	**Aswa** *R* Uganda
80B3	**Aswân** Egypt
95C2	**Aswân High Dam** Egypt
95C2	**Asyût** Egypt
92C3	**As Zilaf** Syria
97C4	**Atakpamé** Togo
71D4	**Atambua** Indon
6E3	**Atangmik** Greenland
8A2	**Atar** Maur
65J5	**Atasu** Kazakhstan
95C3	**Atatisk Baraji** *Res* Turkmenistan
95C3	**Atbara** Sudan
65H4	**Atbasar** Kazakhstan
11A4	**Atchafalaya B** USA
10A3	**Atchison** USA
16B3	**Atco** USA
23A1	**Atenguillo** Mexico
52B2	**Atessa** Italy
46B1	**Ath** Belg
13E2	**Athabasca** Can
5G4	**Athabasca** *R* Can
5H4	**Athabasca L** Can
45B2	**Athenry** Irish Rep
	Athens = Athínai
11B3	**Athens** Georgia, USA
14B3	**Athens** Ohio, USA
19A3	**Athens** Texas, USA
55B3	**Athínai** Greece
41B3	**Athlone** Irish Rep
16C1	**Athol** USA
55B2	**Áthos** *Mt* Greece
45C2	**Athy** Irish Rep
98B1	**Ati** Chad
7A5	**Atikoken** Can
61F3	**Atkarsk** Russian Fed
18B2	**Atkins** USA
23B2	**Atlacomulco** Mexico
11B3	**Atlanta** Georgia, USA
14B2	**Atlanta** Michigan, USA
18A1	**Atlantic** USA
10C3	**Atlantic City** USA
16B2	**Atlantic Highlands** USA
103H8	**Atlantic Indian Basin** Atlantic O
103H7	**Atlantic Indian Ridge** Atlantic O
96C1	**Atlas Saharien** *Mts* Alg
4E4	**Atlin** Can
4E4	**Atlin L** Can
94B2	**'Atlit** Israel
23B2	**Atlixco** Mexico
11B3	**Atmore** USA
101D3	**Atofinandrahana** Madag
12D3	**Atognak I** USA
19A3	**Atoka** USA
23A1	**Atotonilco** Mexico
23B2	**Atoyac** *R* Mexico
32B2	**Atrato** *R* Colombia
91B5	**Attaf** Region, UAE
81C3	**At Ţā'if** S Arabia
94C2	**At Tall** Syria
17A1	**Attalla** USA
7B4	**Attauapiskat** Can
7B4	**Attauapiskat** *R* Can
93D3	**At Taysiyah** *Desert Region* S Arabia
14A2	**Attica** Indiana, USA
46C2	**Attigny** France
15D2	**Attleboro** Massachusetts, USA
76D3	**Attopeu** Laos
92C4	**At Tubayq** *Upland* S Arabia
34B3	**Atuel** *R* Arg
39H7	**Åtvidaberg** Sweden
22B2	**Atwater** USA
49D3	**Aubagne** France
46C2	**Aube** Department, France
49C3	**Aubenas** France
17A1	**Auburn** Alabama, USA
14A2	**Auburn** Indiana, USA
18A1	**Auburn** Nebraska, USA
22B2	**Auburn** California, USA
15C2	**Auburn** New York, USA
20B1	**Auburn** Washington, USA
48C3	**Auch** France
110B1	**Auckland** NZ
105G6	**Auckland Is** NZ
48C3	**Aude** *R* France
7B4	**Auden** Can
47B1	**Audincourt** France
109C1	**Augathella** Aust
57C3	**Augsburg** Germany
106A4	**Augusta** Aust
11B3	**Augusta** Georgia, USA
18A2	**Augusta** Kansas, USA
11B3	**Augusta** Maine, USA
12D3	**Augustine I** USA
58C2	**Augustów** Pol
106A3	**Augustus,Mt** Aust
46A2	**Aumale** France
85D5	**Aurangabad** India
46B2	**Auray** France
48C3	**Aurillac** France
8C3	**Aurora** Colorado, USA
10B2	**Aurora** Illinois, USA
14B3	**Aurora** Indiana, USA
18B2	**Aurora** Mississippi, USA
100A3	**Aus** Namibia
14B2	**Au Sable** USA
10A2	**Austin** Minnesota, USA
21B2	**Austin** Nevada, USA
9D3	**Austin** Texas, USA
106C3	**Australia** Fed. State/ Monarchy
107D4	**Australian Alps** *Mts* Aust
37E4	**Austria** Federal Republic, Europe
46A1	**Authie** *R* France
24B3	**Autlán** Mexico
49C2	**Autun** France
49C2	**Auvergne** Region, France
49C2	**Auxerre** France
46B1	**Auxi-le-Châteaux** France
49C2	**Avallon** France
22C4	**Avalon** USA
7E5	**Avalon Pen** Can
35B2	**Avaré** Brazil
90D3	**Avaz** Iran
33F4	**Aveiro** Brazil
50A1	**Aveiro** Port
27B3	**Avellaneda** Arg
53B2	**Avellino** Italy
46B1	**Avesnes-sur-Helpe** France

39H6 **Avesta** Sweden
52B2 **Avezzano** Italy
44C3 **Aviemore** Scot
111B2 **Aviemore,L** NZ
47B2 **Avigliana** Italy
49C3 **Avignon** France
50B1 **Avila** Spain
50A1 **Avilés** Spain
47D1 **Avisio** R Italy
108B3 **Avoca** R Aust
43C4 **Avon** County, Eng
43D4 **Avon** R Dorset, Eng
43D3 **Avon** R Warwick, Eng
43C4 **Avonmouth** Wales
17B2 **Avon Park** USA
46B2 **Avre** R France
54A2 **Avtovac** Bosnia-Herzegovina
94C2 **A'waj** R Syria
74D4 **Awaji-shima** B Japan
99E2 **Awarē** Eth
111A2 **Awarua Pt** NZ
99E2 **Awash** Eth
99E2 **Awash** R Eth
75B1 **Awa-shima** I Japan
111B2 **Awatere** R NZ
95A2 **Awbārī** Libya
98C2 **Aweil** Sudan
95B2 **Awjilah** Libya
96A2 **Awserd** Well Mor
6A2 **Axel Heiburg I** Can
43C4 **Axminster** Eng
75B1 **Ayabe** Japan
29E3 **Ayacucho** Arg
32C6 **Ayacucho** Peru
65K5 **Ayaguz** Kazakhstan
82C2 **Ayakkum Hu** L China
50A2 **Ayamonte** Spain
63F2 **Ayan** Russian Fed
92A2 **Ayaviri** Peru
55C3 **Áyios Evstrátios** I Greece
43D4 **Aylesbury** Eng
13D2 **Aylmer,Mt** Can
94C2 **'Ayn al Fijah** Syria
93D2 **Ayn Zālah** Iraq
95B2 **Ayn Zuwayyah** Well Libya
99D2 **Ayod** Sudan
107D2 **Ayr** Aust
42B2 **Ayr** Scot
42B2 **Ayr** R Scot
42B2 **Ayre,Pt of** Eng
54C2 **Aytos** Bulg
76C3 **Aytthaya** Thai
23A1 **Ayutla** Mexico
55C3 **Ayvacik** Turk
55C3 **Ayvalik** Turk
86A1 **Azamgarh** India
97B3 **Azaouad** Desert Region Mali
97D3 **Azare** Nig
92C2 **A'Zāz** Syria
Azbine = Aïr
65F5 **Azerbaijan** Republic, Russian Fed
32B4 **Azogues** Ecuador
Azores = Açores
98C1 **Azoum** R Chad
60E4 **Azov, Sea of** Russian Fed/Ukraine
Azovskoye More = Azov, Sea of
96B1 **Azrou** Mor
34D3 **Azucena** Arg
32A2 **Azuero,Pen de** Panama
29E3 **Azúl** Arg
94C2 **Az-Zabdani** Syria
91C5 **Az Zāhirah** Mts Oman
95A2 **Az Zahra** Iraq
96A2 **Azzeffal** R Maur
93E3 **Az Zubayr** Iraq

B

94B2 **Ba'abda** Leb
92C3 **Ba'albek** Leb
94B3 **Ba'al Hazor** Mt Israel
99E2 **Baardheere** Somalia
54C2 **Babadag** Rom
92A1 **Babaeski** Turk
32B4 **Babahoyo** Ecuador
81C4 **Bab al Mandab** Str Djibouti/Yemen
71D4 **Babar** I Indon
99D3 **Babati** Tanz
60E2 **Babayevo** Russian Fed
14B2 **Baberton** USA
13B1 **Babine** R Can
5F4 **Babine L** Can
90B2 **Bābol** Iran
79B2 **Babuyan** Is Phil
79B2 **Babuyan Is** Phil
31C2 **Bacabal** Brazil
71D4 **Bacan** I Indon
60C4 **Bačau** Rom
71C4 **Bac Can** Viet
108B3 **Bacchus Marsh** Aust
82B2 **Bachu** China
4J3 **Back** R Can
12J2 **Backbone Ranges** Mts Can
76D1 **Bac Ninh** Viet
79B3 **Bacolod** Phil
79B3 **Baco,Mt** Phil
87B2 **Badagara** India
72A1 **Badain Jaran Shamo** Desert China
50A2 **Badajoz** Spain
51C1 **Badalona** Spain
93D3 **Badanah** S Arabia
46D2 **Bad Bergzabern** Germany
46D1 **Bad Ems** Germany
47C1 **Baden** Switz
57B3 **Baden-Baden** Germany
57B3 **Baden-Württemberg** State, Germany
57C3 **Badgastein** Austria
22C2 **Badger** USA
57B2 **Bad-Godesberg** Germany
57B2 **Bad Hersfeld** Germany
46D1 **Bad Honnef** Germany
85B4 **Badin** Pak
52B1 **Bad Ischl** Austria
93C3 **Badiyat ash Sham** Desert Region Jordan/Iraq
57B3 **Bad-Kreuznach** Germany
46D1 **Bad Nevenahr-Ahrweiler** Germany
47C1 **Bad Ragaz** Switz
57C3 **Bad Tolz** Germany
87C3 **Badulla** Sri Lanka
50B2 **Baena** Spain
97A3 **Bafatá** Guinea-Bissau
4H2 **Baffin** Region Can
6C2 **Baffin B** Greenland/Can
6C2 **Baffin I** Can
98B2 **Bafia** Cam
97A3 **Bafing** R Mali
97A3 **Bafoulabé** Mali
98B2 **Bafoussam** Cam
90C3 **Bāfq** Iran
60E5 **Bafra Burun** Pt Turk
91C4 **Bāft** Iran
98C2 **Bafwasende** Zaïre
86A1 **Bagaha** India
87B1 **Bāgalkot** India
99D3 **Bagamoyo** Tanz
29F2 **Bagé** Brazil
93D3 **Baghdād** Iraq
86B2 **Bagherhat** Bang
91C3 **Bāghin** Iran
84B1 **Baghlan** Afghan
49C3 **Bagnols-sur-Cèze** France
97B3 **Bagoé** R Mali
79B2 **Baguio** Phil
86B1 **Bāhādurābād** India
11C4 **Bahamas,The** Is Caribbean S
86B2 **Baharampur** India
92A4 **Bahariya Oasis** Egypt
84C3 **Bahawalpur** Pak
84C3 **Bahawalpur** Province, Pak
85C3 **Bahawalnagar** Pak
Bahia = Salvador
31C4 **Bahia** State, Brazil
29D3 **Bahía Blanca** Arg
29D3 **Bahía Blanca** B Arg
34A3 **Bahía Concepción** B Chile
35C2 **Bahía da Ilha Grande** B Brazil
24B2 **Bahía de Banderas** B Mexico
24C2 **Bahía de Campeche** B Mexico
25D3 **Bahía de la Ascension** B Mexico
24B3 **Bahía de Petacalco** B Mexico
96A2 **Bahía de Rio de Oro** B Mor
35C2 **Bahía de Sepetiba** B Brazil
29C6 **Bahía Grande** B Arg
9B4 **Bahía Kino** Mexico
24A2 **Bahía Magdalena** B Mexico
24A2 **Bahía Sebastia Vizcaíno** B Mexico
86A1 **Bahraich** India
80D3 **Bahrain** Sheikdom, Arabian Pen
93D3 **Bahr al Milh** L Iraq
98C2 **Bahr Aouk** R Chad/CAR
Bahrat Lut = Dead S
98C2 **Bahr al Arab** Watercourse Sudan
99D2 **Bahr el Ghazal** R Sudan
98B1 **Bahr el Ghazal** Watercourse Chad
101H1 **Baía de Maputo** B Mozam
31B2 **Baia de Marajó** B Brazil
101D2 **Baía de Pemba** B Mozam
31C2 **Baia de São Marcos** B Brazil
50A2 **Baia de Setúbal** B Port
31D4 **Baía de Todos os Santos** B Brazil
100A2 **Baia dos Tigres** Angola
60B4 **Baia Mare** Rom
98B2 **Baïboukoum** Chad
69E2 **Baicheng** China
101E2 **Baie Antongila** B Madag
7D5 **Baie-Comeau** Can
72B3 **Baihe** China
72C3 **Bai He** R China
93D3 **Ba'iji** Iraq
86A2 **Baikunthpur** India
Baile Atha Cliath = Dublin
86A2 **Bāïlesti** Rom
46B1 **Bailleul** France
72A3 **Baima** China
17B1 **Bainbridge** USA
12B2 **Baird Inlet** USA
4B3 **Baird Mts** USA
72D1 **Bairin Youqi** China
72D1 **Bairin Zuoqi** China
107D4 **Bairnsdale** Aust
79B4 **Bais** Phil
54A1 **Baja** Hung
9B3 **Baja California** State, Mexico
24A1 **Baja California** Pen Mexico
61J2 **Bakal** Russian Fed
98C2 **Bakala** CAR
97A3 **Bakel** Sen
8C2 **Baker** Montana, USA
8B2 **Baker** Oregon, USA
6A3 **Baker Foreland** Pt Can
4J3 **Baker L** Can
4J3 **Baker Lake** Can
8A2 **Baker,Mt** USA
9B3 **Bakersfield** USA
90C2 **Bakharden** Turkmenistan
90C2 **Bakhardok** Turkmenistan
60D3 **Bakhmach** Ukraine
38C1 **Bakkaflói** B Iceland
99D2 **Bako** Eth
98C2 **Bakouma** CAR
65F5 **Baku** Azerbaijan
Baky = Bakū
92B2 **Balā** Turk
79A4 **Balabac** I Phil
70C3 **Balabac** Str Malay
78C2 **Balaikarangan** Indon
108A2 **Balaklava** Aust
61G3 **Balakovo** Russian Fed
86A2 **Balangir** India
61F3 **Balashov** Russian Fed
86B2 **Balasore** India
80B3 **Balat** Egypt
52C1 **Balaton** L Hung
45C2 **Balbriggan** Irish Rep
29E3 **Balcarce** Arg
54C2 **Balchik** Bulg
111B3 **Balclutha** NZ
18B2 **Bald Knob** USA
17B1 **Baldwin** USA
9C3 **Baldy Peak** Mt USA
Balearic Is = Islas Baleares
78C2 **Baleh** R Malay
79B2 **Baler** Phil
61H2 **Balezino** Russian Fed
106A1 **Bali** I Indon
92A2 **Balikesir** Turk
93C2 **Balikh** R Syria
78D3 **Balikpapan** Indon
79B2 **Balintang Chan** Phil
78C4 **Bali S** Indon
35A1 **Baliza** Brazil
84B1 **Balkh** Afghan
65J5 **Balkhash** Kazakhstan
44B3 **Ballachulish** Scot
45B2 **Ballaghaderreen** Irish Rep
42B2 **Ballantrae** Scot
4G2 **Ballantyne Str** Can
87B2 **Ballapur** India
107D4 **Ballarat** Aust
44C3 **Ballater** Scot
112C7 **Balleny Is** Ant
86A1 **Ballia** India
109D1 **Ballina** Aust
41B3 **Ballina** Irish Rep
45B2 **Ballinasloe** Irish Rep
45B2 **Ballinrobe** Irish Rep
55A2 **Ballsh** Alb
45B1 **Ballycastle** Aust
45C1 **Ballycastle** N Ire
45C1 **Ballymena** N Ire
45C1 **Ballymoney** N Ire
45B1 **Ballyshannon** Irish Rep
45B2 **Ballyvaghan** Irish Rep
108B3 **Balmoral** Aust
34C2 **Balnearia** Arg
84B3 **Balochistān** Region, Pak
100A2 **Balombo** Angola
109C1 **Balonn** R Aust
85C3 **Balotra** India
86A1 **Balrāmpur** India
107D4 **Balranald** Aust
31B3 **Balsas** Brazil
23B2 **Balsas** Mexico
24B3 **Balsas** R Mexico
60C4 **Balta** Ukraine
39H7 **Baltic S** N Europe

92B3 **Baltim** Egypt
45B3 **Baltimore** Irish Rep
10C3 **Baltimore** USA
86B1 **Bālurghāt** India
61H4 **Balykshi** Kazakhstan
91C4 **Bam** Iran
98B1 **Bama** Nig
97B3 **Bamako** Mali
98C2 **Bambari** CAR
17B1 **Bamberg** USA
57C3 **Bamberg** Germany
98C2 **Bambili** Zaire
35B2 **Bambui** Brazil
98B2 **Bamenda** Cam
13C3 **Bamfield** Can
98B2 **Bamingui** *R* CAR
98B2 **Bamingui Bangoran** *National Park* CAR
84B2 **Bamiyan** Afghan
91D4 **Bampur** Iran
91D4 **Bampur** *R* Iran
98C2 **Banalia** Zaire
97B3 **Banamba** Mali
76C3 **Ban Aranyaprathet** Thai
76C2 **Ban Ban** Laos
77C4 **Ban Betong** Thai
45C1 **Banbridge** N Ire
43D3 **Banbury** Eng
25D3 **Banchory** Scot
25D3 **Banco Chinchorro** *Is* Mexico
15C1 **Bancroft** Can
81B4 **Bānda** India
70A3 **Banda Aceh** Indon
97B4 **Bandama** *R* Ivory Coast
91C4 **Bandar Abbās** Iran
90A2 **Bandar Anzali** Iran
99F2 **Bandarbeyla** Somalia
91B4 **Bandar-e Daylam** Iran
91B4 **Bandar-e Lengheh** Iran
91B4 **Bandar-e Māqām** Iran
91B4 **Bandar-e Rig** Iran
90B2 **Bandar-e Torkoman** Iran
91A3 **Bandar Khomeyni** Iran
78C2 **Bandar Seri Begawan** Brunei
71D4 **Banda S** Indon
91C4 **Band Boni** Iran
35C2 **Bandeira** Brazil
97B3 **Bandiagara** Mali
60C5 **Bandirma** Turk
45B3 **Bandon** Irish Rep
98B3 **Bandundu** Zaire
78B4 **Bandung** Indon
25E2 **Banes** Cuba
13D2 **Banff** Can
44C3 **Banff** Scot
5G4 **Banff** *R* Can
13D2 **Banff Nat Pk** Can
87B2 **Bangalore** India
98C2 **Bangassou** CAR
70C3 **Banggi** *I* Malay
95B1 **Banghāzī** Libya
77B3 **Bang Hieng** *R* Laos
78B3 **Bangka** *I* Indon
78A3 **Bangko** Indon
76C3 **Bangkok** Thai
82C3 **Bangladesh** Republic, Asia
84D2 **Bangong Co** *L* China
10D2 **Bangor** Maine, USA
45D1 **Bangor** N Ire
16B2 **Bangor** Pennsylvania, USA
42B3 **Bangor** Wales
78D3 **Bangsalsembera** Indon
76B3 **Bang Saphan Yai** Thai
79B2 **Bangued** Phil
98B2 **Bangui** CAR
100C2 **Bangweulu L** Zambia
77C4 **Ban Hat Yai** Thai
76C2 **Ban Hin Heup** Laos
76C1 **Ban Houei Sai** Laos
76B3 **Ban Hua Hin** Thai

97B3 **Bani** *R* Mali
97C3 **Bani Bangou** Niger
95A1 **Bani Walid** Libya
92C2 **Bāniyās** Syria
94B2 **Baniyas** Syria
52C2 **Banja Luka** Bosnia-Herzegovina
78C3 **Banjarmasin** Indon
77B4 **Ban Kantang** Thai
76D2 **Ban Khemmarat** Laos
77B4 **Ban Khok Kloi** Thai
71F5 **Banks I** Aust
5E4 **Banks I** British Columbia, Can
4F2 **Banks I** Northwest Territories, Can
20C1 **Banks L** USA
111B2 **Banks Pen** NZ
109C4 **Banks Str** Aust
86B2 **Ban Mae Sariang** Thai
76B2 **Ban Mae Sot** Thai
76B2 **Ban Me Thuot** Viet
45C1 **Bann** *R* N Ire
77B4 **Ban Na San** Thai
84C2 **Bannu** Pak
34A3 **Baños Maule** Chile
76C2 **Ban Pak Neun** Laos
77C4 **Ban Pak Phanang** Thai
76D3 **Ban Ru Kroy** Camb
76B3 **Ban Sai Yok** Thai
76B3 **Ban Sattahip** Thai
59B3 **Banská Bystrica** Slovakia
85C4 **Bānswāra** India
77B4 **Ban Tha Kham** Thai
76D2 **Ban Thateng** Laos
76C2 **Ban Tha Tum** Thai
41B3 **Bantry** Irish Rep
41A3 **Bantry B** Irish Rep
76D3 **Ban Ya Soup** Viet
78C4 **Banyuwangi** Indon
72C3 **Baofeng** China
76A2 **Bao Ha** Viet
72B3 **Baoji** China
76D3 **Bao Loc** Viet
68B4 **Baoshan** China
72C1 **Baotou** China
87C1 **Bāpatla** India
54A2 **Bapaume** France
32J7 **Baquerizo Morena** Ecuador
54A2 **Bar** Montenegro, Yugos
99D1 **Bara** Sudan
99E2 **Baraawe** Somalia
78D3 **Barabai** Indon
86A1 **Bāra Banki** India
65J4 **Barabinsk** Russian Fed
65J4 **Barabinskaya Step** *Steppe* Kazakhstan/Russian Fed
50B1 **Baracaldo** Spain
26C2 **Baracoa** Cuba
26C2 **Baradá** *R* Syria
109C2 **Baradine** Aust
87A1 **Bārāmati** India
84C2 **Baramula** Pak
85D3 **Bārān** India
79B3 **Baranas** Phil
4E4 **Baranof I** USA
60C3 **Baranovichi** Belorussia
108A2 **Baratta** Aust
86B1 **Barauni** India
31C6 **Barbacena** Brazil
27F4 **Barbados** *I* Caribbean S
51C1 **Barbastro** Spain
101H1 **Barberton** S Africa
48B2 **Barbezieux** France
32C2 **Barbosa** Colombia
27E3 **Barbuda** *I* Caribbean S
107D2 **Barcaldine** Aust
Barce = Al Marj
53C3 **Barcellona** Italy
51C1 **Barcelona** Spain

33E1 **Barcelona** Ven
107D3 **Barcoo** *R* Aust
34B3 **Barda del Medio** Arg
95A2 **Bardai** Chad
29C3 **Bardas Blancas** Arg
88B1 **Barddhamān** India
59C3 **Bardejov** Slovakia
47C2 **Bardi** Italy
47B2 **Bardonecchia** Italy
43B3 **Bardsey** *I* Wales
84D3 **Bareilly** India
64D2 **Barentsøya** *I* Barents S
64E2 **Barents S** Russian Fed
95C3 **Barentu** Eritrea
86A2 **Bargarh** India
47B2 **Barge** Italy
63D2 **Barguzin** Russian Fed
63D2 **Barguzin** *R* Russian Fed
86B2 **Barhi** India
53C2 **Bari** Italy
51D2 **Barika** Alg
32C2 **Barinas** Ven
86B2 **Baripāda** India
85C4 **Bari Sādri** India
86C2 **Barisal** Bang
78C3 **Barito** *R* Indon
95A2 **Barjuj** *Watercourse* Libya
73A3 **Barkam** China
18C2 **Barkley, L** USA
13B3 **Barkley Sd** Can
100B4 **Barkly East** S Africa
106C2 **Barkly Tableland** *Mts* Aust
46C2 **Bar-le-Duc** France
106A3 **Barlee, L** Aust
106A3 **Barlee Range** *Mts* Aust
53C2 **Barletta** Italy
85C3 **Bārmer** India
108B2 **Barmera** Aust
43B3 **Barmouth** Wales
42D2 **Barnard Castle** Eng
84A2 **Barnaul** Russian Fed
16B3 **Barnegat** USA
16B3 **Barnegat B** USA
6C2 **Barnes Icecap** Can
17B1 **Barnesville** Georgia, USA
14B3 **Barnesville** Ohio, USA
43D3 **Barnsley** Eng
43B4 **Barnstaple** Eng
97C4 **Baro** Nig
86C1 **Barpeta** India
32D1 **Barquisimeto** Ven
31C4 **Barra** Brazil
44A3 **Barra** *I* Scot
109D2 **Barraba** Aust
23A2 **Barra de Navidad** Mexico
35C2 **Barra de Piraí** Brazil
35A1 **Barragem de São Simão** *Res* Brazil
35A1 **Barra do Garças** Brazil
35B1 **Barragem Agua Vermelha** *Res* Brazil
50A2 **Barragem do Castelo do Bode** *Res* Port
50A2 **Barragem do Maranhão** *Res* Port
35A2 **Barragem Três Irmãos** *Res* Brazil
31C6 **Barra Mansa** Brazil
32B6 **Barranca** Peru
32C2 **Barrancabermeja** Colombia
33E2 **Barrancas** Ven
30E4 **Barranqueras** Arg
32C1 **Barranquilla** Colombia
44A3 **Barra,Sound of** *Chan* Scot
16C1 **Barre** USA
34B2 **Barreal** Arg
31C4 **Barreiras** Brazil
50A2 **Barreiro** Port

31D3 **Barreiros** Brazil
107D5 **Barren,C** Aust
12D3 **Barren Is** USA
31B6 **Barretos** Brazil
13E2 **Barrhead** Can
14C2 **Barrie** Can
13C2 **Barriere** Can
100D2 **Barrier Range** *Mts* Aust
107E4 **Barrington,Mt** Aust
27N2 **Barrouallie** St Vincent and the Grenadines
4C2 **Barrow** USA
45C2 **Barrow** *R* Irish Rep
106C3 **Barrow Creek** Aust
106A3 **Barrow I** Aust
42C2 **Barrow-in-Furness** Eng
4C2 **Barrow,Pt** USA
6A2 **Barrow Str** Can
15C1 **Barry's Bay** Can
87B1 **Barsi** India
9B3 **Barstow** USA
49C2 **Bar-sur-Aube** France
33F2 **Bartica** Guyana
92B1 **Bartın** Turk
107D2 **Bartle Frere,Mt** Aust
9D3 **Bartlesville** USA
101C3 **Bartolomeu Dias** Mozam
58C2 **Bartoszyce** Pol
78C4 **Barung** *I* Indon
85C4 **Barwāh** India
85C4 **Barwāni** India
109C1 **Barwon** *R* Aust
61G3 **Barysh** Russian Fed
98B2 **Basankusu** Zaire
34D2 **Basavilbaso** Arg
79B1 **Basco** Phil
52A1 **Basel** Switz
53C2 **Basento** *R* Italy
13E2 **Bashaw** Can
79B1 **Bashi Chan** Phil
61H3 **Bashkortostan** Russian Fed
79B4 **Basilan** *I* Phil
43E4 **Basildon** Eng
43E4 **Basingstoke** Eng
8B2 **Basin Region** USA
93E3 **Basra** Iraq
46D2 **Bas-Rhin** Department, France
76D3 **Bassac** *R* Camb
13E2 **Bassano** Can
52B1 **Bassano** Italy
47D2 **Bassano del Grappa** Italy
97C4 **Bassari** Togo
101C3 **Bassas da India** *I* Mozam Chan
76A2 **Bassein** Burma
27E3 **Basse Terre** Guadeloupe
97C4 **Bassila** Benin
22C2 **Bass Lake** USA
107D4 **Bass Str** Aust
39G7 **Båstad** Sweden
91B4 **Bastak** Iran
86A1 **Basti** India
52A2 **Bastia** Corse
53C3 **Bastogne** Belg
19B3 **Bastrop** Louisiana, USA
19A3 **Bastrop** Texas, USA
98A2 **Bata** Eq Guinea
78C3 **Batakan** Indon
84D2 **Batala** India
68B3 **Batang** China
98B2 **Batangafo** CAR
79B1 **Batan Is** Phil
35B2 **Batatais** Brazil
15C2 **Batavia** USA
109D3 **Batemans Bay** Aust
17B1 **Batesburg** USA
18B2 **Batesville** Arkansas, USA
19C3 **Batesville** Mississippi, USA
43C4 **Bath** Eng
15C2 **Bath** New York, USA
98B1 **Batha** *R* Chad
107D4 **Bathurst** Aust
7D5 **Bathurst** Can

4F2 Bathurst,C Can	Bear I = Bjørnøya	84B1 Belchiragh Afghan	97C3 Bembéréke Benin
106C2 Bathurst I Aust	22B1 Bear Valley USA	61H3 Belebey Russian Fed	10A2 Bemidji USA
4H2 Bathurst I Can	8D2 Beatrice USA	99E2 Beled Weyne Somalia	39G6 Bena Nor
4H3 Bathurst Inlet B Can	44C2 Beatrice Oilfield N Sea	31B2 Belém Colombia	98C3 Bena Dibele Zaïre
97B3 Batié Burkina	13C1 Beatton R Can	32B3 Belén Colombia	108C3 Benalla Aust
90B3 Bāttāq-e-Gavkhūnī Salt Flat Iran	5F4 Beatton River Can	34D2 Belén Urug	8A2 Ben Attow Mt Scot
109C3 Batlow Aust	29E6 Beauchene Is Falkland Is	9C3 Belen USA	50A1 Benavente Spain
93D2 Batman Turk	109D1 Beaudesert Aust	45D1 Belfast N Ire	44A3 Benbecula I Scot
96C1 Batna Alg	1B5 Beaufort S Can	101H1 Belfast S Africa	106A4 Bencubbin Aust
11A3 Baton Rouge USA	100B4 Beaufort West S Africa	45D1 Belfast Lough Estuary N Ire	8A2 Bend USA
94B1 Batroun Leb	15D1 Beauharnois Can	99D1 Bélfodiyo Eth	8A2 Ben Dearg Mt Scot
76C3 Battambang Camb	44B3 Beauly Scot	42D2 Belford Eng	60C4 Bendery Moldova
87C3 Batticaloa Sri Lanka	21B3 Beaumont California, USA	49D2 Belfort France	107D4 Bendigo Aust
13F2 Battle R Can	11A3 Beaumont Texas, USA	87A1 Belgaum India	57C3 Benešov Czech Republic
108J2 Battle Creek USA	49C2 Beaune France	56A2 Belgium Kingdom, N W Europe	53B2 Benevento Italy
7E4 Battle Harbour Can	48C2 Beauvais France	60E3 Belgorod Russian Fed	83C4 Bengal,B of Asia
20C2 Battle Mountain USA	13F1 Beauval Can	60D4 Belgorod Dnestrovskiy Ukraine	96D1 Ben Gardane Tunisia
78D2 Batukelau Indon	12E1 Beaver Alaska, USA	Belgrade = Beograd	72D3 Bengbu China
65F5 Batumi Georgia	13F2 Beaver R Saskatchewan, Can	95A2 Bel Hedan Libya	78A3 Bengkalis Indon
77C5 Batu Pahat Malay	4D3 Beaver Creek Can	78B3 Belinyu Indon	78A3 Bengkulu Indon
78A3 Baturaja Indon	12E1 Beaver Creek USA	78B3 Belitung I Indon	100A2 Benguela Angola
94B2 Bat Yam Israel	18C2 Beaver Dam Kentucky, USA	25D3 Belize Belize	92B3 Benha Egypt
78D2 Baubau Indon	13E2 Beaverhill L Can	25D3 Belize Republic, Cent America	44B2 Ben Hope Mt Scot
97C3 Bauchi Nig	14A1 Beaver I USA	48C2 Bellac France	99C2 Beni Zaïre
47B2 Bauges Mts France	18B2 Beaver L USA	5F4 Bella Coola Can	32D6 Beni R Bol
7E4 Bauld,C Can	13D2 Beaverlodge Can	47C2 Bellagio Italy	96B1 Beni Abbès Alg
47B1 Baumes-les-Dames France	85C3 Beawar India	19A4 Bellaire USA	51C1 Benicarló Spain
63D2 Baunt Russian Fed	34B2 Beazley Arg	47C1 Bellano Italy	7A5 Benidji USA
31B6 Bauru Brazil	35B2 Bebedouro Brazil	87B1 Bellary India	51B2 Benidorm Spain
35A1 Baus Brazil	43E3 Beccles Eng	109C1 Bellata Aust	51C2 Beni Mansour Alg
57C2 Bautzen Germany	54B1 Bečej Serbia, Yugos	47B2 Belledonne Mts France	95C2 Beni Mazar Egypt
78C4 Baween I Indon	96B1 Béchar Alg	9D2 Belle Fourche USA	96B1 Beni Mellal Mor
95B2 Bawiti Egypt	12C3 Becharof L USA	49D2 Bellegarde France	97C4 Benin Republic, Africa
97B3 Bawku Ghana	11B3 Beckley USA	17B2 Belle Glade USA	97C4 Benin City Nig
76B2 Bawlake Burma	43D3 Bedford County, Eng	7E4 Belle I Can	97C4 Benin,B of Africa
82D2 Bawlen Aust	43D3 Bedford Eng	48B2 Belle-Île I France	44B2 Ben Klibreck Mt Scot
17B1 Baxley USA	14A3 Bedford Indiana, USA	7E4 Belle Isle,Str of Can	44B3 Ben Lawers Mt UK
25E2 Bayamo Cuba	27M2 Bedford Pt Grenada	7C5 Belleville Can	44C3 Ben Lomond Mt Aust
78D4 Bayan Indon	22B1 Beechey Pt USA	18A2 Belleville Kansas, USA	44C3 Ben Macdui Mt Scot
68C2 Bayandzürh Mongolia	109C3 Beechworth Aust	20B1 Bellevue Washington, USA	44B2 Ben More Assynt Mt Scot
68B3 Bayan Har Shan Mts China	109D1 Beenleigh Aust	109D2 Bellingen Aust	111B2 Benmore,L NZ
72A1 Bayan Mod China	92B3 Beersheba Israel	8A2 Bellingham USA	44B3 Ben Nevis Mt Scot
72B1 Bayan Obo China	Beer Sheva = Beersheba	112C2 Bellingshausen Base Ant	15D2 Bennington USA
47A2 Bayard P France	94B3 Beer Sheva R Israel	112C3 Bellingshausen S Ant	94B2 Bennt Jbaïl Leb
12J3 Bayard,Mt Can	9D4 Beeville USA	52A1 Bellinzona Switz	98B2 Bénoué R Cam
63D3 Bayasgalant Mongolia	98C2 Befale Zaïre	32B2 Bello Colombia	9B3 Benson Arizona, USA
79B3 Baybay Phil	101D2 Befandriana Madag	107F2 Bellona Reefs Nouvelle Calédonie	99C2 Bentiu Sudan
93D1 Bayburt Turk	109C3 Bega Aust	22B1 Bellota USA	19B3 Benton Arkansas, USA
10B2 Bay City Michigan, USA	91B3 Behbehān Iran	18C2 Bellows Falls USA	18C2 Benton Kentucky, USA
19A4 Bay City Texas, USA	12H3 Behm Canal Sd USA	6B3 Bell Pen Can	14A2 Benton Harbor USA
92B2 Bay Dağlari Turk	90B2 Behshahr Iran	52B1 Belluno Italy	97C4 Benue R Nig
64H3 Baydaratskaya Guba B Russian Fed	84B2 Behsud Afghan	29D2 Bell Ville Arg	44B3 Benwee Hd C Irish Rep
99E2 Baydhabo Somalia	69E2 Bei'an China	31D5 Belmonte Brazil	44B3 Ben Wyvis Mt Scot
48B2 Bayeux France	73B5 Beihai China	25D3 Belmopan Belize	72E1 Benxi China
47D1 Bayerische Alpen Mts Germany	72D2 Beijing China	45B1 Belmullet Irish Rep	54B2 Beograd Serbia, Yugos
57C3 Bayern State, Germany	76E1 Beiliu China	31B6 Belogorsk Russian Fed	86A2 Beohari India
92C3 Bāyir Jordan	73B4 Beipan Jiang R China	101D3 Beloha Madag	74C4 Beppu Japan
63C2 Baykalskiy Khrebet Mts Russian Fed	72E1 Beipiao China	31C5 Belo Horizonte Brazil	53A2 Berat Alb
63B1 Baykit Russian Fed	Beira = Sofala	10B2 Beloit Wisconsin, USA	95C3 Berber Sudan
63B3 Baylik Shan Mts China/Mongolia	92C3 Beirut Leb	64E3 Belomorsk Russian Fed	99E1 Berbera Somalia
61J3 Baymak Russian Fed	68B2 Bei Shan Mts China	61J3 Beloretsk Russian Fed	98B2 Berbérati CAR
79B2 Bayombong Phil	94B2 Beit ed Dine Leb	Belorussia Republic, Europe	46A1 Berck France
48B3 Bayonne France	94B3 Beit Jala Israel	60C3 Beloye More S Russian Fed	60C4 Berdichev Ukraine
57C3 Bayreuth Germany	50A2 Beja Port	60E1 Beloye Ozero L Russian Fed	60E4 Berdyansk Ukraine
19C3 Bay St Louis USA	96C1 Beja Tunisia	60E1 Belozersk Russian Fed	97B4 Berekum Ghana
15C2 Bay Shore USA	96C1 Bejaia Alg	14B3 Belpre USA	22B2 Berenda USA
15C1 Bays,L of Can	50A1 Béjar Spain	108A2 Beltana Aust	5J4 Berens R Can
68A2 Baytik Shan Mts China	90C3 Bejestān Iran	19A3 Belton USA	5J4 Berens River Can
Bayt Lahm = Bethlehem	59C3 Békéscsaba Hung	59D3 Bel'tsy Moldova	108A1 Beresford Aust
19B4 Baytown USA	101D3 Bekily Madag	16B2 Belvidere New Jersey, USA	59C3 Berettyóujfalu Hung
50B2 Baza Spain	86A1 Bela India	98B3 Bembe Angola	58D2 Bereza Belorussia
59D3 Bazaliya Ukraine	85B3 Bela Pak		59C3 Berezhany Ukraine
48B3 Bazas France	78C2 Belaga Malay		65G4 Berezniki Russian Fed
73B3 Bazhong China	16A3 Bel Air USA		60D4 Berezovka Ukraine
91D4 Bazmān Iran	87B1 Belamoalli India		64H3 Berezovo Russian Fed
94C1 Bcharré Leb	71D3 Belang Indon		92A2 Bergama Turk
16B3 Beach Haven USA	70A3 Belangpidie Indon		52A1 Bergamo Italy
43E4 Beachy Head Eng	Belarus = Belorussia		39F6 Bergen Nor
16C2 Beacon USA	Belau = Palau Is.		46C1 Bergen op Zoom Neth
101D2 Bealanana Madag	101C3 Bela Vista Mozam		48C3 Bergerac France
18B1 Beardstown USA	70A3 Belawan Indon		46D1 Bergisch-Gladbach Germany
	61J2 Belaya R Ukraine		12F2 Bering Gl USA
	6A2 Belcher Chan Can		
	7C4 Belcher Is Can		

1C6 Bering Str USA/
  Russian Fed
91C4 Berizak Iran
50B2 Berja Spain
8A3 Berkawn Ant
112B2 Berkner I Ant
54B2 Berkovitsa Bulg
43D4 Berkshire County,
  Eng
16C1 Berkshire Hills USA
13D2 Berland R Can
56C2 Berlin Germany
56C2 Berlin State,
  Germany
15D2 Berlin New
  Hampshire, USA
30D3 Bermejo Bol
30D4 Bermejo R Arg
3M5 Bermuda I Atlantic O
52A1 Bern Switz
16B2 Bernasville USA
34C3 Bernasconi Arg
56C2 Bernburg Germany
47B1 Berner Oberland Mts
  Switz
6B2 Bernier B Can
57C3 Berounka R
  Czech Republic
108B2 Berri Aust
96C1 Berriane Alg
48C2 Berry Region, France
22A1 Berryessa,L USA
11C4 Berry Is The
  Bahamas
98B2 Bertoua Cam
45B2 Bertraghboy B
  Irish Rep
15C2 Berwick USA
42C2 Berwick-upon-Tweed
  Eng
43C3 Berwyn Mts Wales
101B2 Besalampy Madag
90C2 Besançon France
59C3 Beskidy Zachodnie
  Mts Pol
93C2 Besni Turk
94B3 Besor R Israel
11B3 Bessemer USA
101D2 Betafo Madag
50A1 Betanzos Spain
94B3 Bet Guvrin Israel
101G1 Bethal S Africa
100A3 Bethanie Namibia
18B1 Bethany Missouri,
  USA
18A2 Bethany Oklahoma,
  USA
4B3 Bethel Alaska, USA
16C2 Bethel Connecticut,
  USA
14B2 Bethel Park USA
15C3 Bethesda USA
94B3 Bethlehem Israel
101G1 Bethlehem S Africa
15C2 Bethlehem USA
48C1 Bethune France
101D3 Betioky Madag
108B1 Betoota Aust
98B2 Betou Congo
82A1 Betpak Dala Steppe
  Kazakhstan
101D3 Betroka Madag
7D5 Betsiamites Can
86A1 Bettiah India
12D1 Bettles USA
47C2 Bettola Italy
85D3 Bétul R India
46D1 Betzdorf Germany
12C3 Beverley,L USA
16D1 Beverly USA
21B3 Beverly Hills USA
97B4 Beyla Guinea
87B2 Beypore India
91C4 Beyram Iran
94B2 Beyşehir Turk
92B2 Beyşehir Gölü L Turk
94B2 Beyt Shean Israel
47C1 Bezau Austria
60E2 Bezhetsk
  Russian Fed
49C3 Béziers France
90C2 Bezmein
  Turkmenistan

63C2 Beznosova
  Russian Fed
86B1 Bhadgaon Nepal
87C1 Bhadrachalam India
86B2 Bhadrakh India
84B3 Bhadra Res India
87B2 Bhadravati India
84B3 Bhag Pak
88B1 Bhagalpur India
84C2 Bhakkar Pak
82D3 Bhamo Burma
85D4 Bhandara India
85D3 Bharatpur India
85C4 Bharuch India
86B2 Bhatiapara Ghat
  Bang
84C2 Bhatinda India
87A2 Bhatkal India
86B2 Bhatpara India
85C4 Bhavnagar India
84C2 Bhera Pak
86A1 Bheri R Nepal
86A2 Bhilai India
85C3 Bhilwara India
87C1 Bhimavaram India
85D3 Bhind India
84D3 Bhiwani India
87B1 Bhongir India
86B2 Bhopal India
86B2 Bhubaneshwar India
85B4 Bhuj India
85D4 Bhusawal India
82C3 Bhutan Kingdom,
  Asia
71E4 Biak I Indon
58C2 Biala Podlaska Pol
58B2 Bialograd Pol
58C2 Bialystok Pol
38A1 Biargtangar C
  Iceland
90C2 Biarjmand Iran
48B3 Biarritz France
47C1 Biasca Switz
92B4 Biba Egypt
74E2 Bibai Japan
100A2 Bibala Angola
57B3 Biberach Germany
97B4 Bibiani Ghana
54C1 Bicaz Rom
97C4 Bida Nig
87B1 Bidar India
101D2 Bidbid Oman
43B4 Bideford Eng
43B4 Bideford B Eng
96C2 Bidon 5 Alg
58C2 Biebrza Pol
52A1 Biel Switz
59B2 Bielawa Pol
56B2 Bielefeld Germany
47B1 Bieler See L Switz
52A1 Biella Italy
58C2 Bielsk Podlaski Pol
76D3 Bien Hoa Viet
53B2 Biferno R Italy
52A1 Biga Turk
55C3 Bigadiç Turk
11C3 Big Black R USA
18A1 Big Blue R USA
17B2 Big Cypress Swamp
  USA
4D3 Big Delta USA
49D2 Bigent Germany
13F2 Biggar Can
5H4 Biggar Kindersley
  Can
109D1 Biggenden Aust
12G3 Biggar,Mt Can
8C2 Bighorn R USA
76C3 Bight of Bangkok B
  Thai
97C4 Bight of Benin B W
  Africa
97C4 Bight of Biafra B
  Cam
6C3 Big I Can
47C1 Bignasco Switz
97A3 Bignona Sen
21B2 Big Pine USA
21B3 Big Pine Key USA
22C3 Big Pine Mt USA
14A2 Big Rapids USA
5H4 Big River Can
9C3 Big Spring USA
7A4 Big Trout L Can

7B4 Big Trout Lake Can
52C2 Bihać Bosnia-
  Herzegovina
86B1 Bihar India
86B2 Bihar State, India
99D3 Biharamulo Tanz
60B4 Bihor Mt Rom
87B1 Bijapur India
87C1 Bijapur India
90A2 Bijar Iran
86A1 Bijauri Nepal
54A2 Bijeljina Bosnia-
  Herzegovina
73B4 Bijie China
85D3 Bijnor India
86B1 Bijnot Pak
84C3 Bikaner India
94B2 Bikfaya Leb
69F2 Bikin Russian Fed
98C3 Bikoro Zaïre
85C3 Bilara India
84D2 Bilaspur India
86A2 Bilaspur India
76B3 Bilauktaung Range
  Mts Thai
50B1 Bilbao Spain
  Bilbo = Bilbao
59B3 Bílé R
  Czech Republic
54A2 Bileća Bosnia-
  Herzegovina
92B1 Bilecik Turk
98C2 Bili R Zaïre
79B3 Biliran I Phil
8C2 Billings USA
95A3 Bilma Niger
11B3 Biloxi USA
98C1 Biltine Chad
85D4 Bina-Etawa India
79B3 Binalbagan Phil
101C2 Bindura Zim
100B2 Binga Zim
101C2 Binga,Mt Zim
109D1 Bingara Aust
57D3 Bingen Germany
10C2 Binghamton USA
78B1 Bingkor Malay
93D2 Bingöl Turk
72D3 Binhai China
78A2 Bintan I Indon
78A3 Bintulu Malay
78C2 Bintulu Malay
29B3 Bío Bío R Chile
102J4 Bioko I Atlantic O
87B1 Bir India
95B2 Bir Abu Husein Well
  Egypt
95B2 Bi'r al Harash Well
  Libya
98C1 Birao CAR
86B1 Biratnagar Nepal
12E1 Birch Creek USA
108B3 Birchip Aust
5G4 Birch Mts Can
7A4 Bird Can
106C2 Birdsville Aust
106C2 Birdum Aust
86A1 Birganj Nepal
93F3 Bir Gifgafa Well
  Egypt
94A3 Bir Hasana Well
  Egypt
35A2 Birigui Brazil
90C3 Birjand Iran
92B4 Birkat Qarun L Egypt
46D2 Birkenfeld Germany
42C3 Birkenhead Eng
60C4 Birlad Rom
93F3 Bir Lahfan Well
  Egypt
43C3 Birmingham Eng
11B3 Birmingham USA
95B2 Bir Misâha Well
  Egypt
96A2 Bir Moghrein Maur
97C3 Birni Kebbi Nig
97C3 Birni N'Konni Nig
69F2 Birobidzhan
  Russian Fed
45C2 Birr Irish Rep
51C2 Bir Rabalou Alg
109C1 Birrie R Aust
44C2 Birsay Scot
61J2 Birsk Russian Fed

95B2 Bîr Tarfâwi Well
  Egypt
63B2 Biryusa Russian Fed
39J7 Birzai Lithuania
96B2 Bir Zreigat Well
  Maur
48A2 Biscay,B of France/
  Spain
17B2 Biscayne B USA
46D2 Bischwiller France
73B4 Bishan China
82B1 Bishkek Kirghizia
42D2 Bishop USA
43E4 Bishop's Stortford
  Eng
86A2 Bishrampur India
96C1 Biskra Alg
79C4 Bislig Phil
8C2 Bismarck USA
90A3 Bisotun Iran
97A3 Bissau Guinea-
  Bissau
10A1 Bissett Can
5G4 Bistcho L Can
54C1 Bistrita R Rom
99B2 Bitam Gabon
57B3 Bitburg Germany
46D2 Bitche France
93D2 Bitlis Turk
55B2 Bitola Macedonia
56C2 Bitterfeld Germany
100A4 Bitterfontein S Africa
92B3 Bitter Lakes Egypt
8B2 Bitterroot Range Mts
  USA
74D3 Biwa-ko L Japan
99E1 Biyo Kaboba Eth
65K4 Biysk Russian Fed
96C1 Bizerte Tunisia
51C2 Bj bou Arréridj Alg
52C1 Bjelovar Croatia
96B2 Bj Flye Ste Marie Alg
64C2 Bjørnøya I Parents S
12F1 Black R USA
18B2 Black R USA
107D3 Blackall Aust
42C3 Blackburn Eng
4D3 Blackburn,Mt USA
13E2 Black Diamond Can
5H5 Black Hills USA
44B3 Black Isle Pen Scot
27H1 Blackman's
  Barbados
43C4 Black Mts Wales
43C3 Blackpool Eng
27H1 Black River Jamaica
8C2 Black Rock Desert
  USA
65E5 Black S Asia/Europe
45B3 Blacksod B Irish Rep
109D2 Black Sugarloaf Mt
  Aust
97B3 Black Volta R Ghana
41B3 Blackwater R
  Irish Rep
18A2 Blackwell USA
54B2 Blagoevgrad Bulg
63E2 Blagoveshchensk
  Russian Fed
20B1 Blaine USA
44C3 Blair Atholl Scot
44C3 Blairgowrie Scot
11B3 Blakely USA
108A1 Blanche,L Aust
34A2 Blanco R Arg
34B1 Blanco R Arg
8A2 Blanco,C USA
27E4 Blanc Sablon Can
43C4 Blandford Forum
  Eng
46A2 Blangy-sur-Bresle
  France
101C2 Blantyre Malawi
48B2 Blaye France
109C2 Blayney Aust
111B2 Blenheim NZ
96C1 Blida Alg
14B1 Blind River Can
108A2 Blinman Aust
78C4 Blitar Indon
15D2 Block I USA
16D2 Block Island Sd USA

Bloemfontein

101G1 **Bloemfontein**
S Africa
101G1 **Bloemhof** S Africa
101G1 **Bloemhof Dam** *Res*
S Africa
33F3 **Blommesteinmeer** *L*
Surinam
38A1 **Blonduós** Iceland
45B1 **Bloody Foreland** *C*
Irish Rep
14A3 **Bloomfield** Indiana,
USA
18B1 **Bloomfield** Iowa,
USA
10B2 **Bloomington** Illinois,
USA
14A3 **Bloomington**
Indiana, USA
16A2 **Bloomsburg** USA
78C4 **Blora** Indon
6H3 **Blosseville Kyst** *Mts*
Greenland
57B3 **Bludenz** Austria
11B3 **Bluefield** USA
26B3 **Blue Mountain Peak**
Mt Jamaica
16A2 **Blue Mt** USA
109D2 **Blue Mts** Aust
27J1 **Blue Mts** Jamaica
8A2 **Blue Mts** USA
Blue Nile = Bahr el
Azraq
99D1 **Blue Nile** *R* Sudan
4G3 **Bluenose L** Can
11B3 **Blue Ridge Mts** USA
13D2 **Blue River** Can
45B1 **Blue Stack** *Mt*
Irish Rep
111A3 **Bluff** NZ
106A4 **Bluff Knoll** *Mt* Aust
30G4 **Blumenau** Brazil
49D2 **Blunau** Austria
20B2 **Bly** USA
12E3 **Blying Sd** USA
42D2 **Blyth** Eng
9B3 **Blythe** USA
11B3 **Blytheville** USA
97A4 **Bo** Sierra Leone
79B3 **Boac** Phil
72D2 **Boading** China
14B2 **Boardman** USA
63C3 **Boatou** China
33E3 **Boa Vista** Brazil
97A4 **Boa Vista** *I Cape*
Verde
76E1 **Bobai** China
47C2 **Bóbbio** Italy
97B3 **Bobo Dioulasso**
Burkina
60C3 **Bobruysk** Belorussia
17B2 **Boca Chica Key** *I*
USA
32D5 **Bôca do Acre** Brazil
35C1 **Bocaiúva** Brazil
98B2 **Bocaranga** CAR
17B2 **Boca Raton** USA
59C3 **Bochnia** Pol
56B2 **Bocholt** Germany
46D1 **Bochum** Germany
100A2 **Bocoio** Angola
98B2 **Boda** CAR
63D2 **Bodaybo**
Russian Fed
21A2 **Bodega Head** *Pt*
USA
95A3 **Bodélé** *Region* Chad
38J5 **Boden** Sweden
47C1 **Bodensee** *L* Switz/
Germany
87B1 **Bodhan** India
87B2 **Bodināyakkanūr**
India
43B4 **Bodmin** Eng
43B4 **Bodmin Moor**
Upland Eng
38G5 **Bodø** Nor
55C3 **Bodrum** Turk
98C3 **Boende** Zaïre
97A3 **Boffa** Guinea
76B2 **Bogale** Burma
19C3 **Bogalusa** USA
109C2 **Bogan** *R* Aust
97B3 **Bogandé** Burkina

6H3 **Bogarnes** Iceland
92C2 **Boğazlıyan** Turk
61K2 **Bogdanovich**
Russian Fed
68A2 **Bogda Shan** *Mt*
China
100A3 **Bogenfels** Namibia
109D1 **Boggabilla** Aust
109C2 **Boggabri** Aust
45B2 **Boggeragh Mts**
Irish Rep
79B3 **Bogo** Phil
109C3 **Bogong,Mt** Aust
78B4 **Bogor** Indon
61H2 **Bogorodskoye**
Russian Fed
32C3 **Bogotá** Colombia
63A2 **Bogotol** Russian Fed
86B2 **Bogra** Bang
72D2 **Bo Hai** *B* China
46B2 **Bohain-en-**
Vermandois France
72D2 **Bohai Wan** *B* China
57C3 **Böhmer-Wald**
Upland Germany
79B4 **Bohol** *I* Phil
79B4 **Bohol S** Phil
35A1 **Bois** *R* Brazil
14B1 **Bois Blanc I** USA
8B2 **Boise** USA
96A2 **Bojador,C** Mor
79B2 **Bojeador,C** Phil
90C2 **Bojnūrd** Iran
97A3 **Boké** Guinea
109C1 **Bokhara** *R* Aust
39F7 **Boknafjord** *Inlet* Nor
98B3 **Boko** Congo
76C3 **Bokor** Camb
98C3 **Bokungu** Zaïre
98B1 **Bol** Chad
23A1 **Bolaános** Mexico
97A3 **Bolama** Guinea-
Bissau
23A1 **Bolanos** *R* Mexico
48C2 **Bolbec** France
97B4 **Bole** Ghana
59B2 **Boleslawiec** Pol
97B3 **Bolgatanga** Ghana
60C4 **Bolgrad** Ukraine
34C3 **Bolívar** Arg
18C2 **Bolívar** Missouri,
USA
18C2 **Bolívar** Tennessee,
USA
30C2 **Bolivia** Republic,
S America
38H6 **Bollnas** Sweden
109C1 **Bollon** Aust
32C2 **Bolívar** *Mt* Ven
52B2 **Bologna** Italy
60D2 **Bologoye**
Russian Fed
69F2 **Bolon'** Russian Fed
61G3 **Bol'shoy Irgiz** *R*
Russian Fed
74C2 **Bol'shoy Kamen**
Russian Fed
Bol'shoy Kavkaz
=Caucasus
61G4 **Bol'shoy Uzen** *R*
Kazakhstan
9C4 **Bolson de Mapimi**
Desert Mexico
43C3 **Bolton** Eng
92B1 **Bolu** Turk
38A1 **Bolungarvik** Iceland
92B2 **Bolvadin** Turk
52B1 **Bolzano** Italy
98B3 **Boma** Zaïre
109C3 **Bombala** Aust
87A1 **Bombay** India
99C2 **Bombo** Uganda
35B1 **Bom Despacho** Brazil
86C1 **Bomdila** India
97A4 **Bomi Hills** Lib
31C4 **Bom Jesus da Lapa**
Brazil
63E2 **Bomnak** Russian Fed
99C2 **Bomokandi** *R* Zaïre
98C2 **Boma** *R* CAR/Zaïre
27D4 **Bonaire** *I*
Caribbean S
29D3 **Bona,Mt** USA
25D3 **Bonanza** Nic

7E5 **Bonavista** Can
108A2 **Bon Bon** Aust
98C2 **Bondo** Zaïre
97B4 **Bondoukou** Ivory
Coast
Bône = 'Annaba
33E3 **Bonfim** Guyana
98C2 **Bongandanga** Zaïre
98B1 **Bongor** Chad
19A3 **Bonham** USA
53A2 **Bonifacio** Corse
52A2 **Bonifacio,Str of** *Chan*
Medit S
Bonin Is = Ogasawara·
Gunto
17B2 **Bonita Springs** USA
57B2 **Bonn** Germany
20C1 **Bonners Ferry** USA
12H1 **Bonnet Plume** *R* Can
13E2 **Bonnyville** Can
97A4 **Bonthe** Sierra Leone
99E1 **Booaaso** Somalia
108B2 **Booligal** Aust
19D1 **Boonah** Aust
15C2 **Boonville** USA
109C2 **Boorowa** Aust
6A2 **Boothia,G of** Can
6A2 **Boothia Pen** Can
98B3 **Booué** Gabon
108A1 **Bopeechee** Aust
99D2 **Bor** Sudan
92B2 **Bor** Turk
54B2 **Bor** Serbia, Yugos
8B2 **Borah Peak** *Mt* USA
39G7 **Borås** Sweden
91B4 **Borāzjan** Iran
108A3 **Borda,C** Aust
48B3 **Bordeaux** France
4G2 **Borden I** Can
6B2 **Borden Pen** Can
16B2 **Bordentown** USA
42C2 **Borders** Region, Scot
108B3 **Bordertown** Aust
96C2 **Bordj Omar Dris** Alg
8D1 **Borens River** Can
38A2 **Borgarnes** Iceland
9C3 **Borger** USA
39H7 **Borgholm** Sweden
47C2 **Borgo Valsugana**
Italy
59C3 **Borislav** Ukraine
61F3 **Borisoglebsk**
Russian Fed
60C3 **Borisov** Belorussia
60E3 **Borisovka**
Russian Fed
95A3 **Borkou** *Region* Chad
39H6 **Borlänge** Sweden
47C2 **Bormida** Italy
47D1 **Bórmio** Italy
67F5 **Borneo** *I* Malay/
Indon
39H7 **Bornholm** *I* Den
55C3 **Bornova** Turk
98C2 **Boro** *R* Sudan
79B3 **Borongo** Burkina
60D2 **Borovichi**
Russian Fed
106C2 **Borroloola** Aust
54B1 **Borsa** Rom
90A3 **Borūjen** Iran
90B3 **Borūjerd** Iran
58B2 **Bory Tucholskie**
Region, Pol
63D2 **Borzya** Russian Fed
73B5 **Bose** China
60D2 **Borovichi**
Russian Fed
106C2 **Borroloola** Aust

54B2 **Botevgrad** Bulg
101G1 **Bothaville** S Africa
64C3 **Bothnia,G of**
Sweden/Fin
100B3 **Botletli** *R* Botswana
60C4 **Botosani** Rom
100B3 **Botswana** Republic,
Africa
53C3 **Botte Donato** *Mt*
Italy
46D1 **Bottrop** Germany
35B2 **Botucatu** Brazil
7E5 **Botwood** Can
98B2 **Bouar** CAR
96B1 **Bouárfa** Mor
98B2 **Bouca** CAR
51C2 **Boufarik** Alg
Bougie = Bejaia
97B3 **Bougouni** Mali
46C2 **Bouillon** France
96B2 **Bou Izakarn** Mor
46D2 **Boulay-Moselle**
France
8C2 **Boulder** Colorado,
USA
9B3 **Boulder City** USA
22A2 **Boulder Creek** USA
48C1 **Boulogne** France
98B2 **Boumba** *R* CAR
97B4 **Bouna** Ivory Coast
8B3 **Boundary Peak** *Mt*
USA
97B4 **Boundiali** Ivory Coast
107F3 **Bourail** Nouvelle
Calédonie
97B3 **Bourem** Mali
49D2 **Bourg** France
49D2 **Bourg de Péage**
France
49C2 **Bourges** France
48C3 **Bourg-Madame**
France
49C2 **Bourgogne** Region,
France
47B2 **Bourg-St-Maurice**
France
108C2 **Bourke** Aust
43D4 **Bournemouth** Eng
96C1 **Bou Saâda** Alg
98B1 **Bousso** Chad
97A3 **Boutilimit** Maur
103J7 **Bouvet I** Atlantic O
34D2 **Bovril** Arg
13E2 **Bow** *R* Can
107D2 **Bowen** Aust
19A3 **Bowie** Texas, USA
9B3 **Bow Island** Can
11B3 **Bowling Green**
Kentucky, USA
18B2 **Bowling Green**
Missouri, USA
14B2 **Bowling Green** Ohio,
USA
15C3 **Bowling Green**
Virginia, USA
15C2 **Bowmanville** Can
109D2 **Bowral** Aust
13C2 **Bowron** *R* Can
72D3 **Bo Xian** China
72D2 **Boxing** China
92B1 **Boyabat** Turk
98B2 **Boyali** CAR
5J4 **Boyd** Can
16B2 **Boyertown** USA
13E2 **Boyle** Can
18B2 **Boyne** *R* Irish Rep
45C2 **Boyne** *R* Irish Rep
17B2 **Boynton Beach** USA
98C2 **Boyoma Falls** Zaïre
55C3 **Bozca Ada** *I* Turk
55C3 **Boz Dağları** *Mts*
Turk
8B2 **Bozeman** USA
98B2 **Bozene** Zaïre
98B2 **Bozoum** CAR
47B2 **Bra** Italy
52C2 **Brač** *I* Croatia
15C1 **Bracebridge** Can
95A2 **Brach** Libya
38H6 **Bräcke** Sweden
17B2 **Bradenton** USA

42D3 Bradford Eng
44E1 Brae Scot
44E1 Braemar Scot
50A1 Braga Port
34C3 Bragado Arg
50A1 Braga Port
31B2 Bragança Brazil
35B2 Bragança Paulista Brazil
86C2 Brahman-Baria Bang
86B2 Brahmani R India
86C1 Brahmaputra R India
7E5 Braie Verte Can
60C4 Brăila Rom
10A2 Brainerd USA
97A3 Brakna Region, Maur
5F4 Bralorne Can
14C2 Brampton Can
33E3 Branco R Brazil
100A3 Brandberg Mt Namibia
10B2 Brandon Can
56C2 Brandenburg Germany
56C2 Brandenburg State, Germany
101G1 Brandfort S Africa
8D2 Brandon USA
100B4 Brandvlei S Africa
57C2 Brandys nad Lebem Czech Republic
58B2 Braniewo Pol
10B2 Brantford Can
100B3 Branxholme Aust
7D5 Bras D'Or L Can
35C1 Brasila de Minas Brazil
32D6 Brasiléia Brazil
31B5 Brasilia Brazil
54C1 Brasov Rom
78D1 Brassay Range Mts Malay
59B3 Bratislava Slovakia
63C2 Bratsk Russian Fed
15D2 Brattleboro USA
56C2 Braunschweig Germany
97A4 Brava I Cape Verde
9B3 Brawley USA
45C2 Bray Irish Rep
6C3 Bray U
13D2 Brazeau R Can
13D2 Brazeau,Mt Can
28D4 Brazil Republic, S America
103G5 Brazil Basin Atlantic O
9D3 Brazos R USA
98B3 Brazzaville Congo
57C3 Brdy Upland Czech Republic
111A3 Breaksea Sd NZ
110B1 Bream B NZ
78B4 Brebes Indon
44C3 Brechin Scot
46C1 Brecht Belg
59B3 Břeclav Czech Republic
43C4 Brecon Wales
43C4 Brecon Beacons Mts Wales
43B3 Brecon Beacons Nat Pk Wales
56A2 Breda Neth
100B4 Bredasdorp S Africa
38H6 Bredbyn Sweden
61J3 Bredy Russian Fed
15C2 Breezewood USA
47C1 Bregenz Austria
47C1 Bregenzer Ache R Austria
38A1 Breiðafjörður B Iceland
47C2 Brembo R Italy
17A1 Bremen USA
56B2 Bremen Germany
56B2 Bremerhaven Germany
20B1 Bremerton USA
19A3 Brenham USA
57C3 Brenner P Austria/Italy
47D2 Breno Italy
47D2 Brenta R Italy
22B2 Brentwood USA

52B1 Brescia Italy
Breslau = Wrocław
47D1 Bressanone Italy
44E1 Bressay I Scot
48B2 Bressuire France
52C1 Brest Belorussia
48B2 Brest France
48B2 Bretagne Region, France
46B2 Breteuil France
16B2 Breton Woods USA
110B1 Brett,C NZ
109C1 Brewarrina Aust
16C2 Brewster New York, USA
20C1 Brewster Washington, USA
101G1 Breyten S Africa
52C1 Brežice Slovenia
98C2 Bria CAR
49D3 Briancon France
49C2 Briare France
21B2 Bridgeport California, USA
15D2 Bridgeport Connecticut, USA
19A3 Bridgeport Texas, USA
22C1 Bridgetown Res USA
16B3 Bridgeton USA
27F4 Bridgetown Barbados
7D5 Bridgewater Can
16D2 Bridgewater USA
43C4 Bridgwater Eng
43C4 Bridgwater B Eng
42D2 Bridlington Eng
109C4 Bridport Aust
47B1 Brienzer See L Switz
46C2 Briey France
52A1 Brig Switz
8B2 Brigham City USA
109C3 Bright Aust
43D4 Brighton Eng
46E1 Brilon Germany
55A2 Brindisi Italy
19B3 Brinkley USA
107E3 Brisbane Aust
15D2 Bristol Connecticut, USA
43C4 Bristol Eng
15D2 Bristol Pennsylvania, USA
16D2 Bristol Rhode Island, USA
11B3 Bristol Tennessee, USA
12B3 Bristol B USA
43B4 Bristol Chan Eng/Wales
4D3 British Mts USA
5F4 British Columbia Province, Can
6B1 British Empire Range Mts Can
101G1 Brits S Africa
100B4 Britstown S Africa
48C2 Brive France
59B3 Brno Czech Republic
17B1 Broad R USA
7C4 Broadback R Can
44A2 Broad Bay Inlet Scot
44B3 Broadford Scot
5H4 Brochet Can
4G2 Brock I Can
15C2 Brockport USA
16D1 Brockton USA
15C2 Brockville Can
16C2 Brodeur Pen Can
42B2 Brodick Scot
58B2 Brodnica Pol
60C3 Brody Ukraine
19B3 Broken Bow Oklahoma, USA
19B3 Broken Bow L USA
107D4 Broken Hill Aust
47C2 Broni Italy
38G5 Brønnøysund Nor
16C2 Bronx Borough, New York, USA
79A4 Brooke's Point Phil
18B2 Brookfield Missouri, USA
11A3 Brookhaven USA

20B2 Brookings Oregon, USA
8D2 Brookings South Dakota, USA
16D1 Brookline USA
16C2 Brooklyn Borough, New York, USA
5G4 Brooks Can
12C3 Brooks,L USA
12A1 Brooks Mt USA
4C3 Brooks Range Mts USA
17B2 Brooksville USA
109D1 Brooloo Aust
109D2 Broome Aust
44C2 Brora Scot
20B2 Brothers USA
95A3 Broulkou Chad
13E3 Browning USA
9D4 Brownsville USA
9D3 Brownwood USA
46B1 Bruay-en-Artois France
106A3 Bruce,Mt Aust
14B1 Bruce Pen Can
59B3 Brück an der Mur Austria
Bruges = Brugge
46B1 Brugge Belg
46D1 Brühl Germany
78C2 Brunei Sultanate, S E Asia
52B1 Brunico Italy
111B2 Bruny I Aust
11B3 Brunswick Georgia, USA
18B2 Brunswick Mississippi, USA
29B6 Brunswick,Pen de Chile
109C4 Bruny I Aust
61F1 Brusenets Russian Fed
26A3 Brus Laguna Honduras
Brüssel = Bruxelles
56A2 Bruxelles Belg
9D3 Bryan USA
108A2 Bryan,Mt Aust
60D3 Bryansk Russian Fed
19B3 Bryant USA
59B2 Brzeg Pol
93E4 Būbiyan I Kuwait/Iraq
99D3 Bubu R Tanz
32C2 Bucaramanga Colombia
44D3 Buchan Oilfield N Sea
97A4 Buchanan Lib
44D3 Buchan Deep N Sea
6C2 Buchan G Can
40C2 Buchan Ness Pen Scot
7E5 Buchans Can
34C2 Buchardo Arg
Bucharest = Bucureşti
47C1 Buchs Switz
43D3 Buckingham Eng
12B1 Buckland USA
12B1 Buckland R USA
108A2 Buckleboo Aust
98B3 Buco Zau Congo
54C2 Bucureşti Rom
59B3 Budapest Hung
84D3 Budaun India
43B4 Bude Eng
19B3 Bude USA
61F5 Budennovsk Russian Fed
54A2 Budva Montenegro, Yugos
98A2 Buéa Cam
22B3 Buellton USA
34B2 Buena Esperanza Arg
32B3 Buenaventura Colombia
23A2 Buenavista Mexico
29E2 Buenos Aires Arg
29D3 Buenos Aires State, Arg
18B2 Buffalo Mississipi, USA

10C2 Buffalo New York, USA
8C2 Buffalo South Dakota, USA
19A3 Buffalo Texas, USA
8C2 Buffalo Wyoming, USA
101I1 Buffalo R S Africa
13E2 Buffalo L Alberta, Can
5G3 Buffalo L Northwest Territories, Can
5H4 Buffalo Narrows Can
17B1 Buford USA
54C2 Buftea Rom
59C2 Bug R Pol/Ukraine
32B3 Buga Colombia
90B2 Bugdayli Turkmenistan
61H3 Bugulma Russian Fed
61H3 Buguruslan Russian Fed
93C2 Buhayrat al Asad Res Syria
41C3 Builth Wells Wales
34A2 Buin Chile
99C3 Bujumbura Burundi
99C3 Bukama Zaire
99C3 Bukavu Zaire
80E2 Bukhara Russian Fed
78C2 Bukit Batubrok Mt Indon
70B4 Bukittinggi Indon
99D3 Bukoba Tanz
78D3 Buku Gandadiwata Mt Indon
71E4 Bula Indon
79B3 Bulan Phil
84D3 Bulandshahr India
100B3 Bulawayo Zim
55C3 Buldan Turk
85D4 Buldana India
68C2 Bulgan Mongolia
54B2 Bulgaria Republic, Europe
47B1 Bulle Switz
111B2 Buller R NZ
109C3 Buller,Mt Aust
106A4 Bullfinch Aust
108B1 Bulloo R Aust
108B1 Bulloo Downs Aust
108B1 Bulloo L Aust
18B2 Bull Shoals Res USA
34A3 Bulnes Chile
71F4 Bulolo PNG
101G1 Bultfontein S Africa
98C2 Bumba Zaire
76B2 Bumphal Dam Thai
99D2 Buna Kenya
106A4 Bunbury Aust
45C1 Buncrana Irish Rep
107E3 Bundaberg Aust
109D2 Bundarra Aust
109D2 Bündi India
45B1 Bundoran Irish Rep
109C1 Bungil R Aust
98B3 Bungo Angola
75A2 Bungo-suidō Str Japan
70B3 Bunguran I Indon
99D2 Bunia Zaire
18B2 Bunker USA
19B3 Bunkie USA
17B2 Bunnell USA
78C3 Buntok Indon
71D3 Buol Indon
94C2 Burāq Syria
34A2 Buran Sudan
99E2 Burao Somalia
79B3 Burauen Phil
80C3 Buraydah S Arabia
21B3 Burbank USA
109C2 Burcher Aust
92B2 Burdur Turk
63F3 Bureinskiy Khrebet Mts Russian Fed
56C2 Burg Germany
54C2 Burgas Bulg
17C1 Burgaw USA
47B1 Burgdorf Switz
100B4 Burgersdorp S Africa
50B1 Burgos Spain
58B1 Burgsvik Sweden

55C3 **Burhaniye** Turk
85D4 **Burhānpur** India
79B3 **Burias** *I* Phil
76C2 **Buriram** Thai
35B1 **Buritis** Brazil
13B2 **Burke Chan** Can
106C2 **Burketown** Aust
97B3 **Burkina** Republic, Africa
15C1 **Burks Falls** Can
8B2 **Burley** USA
10A2 **Burlington** Iowa, USA
16B2 **Burlington** New Jersey, USA
10C2 **Burlington** Vermont, USA
20B1 **Burlington** Washington, USA
83D3 **Burma** Republic, Asia
20B2 **Burney** USA
16A2 **Burnham** USA
107D6 **Burnie** Aust
42C3 **Burnley** Eng
20C2 **Burns** USA
5F4 **Burns Lake** Can
82C1 **Burqin** China
108A2 **Burra** Aust
109D2 **Burragorang,L** Aust
44C2 **Burray** *I* Scot
109C2 **Burren Junction** Aust
109C2 **Burrinjuck Res** Aust
60C5 **Bursa** Turk
80B3 **Bûr Safâga** Egypt
  Bûr Sa'îd = Port Said
14B2 **Burton** USA
43D3 **Burton upon Trent** Eng
38J6 **Burtrask** Sweden
108B2 **Burtundy** Aust
71D4 **Buru** Indon
99C3 **Burundi** Republic, Africa
78A2 **Burung** Indon
63D2 **Buryatskaya Respublika,** Russian Fed
99D1 **Burye** Eth
61H4 **Burynshik** Kazakhstan
43E3 **Bury St Edmunds** Eng
91B4 **Bushehr** Iran
98B3 **Busira** *R* Zaire
58C2 **Buskozdroj** Pol
94C2 **Busrá ash Shām** Syria
106A4 **Busselton** Aust
49D2 **Busto** Italy
52A1 **Busto Arsizio** Italy
79A3 **Busuanga** *I* Phil
98C2 **Buta** Zaire
34B3 **Buta Ranquil** Arg
99C3 **Butare** Rwanda
42B2 **Bute** *I* Scot
69E2 **Butha Qi** China
14C2 **Butler** USA
8B2 **Butte** USA
77C4 **Butterworth** Malay
40B2 **Butt of Lewis** *C* Scot
6D3 **Button Is** Can
79C4 **Butuan** Phil
71D4 **Butung** *I* Indon
61F3 **Buturlinovka** Russian Fed
86A1 **Butwal** Nepal
99E2 **Buulo Barde** Somalia
99E2 **Buur Hakaba** Somalia
61F2 **Buy** Russian Fed
72B1 **Buyant Ovvo** Mongolia
61G5 **Buynaksk** Russian Fed
61D3 **Buyr Nuur** *L* Mongolia
93D2 **Büyük Ağrı** *Mt* Turk
92A2 **Büyük Menderes** *R* Turk
54C1 **Buzău** Rom
54C1 **Buzau** *R* Rom
61H3 **Buzuluk** Russian Fed

16D2 **Buzzards B** USA
54C2 **Byala** Bulg
54B2 **Byala Slatina** Bulg
4H2 **Byam Martin Chan** Can
4H2 **Byam Martin** *I* Can
94B1 **Byblos** Hist Site, Leb
  Byblos = Jubail
58B2 **Bydgoszcz** Pol
39F7 **Bygland** Nor
6C2 **Bylot I** Can
109C2 **Byrock** Aust
22B2 **Byron** USA
109D1 **Byron,C** Aust
59B2 **Bytom** Pol

C

30E4 **Caacupé** Par
100A2 **Caála** Angola
13B2 **Caamano Sd** Can
30E4 **Caazapá** Par
31E3 **Cabedelo** Brazil
50A2 **Cabeza del Buey** Spain
34C3 **Cabildo** Arg
34A2 **Cabildo** Chile
32C1 **Cabimas** Ven
98B3 **Cabinda** Angola
98B3 **Cabinda Province,** Angola
27C3 **Cabo Beata** Dom Rep
51C2 **Cabo Binibeca** *C* Spain
53A3 **Cabo Carbonara** *C* Sardegna
34A3 **Cabo Carranza** *C* Chile
50A2 **Cabo Carvoeiro** *C* Port
9B3 **Cabo Colnett** *C* Mexico
32B2 **Cabo Corrientes** *C* Colombia
24B2 **Cabo Corrientes** *C* Mexico
26B3 **Cabo Cruz** *C* Cuba
50B1 **Cabo de Ajo** *C* Spain
51C1 **Cabo de Caballeria** *C* Spain
51C1 **Cabo de Creus** *C* Spain
50B2 **Cabo de Gata** *C* Spain
29C7 **Cabo de Hornos** *C* Chile
51C2 **Cabo de la Nao** *C* Spain
50A1 **Cabo de Peñas** *C* Spain
51C2 **Cabo de Roca** *C* Port
51C2 **Cabo de Salinas** *C* Spain
35C2 **Cabo de São Tomé** *C* Brazil
35C2 **Cabo de São Vicente** *C* Port
50A2 **Cabo de Sines** *C* Port
51C1 **Cabo de Tortosa** *C* Spain
29C4 **Cabo Dos Bahias** *C* Arg
50A2 **Cabo Espichel** *C* Port
9B4 **Cabo Falso** *C* Mexico
51B2 **Cabo Ferrat** *C* Alg
50A1 **Cabo Finisterre** *C* Spain
51C1 **Cabo Formentor** *C* Spain
35C2 **Cabo Frio** Brazil
35C2 **Cabo Frio** *C* Brazil
26A4 **Cabo Gracias a Dios** Honduras
31B2 **Cabo Maguarinho** *C* Brazil
50A2 **Cabo Negro** *C* Mor
109D1 **Caboolture** Aust
33G3 **Cabo Ortegal** *C* Spain
21B3 **Cabo Punta Banda** *C* Mexico
101C2 **Cabora Bassa Dam** Mozam

24A1 **Caborca** Mexico
24C2 **Cabo Rojo** *C* Mexico
23B1 **Cabos** Mexico
29C6 **Cabo San Diego** *C* Arg
32A4 **Cabo San Lorenzo** *C* Ecuador
53A3 **Cabo Teulada** *C* Sardegna
50A2 **Cabo Trafalgar** *C* Spain
50B2 **Cabo Tres Forcas** *C* Mor
29C5 **Cabo Tres Puntas** *C* Arg
7D5 **Cabot Str** Can
50B2 **Cabra** Spain
50A1 **Cabreira** *Mt* Port
51C2 **Cabrera** *I* Spain
34A3 **Cabrero** Chile
51B2 **Cabriel** *R* Spain
23B2 **Cacahuamilpa** Mexico
54B2 **Cacak** Serbia, Yugos
23B2 **C A Carillo** Mexico
30E2 **Cáceres** Brazil
50A2 **Caceres** Spain
18B2 **Cache** *R* USA
13J2 **Cache Creek** Can
30C4 **Cachi** Arg
33G5 **Cachoeira** Brazil
31D4 **Cachoeira** Brazil
35A1 **Cachoeira Alta** Brazil
31D3 **Cachoeira de Paulo Afonso** *Waterfall* Brazil
29F2 **Cachoeira do Sul** Brazil
31C6 **Cachoeiro de Itapemirim** Brazil
22C3 **Cachuma,L** USA
100A2 **Cacolo** Angola
100A2 **Caconda** Angola
35A1 **Caçu** Brazil
100A2 **Caculuvar** *R* Angola
59B3 **Cadca** Slovakia
43C3 **Cader Idris** *Mts* Wales
10B2 **Cadillac** USA
79B3 **Cadiz** Phil
50A2 **Cadiz** USA
48B2 **Caen** France
43B3 **Caernarfon** Wales
43B3 **Caernarfon B** Wales
94B2 **Caesarea** *Hist Site,* Israel
31C4 **Caetité** Brazil
92B2 **Caga Tepe** Turk
79B2 **Cagayan** *R* Phil
79B4 **Cagayan Is** Phil
53A3 **Cagliari** Sardegna
27D3 **Caguas** Puerto Rico
45B3 **Caha Mts** Irish Rep
45A3 **Cahersiveen** Irish Rep
45C2 **Cahir** Irish Rep
45C2 **Cahore Pt** Irish Rep
48C3 **Cahors** France
110C2 **Caia** Mozam
100B2 **Caianda** Angola
35A1 **Caiapó** *R* Brazil
35A1 **Caiapônia** Brazil
31D3 **Caicó** Brazil
26C2 **Caicos Is** Caribbean S
11C4 **Caicos Pass** The Bahamas
12C2 **Cairn Mt** USA
44C3 **Cairngorms** *Mts* Scot
107D2 **Cairns** Aust
92B3 **Cairo** Egypt
11B3 **Cairo** USA
108B1 **Caiwarro** Aust
32B5 **Cajabamba** Peru
32B5 **Cajamarca** Peru
27D5 **Calabozo** Ven
27D6 **Calafat** Rom
29B6 **Calafate** Arg
79B3 **Calagua Is** Phil
51B1 **Calahorra** Spain
48C1 **Calais** France

30C3 **Calama** Chile
32C3 **Calamar** Colombia
79A3 **Calamian Group** *Is* Phil
98B3 **Calandula** Angola
70A3 **Calang** Indon
95B2 **Calanscio Sand Sea** Libya
79B3 **Calapan** Phil
54C2 **Calarasi** Rom
51B1 **Calatayud** Spain
79B3 **Calbayog** Phil
19B4 **Calcasieu L** USA
86B2 **Calcutta** India
50A2 **Caldas da Rainha** Port
31B5 **Caldas Novas** Brazil
30B4 **Caldera** Chile
8B2 **Caldwell** USA
34C2 **Caleta Olivia** Arg
9B3 **Calexico** USA
5G4 **Calgary** Can
17B1 **Calhoun** USA
17B1 **Calhoun Falls** USA
32B3 **Cali** Colombia
87B2 **Calicut** India
8B3 **Caliente** Nevada, USA
8A3 **California** State, USA
22C3 **California Aqueduct** USA
87B2 **Calimera,Pt** India
34B2 **Calingasta** Arg
22A1 **Calistoga** USA
108B1 **Callabonna** *R* Aust
108A1 **Callabonna,L** Aust
15C1 **Callander** Can
44B3 **Callander** Scot
108B1 **Callanna** Aust
32B6 **Callao** Peru
13E1 **Calling L** Can
13B2 **Calvert I** Can
52A2 **Calvi** Corse
23A1 **Calvillo** Mexico
100A4 **Calvinia** S Africa
25E2 **Camagüey** Cuba
25E2 **Camagüey,Arch de** *Is* Cuba
32B6 **Camaná** Peru
30B2 **Camargo** Bol
22C3 **Camarillo** USA
29C4 **Camarones** Arg
20B1 **Camas** USA
98B3 **Camaxilo** Angola
98B3 **Cambatela** Angola
76C3 **Cambodia** Republic, S E Asia
43B4 **Camborne** Eng
49C1 **Cambrai** France
43C3 **Cambrian Mts** Wales
14B2 **Cambridge** Can
43E3 **Cambridge** Eng
27H1 **Cambridge** Jamaica
15C3 **Cambridge** Maryland, USA
15D2 **Cambridge** Massachussets, USA
110C1 **Cambridge** NZ
14B2 **Cambridge** Ohio, USA
4H3 **Cambridge Bay** Can
60E5 **Cam Burun** *Pt* Turk
11A3 **Camden** Arkansas, USA
109D2 **Camden** Aust
15D3 **Camden** New Jersey, USA
17B1 **Camden** South Carolina, USA
18B2 **Cameron** Missouri, USA

19A3 **Cameron** Texas, USA
4H2 **Cameron** I Can
111A3 **Cameron Mts** NZ
98A2 **Cameroon** Federal Republic, Africa
4A2 **Cameroun** Mt Cam
31B2 **Cametá** Brazil
79B4 **Camiguin** I Phil
79B2 **Camiling** Phil
17B1 **Camilla** USA
22B1 **Camino** USA
30D3 **Camiri** Bol
31C2 **Camocim** Brazil
98C3 **Camissombo** Angola
106C2 **Camooweal** Aust
34D2 **Campana** Arg
29A5 **Campana** I Chile
13B2 **Campania** I Can
111B2 **Campbell,C** NZ
105G6 **Campbell** I NZ
4E3 **Campbell,Mt** Can
84C2 **Campbellpore** Pak
5F5 **Campbell River** Can
7D5 **Campbellton** Can
109D2 **Campbelltown** Aust
42B2 **Campbeltown** Scot
25C3 **Campeche** Mexico
108B3 **Camperdown** Aust
31D3 **Campina Grande** Brazil
31B6 **Campinas** Brazil
35B1 **Campina Verde** Brazil
98A2 **Campo** Cam
53B2 **Campobasso** Italy
35B2 **Campo Belo** Brazil
35B1 **Campo Florido** Brazil
30D4 **Campo Gallo** Arg
30F3 **Campo Grande** Brazil
31C2 **Campo Maior** Brazil
30F3 **Campo Mourão** Brazil
35C2 **Campos** Brazil
35B1 **Campos Altos** Brazil
47D1 **Campo Tures** Italy
76D3 **Cam Ranh** Viet
5G4 **Camrose** Can
100A2 **Camucuio** Angola
27K1 **Canaan** Tobago
16C1 **Canaan** USA
100A2 **Canacupa** Angola
2F3 **Canada** Dominion, N America
29D2 **Cañada de Gomez** Arg
9C3 **Canadian** R USA
60C5 **Canakkale** Turk
34B3 **Canalejas** Arg
13D2 **Canal Flats** Can
24A1 **Cananea** Mexico
102G3 **Canary Basin** Atlantic O
Canary Is = Islas Canarias
23A2 **Canas** Mexico
24B2 **Canatlán** Mexico
11B4 **Canaveral,C** USA
31D5 **Canavieiras** Brazil
107D4 **Canberra** Aust
20B2 **Canby** California, USA
55C3 **Candarli Körfezi** B Turk
16C2 **Candlewood,L** USA
29E2 **Canelones** Urug
18A2 **Caney** USA
100A2 **Cangamba** Angola
100B2 **Cangombe** Angola
72D2 **Cangzhou** China
7D4 **Caniapiscau** R Can
53B3 **Canicattì** Italy
31D2 **Canindé** Brazil
92B1 **Çankırı** Turk
13D2 **Canmore** Can
44A3 **Canna** I Scot
87B2 **Cannanore** India
49D3 **Cannes** France
109C3 **Cann River** Aust
30F4 **Canoas** Brazil
13F1 **Canoe L** Can
9C3 **Canon City** USA

108B2 **Canopus** Aust
5H4 **Canora** Can
109C2 **Canowindra** Aust
45C2 **Cansore Pt** Irish Rep
43E4 **Canterbury** Eng
111B2 **Canterbury Bight** B NZ
111B2 **Canterbury Plains** NZ
77D4 **Can Tho** Viet
Canton = Guangzhou
19C3 **Canton** Mississippi, USA
18B1 **Canton** Missouri, USA
10B2 **Canton** Ohio, USA
12E2 **Cantwell** USA
20C2 **Canyon City** USA
12J2 **Canyon Range** Mts Can
20B2 **Canyonville** USA
98C3 **Canzar** Angola
76D1 **Cao Bang** Viet
31B2 **Capanema** Brazil
35B2 **Capão Bonito** Brazil
48B3 **Capbreton** France
24B2 **Cap Corrientes** C Mexico
52A2 **Cap Corse** C Corse
48B2 **Cap de la Hague** C France
15D1 **Cap-de-la-Madeleine** Can
6C3 **Cap de Nouvelle-France** C Can
51C2 **Capdepera** Spain
23A2 **Cap de Tancitiario** C Mexico
109C4 **Cape Barren I** Aust
103J6 **Cape Basin** Atlantic O
7E6 **Cape Breton I** Can
97B4 **Cape Coast** Ghana
15D2 **Cape Cod B** USA
6C3 **Cape Dorset** Can
17C1 **Cape Fear** R USA
11C3 **Cape Girardeau** USA
6B3 **Cape Henrietta Maria** Can
Cape Horn = Cabo de Hornos
104E3 **Cape Johnston Depth** Pacific O
35C1 **Capelinha** Brazil
44A2 **Cape Lisburne** USA
100A2 **Capelongo** Angola
15D3 **Cape May** USA
5F5 **Cape Mendocino** USA
98B3 **Capenda Camulemba** Angola
4F2 **Cape Perry** Can
7A4 **Cape Tatnam** Can
100A4 **Cape Town** S Africa
102G4 **Cape Verde** Is Atlantic O
102G4 **Cape Verde Basin** Atlantic O
12F3 **Cape Yakataga** USA
107D2 **Cape York Pen** Aust
46A1 **Cap Gris Nez** C France
26C3 **Cap-Haïtien** Haiti
31B2 **Capim** R Brazil
112C2 **Capitán Arturo Prat** Base Ant
27P2 **Cap Moule à Chique** C St Lucia
53C3 **Capo Isola de Correnti** C Italy
53C3 **Capo Rizzuto** C Italy
55A3 **Capo Santa Maria di Leuca** C Italy
53B3 **Capo San Vito** Italy
53C3 **Capo Spartivento** C Italy
27P2 **Cap Pt** St Lucia
53B2 **Capri** I Italy
100B2 **Caprivi Strip** Region, Namibia
52A2 **Capo Rosso** C Corse
102I14 **Cap Vert** C Sen
32C4 **Caquetá** R Colombia
54B2 **Caracal** Rom

33E3 **Caracaraí** Brazil
32D1 **Caracas** Ven
29B3 **Caraguatatuba** Brazil
29B3 **Carahue** Chile
35C1 **Caraí** Brazil
35C2 **Carandaí** Brazil
31C6 **Carangola** Brazil
54B1 **Caransebeş** Rom
108A2 **Carappee Hill** Mt Aust
26A3 **Caratasca** Honduras
35C1 **Caratinga** Brazil
51B2 **Caravaca** Spain
35D1 **Caravelas** Brazil
18C2 **Carbondale** Illinois, USA
53A3 **Carbonia** Sardegna
7E5 **Carborear** Can
5G4 **Carcajou** Can
99E1 **Carcar Mts** Somalia
48C3 **Carcassonne** France
4E3 **Carcross** Can
22B2 **Cárdenas** Mexico
25D2 **Cárdenas** Cuba
23B1 **Cárdenas** Mexico
43C4 **Cardiff** Wales
43B3 **Cardigan** Wales
43B3 **Cardigan B** Wales
13C2 **Cardston** Can
54B1 **Carei** Rom
33F4 **Careiro** Brazil
34A2 **Carén** Chile
14B2 **Carey** USA
48B2 **Carhaix-Plouguer** France
29D3 **Carhué** Arg
31C6 **Cariacica** Brazil
5J4 **Caribou** Can
5G4 **Caribou Mts** Alberta, Can
7F2 **Caribou Mts** British Columbia, Can
79B3 **Carigara** Phil
46C2 **Carignan** France
33E1 **Caripito** Ven
15C1 **Carleton Place** Can
101D1 **Carletonville** S Africa
18C2 **Carlinville** USA
42C2 **Carlisle** Eng
15C2 **Carlisle** USA
34C3 **Carlos** Arg
35C1 **Carlos Chagas** Brazil
45C2 **Carlow** County, Irish Rep
45C2 **Carlow** Irish Rep
21B3 **Carlsbad** California, USA
9C3 **Carlsbad** New Mexico, USA
5H5 **Carlyle** Can
12G2 **Carmacks** Can
47B2 **Carmagnola** Italy
43B4 **Carmarthen** Wales
43B4 **Carmarthen B** Wales
22B1 **Carmel** California, USA
16C2 **Carmel** New York, USA
94B2 **Carmel,Mt** Israel
34D2 **Carmelo** Urug
22B2 **Carmel Valley** USA
9M **Carmen** I Mexico
29D4 **Carmen de Patagones** Arg
18C2 **Carmi** USA
21A2 **Carmichael** USA
35B1 **Carmo do Paranaiba** Brazil
50A2 **Carmona** Spain
106A3 **Carnarvon** Aust
100B4 **Carnarvon** S Africa
35D1 **Carncacá** Brazil
45C1 **Carndonagh** Irish Rep
106B3 **Carnegie,L** Aust
98B2 **Carnot** CAR
17B2 **Carol City** USA
31B3 **Carolina** Brazil
101H1 **Carolina** S Africa
1/C1 **Carolina Beach** USA
104F3 **Caroline Is** Pacific O
60B4 **Carpathians** Mts E Europe

59D3 **Carpatii Orientali** Mts Rom
106C2 **Carpentaria,G of** Aust
83C5 **Carpenter Ridge** Indian O
49D3 **Carpentras** France
52C2 **Carpi** Italy
22C3 **Carpinteria** USA
17B2 **Carrabelle** USA
52B2 **Carrara** Italy
41B3 **Carrauntoohill** Mt Irish Rep
45C2 **Carrickmacross** Irish Rep
45B2 **Carrick on Shannon** Irish Rep
45C2 **Carrick-on-Suir** Irish Rep
108C2 **Carrieton** Aust
8D2 **Carrington** USA
50B1 **Carrión** R Spain
10A2 **Carroll** USA
17A1 **Carrollton** Georgia, USA
14A3 **Carrollton** Kentucky, USA
18B2 **Carrollton** Missouri, USA
18C2 **Carruthersville** USA
60E5 **Carsamba** Turk
92B2 **Carsamba** R Turk
8B3 **Carson City** USA
14B2 **Carsonville** USA
26B4 **Cartagena** Colombia
51B2 **Cartagena** Spain
32B3 **Cartago** Colombia
25D4 **Cartago** Costa Rica
111C2 **Carterton** NZ
18B2 **Carthage** Missouri, USA
15C2 **Carthage** New York, USA
19B3 **Carthage** Texas, USA
18B2 **Cartier I** Timor S
7E4 **Cartwright** Can
31D3 **Caruaru** Brazil
33E1 **Carúpano** Ven
46B1 **Carvin** France
34A2 **Casablanca** Chile
96B1 **Casablanca** Mor
35B2 **Casa Branca** Brazil
9B3 **Casa Grande** USA
52A1 **Casale Monferrato** Italy
47D2 **Casalmaggiore** Italy
34C3 **Casares** Arg
13C3 **Cascade Mts** Can/USA
111A2 **Cascade Pt** NZ
8A2 **Cascade Range** Mts USA
30F3 **Cascavel** Brazil
53B2 **Caserta** Italy
112C9 **Casey** Base Ant
45C2 **Cashel** Irish Rep
107E3 **Casilda** Arg
10C2 **Casino** Aust
32B5 **Casma** Peru
51B1 **Caspe** Spain
8C2 **Casper** USA
61G4 **Caspian Depression** Region Kazakhstan
65G6 **Caspian S** Asia/Europe
14C3 **Cass** USA
100B2 **Cassamba** Angola
46B1 **Cassel** France
12J3 **Cassiar** Can
35A1 **Cassiar Mts** Can
35A1 **Cassilândia** Brazil
53B2 **Cassino** Italy
22C3 **Castaic** USA
34B2 **Castaño** R Arg
47D2 **Castelfranco** Italy
49D3 **Castellane** France
34D3 **Castelli** Arg
51B2 **Castellón de la Plana** Spain
31C3 **Castelo** Brazil
50A2 **Castelo Branco** Port
48C3 **Castelsarrasin** France
53B3 **Castelvetrano** Italy
108B3 **Casterton** Aust

Castilla La Nueva

50B2 **Castilla La Nueva** Region, Spain
50B1 **Castilla La Vieja** Region, Spain
41B3 **Castlebar** Irish Rep
44A3 **Castlebay** Scot
42C2 **Castle Douglas** Scot
20C1 **Castlegar** Can
45B2 **Castleisland** Irish Rep
108B3 **Castlemain** Aust
45B2 **Castlerea** Irish Rep
109C2 **Castlereagh** Aust
48C3 **Castres-sur-l'Agout** France
27E4 **Castries** St Lucia
29B4 **Castro** Arg
30F3 **Castro** Brazil
31D4 **Castro Alves** Brazil
53C3 **Castrovillari** Italy
22B2 **Castroville** USA
111A2 **Caswell Sd** NZ
25E2 **Cat** / The Bahamas
79B3 **Catabalogan** Phil
32A5 **Catacaos** Peru
35C2 **Cataguases** Brazil
19B3 **Catahoula L** USA
35B1 **Catalão** Brazil
51C1 **Cataluña** Region, Spain
30C4 **Catamarca** Arg
30C4 **Catamarca** State, Arg
101C2 **Catandica** Mozam
79B3 **Catanduanes** / Phil
31B6 **Catanduva** Brazil
53C3 **Catania** Italy
53C3 **Catanzaro** Italy
79B3 **Catarman** Phil
108A2 **Catastrophe,C** Aust
26C5 **Catatumbo** R Ven
16A2 **Catawissa** USA
23B2 **Catemaco** Mexico
49D3 **Cater** Corse
52A2 **Cateraggio** Corse
98B3 **Catete** Angola
97A3 **Catio** Guinea-Bissau
7A4 **Cat Lake** Can
13D3 **Catlegar** Can
107E3 **Cato** / Aust
25D2 **Catoche,C** Mexico
15C3 **Catoctin Mt** USA
34C3 **Catrilo** Arg
15D2 **Catskill** USA
15D2 **Catskill Mts** USA
32C2 **Cauca** R Colombia
31D2 **Caucaia** Brazil
32B2 **Caucasia** Colombia
65F5 **Caucasus** Mts Georgia
46B1 **Caudry** France
98B3 **Caungula** Angola
29B3 **Cauquenes** Chile
87B2 **Cauvery** R India
49D3 **Cavaillon** France
47D1 **Cavalese** Italy
97B4 **Cavally** R Lib
45C2 **Cavan** County, Irish Rep
45C2 **Cavan** Irish Rep
79B3 **Cavite** Phil
31C2 **Caxias** Brazil
32C4 **Caxias** Brazil
30F4 **Caxias do Sul** Brazil
98B3 **Caxito** Angola
17B1 **Cayce** USA
93D1 **Çayeli** Turk
33G3 **Cayenne** French Guiana
46A1 **Cayeux-sur-Mer** France
25E3 **Cayman Brac** /, Caribbean S
26A3 **Cayman Is** Caribbean S
26A3 **Cayman Trench** Caribbean S
99E2 **Caynabo** Somalia
25E2 **Cayo Romano** / Cuba
25D3 **Cayos Miskitos** Is Nic
26A2 **Cay Sal** / Caribbean S
100B2 **Cazombo** Angola
Ceará = Fortaleza

31C3 **Ceara** State, Brazil
79B3 **Cebu** Phil
79B3 **Cebu** / Phil
16B3 **Cecilton** USA
52B2 **Cecina** Italy
8B3 **Cedar City** USA
19A3 **Cedar Creek Res** USA
5J4 **Cedar L** Can
10A2 **Cedar Rapids** USA
17A1 **Cedartown** USA
24A2 **Cedros** / Mexico
106C4 **Ceduna** Aust
99E2 **Ceelbuur** Somalia
99E1 **Ceerigabo** Somalia
53B3 **Cefalù** Italy
59B3 **Cegléd** Hung
100A2 **Cela** Angola
24B2 **Celaya** Mexico
70C3 **Celebes S** S E Asia
14B2 **Celina** USA
52C1 **Celje** Slovenia
56C2 **Celle** Germany
71E4 **Cendrawasih** Pen Indon
47C2 **Ceno** R Italy
19B3 **Center** USA
16C2 **Center Moriches** USA
17A1 **Center Point** USA
47D2 **Cento** Italy
44B3 **Central** Region, Scot
98B2 **Central African Republic** Africa
16D2 **Central Falls** USA
18C2 **Centralia** Illinois, USA
8A2 **Centralia** Washington, USA
20B2 **Central Point** USA
71F4 **Central Range** Mts PNG
16A3 **Centreville** Maryland, USA
78C4 **Cepu** Indon
71D4 **Ceram Sea** Indon
34C3 **Cereales** Arg
31B5 **Ceres** Brazil
100A4 **Ceres** S Africa
22B2 **Ceres** USA
48C2 **Cergy-Pontoise** France
53C2 **Cerignola** Italy
60C5 **Cernavodă** Rom
9C4 **Cerralvo** / Mexico
23A1 **Cerritos** Mexico
34B2 **Cerro Aconcagua** Mt Arg
23B1 **Cerro Azul** Mexico
34A3 **Cerro Campanario** Mt Chile
34C2 **Cerro Champaqui** Mt Arg
23A2 **Cerro Cuachaia** Mt Arg
23B2 **Cerro de Astillero** Mexico
34B2 **Cerro de Olivares** Mt Arg
32B6 **Cerro de Pasco** Peru
27D3 **Cerro de Punta** Mt Puerto Rico
23A2 **Cerro El Cantado** Mt Mexico
34B3 **Cerro El Nevado** Mt Arg
23A2 **Cerro Grande** Mts Mexico
34A2 **Cerro Juncal** Mt Arg/Chile
23A1 **Cerro la Ardilla** Mts Mexico
34B1 **Cerro las Tortolas** Mt Chile
23A2 **Cerro Laurel** Mt Mexico
34A2 **Cerro Mercedario** Mt Arg
34A3 **Cerro Mora** Mt Chile
27C4 **Cerron** Mt Ven
34B3 **Cerro Payún** Mt Arg

23B2 **Cerro Penón del Rosario** Mt Mexico
34B2 **Cerro Sosneado** Mt Arg
23A2 **Cerro Teotepec** Mt Mexico
34B2 **Cerro Tupungato** Mt Arg
23B2 **Cerro Yucuyacau** Mt Mexico
47C2 **Cervo** R Italy
52B2 **Cesena** Italy
60B2 **Cēsis** Latvia
57C3 **České Budějovice** Czech Republic
59B3 **Českomoravská Vysocina** Mts Czech Republic
55C3 **Çeşme** Turk
107E4 **Cessnock** Aust
52C2 **Cetina** R Croatia
96B1 **Ceuta** N W Africa
92C2 **Ceyhan** Turk
92C2 **Ceyhan** R Turk
93C2 **Ceylanpinar** Turk
Ceylon = Sri Lanka
63B2 **Chaa-Khol** Russian Fed
48C2 **Châteaudun** France
47B1 **Chablais** Region, France
34C2 **Chacabuco** Arg
32B5 **Chachapoyas** Peru
34B3 **Chacharramendi** Arg
84C3 **Chachran** Pak
30D4 **Chaco** State, Arg
98B1 **Chad** Republic, Africa
98B1 **Chad** L C Africa
34B3 **Chadileuvu** R Arg
82C2 **Chadron** USA
18C2 **Chaffee** USA
85A3 **Chagai** Pak
63F2 **Chagda** Russian Fed
84B2 **Chaghcharan** Afghan
104B4 **Chagos Arch** Indian O
27L1 **Chaguanas** Trinidad
91D4 **Chah Bahār** Iran
76C2 **Chai Badan** Thai
76C3 **Chaine des Cardamomes** Mts Camb
98C4 **Chaine des Mitumba** Mts Zaïre
76C2 **Chaiyaphum** Thai
34D2 **Chajari** Arg
84C2 **Chakwal** Pak
30A2 **Chala** Peru
100C2 **Chalabesa** Zambia
84B2 **Chalap Dalam** Mts Afghan
73C4 **Chaling** China
85C2 **Chālisgaon** India
12F1 **Chalkyitsik** USA
46C2 **Challerange** France
46C2 **Châlons sur Marne** France
47C2 **Chalon sur Saône** France
57C3 **Cham** Germany
84B2 **Chaman** Pak
84D2 **Chamba** India
87B1 **Chamba** R India
15C3 **Chambersburg** USA
49D2 **Chambéry** France
46B2 **Chambly** France
85A3 **Chambor Kalat** Pak
84B3 **Chamgordan** Iran
34B2 **Chamical** Arg
47B2 **Chamonix** France
86A2 **Champa** India
49C2 **Champagne** Region, France
101G1 **Champagne Castle** Mt Lesotho
47A1 **Champagnole** France
18B2 **Champaign** USA
76D3 **Champassak** Laos
10C2 **Champlain,L** USA
87B2 **Chāmrājnagar** India
30B4 **Chañaral** Chile
34A3 **Chanco** Chile
4D3 **Chandalar** R USA

4D3 **Chandalar** R USA
84D2 **Chandigarh** India
86C2 **Chandpur** Bang
85D5 **Chandrapur** India
91D4 **Chānf** Iran
101C2 **Changara** Mozam
74B2 **Changbai** China
69E2 **Changchun** China
73C4 **Changde** China
68E4 **Chang-hua** Taiwan
76D2 **Changjiang** China
73D3 **Chang Jiang** R China
74B2 **Changjin** N Korea
73C4 **Changsha** China
72E3 **Changshu** China
74A2 **Changtu** China
73C4 **Changwu** China
74B3 **Changwon** N Korea
72C2 **Changzhi** China
73E3 **Changzhou** China
48B2 **Channel Is** Europe
9B3 **Channel Is** USA
7E5 **Channel Port-aux-Basques** Can
76C3 **Chanthaburi** Thai
46B2 **Chantilly** France
18A2 **Chanute** USA
73D5 **Chao'an** China
73D3 **Chao Hu** L China
76C2 **Chao Phraya** R Thai
72E1 **Chaoyang** China
31C4 **Chapada Diamantina** Mts Brazil
31C2 **Chapadinha** Brazil
23A1 **Chapala** Mexico
23A1 **Chapala,Lac de** L Mexico
61H3 **Chapayevo** Kazakhstan
30F4 **Chapecó** Brazil
27H1 **Chapeltown** Jamaica
7B5 **Chapleau** Can
61E3 **Chaplygin** Russian Fed
112C3 **Charcot I** Ant
80E2 **Chardzhou** Turkmenistan
48C2 **Charente** R France
98B1 **Chari** R Chad
98B1 **Chari Baguirmi** Region, Chad
84B1 **Charikar** Afghan
18B1 **Chariton** R USA
33F2 **Charity** Guyana
85D3 **Charkhāri** India
46C1 **Charleroi** Belg
18C2 **Charleston** Illinois, USA
17C1 **Charleston** S Carolina, USA
11C3 **Charleston** S Carolina, USA
10B3 **Charleston** W Virginia, USA
98C3 **Charlesville** Zaïre
107D3 **Charleville** Aust
49C2 **Charleville-Mézières** France
14A1 **Charlevoix** USA
14B2 **Charlotte** Michigan, USA
11B3 **Charlotte** N Carolina, USA
17B2 **Charlotte Harbor** B USA
10C3 **Charlottesville** USA
7D5 **Charlottetown** Can
27K1 **Charlotteville** Tobago
108B3 **Charlton** Aust
10C1 **Charlton I** Can
84C2 **Charsadda** Pak
107D3 **Charters Towers** Aust
48C2 **Chartres** France
23A2 **Chascomús** Arg
13D2 **Chase** Can
48B2 **Châteaubriant** France
48C2 **Châteaudun** France
48B2 **Châteaulin** France
48C2 **Châteauroux** France

46D2 **Château-Salins** France
49C2 **Château-Thierry** France
46C1 **Châtelet** Belg
48C2 **Châtellerault** France
43E4 **Chatham** Eng
7D5 **Chatham** New Brunswick, Can
16C1 **Chatham** New York, USA
14B2 **Chatham** Ontario, Can
13A2 **Chatham Sd** Can
12H3 **Chatham Str**
49C2 **Châtillon** France
47B2 **Châtillon** Italy
16B3 **Chatsworth** USA
17B1 **Chattahoochee**
17A1 **Chattahoochee** *R* USA
11B3 **Chattanooga** USA
76A1 **Chauk** Burma
49D2 **Chaumont** France
46B2 **Chauny** France
77D3 **Chau Phu** Viet
50A1 **Chaves** Port
61H2 **Chaykovskiy** Russian Fed
50B2 **Chazaouet** Alg
34C2 **Chazón** Arg
32C2 **Chcontá** Colombia
57C2 **Cheb** Czech Republic
65F4 **Cheboksary** Russian Fed
10B2 **Cheboygan** USA
74B3 **Chech'on** S Korea
85C3 **Chechro** Pak
18A2 **Checotah** USA
76A2 **Cheduba** *I* Burma
108B1 **Chegele** Aust
96B2 **Chegga** Maur
100C2 **Chegutu** Zim
20C1 **Chehalis** USA
74B4 **Cheju** S Korea
74B4 **Cheju do** *I* S Korea
74B4 **Cheju-haehyŏp** *Str* S Korea
63F2 **Chekunda** Russian Fed
20B1 **Chelan,L** USA
90B2 **Cheleken** Turkmenistan
34B3 **Chelforo** Arg
80D1 **Chelkar** Kazakhstan
59C2 **Chełm** Pol
58B2 **Chełmno** Pol
43E4 **Chelmsford** Eng
43C4 **Cheltenham** Eng
65H4 **Chelyabinsk** Russian Fed
101C2 **Chemba** Mozam
57C2 **Chemnitz** Germany
84D2 **Chenab** *R* India/Pak
96B2 **Chenachane** Alg
20C1 **Cheney** USA
18A2 **Cheney Res** USA
72D1 **Chengde** China
73A3 **Chengdu** China
72E2 **Chengshan Jiao** *Pt* China
73C4 **Chenxi** China
73C4 **Chen Xian** China
73D3 **Chen Xian** China
32B5 **Chepén** Peru
34B2 **Chepes** Arg
48C2 **Cher** *R* France
23A2 **Cheran** Mexico
17C1 **Cheraw** USA
48B2 **Cherbourg** France
96C1 **Cherchell** Alg
63C2 **Cheremkhovo** Russian Fed
60E2 **Cherepovets** Russian Fed
60D4 **Cherkassy** Ukraine
61F5 **Cherkessk** Russian Fed
60D3 **Chernigov** Ukraine
60D3 **Chernobyl** Ukraine
60C4 **Chernovtsy** Ukraine
61J2 **Chernushka** Russian Fed

60B3 **Chernyakhovsk** Russian Fed
61G4 **Chernyye Zemli** Region, Russian Fed
18A2 **Cherokees,L o'the** USA
34A3 **Cherquenco** Chile
86C1 **Cherrapunji** India
60C3 **Cherven'** Belorussia
59C2 **Chervonograd** Ukraine
10C3 **Chesapeake** *B* USA
42C3 **Cheshire** County, Eng
16C1 **Cheshire** USA
64F3 **Chëshskaya Guba** *B* Russian Fed
21A1 **Chester** California, USA
42C3 **Chester** Eng
18C2 **Chester** Illinois, USA
16C1 **Chester** Massachusets, USA
15C3 **Chester** Pennsylvania, USA
17B1 **Chester** S Carolina, USA
16A3 **Chester** *R* USA
42D3 **Chesterfield** Eng
6A3 **Chesterfield Inlet** Can
16A3 **Chestertown** USA
2503 **Chetumal** Mexico
13C1 **Chetwynd** Can
12A2 **Chevak** USA
111B2 **Cheviot** NZ
40C2 **Cheviots** *Hills* Eng/Scot
13D3 **Chewelah** USA
8C2 **Cheyenne** USA
86A1 **Chhapra** India
85D4 **Chhatarpur** India
85D4 **Chhindwāra** India
86B1 **Chhukha** Bhutan
73E5 **Chia'i** Taiwan
100A2 **Chiange** Angola
76C2 **Chiang Kham** Thai
76B2 **Chiang Mai** Thai
47C1 **Chiavenna** Italy
74E3 **Chiba** Japan
86B2 **Chibāsa** India
100A2 **Chibia** Angola
7C4 **Chibougamou** Can
75A1 **Chiburi-jima** *I* Japan
101C3 **Chibuto** Mozam
10B2 **Chicago** USA
14A2 **Chicago Heights** USA
12G3 **Chichagof I** USA
43D4 **Chichester** Eng
75B1 **Chichibu** Japan
69G4 **Chichi-jima** *I* Japan
11B3 **Chickamauga L** USA
13C3 **Chickasaway** *R* USA
9D3 **Chickasha** USA
12F2 **Chicken** USA
32J45 **Chiclayo** Peru
8A3 **Chico** USA
29C4 **Chico** *R* Arg
101C2 **Chicoa** Mozam
15D2 **Chicopee** USA
7C5 **Chicoutimi** Can
101C3 **Chicualacuala** Mozam
87B2 **Chidambaram** India
6D3 **Chidley,C** Can
17B2 **Chiefland** USA
99C3 **Chiengi** Zambia
47B2 **Chieri** Italy
46C2 **Chiers** *R* France
47C1 **Chiesa** Italy
47D2 **Chiese** *R* Italy
52B2 **Chieti** Italy
72D1 **Chifeng** China
12C3 **Chiginigak,Mt** USA
12C3 **Chigmit Mts** USA
23B2 **Chignahuapan** Mexico
12C3 **Chignik** USA
24B2 **Chihuahua** Mexico
87B2 **Chik Ballapur** India
87B2 **Chikmagalūr** India
12C2 **Chikuminuk L** USA

101C2 **Chikwawa** Malawi
76A1 **Chi-kyaw** Burma
87C1 **Chilakalūrupet** India
23B2 **Chilapa** Mexico
87B3 **Chilaw** Sri Lanka
28B6 **Chile** Republic
34B2 **Chilecito** Mendoza, Arg
100D2 **Chililabombwe** Zambia
86B2 **Chilka** *L* India
13C2 **Chilko** *R* Can
5F4 **Chilko** *L* Can
13C2 **Chilkotin** *R* Can
34A3 **Chillán** Chile
34D3 **Chillar** Arg
18B2 **Chillicothe** Missouri, USA
14B3 **Chillicothe** Ohio, USA
13C3 **Chilliwack** Can
86B1 **Chilmari** India
101C2 **Chilongozi** Zambia
20B2 **Chiloquin** USA
24C3 **Chilpancingo** Mexico
43D4 **Chiltern Hills** *Upland* Eng
14A2 **Chilton** USA
101C2 **Chilumba** Malawi
69E4 **Chi-lung** Taiwan
101C2 **Chilwa** *L* Malawi
101C2 **Chimanimani** Zim
46C1 **Chimay** Belg
65G5 **Chimbay** Uzbekistan
32B4 **Chimborazo** *Mt* Ecuador
32B5 **Chimbote** Peru
65H5 **Chimkent** Kazakhstan
101C2 **Chimoio** Mozam
67E3 **China** Republic, Asia
China National Republic = Taiwan
25D3 **Chinandega** Nic
32B6 **Chincha Alta** Peru
109D1 **Chinchilla** Aust
101C2 **Chinde** Mozam
86C2 **Chindwin** *R* Burma
100B2 **Chingola** Zambia
100A2 **Chinguar** Angola
96A2 **Chinguetti** Maur
74B3 **Chinhae** S Korea
100C2 **Chinhoyi** Zim
12D3 **Chiniak,C** USA
84C2 **Chiniot** Pak
74B3 **Chinju** S Korea
98C2 **Chinko** *R* CAR
75B1 **Chino** Japan
101C2 **Chinsali** Zambia
52B1 **Chioggia** Italy
101C2 **Chipata** Zambia
101C3 **Chipinge** Zim
87A1 **Chiplūn** India
43C4 **Chippenham** Eng
10A2 **Chippewa Falls** USA
32A4 **Chira** *R* Peru
87C1 **Chirāla** India
101C3 **Chiredzi** Zim
95A2 **Chirfa** Niger
32A2 **Chiriquí** *Mt* Panama
54C2 **Chirpan** Bulg
32A2 **Chirripo Grande** *Mt* Costa Rica
100B2 **Chirundu** Zim
100B2 **Chisamba** Zambia
7C4 **Chisasibi** Can
73B4 **Chishui He** *R* China
Chişinău = Kishinev
47B2 **Chisone** *R* Italy
61H2 **Chistopol** Russian Fed
68D1 **Chita** Russian Fed
100A2 **Chitado** Angola
100A2 **Chitembo** Angola
12F2 **Chitina** USA
12F2 **Chitina** *R* USA
87B2 **Chitradurga** India
84C1 **Chitral** Pak
32A2 **Chitré** Panama
86C2 **Chittagong** Bang
85C4 **Chittaurgarh** India
87B2 **Chittoor** India
100B2 **Chiume** Angola
47D1 **Chiusa** Italy

47B2 **Chivasso** Italy
100C2 **Chivhu** Zim
29D2 **Chivilcoy** Arg
100C2 **Chivu** Zim
75A1 **Chizu** Japan
29C3 **Choele Choel** Arg
34C3 **Choique** Arg
24B2 **Choix** Mexico
58B2 **Chojnice** Pol
99D1 **Choke Mts** Eth
48B2 **Cholet** France
23B2 **Cholula** Mexico
100B2 **Choma** Zambia
86B1 **Chomo Yummo** *Mt* China/India
57C2 **Chomutov** Czech Republic
63C1 **Chona** *R* Russian Fed
74B3 **Ch'ŏnan** S Korea
76C3 **Chon Buri** Thai
32A4 **Chone** Ecuador
74B2 **Ch'ŏngjin** N Korea
74B3 **Chongju** S Korea
74B3 **Ch'ŏngju** S Korea
100A2 **Chongoroi** Angola
73B4 **Chongqing** China
74B3 **Ch'ŏngup** S Korea
74B3 **Chŏnju** S Korea
86B1 **Chooyu** *Mt* China/Nepal
59D3 **Chortkov** Ukraine
74B3 **Ch'ŏrwŏn** N Korea
59B2 **Chorzow** Pol
74E3 **Choshi** Japan
34A3 **Chos-Malal** Arg
58B2 **Choszczno** Pol
86A2 **Chotanāgpur** Region, India
96C1 **Chott Melrhir** Alg
22B2 **Chowchilla** USA
63D3 **Choybalsan** Mongolia
6A3 **Chrantrey Inlet** *B* Can
111B2 **Christchurch** NZ
101G1 **Christiana** S Africa
6D2 **Christian,C** Can
12H3 **Christian Sd** Can
6E3 **Christianshåb** Greenland
104D4 **Christmas I** Indian O
65J5 **Chu** Kazakhstan
65J5 **Chu** *R* Kazakhstan
29C4 **Chubut** State, Arg
29C4 **Chubut** *R* Arg
60D2 **Chudovo** Russian Fed
Chudskoye Ozero = Peipus, Lake
4D3 **Chugach Mts** USA
12E2 **Chugiak** USA
75A1 **Chūgoku-sanchi** *Mts* Japan
29F2 **Chui** Brazil
29B3 **Chuillán** Chile
77C5 **Chukai** Malay
76C1 **Chu Lai** Viet
21B3 **Chula Vista** USA
12E2 **Chulitna** USA
63E2 **Chulman** Russian Fed
32A5 **Chulucanas** Peru
30C2 **Chulumani** Bol
65K4 **Chulym** Russian Fed
63A2 **Chulym** *R* Russian Fed
63B2 **Chulym** *R* Russian Fed
84D2 **Chumar** India
63F2 **Chumikan** Russian Fed
77B3 **Chumphon** Thai
74B3 **Ch'unch'ŏn** S Korea
86B2 **Chunchura** India
74B3 **Ch'ungju** S Korea
Chungking = Chongqing
99D3 **Chunya** Tanz
63C1 **Chunya** *R* Russian Fed
27L1 **Chupara Pt** Trinidad
30C3 **Chuquicamata** Chile
52A1 **Chur** Switz

86C2 Churāchāndpur India	17A1 Clanton USA	16B2 Clinton New Jersey, USA	32A4 Cojimies Ecuador
7A4 Churchill Can	100A4 Clanwilliam S Africa	4H3 Clinton-Colden L Can	107D4 Colac Aust
7D4 Churchill R Labrador, Can	45C2 Clara Irish Rep	24B3 Clipperton I Pacific O	31C5 Colatina Brazil
7A4 Churchill R Manitoba, Can	34D3 Claraz Arg	30C2 Cliza Bol	112B6 Colbeck,C Ant
7A4 Churchill,C Can	45B2 Clare County, Irish Rep	45B3 Clonakilty Irish Rep	43E4 Colchester Eng
7D4 Churchill Falls Can	14B2 Clare USA	107D3 Cloncurry Aust	16C2 Colchester USA
5H4 Churchill L Can	45A2 Clare I Irish Rep	45C1 Clones Irish Rep	47B1 Col de la Faucille France
84C3 Chūru India	75D2 Claremont USA	45C2 Clonmel Irish Rep	13E2 Cold L Can
23A2 Churumuco Mexico	18A2 Claremore USA	10A2 Cloquet USA	52A1 Col du Grand St Bernard P Italy/Switz
61J2 Chusovoy Russian Fed	45B2 Claremorris Irish Rep	12C2 Cloudy Mt USA	47B2 Col du Lautaret P France/Italy
61G2 Chuvashskaya Respublika, Russian Fed	109D1 Clarence R Aust	22C2 Clovis California, USA	52A1 Col du Mont Cenis P France/Italy
68B4 Chuxiong China	111B2 Clarence R NZ	9C3 Clovis New Mexico, USA	14B2 Coldwater USA
76D3 Chu Yang Sin Mt Viet	27C4 Clarence Str Aust	54B1 Cluj Rom	12F1 Coleen R USA
78B4 Cianjur Indon	12H3 Clarence Str USA	54B1 Cluj-Napoca Rom	14B2 Coleman Michigan, USA
47D2 Ciano d'Enza Italy	19B3 Clarendon USA	47B1 Cluses France	101G1 Colenso S Africa
35A2 Cianorte Brazil	7E5 Clarenville Can	25C3 Clusone Italy	45C1 Coleraine N Ire
58C2 Ciechanów Pol	5G4 Claresholm Can	111A3 Clutha R NZ	111B2 Coleridge,L NZ
25E2 Ciego de Avila Cuba	15C2 Clarion Pennsylvania, USA	43C3 Clwyd County, Wales	100B4 Colesberg S Africa
32C1 Ciénaga Colombia	24A3 Clarión I Mexico	6D2 Clyde Can	22C1 Coleville USA
25D2 Cienfuegos Cuba	15C2 Clarion R USA	111A3 Clyde NZ	21A2 Colfax California, USA
59B3 Cieszyn Pol	105J3 Clarion Fracture Zone Pacific O	42B2 Clyde R Scot	19B3 Colfax Louisiana, USA
51B2 Cieza Spain	11B3 Clark Hill Res USA	23A2 Coahuayana Mexico	20C1 Colfax Washington, USA
92B2 Cihanbeyli Turk	14B2 Clark,Pt Can	23A2 Coalcoman Mexico	24B3 Colima Mexico
23A2 Cihuatlán Mexico	21B2 Clarksburg USA	13E2 Coaldale Can	23A2 Colima State, Mexico
78B4 Cijulang Indon	11A3 Clarksdale USA	21B2 Coaldale USA	34A2 Colina Chile
78B4 Cilacap Indon	12C3 Clarks Point USA	21A2 Coalinga USA	44A3 Coll I Scot
54C1 Cîmpina Rom	20C1 Clarkston USA	33E5 Coari R Brazil	109C1 Collarenebri Aust
51C1 Cinca R Spain	18B2 Clarksville Arkansas, USA	17A1 Coastal Plain USA	52A2 Colle de Tende P France/Italy
52C2 Cinčer Mt Bosnia-Herzegovina	35A1 Claro R Brazil	4E4 Coast Mts Can	12E2 College USA
10B3 Cincinnati USA	29D3 Claromecó Arg	8A1 Coast Ranges Mts USA	17B1 College Park Georgia, USA
54B1 Cindrelu Mt Rom	18A2 Clay Center USA	42B2 Coatbridge Scot	16A3 College Park Washington, USA
55C3 Cine R Turk	44D2 Claymore Oilfield N Sea	23B2 Coatepec Mexico	19A3 College Station USA
46C1 Ciney Belg	13B3 Clayoquot Sd Can	16B3 Coatesville USA	106A4 Collie Aust
34B3 Cipolletti Arg	9C3 Clayton New Mexico, USA	15D1 Coaticook Can	106B2 Collier B Aust
4D3 Circle Alaska, USA	15C2 Clayton New York, USA	6B3 Coats I Can	46A1 Collines de L'Artois Mts France
14B3 Circleville USA	41B3 Clear C Irish Rep	112B1 Coats Land Region, Ant	46B2 Collines De Thiérache France
78B4 Cirebon Indon	45C2 Cleare,C USA	25C3 Coatzacoalcos Mexico	14B2 Collingwood Can
43D4 Cirencester Eng	13D1 Clear Hills Mts Can	25C3 Cobalt Can	110B2 Collingwood NZ
47D2 Citadella Italy	21A2 Clear L USA	25C3 Cobán Guatemala	19C3 Collins Mississippi, USA
24C3 Citlaltepetl Mt	20B2 Clear Lake Res USA	107D4 Cobar Aust	4H2 Collinson Pen Can
100A4 Citrusdal S Africa	13D2 Clearwater Can	109C3 Cobargo Aust	107D3 Collinsville Aust
52B2 Città del Vaticano Italy	11B4 Clearwater USA	45B3 Cobh Irish Rep	18C2 Collinsville Illinois, USA
52B2 Città di Castello Italy	13E1 Clearwater R Can	51B2 Cobo de Palos C Spain	18A2 Collinsville Oklahoma, USA
24B2 Ciudad Acuña Mexico	13C2 Clearwater L Can	7C5 Cobourg Can	34A3 Collipulli Chile
23A2 Ciudad Altamirano Mexico	9D3 Cleburne USA	106C2 Cobourg Pen Aust	49D2 Colmar France
33E2 Ciudad Bolivar Ven	44D2 Cleeton Oilfield North Sea	57C2 Coburg Germany	Cologne = Köln
24B2 Ciudad Camargo Mexico	22B1 Clements Can	32B4 Coca Ecuador	35B2 Colômbia Brazil
25C3 Ciudad del Carmen Mexico	79A3 Cleopatra Needle Mt Phil	17B2 Coca USA	32B3 Colombia Republic, S America
23B1 Ciudad del Maiz Mexico	107D3 Clermont Aust	30D2 Cochabamba Bol	15C3 Colombia USA
51C1 Ciudadela Spain	46B2 Clermont France	46D1 Cochem Germany	87B3 Colombo Sri Lanka
33E2 Ciudad Guayana Ven	46C2 Clermont-en-Argonne France	87B3 Cochin India	25D2 Colón Panama
24B3 Ciudad Guzman Mexico	49C2 Clermont-Ferrand France	13E2 Cochrane Alberta, Can	32B2 Colón Panama
23A2 Ciudad Hidalgo Mexico	46D1 Clervaux Germany	7C5 Cochrane Ontario, Can	29E2 Colonia Urug
24B1 Ciudad Juárez Mexico	47D1 Cles Italy	108B2 Cockburn Aust	34D2 Colonia del Sacramento Urug
9C4 Ciudad Lerdo Mexico	108A2 Cleve Aust	16A3 Cockeysville USA	34B3 Colonia 25 de Mayo Arg
24C2 Ciudad Madero Mexico	42D2 Cleveland County, Eng	27H1 Cockpit Country,The Jamaica	29C5 Colonia Las Heras Arg
23B2 Ciudad Mendoza Mexico	19B3 Cleveland Mississippi, USA	25D3 Coco R Honduras/Nic	44A3 Colonsay I Scot
24B2 Ciudad Obregon Mexico	12D2 Cleveland Ohio, USA	98A2 Cocobeach Gabon	23A1 Colontlán Mexico
27C4 Ciudad Ojeda Ven	11B3 Cleveland Tennessee, USA	27L1 Cocos B Trinidad	27E5 Coloradito Ven
33E2 Ciudad Piar Ven	19B3 Cleveland Texas, USA	104C4 Cocos Is Indian O	8C3 Colorado State, USA
50B2 Ciudad Real Spain	41B3 Clew B Irish Rep	23A1 Cocula Mexico	9B3 Colorado R Arizona, USA
50A1 Ciudad Rodrigo Spain	45A2 Clifden Irish Rep	10C2 Cod,C USA	29D3 Colorado R Buenos Aires, Arg
24C2 Ciudad Valles Mexico	109D1 Clifton Aust	111A3 Codfish I NZ	9D3 Colorado R Texas, USA
24C2 Ciudad Victoria Mexico	16B2 Clifton New Jersey, USA	64D1 Cod I Can	9B3 Colorado Plat USA
52B2 Civitavecchia Italy	108A1 Clifton Hills Aust	47E2 Codigoro Italy	8C3 Colorado Springs USA
93D2 Cizre Turk	13F3 Climax Can	31C2 Codó Brazil	22D3 Colton USA
45D4 Clacton-on-Sea Eng	9D3 Clinton Arkansas, USA	47C2 Codogno Italy	16A3 Columbia Maryland, USA
5G4 Claire,L Can	5F4 Clinton Can	8C2 Cody USA	
14C2 Clairton USA	16C2 Clinton Connecticut, USA	56B2 Coesfeld Germany	
47A1 Clairvaux France	16D1 Clinton Massachusetts, USA	8B2 Coeur d'Alene USA	
	19B3 Clinton Mississippi, USA	9D3 Coffeyville USA	
	18B2 Clinton Missouri, USA	108A2 Coffin B Aust	
		109D2 Coff's Harbour Aust	
		23B2 Cofre de Perote Mt Mexico	
		48B2 Cognac France	
		15D2 Cohoes USA	
		108A3 Cohuna Aust	
		29B5 Coihaique Chile	
		87B2 Coimbatore India	
		50A1 Coimbra Port	

19C3 Columbia Mississippi, USA
10A3 Columbia Missouri, USA
15C2 Columbia Pennsylvania, USA
11B3 Columbia S Carolina, USA
11B3 Columbia Tennessee, USA
13D2 Columbia R Can
8A2 Columbia R Can
5G4 Columbia Mt Can
20C1 Columbia Plat USA
11B3 Columbus Georgia, USA
14A3 Columbus Indiana, USA
11B3 Columbus Mississippi, USA
8D2 Columbus Nebraska, USA
10B2 Columbus Ohio, USA
19A4 Columbus Texas, USA
20C1 Colville USA
4C3 Colville R USA
110C1 Colville R NZ
4F3 Colville L Can
108A1 Colwyn Bay Wales
47E2 Comacchio Italy
22B1 Comanche Res USA
112C2 Comandante Ferraz Base Ant
25D3 Comayagua Honduras
34A2 Combarbalá Chile
45C2 Comeragh Mts
86C2 Comilla Bang
25C3 Comitán Mexico
46C2 Commercy France
6B3 Committees B Can
52A1 Como Italy
29C5 Comodoro Rivadavia Arg
23A1 Comonfort Mexico
87B3 Comorin,C India
101D2 Comoros Is Indian O
49C2 Compiègne France
23A1 Compostela Mexico
34B2 Comte Salas Arg
86C1 Cona China
97A4 Conakry Guinea
34B2 Concarán Arg
48B2 Concarneau France
35D1 Conceição da Barra Brazil
31B3 Conceição do Araguaia Brazil
35C1 Conceição do Mato Dentro Brazil
29B3 Concepción Chile
30E3 Concepción Par
29E2 Concepción R Arg
24B2 Concepción del Oro Mexico
34D2 Concepcion del Uruguay Arg
9A3 Conception,Pt USA
35B2 Conchas Brazil
9C4 Conchos R Mexico
21A2 Concord California, USA
10C2 Concord New Hampshire, USA
29E2 Concordia Arg
8D3 Concordia USA
20B1 Concrete USA
109D1 Condamine Aust
107D4 Condobolin Aust
20B1 Condon USA
46C1 Condroz Mts Belg
17A1 Conecuh R USA
47E2 Conegliano Italy
89F8 Congo Republic, Africa
89F8 Congo,R R Congo
Congo,R = Zaire
14B1 Coniston Can
45B2 Connacht Region, Irish Rep
14B2 Conneaut USA

10C2 Connecticut State, USA
15D2 Connecticut R USA
15C2 Connellsville USA
45B2 Connemara,Mts of Irish Rep
14A3 Connersville USA
108B2 Conoble Aust
18A3 Conroe USA
35C2 Conselheiro Lafaiete Brazil
77D4 Con Son Is Viet
Constance,L = Bodensee
60C5 Constanta Rom
96C1 Constantine Alg
12C3 Constantine,C USA
29B3 Constitución Chile
13F3 Consul Can
47E2 Contarina Italy
31C4 Contas R Brazil
23B2 Contreras Mexico
4H3 Contwoyto L Can
11A3 Conway Arkansas, USA
15D2 Conway New Hampshire, USA
17C1 Conway South Carolina, USA
108A1 Conway,L Aust
42C3 Conwy Wales
106C3 Coober Pedy Aust
110B2 Cook Str NZ
13B2 Cook,C Can
105H4 Cook Inlet B USA
111B2 Cook,Mt NZ
107D2 Cooktown Aust
109C2 Coolabah Aust
109C2 Cooladdi Aust
109C2 Coolah Aust
109C2 Coolamon Aust
106B4 Coolgardie Aust
109C2 Coonabarabran Aust
109C2 Coonamble Aust
108A2 Coonbah Aust
108A2 Coondambo Aust
32D1 Coqo India
87B2 Coonoor India
108B1 Cooper Basin Aust
106C3 Cooper Creek Aust
108B1 Cooper Creek Aust
111C1 Coorong,The Aust
109D1 Cooroy Aust
20B2 Coos B USA
20B2 Coos Bay USA
107D4 Cootamundra Aust
45C1 Cootehill Irish Rep
23B2 Copala Mexico
23B2 Copalillo Mexico
Copenhagen = København
30B4 Copiapó Chile
47D2 Copparo Italy
12F2 Copper R USA
4D3 Copper Centre USA
14B1 Copper Cliff Can
Coppermine = Qurlurtuuq
4G3 Coppermine R Can
Coquihalluille = Mbandaka
30B4 Coquimbo Chile
54B2 Corabia Rom
17B2 Coral Gables USA
6B3 Coral Harbour Can
107D2 Coral S Aust/PNG
104F4 Coral Sea Basin Pacific O
107E2 Coral Sea Island Territories Aust
108B3 Corangamite,L Aust
33F3 Corantijn R Surinam/ Guyana
46B2 Corbeil-Essonnes France
50A1 Corcubión Spain
11B3 Cordele USA
50A1 Cordillera Cantabrica Mts Spain
26C3 Cordillera Central Mts Dom Rep

79B2 Cordillera Central Mts Phil
34B2 Cordillera de Ansita Mts Arg
32B5 Cordillera de los Andes Mts Arg
30C4 Cordillera del Toro Mt Arg
32C2 Cordillera de Merida Ven
34A3 Cordillera de Viento Mts Arg
25D3 Cordillera Isabella Mts Nic
32B3 Cordillera Occidental Mts Colombia
32B3 Cordillera Oriental Mts Colombia
108B1 Cordillo Downs Aust
29D2 Córdoba Arg
24C3 Córdoba Mexico
50B2 Córdoba Spain
29D2 Córdoba State, Arg
4D3 Cordova USA
109D2 Coricudgy,Mt Aust
53C3 Corigliano Calabro Italy
11B3 Corinth Mississippi, USA
31C5 Corinto Brazil
45B2 Cork County, Irish Rep
41B3 Cork Irish Rep
92A1 Çorlu Turk
31C5 Cornel Fabriciano Brazil
35A2 Cornelio Procópio Brazil
7E5 Corner Brook Can
109C3 Corner Inlet B Aust
15C2 Corning USA
7C5 Cornwall County, Eng
43B4 Cornwall,C Eng
4H2 Cornwall I Can
6A2 Cornwallis I Can
2Co Ven
31C2 Coroatá Brazil
30C2 Coroico Bol
35B1 Coromandel Brazil
87C2 Coromandel Coast India
110C1 Coromandel Pen NZ
110C1 Coromandel Range Mts NZ
22D4 Corona California, USA
13E2 Coronation Can
4G3 Coronation G Can
34C2 Coronda Arg
34D3 Coronel Brandsen Arg
34C3 Coronel Dorrego Arg
35C1 Coronel Fabriciano Brazil
30E4 Coronel Oviedo Par
29D3 Coronel Pringles Arg
34C3 Coronel Suárez Arg
34D3 Coronel Vidal Arg
30B2 Coropuna Mt Peru
109C3 Corowa Aust
49D3 Corps France
9D4 Corpus Christi USA
9D4 Corpus Christi,L USA
79B3 Corregidor i Phil
35A1 Corrente R Mato Grosso, Brazil
30E4 Corrientes Arg
30E4 Corrientes State, Arg
19B3 Corrigan USA
106A4 Corrigin Aust
107E2 Corringe Is Aust
35C2 Corryong Aust
52A2 Corse I Medit S
42B2 Corsewall Pt Scot
Corsica = Corse
9D3 Corsicana USA
52A2 Corte Corse
9C3 Cortez USA
52B1 Cortina d'Ampezzo Italy

15C2 Cortland USA
23A2 Coruca de Catalan Mexico
93D1 Çoruh R Turk
60E5 Çorum Turk
30E2 Corumbá Brazil
35B1 Corumbaíba Brazil
35B1 Corumbaíba Brazil
20B2 Corvallis USA
96A1 Corvo i Açores
43C3 Corwen Wales
23B2 Coscomatopec Mexico
53C3 Cosenza Italy
101D1 Cosmoledo Is Seychelles
34C2 Cosquín Arg
51B2 Costa Blanca Region, Spain
51C1 Costa Brava Region, Spain
50B2 Costa de la Luz Region, Spain
50B2 Costa del Sol Region, Spain
22D4 Costa Mesa USA
25D3 Costa Rica Republic, Cent America
79B4 Cotabato Phil
30C3 Cotagaita Bol
49D3 Côte d'Azur Region, France
46C2 Côtes de Meuse Mts France
97C4 Cotonou Benin
32B4 Cotopaxi Mt Ecuador
43C4 Cotswold Hills Upland Eng
20B2 Cottage Grove USA
56C2 Cottbus Germany
108A3 Couedic,C du Aust
20C1 Couer d'Alene L USA
46B2 Coulommiers France
16C1 Coulonge R Can
22B2 Coulterville USA
4B3 Council USA
8D2 Council Bluffs USA
58C1 Courland Lagoon Lg Lithuania/Russian Fed
47B2 Courmayeur Italy
13B3 Courtenay Can
Courtrai = Kortrijk
48B2 Coutances France
43D3 Coventry Eng
50A1 Covilhã Spain
17B1 Covington Georgia, USA
19B3 Covington Louisiana, USA
109C2 Cowal,L Aust
108B3 Cowangie Aust
15D1 Cowansville Can
108A1 Coward Springs Aust
108A2 Cowell Aust
108C3 Cowes Aust
20B1 Cowichan L Can
20B1 Cowlitz R USA
109C2 Cowra Aust
30F2 Coxim Brazil
16C1 Coxsackie USA
86C2 Cox's Bazar Bang
22B2 Coyote USA
23A2 Coyuca de Benitez Mexico
59B2 Cracow Pol
108B4 Cradock S Africa
8C2 Craig USA
57C3 Crailsheim Germany
54B2 Craiova Rom
15D2 Cranberry L USA
5G5 Cranbrook Can
20C2 Crane Oregon, USA
16D2 Cranston USA
20B2 Crater L USA
20B2 Crater Lake Nat Pk USA
31C3 Crateús Brazil
31D3 Crato Brazil
14A2 Crawfordsville USA
17B1 Crawfordville USA
43D4 Crawley Eng
5H4 Cree L Can
46B2 Creil France

Crema

47C2 Crema Italy
52B1 Cremona Italy
46B2 Crépy-en-Valois France
52B2 Cres I Yugos
20B2 Crescent City USA
34C2 Crespo Arg
13D3 Creston Can
18B1 Creston USA
17A1 Crestview USA
108B3 Creswick Aust
47A1 Crêt de la Neige Mt France
Crete = Kriti
18A1 Crete USA
55B3 Crete,S of Greece
48C2 Creuse R France
43C3 Crewe Eng
44B3 Crianlarich Scot
30G4 Criciuma Brazil
44C3 Crieff Scot
12G3 Crillon,Mt USA
35B1 Cristalina Brazil
52C1 Croatia Republic, Europe
78D1 Crocker Range Mts Malay
19A3 Crockett USA
106C2 Croker I Aust
44C3 Cromarty Scot
43E3 Cromer Eng
111A3 Cromwell NZ
11C4 Crooked I The Bahamas
13C2 Crooked R Can
8D2 Crookston USA
109C2 Crookwell Aust
109D1 Croppa Creek Aust
11A3 Crossett USA
12G3 Cross Sd USA
53C3 Crotone Italy
19B3 Crowley USA
27K1 Crown Pt Tobago
109D1 Crows Nest Aust
107D2 Croydon Aust
43D4 Croydon Eng
104B5 Crozet Basin Indian O
4F2 Crozier Chan Can
30F4 Cruz Alta Brazil
25E3 Cruz,C Cuba
29D2 Cruz del Eje Arg
32C5 Cruzeiro Arg
30C2 Cruzeiro do Sul Brazil
13C1 Crysdale,Mt Can
108A2 Crystal Brook Aust
18B2 Crystal City Missouri, USA
14A1 Crystal Falls USA
101C2 Cuamba Mozam
100B2 Cuando R Angola
100A2 Cuangar Angola
Cuango,R = Kwango,R
34C2 Cuarto R Arg
24B2 Cuauhtémoc Mexico
23B2 Cuautla Mexico
25D2 Cuba Republic, Caribbean S
100A2 Cubango R Angola
100A2 Cuchi Angola
100A2 Cuchi R Angola
34C3 Cuchillo Co Arg
32D3 Cucuí Brazil
32C2 Cúcuta Colombia
87B2 Cuddalore India
87B2 Cuddapah India
106A3 Cue Aust
32B4 Cuenca Ecuador
51B1 Cuenca Spain
24C3 Cuernavaca Mexico
19A4 Cuero USA
30E2 Cuiabá Brazil
30E2 Cuiabá R Brazil
23B2 Cuicatlan Mexico
35C1 Cuieté Brazil
44A3 Cuillin Hills Mts Scot
98B3 Cuilo R Angola
100A2 Cuito R Angola
100A2 Cuito Cunavale Angola
23A2 Cuitzeo Mexico
77D3 Cu Lao Hon I Viet
109C3 Culcairn Aust

109C1 Culgoa R Aust
24B2 Culiacán Mexico
79A3 Culion I Phil
17A1 Cullman USA
47A2 Culoz France
15C3 Culpeper USA
32J7 Culpepper I Ecuador
17B2 Culter Ridge USA
11B2 Culverden NZ
33E1 Cumaná Ven
10C3 Cumberland Maryland, USA
11B3 Cumberland R USA
6D3 Cumberland Pen Can
6D3 Cumbernauld Sd Can
42C2 Cumbria Eng
21A2 Cummings USA
108A2 Cummins Aust
44C3 Cumnock Scot
34A3 Cunco Chile
100A2 Cunene R Angola/Namibia
52A2 Cuneo Italy
107D3 Cunnamulla Aust
44C3 Cupar Scot
54B2 Cuprija Serbia, Yugos
27D4 Curaçao I Caribbean S
34A3 Curacautin Chile
34B3 Curaco R Arg
34A3 Curanilahue Chile
34A3 Curepto Chile
29B2 Curicó Chile
30G4 Curitiba Brazil
108A2 Curnamona Aust
100A2 Curoca R Angola
31C5 Curvelo Brazil
18A2 Cushing USA
13D2 Cutbank R Can
17B1 Cuthbert USA
34B3 Cutral-Có Arg
86B2 Cuttack India
100A2 Cuvelai Angola
56B2 Cuxhaven Germany
14B2 Cuyahoga Falls USA
79B3 Cuyo Is Phil
32C6 Cuzco Peru
99C3 Cyangugu Zaire
Cyclades = Kikládhes
13F5 Cypress Hills Mts Can
92B3 Cyprus Republic, Medit S
6D3 Cyrus Field B Can
59B3 Czech Republic Republic, Europe
59B2 Częstochowa Pol

D

76C1 Da R Viet
69E2 Da'an China
94C3 Dab'a Jordan
27C4 Dabajuro Ven
99E2 Dabaro Somalia
73B3 Daba Shan Mts China
99D1 Dabat Eth
85C4 Dabhoi India
73C3 Dabie Shan Mts China
97A3 Dabola Guinea
97B4 Daboya Ivory Coast
59B2 Dabrowa Gorn Pol
57C3 Dachau Germany
52B1 Dachstein Mt Austria
73A3 Dada He R China
17B2 Dade City USA
84B3 Dadhar Pak
85B3 Dadu Pak
68C3 Dadu He R China
79B3 Daet Phil
73B4 Dafang China
76B2 Daga R Burma
99E2 Dagana Eth
97A3 Dagana Eth
65F5 Dagestanskaya Respublic, Russian Fed
79B2 Dagupan Phil
92B4 Dahab Egypt
63E3 Da Hinggan Ling Mts China
17B1 Dahlonega USA

85C4 Dāhod India
86A1 Dailekh Nepal
34C2 Daireaux Arg
69F4 Daitō Is Pacific O
106C3 Dajarra Aust
97A3 Dakar Sen
95B2 Dakhla Oasis Egypt
97C3 Dakoro Niger
54B2 Dakovica Serbia, Yugos
54A1 Dakovo Croatia
100B2 Dala Angola
97A3 Dalaba Guinea
72D1 Dalai Nur L China
68C2 Dalandzadgad Mongolia
79B3 Dalangaman Is Phil
76D3 Da Lat Viet
72A1 Dalay Mongolia
107E3 Dalby Aust
39F7 Dalen Nor
42C2 Dales,The Upland Eng
17A1 Daleville USA
9C3 Dalhart USA
4E2 Dalhousie,C Can
72E2 Dalian China
9D3 Dallas USA
20B1 Dalles,The USA
5E4 Dall I USA
86A2 Dalli Rajhara India
97C3 Dallol R Niger
97C3 Dallol Bosso R Niger
52C2 Dalmatia Region Bosnia-Herzegovnia
69F2 Dal'nerechensk Russian Fed
97B4 Daloa Ivory Coast
73B4 Dalou Shan Mts China
86A2 Dāltenganj India
17B1 Dalton Georgia, USA
16C1 Dalton Massachusetts, USA
106C2 Daly R Aust
21A2 Daly City USA
106C2 Daly Waters Aust
79B4 Damaguete Phil
85C4 Daman India
92B3 Damanhûr Egypt
71D4 Damar I Indon
98B2 Damara CAR
92C3 Damascus Syria
16A3 Damascus USA
97D3 Damaturu Nig
90B2 Damavand Iran
98B3 Damba Angola
87C3 Dambulla Sri Lanka
90B2 Damghan Iran
85D4 Damoh India
99E2 Damot Eth
94B2 Damour Leb
106A3 Dampier Aust
94B3 Danā Jordan
22C2 Dana,Mt USA
97B4 Danané Lib
76D2 Da Nang Viet
79B3 Danao Phil
70A3 Danau Tobu L Indon
71D4 Danau Tuwuti L Indon
73A3 Danbu China
15D2 Danbury USA
86A1 Dandeldhura Nepal
87A1 Dandeli India
108C3 Dandenong Aust
74A2 Dandong China
100A4 Danger Pt S Africa
99D1 Dangila Eth
6D1 Danguard Jenson Land Region Can
7E4 Daniels Harbour Can
6G3 Dannebrogs Øy I Greenland
110C2 Dannevirke NZ
87C1 Dantewāra India
10B2 Danube = Donau
10B2 Danville Illinois, USA
11B3 Danville Kentucky, USA
16A2 Danville Pennsylvania, USA

11C3 Danville Virginia, USA
Danzig = Gdańsk
73C4 Dao Xian China
73B4 Daozhen China
79B4 Dapiak,Mt Phil
79B4 Dapitan Phil
66C2 Da Qaidam China
69C2 Daqing China
94C2 Dar'a Syria
91B4 Dārāb Iran
91A4 Daraj Libya
90B3 Dārān Iran
92C3 Dar'ā Salkhad Syria
86B1 Darbhanga India
22C1 Dardanelle USA
18B2 Dardanelle,C USA
Dar-el-Beïda = Casablanca
99D3 Dar es Salaam Tanz
110B1 Dargaville NZ
17B1 Darien USA
86B1 Darjeeling = Dārjiling
86B1 Dārjiling India
107D4 Darling R Aust
109C1 Darling Downs Aust
6C1 Darling Pen Can
108B2 Darlington Aust
42D2 Darlington Eng
17C1 Darlington USA
57B3 Darmstadt Germany
95B1 Darnah Libya
108B2 Darnick Aust
4F3 Darnley B Can
112C10 Darnley,C Ant
51B1 Daroca Spain
98C2 Dar Rounga Region, CAR
43C4 Dart R Eng
41C3 Dartmoor Moorland Eng
43C4 Dartmoor Nat Pk Eng
7D5 Dartmouth Can
43C4 Dartmouth Eng
7D7 Daru PNG
52C1 Daruvar Croatia
106C2 Darwin Aust
91B4 Daryacheh-ye Bakhtegan L Iran
91B4 Daryacheh-ye Mahārlū L Iran
90B3 Daryacheh-ye Namak Salt Flat Iran
90D3 Daryacheh-ye-Sistan Salt L Iran/Afghan
91B4 Daryacheh-ye Tashk L Iran
80C2 Daryacheh-ye Orūmiyeh L Iran
91C4 Darzin Iran
91B4 Das I UAE
73C3 Dashennonglia Mt China
90C2 Dasht Iran
90B3 Dasht-e-Kavir Salt Desert Iran
90C3 Dasht-e-Lut Salt Desert Iran
90D3 Dasht-e-Naomid Desert Region Iran
85D3 Datia India
72A2 Datong China
72C1 Datong China
72A2 Datong He R China
39K7 Datu Piang Phil
39K7 Daugava R Latvia
60C2 Daugavpils Latvia
6D1 Dauguard Jensen Land Greenland
84A1 Dauiatabad Afghan
85D3 Daulpur India
46D1 Daun Germany
87A1 Daund India
5H4 Dauphin Can
16A2 Dauphin USA
49D2 Dauphiné Region, France
97C3 Daura Nig
85D3 Dausa India
87B2 Dāvangere India
79C4 Davao Phil
79C4 Davao G Phil
22A2 Davenport California, USA

10A2 Davenport Iowa, USA
32A2 David Panama
4D3 Davidson Mts USA
21A2 Davis USA
112C10 Davis Base Ant
7D4 Davis Inlet Can
6E3 Davis Str Greenland/Can
61J3 Davlekanovo Russian Fed
47C1 Davos Switz
99E2 Dawa R Eth
73A4 Dawan China
84B2 Dawat Yar Afghan
Dawei = Tavoy
91B4 Dawhat Salwah B Qatar/S Arabia
76B2 Dawna Range Mts Burma
4E3 Dawson Can
17B1 Dawson Georgia, USA
107D3 Dawson R Aust
5F4 Dawson Creek Can
13D2 Dawson,Mt Can
12G2 Dawson Range Mts Can
73A3 Dawu China
73C3 Dawu China
48B3 Dax France
73B3 Daxian China
73B5 Daxin China
73A3 Daxue Shan Mts China
73C4 Dayong China
94C2 Dayr 'Ali Syria
94C1 Dayr 'Atiyah Syria
93D2 Dayr az Zawr Syria
10B3 Dayton Ohio, USA
19B4 Dayton Texas, USA
20C1 Dayton Washington, USA
11B4 Daytona Beach USA
73C4 Dayu China
78D3 Dayu Indon
72D2 Da Yunhe R China
20C2 Dayville USA
73A3 Dazhu China
100B4 De Aar S Africa
26C2 Deadman's Cay The Bahamas
92C3 Dead S Israel/Jordan
24G1 Deal Eng
101G1 Dealesville S Africa
13B2 Dean R Can
13B2 Dean Chan Can
34C2 Deán Funes Arg
14B2 Dearborn USA
4F3 Dease Arm B Can
4E4 Dease Lake Can
9B3 Death V USA
48C2 Deauville France
97B4 Debakala Ivory Coast
12B2 Debauch Mt USA
27L1 Débé Trinidad
59C2 Debica Pol
58C2 Deblin Pol
97B3 Débo,L Mali
59C3 Debrecen Hung
99D2 Debre Birhan Eth
99D1 Debre Markos Eth
99D1 Debre Tabor Eth
11B3 Decatur Alabama, USA
17B1 Decatur Georgia, USA
10B3 Decatur Illinois, USA
14B2 Decatur Indiana, USA
48C3 Decazeville France
73A4 Dechang China
97B3 Dédougou Burkina
101C2 Dedza Malawi
42B2 Dee R Dumfries and Galloway, Scot
42C3 Dee R Eng/Wales
44C3 Dee R Grampian, Scot
15C1 Deep River Can
16C2 Deep River USA
109D1 Deepwater Aust
7E5 Deer Lake Can
8B2 Deer Lodge USA

34D3 Defferrari Arg
17A1 De Funiak Springs USA
68B3 Dêgê China
99E1 Degeh Bur Eth
106A3 De Grey R Aust
91B3 Deh Bid Iran
84B1 Dehi Afghan
96D1 Dehibat Tunisia
87B3 Dehiwala-Mt Lavinia Sri Lanka
90A3 Dehloran Iran
84D2 Dehra Dün India
86A2 Dehri India
98C2 Deim Zubeir Sudan
94B2 Deir Abu Sa'id Jordan
94C1 Deir el Ahmar Leb
60B4 Dej Rom
19B3 De Kalb Texas, USA
63G2 De Kastri Russian Fed
98C3 Dekese Zaïre
98B2 Dekoa CAR
106B1 Dekusi Indon
98B3 Delano USA
10C3 Delaware State, USA
14B2 Delaware USA
15C2 Delaware R USA
10C3 Delaware B USA
109C3 Delegate Aust
47B1 Delémont Switz
101D2 Delgado C Mozam
84D3 Delhi India
15D2 Delhi New York, USA
92B1 Delice Turk
24B2 Delicias Mexico
90B3 Delijān Iran
47B1 Delle France
22D4 Del Mar USA
39F8 Delmenhorst Germany
4B3 De Long Mts USA
109C4 Deloraine Aust
5Hb Deloraine Can
17B2 Delray Beach USA
9C4 Del Rio USA
8B3 Delta USA
12E2 Delta R USA
12E2 Delta Junction USA
99D2 Dembi Dolo Eth
46C1 Demer R Belg
9C3 Deming USA
54C2 Demirköy Turk
49C1 Denain France
82A2 Denau Uzbekistan
42C3 Denbigh Wales
12B2 Denbigh,C USA
78B3 Dendang Indon
46C1 Dendermond Belg
90D2 Dendi Mt Eth
46B1 Dendre R Belg
72B1 Dengkou China
72C3 Deng Xian China
27H1 Denham,Mt Jamaica
56A2 Den Helder Neth
51C2 Denia Spain
107D4 Deniliquin Aust
20C2 Denio USA
9D3 Denison Texas, USA
12D3 Denison,Mt USA
92A2 Denizli Turk
39F7 Denmark Kingdom, Europe
1C1 Denmark Str Greenland/Iceland
27P2 Dennery St Lucia
78D4 Denpasar Indon
16B3 Denton Maryland, USA
9D3 Denton Texas, USA
107E1 D'Entrecasteaux Is PNG
47B1 Dents du Midi Mt Switz
8C3 Denver USA
9RB7 Déo R Cam
86B2 Deoghar India
85C5 Deolāli India
84D1 Deosai Plain India

95B3 Dépression du Mourdi Chad
19B3 De Queen USA
84C3 Dera Pak
84C2 Dera Bugti Pak
84C2 Dera Ismail Khan Pak
106B2 Derby Eng
16C2 Derby Connecticut, USA
43D3 Derby County, Eng
43D3 Derby Eng
18A2 Derby Kansas, USA
60E3 Dergachi Ukraine
19B3 De Ridder USA
Derna = Darnah
95C3 Derudeb Sudan
109C4 Derwent Bridge Aust
34B2 Desaguadero Arg
34B2 Desaguadero R Arg
30C2 Desaguadero R Bol
21B3 Descanso Mexico
20B2 Deschutes R USA
99D1 Desē Eth
29C5 Deseado Arg
29C5 Deseado R Arg
47D2 Desenzano Italy
96A1 Deserta Grande I Medeira
30C4 Desierto de Atacama Desert Chile
18B2 Desloge USA
10A2 Des Moines Iowa, USA
60D3 Desna R Russian Fed
29B6 Desolación I Chile
14A2 Des Plaines USA
56C2 Dessau Germany
12G2 Destruction Bay Can
46A1 Desvres France
54B1 Deta Rom
100B2 Dete Zim
10C2 Detroit USA
76D3 Det Udom Thai
54B1 Deva Rom
56B2 Deventer Neth
44C3 Deveron R Scot
85C3 Devikot India
7D4 Devil Postpile Nat Mon USA
22C1 Devils Gate P USA
8D2 Devils Lake USA
12H3 Devils Paw Mt Can
85D3 Devli India
51B2 Devoll R Alb
43B4 Devon County, Eng
6A2 Devon I Can
107D5 Devonport Aust
86C1 Dewangiri Bhutan
85D4 Dewās India
101G1 Dewetsdorp S Africa
11B3 Dewey Res USA
19B3 De Witt USA
16C3 Dexter Missouri, USA
73A3 Deyang China
91A4 Deyhük Iran
90A3 Dezfül Iran
72D2 Dezhou China
91B4 Dezh Shāhpür Iran
91A4 Dhahran S Arabia
86C2 Dhäkä Bang
87B2 Dhamavaram India
86A2 Dhamtari India
86B2 Dhanbād India
86A1 Dhangarhi Nepal
86B1 Dhankuta Nepal
85D4 Dhar India
87B2 Dharmapuri India
84D2 Dharmshala India
97B3 Dhar Oualata Desert Region Maur
86A1 Dhaulagiri Mt Nepal
86B2 Dhenkānāi India
94B3 Dhibah Jordan
55C3 Dhikti Ori Mt Greece
55C3 Dhodhekánisos = Greece
55B3 Dhomokós Greece
87B1 Dhone India

85C4 Dhoraji India
85C4 Dhrāngadhra India
86B1 Dhubri India
85C4 Dhule India
22B2 Diablo,Mt USA
21A2 Diablo Range Mts USA
34C2 Diamante Arg
34B2 Diamante R Arg
31C5 Diamantina Brazil
107D3 Diamantina R Aust
86B2 Diamond Harbours India
22B1 Diamond Springs USA
91C4 Dibā UAE
98C3 Dibaya Zaïre
86C1 Dibrugarh India
8C2 Dickinson USA
15C2 Dickson City USA
93D2 Dicle R Turk
13E2 Didsbury Can
85C3 Didwāna India
97B3 Diebougou Burkina
46D2 Diekirch Lux
97B3 Diéma Mali
76C1 Dien Bien Phu Viet
56B2 Diepholz Germany
48C2 Dieppe France
46C1 Diest Belg
46D2 Dieuze France
7D5 Digby Can
49D3 Digne-les-Bains France
49C2 Digoin France
79C4 Digos Phil
71E4 Digul R Indon
86C1 Dihang R India
Dijlah = Tigris
48C2 Dijon France
98B2 Dik Chad
99E1 Dikhil Djibouti
46B1 Diksmuide Belg
18I0 Dikson Russian Fed
82A2 Dilaram Afghan
106B1 Dili Indon
76D3 Di Linh Viet
56B2 Dillenburg Germany
99C1 Dilling Sudan
12C3 Dillingham USA
8B2 Dillon USA
16A2 Dillsburg USA
100B2 Dilolo Zaïre
Dimashq = Damascus
98C3 Dimbelenge Zaïre
97B4 Dimbokro Ivory Coast
54C2 Dimitrovgrad Bulg
61G3 Dimitrovgrad Russian Fed
94B3 Dimona Israel
79C3 Dinagat I Phil
86B1 Dinajpur India
48B2 Dinan France
46C1 Dinant Belg
92B2 Dinar Turk
99D1 Dinder R Sudan
87B2 Dindigul India
72B2 Dingbian China
86B1 Dinggyê China
41A3 Dingle Irish Rep
41A3 Dingle B Irish Rep
97A3 Dinguiraye Guinea
44B3 Dingwall Scot
72A2 Dingxi China
72D2 Ding Xian China
22C2 Dinuba USA
97A3 Dioulboulou Sen
86C1 Diphu India
99E2 Diré Dawa Eth
3K Dirk Hartog I Aust
95A3 Dirkou Niger
109C1 Dirranbandi Aust
99E2 Dirri Somalia
29G8 Disappointment,C South Georgia
20B1 Disappointment,L USA
106B3 Disappointment,L Aust
108B3 Discovery B Aust

Discovery Tablemount

103J7 Discovery Tablemount Atlantic Ocean
47C1 Disentis Muster Switz
6E3 Disko Greenland
6E3 Disko Bugt B Greenland
6E3 Diskorjord Greenland
58D1 Disna R Belorussia
35B1 Distrito Federal Federal District, Brazil
85C4 Diu India
79C4 Diuat Mts Phil
31C6 Divinópolis Brazil
61F4 Divnoye Russian Fed
93C2 Divriği Turk
22B1 Dixon California, USA
5E4 Dixon Entrance Sd Can/USA
13D1 Dixonville Can
93E3 Diyālā R Iraq
65F6 Diyarbakir Turk
90A3 Diz R Iran
98B2 Dja R Cam
96C1 Djadi R Alg
95A2 Djado,Plat du Niger
98B3 Djambala Congo
96C2 Djanet Alg
50A2 Djebel Bouhalla Mt Mor
96C1 Djelfa Alg
98C2 Djéma CAR
97B3 Djenné Mali
97B3 Djibo Burkina
99E1 Djibouti Djibouti
99E1 Djibouti Republic, E Africa
98C2 Djolu Zaire
97C4 Djougou Benin
99D2 Djugu Zaire
38C2 Djúpivogur Iceland
51C2 Djurdjura Mts Alg
60E2 Dmitrov Russian Fed
Dnepr = Dnieper
60D4 Dneprodzerzhinsk Ukraine
60E4 Dnepropetrovsk Ukraine
60C3 Dneprovskaya Nizmennost' Region, Belorussia
Dnestr = Dniester
72C2 Dnieper R Ukraine
60B4 Dniester R Ukraine
60D2 Dno Russian Fed
98B2 Doba Chad
58C1 Dobele Latvia
34C3 Doblas Arg
71E4 Dobo Indon
54A2 Doboj Bosnia-Herzegovina
54B2 Dobreta-Turnu-Severin Rom
54C2 Dobrich Bulg
60D3 Dobrush Belorussia
31C5 Doce R Brazil
30D3 Doctor R P Peña Arg
87B2 Dod India
87B2 Doda Balta Mt India
Dodecanese = Sporádhes
9C3 Dodge City USA
99D3 Dodoma Tanz
75A1 Dōgo I Japan
97C3 Dogondoutchi Niger
93D2 Doğubayazit Turk
91B4 Doha Qatar
7C5 Dolbeau Can
49D2 Dôle France
43C3 Dolgellau Wales
47D1 Dolomitiche Mts Italy
29E3 Dolores Arg
34D2 Dolores Urug
23A1 Dolores Hidalgo Mexico
4G3 Dolphin and Union Str Can
29E6 Dolphin,C Falkland Is
71E4 Dom Mt Indon
65G4 Dombarovskiy Russian Fed

38F6 Dombås Nor
46D2 Dombasle-sur-Meurthe France
54A1 Dombóvár Hung
48B2 Domfront France
27E3 Dominica I Caribbean S
27C3 Dominican Republic Caribbean S
6C3 Dominion,C Can
7E4 Domino Can
68D1 Domna Russian Fed
52A1 Domodossola Italy
78D4 Dompu Indon
29B3 Domuyo Mt Arg
109D1 Domville,Mt Aust
44C3 Don R Scot
61F4 Don R Russian Fed
45C1 Donaghadee N Ire
57C3 Donau R Germany
57C3 Donauwörth Germany
50A2 Don Benito Spain
42D3 Doncaster Eng
98B3 Dondo Angola
101C2 Dondo Mozam
87C3 Dondra Head C Sri Lanka
45B1 Donegal County, Irish Rep
40B3 Donegal Irish Rep
40B3 Donegal B Irish Rep
45B1 Donegal Mts Irish Rep
60E4 Donetsk Ukraine
73C4 Dong'an China
106A3 Dongara Aust
73A4 Dongchuan China
76D2 Dongfang China
74B2 Dongfeng China
70C4 Donggala Indon
68B3 Donggi Cona L China
74A3 Donggou China
73C5 Donghai Dao I China
72A1 Dong He R China
76D2 Dong Hoi Viet
73C5 Dong Jiang R China
95C3 Dongola Sudan
73D5 Dongshan China
68D4 Dongsha Qundao I China
72C2 Dongsheng China
72E3 Dongtai China
73C4 Dongting Hu L China
73B5 Dongxing China
73D3 Dongzhi China
18B2 Doniphan USA
54A2 Donji Vakuf Bosnia-Herzegovina
38G5 Dönna I Nor
21A2 Donner R USA
46D2 Donnersberg Mt Germany
101G1 Donnybrook S Africa
Donostia = San Sebastian
22B2 Don Pedro Res USA
12D1 Doonerak,Mt USA
79B4 Dopolong Phil
73A3 Do Qu R China
47B2 Dora Baltea R Italy
49D2 Dorbirn Austria
43C4 Dorchester Eng
6C3 Dorchester,C Can
48C2 Dordogne R France
56A2 Dordrecht Neth
13F2 Dore L Can
13F2 Dore Lake Can
97B3 Dori Burkina
46B2 Dormans France
57B3 Dornbirn Austria
44C3 Dornoch Scot
44C3 Dornoch Firth Estuary Scot
38H6 Dorotea Sweden
109D2 Dorrigo Aust
20B2 Dorris USA
43C4 Dorset County, Eng
46D1 Dorsten Germany
56B2 Dortmund Germany
98C2 Doruma Zaire
63D2 Dosatuy Russian Fed
84B1 Doshi Afghan

22B2 Dos Palos USA
97C3 Dosso Niger
65G5 Dossor Kazakhstan
11B3 Dothan USA
49C1 Douai France
98A2 Douala Cam
109D1 Double Island Pt Aust
49D2 Doubs R France
111A3 Doubtful Sd NZ
97B3 Douentza Mali
9C3 Douglas Arizona, USA
42B2 Douglas Eng
17B1 Douglas Georgia, USA
8C2 Douglas Wyoming, USA
12A1 Douglas,C USA
13B2 Douglas Chan Can
12D3 Douglas,Mt USA
46B1 Doullens France
45C1 Doun County, N Ire
76D3 Dourados Brazil
50A1 Douro R Port
15C3 Dover Delaware, USA
43E4 Dover Eng
15D2 Dover New Hampshire, USA
16B2 Dover New Jersey, USA
14B2 Dover Ohio, USA
42D3 Dover R Eng
41D3 Dover,Str of UK/France
16B3 Downington USA
42B2 Downpatrick N Ire
13C2 Downton,Mt Can
16B2 Doylestown USA
75A1 Dōzen I Japan
34A2 Dr'aa R Mor
35A2 Dracena Brazil
16D1 Dracut USA
49D3 Draguignan France
101C3 Drakensberg Mts S Africa
101G1 Drakensberg Mt S Africa
103E7 Drake Pass Pacific/Atlantic O
55B2 Dráma Greece
39G7 Drammen Nor
38A1 Drangajökull Iceland
52C1 Drava R Slovenia
13D2 Drayton Valley Can
49C2 Dreaux France
57C2 Dresden Germany
48C2 Dreux France
20C2 Drewsey USA
58D1 Drin R Alb
54B2 Drina R Bosnia-Herzegovina/Serbia
58D1 Drissa R Belorussia
41B3 Drogheda Irish Rep
59C3 Drogobych Ukraine
112B12 Dronning Maud Land Region, Ant
30D3 Dr P.P. Pená Par
13E2 Drumheller Can
14B1 Drummond I USA
15D1 Drummondville Can
58C2 Druskininksi Lithuania
12G3 Dry B USA
7A5 Dryden Can
27H1 Dry Harbour Mts Jamaica
76B3 Duang I Burma
91C4 Dubai UAE
5H3 Dubawnt R Can
4H3 Dubawnt L Can
107D4 Dubbo Aust
45C2 Dublin County, Irish Rep
17B1 Dublin USA
60E2 Dubna Russian Fed
60C3 Dubno Ukraine
15C2 Du Bois USA
13B2 Dubose,Mt Can
58D2 Dubrovica Ukraine
54A2 Dubrovnik Croatia
10A2 Dubuque USA

46D2 Dudelange Lux
1C10 Dudinka Russian Fed
43C3 Dudley Eng
97B4 Duekoué Ivory Coast
50B1 Duero R Spain
44C3 Dufftown Scot
52B2 Dugi Otok I Croatia
56B2 Duisburg Germany
93E3 Dūkan Iraq
99D2 Duk Faiwil Sudan
91B4 Dukhān Qatar
73A4 Dukou China
68B3 Dulan China
34C2 Dulce R Arg
78C2 Dulit Range Mts Malay
86C2 Dullabchara India
10A2 Duluth USA
92C2 Dūmā Syria
78A2 Dumai Indon
79A3 Dumaran I Phil
9C3 Dumas USA
94C2 Dumayr Syria
42B2 Dumbarton Scot
42B2 Dumfries Scot
Dumfries and Galloway Region, Scot
86B2 Dumka India
15C1 Dumoine,L Can
112C8 Dumont d'Urville Base Ant
95C1 Dumyat Egypt
54C2 Dunărea R Rom
45C2 Dunary Head R Irish Rep
54B2 Dunav R Bulg
59D3 Dunayevtsy Ukraine
13D3 Duncan Can
16A2 Duncannon USA
44C2 Duncansby Head C Scot
45C1 Dundalk Irish Rep
45C2 Dundalk USA
45C2 Dundalk B Irish Rep
6D2 Dundas Greenland
13C3 Dundas Pen Can
71E5 Dundas Str Aust
101H1 Dundee S Africa
44C3 Dundee Scot
108B1 Dundoo Aust
42B2 Dundrum B N Ire
111B3 Dunedin NZ
17B2 Dunedin USA
109C2 Dunedoo Aust
44C3 Dunfermline Scot
85C4 Dungarpur India
45C2 Dungarvan Irish Rep
43E4 Dungeness Eng
109D2 Dungog Aust
99C2 Dungu Zaire
95C2 Dungunab Sudan
68B2 Dunhuang China
46B1 Dunkerque France
99D1 Dunkur Eth
15C2 Dunkirk USA
97B4 Dunkwa Ghana
41B3 Dun Laoghaire Irish Rep
45B3 Dunmanway Irish Rep
26B1 Dunmore Town The Bahamas
44C2 Dunnet Head Pt Scot
20B2 Dunsmuir USA
111A2 Dunstan Mts NZ
46C2 Dun-sur-Meuse France
72D1 Duolun China
18C2 Du Quoin USA
94B3 Dura Israel
49D3 Durance R France
23A2 Durango Mexico
50B1 Durango Spain
9C3 Durango USA
29E2 Durano Urug
9D3 Durant USA
94C1 Duraykish Syria
101H1 Durban S Africa
46D1 Düren Germany
86A2 Durg India
86B2 Durgapur India
42D2 Durham County, Eng

42D2 Durham Eng
11C3 Durham N Carolina, USA
16D1 Durham New Hampshire, USA
108B1 Durham Downs Aust
54A2 Durmitor Mt Montenegro, Yugos
44B2 Durness Scot
55A2 Durrës Alb
108B1 Durrie Aust
45A3 Dursey I Irish Rep
55C3 Dursunbey Turk
110B2 D'Urville I NZ
90D2 Dushak Turkmenistan
73B4 Dushan China
82A2 Dushanbe Tajikistan
111A3 Dusky Sd NZ
56B2 Düsseldorf Germany
73B4 Duyun China
92B1 Düzce Turk
60C2 Dvina R Latvia
84B2 Dwãrka India
6D3 Dyer,C Can
11B3 Dyersburg USA
43B3 Dyfed County, Wales
61F5 Dykh Tau Mt Russian Fed
108B1 Dynevor Downs Aust
68B2 Dzag Mongolia
63C3 Dzamin Üüd Mongolia
101D2 Dzaoudzi Mayotte
68B2 Dzarin Üüd Mongolia
68B2 Dzavhan Gol R Mongolia
80E1 Dzhezkazgan Kazakhstan
61F2 Dzerzhinsk Russian Fed
63E2 Dzhalinda Russian Fed
65J5 Dzhambul Kazakhstan
60D4 Dzhankoy Ukraine
65H4 Dzhezkazgan Kazakhstan
84B1 Dzhilikul' Tajikistan
65J5 Dzhungarskiy Alatau Mts Kazakhstan
59B2 Dzierzoniow Pol
82C1 Dzüyl Mongolia
82C1 Dzungaria Basin, China

E

7B4 Eabamet L Can
12F2 Eagle Alaska, USA
20B2 Eagle L California, USA
19A3 Eagle Mountain L USA
9C4 Eagle Pass USA
4E3 Eagle Plain Can
12E2 Eagle River USA
21B2 Earlimart USA
17B1 Easley USA
15C2 East Aurora USA
43E4 Eastbourne Eng
14A2 East Chicago USA
69E3 East China Sea China/Japan
83B4 Eastern Ghats Mts India
29E6 East Falkland I Falkland Is
12E1 East Fork R USA
21B2 Eastgate USA
16C1 Easthampton USA
16C2 East Hampton USA
14A2 East Lake USA
14B2 East Liverpool USA
100B4 East London S Africa
7C4 Eastmain Can
7C4 Eastmain R Can
17B1 Eastman USA
15C3 Easton Maryland, USA
15C2 Easton Pennsylvania, USA
16B2 East Orange USA

105L4 East Pacific Ridge Pacific O
17B1 East Point USA
42D3 East Retford Eng
11A3 East St Louis USA
1B7 East Siberian S Russian Fed
43E4 East Sussex County. Eng
17B1 Eatonton USA
10A2 Eau Claire USA
71F3 Eauripik I Pacific O
23B1 Ebano Mexico
98B2 Ebebiyin Eq Guinea
56C2 Eberswalde Germany
73A4 Ebian China
65K5 Ebinur L China
53C2 Eboli Italy
98B2 Ebolowa Cam
51B1 Ebro R Spain
92A1 Eceabat Turk
96C1 Ech Cheliff Alg
72D2 Eching China
20C1 Echo USA
4G3 Echo Bay Can
46D2 Echternach Lux
108B3 Echuca Aust
50A2 Ecija Spain
6B2 Eclipse Sd Can
32B4 Ecuador Republic, S America
99E1 Ed Eritrea
44C2 Eday I Scot
99C1 Ed Da'ein Sudan
95C3 Ed Damer Sudan
95C3 Ed Debba Sudan
44B2 Edrachillis B Scot
99D1 Ed Dueim Sudan
109C4 Eddystone Pt Aust
98A2 Edea Cam
109C3 Eden Aust
42C2 Eden R Eng
101G1 Edenburg S Africa
111A3 Edendale NZ
46E2 Edenkoben Germany
46E1 Eder R Germany
6D3 Edgell I Can
64D2 Edgeoya I Barents S
16A3 Edgewood USA
94B3 Edh Dhahiriya Israel
55B2 Edhessa Greece
44C3 Edinburgh Scot
60C5 Edirne Turk
17B1 Edisto R USA
13D2 Edith Cavell,Mt Can
20B1 Edmonds USA
5G4 Edmonton Can
7D5 Edmundston Can
19A4 Edna USA
12H3 Edna Bay USA
52B1 Edolo Italy
94B3 Edom Region, Jordan
92A2 Edremit Turk
55C3 Edremit Körfezi B Turk
68B2 Edrengiyn Nuruu Mts Mongolia
5G4 Edson Can
34C3 Eduardo Castex Arg
12J2 Eduni,Mt Can
108B3 Edward R Aust
99C3 Edward,L Uganda/Zaire
108A1 Edwards Creek Aust
9C3 Edwards Plat USA
18C2 Edwardsville USA
12H3 Edziza,Mt Can
12B2 Eek USA
46B1 Eeklo Belg
10B3 Effingham USA
6E3 Egedesminde Greenland
12C3 Egegik USA
59C3 Eger Hung
39F7 Egersund Nor
16B3 Egg Harbor City USA
16B2 Eglinton I Can
110B1 Egmont,C NZ
110B1 Egmont,Mt NZ
92B2 Eğridir Gölü L Turk
95B2 Egypt Republic, Africa

50B1 Eibar Spain
49C2 Eibeuf France
46D1 Eifel Region, Germany
44A3 Eigg I Scot
83B5 Eight Degree Chan Indian O
106B4 Eighty Mile Beach Aust
108C3 Eildon,L Aust
56B2 Eindhoven Neth
47C1 Einsiedeln Switz
94B3 Ein Yahav Israel
57C2 Eisenach Germany
57C3 Eisenerz Austria
46D1 Eitorf Germany
72A1 Ejin qi China
23B2 Ejutla Mexico
110C2 Eketahuna NZ
65J4 Ekibastuz Kazakhstan
63F2 Ekimchan Russian Fed
92B3 Ek Mahalla el Kubra Egypt
39H7 Eksjo Sweden
10B1 Ekwen R Can
92A3 El'Alamein Egypt
92B3 El'Arish Egypt
92B4 Elat Israel
95B3 El'Atrun Oasis Sudan
93C2 Elazig Turk
92C3 El Azraq Jordan
52B2 Elba I Italy
32C1 El Banco Colombia
52B2 Elbasan Alb
27D5 El Baúl Ven
57C2 Elbe R Germany
94C1 El Bega'a R Leb
14A2 Elberta USA
8C3 Elbert,Mt USA
17B1 Elberton USA
92C2 Elbistan Turk
58B2 Elblag Pol
29B4 El Bolson Arg
61F5 Elbrus Mt Russian Fed
Elburz Mts = Reshteh-ye Alborz
21B3 El Cajon USA
19A4 El Campo USA
51B2 Elche Spain
51B2 Elda Spain
32B3 El Diviso Colombia
96B2 El Djouf Desert Region Maur
18B2 Eldon USA
11A3 El Dorado Arkansas, USA
35B2 Eldorado Brazil
9D3 El Dorado Kansas, USA
24B2 El Dorado Mexico
33E2 El Dorado Ven
99D2 Eldoret Kenya
22C1 Eleanor,L USA
96B2 El Eglab Region, Alg
50B1 El Escorial Spain
93D2 Eleşkirt Turk
11C4 Eleuthera I The Bahamas
92B4 El Faiyûm Egypt
98B2 El Fasher Sudan
98C1 El Fasher Sudan
92B4 El Fashn Egypt
50A1 El Ferrol del Caudillo Spain
99C1 El Fula Sudan
96C1 El Gassi Alg
99D1 El Geteina Sudan
99D1 El Gezira Region, Sudan
94B3 El Ghor V Israel/Jordan
10B2 Elgin Illinois, USA
44C3 Elgin Scot
92B3 El Giza Egypt
99C1 El Golea Alg
99D2 Elgon,Mt Uganda/Kenya
99E2 El Goran Eth
23A2 El Grullo Mexico

96B2 El Guettara Well Mali
96B2 El Haricha Desert Region Mali
92A4 El Harra Egypt
51C2 El Harrach Alg
99D1 El Hawata Sudan
23B1 El Hlgo Mexico
34A3 El Huecu Arg
92B4 El Igma Desert Region Egypt
12B2 Elim USA
4H2 Elira,C Can
Elisabethville = Lubumbashi
39K6 Elisenvaara Fin
El Iskandariya = Alexandria
61F4 Elista Russian Fed
106C4 Elizabeth Aust
15D2 Elizabeth USA
11C3 Elizabeth City USA
17C1 Elizabethtown N Carolina, USA
16A2 Elizabethtown Pennsylvania, USA
96B1 El Jadida Mor
92C3 El Jafr Jordan
99D1 El Jebelein Sudan
96D1 El Jem Tunisia
58C2 Elk Pol
16B3 Elk R Maryland, USA
14B3 Elk R W Virginia, USA
95C3 El Kamlin Sudan
22B1 Elk Grove USA
El Khalil = Hebron
80B3 El Khârga Egypt
80B3 El Khârga Oasis Egypt
14A2 Elkhart USA
96B2 El Khenachich Desert Region Mali
54C2 Elkhovo R Bulg
14C3 Elkins USA
8B2 Elko USA
16B3 Elkton USA
92B3 El Kuntilla Egypt
99C1 El Lagowa Sudan
4H2 Ellef Ringnes I Can
8A2 Ellensburg USA
6B2 Ellesmere I Can
111B2 Ellesmere,L NZ
16A3 Ellicott City USA
100B4 Elliot S Africa
7B5 Elliot Lake Can
94B3 El Lisan Pen Jordan
112B3 Ellsworth Land Ant
95B1 El Maghra L Egypt
92B3 El Mansûra Egypt
16B3 Elmer USA
96B2 El Merelé Desert Region Maur
34B2 El Milagro Arg
94B1 El Mina Leb
92B4 El Minya Egypt
22B1 Elmira California, USA
10C2 Elmira New York, USA
96B2 El Mreitî Well Maur
56B2 Elmshorn Germany
98C1 El Mugläd Sudan
96B2 El Mzereb Well Mali
79A3 El Nido Phil
99D1 El Obeid Sudan
23A2 El Oro Mexico
99C1 El Oued Alg
21A2 El Porta USA
22C2 El Portal USA
50A2 El Puerto del Sta Maria Spain
El Qâhira = Cairo
El Quds = Jerusalem
94B3 El Quseima Egypt
9D3 El Reno USA
4C3 Elsa Can
25D3 El Salvador Republic, Cent America
22D4 Elsinore L USA
34B3 El Sosneade Arg

Elsterwerde

57C2 Elsterwerde Germany
El Suweis = Suez
50A1 El Teleno Mt Spain
110B1 Eltham NZ
33E2 El Tigre Ven
92B4 El Tîh Desert Region Egypt
34C2 El Tio Arg
20C1 Eltopia USA
92B4 El Tur Egypt
87C1 Eluru India
50A2 Elvas Port
32C5 Elvira Brazil
34A2 El Volcán Chile
14A2 Elwood USA
43E3 Ely Eng
10A2 Ely Minnesota, USA
8B3 Ely Nevada, USA
14B2 Elyria USA
90B2 Emämrud Iran
84B1 Emäm Säheb Afghan
58B1 Eman R Sweden
61J4 Emba Kazakhstan
61J4 Emba R Kazakhstan
29C3 Embalse Cerros Colorados L Arg
51B2 Embalse de Alarcón Res Spain
50A2 Embalse de Alcántara Res Spain
50A1 Embalse de Almendra Res Spain
50A2 Embalse de Garcia de Sola Res Spain
33E2 Embalse de Guri L Ven
51B1 Embalse de Mequinenza Res Spain
50A1 Embalse de Ricobayo Res Spain
29E2 Embalse de Rio Negro Res Urug
29C3 Embalse El Chocón L Arg
29C4 Embalse Florentine Ameghino L Arg
50A1 Embalse Gabriel y Galan Res Spain
30D3 Embarcación Arg
5G4 Embarras Portage Can
47B2 Embrun France
99D3 Embu Kenya
56B2 Emden Germany
73A4 Emei China
107D3 Emerald Aust
7D4 Emeri Can
5J5 Emerson Can
21B1 Emigrant P USA
95A3 Emi Koussi Mt Chad
34B3 Emilo Mitre Arg
92B2 Emirdağ Turk
16B2 Emmaus USA
56B2 Emmen Neth
20C2 Emmett USA
16A3 Emmitsburg USA
12B2 Emmonak USA
9C4 Emory Peak Mt USA
24A2 Empalme Mexico
101H1 Empangeni S Africa
30E4 Empedrado Arg
105G1 Emperor Seamount Chain Pacific O
18A2 Emporia Kansas, USA
56B2 Ems R Germany
42B2 Enard B Scot
23A1 Encarnación Mexico
30E4 Encarnación Par
97B4 Enchi Ghana
28C4 Encinitas USA
35C1 Encruzilhada Brazil
106B1 Endeh Indon
13D2 Enderby Can
112C11 Enderby Land Region, Ant
15C2 Endicott USA
12D1 Endicott Mts USA
47D1 Engadin Mts Switz
79B2 Engaño,C Phil
94B3 En Gedi Israel

47C1 Engelberg Switz
78A4 Enggano I Indon
41C3 England Country, UK
7E4 Englee Can
41C3 English Channel Eng/France
97B3 Enji Well Maur
39H7 Enkoping Sweden
53B3 Enna Italy
99C1 En Nahud Sudan
95B3 Ennedi Region Chad
109C1 Enngonia Aust
41B3 Ennis Irish Rep
19A3 Ennis Texas, USA
45C2 Enniscorthy Irish Rep
45C1 Enniskillen N Ire
45B2 Ennistimon Irish Rep
94B2 Enn Nâqoûra Leb
57C3 Enns R Austria
39F8 Enschede Neth
24A1 Ensenada Mexico
73B3 Enshi China
99D2 Entebbe Uganda
17A1 Enterprise Alabama, USA
20C1 Enterprise Oregon, USA
97C4 Enugu Nig
75B1 Enzan Japan
49C2 Epernay France
16A2 Ephrata Pennsylvania, USA
20C1 Ephrata Washington, USA
49D2 Épinal France
46A2 Epte R France
100A3 Epukiro Namibia
29B4 Epu pel Arg
90B3 Eqlid Iran
89D7 Equator
98A2 Equatorial Guinea Republic, Africa
47C2 Erbaa Italy
46D2 Erbeskopf Mt Germany
34A3 Ercilla Chile
93D2 Erciş Turk
92C2 Erciyas Daglari Mt Turk
74B2 Erdaobaihe China
72C1 Erdene Mongolia
68C2 Erdenet Mongolia
95B3 Erdi Region Chad
30F4 Erechim Brazil
92B1 Ereğli Turk
92B2 Ereğli Turk
68D2 Erenhot China
50B1 Eresma R Spain
46D1 Erft R Germany
57C2 Erfurt Germany
93C2 Ergani Turk
96B2 Erg Chech Desert Region Alg
95A3 Erg du Djourab Desert Chad
97D3 Erg Du Ténéré Desert Region Niger
97B2 Ergene R Turk
96B2 Erg Iguidi Region Alg
58D1 Ergli Latvia
98B1 Erguig R Chad
68D1 Ergun' R China/Russian Fed
63E2 Ergun Zuoqi China
95C3 Eriba Sudan
10C2 Erie USA
10B2 Erie,L Can/USA
44A3 Eriskay I Scot
99D1 Eritrea Republic,Africa
46D1 Erkelenz Germany
57C3 Erlangen Germany
19B3 Erling,L USA
101G1 Ermelo S Africa
87B3 Ernäkulam India
87B2 Erode India
108B1 Eromanga Aust
96B1 Er Rachidia Mor
99D1 Er Rahad Sudan
101C2 Errego Mozam
40B2 Errigal Mt Irish Rep
41A3 Erris Head Pt Irish Rep
99D1 Er Roseires Sudan

94B2 Er Rummân Jordan
57C2 Erzgebirge Upland Germany
93C2 Erzincan Turk
93C2 Erzurum Turk
48C3 Esara R Spain
56B1 Esbjerg Den
9C4 Escalón Mexico
10B2 Escanaba USA
25C3 Escárcega Mexico
46C2 Esch Lux
21B3 Escondido USA
24B2 Escuinapa Mexico
25C3 Escuintla Guatemala
98B2 Eséka Cam
51C1 Esera R Spain
90B3 Esfahân Iran
101H1 Eshowe S Africa
111C5 Eskdale NZ
38C1 Eskifjörður Iceland
39H7 Eskilstuna Sweden
4E3 Eskimo L Can
7A3 Eskimo Point Can
92B2 Eskisehir Turk
50A1 Esla R Spain
29A5 Esmeralda Chile
32B3 Esmeraldas Ecuador
26B2 Esmerelda Cuba
52J0 Espalion France
14B1 Espanola USA
32J7 Española I Ecuador
106B4 Esperance Aust
34C2 Esperanza Arg
112C2 Esperanza Base Ant
35C1 Espírito Santo State, Brazil
101C3 Espungabera Mozam
29B4 Esquel Arg
20B1 Esquimalt Can
34D2 Esquina Arg
94C2 Es Samra Jordan
96A2 Es Semara Mor
56B2 Essen Germany
33F3 Essequibo R Guyana
43E4 Essex County, Eng
15D2 Essexville USA
57B3 Esslingen Germany
46B2 Essonne France
31D4 Estância Brazil
101G1 Estcourt S Africa
47B2 Este Italy
46C2 Esternay France
30D3 Esteros Par
5H5 Estevan Can
17B1 Estill USA
60B2 Estonia Republic, Europe
29B6 Estrecho de Magallanes Str Chile
50A2 Estremoz Port
59B3 Esztergom Hung
108A1 Etadunna Aust
46C2 Etam France
48C2 Étampes France
85D3 Etäwah India
99D2 Ethiopia Republic, Africa
23B2 Etla Mexico
53B3 Etna Mt Italy
12H3 Etolin I USA
12A2 Etolin Str USA
6C2 Eton Can
100A2 Etosha Nat Pk Namibia
100A2 Etosha Pan Salt L Namibia
17B1 Etowah R USA
46D2 Ettelbruck Lux
109C2 Euabalong Aust
14B2 Euclid USA
109C3 Eucumbene,L Aust
108A2 Eudunda Aust
19A2 Eufala L USA
17A1 Eufaula USA
8A2 Eugene USA
108C1 Eulo Aust
19B3 Eunice Louisiana, USA
46D1 Eupen Germany
93D3 Euphrates R Iraq
19C3 Eupora USA

48C2 Eure R France
20B2 Eureka California, USA
6B1 Eureka Can
8A2 Eureka Nevada, USA
8B2 Eureka Sd Can
108C3 Euroa Aust
109C1 Eurombah R Aust
101D3 Europa I Mozam Chan
78B2 Euskirchen Germany
13B2 Eutsuk L Can
13D2 Evansburg Can
6B1 Evans,C Can
7C4 Evans,L Can
6B3 Evans Str Can
14A2 Evanston Illinois, USA
8B2 Evanston Wyoming, USA
11B3 Evansville Indiana, USA
101G1 Evaton S Africa
106C4 Everard,L Aust
82C3 Everest,Mt China/Nepal
8A2 Everett Washington, USA
16C1 Everett USA
11B4 Everglades,The Swamp USA
43D3 Evesham Eng
98B2 Evinayong Eq Guinea
39F7 Evje Nor
47B1 Evolène Switz
50A2 Évora Port
48C2 Evreux France
55B3 Evvoia I Greece
98B3 Ewo Congo
22C1 Excelsior Mt USA
18B2 Excelsior Springs USA
21B2 Exeter California, USA
43C4 Exeter Eng
15D2 Exeter New Hampshire, USA
43C4 Exmoor Nat Pk Eng
43C4 Exmouth Eng
50A2 Extremadura Region, Spain
25E2 Exuma Sd The Bahamas
99D3 Eyasi L Tanz
42C2 Eyemouth Scot
99E2 Eyl Somalia
106C3 Eyre Creek R Aust
106C3 Eyre,L Aust
106C4 Eyre Pen Aust
79B3 Eyte I Phil
23A1 Eztalan Mexico
55C3 Ezine Turk

F
4G3 Faber L Can
39G7 Fåborg Den
52B2 Fabriano Italy
95A3 Fachi Niger
95B3 Fada Chad
97C3 Fada N'Gourma Burkina
52B2 Faenza Italy
6E3 Faeringehavn Greenland
98B2 Fafa R CAR
99E2 Fafan R Eth
54B1 Fǎgǎraş Rom
46C1 Fagnes Region, Belg
97B3 Faguibine,L Mali
91C5 Fahud Oman
96A1 Faiol I Açores
4G3 Fairbanks USA
14B3 Fairborn USA
8D2 Fairbury USA
16A3 Fairfax USA
21A2 Fairfield California, USA
16C2 Fairfield Connecticut, USA
14B3 Fairfield Ohio, USA
45C1 Fair Head Pt N Ire
40C2 Fair Isle I Scot
111B2 Fairlie NZ

14B3	**Fairmont** W Virginia, USA
13D1	**Fairview** Can
4E4	**Fairweather,Mt** USA
71F3	**Fais** I Pacific O
84C2	**Faisalabad** Pak
8C2	**Faith** USA
44E1	**Faither,The** Pen Scot
86A1	**Faizābād** India
43E3	**Fakenham** Eng
39G7	**Fakoping** Sweden
86C2	**Fakam** Burma
24C2	**Falcon Res** Mexico/USA
97A3	**Falémé** R Mali/Sen
39G7	**Falkenberg** Sweden
42C1	**Falkirk** Scot
29D6	**Falkland Is** Dependency, S Atlantic
29E6	**Falkland Sd** Falkland Is
22D4	**Fallbrook** USA
8B3	**Fallon** USA
15D2	**Fall River** USA
18A1	**Falls City** USA
43B4	**Falmouth** Eng
27H1	**Falmouth** Jamaica
16D2	**Falmouth** Massachusetts, USA
100A4	**False B** S Africa
24A2	**Falso,C** Mexico
56C2	**Falster** I Den
54C1	**Fălticeni** Rom
39H6	**Falun** Sweden
92B2	**Famagusta** Cyprus
46C1	**Famenne** Region, Belg
76B2	**Fang** Thai
99D2	**Fangak** Sudan
73E5	**Fang liao** Taiwan
52B2	**Fano** Italy
112C3	**Faraday** Base Ant
99C2	**Faradje** Zaïre
101D3	**Farafangana** Madag
95B2	**Farafra Oasis** Egypt
80E2	**Farah** Afghan
71F2	**Farallon de Medinilla** I Pacific O
97A3	**Faranah** Guinea
71F3	**Faraulep** I Pacific O
43D4	**Fareham** Eng
	Farewell,C = Kap Farvel
107G5	**Farewell,C** NZ
110B2	**Farewell Spit** Pt NZ
8D2	**Fargo** USA
94B2	**Fari'a** R Israel
10A2	**Faribault** USA
86B2	**Faridpur** Bang
90C2	**Farīmān** Iran
18B2	**Farmington** Missouri, USA
9C3	**Farmington** New Mexico, USA
22B2	**Farmington Res** USA
42D2	**Farne Deep** N Sea
13D2	**Farnham,Mt** USA
12H2	**Faro** Can
50A2	**Faro** Port
39H7	**Fåro** I Sweden
89K9	**Farquhar** Is Indian O
44B3	**Farrar** R Scot
14B2	**Farrell** USA
55B3	**Fársala** Greece
91B4	**Fasa** Iran
45B3	**Fastnet Rock** Irish Rep
60C3	**Fastov** Ukraine
86A1	**Fatehpur** India
13D1	**Father** Can
30F2	**Fatima du Sul** Brazil
101G1	**Fauresmith** S Africa
47B2	**Faverges** France
7B4	**Fawn** R Can
38H6	**Fax** R Sweden
38A2	**Faxaflói** B Iceland
95A3	**Faya** Chad
11A3	**Fayette** USA Arkansas, USA
11C3	**Fayetteville** N Carolina, USA
93E4	**Faylakah** I Kuwait
84C2	**Fāzilka** India
96A2	**Fdêrik** Maur
11C3	**Fear,C** USA
21A2	**Feather Middle Fork** R USA
48C2	**Fécamp** France
34D2	**Federación** Arg
34D2	**Federal** Arg
71F3	**Federated States of Micronesia** Is Pacific O
56C2	**Fehmarn** I Germany
32C5	**Feijó** Brazil
73C5	**Feilai Xai Bei Jiang** R China
110C2	**Feilding** NZ
100C2	**Feira** Zambia
31D4	**Feira de Santan** Brazil
92C2	**Feke** Turk
57B3	**Feldkirch** Austria
34D2	**Feliciano** R Arg
41D3	**Felixstowe** Eng
47D1	**Feltre** Italy
38G6	**Femund** L Nor
74A2	**Fengcheng** China
73B4	**Fengdu** China
72D1	**Fenging** China
73B3	**Fengjie** China
72B3	**Feng Xian** China
72C1	**Fengzhen** China
72C2	**Fen He** R China
101D2	**Fenoarivo Atsinanana** Madag
60E5	**Feodosiya** Ukraine
90C3	**Ferdow** Iran
46B2	**Fère-Champenoise** France
82B2	**Fergana** Uzbekistan
45C1	**Fermanagh** County, N Ire
45B2	**Fermoy** Irish Rep
47D1	**Fern** Mt Austria
32J7	**Fernandina** I Ecuador
17B1	**Fernandina Beach** USA
103G5	**Fernando de Noronha** I Atlantic O
35A2	**Fernandópolis** Brazil
20B1	**Ferndale** USA
21B2	**Fernley** USA
52B2	**Ferrara** Italy
32B5	**Ferreñafe** Peru
19B3	**Ferriday** USA
96B1	**Fés** Mor
18B2	**Festus** USA
54C2	**Fetesti** Rom
92A2	**Fethiye** Turk
61H5	**Fetisovo** Kazakhstan
44E1	**Fetlar** I Scot
84C1	**Feyzabad** Afghan
101D3	**Fianarantsoa** Madag
99D2	**Fichê** Eth
101G1	**Ficksburg** S Africa
47D2	**Fidenza** Italy
55A2	**Fier** Alb
47D1	**Fiera Di Primeiro** Italy
44C3	**Fife** Region, Scot
44C3	**Fife Ness** Pen Scot
48C3	**Figeac** France
50A1	**Figueira da Foz** Port
51C1	**Figueras** Spain
	Figueres = Figueras
96B1	**Figuig** Mor
105G4	**Fiji** Is Pacific O
30D3	**Filadelfia** USA
54B2	**Filiaşi** Rom
55B3	**Filiatrá** Greece
53B3	**Filicudi** I Italy
21B3	**Fillmore** California, USA
44B3	**Findhorn** R Scot
10B2	**Findlay** USA
13D2	**Findlay,Mt** USA
15C2	**Finger Lakes** USA
101C2	**Fingoè** Mozam
92B2	**Finike** Turk
106C3	**Finke** R Aust
108A1	**Finke Flood Flats** Aust
64D3	**Finland** Republic, N Europe
39J7	**Finland,G of** N Europe
5F4	**Finlay** R Can
5F4	**Finlay Forks** Can
108C3	**Finley** Aust
38H5	**Finnsnes** Nor
71F4	**Finschhafen** PNG
47C1	**Finsteraarhorn** Mt Switz
56C2	**Finsterwalde** Austria
45C1	**Fintona** N Ire
111A3	**Fiordland Nat Pk** NZ
94B2	**Fiq** Syria
93C2	**Firat** R Turk
22B2	**Firebaugh** USA
52B2	**Firenze** Italy
34C2	**Firmat** Arg
85D3	**Firozābād** India
84C2	**Firozpur** India
39H7	**Firspang** Sweden
44C3	**Firth of Clyde** Estuary Scot
44C3	**Firth of Forth** Estuary Scot
44A3	**Firth of Lorn** Estuary Scot
40C2	**Firth of Tay** Estuary Scot
91B4	**Firūzābād** Iran
100A3	**Fish** R Namibia
22C2	**Fish Camp** USA
16C2	**Fishers** I USA
68B3	**Fisher Str** Can
43B4	**Fishguard** Wales
43E3	**Fiskenaesset** Greenland
46B2	**Fismes** France
15D2	**Fitchburg** USA
44E2	**Fitful Head** Pt Scot
17B1	**Fitzgerald** USA
106B2	**Fitzroy** R Aust
108B2	**Fitzroy Crossing** Aust
14B1	**Fitzwilliam** I Can
	Hume = Rijeka
99C3	**Fizi** Zaïre
9B3	**Flagstaff** USA
42D2	**Flamborough Head** C Eng
8C2	**Flaming Gorge Res** USA
44A2	**Flannan Isls** Is Scot
12J2	**Flat** R Can
13E3	**Flathead** R USA
8B2	**Flathead L** USA
18B2	**Flat River** USA
8A2	**Flattery,C** USA
42C3	**Fleetwood** Eng
39F7	**Flekkefjord** Nor
69G4	**Fleming Deep** Pacific O
16B2	**Flemington** USA
56B2	**Flensburg** Germany
47B1	**Fleurier** Switz
106C4	**Flinders** I Aust
107D2	**Flinders** R Aust
107D2	**Flinders** I Aust
106C4	**Flinders Range** Mts Aust
5H4	**Flin Flon** Can
10B2	**Flint** USA
42C3	**Flint** Wales
46B1	**Flixecourt** France
17A1	**Florala** USA
	Florence = Firenze
11B3	**Florence** Alabama, USA
18A2	**Florence** Kansas, USA
20B2	**Florence** Oregon, USA
11C3	**Florence** S Carolina, USA
32B3	**Florencia** Colombia
46C2	**Florenville** Belg
25D3	**Flores** Guatemala
96A1	**Flores** I Açores
106B1	**Flores** I Indon
14D3	**Flores** R Arg
70C4	**Flores S** Indon
31C3	**Floriano** Brazil
30G4	**Florianópolis** Brazil
25D2	**Florida** State, USA
29E2	**Florida** Urug
17B2	**Florida B** USA
52B2	**Florida City** USA
107E1	**Florida** Is Solomon Is
11B4	**Florida Keys** Is USA
11B4	**Florida,Strs of** USA
55B2	**Flórina** Greece
38F6	**Florø** Nor
47D1	**Fluchthorn** Mt Austria
54C1	**Focsani** Rom
53C2	**Foggia** Italy
97A4	**Fogo** I Cape Verde
48C3	**Foix** France
6C3	**Foley** I Can
52B2	**Foligno** Italy
43E4	**Folkestone** Eng
17B1	**Folkston** USA
52B2	**Follonica** Italy
22B1	**Folsom** USA
22B1	**Folsom L** L USA
5H4	**Fond-du-Lac** Can
10B2	**Fond du Lac** USA
48C2	**Fontainebleau** France
18B2	**Fontenac** USA
48B2	**Fontenay-le-Comte** France
52C1	**Fonyód** Hung
12D2	**Foochow = Fuzhou**
46D2	**Forbach** France
109C2	**Forbes** Aust
96A4	**Forcados** Nig
38F6	**Forde** Nor
108C1	**Fords Bridge** Aust
19B3	**Fordyce** USA
97A4	**Forecariah** Guinea
6G3	**Forel,Mt** Greenland
14B2	**Forest** Can
17B1	**Forest Park** USA
22A1	**Forestville** USA
44C3	**Forfar** Scot
46A2	**Forges-les-Eaux** France
20B1	**Forks** USA
52B2	**Forlì** Italy
51C2	**Formentera** I Spain
53B2	**Formia** Italy
96A1	**Formigas** I Açores
	Formosa = Taiwan
30E4	**Formosa** Arg
31B5	**Formosa** Brazil
30D3	**Formosa** State, Arg
73D5	**Formosa Str** Taiwan/China
47D2	**Fornovo di Taro** Italy
38D3	**Føroyar** Is N Atlantic O
44C3	**Forres** Scot
106B4	**Forrest** Aust
11A3	**Forrest City** USA
107D2	**Forsayth** Aust
39J6	**Forssa** Fin
109D2	**Forster** Aust
18B2	**Forsyth** Missouri, USA
84C3	**Fort Abbas** Pak
7B4	**Fort Albany** Can
31D2	**Fortaleza** Brazil
44B3	**Fort Augustus** Scot
100B4	**Fort Beaufort** S Africa
21A2	**Fort Bragg** USA
8C2	**Fort Collins** USA
15C1	**Fort Coulogne** Can
27E4	**Fort de France** Martinique
17A1	**Fort Deposit** USA
17B2	**Fort Dodge** USA
106A3	**Fortescue** R Aust
7A5	**Fort Frances** Can
4F3	**Fort Franklin** Can
6G4	**Fort Good Hope** Can
108B1	**Fort Grey** Aust
4F3	**Forth** R Scot
7B4	**Fort Hope** Can
34B3	**Fortín Uno** Arg
8C2	**Fort Laird** Can
90C1	**Fort Lallemand** Alg
	Fort Lamy = Ndjamena
11B4	**Fort Lauderdale** USA
4F3	**Fort Liard** Can

Fort Mackay

5G4 Fort Mackay Can
5G5 Fort Macleod Can
5G4 Fort McMurray Can
4E3 Fort McPherson Can
18B2 Fort Madison USA
8C2 Fort Morgan USA
11B4 Fort Myers USA
5F4 Fort Nelson Can
4F3 Fort Norman Can
17A1 Fort Payne USA
8C2 Fort Peck Res USA
11B4 Fort Pierce USA
4G3 Fort Providence Can
5G3 Fort Resolution Can
98B3 Fort Rousset Congo
5F4 Fort St James Can
13C1 Fort St John Can
13E2 Fort Saskatchewan Can
18B2 Fort Scott USA
4E3 Fort Selkirk Can
7B4 Fort Severn Can
61H5 Fort Shevchenko Kazakhstan
4F3 Fort Simpson Can
5G3 Fort Smith Can
4G3 Fort Smith Region, Can
11A3 Fort Smith USA
9C3 Fort Stockton USA
20B2 Fortuna California, USA
5G4 Fort Vermillion Can
17A1 Fort Walton Beach USA
10B2 Fort Wayne USA
44B3 Fort William Scot
9D3 Fort Worth USA
12F2 Fortymile R USA
12E1 Fort Yukon USA
73C5 Foshan China
47B2 Fossano Italy
12G3 Foster,Mt USA
98B3 Fougamou Gabon
48B2 Fougeres France
44D1 Foula I Scot
43E4 Foulness I Eng
111B2 Foulwind,C NZ
98B2 Foumban Cam
49C1 Fourmies France
55C3 Fournoi I Greece
97A3 Fouta Djallon Mts Guinea
111B3 Foveaux Str NZ
43B4 Fowey Eng
13D2 Fox Creek Can
6B3 Foxe Basin G Can
6C3 Foxe Chan Can
6C3 Foxe Pen Can
110C2 Foxton NZ
13F2 Fox Valley Can
45B2 Foynes Irish Rep
100A2 Foz do Cuene Angola
30F4 Foz do Iguaçu Brazil
16A2 Frackville USA
34B2 Fraga Arg
16D1 Framingham USA
31B6 Franca Brazil
49C2 France Republic, Europe
10A2 Frances Can
12J2 Frances R Can
49D2 Franche Comté Region, France
100B3 Francistown Botswana
13B2 Francois L Can
14A2 Frankfort Indiana, USA
11B3 Frankfort Kentucky, USA
101G1 Frankfort S Africa
57B2 Frankfurt Germany
46E1 Frankfurt am Main Germany
56C2 Frankfurt-an-der-Oder Germany
57C3 Fränkische Alb Upland Germany
14A3 Franklin Indiana, USA
19B4 Franklin Louisiana, USA

16D1 Franklin Massachusetts, USA
16B2 Franklin New Jersey, USA
14C2 Franklin Pennsylvania, USA
4F2 Franklin B Can
20C1 Franklin D Roosevelt L USA
4F3 Franklin Mts Can
4J2 Franklin Str Can
111B2 Franz Josef Glacier NZ
Franz-Joseph-Land = Zemlya Frantsa Iosifa
5F5 Fraser R Can
44C3 Fraserburgh Scot
107E3 Fraser I Aust
13B2 Fraser L Can
47B1 Frasne France
47C1 Frauenfeld Switz
34D2 Fray Bentos Urug
16B3 Frederica USA
56B1 Fredericia Den
15C3 Frederick Maryland, USA
15C3 Fredericksburg Virginia, USA
12H3 Frederick Sd Can
18B2 Fredericktown USA
7D5 Fredericton Can
6E3 Frederikshab Greenland
39G7 Frederikshavn Den
15C2 Fredonia USA
39G7 Fredrikstad Nor
16B2 Freehold USA
26B1 Freeport The Bahamas
19A4 Freeport Texas, USA
97A4 Freetown Sierra Leone
57B3 Freiburg Germany
57B3 Freistadt Austria
106A4 Fremantle Aust
22B2 Fremont California, USA
18A1 Fremont Nebraska, USA
14B2 Fremont Ohio, USA
33G3 French Guiana Dependency, S-America
109C4 Frenchmans Cap Mt Aust
105J4 French Polynesia Is Pacific O
24B2 Fresnillo Mexico
8B3 Fresno USA
22C2 Fresno R USA
47A1 Fretigney France
46B1 Frévent France
109C4 Freycinet Pen Aust
97A3 Fria Guinea
22C2 Friant USA
22C2 Friant Dam USA
52A1 Fribourg Switz
57B3 Friedrichshafen Germany
6D3 Frobisher B Can
6D3 Frobisher Bay Can
5H4 Frobisher L Can
61F4 Frolovo Russian Fed
43C4 Frome Eng
108A1 Frome R Aust
43C4 Frome,R Eng
106C4 Frome,L Aust
25C3 Frontera Mexico
15C3 Front Royal USA
53B2 Frosinone Italy
73C5 Fuchuan China
73E4 Fuding China
24B2 Fuerte R Mexico
30E3 Fuerte Olimpo Par
96A2 Fuerteventura I Canary Is
72C2 Fugu China
68A2 Fuhai China
91C4 Fujairah UAE
75B1 Fuji Japan
73D4 Fujian Province, China
69F2 Fujin China

75B1 Fujinomiya Japan
74D3 Fuji-san Mt Japan
75B1 Fujisawa Japan
75B1 Fuji-Yoshida Japan
63A3 Fukang China
74C3 Fukuchiyima Japan
74D3 Fukui Japan
74C4 Fukuoka Japan
74E3 Fukushima Japan
75B2 Fukuyama Japan
57B2 Fulda Germany
57B2 Fulda R Germany
73B4 Fuling China
27J1 Fullarton Trinidad
22D4 Fullerton USA
18C2 Fulton Kentucky, USA
15C2 Fulton New York, USA
46C1 Fumay France
75C1 Funabashi Japan
96A1 Funchal Madeira
35C1 Fundão Brazil
7D5 Fundy,B of Can
101C3 Funhalouro Mozam
72D3 Funing China
73B5 Funing China
97C3 Funtua Nig
73D4 Fuqing China
101C2 Furancungo Mozam
91C4 Fürg Iran
47C1 Furka P Switz
107D5 Furneaux Group Is Aust
56C2 Fürstenwalde Germany
57C3 Fürth Germany
74D3 Furukawa Japan
6B3 Fury and Hecla St Can
74A2 Fushun Liaoning, China
73A4 Fushun Sichuan, China
74B2 Fusong China
57C3 Füssen Germany
72E2 Fu Xian China
73C4 Fuxin China
72D3 Fuyang China
72E1 Fuyuan Liaoning, China
73A4 Fuyuan Yunnan, China
68A2 Fuyun China
73D4 Fuzhou China
56C1 Fyn I Den

G

99E2 Gaalkacyo Somalia
21B2 Gabbs USA
100A2 Gabela Angola
96D1 Gabe's Tunisia
22B2 Gabilan Range Mts USA
98B3 Gabon Republic, Africa
100B3 Gaborone Botswana
54C2 Gabrovo Bulg
91B3 Gach Sārān Iran
17A1 Gadsden Alabama, USA
10A1 Gads L Can
53B2 Gaeta Italy
71F3 Gaferut I Pacific O
96C1 Gafsa Tunisia
60D2 Gagarin Russian Fed
97B4 Gagnoa Ivory Coast
7D4 Gagnon Can
61F5 Gagra Georgia
86B1 Gaibanda India
29C4 Gaimán Arg
17B2 Gainesville Florida, USA
17B1 Gainesville Georgia, USA
19A3 Gainesville Texas, USA
42D3 Gainsborough Eng
108A2 Gairdner,L Aust
44B3 Gairloch Scot
16A3 Gaithersburg USA
87B1 Gajendragarh India
73D4 Ga Jiang R China
99D3 Galana R Kenya

103D5 Galapagos Is Pacific O
42C2 Galashiels Scot
54C1 Galaţi Rom
4C3 Galena Alaska, USA
18A2 Galena Kansas, USA
27L1 Galeota Pt Trinidad
27L1 Galera Pt Trinidad
10A2 Galesburg USA
15C2 Galeton USA
61F2 Galich Russian Fed
50A1 Galicia Region, Spain
Galilee,S of = Tiberias,L
27J1 Galina Pt Jamaica
90D1 Gallabat Sudan
47C2 Gallarate Italy
87C3 Galle Sri Lanka
51B1 Gállego R Spain
Gallipoli = Gelibolu
55A2 Gallipoli Italy
38J5 Gällivare Sweden
42B2 Galloway District
42B2 Galloway,Mull of C Scot
18B2 Gallup USA
22B1 Galt USA
96A2 Galtat Zemmour Mor
25C2 Galveston USA
25C3 Galveston B USA
34C2 Galvez Arg
49D3 Galvi Corse
45B2 Galway County, Irish Rep
41B3 Galway Irish Rep
41B3 Galway B Irish Rep
86B1 Gamba China
97B3 Gambaga Ghana
4A3 Gambell USA
97A3 Gambia R The Gambia/Sen
97A3 Gambia,The Republic, Africa
98B3 Gamboma Congo
100A2 Gambos Angola
87C3 Gampola Sri Lanka
99E2 Ganale Dorya R Eth
15C2 Gananoque Can
Gand = Gent
100A2 Ganda Angola
98C3 Gandajika Zaïre
84B3 Gandava Pak
85C4 Gändhidham India
85C4 Gändhinagar India
85D4 Gändhi Sägar L India
51B2 Gandia Spain
86B2 Ganga R India
85C3 Ganganar India
86C2 Gangaw Burma
72A2 Gangca China
82C2 Gangdise Shan Mts China
Ganges = Ganga
86B1 Gangtok India
72B3 Gangu China
8C2 Gannett Peak Mt USA
72B2 Ganquan China
108A3 Gantheaume C Aust
39K8 Gantsevichi Belorussia
73D4 Ganzhou China
97C3 Gao Mali
72C2 Gaoping China
97B3 Gaoua Burkina
97A3 Gaoual Guinea
72D3 Gaoyou Hu L China
73C5 Gaozhou China
49D3 Gap France
79B2 Gapan Phil
84D2 Gar China
109C1 Garah Aust
31D3 Garanhuns Brazil
21A1 Garberville USA
35B2 Garça Brazil
35A2 Garcias Brazil
47D2 Garda Italy
9C3 Garden City USA
14A1 Garden Pen USA
34D3 Gardey Arg
84B2 Gardez Afghan

Godoy Cruz

16C2 **Gardiners I** USA
16D1 **Gardner** USA
47D2 **Gardone** Italy
47D2 **Gargano** Italy
85D4 **Garhäkota** India
61K2 **Gari** Russian Fed
100A4 **Garies** S Africa
99D3 **Gariesa** Konya
19A3 **Garland** USA
57C3 **Garmisch-Partenkirchen** Germany
90B2 **Garmsar** Iran
18A2 **Garnett** USA
8B2 **Garnett Peak** Mt USA
48C3 **Garonne** R France
44B3 **Garry** R Scot
78B4 **Garut** Indon
86A2 **Garwa** India
14A2 **Gary** USA
82C2 **Garyarsa** China
4H3 **Gary L** Can
19A3 **Garza-Little Elm** Res USA
90B2 **Gasan Kuli** Turkmenistan
48B3 **Gascogne** Region, France
18B2 **Gasconade** R USA
106A3 **Gascoyne** R Aust
98B2 **Gashaka** Nig
97D3 **Gashua** Nig
10D2 **Gaspé** Can
10D2 **Gaspé,C. de** Can
94A1 **Gata,C** Cyprus
60C2 **Gatchina** Russian Fed
42D2 **Gateshead** Eng
19A3 **Gatesville** USA
15C1 **Gatineau** Can
15C1 **Gatineau** R Can
109D1 **Gatton** Aust
86C1 **Gauhāti** India
58C1 **Gauja** R Latvia
86A1 **Gauri Phanta** India
22B3 **Gaviota** USA
39H6 **Gävle** Sweden
108A2 **Gawler Ranges** Mts Aust
72A1 **Gaxun Nur** L China
86A2 **Gaya** India
97C3 **Gaya** Niger
14B1 **Gaylord** USA
109D1 **Gayndah** Aust
61H1 **Gayny** Russian Fed
60C4 **Gaysin** Ukraine
92B3 **Gaza** Israel
92C2 **Gaziantep** Turk
97B4 **Gbaringa** Lib
58B2 **Gdańsk** Pol
58B2 **Gdańsk,G of** Pol
39K7 **Gdov** Russian Fed
58B2 **Gdynia** Pol
94A3 **Gebel Halâl** Mt Egypt
95C2 **Gebel Hamata** Mt Egypt
92B4 **Gebel Katherina** Mt Egypt
94A3 **Gebel Libni** Mt Egypt
94A3 **Gebel Maghâra** Mt Egypt
99D1 **Gedaref** Sudan
55C2 **Gediz** R Turk
56C2 **Gedser** Den
46C1 **Geel** Belg
108B3 **Geelong** Aust
109C4 **Geeveston** Aust
97D3 **Geidam** Nig
46D1 **Geilenkirchen** Germany
99D3 **Geita** Tanz
73A5 **Gejiu** China
53B3 **Gela** Italy
99E2 **Geladī** Eth
46D1 **Geldern** Germany
55C2 **Gelibolu** Turk
92B2 **Gelidonya Burun** Turk
46D1 **Gelsenkirchen** Germany
39F8 **Gelting** Germany

77C5 **Gemas** Malay
46C1 **Gembloux** Belg
98B2 **Gemena** Zaire
92C2 **Gemerek** Turk
92A1 **Gemlik** Turk
52B1 **Gemona** Italy
100B3 **Gemsbok** Nat Pk Botswana
98C1 **Geneina** Sudan
34C3 **General Acha** Arg
34C3 **General Alvear** Buenos Aires, Arg
34B2 **General Alvear** Mendoza, Arg
34C2 **General Arenales** Arg
34D3 **General Belgrano** Arg
112B2 **General Belgrano** Base Ant
112C2 **General Bernardo O'Higgins** Base Ant
34D3 **General Conesa** Buenos Aires, Arg
30D3 **General Eugenio A Garay** Par
34D3 **General Guido** Arg
34C3 **General La Madrid** Arg
34C2 **General Levalle** Arg
30C4 **General Manuel Belgrano** Mt Arg
34D3 **General Paz** Buenos Aires, Arg
34C2 **General Pico** Arg
34D3 **General Pirán** Arg
29C3 **General Roca** Arg
112C3 **General San Martin** Base Ant
79C4 **General Santos** Phil
34C3 **General Viamonte** Arg
34C3 **General Villegas** Arg
15C2 **Genesee** R USA
15C2 **Geneseo** USA
Geneva = Genève
18A1 **Geneva** Nebraska, USA
15C2 **Geneva** New York, USA
Geneva,L of = LacLéman
52A1 **Genève** Switz
50B2 **Genil** R Spain
Genoa = Genova
52A2 **Genova** Italy
46B1 **Gent** Belg
78B4 **Genteng** Indon
56C2 **Genthin** Germany
93E1 **Geokchay** Azerbaijan
100B4 **George** S Africa
7D4 **George** R Can
109C2 **George,L** Aust
17B2 **George,L** Florida, USA
15D2 **George,L** New York, USA
111A2 **George Sd** NZ
109C4 **George Town** Aust
15C3 **Georgetown** Delaware, USA
33F2 **Georgetown** Guyana
14B3 **Georgetown** Kentucky, USA
77C4 **George Town** Malay
27N2 **Georgetown** St Vincent and the Grenadines
17C1 **Georgetown** S Carolina, USA
19A3 **Georgetown** Texas, USA
97A3 **Georgetown** The Gambia
112C8 **George V Land** Region, Ant
65F5 **Georgia** Republic, Europe
112C12 **Georg Forster** Base Ant
17B1 **Georgia** State, USA

14B1 **Georgian B** Can
13C3 **Georgia,Str of** Can
106C3 **Georgina** R Aust
61F5 **Georgiyevsk** Russian Fed
57C2 **Gera** Germany
46B1 **Geraardsbergen** Belg
111B2 **Geraldine** NZ
106A3 **Geraldton** Aust
10B2 **Geraldton** Can
94B3 **Gerar** R Israel
4C3 **Gerdine,Mt** USA
12E2 **Gerdova Peak** Mt USA
77C4 **Gerik** Malay
60B4 **Gerlachovsky** Mt Pol
13C1 **Germanson Lodge** Can
56C2 **Germany** Republic, Europe
101G1 **Germiston** S Africa
46D1 **Gerolstein** Germany
51C1 **Gerona** Spain
46E1 **Geseke** Germany
51C0 **Getafe** Spain
50B1 **Getafe** Spain
14C3 **Gettysburg** Pennsylvania, USA
93D2 **Gevaş** Turk
55B2 **Gevgelija** Macedonia
47B1 **Gex** France
94C2 **Ghabāghib** Syria
96C1 **Ghadāmis** Libya
90B2 **Ghaem Shahr** Iran
86A1 **Ghāghara** R India
97B4 **Ghana** Republic, Africa
100B3 **Ghanzi** Botswana
96C1 **Ghardaia** Alg
95A1 **Gharyan** Libya
95A2 **Ghāt** Libya
84D3 **Ghāziäbäd** India
84C3 **Ghazi Khan** Pak
84B2 **Ghazni** Afghan
54C1 **Gheorgheni** Rom
84E4 **Ghudamis** Alg
90D3 **Ghurian** Afghan
95B2 **Gialo** Libya
99E2 **Giamame** Somalia
53C3 **Giarre** Italy
100A3 **Gibeon** Namibia
50A2 **Gibraltar** Colony, SW Europe
50A2 **Gibraltar,Str of** Spain/Africa
106B3 **Gibson Desert** Aust
20B1 **Gibsons** Can
87B1 **Giddalür** India
57B2 **Giessen** Germany
17B2 **Gifford** USA
74D3 **Gifu** Japan
42B2 **Gigha** I Scot
52B2 **Giglio** I Italy
50A1 **Gijón** Spain
107D2 **Gilbert** R Aust
13C2 **Gilbert,Mt** Can
101C2 **Gilé** Mozam
94B2 **Gilead** Region, Jordan
95B2 **Gilf Kebir Plat** Egypt
109C2 **Gilgandra** Aust
84C1 **Gilgit** Pak
84C1 **Gilgit** R Pak
108C2 **Gilgunnia** Aust
7A4 **Gillam** Can
108A2 **Gilles** L Aust
13B2 **Gill I** Can
14A1 **Gills Rock** USA
14A2 **Gilman** USA
22B2 **Gilroy** USA
8D1 **Gimli** Can
101H1 **Gingindlovu** S Africa
79C4 **Gingoog** Phil
99E2 **Ginir** Eth
55B3 **Gióna** Mt Greece
105A3 **Gippsland** Mts Aust
14B2 **Girard** USA
32C3 **Girardot** Colombia
44C3 **Girdle Ness** Pen Scot
93C1 **Gresun** Turk
85C4 **Gir Hills** India
98B2 **Giri** R Zaire

86B2 **Giridïh** India
Girona = Gerona
48B2 **Gironde** R France
42B2 **Girvan** Scot
111C2 **Gisborne** NZ
46A2 **Gisors** France
99C3 **Gitega** Burundi
Giuba,R = Juba,R
54C2 **Giurgiu** Rom
46C1 **Givet** Belg
58B2 **Gizycko** Pol
55B2 **Gjirokastër** Alb
4J3 **Gjoatlaven** Can
39G6 **Gjøvik** Nor
7D5 **Glace Bay** Can
12G3 **Glacier Bay Nat Mon** USA
13E3 **Glacier Nat Pk** USA/Can
20B1 **Glacier Peak** Mt USA
6B2 **Glacier Str** Can
107E3 **Gladstone** Queensland, Aust
109C4 **Gladstone** S Aust, Aust
109C4 **Gladstone** Tasmania, Aust
14A1 **Gladstone** USA
38A1 **Glama** Mt Iceland
39G7 **Glåma** R Nor
46D2 **Glan** R Germany
47C1 **Glärner** Mts Switz
47C1 **Glärus** Switz
18A2 **Glasco** USA
8C2 **Glasgow** Montana, USA
42B2 **Glasgow** Scot
16B3 **Glasboro** USA
43C4 **Glastonbury** Eng
61H2 **Glazov** Russian Fed
59B3 **Gleisdorf** Austria
110C1 **Glen Afton** NZ
16A3 **Glen Burnie** USA
101H1 **Glencoe** S Africa
9B3 **Glendale** Arizona, USA
22C3 **Glendale** California, USA
12E2 **Glenhallen** USA
109D1 **Glen Innes** Aust
109C2 **Glenmorgan** Aust
16A3 **Glen Rock** USA
19A3 **Glen Rose** USA
44C3 **Glenrothes** UK
15D2 **Glens Falls** USA
45B1 **Glenties** Irish Rep
19B3 **Glenwood** Arkansas, USA
8C3 **Glenwood Springs** USA
39F6 **Glittertind** Mt Nor
59B2 **Gliwice** Pol
9B3 **Globe** USA
58B2 **Glogów** Pol
38G5 **Glomfjord** Nor
109D2 **Gloucester** Aust
43C4 **Gloucester** Eng
16D1 **Gloucester** USA
58D1 **Glubokoye** Belorussia
60D3 **Glukhov** Russian Fed
59B3 **Gmünd** Austria
57C3 **Gmunden** Austria
58B2 **Gniezno** Pol
100A3 **Goabeg** Namibia
87A1 **Goa, Daman and Diu** Union Territory, India
86C1 **Goälpära** India
99D2 **Goba** Eth
100A3 **Gobabis** Namibia
34C2 **Gobernador Crespo** Arg
34B3 **Gobernador Duval** Arg
72B1 **Gobi** Desert China/Mongolia
75B2 **Gobo** Japan
87B1 **Godag** India
87C1 **Godävari** R India
14B2 **Goderich** Can
6E3 **Godhavn** Greenland
85C4 **Godhra** India
34B2 **Godoy Cruz** Arg

Gods L

7A4 **Gods L** Can
6E3 **Godthab** Greenland
**Godwin Austen =
K2**
35B1 **Goiandira** Brazil
35B1 **Goianésia** Brazil
35B1 **Goiânia** Brazil
35A1 **Goiás** Brazil
31B4 **Goiás** State, Brazil
35A2 **Goio-Erê** Brazil
99D2 **Gojab** R Eth
55C2 **Gökçeada** R Turk
55C3 **Gökova Körfezi** B Turk
92C2 **Göksun** Turk
63C3 **Gol** R Mongolia
86C1 **Golâghât** India
93C2 **Gôlbasi** Turk
20C2 **Golconda** USA
20B2 **Gold Beach** USA
109D1 **Gold Coast** Aust
13D2 **Golden** Can
110B2 **Golden** B NZ
20B1 **Goldendale** USA
22A2 **Golden Gate** Chan USA
19B4 **Golden Meadow** USA
21B2 **Goldfield** USA
13B3 **Gold River** Can
56C2 **Goleniów** Pol
22C3 **Goleta** USA
52A2 **Golfe d'Ajaccio** G Corse
96D1 **Golfe de Gabes** G Tunisia
**Golfe de Gascogne =
Biscay,Bay of**
52A2 **Golfe de St Florent** G Corse
48B2 **Golfe de St-Malo** G France
49C3 **Golfe du Lion** G France
29B4 **Golfo Corcovado** G Chile
50B2 **Golfo de Almeira** G Spain
29B4 **Golfo de Ancud** G Chile
25D2 **Golfo de Batabano** G Cuba
50A2 **Golfo de Cadiz** G Spain
53A3 **Golfo de Cagliari** G Sardegna
24A1 **Golfo de California** G Mexico
25D4 **Golfo de Chiriqui** G Panama
25D3 **Golfo de Fonseca** Honduras
26B2 **Golfo de Guacanayabo** G Cuba
32A4 **Golfo de Guayaquil** G Ecuador
26B5 **Golfo de Darien** G Colombia/Panama
32A2 **Golfo de los Mosquitos** G Panama
25D3 **Golfo del Papagaya** G Nic
51B2 **Golfo de Mazarrón** G Spain
25D4 **Golfo de Nicoya** G Costa Rica
53A3 **Golfo de Oristano** G Sardegna
25E4 **Golfo de Panamá** G Panama
25D3 **Golfo de Papagayo** G Costa Rica
27E4 **Golfo de Paria** G Ven
29B5 **Golfo de Penas** G Chile
49D3 **Golfo de St Florent** Corse
51C1 **Golfo de San Jorge** G Spain
24C3 **Golfo de Tehuantepec** G Mexico

32B3 **Golfo de Torugas** G Colombia
32B2 **Golfo de Uraba** G Colombia
51C2 **Golfo de Valencia** G Spain
27C4 **Golfo de Venezuela** G Ven
52A2 **Golfo di Genova** G Italy
53C3 **Golfo di Policastro** G Italy
53C3 **Golfo di Squillace** G Italy
53C2 **Golfo di Taranto** G Italy
52B1 **Golfo di Venezia** G Italy
25D4 **Golfo Dulce** G Costa Rica
29C5 **Golfo San Jorge** G Arg
29D4 **Golfo San Matias** G Arg
68B3 **Golmud** China
99E2 **Golocha** Eth
12B2 **Golovin** B USA
74F2 **Golovnino** Russian Fed
99C3 **Goma** Zaïre
97D3 **Gombe** Nig
60D3 **Gombi** Nig
96A2 **Gomera** R Canary Is
24B2 **Gómez Palacio** Mexico
63E2 **Gonam** R Russian Fed
90C2 **Gonbad-e Kāvūs** Iran
86A1 **Gonda** India
85C4 **Gondal** India
99D1 **Gonder** Eth
92A1 **Gönen** Turk
55C3 **Gonen** R Turk
73A4 **Gongga Shan** Mt China
72A2 **Gonghe** China
97D3 **Gongola** R Nig
22B2 **Gonzales** California, USA
19A4 **Gonzales** Texas, USA
34C3 **Gonzalez Chaves** Arg
13C2 **Good Hope Mt** Can
8C2 **Goodland** USA
12B3 **Goodnews Bay** USA
109C1 **Goodooga** R Aust
42D3 **Goole** Eng
108C2 **Goolgowi** Aust
108A3 **Goolwa** Aust
106A4 **Goomalling** Aust
108C2 **Goombalie** Aust
109D1 **Goomer** Aust
109D1 **Goomeri** Aust
109D1 **Goondiwindi** Aust
7E4 **Goose Bay** Can
17C1 **Goose Creek** USA
20B2 **Goose L** USA
87B1 **Gooty** India
63C2 **Gora Munku Sardyk** Mt Mongolia/Russian Fed
64H3 **Gora Narodnaya** Mt Russian Fed
64G3 **Gora Tel'pos-iz** Russian Fed
54A2 **Goražde** Bosnia-Herzegovina
4D3 **Gordon L** Can
13E1 **Gordon L** Can
15C3 **Gordonsville** USA
98B2 **Goré** Chad
99D2 **Goré** Eth
111A3 **Gore** NZ
63F2 **Gore Topko** Mt Russian Fed
45C2 **Gorey** Irish Rep
90B2 **Gorgān** Iran
93E2 **Goris** Armenia
52B1 **Gorizia** Italy
**Gor'kiy = Nizniy
Novgorod**
61F2 **Gor'kovskoye Vodokhranilische** Res Russian Fed

57C2 **Görlitz** Germany
60E4 **Gorlovka** Ukraine
22C3 **Gorman** USA
54C2 **Gorna Orjahovica** Bulg
68A1 **Gorno-Altaysk** Russian Fed
69G2 **Gornozavodsk** Russian Fed
61F2 **Gorodets** Russian Fed
59C3 **Gorodok** Ukraine
59D3 **Gorodok** Ukraine
71F4 **Goroka** PNG
86A1 **Gorokhpur** India
101C2 **Gorongosa** Mozam
71D3 **Gorontalo** Indon
61K2 **Goro Yurma** Mt Russian Fed
45B2 **Gort** Irish Rep
63C2 **Goryachinsk** Russian Fed
59D3 **Goryn'** R Ukraine
59C2 **Góry Swietokrzyskie** Upland Pol
64G3 **Gory Tel'pos-iz'** Mt Russian Fed
39H8 **Gorzów Wielkopolski** Pol
74E2 **Goshogawara** Japan
54C2 **Gospić** Croatia
54B2 **Gostivar** Macedonia
58B2 **Gostynin** Pol
38G7 **Göteborg** Sweden
99E2 **Gotèl** Mts Nig
39H7 **Gotland** I Sweden
74B4 **Gotō-retto** I Japan
39H7 **Gotska Sandön** I Sweden
74C3 **Gōtsu** Japan
98B1 **Goudoumaria** Niger
107J **Gough I** Atlantic O
109C2 **Goulburn** Aust
97B3 **Goumbou** Mali
97B3 **Goundam** Mali
98B1 **Gouré** Niger
97B3 **Gourma Rharous** Mali
46A2 **Gournay-en-Bray** France
95A3 **Gouro** Chad
71E5 **Gove Pen** Aust
60B4 **Goverla** Mt Ukraine
35C1 **Governador Valadares** Brazil
86A2 **Govind Ballabh Paht Sāgar** L India
15C2 **Gowanda** USA
84B3 **Gowārān** Afghan
30E4 **Goya** Arg
98C1 **Goz-Beida** Chad
53B3 **Gozo** I Medit S
95C3 **Goz Regeb** Sudan
100B4 **Graaff-Reinet** S Africa
15C1 **Gracefield** Can
109D1 **Grafton** Aust
8D2 **Grafton** N Dakota, USA
14B3 **Grafton** W Virginia, USA
5E4 **Graham I** Can
13C1 **Graham** R Can
13E1 **Graham L** Can
100B4 **Grahamstown** S Africa
31B3 **Grajaú** Brazil
58C2 **Grajewo** Pol
55B2 **Grámmos** Mt Greece/Alb
44C3 **Grampian** Region, Scot
44B3 **Grampian Mts** Scot
32C3 **Granada** Colombia
50B2 **Granada** Spain
50B2 **Granada** Nic
15D1 **Granby** Can
96A2 **Gran Canaria** I Canary Is
30D4 **Gran Chaco** Region Arg
14A2 **Grand** R Michigan, USA

18B1 **Grand** R Missouri, USA
27Q2 **Grand B** Dominica
11C4 **Grand Bahama** I The Bahamas
7E5 **Grand Bank** Can
102F2 **Grand Banks** Atlantic O
97B4 **Grand Bassam** Ivory Coast
9B3 **Grand Canyon** USA
26A3 **Grand Cayman** I Caribbean S
13E2 **Grand Centre** Can
20C1 **Grand Coulee** USA
34B3 **Grande** R Arg
31C4 **Grande** R Bahia, Brazil
35B1 **Grande** R Minas Gerais/São Paulo, Brazil
13D2 **Grande Cache** Can
47A2 **Grande Chartreuse** Region, France
101D2 **Grande Comore** I Comoros
13D1 **Grande Prairie** Can
19A3 **Grande Prairie** USA
95A3 **Grand Erg de Bilma** Desert Niger
96B2 **Grand erg Occidental** Mts Alg
96C2 **Grand erg Oriental** Mts Alg
7C4 **Grande Rivière de la Baleine** R Can
20C1 **Grande Ronde** R USA
7D5 **Grand Falls** New Brunswick, Can
7E5 **Grand Falls** Newfoundland, Can
20C1 **Grand Forks** Can
8D2 **Grand Forks** USA
16B1 **Grand Gorge** USA
14A2 **Grand Haven** USA
19C3 **Grand Isle** USA
19B4 **Grand L** USA
15D1 **Grand Mère** Can
50A2 **Grândola** Port
5J4 **Grand Rapids** Can
14A2 **Grand Rapids** Michigan, USA
10A2 **Grand Rapids** Minnesota, USA
47B2 **Grand St Bernard** P Italy/Switz
8B2 **Grand Teton** Mt USA
8B2 **Grand Teton Nat Pk** USA
46A2 **Grandvilliers** France
25D1 **Grangeburg** USA
51C1 **Granollers** Spain
52A1 **Gran Paradiso** Mt Italy
47D1 **Gran Pilastro** Mt Austria/Italy
43D3 **Grantham** Eng
21B2 **Grant,Mt** USA
44C3 **Grantown-on-Spey** Scot
9C3 **Grants** USA
20B2 **Grants Pass** USA
48B2 **Granville** France
48B2 **Granville L** Can
35C1 **Grão Mogol** Brazil
49D3 **Grasse** France
21A2 **Grass Valley** USA
5H5 **Gravelbourg** Can
46B1 **Gravelines** France
100C3 **Gravelotte** S Africa
15C2 **Gravenhurst** Can
109D1 **Gravesend** Aust
12H3 **Gravina I** USA
12B2 **Grayling** USA
20B1 **Grays Harbor** B USA
14B3 **Grayson** USA
18C2 **Grayville** USA
59B3 **Graz** Austria
27H1 **Great** R Jamaica
11C4 **Great Abaco** I The Bahamas

106B4 **Great Australian Bight** *G* Aust
16B3 **Great B** New Jersey, USA
25E2 **Great Bahama Bank** The Bahamas
110C1 **Great Barrier I** NZ
107D2 **Great Barrier Reef** *Is* Aust
16C1 **Great Barrington** USA
4F3 **Great Bear L** Can
9D2 **Great Bend** USA
107D3 **Great Dividing Range** *Mts* Aust
42D2 **Great Driffield** Eng
16B3 **Great Egg Harbor** *B* USA
112B10 **Greater Antarctic** Region, Ant
26B2 **Greater Antilles** *Is* Caribbean S
43D4 **Greater London** Metropolitan County, Eng
43C3 **Greater Manchester** County, Eng
25E2 **Greater Exuma** *I* The Bahamas
8B2 **Great Falls** USA
44B3 **Great Glen** *V* Scot
86B1 **Great Himalayan Range** *Mts* Asia
11C4 **Great Inagua** *I* The Bahamas
100B4 **Great Karroo** *Mts* S Africa
109C4 **Great L** Aust
100A3 **Great Namaland** Region, Namibia
42C3 **Great Ormes Head** *C* Wales
11C4 **Great Ragged** *I* The Bahamas
99D3 **Great Ruaha** *R* Tanz
15D2 **Great Sacandaga L** USA
8B2 **Great Salt L** USA
95B2 **Great Sand Sea** Libya/Egypt
106B3 **Great Sandy Desert** Aust
8A2 **Great Sandy Desert** USA
Great Sandy I = **Fraser I**
4G3 **Great Slave L** Can
16C2 **Great South B** USA
106B3 **Great Victoria Desert** Aust
112C2 **Great Wall** *Base* Ant
72B2 **Great Wall** China
43E3 **Great Yarmouth** Eng
94B1 **Greco,C** Cyprus
55B3 **Greece** Republic, Europe
15C2 **Greece** USA
8C2 **Greeley** USA
6B1 **Greely Fjord** Can
14A1 **Green B** USA
14A2 **Green Bay** USA
14A3 **Greencastle** Indiana, USA
16C1 **Greenfield** Massachusetts, USA
14A2 **Greenfield** Wisconsin, USA
13F2 **Green Lake** Can
6F2 **Greenland** Dependency, N Atlantic O
102H1 **Greenland Basin** Greenland S
1B1 **Greenland S** Greenland
42B2 **Greenock** Scot
16C2 **Greenport** USA
16B3 **Greensboro** Maryland, USA
11C3 **Greensboro** N Carolina, USA
15C2 **Greensburg** Pennsylvania, USA
44B3 **Greenstone** *Pt* Scot

18C2 **Greenup** USA
17A1 **Greenville** Alabama, USA
97B4 **Greenville** Lib
19B3 **Greenville** Mississippi, USA
16D1 **Greenville** N Hampshire, USA
14B2 **Greenville** Ohio, USA
17B1 **Greenville** S Carolina, USA
19A3 **Greenville** Texas, USA
43E4 **Greenwich** Eng
16C2 **Greenwich** USA
16B3 **Greenwood** Delaware, USA
19B3 **Greenwood** Mississippi, USA
17B1 **Greenwood** S Carolina, USA
18B2 **Greers Ferry L** USA
108A1 **Gregory,L** Aust
107D2 **Gregory Range** *Mts* Aust
56C2 **Greifswald** Germany
64F3 **Gremikha** Russian Fed
56C1 **Grená** Den
19C3 **Grenada** USA
27E4 **Grenada** *I* Caribbean S
109C2 **Grenfell** Aust
49D2 **Grenoble** France
27M2 **Grenville** Grenada
107D2 **Grenville,C** PNG
20B1 **Gresham** USA
78C4 **Gresik** Jawa, Indon
78A3 **Gresik** Sumatera, Indon
19B4 **Gretna** USA
111B2 **Grey** *R* NZ
12G2 **Grey Hunter Pk** *Mt* Can
7E4 **Grey Is** Can
16C1 **Greylock,Mt** USA
111B2 **Greymouth** NZ
107D3 **Grey Range** *Mts* Aust
45C2 **Greystones** Irish Rep
101H1 **Greytown** S Africa
101F1 **Griekwastad** S Africa
17B1 **Griffin** USA
108C2 **Griffith** Aust
107D5 **Grim,C** Aust
42D3 **Grimsby** Can
42D3 **Grimsby** Eng
38B1 **Grímsey** *I* Iceland
13D1 **Grimshaw** Can
39F7 **Grimstad** Nor
47C1 **Grindelwald** Switz
6A2 **Grinnell Pen** Can
6B2 **Grise Fjord** Can
58B1 **Grobina** Latvia
58C2 **Grodno** Belorussia
86A1 **Gromati** *R* India
56B2 **Groningen** Neth
106C2 **Groote Eylandt** *I* Aust
100A2 **Grootfontein** Namibia
100B3 **Grootvloer** *Salt L* S Africa
27P2 **Gros Islet** St Lucia
46E1 **Grosser Feldberg** *Mt* Germany
52B2 **Grosseto** Italy
46E2 **Gross-Gerau** Germany
57C3 **Grossglockner** *Mt* Austria
47E1 **Gross Venediger** *Mt* Austria
12C3 **Grosvenor,L** USA
22B2 **Groveland** USA
21A2 **Grover City** USA
15D2 **Groveton** USA
61G6 **Groznyy** Russian Fed
58B2 **Grudziądz** Pol
100A3 **Grünau** Namibia
44E2 **Grutness** Scot
61F3 **Gryazi** Russian Fed

61E2 **Gryazovets** Russian Fed
29G8 **Grytviken** South Georgia
45A2 **Gt Blasket** *I* Irish Rep
35C2 **Guaçuí** Brazil
23A1 **Guadalajara** Mexico
50B1 **Guadalajara** Spain
107E1 **Guadalcanal** *I* Solomon Is
50B2 **Guadalimar** *R* Spain
51B1 **Guadalope** *R* Spain
50B2 **Guadalqivir** *R* Spain
24B2 **Guadalupe** Mexico
3G6 **Guadalupe** *I* Mexico
27E3 **Guadeloupe** *I* Caribbean S
50B2 **Guadian** *R* Spain
50A2 **Guadiana** *R* Port
50B2 **Guadix** Spain
32D6 **Guajará Mirim** Brazil
32C1 **Guajira,Pen de** Colombia
32B4 **Gualaceo** Ecuador
34D2 **Gualeguay** Arg
34D2 **Gualeguaychú** Arg
71F2 **Guam** *I* Pacific O
34C3 **Guamini** Arg
77C5 **Gua Musang** Malay
23A1 **Guanajuato** Mexico
23A1 **Guanajuato** State, Mexico
32D2 **Guanare** Ven
25D2 **Guane** Cuba
73C5 **Guangdong** Province, China
73A3 **Guanghan** China
72C3 **Guanghua** China
73A4 **Guangmao Shan** *Mt* China
73B5 **Guangnan** China
73A3 **Guangyuan** China
73D4 **Guangze** China
67F3 **Guangzhou** China
35C1 **Guanhães** Brazil
32D3 **Guania** *R* Colombia
27E5 **Guanipa** *R* Ven
26B2 **Guantánamo** Cuba
72D1 **Guanting Shuiku** *Res* China
73B5 **Guanxi** Province, China
73A3 **Guan Xian** China
32B2 **Guapa** Colombia
33E6 **Guaporé** *R* Brazil/Bol
30C2 **Guaqui** Bol
32B4 **Guaranda** Ecuador
30F4 **Guarapuava** Brazil
35B2 **Guaratinguetá** Brazil
50A1 **Guarda** Port
35B1 **Guarda Mor** Brazil
9C4 **Guasave** Mexico
47D2 **Guastalla** Italy
25C3 **Guatemala** Guatemala
25C3 **Guatemala** Republic, Cent America
34C3 **Guatraché** Arg
32C3 **Guaviare** *R* Colombia
35B2 **Guaxupé** Brazil
27L1 **Guayaguayare** Trinidad
32A4 **Guayaquil** Ecuador
24A2 **Guaymas** Mexico
34D2 **Guayquiraro** *R* Arg
100B2 **Guba** Zaïre
99E2 **Guban** *Region* Somalia
79B3 **Gubat** Phil
56C2 **Gubin** Pol
87B2 **Güdür** India
14B2 **Guelph** Can
26A2 **Guenabacoa** Cuba
98C1 **Guéréda** Chad
48C2 **Guéret** France
48B2 **Guernsey** *I* UK
23A2 **Guerrero** State, Mexico
99D2 **Gughe** *Mt* Eth
63E2 **Gugigu** China
71F2 **Guguan** *I* Pacific O
109C2 **Guiargambone** Aust

73C4 **Guidong** China
97B4 **Guiglo** Ivory Coast
73C5 **Gui Jiang** *R* China
43D4 **Guildford** Eng
73C4 **Guilin** China
47B2 **Guillestre** France
72A3 **Guinan** China
97A3 **Guinea** Republic, Africa
102H4 **Guinea Basin** Atlantic O
97A3 **Guinea-Bissau** Republic, Africa
97C4 **Guinea,G of** W Africa
26A2 **Güines** Cuba
97B3 **Guir** *Well* Mali
84C2 **Guiranwala** Pak
33E1 **Güiria** Ven
46B2 **Guise** France
87B1 **Guledagudda** India
87B1 **Gulbarga** India
58D1 **Gulbene** Latvia
80D3 **Gulf,The** S W Asia
109C2 **Gulgong** Aust
73B4 **Gulin** China
12E2 **Gulkana** USA
13E2 **Gull L** Can
13F2 **Gull Lake** Can
55C3 **Güllük Körfezi** *B* Turk
99D2 **Gulu** Uganda
109C1 **Gulugaba** Aust
97C3 **Gumel** Nig
46D1 **Gummersbach** Germany
86A2 **Gumpla** India
93C1 **Gümüşhane** Turk
85D4 **Guna** India
99D1 **Guna** *Mt* Eth
109C3 **Gundagai** Aust
98B3 **Gungu** Zaïre
6H3 **Gunnbjørn Fjeld** *Mt* Greenland
109D2 **Gunnedah** Aust
87B1 **Guntakal** India
17A1 **Guntersville** USA
17A1 **Guntersville L** USA
87C1 **Guntür** India
77C5 **Gunung Batu Putch** *Mt* Malay
78D3 **Gunung Besar** *Mt* Indon
78D2 **Gunung Bulu** *Mt* Indon
78A3 **Gunung Gedang** *Mt* Indon
78C2 **Gunung Lawit** *Mt* Malay
78C4 **Gunung Lawu** *Mt* Indon
78D2 **Gunung Menyapa** *Mt* Indon
78D2 **Gunung Niapa** *Mt* Indon
78A3 **Gunung Patah** *Mt* Indon
78C4 **Gunung Raung** *Mt* Indon
78A3 **Gunung Resag** *Mt* Indon
78D3 **Gunung Sarempaka** *Mt* Indon
78C4 **Gunung Sumbing** *Mt* Indon
77C5 **Gunung Tahan** *Mt* Malay
78A2 **Gunung Talakmau** *Mt* Indon
100A2 **Gunza** Angola
72D3 **Guoyang** China
84D2 **Gurdaspur** India
84D3 **Gurgaon** India
86A1 **Gurkha** Nepal
92C2 **Gürün** Turk
31B2 **Gurupi** *R* Brazil

100C2 **Guruve** Zim
72A1 **Gurvan Sayhan Uul**
  Upland Mongolia
61H4 **Gur'yev** Kazakhstan
97C3 **Gusau** Nig
58C2 **Gusev** Russian Fed
74A3 **Gushan** China
61F2 **Gus'khrustalnyy**
  Russian Fed
12G3 **Gustavus** USA
22B2 **Gustine** USA
11B3 **Guston** USA
56B2 **Gütersloh** Germany
18C2 **Guthrie** Kentucky,
  USA
18A2 **Guthrie** Oklahoma,
  USA
23B1 **Gutiérrez Zamora**
  Mexico
33F3 **Guyana** Republic,
  S America
102F4 **Guyana Basin**
  Atlantic O
72C1 **Guyang** China
48B3 **Guyenne** Region,
  France
9C3 **Guymon** USA
109D2 **Guyra** Aust
72B2 **Guyuan** China
109C2 **Gwabegar** Aust
85D3 **Gwalior** India
100B3 **Gwanda** Zaïre
98C2 **Gwane** Zaïre
82A3 **Gwardar** Pak
45B1 **Gweebarra B**
  Irish Rep
89G9 **Gwelo** Zim
43C4 **Gwent** County,
  Wales
100B2 **Gweru** Zim
109C1 **Gwydir** *R* Aust
43C3 **Gwynedd** Wales
65F5 **Gyandzha**
  Azerbaijan
86B1 **Gyangzê** China
68B3 **Gyaring Hu** *L* China
64J2 **Gydanskiy Poluostrov**
  Pen Russian Fed
86B1 **Gyirong** China
6F3 **Gyldenløues**
  Greenland
109D1 **Gympie** Aust
59B3 **Gyöngyös** Hung
59B3 **Györ** Hung

H

38K6 **Haapajärvi** Fin
60B2 **Haapsalu** Estonia
56A2 **Haarlem** Neth
46D1 **Haarstrang** Region,
  Germany
25D2 **Habana** Cuba
86C2 **Habiganj** Bang
74D4 **Hachijō-jima** *I* Japan
75B1 **Hachiman** Japan
74E2 **Hachinohe** Japan
75B1 **Hachioji** Japan
16B2 **Hacketstown** USA
108A2 **Hack,Mt** *Mt* Aust
42C2 **Haddington** Scot
108B1 **Haddon Corner** Aust
108B1 **Haddon Downs** Aust
97D3 **Hadejia** Nig
97C3 **Hadejia** *R* Nig
94B2 **Hadera** Israel
56B1 **Haderslev** Den
81D4 **Hadiboh** Socotra
4H2 **Hadley B** Can
73B5 **Hadong** Vietnam
81C4 **Hadramawt** Region,
  Yemen
56C1 **Hadsund** Den
74B3 **Haeju** N Korea
91A4 **Hafar al Bātin**
  S Arabia
6D2 **Haffners Bjerg** *Mt*
  Greenland
84C2 **Hafizabad** Pak
86C1 **Hāflong** India
38A1 **Hafnafjördur** Iceland
12B3 **Hagemeister** *I* USA
56B2 **Hagen** Germany
15C3 **Hagerstown** USA
75A2 **Hagi** Japan

73A5 **Ha Giang** Vietnam
46D2 **Hagondange** France
45B2 **Hags Hd** *C* Irish Rep
46D2 **Haguenau** France
96A2 **Hagunia** *Well* Mor
69G4 **Haha-jima** *I* Japan
68B3 **Hah Xil Hu** *L* China
74A2 **Haicheng** China
76D1 **Hai Duong** Viet
94B2 **Haifa** Israel
94B2 **Haifa,B of** Israel
72D2 **Hai He** *R* China
73C5 **Haikang** China
76E1 **Haikou** China
80C3 **Ha'il** S Arabia
86C2 **Hailākāndi** India
63D3 **Hailar** China
74B2 **Hailong** China
69E2 **Hailun** China
38J5 **Hailuoto** *I* Fin
76D2 **Hainan** *I* China
12G3 **Haines** USA
12G2 **Haines Junction**
  Can
59B3 **Hainfeld** Austria
73B5 **Haiphong** Vietnam
26C3 **Haiti** Republic,
  Caribbean S
95C3 **Haiya** Sudan
72A2 **Haiyan** China
72B2 **Haiyuan** China
72D3 **Haizhou Wan** *B*
  China
59C3 **Hajdúböszörmény**
  Hung
75B1 **Hajiki-saki** *Pt* Japan
86C2 **Haka** Burma
21C4 **Hakalau** Hawaiian Is
93D2 **Hakkâri** Turk
74E2 **Hakodate** Japan
   Hakwa = Haka
75B1 **Hakui** Japan
75B1 **Haku-san** *Mt* Japan
92C2 **Halab** Syria
93E3 **Halabja** Iraq
95C2 **Halaib** Sudan
94C1 **Halba** Leb
68B2 **Halban** Mongolia
56B2 **Halberstadt**
  Germany
79B3 **Halcon,Mt** Phil
39G7 **Halden** Nor
86B2 **Haldia** India
84D3 **Haldwāni** India
13C1 **Halfway** *R* Can
7D5 **Halifax** Can
42D3 **Halifax** Eng
6D1 **Hall Bals** *Sd* Can
6B3 **Hall Beach** Can
46C1 **Halle** Belg
56C2 **Halle** Germany
112B1 **Halley** *Base* Ant
39F6 **Hallingdal** *R* Nor
6D3 **Hall Pen** Can
106B2 **Hall's Creek** Aust
71D3 **Halmahera** *I* Indon
39G7 **Halmstad** Sweden
56B2 **Haltern** Germany
38J5 **Halti** *Mt* Nor
42C2 **Haltwhistle** Eng
91B4 **Halul** *I* Qatar
94B3 **Haluza** *Hist Site*
  Israel
75A2 **Hamada** Japan
96C2 **Hamada de Tinrhert**
  Desert Region Alg
96B2 **Hamada du Dra**
  Upland Alg
90A3 **Hamadān** Iran
96C2 **Hamada Tounassine**
  Region, Alg
92C2 **Hamāh** Syria
75B2 **Hamamatsu** Japan
39G6 **Hamar** Nor
87C3 **Hambantota**
  Sri Lanka
19B3 **Hamburg** Arkansas,
  USA
18A1 **Hamburg** Iowa, USA
16B2 **Hamburg**
  Pennsylvania, USA
56B2 **Hamburg** Germany
16C2 **Hamden** USA
39J6 **Hämeenlinna** Fin

106A3 **Hamersley Range**
  Mts Aust
74B2 **Hamgyong Sanmaek**
  Mts N Korea
74B2 **Hamhŭng** N Korea
72C2 **Hami** China
94B1 **Hamidiyah** Syria
108B3 **Hamilton** Aust
14C2 **Hamilton** Can
110C1 **Hamilton** NZ
18B3 **Hamilton** Ohio, USA
42B2 **Hamilton** Scot
22B2 **Hamilton,Mt** USA
38K6 **Hamina** Fin
86A1 **Hamirpur** India
56B2 **Hamm** Germany
95A2 **Hammādah al Hamra**
  Upland Libya
38H6 **Hammerdal** Sweden
38H5 **Hammerfest** Nor
18B2 **Hammond** Illinois,
  USA
19B3 **Hammond** Louisiana,
  USA
16B3 **Hammonton** USA
111B3 **Hampden** NZ
43D4 **Hampshire** County,
  Eng
19B3 **Hampton** Arkansas,
  USA
91C4 **Hāmūn-e Jaz Mūrian**
  L Iran
84B3 **Hamun-i-Lora** *Salt L*
  Pak
21C4 **Hana** Hawaiian Is
21C4 **Hanalei** Hawaiian Is
74E3 **Hanamaki** Japan
72C2 **Hancheng** China
73C3 **Hanchuan** China
15C3 **Hancock** Maryland,
  USA
10B2 **Hancock** Michigan,
  USA
75B2 **Handa** Japan
72C2 **Handan** China
99D3 **Handeni** Tanz
72B2 **Hanggin Qi** China
39J7 **Hangö** Fin
73E3 **Hangzhou** China
73E3 **Hangzhou Wan** *B*
  China
111B2 **Hanmer Springs** NZ
13E2 **Hanna** Can
18B2 **Hannibal** USA
56B2 **Hannover** Germany
39G7 **Hanöbukten** *B*
  Sweden
76D1 **Hanoi** Viet
16A3 **Hanover** USA
29B6 **Hanover** *I* Chile
72B3 **Han Shui** China
73B3 **Han Shui** *R* China
85D3 **Hānsi** India
68C2 **Hantay** Mongolia
72B3 **Hanzhong** China
86B2 **Hāora** India
92C4 **Haql** S Arabia
91A5 **Haradh** S Arabia
76E2 **Hara Fanna** Eth
75C1 **Haramachi** Japan
101C2 **Harare** Zim
98C1 **Harazé** Chad
14B2 **Harbor Beach** USA
85D4 **Harda** India
39F6 **Hardangerfjord** *Inlet*
  Nor
46D2 **Hardt** Region,
  Germany
108A2 **Hardwicke B** Aust
18B2 **Hardy** USA
99E2 **Harēr** Eth
99E2 **Hargeysa** Somalia
94B3 **Har Hakippa** *Mt*
  Israel
68B3 **Harhu** *L* China
78A3 **Hari** *R* Indon
75A2 **Harima-nada** *B*
  Japan
56B2 **Harlingen** Neth
9D4 **Harlingen** USA
43E4 **Harlow** Eng
94B2 **Har Meron** *Mt* Israel

20C2 **Harney Basin** USA
20C2 **Harney L** USA
38H6 **Härnosand** Sweden
63B3 **Har Nuur** *L* Mongolia
97B4 **Harper** Lib
12F2 **Harper,Mt** USA
15C3 **Harpers Ferry** USA
94B3 **Har Ramon** *Mt*
  Israel
7C4 **Harricanaw** *R* Can
16B3 **Harrington** USA
7E4 **Harrington Harbour**
  Can
44A3 **Harris** *District* Scot
18C2 **Harrisburg** Illinois,
  USA
16A2 **Harrisburg**
  Pennsylvania, USA
101G1 **Harrismith** S Africa
18B2 **Harrison** USA
13C3 **Harrisonburg** USA
7E4 **Harrison,C** Can
18B2 **Harrisonville** USA
44A3 **Harris,Sound of** *Chan*
  Scot
14B2 **Harrisville** USA
42D3 **Harrogate** Eng
94B2 **Har Saggi** *Mt* Israel
38H5 **Harstad** Nor
12G2 **Hart** *R* Can
39F6 **Hårteigen** *Mt* Nor
16C2 **Hartford** Connecticut,
  USA
14A2 **Hartford** Michigan,
  USA
18A2 **Hart,L** Aust
43B4 **Hartland Pt** Eng
42D2 **Hartlepool** Eng
19A3 **Hartshorne** USA
17B1 **Hartwell Res** USA
101F1 **Hartz** *R* S Africa
68B2 **Har Us Nuur** *L*
  Mongolia
43E4 **Harwich** Eng
84D3 **Haryāna** State, India
94B3 **Hāsā** Jordan
94B2 **Hāsbaiya** Leb
43D4 **Haselmere** Eng
75B2 **Hashimoto** Japan
90A2 **Hashtpar** Iran
90A2 **Hashtrūd** Iran
87B2 **Hassan** India
56B2 **Hasselt** Belg
96C2 **Hassi Inifel** Alg
96B2 **Hassi Mdakane** *Well*
  Alg
96C1 **Hassi Messaoud** Alg
108C3 **Hastings** Aust
43E4 **Hastings** Eng
8D2 **Hastings** Nebraska,
  USA
110C1 **Hastings** NZ
108B2 **Hatfield** Aust
12B1 **Hatham Inlet** USA
78B3 **Hatibis** India
76D2 **Ha Tinh** Viet
108B2 **Hattah** Aust
11C3 **Hatteras,C** USA
19C3 **Hattiesburg** USA
76D3 **Hau Bon** Viet
99E2 **Haud** Region, Eth
110C1 **Hauhungaroa Range**
  Mts NZ
13F1 **Hautain** *R* Can
110B1 **Hauraki G** NZ
111A3 **Hauroko,L** NZ
47C1 **Hausstock** *Mt* Switz
96B1 **Haut Atlas** *Mts* Mor
98C2 **Haute Kotto** Region,
  CAR
46C1 **Hautes Fagnes** *Mts*
  Belg
46B1 **Hautmont** Belg
46B1 **Hauts Plateaux** *Mts*
  Alg
90D3 **Hauzdar** Iran
18B1 **Havana** USA
  Havana = Habana
87B3 **Havankulam**
  Sri Lanka

110C1 **Havelock North** NZ
43B4 **Haverfordwest** Wales
16D1 **Haverhill** USA
87B2 **Havrī** India
16C2 **Haverstraw** USA
59B3 **Havlíčkův Brod** Czech Republic
8C2 **Havre** USA
16A3 **Havre de Grace** USA
7D4 **Havre-St-Pierre** Can
54C2 **Havsa** Turk
21C4 **Hawaii** I Hawaiian Is
21C4 **Hawaii Volcanoes Nat Pk** Hawaiian Is
111A2 **Hawea,L** NZ
110B1 **Hawera** NZ
42C2 **Hawick** Scot
111A2 **Hawkdun Range** Mts NZ
110C1 **Hawke B** NZ
109D2 **Hawke,C** Aust
108A2 **Hawker** Aust
76B1 **Hawng Luk** Burma
93D3 **Hawr al Habbaniyah** L Iraq
93E3 **Hawr al Hammār** L Iraq
21B2 **Hawthorne** USA
108B2 **Hay** Aust
5G3 **Hay** R Can
18A2 **Hay River** Can
22A2 **Hayward** California, USA
86B2 **Hazārībāg** India
46B1 **Hazebrouck** France
19B3 **Hazelhurst** USA
4G? **Hazel Str** Can
5F4 **Hazelton** Can
13B1 **Hazelton Mts** Can
6C1 **Hazen L** Can
94B3 **Hazeva** Israel
16B2 **Hazleton** USA
22A1 **Healdsburg** USA
108C3 **Healesville** Aust
12E2 **Healy** USA
104B6 **Heard I** Indian O
19A3 **Hearne** USA
10B2 **Hearst** Can
72D2 **Hebei** Province, China
109C1 **Hebel** Aust
72C2 **Hebi** China
72C2 **Hebian** China
7D4 **Hebron** Can
94B3 **Hebron** Israel
18A1 **Hebron** Nebraska, USA
5E4 **Hecate** Str Can
12H3 **Heceta I** USA
73B5 **Hechi** China
4G2 **Hecla and Griper B** Can
111C2 **Hector,Mt** NZ
38G6 **Hede** Sweden
39H6 **Hedemora** Sweden
20C1 **He Devil Mt** USA
56B2 **Heerenveen** Neth
46C1 **Heerlen** Neth
Hefa = Haifa
73D3 **Hefei** China
73B4 **Hefeng** China
69F2 **Hegang** China
75B1 **Hegura-jima** I Japan
94B3 **Heidan** R Jordan
56B2 **Heide** Germany
101G1 **Heidelberg** Transvaal, S Africa
57B3 **Heidelberg** Germany
63E2 **Heihe** China
101G1 **Heilbron** S Africa
57B3 **Heilbronn** Germany
56C2 **Heiligenstadt** Germany
38K6 **Heinola** Fin
73B4 **Hejiang** China
6J3 **Hekla** Mt Iceland

76C1 **Hekou** Viet
73A5 **Hekou Yaozou Zizhixian** China
72B2 **Helan** China
72B2 **Helan Shan** Mt China
19B3 **Helena** Arkansas, USA
8B2 **Helena** Montana, USA
22D3 **Helendale** USA
71E3 **Helen Reef** I Pacific O
44B3 **Helensburgh** Scot
91B4 **Helleh** R Iran
51B2 **Hellín** Spain
20C1 **Hells Canyon** R USA
46D1 **Hellweg** Region, Germany
22B2 **Helm** USA
80E2 **Helmand** R Afghan
100A3 **Helmeringhausen** Namibia
46C1 **Helmond** Neth
44C2 **Helmsdale** Scot
74B2 **Helong** China
39G7 **Helsingborg** Sweden
Helsingfors = Helsinki
56C1 **Helsingør** Den
38J6 **Helsinki** Fin
43B4 **Helston** Eng
92B4 **Helwân** Egypt
19A3 **Hempstead** USA
39H7 **Hemse** Sweden
72A3 **Henan** China
72C3 **Henan** Province, China
110B1 **Hen and Chicken Is** NZ
14A3 **Henderson** Kentucky, USA
9B3 **Henderson** Nevada, USA
19B3 **Henderson** Texas, USA
73E5 **Heng-ch'un** Taiwan
68B4 **Hengduan Shan** Mts China
56B2 **Hengelo** Neth
72B2 **Hengshan** China
72B2 **Hengshui** China
76D1 **Heng Xian** China
73C4 **Hengyang** China
77A4 **Henhoaha** Nicobar Is
43D4 **Henley-on-Thames** Eng
16B3 **Henlopen,C** USA
7B4 **Henrietta Maria,C** Can
18A2 **Henryetta** USA
112C2 **Henryk Arctowski** Base Ant
6D3 **Henry Kater Pen** Can
68C2 **Hentiyn Nuruu** Mts Mongolia
76B2 **Henzada** Burma
73B5 **Hepu** China
80E2 **Herat** Afghan
5H4 **Herbert** Can
110C2 **Herbertville** NZ
46E1 **Herborn** Germany
26A4 **Heredia** Costa Rica
43C3 **Hereford** Eng
43C3 **Hereford & Worcester** County, Eng
46C1 **Herentals** Belg
47B1 **Héricourt** France
18A2 **Herington** USA
111A3 **Heriot** NZ
47C1 **Herisau** Switz
15D2 **Herkimer** USA
44E1 **Herma Ness** Pen Scot
109C2 **Hermidale** Aust
111B2 **Hermitage** NZ
Hermon,Mt = Jebel ash Shaykh
24A2 **Hermosillo** Mexico
16A2 **Herndon** Pennsylvania, USA
22C2 **Herndon** California, USA
46D1 **Herne** Germany
56B1 **Herning** Den

90A2 **Herowābad** Iran
50A2 **Herrera del Duque** Spain
16A2 **Hershey** USA
43D4 **Hertford** County, Eng
94B2 **Herzliyya** Israel
46C1 **Hesbaye** Region, Belg
46B1 **Hesdin** France
72B2 **Heshui** China
22D3 **Hesperia** USA
12H2 **Hess** R Can
57B2 **Hessen** State, Germany
22C2 **Hetch Hetchy Res** USA
42C2 **Hexham** Eng
73C5 **He Xian** China
73C5 **Heyuan** China
108B3 **Heywood** Aust
72B2 **Heze** China
17B2 **Hialeah** USA
10A2 **Hibbing** USA
110C1 **Hicks Bay** NZ
109C3 **Hicks,Pt** Aust
23B1 **Hidalgo** State, Mexico
24B2 **Hidalgo del Parral** Mexico
35B1 **Hidrolândia** Brazil
96A2 **Hierro** I Canary Is
75C1 **Higashine** Japan
74D4 **Higashi-suidō** Str Japan
20B2 **High Desert** USA
19B4 **High Island** USA
44B3 **Highland** Region, Scot
22C3 **Highland Peak** Mt USA
16B2 **Highlands Falls** USA
11B3 **High Point** USA
13D1 **High Prairie** Can
5G4 **High River** Can
15B2 **High Springs** USA
16B2 **Hightstown** USA
43D4 **High Wycombe** Eng
39J7 **Hiiumaa** I Estonia
80B3 **Hijaz** Region, S Arabia
75B2 **Hikigawa** Japan
75B1 **Hikone** Japan
110B1 **Hikurangi** NZ
9C4 **Hildago** Mexico
9C4 **Hildago del Parral** Mexico
56B2 **Hildesheim** Germany
27R3 **Hillaby,Mt** Barbados
56C1 **Hillerød** Den
14B3 **Hillsboro** Ohio, USA
20B1 **Hillsboro** Oregon, USA
19A3 **Hillsboro** Texas, USA
44E1 **Hillswick** Scot
21C4 **Hilo** Hawaiian Is
93C2 **Hilvan** Turk
46C1 **Hilversum** Neth
84D2 **Himachal Pradesh** State, India
82B3 **Himalaya** Mts Asia
85C4 **Himatnagar** India
74E6 **Himeji** Japan
74D3 **Himi** Japan
92C3 **Hims** Syria
12E2 **Hinchinbrook Entrance** USA
12E2 **Hinchinbrook I** USA
85D3 **Hindaun** India
84B1 **Hindu Kush** Mts Afghan
87B2 **Hindupur** India
13D1 **Hines Creek** Can
85D4 **Hinganghāt** India
69E2 **Hinggan Ling** Upland China
85B3 **Hingol** R Pak
85D5 **Hingoli** India
38H5 **Hinnøya** I Nor
16C1 **Hinsdale** USA
13D2 **Hinton** Can
34B2 **Hipolito Itrogoyen** Arg

86A2 **Hirakud Res** India
92B2 **Hirfanli Baraji** Res Turk
87B2 **Hirihar** India
74E2 **Hirosaki** Japan
74C4 **Hiroshima** Japan
46C2 **Hirson** France
54C2 **Hîrşova** Rom
56B1 **Hirtshals** Den
84D3 **Hisār** India
26C3 **Hispaniola** I Caribbean S
94C1 **Hisyah** Syria
93D3 **Hit** Iraq
74E3 **Hitachi** Japan
75C1 **Hitachi-Ota** Japan
43D4 **Hitchin** Eng
38F6 **Hitra** I Nor
75A2 **Hiuchi-nada** B Japan
75A2 **Hiwasa** Japan
56B1 **Hjørring** Den
76B1 **Hka** R Burma
97C4 **Ho** Ghana
76D1 **Hoa Binh** Viet
76D3 **Hoa Da** Viet
109C4 **Hobart** Aust
9C3 **Hobbs** USA
56B1 **Hobro** Den
13C2 **Hobson L** Can
99E2 **Hobyo** Somalia
76D3 **Ho Chi Minh** Viet
57C3 **Hochkonig** Mt Austria
54B1 **Hódmezö'hely** Hung
59B3 **Hodonín** Czech Republic
74B2 **Hoeryong** N Korea
57C2 **Hof** Germany
38B2 **Hofsjökull** Mts Iceland
74C4 **Hôfu** Japan
96C2 **Hoggar** Upland Alg
46D1 **Hohe Acht** Mt Gormany
72C1 **Hohhot** China
6J3 **Höhn** Iceland
68B3 **Hoh Sai Hu** L China
82C2 **Hoh Xil Shan** Mts China
99D2 **Hoima** Uganda
86C1 **Hojāi** India
75A2 **Hojo** Japan
110B1 **Hokianga Harbour** B NZ
111B2 **Hokitika** NZ
74E2 **Hokkaido** Japan
90C2 **Hokmābād** Iran
109C3 **Holbrook** Aust
9B3 **Holbrook** USA
19A2 **Holdenville** USA
87B2 **Hole Narsipur** India
27R3 **Holetown** Barbados
26B2 **Holguín** Cuba
111B2 **Holitika** NZ
12C2 **Holitna** USA
59B3 **Hollabrunn** Austria
14A2 **Holland** USA
22B2 **Hollister** USA
19C3 **Holly Springs** USA
22C3 **Hollywood** California, USA
17B2 **Hollywood** Florida, USA
4G2 **Holman Island** Can
38J6 **Holmsund** Sweden
94B2 **Holon** Israel
56B1 **Holstebro** Den
6E3 **Holsteinborg** Greenland
14B2 **Holt** USA
18A2 **Holton** USA
12C2 **Holy Cross** USA
43B3 **Holyhead** Wales
42D2 **Holy I** Eng
43B3 **Holy I** Wales
16C1 **Holyoke** USA
86C2 **Homalin** Burma
6D3 **Home B** Can
12D3 **Homer** Alaska, USA
19B3 **Homer** Louisiana, USA
111A2 **Homer Tunnel** NZ
17B1 **Homerville** USA

17B2 **Homestead** USA
17A1 **Homewood** USA
87B1 **Homnābād** India
101C3 **Homoine** Mozam
25D3 **Honda** R Mexico
25D3 **Honduras** Republic,
Cent America
25D3 **Honduras,G of**
Honduras
39G6 **Hønefoss** Nor
15C2 **Honesdale** USA
21A1 **Honey L** USA
76C1 **Hong** R Viet
76D1 **Hon Gai** Viet
73A4 **Honggou** China
73C4 **Hong Hu** L China
72B2 **Honghui** China
73C4 **Hongjiang** China
73C5 **Hong Kong** Colony,
S E Asia
68D2 **Hongor** Mongolia
73B5 **Hongshui He** R
China
72A3 **Hongyuan** China
72D3 **Hongze Hu** L China
107E1 **Honiara** Solomon Is
77C4 **Hon Khoai** I Camb
76D3 **Hon Lan** I Viet
38K4 **Hönningsväg** Nor
21C4 **Honolulu** Hawaiian Is
77C4 **Hon Panjang** I Viet
74D3 **Honshu** I Japan
20B1 **Hood,Mt** USA
20B1 **Hood River** USA
45C2 **Hook Head** C
Irish Rep
12G3 **Hoonah** USA
12A2 **Hooper Bay** USA
101G1 **Hoopstad** S Africa
56A2 **Hoorn** Neth
20B2 **Hoover Dam** USA
12E2 **Hope** Alaska, USA
19B3 **Hope** Arkansas, USA
13C3 **Hope** Can
7D4 **Hopedale** Can
64D2 **Hopen** I Barents S
6D3 **Hopes Advance,C**
Can
108B3 **Hopetoun** Aust
100B3 **Hopetown** S Africa
18C2 **Hopkinsville** USA
20B1 **Hoquiam** USA
93D1 **Horasan** Turk
99F1 **Hordiyo** Somalia
47C1 **Horgen** Switz
105H5 **Horizon Depth**
Pacific O
91C4 **Hormuz,Str of** Oman/
Iran
59B3 **Horn** Austria
6H3 **Horn** C Iceland
38H5 **Hornavan** L Sweden
19B3 **Hornbeck** USA
20B2 **Hornbrook** USA
111B2 **Hornby** NZ
7B5 **Hornepayne** Can
4F3 **Horn Mts** Can
42D3 **Hornsea** Eng
72B1 **Horn Uul** Mt
Mongolia
30E3 **Horqueta** Par
15C2 **Horseheads** USA
56C1 **Horsens** Den
20B1 **Horseshoe Bay** Can
108B3 **Horsham** Aust
43D4 **Horsham** Eng
39G7 **Horten** Nor
4F3 **Horton** R Can
78C2 **Hose Mts** Malay
85D4 **Hoshangābād** India
84D2 **Hoshiārpur** India
87B1 **Hospet** India
29C7 **Hoste** I Chile
72B2 **Hotan** China
19B3 **Hot Springs**
Arkansas, USA
8C2 **Hot Springs** S.
Dakota, USA
4G3 **Hottah** Can
46A2 **Houdan** France
72C2 **Houma** China
19B4 **Houma** USA
16C2 **Housatonic** R USA
13B2 **Houston** Can

19C3 **Houston** Mississippi,
USA
19A4 **Houston** Texas, USA
106A3 **Houtman** Is Aust
68B2 **Hovd** Mongolia
68C1 **Hövsgöl Nuur** L
Mongolia
14A2 **Howard City** USA
12C1 **Howard P** USA
109C3 **Howe,C** Aust
101H1 **Howick** S Africa
44C2 **Hoy** I Scot
39F6 **Høyanger** Nor
59B2 **Hradec-Králové**
Czech Republic
59B3 **Hranice**
Czech Republic
59B3 **Hron** R Slovakia
73E5 **Hsin-chu** Taiwan
73E5 **Hsüeh Shan** Mt
Taiwan
72B2 **Huachi** China
32B6 **Huacho** Peru
72C1 **Huade** China
72D3 **Huaibei** China
72D3 **Huaibin** China
73C4 **Huai He** R China
73C4 **Huaihua** China
73C5 **Huaiji** China
72D3 **Huainan** China
69E4 **Hua-lien** Taiwan
32B5 **Huallaga** R Peru
32B5 **Huallanca** Peru
32B5 **Huamachuco** Peru
100A2 **Huambo** Angola
30C2 **Huanay** Bol
32B5 **Huancabamba** Peru
32B6 **Huancavelica** Peru
32B6 **Huancayo** Peru
73D3 **Huangchuan** China
Huang Hai = Yellow S
72D2 **Huang He** R China
72B2 **Huangling** China
76D2 **Huangliu** China
73C3 **Huangpi** China
73D4 **Huangshan** China
73D3 **Huangshi** China
34C3 **Huanguelén** Arg
73E4 **Huangyan** China
74B2 **Huanren** China
32B5 **Huánuco** Peru
30C2 **Huanuni** Bol
72B2 **Huan Xian** China
32B5 **Huaráz** Peru
32B6 **Huarmey** Peru
32B5 **Huascarán** Mt Peru
30B4 **Huasco** Chile
23B2 **Huatusco** Mexico
23B1 **Huauchinango**
Mexico
23B2 **Huautla** Mexico
72C2 **Hua Xian** China
24B2 **Huayapan** R Mexico
73C3 **Hubei** Province,
China
87B1 **Hubli** India
34C3 **Hucal** Arg
74A2 **Huch'ang** N Korea
42D3 **Huddersfield** Eng
39H6 **Hudiksvall** Sweden
17B2 **Hudson** Florida,
USA
14B2 **Hudson** Michigan,
USA
16C1 **Hudson** New York,
USA
16C1 **Hudson** R USA
7B4 **Hudson B** Can
5H4 **Hudson Bay** Can
13C1 **Hudson's Hope** Can
6C3 **Hudson Str** Can
76D2 **Hue** Viet
23B1 **Huejutla** Mexico
50A2 **Huelva** Spain
23A2 **Hueramo** Mexico
51B2 **Húercal Overa** Spain
51B1 **Huesca** Spain
23B2 **Huextla** Hist Site
Mexico
107D3 **Hughenden** Aust
12D1 **Hughes** Aust
86B2 **Hugli** R India
19A3 **Hugo** USA
73D4 **Hui'an** China

110C1 **Huiarau Range** Mts
NZ
74B2 **Huich'ŏn** N Korea
74B2 **Huifa He** R China
32B3 **Huila** Mt Colombia
73D5 **Huilai** China
73A4 **Huili** China
74B2 **Huinan** China
34C2 **Huinca Renancó** Arg
25C3 **Huixtla** Mexico
73A4 **Huize** China
73C5 **Huizhou** China
23B2 **Hujuápan de Léon**
Mexico
69F2 **Hulin** China
15C1 **Hull** Can
42D3 **Hull** Eng
33E5 **Humaitá** Brazil
100B4 **Humansdorp** S Africa
42D3 **Humber** R Eng
42D3 **Humberside** County,
Eng
5H4 **Humboldt** Can
20C2 **Humboldt** R USA
20B2 **Humboldt B** USA
6D2 **Humboldt Gletscher**
Gl Greenland
21B2 **Humboldt L** USA
11C1 **Humeburn** Aust
109C3 **Hume,L** Aust
100A2 **Humpata** Angola
22C2 **Humphreys** USA
38A1 **Húnaflói** B Iceland
73C4 **Hunan** Province,
China
74C2 **Hunchun** China
13C2 **Hundred Mile House**
Can
54B1 **Hunedoara** Rom
59B3 **Hungary**
Republic, Europe
108B1 **Hungerford** Aust
74B2 **Hüngnam** N Korea
74B2 **Hunjiang** China
46D2 **Hunsrück** Mts,
Germany
109C3 **Hunter** R Aust
13B2 **Hunter** I Can
109C4 **Hunter Is** Aust
12D2 **Hunter,Mt** USA
14A3 **Huntingburg** USA
43D3 **Huntingdon** Eng
14A2 **Huntingdon** Indiana,
USA
14B3 **Huntington** W
Virginia, USA
22C4 **Huntington Beach**
USA
22C2 **Huntington L** USA
110C1 **Huntly** NZ
44C3 **Huntly** Scot
12J2 **Hunt,Mt** Can
108A1 **Hunt Pen** Aust
17A1 **Huntsville** Alabama,
USA
15C1 **Huntsville** Can
19A3 **Huntsville** Texas,
USA
76D2 **Huong Khe** Viet
71F4 **Huon Peninsula** Pen
PNG
109C4 **Huonville** Aust
14B1 **Hurd,C** Can
80B3 **Hurghada** Egypt
8D2 **Huron** S. Dakota,
USA
14B1 **Huron,L** Can/USA
34A2 **Hurtado** Chile
111B2 **Hurunui** R NZ
38B1 **Husavik** Iceland
54C1 **Huşi** Rom
39G7 **Huskvarna** Sweden
12C1 **Huslia** USA
94B2 **Husn** Jordan
56B2 **Husum** Germany
19C3 **Hutchinson** USA
72D2 **Hutuo He** R China
46C1 **Huy** Belg
72A2 **Huzhu** China
52C2 **Hvar** I Croatia
100B2 **Hwange** Zim

100B2 **Hwange Nat Pk** Zim
15D2 **Hyannis** USA
68B2 **Hyaryas Nuur** L
Mongolia
5E4 **Hydaburg** Can
16C2 **Hyde Park** USA
87B1 **Hyderābād** India
85B3 **Hyderabad** Pak
49D3 **Hyères** France
12J2 **Hyland** R Can
8B2 **Hyndman Peak** Mt
USA
38K6 **Hyrynsalmi** Fin
13D1 **Hythe** Can
74C4 **Hyūga** Japan
39J6 **Hyvikää** Fin

I

31C4 **Iaçu** Brazil
54C2 **Ialomiţa** R Rom
54C1 **Iaşi** Rom
97C4 **Ibadan** Nig
32B3 **Ibagué** Colombia
54B2 **Ibar** R Montenegro/
Serbia, Yugos
32B3 **Ibarra** Ecuador
35B1 **Ibiá** Brazil
30E4 **Ibicuí** R Brazil
34D2 **Ibicuy** Arg
51C2 **Ibiza** Spain
51C2 **Ibiza** I Spain
101D2 **Ibo** Mozam
31C4 **Ibotirama** Brazil
91C5 **'Ibri** Oman
32B6 **Ica** Peru
32D4 **Icá** R Brazil
32D3 **Icana** Brazil
38A1 **Iceland** Republic,
N Atlantic O
13C2 **Ice Mt** Can
87A1 **Ichalkaranji** India
75B1 **Ichihara** Japan
74E3 **Ichinoseki** Japan
12F3 **Icy B** USA
4B2 **Icy C** USA
19B3 **Idabell** USA
8B2 **Idaho Falls** USA
20B2 **Idanha** USA
46D2 **Idar Oberstein**
USA
95A2 **Idehan Marzūg**
Desert Libya
95A2 **Idehan Ubari** Desert
Libya
96C2 **Idelès** Alg
68B2 **Iderlym Gol** R
Mongolia
95C2 **Idfu** Egypt
55B3 **Idhi Óros** Mt Greece
55B3 **Idhra** I Greece
98B3 **Idiofa** Zaire
12C2 **Iditarod** USA
92C2 **Idlib** Syria
39K7 **Idritsa** Russian Fed
100B4 **Idutywa** S Africa
55C3 **Ieràpetra** Greece
46B1 **Ieper** Belg
63D2 **Iet Oktyobr'ya**
Russian Fed
99D3 **Ifakara** Tanz
71F3 **Ifalik** I Pacific O
101D3 **Ifanadiana** Madag
97C4 **Ife** Nig
97C3 **Iférouane** Niger
78C2 **Igan** Malay
35B2 **Igarapava** Brazil
93E2 **Igdir** Iran
39H6 **Iggesund** Sweden
34B2 **Iglesia** Arg
53A3 **Iglesias** Sardegna
6B3 **Igloolik** Can
10A2 **Ignace** Can
55B3 **Igoumenitsa** Greece
61H2 **Igra** Russian Fed
23B2 **Iguala** Mexico
35B2 **Iguape** Brazil
35B2 **Iguatama** Brazil
31D3 **Iguatu** Brazil
98A3 **Iguéla** Gabon
101D3 **Ihosy** Madag
74D3 **Iida** Japan
75B1 **Iide-san** Mt Japan
38K6 **Iisalmi** Fin

Islas de Margarita

75A2 Iizuka *Japan*
97C4 Ijebu Ode *Nig*
56B2 Ijsselmeer *S* Neth
55C3 Ikaria *I* Greece
74E2 Ikeda *Japan*
98C3 Ikela *Zaire*
54B2 Ikhtiman *Bulg*
12D3 Ikolik,C *USA*
10D2 Ikopa *R* Madag
79B2 Ilagan *Phil*
90A3 Ilam *Iran*
47C1 Ilanz *Switz*
13F1 Île a la Crosse *Can*
13F1 Île a la Crosse,L *Can*
89G8 Ilebo *Zaire*
96D1 Île de Jerba *I* Tunisia
48B2 Île de Noirmoutier *I* France
107F3 Île des Pins *I* Nouvelle Calédonie
48B2 Île d'Ouessant *I* France
48B2 Île d'Yeu *I* France
61J3 Ilek *R* Russian Fed
107F2 Îles Bélép *Nouvelle Calédonie*
107E2 Îles Chesterfield *Nouvelle Calédonie*
49D3 Îles d'Hyères *Is* France
43B4 Ilfracombe *Eng*
92B1 Ilgaz Dağları *Mts* Turk
33G3 Ilha Bazaruto *I* Mozam
33G3 Ilha da Maracá *I* Brazil
33G4 Ilha de Marajó *I* Brazil
35B2 Ilha de São Sebastião *I* Brazil
33G6 Ilha do Bananal *Region* Brazil
35C2 Ilha Grande *I* Brazil
35B2 Ilha Santo Amaro *I* Brazil
96A1 Ilhas Selvegens *I* Atlantic O
35A2 Ilha Solteira Dam *Brazil*
31D4 Ilhéus *Brazil*
12C3 Iliamna L *USA*
12D2 Iliamna V *USA*
79B4 Iligan *Phil*
63C2 Ilim *R* Russian Fed
75C1 Ilim *Russian Fed*
63G3 Il'inskiy *Russian Fed*
55B3 Iliodhrómia *I* Greece
79B4 Ilana B *Phil*
34A2 Illapel *Chile*
34A2 Illapel *R* Chile
97C3 Illéla *Niger*
47D1 Iller *R* Germany
4C4 Illiamna L *USA*
10A2 Illinois *State, USA*
18B2 Illinois *R* USA
38L6 Illizi *Alg*
30B2 Ilo *Peru*
79B3 Iloilo *Phil*
38L6 Ilomantsi *Fin*
97C4 Ilorin *Nig*
75A2 Imabari *Japan*
75B1 Imaichi *Japan*
60C1 Imatra *Fin*
30G4 Imbituba *Brazil*
99E2 Imi *Eth*
20C2 Imlay *USA*
47D1 Immenstadt *Germany*
52B2 Imola *Italy*
31B3 Imperatriz *Brazil*
22A2 Imperial *USA*
98B2 Impfondo *Congo*
86C2 Imphal *India*
47D1 Imst *Austria*
12B1 Imuruk L *USA*
75B1 Ina *Japan*
96C2 In Afahleleh *Well* Alg
75B2 Inamba-jima *I* Japan
96C2 In Amenas *Alg*
38K5 Inari *Fin*
38K5 Inarijärvi *L* Fin

75C1 Inawashiro-ko *L* Japan
96C2 In Belbel *Alg*
60E5 Ince Burun *Pt* Turk
92B2 Incekum Burun *Pt* Turk
74B3 Inch'ón *S* Korea
96B2 In Dagouher *Well* Mali
31A2 Indaiá *R* Brazil
38H6 Indals *R* Sweden
21B2 Independence California, USA
18A2 Independence Kansas, USA
18B2 Independence Missouri, USA
78A3 Inderagiri *R* Indon
61H4 Inderborskiy Kazakhstan
83B3 India *Federal Republic, Asia*
14A2 Indiana *State, USA*
15C2 Indiana *USA*
104C6 Indian-Antarctic Ridge *Indian O*
14A3 Indianapolis *USA*
Indian Desert = Thar Desert
7E4 Indian Harbour *Can*
104B4 Indian *R* USA
18B1 Indianola *Iowa, USA*
19B3 Indianola *Mississippi, USA*
35B1 Indianópolis *Brazil*
76D2 Indo China *Region, S E Asia*
70A4 Indonesia *Republic, S E Asia*
85D4 Indore *India*
78B4 Indramayu *Indon*
48C2 Indre *R* France
85B3 Indus *R* Pak
60D5 Inebu *Turk*
96C2 In Ebeuyi *Well* Alg
92A1 Inegöl *Turk*
96D2 In Ezzane *Alg*
97C3 Ingal *Niger*
14B2 Ingersoll *Can*
107D2 Ingham *Aust*
6D2 Inglefield Land *Region* Can
110B1 Inglewood *NZ*
109D1 Inglewood *USA*
22C4 Inglewood *USA*
108B3 Inglewood *Victoria, Aust*
38B2 Ingólfshöfði *I* Iceland
57C3 Ingolstadt *Germany*
86B2 Ingrāj Bāzār *India*
96C3 In-Guezzam *Well* Alg
101C3 Inhambane *Mozam*
101C3 Inharrime *Mozam*
35B1 Inhumas *Brazil*
32D3 Inírida *R* Colombia
45A2 Inisbofin *I* Irish Rep
45A1 Inishkea *I* Irish Rep
45B2 Inishmaan *I* Irish Rep
45B2 Inishmore *I* Irish Rep
45B1 Inishmurray *I* Irish Rep
45C1 Inishowen *District, Irish Rep*
45A1 Inishshark *I* Irish Rep
45A2 Inishturk *I* Irish Rep
109C1 Injune *Aust*
12H3 Inklin *Can*
12H3 Inklin *R* Can
12C1 Inland L *USA*
47D1 Inn *R* Austria
108B1 Innamincka *Aust*
68C2 Inner Mongolia *Autonomous Region, China*
107D2 Innisfail *Aust*
12C2 Innoko *R* USA
57C3 Innsbruck *Austria*
98B3 Inongo *Zaire*
58B2 Inowrocław *Pol*
96C2 In Salah *Alg*
47B1 Interlaken *Switz*

24C3 Intexpec *Mexico*
47C2 Intra *Italy*
78D3 Intu *Indon*
75C1 Inubo-saki *C* Japan
7C4 Inukjuak *Can*
4E3 Inuvik *Can*
4F3 Inuvik *Region* Can
14B3 Inveraray *Scot*
11A3 Invercargill *NZ*
109D1 Inverell *Aust*
13D2 Invermere *Can*
44D3 Inverness *Scot*
44C3 Inverurie *Scot*
108A3 Investigator Str *Aust*
69E4 Inya *R* Russian Fed
22B2 Inyokern *USA*
98B3 Inzia *R* Zaire
55A3 Ioánnina *Greece*
18A2 Iola *USA*
44A3 Iona *I* Scot
100A2 Iôna Nat Pk *Angola*
20C1 Ione *USA*
Ionian Is = Ionioi Nísoi
55A3 Ionian S *Italy/Greece*
55B3 Ionioi Nísoi *Greece*
55C3 Ios *I* Greece
10A2 Iowa *R* USA
10A2 Iowa *State, USA*
10A2 Iowa City *USA*
35B1 Ipameri *Brazil*
35C1 Ipanema *Brazil*
61F4 Ipatovo *Russian Fed*
32B3 Ipiales *Colombia*
77C5 Ipoh *Malay*
31A4 Iporá *Brazil*
55C2 Ipsala *Turk*
109D1 Ipswich *Aust*
43E3 Ipswich *Eng*
16D1 Ipswich *USA*
103D3 Ipu *Brazil*
32C4 Iquitos *Peru*
55C3 Iráklion *Greece*
80D2 Iran *Republic, S W Asia*
91D4 Iranshahr *Iran*
23A1 Irapuato *Mexico*
93D3 Iraq *Republic, S W Asia*
95A2 Irá Wan *Watercourse* Libya
94B2 Irbid *Jordan*
61K2 Irbit *Russian Fed*
36C3 Ireland *Republic, NW Europe*
33F3 Ireng *R* Guyana
71E4 Irian Jaya *Province, Indon*
95A2 Iri *S* Korea
71E4 Irian Jaya *Province, Indon*
95A2 Iriba *Chad*
99D3 Iringa *Tanz*
69E4 Iriomote *I* Japan
23A1 Irapuato *Mexico*
33F3 Iris B *Africa*
42B3 Irish Sea *Eng/Irish Rep*
12D1 Irkillik *R* Can
63C2 Irkutsk *Russian Fed*
65J4 Irlysh *R* Kazakhstan
108A2 Iron Knob *Aust*
14A1 Iron Mountain *USA*
107D2 Iron Range *Aust*
14A1 Iron River *USA*
14B3 Irontown *USA*
10A2 Ironwood *USA*
15B2 Iroquois Falls *Can*
75B2 Iro-zaki *C* Japan
76A2 Irrawaddy,Mouths of the *Burma*
65H4 Irtysh *R* Russian Fed
51B1 Irun *Spain*
42B2 Irvine *Scot*
19A3 Irving *USA*
79B4 Isabela *Phil*
32J7 Isabela *I* Ecuador
4H2 Isachsen *Can*
4H2 Isachsen,C *Can*
6H3 Ísafjörður *Iceland*
74C4 Isahaya *Japan*
98C2 Isangi *Zaire*
47D1 Isar *R* Germany
47D1 Isarco *R* Italy
44E1 Isbister *Scot*
47D1 Ischgl *Austria*
53B2 Ischia *I* Italy

75B2 Ise *Japan*
47D2 Iseo *Italy*
46D1 Iserlohn *Germany*
53B2 Isernia *Italy*
75B2 Ise-wan *B* Japan
69E4 Ishigaki *I* Japan
74E2 Ishikari *R* Japan
74E2 Ishikari-wan *B* Japan
74E3 Ishim *Russian Fed*
65H4 Ishim *R* Kazakhstan
74E3 Ishinomaki *Japan*
75C1 Ishioka *Japan*
84C1 Ishkashim *Afghan*
65J4 Isil'kul *Russian Fed*
99D2 Isiolo *Kenya*
98C2 Isiro *Zaire*
92C2 Iskenderun *Turk*
92C2 Iskenderun Körfezi *B* Turk
93B1 İskilip *Turk*
65K4 Iskitim *Russian Fed*
54B2 Iskur *R* Bulg
12H3 Iskut *R* Can/USA
23B2 Isla *Mexico*
34C3 Isla Bermejo *I* Arg
32A2 Isla Blanquilla *Ven*
32A2 Isla Coiba *I* Panama
9B4 Isla de Cedros *I* Mexico
29B4 Isla de Chiloé *I* Chile
25D2 Isla de Cozumel *I* Mexico
26C3 Isla de la Gonâve *Cuba*
26A2 Isla de la Juventud *I* Cuba
29B4 Isla de las Lechiguanas *I* Arg
3K8 Isla del Coco *I* Costa Rica
25D3 Isla del Maíz *I* Caribbean S
23B1 Isla de Lobos *I* Mexico
29C2 Isla de los Estados *I* Arg
28E2 Isla de Marajó *I* Brazil
105L5 Isla de Pascua *I* Pacific O
26A4 Isla de Providencia *I* Caribbean S
26A4 Isla de San Andres *I* Caribbean S
30G4 Isla de Santa Catarina *I* Brazil
33G2 Isla du Diable *I* French Guiana
31E2 Isla Fernando de Noronha *I* Brazil
29C6 Isla Grande de Tierra del Fuego *I* Arg/Chile
27D6 Isla Tortuga *I* Ven
84C2 Islamabad *Pak*
24A2 Isla Magdalena *I* Mexico
27E4 Isla Margarita *Ven*
34A3 Isla Mocha *Chile*
17B2 Islamorada *USA*
10A1 Island L *Can*
108A2 Island Lg *Aust*
110B1 Islands,B of *NZ*
32A4 Isla Puná *I* Ecuador
103D6 Isla San Ambrosia *I* Pacific O
103D6 Isla San Felix *I* Pacific O
24A2 Isla Santa Margarita *I* Mexico
34A3 Isla Santa Maria *I* Chile
51C2 Islas Baleares *Is* Spain
96A2 Islas Canarias *Is* Atlantic O
51C2 Islas Columbretes *Is* Spain
25D3 Islas de la Bahia *Is* Honduras
26A4 Islas del Maíz *Is* Caribbean S
33E1 Islas de Margarita *Is* Ven

Kalahari Desert

100B3 Kalahari Desert Botswana
38J6 Kalajoki Fin
63D2 Kalakan Russian Fed
70A3 Kalakepen Indon
84C1 Kalam Pak
55B3 Kalámai Greece
10B2 Kalamazoo USA
84B3 Kalat Pak
92B1 Kalecik Turk
78D3 Kalemie R / Indon
99C3 Kalémié Zaïre
38L5 Kalevala Russian Fed
86C2 Kalewa Burma
12D2 Kalgin I USA
106B4 Kalgoorlie Aust
78B4 Kalianda Indon
78J3 Kalibo Phil
98C3 Kalima Zaïre
78C3 Kalimantan Province, Indon
55C3 Kálimnos I Greece
86B1 Kālimpang India
60B3 Kaliningrad Russian Fed
60C3 Kalinkovichi Belorussia
88Z Kalispell USA
58B2 Kalisz Pol
99D3 Kaliua Tanz
38J5 Kalix R Sweden
100A3 Kalkfeld Namibia
100A3 Kalkrand Namibia
108A1 Kalkoopah R Aust
38K6 Kallávesi L Fin
55C3 Kallonis Kólpos B Greece
39H7 Kalmar Sweden
61G4 Kalmytskaya Respublika, Russian Fed
100B2 Kalomo Zambia
18B1 Kalona USA
13B2 Kalone Peak Mt Can
87A2 Kalpeni I India
85D3 Kālpi India
53A3 Kalat Khasba Tunisia
12B2 Kalskag USA
12C2 Kaltag USA
62A3 Kaluga Russian Fed
39G7 Kalundborg Den
59C3 Kalush Ukraine
87B2 Kalyandurg India
60E2 Kalyazin Russian Fed
61H1 Kama R Russian Fed
74E3 Kamaishi Japan
84C2 Kamalia Pak
110C1 Kamanawa Mts NZ
100A2 Kamanjab Namibia
84D2 Kamat Mt India
87B3 Kamban India
61H2 Kambarka Russian Fed
97A4 Kambia Sierra Leone
59D3 Kamenets Podolskiy Ukraine
61F3 Kamenka Russian Fed
65K4 Kamen-na-Obi Russian Fed
61K2 Kamensk-Ural'skiy Russian Fed
5H3 Kamilukuak L Can
98C3 Kamina Zaïre
7A3 Kaminak L Can
75C1 Kaminoyama Japan
5F4 Kamloops Can
93E1 Kamo Armenia
75C1 Kamogawa Japan
99D2 Kampala Uganda
77C5 Kampar Malay
78A2 Kampar R Indon
56B2 Kampen Neth
76B2 Kamphaeng Phet Thai
77C3 Kampot Camb
91D4 Kamsack Can
61J2 Kamskoye Vodokhranilishche Res Russian Fed
85D4 Kämthi India
61G3 Kamyshin Russian Fed

61K2 Kamyshlov Russian Fed
7C4 Kanaaupscow R Can
99C3 Kananga Zaïre
61G2 Kanash Russian Fed
75B1 Kanayama Japan
74D3 Kanazawa Japan
4C3 Kanbisha US
87B2 Kanchipuram India
84B2 Kandahar Afghan
64E3 Kandalaksha Russian Fed
38L5 Kandalakshskaya Guba B Russian Fed
97C3 Kandi Benin
109C2 Kandos Aust
87C3 Kandy Sri Lanka
15C2 Kane USA
6C1 Kane Basin B Can
98B1 Kanem Desert Region Chad
97B3 Kangaba Mali
92C2 Kangal Turk
6E3 Kangâmiut Greenland
91B4 Kangān Iran
77C4 Kangar Malay
106C4 Kangaroo I Aust
6E3 Kangâtsiaq Greenland
90A3 Kangavar Iran
72C1 Kangbao China
82C3 Kangchenjunga Mt Nepal
73A4 Kangding China
6G3 Kangerdlugssuaq B Greenland
6G3 Kangerdlugssuaq B Greenland
99D2 Kangetet Kenya
74B2 Kanggye N Korea
7D4 Kangiqsualujjuaq Can
6C3 Kangigsujuaq Can
7C3 Kangirsuk Can
74B3 Kangnŭng S Korea
98B2 Kango Gabon
68B4 Kangto Mt China
72B3 Kang Xian China
77C4 Kanh Hung Viet
98C3 Kaniama Zaïre
87B1 Kani Giri India
39J6 Kankaanpää Fin
14A2 Kankakee USA
14A2 Kankakee R USA
97B3 Kankan Guinea
86A2 Kanker India
87B3 Kanniyakuman India
97C3 Kano Nig
74C4 Kanoya Japan
86A1 Kānpur India
9D3 Kansas State, USA
18A2 Kansas R USA
10A3 Kansas City USA
73D5 Kanshi China
63B2 Kansk Russian Fed
97C3 Kantchari Burkina
86B2 Kanthi India
12D2 Kantishna USA
12D2 Kantishna R USA
100B3 Kanye R Botswana
68D4 Kao-hsiung Taiwan
100A2 Kaoka Veld Plain Namibia
97A3 Kaolack Sen
100B2 Kaoma Zambia
21C4 Kapaau Hawaiian Is
98C3 Kapanga Zaïre
6F3 Kap Cort Adelaer C Greenland
6H3 Kap Dalton C Greenland
39H7 Kapellskär Sweden
6F3 Kap Farvel C Greenland
6G3 Kap Gustav Holm C Greenland
100B2 Kapiri Zambia
78C2 Kapit Malay
19B3 Kaplan USA
57C3 Kaplice Czech Republic
77B4 Kapoe Thai
99C3 Kapona Zaïre

52C1 Kaposvár Hung
6C2 Kap Parry C Can
6H3 Kap Ravn C Greenland
78B3 Kapsan R Indon
108A2 Kapunda Aust
84D2 Kapurthala India
78B5 Kapuskasing Can
109D2 Kaputar Mt Aust
93E2 Kapydzhik Mt Armenia
6D2 Kap York C Greenland
92B1 Karabük Turk
55C2 Karacabey Turk
85B4 Karachi Pak
87A1 Karäd India
60E5 Kara Daglari Mt Turk
54C5 Karadeniz Bogazi Sd Turk
68D1 Karaftit Russian Fed
65J5 Karaganda Kazakhstan
65J5 Karagayly Kazakhstan
87B2 Kāraikāl India
90B2 Karaj Iran
94B3 Kara Jordan
65G5 Kara Kalpakskaya Respublika, Uzbekistan
84D1 Karakax He R China
71D3 Karakelong I Indon
84D1 Karakoram Mts India
84D1 Karakoram P India/China
97A3 Karakoro R Maur/Sen
65G6 Karakumy Desert Russian Fed
94B3 Karama Jordan
92B2 Karaman Turk
65K5 Karamay China
111B2 Karamea NZ
111B2 Karamea Bight B NZ
85D4 Kāranja India
92B2 Karapınar Turk
64H2 Kara S Russian Fed
100A3 Karasburg Namibia
38K5 Karasjok Nor
65J4 Karasuk Russian Fed
92C2 Karataş Turk
65H5 Kara Tau Mts Kazakhstan
76B2 Karathuri Burma
74B4 Karatsu Japan
84B1 Karāz Iran
93D3 Karbalā' Iraq
59C3 Karcag Hung
55B3 Kardhitsa Greece
60E2 Karel'skaya Respublika, Russian Fed
38J5 Karesvando Sweden
96B2 Karet Desert Region Maur
64K5 Kargasok Russian Fed
97D3 Kari Nig
100B2 Kariba Zim
100B2 Kariba L Zim/Zambia
100B2 Kariba Dam Zim/Zambia
95C3 Karima Sudan
78B3 Karimata I Indon
86C2 Karimganj Bang
87B1 Karimnagar India
99E1 Karin Somalia
39J6 Karis Fin
99C3 Karishimbe Mt Zaïre
55B3 Káristos Greece
87A2 Kārkal India
71F4 Karkar I PNG
90A3 Karkheh R Iran
60D4 Karkinitskiy Zaliv B Ukraine
63B3 Karlik Shan Mt China
58B2 Karlino Pol
52C1 Karlobag Croatia
52C1 Karlovac Croatia
54B2 Karlovo Bulg
57C2 Karlovy Vary Czech Republic

39G7 Karlshamn Sweden
39G7 Karlskoga Sweden
39H7 Karlskrona Sweden
57B3 Karlsruhe Germany
39G7 Karlstad Sweden
12D3 Karluk USA
86C2 Karnafuli Res Bang
84D3 Karnal India
87A1 Karnataka State, India
54C2 Karnobat Bulg
100B2 Karoi Zim
99D3 Karonga Malawi
95C3 Karora Sudan
78D3 Karossa Indon
55C3 Kárpathos I Greece
6E2 Karrats Fjord Greenland
93D1 Kars Turk
65H4 Karsakpay Kazakhstan
58D1 Kärsava Latvia
65G2 Karshi Uzbekistan
38J6 Karstula Fin
94B1 Kartaba Leb
94B1 Kartal Turk
61K3 Kartaly Russian Fed
90A3 Kärun R Iran
86A1 Karwa India
87A2 Kärwär India
68D1 Karymskoye Russian Fed
94A3 Kasai R Zaïre
100B2 Kasaji Zaïre
101C2 Kasama Zambia
99D3 Kasanga Tanz
87A2 Käsaragod India
5H3 Kasba L Can
100B2 Kasempa Zambia
100B2 Kasenga Zaïre
99E3 Kasese Uganda
90B3 Käshän Iran
12C2 Kashegelok USA
82B2 Kashi China
84D3 Käshipur India
74D3 Kashiwazaki Japan
90C2 Kashmar Iran
84C2 Kashmir State, India
61F3 Kasimov Russian Fed
14C3 Kaskaskia R USA
38J6 Kaskinen Fin
61K2 Kasli Russian Fed
5G5 Kaslo Can
98C3 Kasonga Zaïre
99B3 Kasongo-Lunda Zaïre
55C3 Kásos I Greece
Kaspiyskiy = Lagan'
95C3 Kassala Sudan
56B2 Kassel Germany
96C1 Kasserine Tunisia
100A2 Kassinga Angola
92B1 Kastamonou Turk
55B3 Kastélli Greece
92A2 Kastellorizon I Greece
55B2 Kastoría Greece
54D3 Kástron Greece
74D3 Kasugai Japan
101C2 Kasungu Malawi
84C2 Kasur Pak
100B2 Kataba Zambia
98C3 Katako-kombe Zaïre
12D3 Katalla USA
63G2 Katangli Russian Fed
106A4 Katanning Aust
55B2 Katerini Greece
5E4 Kates Needle Mt Can/USA
82D3 Katha Burma
106C2 Katherine Aust
85C4 Käthiawär Pen India
86B1 Kathmandu Nepal
84D2 Kathua India
86B1 Kätihär India
100B2 Katima Mulilo Namibia
4C4 Katmai,Mt USA
12D3 Katmai Nat Mon USA
86A2 Katni India
109D2 Katoomba Aust
59B2 Katowice Pol
39H7 Katrineholm Sweden

97C3 **Katsina** Nig	
97C4 **Katsina Ala** Nig	
75C1 **Katsuta** Japan	
75C1 **Katsuura** Japan	
75B1 **Katsuyo** Japan	
65H6 **Kattakurgan** Uzbekistan	
39G7 **Kattegat** *Str* Den/Sweden	
21C4 **Kauai** *I* Hawaiian Is	
21C4 **Kauai Chan** Hawaiian Is	
21C4 **Kaulakahi Chan** Hawaiian Is	
21C4 **Kaunakaki** Hawaiian Is	
60B3 **Kaunas** Lithuania	
97C3 **Kaura Namoda** Nig	
38J5 **Kautokeino** Nor	
73J2 **Kavadarci** Macedonia	
55A2 **Kavajë** Alb	
87B2 **Kavali** India	
55B2 **Kaválla** Greece	
85B4 **Kävda** India	
75B1 **Kawagoe** Japan	
75B1 **Kawaguchi** Japan	
110B1 **Kawakawa** NZ	
99C3 **Kawambwa** Zambia	
86A2 **Kawardha** India	
15C2 **Kawartha Lakes** Can	
74D3 **Kawasaki** Japan	
110C1 **Kawerau** NZ	
110B1 **Kawhia** NZ	
73B3 **Kaya** Burkina	
12F3 **Kayak** *I* USA	
78D2 **Kayan** *R* Indon	
87B3 **Käyankulam** India	
97A3 **Kayes** Mali	
92C2 **Kayseri** Turk	
1B8 **Kazach'ye** Russian Fed	
93E1 **Kazakh** Azerbaijan	
65G5 **Kazakhstan** Republic, Asia	
61G2 **Kazan'** Russian Fed	
54C2 **Kazanlŭk** Bulg	
69G4 **Kazan Retto** *Is* Japan	
91B4 **Käzerün** Iran	
61H4 **Kazhim** Russian Fed	
93E1 **Kazi Magomed** Azerbaijan	
59C3 **Kazincbarcika** Hung	
55B3 **Kéa** *I* Greece	
21C4 **Kealaikahiki Chan** Hawaiian Is	
8D2 **Kearney** USA	
93C2 **Keban Baraji** *Res* Turk	
97A3 **Kébémer** Sen	
96C1 **Kebili** Tunisia	
97A3 **Kédougou** Sen	
12J2 **Keele** *R* Can	
12H2 **Keele Pk** *Mt* Can	
21B2 **Keeler** USA	
21B2 **Keene** New Hampshire, USA	
100A3 **Keetmanshoop** Namibia	
18C1 **Keewanee** USA	
6A3 **Keewatin** *Region* Can	
55B3 **Kefallinia** *I* Greece	
94B2 **Kefar Sava** Israel	
97C4 **Keffi** Nig	
38A2 **Keflavik** Iceland	
5G4 **Keg River** Can	
76B1 **Kehsi Mansam** Burma	
108B3 **Keith** Aust	
44C3 **Keith** Scot	
4F3 **Keith Arm** *B* Can	
6D3 **Kekertuk** Can	
85D3 **Kekri** India	
77C5 **Kelang** Malay	
77C4 **Kelantan** *R* Malay	
84B1 **Kelif** Turkmenistan	
92C1 **Kelkit** *R* Turk	
98B3 **Kellé** Congo	

4F2 **Kellet,C** Can	
20C1 **Kellogg** USA	
64D3 **Kelloselka** Fin	
45C2 **Kells** Irish Rep	
42B2 **Kells Range** *Hills* Scot	
58C1 **Kelme** Lithuania	
5C5 **Kelowna** Can	
5F4 **Kelsey Bay** Can	
42C2 **Kelso** Scot	
20B1 **Kelso** USA	
64E3 **Kem'** Russian Fed	
38L6 **Kem'** *R* Russian Fed	
97B3 **Ke Macina** Mali	
13B2 **Kemano** Can	
65K4 **Kemerovo** Russian Fed	
38J5 **Kemi** Fin	
38K5 **Kemi** *R* Fin	
38K5 **Kemijärvi** Fin	
46C1 **Kempen** *Region*, Belg	
26B2 **Kemps Bay** The Bahamas	
109D2 **Kempsey** Aust	
57C3 **Kempten** Germany	
12D2 **Kenai** USA	
12D3 **Kenai Mts** USA	
12D2 **Kenai Pen** USA	
99D2 **Kenamuke Swamp** Sudan	
42C2 **Kendal** Eng	
109D2 **Kendall** Aust	
71D4 **Kendari** Indon	
78C3 **Kendawangan** Indon	
86B2 **Kendräpära** India	
20C1 **Kendrick** USA	
97A4 **Kenema** Sierra Leone	
98B3 **Kenge** Zaire	
76B1 **Kengtung** Burma	
100B3 **Kenhardt** S Africa	
97A3 **Kéniéba** Mali	
96B1 **Kenitra** Mor	
45B3 **Kenmare** Irish Rep	
45B3 **Kenmare** *R* Irish Rep	
19B4 **Kenner** USA	
18C2 **Kennett** USA	
16B3 **Kennett Square** USA	
20C1 **Kennewick** USA	
5F4 **Kenny Dam** Can	
7A5 **Kenora** Can	
10B2 **Kenosha** USA	
43E4 **Kent** County, Eng	
20B1 **Kent** Washington, USA	
14A2 **Kentland** USA	
14B2 **Kenton** USA	
4H3 **Kent Pen** Can	
11B3 **Kentucky** State, USA	
11B3 **Kentucky L** USA	
19B3 **Kentwood** Louisiana, USA	
14A2 **Kentwood** Michigan, USA	
99D2 **Kenya** Republic, Africa	
Kenya,Mt = Kirinyaga	
18B1 **Keokuk** USA	
86A2 **Keonchi** India	
86B2 **Keonjhargarh** India	
71E4 **Kepaluan Tanimbar** *Arch* Indon	
6H3 **Keplavik** Iceland	
59B2 **Kepno** Pol	
78B2 **Kepulauan Anambas** *Arch* Indon	
71E4 **Kepulauan Aru** *Arch* Indon	
78B2 **Kepulauan Badas** *Is* Indon	
71E4 **Kepulauan Banda** *Arch* Indon	
71D4 **Kepulauan Banggai** *I* Indon	
78B2 **Kepulauan Bunguran Seletan** *Arch* Indon	
71E4 **Kepulauan Kai** *Arch* Indon	
71D4 **Kepulauan Leti** *I* Indon	
78A3 **Kepulauan Lingga** *Is* Indon	
70A4 **Kepulauan Mentawi** *Arch* Indon	

78A2 **Kepulauan Riau** *Arch* Indon	
78D4 **Kepulauan Sabalana** *Arch* Indon	
71D3 **Kepulauan Sangihe** *Arch* Indon	
71D4 **Kepulauan Sula** *I* Indon	
71D3 **Kepulauan Talaud** *Arch* Indon	
78B2 **Kepulauan Tambelan** *Is* Indon	
71E4 **Kepulauan Tanimbar** *I* Indon	
71D4 **Kepulauan Togian** *I* Indon	
71D4 **Kepulauan Tukambesi** *Is* Indon	
87B2 **Kerala** State, India	
108B3 **Kerang** Aust	
39K6 **Kerava** Fin	
60E4 **Kerch'** Ukraine	
71F4 **Kerema** PNG	
95C3 **Keren** Eritrea	
104B6 **Kerguelen Ridge** Indian O	
99D3 **Kericho** Kenya	
71A4 **Kerinci** *Mt* Indon	
99D2 **Kerio** *R* Kenya	
80E2 **Kerki** Turkmenistan	
55A3 **Kérkira** Greece	
55A3 **Kérkira** *I* Greece	
21B2 **Kerman** USA	
90A3 **Kermänshäh** Iran	
21B2 **Kern** *R* USA	
13F2 **Kerrobert** Can	
45B2 **Kerry** County, Irish Rep	
17B1 **Kershaw** USA	
78B3 **Kertamulia** Indon	
63D3 **Kerulen** *R* Mongolia	
96B2 **Kerzaz** Alg	
55C2 **Keşan** Turk	
74E3 **Kesennuma** Japan	
38L5 **Kesten'ga** Russian Fed	
42C2 **Keswick** Eng	
65K4 **Ket** *R* Russian Fed	
97C4 **Kéta** Ghana	
56E4 **Ketapang** Indon	
5E4 **Ketchikan** USA	
97C3 **Ketia** Niger	
85B4 **Keti Bandar** Pak	
58C2 **Kętrzyn** Pol	
43D3 **Kettering** Eng	
14B3 **Kettering** USA	
20C1 **Kettle** *R* Can	
20C1 **Kettle River Range** *Mts* USA	
7C3 **Kettlestone B** Can	
90C3 **Kevir-i Namak** *Salt Flat* Iran	
14A2 **Kewaunee** USA	
14B1 **Key Harbour** Can	
17B2 **Key Largo** USA	
11B4 **Key West** USA	
63C2 **Kezhma** Russian Fed	
47C1 **K'félghäza** Hung	
12B2 **Kgun L** USA	
94C2 **Khabab** Syria	
62H3 **Khabarovsk** Russian Fed	
85B3 **Khairpur** Pak	
85B3 **Khairpur** Region, Pak	
100A3 **Khakhea** Botswana	
55C3 **Khálki** *I* Greece	
55B2 **Khalkidhiki** *Pen* Greece	
55B3 **Khalkis** Greece	
61G2 **Khalturin**	
85C4 **Khambhät,G of** India	
85D4 **Khämgaon** India	
76C2 **Kham Keut** Laos	
87C1 **Khammam** India	
90A2 **Khamseh** *Mts* Iran	
76C2 **Khan** *R* Laos	
84B1 **Khanabad** Afghan	
93E3 **Khänaqin** Iraq	
85D4 **Khandwa** India	
84C2 **Khanewal** Pak	

94C3 **Khan ez Zabib** Jordan	
77D4 **Khanh Hung** Viet	
55B3 **Khaniá** Greece	
84C3 **Khanpur** Pak	
65H3 **Khanty-Masiysk** Russian Fed	
94B3 **Khan Yunis** Egypt	
84D1 **Khapalu** India	
68C2 **Khapcheranga** Russian Fed	
61G4 **Kharabali** Russian Fed	
86B2 **Kharagpur** India	
91C4 **Khärän** Iran	
84B3 **Khärän** Pak	
91B4 **Khäränaq** Iran	
91B4 **Khärg** *Is* Iran	
95C2 **Khärga Oasis** Egypt	
85D4 **Khargon** India	
60E4 **Khar'kov** Ukraine	
61F2 **Kharovsk** Russian Fed	
95C3 **Khartoum** Sudan	
95C3 **Khartoum North** Sudan	
74C2 **Khasan** Russian Fed	
95C3 **Khashm el Girba** Sudan	
86C1 **Khasi-Jaintia Hills** India	
54C2 **Khaskovo** Bulg	
1B9 **Khatanga** Russian Fed	
76B3 **Khawsa** Burma	
85C4 **Khed Brahma** India	
51C2 **Khemis** Alg	
96B1 **Khenifra** Mor	
51D2 **Kherrata** Alg	
60D4 **Kherson** Ukraine	
63D2 **Khilok** Russian Fed	
55C3 **Khios** *I* Greece	
55C3 **Khios** *I* Greece	
60C4 **Khmel'nitskiy** Ukraine	
59C3 **Khodorov** Ukraine	
84B1 **Kholm** Afghan	
76D3 **Khong** Laos	
91B4 **Khonj** Iran	
69F2 **Khor** Russian Fed	
91A3 **Khoramshahr** Iran	
91B5 **Khôr Duwayhin** *B* UAE	
84C1 **Khorog** Tajikistan	
90A3 **Khorramäbad** Iran	
90C3 **Khosf** Iran	
84B2 **Khost** Pak	
60C4 **Khotin** Ukraine	
12C1 **Khotol** *Mt* USA	
60C3 **Khoyniki** Belorussia	
63F2 **Khrebet Dzhugdzhur** *Mts* Russian Fed	
90C2 **Khrebet Kopet Dag** *Mts* Turkmenistan	
64H3 **Khrebet Pay-khoy** *Mts* Russian Fed	
82C1 **Khrebet Tarbagatay** *Mts* Kazakhstan	
63E2 **Khrebet Tukuringra** *Mts* Russian Fed	
82A1 **Khudzhand** Tajikistan	
86B2 **Khulna** Bang	
84D1 **Khunjerab** *P* China/India	
90B3 **Khunsar** Iran	
91A4 **Khurays** S Arabia	
86B2 **Khurda** India	
84D3 **Khurja** India	
84C2 **Khushab** Pak	
94B2 **Khushniyah** Syria	
59C3 **Khust** Ukraine	
90A3 **Khut** Sudan	
90D3 **Khuzdar** Pak	
90D3 **Khvāf** Iran	
61G3 **Khvalynsk** Russian Fed	
90C3 **Khvor** Iran	
91B4 **Khvormüj** Iran	
93D2 **Khvoy** Iran	
84C1 **Khwaja Muhammad** *Mts* Afghan	
84C2 **Khyber P** Afghan/Pak	

Kiambi

99C3 Kiambi Zaire
19A3 Kiamichi R USA
12B1 Kiana USA
98B3 Kibangou Congo
99D3 Kibaya Tanz
98C3 Kibombo Zaire
99D3 Kibondo Tanz
99D3 Kibungu Rwanda
55B2 Kičevo Macedonia
5G4 Kicking Horse P Can
97C3 Kidal Mali
43C3 Kidderminster Eng
97A3 Kidira Sen
110C1 Kidnappers,C NZ
56C2 Kiel Germany
59C2 Kielce Pol
56C2 Kieler Bucht B Germany
Kiev = Kiyev
80E2 Kifab Uzbekistan
97A3 Kiffa Maur
89H8 Kigali Rwanda
12A2 Kigluaik Mts USA
99C3 Kigoma Tanz
75B2 Kii-sanchi Mts Japan
74C4 Kii-suido B Japan
54B1 Kikinda Serbia, Yugos
55B3 Kikládhes Is Greece
71F4 Kikori PNG
98B3 Kikwit Zaire
21C4 Kilauea Crater Mt Hawaiian Is
4C3 Kilbuck Mts USA
74B2 Kilchu N Korea
109D1 Kilcoy Aust
45C2 Kildare County, Irish Rep
45C2 Kildare Irish Rep
19B3 Kilgore USA
99D3 Kilifi Kenya
99D3 Kilimanjaro Mt Tanz
99D3 Kilindoni Tanz
92C2 Kilis Turk
45B2 Kilkee Irish Rep
45C2 Kilkenny County, Irish Rep
45C2 Kilkenny Irish Rep
45B2 Kilkieran B Irish Rep
55B2 Kilkis Greece
45B1 Killala B Irish Rep
45B2 Killaloe Irish Rep
109D1 Killarney Aust
41B3 Killarney Irish Rep
19A3 Killeen USA
12D1 Killik R USA
44B3 Killin Scot
55B3 Killini Mt Greece
45B1 Killybegs Irish Rep
42B2 Kilmarnock Scot
61H2 Kil'mez Russian Fed
99D3 Kilosa Tanz
41B3 Kilrush Irish Rep
99C3 Kilwa Zaire
99D3 Kilwa Kisivani Tanz
99D3 Kilwa Kivinje Tanz
108A2 Kimba Aust
12F2 Kimball,Mt USA
13D3 Kimberley Can
101F1 Kimberley S Africa
106B2 Kimberley Plat Aust
74B2 Kimch'aek N Korea
74B3 Kimch'ŏn S Korea
55B3 Kími Greece
60E2 Kimry Russian Fed
70C3 Kinabalu Mt Malay
78D1 Kinabatangan R Malay
14B2 Kincardine Can
13B1 Kincolith Can
19B3 Kinder USA
13F2 Kindersley Can
97A3 Kindia Guinea
98C3 Kindu Zaire
61H3 Kinel' Russian Fed
61F2 Kineshma Russian Fed
109D1 Kingaroy Aust
21A2 King City USA
5F4 Kingcome Inlet Can
7K4 King George Is Can
107D4 King I Aust
13B2 King I Can

106B2 King Leopold Range Mts Aust
9B3 Kingman USA
98C3 Kingombe Zaire
108A2 Kingoonya Aust
22C2 Kingsburg USA
21B2 Kings Canyon Nat Pk USA
108A3 Kingscote Aust
106B2 King Sd Aust
112C2 King Sejong Base Ant
14A1 Kingsford USA
17B1 Kingsland USA
43E3 King's Lynn Eng
16C2 Kings Park USA
8B2 Kings Peak Mt USA
107C4 Kingston Aust
7C5 Kingston Can
25E3 Kingston Jamaica
15D2 Kingston New York, USA
111A3 Kingston NZ
27E4 Kingstown St Vincent and the Grenadines
9D4 Kingsville USA
44B3 Kingussie Scot
4J3 King William I Can
100B4 King William's Town S Africa
98B3 Kinkala Congo
39G7 Kinna Sweden
44D3 Kinnairds Head Pt Scot
75B1 Kinomoto Japan
44C3 Kinross Scot
45B3 Kinsale Irish Rep
99B3 Kinshasa Zaire
78D3 Kintap Indon
42B2 Kintyre Pen Scot
13D1 Kinuso Can
99D2 Kinyeti Mt Sudan
55B3 Kiparissía Greece
55B3 Kiparissiakós Kólpos G Greece
15C1 Kipawa,L Can
99D3 Kipili Tanz
12B3 Kipnuk USA
45C2 Kippure Mt Irish Rep
100B2 Kipushi Zaire
63C2 Kirensk Russian Fed
65J5 Kirghizia Republic, Asia
82B1 Kirgizskiy Khrebet Mts Kirghizia
98B3 Kiri Zaire
105G4 Kiribati Is Pacific O
92B2 Kırıkkale Turk
99D3 Kirinyaga Mt Kenya
60D2 Kirishi Russian Fed
85B3 Kirithar Range Mts Pak
55C3 Kirkağaç Turk
90A2 Kirk Bulag Dāgh Mt Iran
42C2 Kirkby Eng
44C3 Kirkcaldy Scot
42B2 Kirkcudbright Scot
38K5 Kirkenes Nor
7B5 Kirkland Lake Can
112A Kirkpatrick,Mt Ant
10A2 Kirksville USA
93D2 Kirkūk Iraq
44C2 Kirkwall Scot
18B2 Kirkwood USA
60D3 Kirov Russian Fed
61G2 Kirov Russian Fed
93D1 Kirovakan Armenia
61J2 Kirovgrad Russian Fed
60D4 Kirovograd Ukraine
61H2 Kirs Russian Fed
92B2 Kirşehir Turk
56C2 Kiruna Sweden
75B1 Kiryū Japan
98C2 Kisangani Zaire
75B1 Kisarazu Japan
85C3 Kishangarh India
60C4 Kishinev Moldova
75B2 Kishiwada Japan
99D3 Kisii Kenya
99D3 Kisiju Tanz

59B3 Kiskunhalas Hung
65F5 Kislovodsk Russian Fed
99E3 Kismaayo Somalia
75B1 Kiso-sammyaku Mts Japan
97A4 Kissidougou Guinea
17B2 Kissimmee,L USA
99D3 Kisumu Kenya
55B3 Kisvárda Hung
97B3 Kita Mali
65H6 Kitab Uzbekistan
75C1 Kitakata Japan
74A3 Kita-Kyushu Japan
99D2 Kitale Kenya
69G4 Kitalo I Japan
74E2 Kitami Japan
7B5 Kitchener Can
99D2 Kitgum Uganda
55B3 Kíthira I Greece
55B3 Kíthnos I Greece
94A1 Kiti,C Cyprus
4H3 Kitikmeot Region Can
5F4 Kitimat Can
38K5 Kitnen R Fin
15C2 Kitsuki Japan
15C2 Kittanning USA
38J5 Kittilä Fin
99D3 Kitunda Tanz
13B1 Kitwanga Can
100B2 Kitwe Zambia
57C3 Kitzbühel Austria
47E1 Kitzbühler Alpen Mts Austria
57C3 Kitzingen Germany
98C3 Kiumbi Zaire
12B1 Kivalina USA
59D2 Kivercy Ukraine
99C3 Kivu,L Zaire/Rwanda
98C3 Kiwalik USA
60D3 Kiyev Ukraine
61J2 Kizel Russian Fed
92C2 Kizil R Turk
80D2 Kizyl-Arvat Turkmenistan
90B2 Kizyl-Atrek Turkmenistan
57C2 Kladno Czech Republic
57C3 Klagenfurt Austria
60B2 Klaipėda Lithuania
8A2 Klamath R USA
20B2 Klamath R USA
8A2 Klamath,Falls USA
20B2 Klamath Mts USA
57C3 Klatovy Czech Republic
12H3 Klawak USA
94B1 Kleiat Leb
101G1 Klerksdorp S Africa
60E2 Klin Russian Fed
58B1 Klintehamn Sweden
60D3 Klintsy Russian Fed
52C2 Ključ Bosnia-Herzegovina
59B2 Kłodzko Pol
12G2 Klondike R Can/USA
4D3 Klondike Plat Can/USA
59B3 Klosterneuburg Austria
12G2 Kluane Can
12G2 Kluane L Can
12G2 Kluane Nat Pk Can
59B2 Kluczbork Pol
12G3 Klukwan USA
12E2 Klutina L USA
12E2 Knight I USA
43C3 Knighton Wales
52C2 Knin Croatia
106A4 Knob,C Aust
46B1 Knokke-Heist Belg
112C9 Knox Coast Ant
15C2 Knoxville Tennessee, USA
6H3 Knud Ramussens Land Region Greenland
78B3 Koba Indon
6F3 Kobbermirebugt Greenland
74D4 Kobe Japan

56C1 København Den
57B2 Koblenz Germany
60B3 Kobrin Russian Fed
71E4 Kobroör I Indon
12C1 Kobuk R USA
54B2 Kočani Macedonia
76C3 Ko Chang I Thai
86B1 Koch Bihār India
47D1 Kochel Germany
6C3 Koch I Can
Kochi = Cochin
74C4 Kōchi Japan
12D3 Kodiak USA
12D3 Kodiak I USA
87B2 Kodaykkari India
97D3 Kodok Sudan
100A3 Koes Namibia
101G1 Koffiefontein S Africa
97B4 Koforidua Ghana
74D3 Kōfu Japan
75B1 Koga Japan
39G7 Køge Den
84C2 Kohat Pak
84B1 Koh-i-Baba Mts Afghan
84B1 Koh-i-Hisar Mts Afghan
84B2 Koh-i-Khurd Mt Afghan
86C1 Kohima India
84B1 Koh-i-Mazar Mt Afghan
84B3 Kohlu Pak
60C2 Kohtla Järve Estonia
75B1 Koide Japan
12F2 Koidern Can
77A4 Koihoa Is Nicobar Is
74B4 Köje-do I S Korea
65H4 Kokchetav Kazakhstan
39J6 Kokemaki L Fin
38J6 Kokkola Fin
107D1 Kokoda PNG
14A2 Kokomo USA
71E4 Kokonau Indon
65K5 Kokpekty Kazakhstan
7D4 Koksoak R Can
100B4 Kokstad S Africa
76C3 Ko Kut I Thai
38L5 Kola Russian Fed
71D4 Kolaka Indon
77B4 Ko Lanta I Thai
Kollam = Quilon
87B2 Kolār India
87B2 Kolār Gold Fields India
74D3 Kolda Sen
39F7 Kolding Den
87A1 Kolhapur India
12C3 Kolignek USA
59B2 Kolín Czech Republic
56B2 Köln Germany
58B2 Koło Pol
58B2 Kołobrzeg Pol
97B3 Kolokani Mali
60E2 Kolomna Russian Fed
60C4 Kolomyya Ukraine
65K4 Kolpashevo Russian Fed
55B3 Kólpos Merabéllou B Greece
55B2 Kólpos Singitikós G Greece
55B2 Kólpos Strimonikós G Greece
55B2 Kólpos Toronaíos G Greece
38L5 Kol'skiy Poluostrov Pen Russian Fed
38G6 Kolvereid Nor
100B2 Kolwezi Zaire
1C7 Kolyma R Russian Fed
54B2 Kom Mt Bulg/Serbia, Yugos
99D2 Kuma Eth
97D3 Komaduga Gana R Nig
59B3 Komárno Slovakia
101H1 Komati R S Africa
74D3 Komatsu Japan

75A2 **Komatsushima** Japan
64G3 **Komi Respublika,** Russian Fed
70C4 **Komodo** I Indon
71E4 **Komoran** I Indon
75B1 **Komoro** Japan
55C2 **Komotini** Greece
76D3 **Kompong Cham** Camb
76C3 **Kompong Chhnang** Mts Camb
77C3 **Kompong Som** Camb
76C3 **Kompong Thom** Camb
76D3 **Kompong Trabek** Camb
63F2 **Komsomol'sk na Amure** Russian Fed
65H4 **Konda** R Russian Fed
99D3 **Kondoa** Tanz
87B1 **Kondukūr** India
6G3 **Kong Christian IX Land** Region Greenland
6F3 **Kong Frederik VI Kyst** Mts Greenland
64C2 **Kong Karls Land** Is Barents S
78D2 **Kongkemul** Mt Indon
98C3 **Kongolo** Zaire
39F7 **Kongsberg** Den
39G6 **Kongsvinger** Nor
Königsberg = Kaliningrad
58B2 **Konin** Pol
54A2 **Konjic** Bosnia-Herzegovina
61F1 **Konosha** Russian Fed
75B1 **Konosu** Japan
60D3 **Konotop** Ukraine
59C2 **Końskie** Pol
49D2 **Konstanz** Germany
97C3 **Kontagora** Nig
76D3 **Kontum** Viet
92B2 **Konya** Turk
13D3 **Kootenay** R Can
85C5 **Kopargaon** India
6J3 **Köpasker** Iceland
38A2 **Kópavogur** Iceland
52B1 **Koper** Slovenia
80D2 **Kopet Dag** Mts Iran/Turkmenistan
61K2 **Kopeysk** Russian Fed
77C4 **Ko Phangan** I Thai
77B4 **Ko Phuket** I Thai
39H7 **Köping** Sweden
87B1 **Koppal** India
52C1 **Koprivnica** Croatia
85B4 **Korangi** Pak
87C1 **Koraput** India
86A2 **Korba** India
57B2 **Korbach** Germany
4B3 **Korbuk** R USA
55B2 **Korçë** Alb
52C2 **Korčula** I Croatia
72E2 **Korea B** China/Korea
74B4 **Korea Str** S Korea/Japan
59D2 **Korec** Ukraine
92B1 **Körğlu Tepesi** Mt Turk
97B4 **Korhogo** Ivory Coast
85B4 **Kori Creek** India
55B3 **Korinthiakós Kólpos** G Greece
55B3 **Kórinthos** Greece
74E3 **Kōriyama** Japan
61K3 **Korkino** Russian Fed
92B2 **Korkuteli** Turk
82C1 **Korla** China
52C2 **Kornat** I Croatia
60D5 **Köroğlu Tepesi** Mt Turk
99D3 **Korogwe** Tanz
108B3 **Koroit** Aust
71E3 **Koror** Palau Is, Pacific O
93C3 **Körös** R Hung
60C3 **Korosten** Ukraine
95A3 **Koro Toro** Chad

12B3 **Korovin** I USA
69G2 **Korsakov** Russian Fed
39G7 **Korsør** Den
46B1 **Kortrijk** Belg
55C3 **Kós** I Greece
77C4 **Ko Samui** I Thai
58B2 **Koscierzyna** Pol
107D4 **Kosciusko** Mt Aust
12H3 **Kosciusko** I USA
74B4 **Koshikijima-retto** I Japan
59C3 **Košice** Slovakia
74B3 **Kosong** N Korea
54B2 **Kosovo** Aut Republic, Serbia, Yugos
74B3 **Kossou** L Ivory Coast
101G1 **Koster** S Africa
99D1 **Kosti** Sudan
59D2 **Kostopol'** Ukraine
61F2 **Kostroma** Russian Fed
56C2 **Kostrzyn** Pol
39H8 **Koszalin** Pol
85D3 **Kota** India
78A4 **Kotaagung** Indon
78B3 **Kotabaharu** Indon
78D3 **Kotabaru** Indon
77C4 **Kota Bharu** Malay
78A3 **Kotabum** Indon
84C2 **Kot Addu** Pak
78D1 **Kota Kinabalu** Malay
87C1 **Kotapad** India
61G2 **Kotel'nich** Russian Fed
61F4 **Kotel'nikovo** Russian Fed
39K6 **Kotka** Fin
64F3 **Kotlas** Russian Fed
12B2 **Kotlik** USA
54A2 **Kotor** Montenegro, Yugos
60C4 **Kotovsk** Ukraine
85B3 **kotri** Pak
87C1 **Kottagüdem** India
87B3 **Kottayam** India
98C2 **Kotto** R CAR
87B2 **Kottūru** India
12B1 **Kotzebue** USA
4B3 **Kotzebue Sd** USA
97C3 **Kouande** Benin
98C2 **Kouango** CAR
97B3 **Koudougou** Burkina
98B3 **Koulamoutou** Gabon
97B3 **Koulikoro** Mali
97B3 **Koupéla** Burkina
33G2 **Kourou** French Guiana
97B3 **Kouroussa** Guinea
98B1 **Kousséri** Cam
39K6 **Kouvola** Fin
38L5 **Kovdor** Russian Fed
60B3 **Kovel'** Ukraine
Kovno = Kaunas
61F2 **Kovrov** Russian Fed
61F3 **Kovylkino** Russian Fed
60E1 **Kovzha** R Russian Fed
77C4 **Ko Way** I Thai
73C5 **Kowloon** Hong Kong
84B2 **Kowt-e-Ashrow** Afghan
92A2 **Köyceğiz** Turk
38L5 **Koydor** Russian Fed
87A1 **Koyna Res** India
12B2 **Koyuk** USA
12B1 **Koyuk** R USA
12C2 **Koyukuk** R USA
12C1 **Koyukuk** R USA
92C2 **Kozan** Turk
55B3 **Kozani** Greece
Kozhikode = Calicut
61G2 **Koz'modemyansk** Russian Fed
75B2 **Kōzu-shima** I Japan
39F7 **Kragerø** Nor
54B2 **Kragujevac** Serbia, Yugos
77B3 **Kra,Isthmus of** Burma/Malay
Krakatau = Rakata

94C1 **Krak des Chevaliers** Hist Site Syria
Kraków = Cracow
54B2 **Kraljevo** Serbia, Yugos
60E4 **Kramatorsk** Ukraine
38H6 **Kramfors** Sweden
52R1 **Kranj** Slovenia
61G1 **Krasavino** Russian Fed
64G2 **Krasino** Russian Fed
59C2 **Kraśnik** Pol
61G3 **Krasnoarmeysk** Russian Fed
60E5 **Krasnodar** Russian Fed
61J2 **Krasnokamsk** Russian Fed
61K2 **Krasnotur'insk** Russian Fed
61J2 **Krasnoufimsk** Russian Fed
61J3 **Krasnousol'-skiy** Russian Fed
65G3 **Krasnovishersk** Russian Fed
65G5 **Krasnovodsk** Turkmenistan
63B2 **Krasnoyarsk** Russian Fed
59C2 **Krasnystaw** Pol
61G3 **Krasnyy Kut** Russian Fed
60E4 **Krasnyy Luch** Ukraine
61G4 **Krasnyy Yar** Russian Fed
76D3 **Kratie** Camb
6E2 **Kraulshavn** Greenland
56B2 **Krefeld** Germany
60D4 **Kremenchug** Ukraine
60D4 **Kremenchugskoye Vodokhranilische** Res Ukraine
59D2 **Kremenets** Ukraine
98A2 **Kribi** Cam
60D3 **Krichev** Belorussia
47E1 **Krimml** Austria
87B1 **Krishna** R India
87B2 **Krishnagiri** India
86B2 **Krishnanagar** India
39F7 **Kristiansand** Nor
39G7 **Kristianstad** Sweden
64B3 **Kristiansund** Nor
39G7 **Kristinehamn** Sweden
38J6 **Kristiinankaupunki** Fin
55B3 **Kriti** I Greece
60D4 **Krivoy Rog** Ukraine
52B1 **Krk** I Croatia
6G3 **Kronpris Frederik Bjerge** Mts Greenland
39K7 **Kronshtadt** Russian Fed
101G1 **Kroonstad** S Africa
65F5 **Kropotkin** Russian Fed
101G1 **Krugersdorp** S Africa
78A4 **Krui** Indon
55A2 **Kruje** Alb
58C2 **Krupki** Belorussia
12B1 **Krusenstern,C** USA
54B2 **Kruševac** Serbia, Yugos
39K7 **Krustpils** Latvia
12C3 **Kruzof** I USA
65E5 **Krym** Pen Ukraine
60E5 **Krymsk** Russian Fed
58B2 **Krzyz** Pol
96B1 **Ksar El Boukhari** Alg
96B1 **Ksar el Kebir** Mor
70A3 **Kuala** Indon
77C5 **Kuala Dungun** Malay
77C4 **Kuala Kerai** Malay
77C5 **Kuala Kubu Baharu** Malay
77C5 **Kuala Lipis** Malay
77C5 **Kuala Lumpur** Malay
77C4 **Kuala Trengganu** Malay
78D1 **Kuamut** Malay

74A2 **Kuandian** China
77C5 **Kuantan** Malay
93E1 **Kuba** Azerbaijan
71F4 **Kubar** PNG
72D2 **Kuching** Malay
70C3 **Kudat** Malay
78A4 **Kudus** Indon
61H2 **Kudymkar** Russian Fed
57C3 **Kufstein** Austria
90C3 **Kuh Duren** Upland Iran
91C4 **Küh e Bazmān** Mt Iran
90B3 **Küh-e Dinar** Mt Iran
90C2 **Küh-e-Hazār Masjed** Mts Iran
91C4 **Küh-e Jebāl Barez** Iran
90B3 **Küh-e Karkas** Mts Iran
91C4 **Küh-e Laleh Zar** Mt Iran
90A2 **Küh-e Sahand** Mt Iran
91C4 **Kuh e Taftān** Mt Iran
90A2 **Kühhaye Sabalan** Iran
90A3 **Kühhā-ye Zāgros** Mts Iran
38K6 **Kuhmo** Fin
90B3 **Kühpāyeh** Iran
90C3 **Kühpāyeh** Mt Iran
91C4 **Küh ye Bashäkerd** Mts Iran
90A2 **Küh ye Sabalan** Mt Iran
100A3 **Kuibis** Namibia
4B4 **Kuigillingok** USA
77C4 **Kuito** Angola
12H3 **Kuiu** I USA
74E2 **Kuji** Japan
75A2 **Kuju-san** Mt Japan
12C3 **Kukaklek** L USA
54B2 **Kukës** Alb
90A2 **Kül** R Iran
91C4 **Kül** R Iran
55C3 **Kula** Turk
61J4 **Kulakshi** Kazakhstan
99D2 **Kulal,Mt** Kenya
55B2 **Kulata** Bulg
50G2 **Kuldiga** Latvia
61H4 **Kul'sary** Kazakhstan
84D2 **Kulu** India
92B2 **Kulu** Turk
65J4 **Kulunda** Russian Fed
108B2 **Kulwin** Aust
61G5 **Kuma** R Russian Fed
75B1 **Kumagaya** Japan
78C3 **Kumai** Indon
74C4 **Kumamoto** Japan
75B2 **Kumano** Japan
54B2 **Kumanovo** Macedonia
63E2 **Kumara** China
97B4 **Kumasi** Ghana
65F5 **Kumayri** Armenia
98A2 **Kumba** Cam
87B2 **Kumbakonam** India
61J3 **Kumertau** Russian Fed
74B3 **Kümhwa** S Korea
39H7 **Kumla** Sweden
87A2 **Kumta** India
82C1 **Kümüx** China
84C2 **Kunar** R Afghan
39K7 **Kunda** Estonia
87A2 **Kundāpura** India
84B1 **Kunduz** Afghan
89F9 **Kunene** R Angola
39G7 **Kungsbacka** Sweden
63G2 **Kungur** Russian Fed
76B1 **Kunhing** Burma
82B2 **Kunlun Shan** Mts China
73A4 **Kunming** China
74B3 **Kunsan** S Korea
38K6 **Kuopio** Fin
52C1 **Kupa** R Croatia/Bosnia-Herzegovina
106B2 **Kupang** Indon
107D2 **Kupiano** PNG
12H3 **Kupreanof I** USA

Kupyansk

60E1	**Kupyansk** Ukraine	
82C1	**Kuqa** China	
75B1	**Kurabe** Japan	
74C4	**Kurashiki** Japan	
75A1	**Kurayoshi** Japan	
54C2	**Kürdzhali** Bulg	
74C4	**Kure** Japan	
60B2	**Kuressaare** Estonia	
63A1	**Kureyka** *R*	
	Russian Fed	
65H4	**Kurgan** Russian Fed	
88K6	**Kuria Muria Is** Oman	
38J6	**Kurikka** Fin	
	Kuril Is = Kuril'skoye	
	Osrova	
69H2	**Kuril'skiye Ostrova**	
	Russian Fed	
87B1	**Kurnool** India	
75C1	**Kuroiso** Japan	
111B2	**Kurow** NZ	
109D2	**Kurri Kurri** Aust	
60E3	**Kursk** Russian Fed	
	Kurskiy Zaliv =	
	Courland Lagoon	
68A2	**Kuruktag** *R* China	
100B3	**Kuruman** S Africa	
74C4	**Kurume** Japan	
87C3	**Kurunegala**	
	Sri Lanka	
65K5	**Kurunktag** *R* China	
61J2	**Kusa** Russian Fed	
55C3	**Kuşadasi Körfezi** *B*	
	Turk	
55C2	**Kus Golü** *L* Turk	
74D4	**Kushimoto** Japan	
74E2	**Kushiro** Japan	
86B2	**Kushtia** Bang	
61H3	**Kushum** *R*	
	Kazakhstan	
80E3	**Kushra** Afgan	
65G4	**Kushva** Russian Fed	
12B2	**Kuskokwim** *R* USA	
12B3	**Kuskokwim B** USA	
12C2	**Kuskokwim Mts** USA	
86A1	**Kusma** Nepal	
74E2	**Kussharo-ko** *L*	
	Japan	
65H4	**Kustanay**	
	Kazakhstan	
92A2	**Kütahya** Turk	
78D3	**Kutai** *R* Indon	
59B3	**Kutná Hora**	
	Czech Republic	
58B2	**Kutno** Pol	
98B3	**Kutu** Zaïre	
86C2	**Kutubdia I** Bang	
98C1	**Kutum** Sudan	
7D4	**Kuujjuaq** Can	
7C4	**Kuujjuarapik** Can	
38K5	**Kuusamo** Fin	
61J3	**Kuvandyk**	
	Russian Fed	
91G4	**Kuwait** Kuwait	
80C3	**Kuwait** Sheikdom,	
	S W Asia	
75B1	**Kuwana** Japan	
	Kuybyshev = Samara	
65J4	**Kuybyshev**	
	Russian Fed	
61G3	**Kuybyshevskoye**	
	Vodokhranilishche	
	Res Russian Fed	
63C2	**Kuytun** Russian Fed	
60E5	**Kuzey Anadolu**	
	Daglari *Mts* Turk	
61G3	**Kuznetsk**	
	Russian Fed	
38J4	**Kvaenangen** *Sd* Nor	
12C3	**Kvichak** USA	
12C3	**Kvichak** *R* USA	
12B3	**Kvichak B** USA	
38H5	**Kvigtind** *Mt* Nor	
38H5	**Kvikkjokk** Sweden	
99D3	**Kwale** Kenya	
74B3	**Kwangju** S Korea	
98B3	**Kwango** *R* Zaïre	
100B2	**Kwekwe** Zim	
12B2	**Kwethluk** USA	
12B2	**Kwethluk** *R* USA	
58B2	**Kwidzyn** Pol	
71E4	**Kwoka** *Mt* Indon	
108C3	**Kyabram** Aust	
76B2	**Kyaikkami** Burma	
76B2	**Kyaikto** Burma	

68C1	**Kyakhta** Russian Fed	
108A2	**Kyancutta** Aust	
76B1	**Kyaukme** Burma	
76B1	**Kyauk-padaung**	
	Burma	
76A2	**Kyaukpyu** Burma	
40B2	**Kyle of Lochalsh**	
	Scot	
46D1	**Kyll** *R* Germany	
108B3	**Kyneton** Aust	
99D2	**Kyoga** *L* Uganda	
109D1	**Kyogle** Aust	
74B3	**Kyöngju** S Korea	
74D3	**Kyoto** Japan	
	Kyrgyzstan =	
	Kirghizia	
65H4	**Kyshtym**	
	Russian Fed	
74C4	**Kyūshū** *I* Japan	
104E3	**Kyushu-Palau Ridge**	
	Pacific O	
54B2	**Kyustendil** Bulg	
68B1	**Kyzyl** Russian Fed	
65H5	**Kyzylkum** *Desert*	
	Uzbekistan	
65H5	**Kzyl Orda**	
	Kazakhstan	

L

99E2	**Laascaanood**	
	Somalia	
46E1	**Laasphe** Germany	
99E1	**Laasqoray** Somalia	
33E1	**La Asunción** Ven	
96A2	**Laâyoune** Mor	
23A1	**La Barca** Mexico	
97A3	**Labé** Guinea	
59B2	**Labe** *R*	
	Czech Republic	
15D1	**Labelle** Can	
17B2	**La Belle** USA	
12G2	**Laberge,L** Can	
78D1	**Labi** Brunei	
13E2	**la Biche,L** Can	
61F5	**Labinsk** Russian Fed	
94C1	**Laboué** Leb	
34C2	**Laboulaye** Arg	
7D4	**Labrador** *Region*	
	Can	
7D4	**Labrador City** Can	
7E4	**Labrador S**	
	Greenland/Can	
33E5	**Lábrea** Brazil	
78D1	**Labuan** *I* Malay	
78B4	**Labuhan** Indon	
76A2	**Labutta** Burma	
65H3	**Labytnangi**	
	Russian Fed	
7C4	**Lac á L'eau Claire**	
	Can	
46B2	**La Capelle** France	
34C2	**La Carlota** Arg	
79B3	**La Carlota** Phil	
12J1	**Lac Belot** *L* Can	
7C4	**Lac Bienville** *L* Can	
83B4	**Laccadive Is** India	
47B2	**Lac d'Annecy** *L*	
	France	
4G3	**Lac de Gras** *L* Can	
47B1	**Lac de Joux** *L* Switz	
47B1	**Lac de Neuchâtel** *L*	
	Switz	
23A2	**Lac de Patzcuaro** *L*	
	Mexico	
23A2	**Lac de Sayula** *L*	
	Mexico	
4F3	**Lac des Bois** *L* Can	
47A2	**Lac du Bourget** *L*	
	France	
25D3	**La Ceiba** Honduras	
108A3	**Lacepede B** Aust	
48C2	**La Châtre** France	
47B1	**La-Chaux-de-Fonds**	
	Switz	
94B3	**Lachish** *Hist Site*	
	Israel	
107D4	**Lachlan** *R* Aust	
32B2	**La Chorrera** Panama	
15D1	**Lachute** Can	
7D4	**Lac Joseph** *L* Can	
15C2	**Lackawanna** USA	
5G4	**Lac la Biche** Can	
4G3	**Lac la Martre** *L* Can	
5H4	**Lac la Ronge** *L* Can	

52A1	**Lac Léman** *L* Switz/	
	France	
10C1	**Lac Manouane** *I*	
	Can	
15D1	**Lac Megantic** Can	
7C4	**Lac Mistassini** *L* Can	
13E2	**Lacombe** Can	
15D2	**Laconia** USA	
50A1	**La Coruña** Spain	
10A2	**La Crosse** USA	
9C3	**La Cruces** USA	
7A4	**Lac Seul** *L* Can	
18B2	**La Cygne** USA	
84D2	**Ladakh Range** India	
85C3	**Ladnun** India	
73B5	**Ladong** China	
60D1	**Ladozhskoye Ozero** *L*	
	Ukraine	
6B2	**Lady Ann Str** Can	
109C4	**Lady Barron** Aust	
101G1	**Ladybrand** S Africa	
13C3	**Ladysmith** Can	
101G1	**Ladysmith** S Africa	
71F4	**Lae** PNG	
76C3	**Laem Ngop** Thai	
56C1	**Laesø** *I* Den	
10B2	**Lafayette** Indiana,	
	USA	
11A3	**Lafayette** Louisiana,	
	USA	
46B2	**La Fère** France	
46B2	**La-Ferté-sous-Jouarre**	
	France	
97C4	**Lafia** Nig	
97C4	**Lafiagi** Nig	
48B2	**La Flèche** France	
96C1	**La Galite** *I* Tunisia	
61G4	**Lagan** *R* Sweden	
61G4	**Lagan** *R* Sweden	
31D4	**Lagarto** Brazil	
96C1	**Laghouat** Alg	
35C2	**Lagoa de Araruama**	
	Brazil	
29F2	**Lagoa dos Patos** *Lg*	
	Brazil	
35C2	**Lagoa Feia** Brazil	
32B4	**Lago Agrio** Ecuador	
35C1	**Lagoa Juparaná** *L*	
	Brazil	
29D2	**Lagoa mar Chiguita** *L*	
	Arg	
29F2	**Lagoa Mirim** *L*	
	Brazil/Urug	
29B6	**Lago Argentino** *L*	
	Arg	
29B5	**Lago Buenos Aires** *L*	
	Arg	
29B5	**Lago Cochrane** *L*	
	Arg/Chile	
29C5	**Lago Colhué Huapi** *L*	
	Arg	
24B2	**Lago de Chapala** *L*	
	Mexico	
32A2	**Lago de Chiriqui** *L*	
	Panama	
23A2	**Lago de Cuitzeo** *L*	
	Mexico	
29B3	**Lago de la Laja** *L*	
	Chile	
53A2	**Lago del Coghinas** *L*	
	Sardegna	
32C2	**Lago de Maracaibo** *L*	
	Ven	
25D3	**Lago de Nicaragua** *L*	
	Nic	
32A1	**Lago de Perlas** *L* Nic	
52B2	**Lago di Bolsena** *L*	
	Italy	
52A1	**Lago di Bracciano** *L*	
	Italy	
47C2	**Lago d'Idro** *L* Italy	
52B1	**Lago di Como** *L* Italy	
52B1	**Lago di Garda** *L* Italy	
47C2	**Lago di Lecco** *L* Italy	
47C2	**Lago di Lugano** *L*	
	Italy	
47C2	**Lago d'Iseo** *L* Italy	
47C2	**Lago d'Orta** *L* Italy	
29B5	**Lago General Carrera**	
	L Chile	
52A1	**Lago Maggiore** *L*	
	Italy	
29C5	**Lago Musters** *L* Arg	
48B3	**Lagon** France	

29B4	**Lago Nahuel Huapi** *L*	
	Arg	
29B5	**Lago O'Higgins** *L*	
	Chile	
53A2	**Lago Omodeo** *L*	
	Sardegna	
30C2	**Lago Poopó** *L* Bol	
29B4	**Lago Ranco** *L* Chile	
32D6	**Lago Rogaguado** *L*	
	Bol	
97C4	**Lagos** Nig	
50A2	**Lagos** Port	
29B5	**Lago San Martín** *L*	
	Arg/Chile	
24B2	**Lagos de Moreno**	
	Mexico	
30C2	**Lago Titicaca** Bol/	
	Peru	
29B5	**Lago Viedma** *L* Arg	
8B2	**La Grande** USA	
106B2	**Lagrange** Aust	
11B3	**La Grange** Georgia,	
	USA	
14A3	**La Grange** Kentucky,	
	USA	
19A4	**La Grange** Texas,	
	USA	
33E2	**La Gran Sabana** *Mts*	
	Ven	
47B2	**La Grave** France	
48B3	**Lagronño** Spain	
34A3	**Laguna Aluminé** *L*	
	Arg	
21B3	**Laguna Beach** USA	
34C3	**Laguna Colorada**	
	Grande *L* Arg	
79B3	**Laguna de Bay** *Lg*	
	Phil	
25D3	**Laguna de Caratasca**	
	Lg Honduras	
25D4	**Laguna de Chiriquí** *L*	
	Panama	
25D3	**Laguna de Managua**	
	L Nic	
25D3	**Laguna de Nicaragua**	
	L Nic	
26A4	**Laguna de Perlas** *Lg*	
	Nic	
23B1	**Laguna de Pueblo**	
	Viejo *L* Mexico	
24C2	**Laguna de Tamiahua**	
	Lg Mexico	
25C3	**Laguna de Términos**	
	Lg Mexico	
23A1	**Laguna de Yuriria** *L*	
	Mexico	
23B1	**Laguna le Altamira**	
	Mexico	
24C2	**Laguna Madre** *Lg*	
	Mexico	
34C2	**Laguna Mar Chiquita**	
	L Arg	
29B4	**Laguna Nahuel Huapí**	
	L Arg	
34C2	**Laguna Paiva** Arg	
29B4	**Laguna Ranco** Chile	
9C4	**Laguna Seca** Mexico	
23B1	**Laguna Tortugas** *L*	
	Mexico	
70C3	**Lahad Datu** Malay	
78A3	**Lahat** Indon	
38J6	**Lahia** Fin	
90B2	**Lāhijān** Iran	
46D1	**Lahn** *R* Germany	
46D1	**Lahnstein** Germany	
84C2	**Lahore** Pak	
39K6	**Lahti** Fin	
23A2	**La Huerta** Mexico	
98B2	**Laï** Chad	
73B5	**Laibin** China	
76C1	**Lai Chau** Viet	
100B4	**Laingsburg** S Africa	
44B2	**Lairg** Scot	
78A3	**Lais** Indon	
79C4	**Lais** Phil	
72E2	**Laiyang** China	
72D2	**Laizhou Wan** *B*	
	China	
34A3	**Laja** *R* Chile	
30F4	**Lajes** Brazil	
22D4	**La Jolla** USA	
9C3	**La Junta** USA	
109C2	**Lake Cargelligo** Aust	
11A3	**Lake Charles** USA	

17R1 Lake City Florida, USA
17C1 Lake City S Carolina, USA
42C2 Lake District Region, Eng
22D4 Lake Elsinore USA
106C3 Lake Eyre Basin Aust
15C2 Lakefield Can
6D3 Lake Harbour Can
22C3 Lake Hughes USA
16B2 Lakehurst USA
19A4 Lake Jackson USA
13E2 Lake la Biche Can
17B2 Lakeland USA
7A5 Lake of the Woods Can
20B1 Lake Oswego USA
21A2 Lakeport USA
19B3 Lake Providence USA
111B2 Lake Pukaki NZ
109C3 Lakes Entrance Aust
22C2 Lakeshore USA
108B1 Lake Stewart Aust
15C1 Lake Traverse USA
8A2 Lakeview USA
20B1 Lakeview Mt Can
19B3 Lake Village USA
17B2 Lake Wales USA
22C4 Lakewood California, USA
16B2 Lakewood New Jersey, USA
14B2 Lakewood Ohio, USA
17B2 Lake Worth USA
8GA1 Lakhimpur India
85B4 Lakhpat India
84C2 Lakki Pak
55B3 Lakonikós Kólpos G Greece
97B4 Lakota Ivory Coast
38K4 Laksefjord Inlet Nor
38K4 Lakselv Nor
34C2 La Laguna Arg
32A4 La Libertad Ecuador
34A2 La Ligua Chile
50A2 La Línea Spain
85D4 Lalitpur India
5H4 La Loche Can
13F1 La Loche,L Can
46C1 La Louvière Belg
26A4 La Luz Nic
7C5 La Malbaie Can
23B2 La Malinche Mt Mexico
50B2 La Mancha Region, Spain
9C3 Lamar Colorado, USA
18B2 Lamar Missouri, USA
19A4 La Marque USA
98B3 Lambaréné Gabon
32A5 Lambayeque Peru
112B10 Lambert GI Ant
4F2 Lambton,C Can
47C2 Lambro R Italy
76C2 Lam Pao R Thai
50A1 Lamego Port
47B2 La Meije Mt France
32B6 La Merced Peru
21B3 La Mesa USA
55B3 Lamía Greece
42C2 Lammermuir Hills Scot
39G7 Lammhult Sweden
19B3 Lamon B Phil
18B1 Lamoni USA
71F3 Lamotrek I Pacific O
43B3 Lampeter Wales
99E3 Lamu Kenya
47D1 Lana Italy
21C4 Lanai I Hawaiian Is
21C4 Lanai City Hawaiian Is
42C2 Lanark Scot
76B3 Lanbi I Burma
76C1 Lancang R China
42C3 Lancashire County, Eng
21B3 Lancaster California, USA

42C2 Lancaster Eng
18B1 Lancaster Mississippi, USA
15D2 Lancaster New Hampshire, USA
14B3 Lancaster Ohio, USA
10C3 Lancaster Pennsylvania, USA
17B1 Lancaster S Carolina, USA
6B2 Lancaster Sd Can
78B3 Landak R Indon
46E2 Landau Germany
57C3 Landeck Austria
8C2 Lander USA
34C2 Landeta Arg
57C3 Landsberg Germany
4F2 Lands End C Can
43B4 Land's End Pt Eng
57C3 Landshut Germany
39G7 Landskrona Sweden
17A1 Lanett USA
56B2 Langenhagen Germany
47B1 Langenthal Switz
42C2 Langholm Scot
38A2 Langjökull Mts Iceland
77B4 Langkawi I Malay
13C3 Langley Can
108C1 Langlo R Aust
47B1 Langnau Switz
49D2 Langres France
70A3 langsa Indon
68C2 Lang Shan Mts China
76D1 Lang Son Viet
48C3 Languedoc Region, France
29B3 Lanín Mt Arg
79B4 Lanoa,L I Phil
16B2 Lansdale USA
77B4 Lansdowne House Can
16B2 Lansford USA
10B2 Lansing USA
47B2 Lanslebourg France
96A2 Lanzarote I Canary Is
72A2 Lanzhou China
47B2 Lanzo Torinese Italy
79B2 Laoag Phil
76C1 Lao Cai Viet
72D1 Laoha He R China
45C2 Laois County, Irish Rep
46B2 Laon France
32B6 La Oroya Peru
76C2 Laos Republic, S E Asia
49C2 Lapalisse France
32B2 La Palma Panama
96A2 La Palma I Canary Is
34B3 La Pampa State, Arg
33E2 La Paragua Ven
29E2 La Paz Arg
34B2 La Paz Arg
30C2 La Paz Bol
24A2 La Paz Mexico
69G2 La Perouse Str Japan/Russian Fed
23A1 La Piedad Mexico
20B2 La Pine USA
19B3 Laplace USA
23A2 la Placita Mexico
29E2 La Plata Arg
13F1 La Plonge,L Can
1A A2 La Porte USA
39K6 Lappeenranta Fin
38H5 Lappland Region Sweden/Fin
34C3 Laprida Arg
1B8 Laptev S Russian Fed
38J6 Lapua Fin
79B3 Lapu-Lapu Phil
9B4 La Purisima Mexico
95B2 Laqiya Arba'in Well Sudan
30C3 La Quiaca Arg
52B2 L'Aquila Italy
91B4 Lar Iran
96B1 Larache Mor
8C2 Laramie USA

8C2 Laramie Range Mts USA
50B2 Larca Spain
9D4 Laredo USA
91B4 Larestan Region, Iran
Largeau = Faya
47B2 L'Argentière France
17B2 Largo USA
42B2 Largs Scot
90A2 Lārī Iran
30C4 La Rioja Arg
30A2 La Rioja State, Arg
55B3 Lárisa Greece
85B3 Larkana Pak
92B3 Larnaca Cyprus
94A1 Larnaca B Cyprus
45D1 Larne N Ire
50A1 La Robla Spain
46C1 La Roche-en-Ardenne Belg
48B2 La Rochelle France
47B1 La Roche-sur-Foron France
48B2 La Roche-sur-Yon France
51B2 La Roda Spain
27D3 La Romana Dom Rep
5H4 La Ronge Can
5H4 La Ronge,L Can
39F7 Larvik Nor
65J3 Laryak Russian Fed
50B2 La Sagra Mt Spain
15D1 La Salle USA
18C1 La Salle USA
7C5 La Sarre Can
34C1 Las Avispas Arg
34A2 Las Cabras Chile
5G4 Lascombe Can
9C3 Las Cruces USA
26C3 La Selle Mt Haiti
77B2 Lasengmia China
30B4 la Sereña Chile
29E3 Las Flores Arg
76B1 Lashio Burma
53C3 La Sila Mts Italy
90B2 Lāsjerd Iran
34A3 Las Lajas Chile
50A2 Las Marismas Marshland Spain
96A2 Las Palmas de Gran Canaria Canary Is
52A2 La Spezia Italy
29C4 Las Plumas Arg
34C2 Las Rosas Arg
20B2 Lassen Peak Mt USA
20B2 Lassen Volcanic Nat Pk USA
23B2 las Tinai Mexico
98B3 Lastoursville Gabon
52C2 Lastovo I Croatia
24B2 Las Tres Marias Is Mexico
9C3 Las Vegas USA
34C2 Las Varillas Arg
9C3 Las Vegas USA
94B3 Latakia = Al Lādhiqiyah
53B2 Latina Italy
34B2 La Toma Arg
32D1 La Tortuga I Ven
79B2 La Trinidad Phil
109C4 Latrobe Aust
94B3 Latrun Israel
7C5 La Tuque Can
87B1 Latūr India
60B2 Latvia Republic, Europe
107D5 Launceston Aust
43B4 Launceston Eng
26C3 La Unión Chile
25D3 La Unión El Salvador
23A2 La Unión Mexico
32B5 La Unión Peru
107D2 Laura Aust
15C3 Laurel Delaware, USA
16A3 Laurel Maryland, USA
11B3 Laurel Mississippi, USA
17B1 Laurens USA
17C1 Laurinburg USA
52A1 Lausanne Switz
78D3 Laut I Indon
29B5 Lautaro Mt Chile

46D2 Lauterecken Germany
52D1 Laval Can
48B2 Laval France
22B2 Laveaga Peak Mt USA
47C2 Laveno Italy
31B6 Lavras Brazil
4A3 Lavrentiya Russian Fed
101H1 Lavumisa Swaziland
78D1 Lawas Malay
76B1 Lawksawk Burma
18A2 Lawrence Kansas, USA
15D2 Lawrence Massachusetts, USA
111A3 Lawrence NZ
14A3 Lawrenceville Illinois, USA
9D3 Lawton USA
91A5 Layla S Arabia
99D2 Laylo Sudan
23A2 Lázaro Cárdenas Mexico
99E1 Laz Daua Somalia
79B4 Lazi Phil
5C2 Lead USA
13F2 Leader Can
18A2 Leavenworth USA
58B2 Leba Pol
18B2 Lebanon Missouri, USA
20B2 Lebanon Oregon, USA
15C2 Lebanon Pennsylvania, USA
92C3 Lebanon Republic, S W Asia
101C3 Lebombo Mts Mozam/S Africa/Swaziland
50B2 Lehork Pol
16 The Bourg-d'Oisans France
47B1 Le Brassus Switz
29B3 Lebu Chile
47B1 Le Buet Mt France
46B1 Le Cateau France
55A2 Lecce Italy
52A1 Lecco Italy
47D1 Lech R Austria
47D1 Lechtaler Alpen Mts Austria
47A2 Le Creusot France
43C3 Ledbury Eng
13E2 Leduc Can
16C1 Lee USA
45B3 Lee R Irish Rep
43C3 Leek Eng
56B2 Leer Germany
17B2 Leesburg Florida, USA
16A3 Leesburg Virginia, USA
19B3 Leesville USA
109C2 Leeton Aust
56B2 Leeuwarden Neth
106A4 Leeuwin,C Aust
22C2 Lee Vining USA
27E3 Leeward Is Caribbean S
94A1 Lefkara Cyprus
79B3 Legazpi Phil
47D2 Legnago Italy
59B2 Legnica Pol
33F2 Leguan Inlet Guyana
32C4 Leguizamo Colombia
84D2 Leh India
48C2 Le Havre France
16B2 Lehigh R USA
16B2 Lehighton USA
84C2 Leiah Pak
59B3 Leibnitz Austria
43D3 Leicester County, Eng
43D3 Leicester Eng
107C2 Leichhardt R Aust
56A2 Leiden Neth
46B1 Leie R Belg
106C4 Leigh Creek Aust
43D4 Leighton Buzzard Eng

Leine

40

56B2 Leine R Germany
45C2 Leinster Region, Irish Rep
57C2 Leipzig Germany
50A2 Leiria Port
39F1 Leirvik Nor
45B1 Leitrim County, Irish Rep
73C4 Leiyang China
73B5 Leizhou Bandao Pen China
73C5 Leizhou Wan B China
56A2 Lek R Neth
96C1 Le Kef Tunisia
19B3 Leland USA
54A2 Lelija Mt Bosnia-Herzegovina
47B1 Le Locle France
48C2 Le Mans France
6D3 Lemieux Is Can
8C2 Lemmon USA
21B2 Lemoore USA
49C2 Lempdes France
86C2 Lemro R Burma
52C2 Le Murge Region, Italy
63C2 Lena R Russian Fed
38L6 Lendery Russian Fed
73C4 Lengshuijiang China
Leningrad = Sankt-Peterburg
112B7 Leningradskaya Base Ant
61H3 Leninogorsk Tatarskaya Respublika, Russian Fed
68A1 Leninogorsk Kazakhstan
65K4 Leninsk-Kuznetskiy Russian Fed
69F2 Leninskoye Russian Fed
65F6 Lenkoran' Azerbaijan
46E1 Lenne R Germany
7C5 Lennox USA
16C1 Lenoir USA
63D1 Lensk Russian Fed
53B3 Lentini Italy
76B3 Lenya R Burma
52B1 Leoben Austria
43C3 Leominster Eng
16D1 Leominster USA
24B2 Leon Mexico
25D3 León Nic
50A1 Leon Region, Spain
50A1 León Spain
100A3 Leonardville Namibia
106B3 Leonora Aust
35C2 Leopoldina Brazil
Léopoldville = Kinshasa
60C3 Lepel Belorussia
73D4 Leping China
49C2 Le Puy-en-Velay France
98B2 Léré Chad
101G1 Leribe Lesotho
47C2 Lerici Italy
51C1 Lérida Spain
23A1 Lerma R Mexico
47D1 Lermoos Austria
55C3 Léros I Greece
44E1 Lerwick Scot
46A2 Les Andelys France
26C3 Les Cayes Haiti
47B2 Les Ecrins Mt France
73A4 Leshan China
54B2 Leskovac Serbia, Yugos
48B3 Les Landes Region, France
101G1 Leslie S Africa
61H2 Lesnoy Russian Fed
63B2 Lesosibirsk Russian Fed
101G1 Lesotho Kingdom, S Africa
69F2 Lesozavodsk Russian Fed
48B2 Les Sables-d'Olonne France

112A Lesser Antarctica Region, Ant
27D4 Lesser Antilles Is Caribbean S
65F5 Lesser Caucasus Mts Azerbaijan/Georgia
13E1 Lesser Slave L Can
55C3 Lésvos I Greece
58B2 Leszno Pol
86C2 Letha Range Mts Burma
5G5 Lethbridge Can
33F3 Lethem Guyana
59D3 Letichev Ukraine
63D2 Let Oktyobr'ya USA
78B2 Letong Indon
46A1 Le Touquet-Paris-Plage France
76B2 Letpadan Burma
48C1 Le Tréport France
47B1 Leuk Switz
57A2 Leuven Belg
55B3 Levádhia Greece
38G6 Levanger Nor
47B2 Levanna Mt Italy
71D5 Lévêque,C Aust
46D1 Leverkusen Germany
59B3 Levice Slovákia
47D1 Levico Italy
110C2 Levin NZ
7C5 Lévis Can
15D2 Levittown USA
55B3 Lévka-ri Mt Greece
55B3 Levkás Greece
55B3 Levkás I Greece
106B2 Lévêque,C Aust
54C2 Levski Bulg
43E4 Lewes Eng
40B2 Lewis I Scot
16A2 Lewisburg USA
11B2 Lewis R Mts USA
8B2 Lewis Range Mts USA
8B2 Lewiston Idaho, USA
10C2 Lewiston Maine, USA
8C2 Lewistown Montana, USA
15C2 Lewistown Pennsylvania, USA
19B3 Lewisville USA
11B3 Lexington Kentucky, USA
18B2 Lexington Missouri, USA
15C3 Lexington Park USA
79C3 Leyte G Phil
54A2 Lezhe Alb
82D3 Lhasa China
86B1 Lhazê China
70A3 Lhokseumawe Indon
86C1 Lhozhag China
68B4 Lhunze China
Liancourt Rocks = Tok-do
79C4 Lianga Phil
72B3 Liangdang China
73C5 Lianjiang China
73C5 Lianping China
73C5 Lian Xian China
72D3 Lianyungang China
72E1 Liaodong Bandao Pen China
72E1 Liaodong Wan B China
72E1 Liao He R China
72E1 Liaoning Province, China
72E1 Liaoyang China
74B2 Liaoyuan China
4F3 Liard R Can
4F4 Liard River Can
46C2 Liart France
98B2 Libenge Zaïre
9C3 Liberal USA
57C2 Liberec Czech Republic
97A4 Liberia Republic, Africa
18B2 Liberty Missouri, USA

15D2 Liberty New York, USA
19B3 Liberty Texas, USA
48B3 Libourne France
23B2 Libres Mexico
98A2 Libreville Gabon
95A2 Libya Republic, Africa
95B2 Libyan Desert Libya
95B1 Libyan Plat Egypt
53B3 Licata Italy
43D3 Lichfield Eng
101C2 Lichinga Mozam
101G1 Lichtenburg S Africa
14B3 Licking R USA
22B2 Lick Observatory USA
60C3 Lida Belorussia
39G7 Lidköping Sweden
98C2 Lienart Zaïre
52C1 Lienz Austria
60B2 Liepāja Latvia
46C1 Lier Belg
47B1 Liestal Switz
57C3 Liezen Austria
45C2 Liffey R Irish Rep
45C1 Lifford Irish Rep
107F3 Lifu I Nouvelle Calédonie
109C1 Lightning Ridge Aust
46C2 Ligny-en-Barrois France
101C2 Ligonha R Mozam
47C2 Liguria Region, Italy
52A2 Ligurian S Italy
21C4 Lihue Hawaiian Is
100B2 Likasi Zaïre
49C1 Lille France
39G6 Lillehammer Nor
46B1 Lillers France
13C2 Lillooet Can
13C2 Lillooet R Can
101C2 Lilongwe Malawi
79B4 Liloy Phil
54A2 Lim R Montenegro/Serbia, Yugos
32B6 Lima Peru
50A1 Lima Spain
10B2 Lima USA
92B3 Limassol Cyprus
45C1 Limavady N Ire
34B3 Limay R Arg
34B3 Limay Mahuida Arg
98A2 Limbe Cam
101C2 Limbe Malawi
57B2 Limburg W Gem
31B6 Limeira Brazil
45B2 Limerick County, Irish Rep
45B2 Limerick Irish Rep
56B1 Limfjorden L Den
106C2 Limmen Bight B Aust
55C3 Limnos I Greece
31D3 Limoeiro Brazil
48C2 Limoges France
25D4 Limón Costa Rica
8C3 Limon USA
48C2 Limousin Region, France
79A3 Linapacan Str Phil
29B3 Linares Chile
9D4 Linares Mexico
50B2 Linares Spain
68B4 Lincang China
29D2 Lincoln Arg
18A1 Lincoln California, USA
42D3 Lincoln County, Eng
42D3 Lincoln Eng
18C1 Lincoln Illinois, USA
20C0 Lincoln Nebraska, USA
15D2 Lincoln New Hampshire, USA
111B2 Lincoln NZ
80A Lincoln S Greenland

20B2 Lincoln City USA
14B2 Lincoln Park USA
52A2 L'Incudina Mt Corse
57B3 Lindau Germany
33F2 Linden Guyana
39F7 Lindesnes C Nor
99D3 Lindi Tanz
98C2 Lindi R Zaïre
101G1 Lindley S Africa
55C3 Lindos Greece
15C2 Lindsay Can
105J3 Line Is Pacific O
72C2 Linfen China
73D2 Lingao China
79B2 Lingayen Phil
56B2 Lingen Germany
73C4 Lingling China
73B5 Lingshan China
72C2 Lingshi China
97A3 Linguère Sen
73E4 Linhai Rhejiang, China
31D5 Linhares Brazil
72B1 Linhe China
74B2 Linjiang China
39H7 Linköping Sweden
72D2 Linqing China
35B2 Lins Brazil
72A2 Lintao China
47C1 Linthal Switz
68D2 Linxi China
72A2 Linxia China
57C3 Linz Austria
79B3 Lipa Phil
53B3 Lipari I Italy
61E3 Lipetsk Russian Fed
54B1 Lipova Romania
56B2 Lippe R Germany
46E1 Lippstadt Germany
99D2 Lira Uganda
98B3 Liranga Congo
98C2 Lisala Zaïre
50A2 Lisboa Port
Lisbon = Lisboa
45C1 Lisburn N Ire
45B2 Liscannor B Irish Rep
73D4 Lishui China
73C4 Li Shui R China
60E4 Lisichansk Ukraine
48C2 Lisieux France
60E3 Liski Russian Fed
46B2 L'Isle-Adam France
48B2 L'Isle-sur-le-Doubs France
107E3 Lismore Aust
45B2 Listowel Irish Rep
73B5 Litang China
94B2 Litani R Leb
33G3 Litani R Surinam
18C2 Litchfield USA
107E4 Lithgow Aust
60B2 Lithuania Republic, Europe
16A2 Lititz USA
69F2 Litovko Russian Fed
19A3 Little R USA
11C4 Little Abaco I The Bahamas
110C1 Little Barrier I NZ
13E2 Little Bow R Can
25D3 Little Cayman I Caribbean S
16B3 Little Egg Harbor B USA
26C2 Little Inagua I Caribbean S
77A4 Little Nicobar I Nicobar Is
11A3 Little Rock USA
22D3 Littlerock USA
13D2 Little Smoky Can
13D2 Little Smoky R Can
16A3 Littlestown USA
15D2 Littleton New Hampshire, USA
74B2 Liuhe China
73B5 Liuzhou China
55B3 Livanátais Greece
58D1 Līvāni Latvia
12E1 Livengood USA
17B1 Live Oak USA
21A2 Livermore USA
7D5 Liverpool Can
42C3 Liverpool Eng

4E2 Liverpool B Can
42C2 Liverpool B Eng
6C2 Liverpool,C Can
109D2 Liverpool Range Mts Aust
8B2 Livingston Montana, USA
19B3 Livingston Texas, USA
44C4 Livingstone UK
Livingstone = Maramba
19A3 Livingston,L USA
52C2 Livno Bosnia-Herzegovina
60E3 Livny Russian Fed
14B2 Livonia Italy
52B2 Livorno Italy
19D3 Liwale Tanz
52B1 Ljubljana Slovenia
38G5 Ljungan R Sweden
39G7 Ljungby Sweden
39H6 Ljusdal Sweden
38H6 Ljusnan R Sweden
43C4 Llandeilo Wales
43C4 Llandovery Wales
43C3 Llandrindod Wells Wales
42C3 Llandudno Wales
43B4 Llanelli Wales
43C3 Llangollen Wales
9C3 Llano Estacado Plat USA
32C2 Llanos Region, Colombia/Ven
30D2 Llanos de Chiquitos Region, Bol
Lleida = Lérida
50A2 Llerena Spain
43B3 Lleyn Pen Wales
89E7 Llorin Nig
5H4 Lloydminster Can
30C3 Llullaillaco Mt Arg/Chile
30C3 Loa R Chile
49C2 Loan France
98B3 Loange R Zaire
100B3 Lobatse Botswana
89D2 Lobaye R CAR
34D3 Loberia Arg
100A2 Lobito Angola
34D3 Lobos Arg
47B2 Locano Italy
47C1 Locarno Switz
44B3 Loch Awe L Scot
44A3 Lochboisdale Scot
44A3 Loch Bracadale Inlet Scot
44B3 Loch Broom Estuary Scot
42B2 Loch Doon L Scot
44B3 Loch Earn L Scot
44B2 Loch Eriboll Inlet Scot
44B3 Loch Ericht L Scot
44B3 Loches France
44B3 Loch Etive Inlet Scot
44B3 Loch Ewe Inlet Scot
44B3 Loch Fyne Inlet Scot
44B3 Loch Hourn Inlet Scot
44B3 Lochinver Scot
44B2 Loch Katrine L Scot
44B3 Loch Leven L Scot
44C3 Loch Linnhe Inlet Scot
44B3 Loch Lochy L Scot
44B3 Loch Lomond L Scot
44B3 Loch Long Inlet Scot
44A3 Lochmaddy Scot
44B3 Loch Maree L Scot
44A3 Loch Morar L Scot
44C3 Lochnagar Mt Scot
44B3 Loch Ness L Scot
44B3 Loch Rannoch L Scot
44A2 Loch Roag Inlet Scot
44A3 Loch Sheil L Scot
44B2 Loch Shin L Scot
44A3 Loch Snizort Inlet Scot
44B3 Loch Sunart Inlet Scot
44B3 Loch Tay L Scot

44B3 Loch Torridon Inlet Scot
108A2 Lock Aust
42C2 Lockerbie Scot
15C2 Lock Haven USA
15C2 Lockport USA
18D2 Loc Ninh Viet
53C3 Locri Italy
94B3 Lod Israel
108B3 Loddon R Aust
60D1 Lodeynoye Pole Russian Fed
84C3 Lodhran Pak
52A1 Lodi Italy
21A2 Lodi USA
98C3 Lodja Zaire
47B1 Lods France
99D2 Lodwar Kenya
58B2 Łódź Pol
38G5 Lofoten Is Nor
8B2 Logan Utah, USA
4D3 Logan,Mt USA
14A2 Logansport Indiana, USA
19B3 Logansport Louisiana, USA
86A2 Lohardaga India
39J6 Lohja Fin
76B2 Loikaw Burma
39J6 Loimaa Fin
48C2 Loir R France
49C2 Loire R France
32B4 Loja Ecuador
50B2 Loja Spain
38K5 Lokan Tekojärvi Res Fin
46B1 Lokeren Belg
99D2 Lokitaung Kenya
58D1 Loknya Russian Fed
98C3 Lokolo R Zaire
98C3 Lokoro R Zaire
6D3 Loks Land I Can
56C2 Lolland I Den
54B2 Lom Bulg
98C3 Lomami R Zaire
97A4 Loma Mts Sierra Leone/Guinea
47C2 Lombardia Region, Italy
71D4 Lomblen I Indon
78D4 Lombok I Indon
97C4 Lomé Togo
98C3 Lomela Zaire
98C3 Lomela R Zaire
60C? Lomonosov Russian Fed
47B1 Lomont Region, France
21A3 Lompoc USA
58C2 Łomza Pol
87A1 Lonavale India
29B3 Loncoche Chile
7B5 London Can
43D4 London Eng
45C1 Londonderry County, N Ire
45C1 Londonderry N Ire
29B7 Londonderry I Chile
108B2 Londonderry,C Aust
30C4 Londres Arg
30F3 Londrina Brazil
21B2 Lone Pine USA
11C4 Long I The Bahamas
71F4 Long I PNG
78C2 Long Akah Malay
47E1 Longarone Italy
34A3 Longavi Mt Chile
27H2 Long B Jamaica
17C1 Long B USA
9B3 Long Beach California, USA
15D2 Long Beach New York, USA
15D2 Long Branch USA
73D5 Longchuan China
20C2 Long Creek USA
109C4 Longford Aust
45C2 Longford County, Irish Rep
44D3 Long Forties Region N Sea
72D1 Longhua China

7C4 Long I Can
10C2 Long I USA
16C2 Long Island Sd USA
7B4 Longlac Can
73B6 Longlin China
8C2 Longmont USA
78D2 Longnawan Indon
29B3 Longquimay Chile
107D3 Longreach Aust
72A2 Longshou Shan Upland China
42C2 Longtown Eng
15D1 Longueuil Can
34A3 Longuimay Chile
46C2 Longuyon France
11A3 Longview Texas, USA
8A2 Longview Washington, USA
46C2 Longwy France
73A3 Longxi China
77D3 Long Xuyen Viet
73D4 Longyan China
73B5 Longzhou China
47D2 Lonigo Italy
49D2 Lons-le-Saunier France
11C3 Lookout,C USA
99D3 Loolmalasin Mt Tanz
13D1 Loon R Can
45B2 Loop Hd C Irish Rep
76B2 Lop Buri Thai
98A3 Lopez C Gabon
68B2 Lop Nur L China
50A2 Lora del Rio Spain
10D2 Lorain USA
84B2 Loralai Pak
90B3 Lordegan Iran
107E4 Lord Howe I Aust
105G5 Lord Howe Rise Pacific O
6A3 Lord Mayor B Can
9C3 Lordsburg USA
35B2 Lorena Brazil
47E2 Loreo Italy
23A1 Loreto Mexico
48B2 Lorient France
108B3 Lorne Aust
57B3 Lörrach Germany
49D2 Lorraine Region France
9C3 Los Alamos USA
34A2 Los Andes Chile
29B3 Los Angeles Chile
9B3 Los Angeles USA
21A2 Los Banos USA
34b2 Los Carrillos Arg
21A2 Los Gatos USA
52C2 Lošinj I Croatia
29B3 Los Lagos Chile
24B2 Los Mochis Mexico
22B3 Los Olivos USA
34A3 Los Sauces Chile
44C3 Lossiemouth Scot
27E4 Los Testigos Is Ven
29B2 Los Vilos Chile
48C3 Lot R France
34A3 Lota Chile
42C2 Lothian Region, Scot
99D2 Lotikipi Plain Sudan/Kenya
98C3 Loto Zaire
47B1 Lötschberg Tunnel Switz
38K5 Lotta R Fin/Russian Fed
48B2 Loudéac France
97A3 Louga Sen
41B3 Lough Allen L Irish Rep
45C2 Lough Boderg L Irish Rep
45C2 Lough Bowna L Irish Rep
45C1 Lough Carlingford L N Ire
41B3 Lough Conn L Irish Rep
41B3 Lough Corrib L Irish Rep
41B3 Lough Derg L Irish Rep

45C2 Lough Derravaragh L Irish Rep
4H2 Loughead I Can
45C1 Lough Ennell L Irish Rep
41B3 Lough Erne L N Ire
40B2 Lough Foyle Estuary N Ire/Irish Rep
40B3 Lough Neagh L N Ire
45C1 Lough Oughter L Irish Rep
45B2 Loughrea Irish Rep
45C2 Lough Ree L Irish Rep
45C1 Lough Sheelin L Irish Rep
42B2 Lough Strangford L Irish Rep
45C1 Lough Swilly Estuary Irish Rep
14B3 Louisa USA
10C3 Louisa Reef I S E Asia
12E2 Louise,L USA
107E2 Louisiade Arch Solomon Is
11A3 Louisiana State, USA
17B1 Louisville Georgia, USA
11B3 Louisville Kentucky, USA
38L5 Loukhi Russian Fed
48B3 Lourdes France
108C2 Louth Aust
45C2 Louth County, Irish Rep
42D3 Louth Eng
Louvain = Leuven
48C2 Louviers France
60D2 Lovat R Russian Fed
54B2 Lovech Bulg
21B1 Lovelock USA
57B1 Lovere Italy
60C2 Lovington USA
38L5 Lovozero Russian Fed
6B3 Low,C Can
10C2 Lowell Massachusetts, USA
20B2 Lowell Oregon, USA
16D1 Lowell USA
111B2 Lower Hutt NZ
43E3 Lowestoft Eng
58B2 Łowicz Pol
108B2 Loxton Aust
5F4 Loyd George,Mt Can
54A2 Loznica Serbia, Yugos
22A? Loz Reyes Mexico
65H3 Lozva R Russian Fed
100B2 Luacano Angola
98C3 Luachimo Angola
98C3 Lualaba R Zaire
100B2 Luampa Zambia
100B2 Luân Angola
73D3 Lu'an China
98B3 Luanda Angola
100A2 Luando R Angola
100B2 Luanginga R Angola
76C1 Luang Namtha Laos
76C2 Luang Prabang Laos
98B3 Luangue R Angola
100C2 Luangwa R Zambia
72D1 Luan He R China
72D1 Luanping China
100B2 Luanshya Zambia
100B2 Luapula R Zaire
50A1 Luarca Spain
98B3 Lubalo Angola
79B3 Lubang Is Phil
100A2 Lubango Angola
9C3 Lubbock USA
56C2 Lübeck Germany
98C3 Lubefu Zaire
98C3 Lubefu R Zaire
98C3 Lubero Zaire
98C3 Lubilash R Zaire
59C2 Lublin Pol
60C2 Lubny Ukraine
78C2 Lubok Antu Malay
98C3 Lubudi Zaire
98C3 Lubudi R Zaire

78A3	Lubuklinggau Indon
100B2	Lubumbashi Zaire
98C3	Lubutu Zaire
79B3	Lucban Phil
52B2	Lucca Italy
42B2	Luce R Scot
19C3	Lucedale USA
79B3	Lucena Phil
59B3	Lucenec Slovakia
	Lucerne = Luzern
73C5	Luchuan China
56C2	Luckenwalde Germany
101F1	Luckhoff S Africa
86A1	Lucknow India
100B2	Lucusse Angola
46D1	Lüdenscheid Germany
100A3	Lüderitz Namibia
84D2	Ludhiana India
14A2	Ludington USA
43C3	Ludlow Eng
54C2	Ludogorie Upland Bulg
17B1	Ludowici USA
54B1	Luduş Rom
39H6	Ludvika Sweden
57B3	Ludwigsburg Germany
57B3	Ludwigshafen Germany
56C2	Ludwigslust Germany
98C3	Luebo R Zaire
98C3	Luema R Zaire
98C3	Luembe R Angola
100A2	Luena Angola
100B2	Luene R Angola
72B3	Lüeyang China
73D5	Lufeng China
11A3	Lufkin USA
60C2	Luga R Russian Fed
52A1	Lugano Switz
60E4	Lugansk Ukraine
101C2	Lugela R Mozam
101C2	Lugenda R Mozam
50A1	Lugo Spain
54B1	Lugoj Rom
72A3	Luhuo China
98B3	Lui R Angola
100B2	Luiana Angola
100B2	Luiana R Angola
	Luichow Peninsula = Leizhou Bandao
47C2	Luino Italy
98B2	Luionga R Zaire
72B2	Luipan Shan Upland China
100B2	Luishia Zaire
68B4	Luixi China
98C3	Luiza Zaire
34B2	Luján Arg
34D2	Luján Arg
73D3	Lujiang China
98B3	Lukenie R Zaire
64E4	Luki Russian Fed
98B3	Lukolela Zaire
58C2	Luków Pol
98C3	Lukuga R Zaire
100B2	Lukulu Zambia
38J5	Lule R Sweden
38J5	Luleå Sweden
54C2	Lüleburgaz Turk
72C2	Luliang Shan Mts China
19A4	Luling USA
98C2	Lulonga R Zaire
	Luluabourg = Kananga
100B2	Lumbala Kaquengue Angola
11C3	Lumberton USA
78D1	Lumbis Indon
86C1	Lumding India
100B2	Lumeje Angola
111A3	Lumsden NZ
39G7	Lund Sweden
101C2	Lundazi Zambia
43B4	Lundy I Eng
56C2	Lüneburg Germany
46D2	Lunéville France
100B2	Lunga R Zambia
86C2	Lunglei India
100A2	Lungue Bungo R Angola
58D2	Luninec Belorussia
98B3	Luobomo Congo
73B5	Luocheng China
73C5	Luoding China
72C3	Luohe China
72C3	Luo He R Henan, China
72C3	Luo He R Shaanxi, China
73C4	Luoxiao Shan Hills China
72C3	Luoyang China
98B3	Luozi Zaire
100B2	Lupane Zim
101C2	Lupilichi Mozam
	Lu Qu = Tao He
30E4	Luqe Par
45C1	Lurgan N Ire
101C2	Lurio R Mozam
90A3	Luristan Region, Iran
100B2	Lusaka Zambia
98C3	Lusambo Zaire
55A2	Lushnjë Alb
99D3	Lushoto Tanz
68B4	Lushui China
72E2	Lüshun China
43D4	Luton Eng
60C3	Lutsk Ukraine
99E2	Luuq Somalia
99D3	Luwegu R Tanz
100C2	Luwingu Zambia
71D4	Luwuk Indon
46D2	Luxembourg Grand Duchy, N W Europe
73A5	Luxi China
95C2	Luxor Egypt
61G1	Luza Russian Fed
61G1	Luza R Russian Fed
52A1	Luzern Switz
73B5	Luzhai China
73B4	Luzhi China
73B4	Luzhou China
35B1	Luziânia Brazil
79B2	Luzon I Phil
79B1	Luzon Str Phil
59C3	L'vov Ukraine
44C2	Lybster Scot
38H6	Lycksele Sweden
100B3	Lydenburg S Africa
8B3	Lyell,Mt USA
16A2	Lykens USA
43C4	Lyme B Eng
43C4	Lyme Regis Eng
11C3	Lynchburg USA
108A2	Lyndhurst Aust
15D2	Lynn USA
12G3	Lynn Canal Sd USA
17A1	Lynn Haven USA
5H4	Lynn Lake Can
5H3	Lynx L Can
49C2	Lyon France
12G3	Lyon Canal Sd USA
17B1	Lyons Georgia, USA
106A3	Lyons R Aust
47B2	Lys R Italy
61J2	Lys'va Russian Fed
111B2	Lyttelton NZ
13C2	Lytton Can
22A1	Lytton USA
58D2	Lyubeshov Ukraine
60E2	Lyublino Russian Fed

M

76C1	Ma R Viet
94B2	Ma'agan Jordan
94B2	Ma'alot Tarshiha Israel
92C3	Ma'an Jordan
73D3	Ma'anshan China
92C2	Ma'arrat an Nu'mān Syria
46C1	Maas R Neth
46C1	Maaseik Belg
79B3	Maasin Phil
57B2	Maastricht Neth
101C3	Mabalane Mozam
33F2	Mabaruma Guyana
42E3	Mablethorpe Eng
101C3	Mabote Mozam
58C2	Mabrita Belorussia
58D2	M'adel Belorussia
35C2	Macaé Brazil
9D3	McAlester USA
9D4	McAllen USA
101C2	Macaloge Mozam
33G3	Macapá Brazil
35C1	Macarani Brazil
32B4	Macas Ecuador
31D3	Macaú Brazil
73C5	Macau Dependency, China
98C2	M'Bari R CAR
13C2	McBride Can
35C2	McCarthy USA
13A2	McCauley I Can
42C3	Macclesfield Eng
6B1	McClintock B Can
4H2	McClintock Chan Can
16A2	McClure USA
22B2	McClure,L USA
4G2	McClure Str Can
19B3	McComb USA
6C2	McCook USA
6C2	McCullogh,Pt Can
13C1	McCusker,Mt Can
4F4	McDame Can
18B2	McDermitt USA
13E2	Macdonald R Can
106C3	Macdonnell Ranges Mts Aust
50A1	Macedo de Cavaleiros Port
55B2	Macedonia Republic, Europe
31D3	Maceió Brazil
97B4	Macenta Guinea
52B2	Macerata Italy
108A2	Macfarlane,L Aust
19B3	McGehee USA
45B3	MacGillycuddys Reeks Mts Irish Rep
4C3	McGrath USA
35B2	Machado Brazil
101C3	Machaíla Mozam
99D3	Machakos Kenya
32B4	Machala Ecuador
101C3	Machaze Mozam
87B1	Mācherla India
94B2	Machgharab Leb
87C1	Machilipatnam India
32C1	Machiques Ven
32C6	Machu-Picchu Hist Site Peru
101C3	Macia Mozam
109C1	McIntyre R Aust
107D3	Mackay Aust
106B3	Mackay,L Aust
14C2	McKeesport USA
13C1	Mackenzie Can
4F3	Mackenzie R Can
4E3	Mackenzie B Can
4G2	Mackenzie King I Can
4E3	Mackenzie Mts Can
14B1	Mackinac,Str of USA
14B1	Mackinaw City USA
12D2	McKinley,Mt USA
19A3	McKinney USA
6C2	Mackinson Inlet B Can
109D2	Macksville Aust
20B2	Mclaoughlin,Mt USA
109D1	Maclean Aust
100B4	Maclear S Africa
5G4	McLennan Can
13D2	McLeod R Can
4G3	McLeod B Can
106A3	McLeod,L Aust
13C1	McLeod Lake Can
4E3	Macmillan R Can
12H2	Macmillan P Can
20B1	McMinnville Oregon, USA
112B7	McMurdo Base Ant
13D2	McNaughton L Can
18B1	Macomb USA
53A2	Macomer Sardegna
101C2	Macomia Mozam
49C2	Mâcon France
11B3	Macon Georgia, USA
18B2	Macon Missouri, USA
100B2	Macondo Angola
18A2	McPherson USA
104F6	Macquarie Is Aust
109C2	Macquarie R Aust
109C4	Macquarie Harbour B Aust
109D2	Macquarie,L Aust
17B1	McRae USA
112B11	Mac. Robertson Land Region, Ant
45B3	Macroom Irish Rep
96C1	M'Sila Alg
4G3	McTavish Arm B Can
108A1	Macumba R Aust
47C2	Macunaga Italy
45C3	McVicar Arm B Can
93B3	M'yarovár Hung
94B3	Mádabá Jordan
95A3	Madadi Well Chad
89J10	Madagascar I Indian O
95A2	Madama Niger
71F4	Madang PNG
97C3	Madaoua Niger
86C2	Madaripur Bang
90B2	Madau Turkmenistan
15C1	Madawaska R Can
96A1	Madeira I Atlantic O
33E5	Madeira R Brazil
7D5	Madeleine, Isle de la Can
24B2	Madera Mexico
21A2	Madera USA
87A1	Madgaon India
86A1	Madhubani India
86A2	Madhya Pradesh State, India
87B2	Madikeri India
98B3	Madimba Zaire
98B3	Madingo Kayes Congo
98B3	Madingou Congo
10B3	Madison Indiana, USA
10B2	Madison Wisconsin, USA
18C2	Madisonville Kentucky, USA
19A3	Madisonville Texas, USA
78C4	Madiun Indon
99D2	Mado Gashi Kenya
47D1	Madonna Di Campiglio Italy
87C2	Madras India
20B2	Madras USA
29A6	Madre de Dios I Chile
32D6	Madre de Dios R Bol
50B1	Madrid Spain
50B2	Madridejos Spain
75B1	Maebashi Japan
76B3	Mae Khlong R Thai
77B4	Mae Nam Lunang R Thai
76C2	Mae Nam Mun R Thai
76B2	Mae Nam Ping R Thai
101D2	Maevatanana Madag
101G1	Mafeteng Lesotho
109C3	Maffra Aust
99D3	Mafia I Tanz
101G1	Mafikeng S Africa
31B6	Mafra Brazil
92C3	Mafraq Jordan
32C2	Maganguè Colombia
34D3	Magdalena Arg
24A1	Magdalena Mexico
32C2	Magdalena R Colombia
78D1	Magdalena,Mt Malay
56C2	Magdeburg Germany
31C6	Magé Brazil
78C4	Magelang Indon
47C1	Maggia R Switz
92B4	Maghâgha Egypt
45C1	Magherafelt N Ire
55A2	Maglie Italy
61J3	Magnitogorsk Russian Fed
19B3	Magnolia USA
101C2	Magoé Mozam

15D1 Magog Can
23A1 Magosal Mexico
13E2 Magrath Can
7A3 Maguse River Can
76B1 Magwe Burma
90A2 Mahābād Iran
86B1 Mahabharat Range Mts Nepal
87A1 Mahād India
85D4 Mahadeo Hills India
101D2 Mahajanga Madag
100B3 Mahalapye Botswana
86A2 Mahānadi R India
101D2 Mahanoro Madag
16A2 Mahanoy City USA
87A1 Maharashtra State, India
86A2 Māhāsamund India
76C2 Maha Sarakham Thai
101D2 Mahavavy R Madag
87B1 Mahbūbnagar India
96D1 Mahdia Tunisia
87B2 Mahe India
85D4 Mahekar India
101D2 Mahéli I Comoros
86A2 Mahendragarh India
99D3 Mahenge Tanz
86A2 Mahesāna India
110C1 Mahia Pen NZ
85D3 Mahoba India
51C2 Mahón Spain
12J1 Mahony L Can
51D3 Mahrès Tunisia
85C4 Mahuva India
32C1 Maicao Colombia
47B1 Maîche France
43E4 Maidstone Eng
98B1 Maiduguri Nig
86A2 Maihar India
76B3 Mail Kyun I Burma
84A1 Maimana Afghan
14B1 Main Chan Can
98B3 Mai-Ndombe L Zaïre
48B2 Maine Region France
44C2 Mainland I Scot
85D3 Mainpuri India
46A2 Maintenon France
101D2 Maintirano Madag
57B2 Mainz Germany
97A4 Maio I Cape Verde
29C2 Maipó Mt Arg/Chile
34D3 Maipú Arg
32D1 Maiquetía Ven
47B2 Maira R Italy
86C1 Mairābāri India
86C2 Maiskhal I Bang
107E4 Maitland New South Wales, Aust
108A2 Maitland S Australia, Aust
112C1 Maïtri Base Ant
84D3 Maizuru Japan
70C4 Majene Indon
30B2 Majes R Peru
99D2 Maji Eth
72D2 Majia He R China
Majunga = Mahajanga
70C4 Makale Indon
86B1 Makalu Mt China/Nepal
98B2 Makanza Zaïre
52C2 Makarska Croatia
61F2 Makaryev Russian Fed
Makassar = Ujung Pandang
78D3 Makassar Str Indon
61H4 Makat Kazakhstan
97A4 Makeni Sierra Leone
60E4 Makeyevka Ukraine
100B3 Makgadikgadi Salt Pan Botswana
61H5 Makhachkala Russian Fed
99D3 Makindu Kenya
88H5 Makkah S Arabia
7E4 Makkovik Can
59C3 Makó Hung
98B2 Makokou Gabon
110C1 Makorako,Mt NZ

98B2 Makoua Congo
85C3 Makrāna India
85A3 Makran Coast Range Mts Pak
96C1 Makthar Tunisia
93D2 Mākū Iran
98C3 Makumbi Zaïre
74C4 Makurazaki Japan
97C4 Makurdi Nig
79B4 Malabang Phil
87A2 Malabar Coast India
89E7 Malabo Bioko
77C5 Malacca,Str of S E Asia
32C2 Málaga Colombia
50B2 Málaga Spain
101D3 Malaimbandy Madag
107F1 Malaita I Solomon Is
99D2 Malakal Sudan
84C2 Malakand Pak
71E4 Malang Indon
98B3 Malange Angola
97C3 Malanville Benin
39H7 Mälaren L Sweden
34B3 Malargüe Arg
12F3 Malaspina Gl USA
93C2 Malatya Turk
101C2 Malawi Republic, Africa
Malawi,L = Nyasa,L
79C4 Malaybalay Phil
90A3 Malāyer Iran
70B3 Malaysia Federation, S E Asia
93D2 Malazgirt Turk
58B2 Malbork Pol
56C2 Malchin Germany
18C1 Malden USA
83B5 Maldives Is Indian O
104B4 Maldives Ridge Indian O
29F2 Maldonado Urug
47D1 Male Italy
85C4 Malegaon India
59B3 Malé Karpaty Upland Slovakia
101C2 Malema Mozam
84B2 Mālestān Afghan
38H5 Malgomaj L Sweden
95B3 Malha Well Sudan
20C2 Malheur L USA
97B3 Mali Republic, Africa
78D1 Malinau Indon
99E3 Malindi Kenya
Malines = Mechelen
40B2 Malin Head Pt Irish Rep
86A2 Malkala Range Mts India
85D4 Malkāpur India
55C2 Malkara Turk
54C2 Malko Tŭrnovo Bulg
44B3 Mallaig Scot
95C2 Mallawi Egypt
47D1 Málles Venosta Italy
51C2 Mallorca I Spain
42B3 Mallow Irish Rep
38G6 Malm Nor
38J5 Malmberget Sweden
46D1 Malmédy Germany
43C4 Malmesbury Eng
100A4 Malmesbury S Africa
39G7 Malmö Sweden
61G2 Malmyzh Russian Fed
79B3 Malolos Phil
15D2 Malone USA
101G1 Maloti Mts Lesotho
38F6 Måløy Nor
28A2 Malpelo I Colombia
34A2 Malpo R Chile
85D3 Mālpura India
8C2 Malta Montana, USA
53D3 Malta Chan Malta/Italy
53B3 Malta I Medit S
100A3 Maltahöhe Namibia
42D2 Malton Eng
39G6 Malung Sweden
87A1 Malvan India
19B3 Malvern USA
85D4 Malwa Plat India

61G4 Malyy Uzen' R Kazakhstan
63D2 Mama Russian Fed
61H2 Mamadysh Russian Fed
99C2 Mambasa Zaïre
71E4 Mamberamo R Indon
98B2 Mambéré R CAR
89E7 Mamfé Cam
33D6 Mamoré R Bol
97A3 Mamou Guinea
101D2 Mampikony Madag
97B4 Mampong Ghana
94B3 Mamshit Hist Site Israel
100B3 Mamuno Botswana
97B4 Man Ivory Coast
21C4 Mana Hawaiian Is
101D3 Manabo Madag
33E4 Manacapuru Brazil
51C2 Manacor Spain
25D3 Managua Nic
101D3 Manakara Madag
101D3 Mananara Madag
101D3 Mananjary Madag
111A3 Manapouri NZ
111A3 Manapouri,L NZ
86C1 Manas Bhutan
82C1 Manas China
65K5 Manas Hu L China
86A1 Manaslu Mt Nepal
16B2 Manasquan USA
33F4 Manaus Brazil
92B2 Manavgat Turk
93C2 Manbij Syria
42B2 Man,Calf of I Eng
87B1 Mancheral India
15D2 Manchester Connecticut, USA
42C3 Manchester Eng
10C2 Manchester New Hampshire, USA
16A2 Manchester Pennsylvania, USA
69E2 Manchuria Hist Region, China
91B4 Mand R Iran
101C2 Manda Tanz
35A2 Mandaguari Brazil
39F7 Mandal Nor
76B1 Mandalay Burma
68C2 Mandalgovi Mongolia
8C2 Mandan USA
14A2 Mandelona USA
99E2 Mandera Eth
26B3 Mandeville Jamaica
101C2 Mandimba Mozam
86A2 Mandla India
101D2 Mandritsara Madag
85D4 Mandsaur India
53C2 Manduria Italy
85B4 Mandvi India
87B2 Mandya India
47D2 Manerbio Italy
42D3 Manfield Eng
53C2 Manfredonia Italy
98B1 Manga Desert Region Niger
110C1 Mangakino NZ
54C2 Mangalia Rom
98B1 Mangalmé Chad
87A2 Mangalore India
78B3 Manggar Indon
68B3 Mangnia China
101C2 Mangoche Malawi
101D3 Mangoky R Madag
71D4 Mangole I Indon
85B4 Mangral India
63E2 Mangui China
18A1 Manhattan USA
31C6 Manhuaçu Brazil
101D2 Mania R Madag
101C2 Manica Mozam
7D5 Manicouagan R Can
91A4 Manīfah S Arabia
105H4 Manihiki I Pacific O
79B3 Manila Phil
107D2 Manilla Aust
97B3 Maninian Ivory Coast
86C2 Manipur State, India
86C2 Manipur R Burma
92A2 Manisa Turk

41C3 Man,Isle of I Irish S
14A2 Manistee USA
14A2 Manistee R USA
14A1 Manistique USA
5H4 Manitoba Province, Can
5J4 Manitoba,L Can
13F2 Manito L Can
14A1 Manitou Is USA
7B5 Manitoulin I Can
14A2 Manitowoc USA
15C1 Maniwaki Can
32B2 Manizales Colombia
101D3 Manja Madag
106A4 Manjimup Aust
87B1 Manjra R India
10A2 Mankato USA
97B4 Mankono Ivory Coast
12D2 Manley Hot Springs USA
110B1 Manly NZ
85C4 Manmād India
78A3 Manna Indon
108A2 Mannahill Aust
87B3 Mannar Sri Lanka
87B3 Mannar,G of India
87B2 Mannārgudi India
57B3 Mannheim Germany
13D1 Manning Can
17B1 Manning USA
108A2 Mannum Aust
97A4 Mano Sierra Leone
71E4 Manokwari Indon
98C3 Manono Zaïre
76B3 Manoron Burma
75B1 Mano-wan B Japan
74B2 Mano I N Korea
84D3 Mānsa India
100B2 Mansa Zambia
6B3 Mansel I Can
19B2 Mansfield Arkansas, USA
108C3 Mansfield Aust
19B3 Mansfield Louisiana, USA
16D1 Mansfield Massachusetts, USA
10B2 Mansfield Ohio, USA
15C2 Mansfield Pennsylvania, USA
71E2 Mansyu Deep Pacific O
32A4 Manta Ecuador
79A4 Mantalingajan,Mt Phil
32B6 Mantaro R Peru
22B2 Manteca USA
48C2 Mantes France
52B1 Mantova Italy
38J6 Mänttä Fin
61F2 Manturovo Russian Fed
35A2 Manuel Ribas Brazil
79B4 Manukan Phil
110B1 Manukau NZ
71F4 Manus I Pacific O
50B2 Manzanares Spain
25E2 Manzanillo Cuba
24B3 Manzanillo Mexico
63D3 Manzhouli China
94C3 Manzil Jordan
101C3 Manzini Swaziland
98B1 Mao Chad
72A2 Maomao Shan Mt China
73C5 Maoming China
101C3 Mapai Mozam
71E3 Mapia Is Pacific O
79A4 Mapin I Phil
5H5 Maple Creek Can
101H1 Maputo Mozam
101H1 Maputo R Mozam
Ma Qu = Huange He
72A3 Maqu China
86B1 Maquan He R China
98B3 Maquela do Zombo Angola
29C4 Maquinchao Arg
31B2 Marabá Brazil
32C1 Maracaibo Ven
32D1 Maracay Ven
95A2 Marādah Libya
97C3 Maradi Niger
90A2 Marāgheh Iran

99D2 **Maralal** Kenya
107F1 **Maramasike** I Solomon Is
100B2 **Maramba** Zambia
90A2 **Marand** Iran
31B2 **Maranhão** State, Brazil
109C1 **Maranoa** R Aust
32B4 **Marañón** R Peru
7B5 **Marathon** Can
17B2 **Marathon** Florida, USA
78D2 **Maratua** I Indon
23A2 **Maravatio** Mexico
79B4 **Marawi** Phil
34B2 **Marayes** Arg
50B2 **Marbella** Spain
106A3 **Marble Bar** Aust
100B3 **Marblehall** S Africa
16D1 **Marblehead** USA
57B2 **Marburg** Germany
57B2 **Marche** Belg
50A2 **Marchena** Spain
46C1 **Marche-en-Famenne** Belg
32J7 **Marchena** I Ecuador
17B2 **Marco** USA
34C2 **Marcos Juárez** Arg
12E2 **Marcus Baker,Mt** USA
15D2 **Marcy,Mt** USA
84C2 **Mardan** Pak
29E3 **Mar del Plata** Arg
93D2 **Mardin** Turk
99D1 **Mareb** R Eritrea/Eth
16B1 **Margaretville** USA
43E **Margate** Eng
54B1 **Marghita** Rom
109C4 **Maria I** Aust
104F3 **Mariana** Is Pacific O
13E1 **Mariana Lake** Can
104F3 **Marianas Trench** Pacific O
86C1 **Mariāni** India
19B3 **Marianna** Arkansas, USA
17A1 **Marianna** Florida, USA
7G4 **Maria Van Diemen,C** NZ
59B3 **Mariazell** Austria
52C1 **Maribor** Slovenia
99C2 **Maridi** Sudan
112B5 **Marie Byrd Land** Region, Ant
27E3 **Marie Galante** I Caribbean S
39H6 **Mariehamn** Fin
46C1 **Mariembourg** Belg
33G2 **Marienburg** Surinam
100A3 **Mariental** Namibia
39G7 **Mariestad** Sweden
17B1 **Marietta** Georgia, USA
14B3 **Marietta** Ohio, USA
19A3 **Marietta** Oklahoma, USA
27O2 **Marigot** Dominica
60B3 **Marijampole** Lithuania
31B6 **Marília** Brazil
98B3 **Marimba** Angola
79B3 **Marinduque** I Phil
10F3 **Maringá** Brazil
98C2 **Maringa** R Zaire
18C2 **Marion** Arkansas, USA
18C2 **Marion** Illinois, USA
10B2 **Marion** Indiana, USA
10B2 **Marion** Ohio, USA
17C1 **Marion** S Carolina, USA
11B3 **Marion,L** USA
107E2 **Marion Reef** Aust
21B2 **Mariposa** USA
22B2 **Mariposa** R USA
22B2 **Mariposa Res** USA
60C5 **Marista** R Bulg
60E4 **Mariupol'** Ukraine
61G2 **Mariyskaya Respublika,** Russian Fed
94B2 **Marjayoun** Leb

58D2 **Marjina Gorki** Belorussia
94B3 **Marka** Jordan
99E2 **Marka** Somalia
56C1 **Markaryd** Sweden
43C3 **Market Drayton** Eng
43D3 **Market Harborough** Eng
112A **Markham,Mt** Ant
22C1 **Markleeville** USA
16D1 **Marlboro** Massachusetts, USA
107D3 **Marlborough** Aust
46B2 **Marle** France
19A3 **Marlin** USA
48C3 **Marmande** France
55C2 **Marmara Adi** I Turk
92A1 **Marmara,S of** Turk
55C2 **Marmaris** Turk
14B3 **Marmet** USA
52B1 **Marmolada** Mt Italy
12D3 **Marmot B** USA
47A1 **Marnay** France
46B2 **Marne** Department, France
46B2 **Marne** R France
98B2 **Maro** Chad
101D2 **Maroantsetra** Madag
101C2 **Marondera** Zim
33G3 **Maroni** R French Guiana
109D1 **Maroochydore** Aust
98B1 **Maroua** Cam
101D2 **Marovoay** Madag
11B4 **Marquesas Keys** Is USA
10B2 **Marquette** USA
46A1 **Marquise** France
109C2 **Marra** R Aust
101H1 **Marracuene** Mozam
96B1 **Marrakech** Mor
106C3 **Marree** Aust
19A4 **Marrero** USA
101C2 **Marromeu** Mozam
101C2 **Marrupa** Mozam
95C2 **Marsa Alam** Egypt
99D2 **Marsabit** Kenya
53B3 **Marsala** Italy
49D3 **Marseille** France
12B2 **Marshall** Alaska, USA
14A3 **Marshall** Illinois, USA
14B2 **Marshall** Michigan, USA
18B2 **Marshall** Missouri, USA
11A3 **Marshall** Texas, USA
105G3 **Marshall Is** Pacific O
18B2 **Marshfield** Missouri, USA
26B1 **Marsh Harbour** The Bahamas
19B4 **Marsh I** USA
12H2 **Marsh L** Can
76B2 **Martaban,G of** Burma
78A3 **Martapura** Indon
78C3 **Martapura** Indon
15D2 **Martha's Vineyard** I USA
49D2 **Martigny** Switz
59B3 **Martin** Slovakia
111C2 **Martinborough** NZ
34B3 **Martin de Loyola** Arg
23B1 **Martinez de la Torre** Mexico
27E4 **Martinique** I Caribbean S
17A1 **Martin,L** USA
15C3 **Martinsburg** USA
18B2 **Martins Ferry** USA
103G6 **Martin Vaz** I Atlantic O
49D3 **Martiques** France
110C2 **Marton** NZ
50B2 **Martos** Spain
78D1 **Marudi** Malay
84B2 **Maruf** Afghan
75A2 **Marugame** Japan
85B3 **Mārwār** India
65H6 **Mary** Turkmenistan
107E3 **Maryborough** Queensland, Aust
108B3 **Maryborough** Victoria, Aust

5F4 **Mary Henry,Mt** Can
10C3 **Maryland** State, USA
42C2 **Maryport** Eng
21A2 **Marysville** California, USA
18A2 **Marysville** Kansas, USA
20B1 **Marysville** Washington, USA
10A2 **Maryville** USA
18B1 **Maryville** Missouri, USA
95A2 **Marzuq** Libya
Masada = Mezada
94B2 **Mas'adah** Israel
99D3 **Masai Steppe** Upland Tanz
99D3 **Masaka** Uganda
93E2 **Masally** Azerbaijan
74B3 **Masan** S Korea
101C2 **Masasi** Tanz
25D3 **Masaya** Nic
79B3 **Masbate** Phil
79B3 **Masbate** I Phil
96C1 **Mascara** Alg
23A1 **Mascota** Mexico
35D1 **Mascote** Brazil
Maseru Lesotho
68C3 **Mashad** Iran
84B2 **Mashaki** Afghan
90C2 **Mashhad** Iran
98B3 **Masi-Manimba** Zaire
98D1 **Masindi** Uganda
99C3 **Masisi** Zaire
90A3 **Masjed Soleyman** Iran
101E2 **Masoala** C Madag
10A2 **Mason City** USA
91C5 **Masqat** Oman
52B2 **Massa** Italy
10C2 **Massachusetts** State, USA
15D2 **Massachusetts B** USA
98B1 **Massakori** Chad
101C3 **Massangena** Mozam
Massanga = Mits'iwa
15D2 **Massena** USA
98B1 **Massénya** Chad
14B1 **Massey** Can
49C2 **Massif Central** Mts France
98B2 **Massif de l'Adamaoua** Mts Cam
26C3 **Massif de la Hotte** Mts Haiti
101D3 **Massif de l'Isalo** Upland Madag
98C2 **Massif des Bongo** Upland CAR
49D2 **Massif du Pelvoux** Mts France
101D2 **Massif du Tsaratanana** Mt Madag
14B2 **Massilon** USA
97B3 **Massina** Region, Mali
101C3 **Massinga** Mozam
101C3 **Massingir** Mozam
61H4 **Masteksay** Kazakhstan
111C2 **Masterton** NZ
74C4 **Masuda** Japan
100A3 **Masuku** Gabon
100C3 **Masvingo** Zim
92C2 **Maşyāf** Syria
98B3 **Matadi** Zaire
25D3 **Matagalpa** Nic
7C4 **Matagami** Can
9D4 **Matagorda B** USA
110C1 **Matakana I** NZ
100A2 **Matala** Angola
97A3 **Matam** Sen
97C3 **Matameye** Niger
24C2 **Matamoros** Mexico
95B2 **Ma'tan as Sarra** Well Libya
7D5 **Matane** Can
25D2 **Matanzas** Cuba
34A2 **Mataquito** R Chile
87B3 **Matara** Sri Lanka
106A1 **Mataram** Indon

30B2 **Matarani** Peru
51C1 **Mataró** Spain
111A3 **Mataura** NZ
24B2 **Matehuala** Mexico
27L1 **Matelot** Trinidad
53C2 **Matera** Italy
59C3 **Mátészalka** Hung
85D3 **Mathura** India
79C4 **Mati** Phil
78D3 **Matisiri** I Indon
43D3 **Matlock** Eng
33F6 **Mato Grosso** Brazil
33F6 **Mato Grosso** State, Brazil
30E2 **Mato Grosso do Sul** State, Brazil
101H1 **Matola** Mozam
91C5 **Matrah** Oman
95A2 **Matrûh** Egypt
74C3 **Matsue** Japan
74E2 **Matsumae** Japan
74D3 **Matsumoto** Japan
74D4 **Matsusaka** Japan
74C4 **Matsuyama** Japan
7B5 **Mattagami** R Can
15C1 **Mattawa** Can
52A1 **Matterhorn** Mt Italy/ Switz
26C2 **Matthew Town** The Bahamas
16C2 **Mattituck** USA
18C2 **Mattoon** USA
84B2 **Matun** Afghan
27L1 **Matura B** Trinidad
33E2 **Maturín** Ven
86A1 **Mau** India
101A2 **Maúa** Mozam
49C1 **Maubeuge** France
108B2 **Maude** Aust
103J8 **Maud Seamount** Atlantic O
21C4 **Maui** I Hawaiian Is
34A3 **Maule** R Chile
14B2 **Maumee** USA
14B2 **Maumee** R USA
100B2 **Maun** Botswana
21C4 **Mauna Kea** Mt Hawaiian Is
21C4 **Mauna Loa** Mt Hawaiian Is
4F3 **Maunoir** L Can
4F3 **Maunoir,L** Can
48C2 **Mauriac** France
96A2 **Mauritania** Republic, Africa
100E3 **Mauritius** I Indian O
100B2 **Mavinga** Angola
86C2 **Mawlaik** Burma
Mawlamyine = Moulmein
112C10 **Mawson** Base Ant
78B3 **Maya** I Indon
63F2 **Maya** R Russian Fed
93D2 **Mayādīn** Syria
11C4 **Mayaguana** I The Bahamas
27D3 **Mayagüez** Puerto Rico
97C3 **Mayahi** Niger
98C2 **Mayama** Congo
90C2 **Mayamey** Iran
42B2 **Maybole** Scot
10C3 **May,C** USA
109C4 **Maydena** Aust
46D1 **Mayen** Germany
48B2 **Mayenne** France
13D2 **Mayerthorpe** Can
61E5 **Mayfield** USA
61E5 **Maykop** Russian Fed
65H6 **Maymaneh** Afghan
76B1 **Maymyo** Burma
4E3 **Mayo** Can
45B2 **Mayo** County, Irish Rep
16A3 **Mayo** USA
79B3 **Mayon** Mt Phil
51C2 **Mayor** Mt Spain
34C3 **Mayor Buratovich** Arg
110C1 **Mayor I** NZ
30D2 **Mayor P Lagerenza** Par

101D2 **Mayotte** I Indian O
27H2 **May Pen** Jamaica
16B3 **May Point,C** USA
47D1 **Mayrhofen** Austria
16B3 **Mays Landing** USA
98B3 **Maysville** USA
98B3 **Mayumba** Gabon
100B2 **Mazabuka** Zambia
84D1 **Mazar** China
94B3 **Mazār** Jordan
53B3 **Mazara del Vallo** Italy
84B1 **Mazar-i-Sharif** Afghan
24B2 **Mazatlán** Mexico
60B2 **Mazeikiai** Lithuania
94B3 **Mazra** Jordan
101C3 **Mbabane** Swaziland
98B2 **Mbaiki** CAR
99D3 **Mbala** Zambia
100B3 **Mbalabala** Zim
99D2 **Mbale** Uganda
98B2 **Mbalmayo** Cam
98B2 **Mbam** R Cam
101C2 **Mbamba Bay** Tanz
98B2 **Mbandaka** Zaïre
98B3 **Mbanza Congo** Angola
98B3 **Mbanza-Ngungu** Zaïre
99D3 **Mbarara** Uganda
98B2 **Mbènza** Congo
98B2 **Mbère** R Cam
99D3 **Mbeya** Tanz
98B3 **Mbinda** Congo
97A3 **Mbout** Maur
98C3 **Mbuji-Mayi** Zaïre
99D3 **Mbulu** Tanz
96R? **Mcherrah** Region, Alg
101C2 **Mchinji** Malawi
76D3 **Mdrak** Viet
9B3 **Mead,L** USA
5H4 **Meadow Lake** Can
14B2 **Meadville** Can
7E4 **Mealy Mts** Can
109C1 **Meandarra** Aust
5G4 **Meander River** Can
45C2 **Meath** County, Irish Rep
49C2 **Meaux** France
16C1 **Mechanicville** USA
56A2 **Mechelen** Belg
96B1 **Mecheria** Alg
56C2 **Mecklenburg-Vorpommern** State Germany
56C2 **Mecklenburger Bucht** B Germany
101C2 **Meconta** Mozam
101C2 **Mecubúri** Mozam
101D2 **Mecufi** Mozam
101C2 **Mecula** Mozam
70A3 **Medan** Indon
34C3 **Medanos** Arg
34D2 **Medanos** Arg
13E2 **Medecine Hat** Can
32B2 **Medellín** Colombia
96D1 **Medenine** Tunisia
8A2 **Medford** USA
54C2 **Medgidia** Rom
34B2 **Media Agua** Arg
54B1 **Medias** Rom
20C1 **Medical Lake** USA
5G5 **Medicine Hat** Can
35C1 **Medina** Brazil
80B3 **Medina** S Arabia
50B1 **Medinaceli** Spain
50B1 **Medina del Campo** Spain
50B1 **Medina de Rio Seco** Spain
86B2 **Medinipur** India
88E4 **Mediterranean S** Europe
13F2 **Medley** Can
61J3 **Mednogorsk** Russian Fed
86D1 **Mēdog** China
98B2 **Medouneu** Gabon
61F3 **Medvedista** R Russian Fed
64E3 **Medvezh'yegorsk** Russian Fed

106A3 **Meekatharra** Aust
84D3 **Meerut** India
99D2 **Mēga** Eth
55B3 **Megalópolis** Greece
55B3 **Mégara** Greece
86C1 **Meghálaya** State, India
86C2 **Meghna** R Bang
94B2 **Megiddo** Hist Site Israel
91B4 **Mehran** R Iran
90B3 **Mehriz** Iran
35B1 **Meia Ponte** R Brazil
98B2 **Meiganga** Cam
76B1 **Meiktila** Burma
47C1 **Meiringen** Switz
73A4 **Meishan** China
57C2 **Meissen** Germany
73D5 **Mei Xian** China
73D5 **Meizhou** China
30B3 **Mejillones** Chile
98B2 **Mekambo** Gabon
99D1 **Mek'elē** Eth
96B1 **Meknès** Mor
76D3 **Mekong** R Camb
97C3 **Mekrou** R Benin
77C5 **Melaka** Malay
104F4 **Melanesia** Region Pacific O
78C3 **Melawi** R Indon
107D4 **Melbourne** Aust
11B4 **Melbourne** USA
9C4 **Melchor Muzquiz** Mexico
61J3 **Meleuz** Russian Fed
98B1 **Melfi** Chad
5H4 **Melfort** Can
96B1 **Melilla** N W Africa
29B4 **Melimoyu** Mt Chile
34C2 **Melincué** Arg
34A2 **Melipilla** Chile
60E4 **Melitopol'** Ukraine
6D2 **Melville Bugt** B Greenland
99D2 **Melka Guba** Eth
10H1 **Melmoth** S Africa
34C2 **Melo** Arg
29F2 **Melo** Urug
22B2 **Melones** Res USA
12D1 **Melozitna** R USA
47C1 **Mels** Switz
43D3 **Melton Mowbry** Eng
49C2 **Melun** France
5H4 **Melville** Can
27Q2 **Melville,C** Dominica
4F3 **Melville Hills** Mts Can
106C2 **Melville I** Aust
4G2 **Melville I** Can
7E4 **Melville,L** Can
68B3 **Melville Pen** Can
45B1 **Melvin,L** Irish Rep
101D2 **Memba** Mozam
106A1 **Memboro** Indon
57C3 **Memmingen** Germany
78B2 **Mempawan** Indon
11B3 **Memphis** Tennessee, USA
19B3 **Mena** USA
43B3 **Menai Str** Wales
97C3 **Ménaka** Mali
14A2 **Menasha** USA
78C3 **Mendawai** R Indon
49C3 **Mende** France
99D2 **Mendebo** Mts Eth
43C4 **Mendip Hills** Upland Eng
20B2 **Mendocino,C** USA
105J2 **Mendocino Seascarp** Pacific O
22B2 **Mendota** California, USA
29C2 **Mendoza** Arg
29C3 **Mendoza** State, Arg
55C3 **Menemen** Turk
46B1 **Menen** Belg
72D3 **Mengcheng** China
78B3 **Menggala** Indon
76B1 **Menghai** China
73A5 **Mengla** China
76B1 **Menglian** China
73A5 **Mengzi** China
107D4 **Menindee** Aust

108B2 **Menindee L** Aust
108A3 **Meningie** Aust
14A1 **Menominee** USA
14A2 **Menomonee Falls** USA
100A2 **Menongue** Angola
51C1 **Menorca** I Spain
12F2 **Mentasta Mts** USA
78B3 **Mentok** Indon
14B2 **Mentor** USA
46B2 **Ménu** France
72A2 **Menyuan** China
61H2 **Menzelinsk** Russian Fed
56B2 **Meppen** Germany
78D2 **Merah** Indon
18B2 **Meramec** R USA
52B1 **Merano** Italy
71F4 **Merauke** Indon
8A3 **Merced** USA
22B2 **Merced** R USA
29B2 **Mercedario** Mt Chile
29C2 **Mercedes** Arg
29E2 **Mercedes** Buenos Aires, Arg
30E4 **Mercedes** Corrientes, Arg
29E2 **Mercedes** Urug
110C1 **Mercury B** NZ
110C1 **Mercury Is** NZ
4F2 **Mercy,C** Can
6D3 **Mercy,C** Can
99E2 **Meregh** Somalia
76B3 **Mergui** Burma
76B3 **Mergui Arch** Burma
25D2 **Mérida** Mexico
50A2 **Mérida** Spain
32C2 **Mérida** Ven
11B3 **Meridian** USA
109C3 **Merimbula** Aust
108B2 **Meringur** Aust
98C3 **Morowe** Sudan
106A4 **Merredin** Aust
44B2 **Merrick** Mt Scot
14A2 **Merrillville** USA
13C2 **Merritt** Can
17B2 **Merritt Island** USA
99E1 **Mersa Fatma** Eritrea
61E4 **Mers el Kebir** Alg
42C3 **Mersey** R Eng
42C3 **Merseyside** Metropolitan County, Eng
92B2 **Mersin** Turk
77C5 **Mersing** Malay
85C3 **Merta** India
43C4 **Merthyr Tydfil** Wales
50A2 **Mertola** Port
99D3 **Meru** Mt Tanz
60E5 **Merzifon** Turk
46D2 **Merzig** Germany
9B3 **Mesa** USA
46E1 **Meschede** Germany
93D1 **Mescit Dağ** Mt Turk
99C2 **Meshra Er Req** Sudan
47C1 **Mesocco** Switz
55B3 **Mesolóngion** Greece
19B4 **Mesquite** Texas, USA
101C2 **Messalo** R Mozam
53C3 **Messina** Italy
100B3 **Messina** S Africa
55B3 **Messini** Greece
55B3 **Messiniakós Kólpos** G Greece
54B2 **Mesta** R Bulg
52B1 **Mestre** Italy
32C3 **Meta** R Colombia
60D2 **Meta** R Russian Fed
32D2 **Meta** R Ven
6C3 **Meta Incognito Pen** Can
19B4 **Metairie** USA
20C1 **Metaline Falls** USA
30D4 **Metán** Arg
101C2 **Matangula** Mozam
53C2 **Metaponto** Italy
44C3 **Methil** Scot
16D1 **Methuen** USA
111B2 **Methven** NZ
12H3 **Metlakatla** USA

18C2 **Metropolis** USA
87B2 **Mettür** India
49D2 **Metz** France
70A3 **Meulaboh** Indon
46A2 **Meulan** France
46C2 **Meuse** Department, France
49D2 **Meuse** R France
19A3 **Mexia** USA
24A1 **Mexicali** Mexico
24B2 **México** Federal Republic, Cent America
24C3 **México** Mexico
23A2 **México** State, Mexico
18B2 **México** USA
24C2 **México,G of** Cent America
94B3 **Mezada** Hist Site Israel
23B2 **Mezcala** Mexico
64F3 **Mezen'** Russian Fed
64G2 **Mezhdurskariy, Ostrov** I Russian Fed
85D4 **Mhow** India
23B2 **Miahuatlán** Mexico
11B4 **Miami** Florida, USA
18B2 **Miami** Oklahoma, USA
11B4 **Miami Beach** USA
90A2 **Mianeh** Iran
101D2 **Miandrivazo** Madag
90A2 **Miāneh** Iran
84C2 **Mianwali** Pak
73A3 **Mianyang** China
73C3 **Mianyang** China
73A3 **Mianzhu** China
72E2 **Miaodao Qundao** Arch China
73B4 **Miao Ling** Upland China
61K3 **Miass** Russian Fed
59C3 **Michalovce** Slovakia
27D3 **Miches** Dom Rep
10B2 **Michigan** State, USA
14A2 **Michigan City** USA
10B2 **Michigan,L** USA
7B5 **Michipicoten I** Can
23A2 **Michoacán** State, Mexico
54C2 **Michurin** Bulg
61F3 **Michurinsk** Russian Fed
104F3 **Micronesia** Region Pacific O
78B2 **Midai** I Indon
102F4 **Mid Atlantic Ridge** Atlantic O
46B1 **Middelburg** Neth
20B2 **Middle Alkali L** USA
16D2 **Middleboro** USA
100B4 **Middleburg** Cape Province, S Africa
16A2 **Middleburg** Pennsylvania, USA
101G1 **Middleburg** Transvaal, S Africa
16B1 **Middleburgh** USA
15D2 **Middlebury** USA
11B3 **Middlesboro** USA
42D2 **Middlesbrough** Eng
16C2 **Middletown** Connecticut, USA
16B3 **Middletown** Delaware, USA
15D2 **Middletown** New York, USA
14B3 **Middletown** Ohio, USA
16A2 **Middletown** Pennsylvania, USA
96B1 **Midelt** Mor
43C4 **Mid Glamorgan** County, Wales
104B4 **Mid Indian Basin** Indian O
104B4 **Mid Indian Ridge** Indian O
/C5 **Midland** Can
14B2 **Midland** Michigan, USA
9C3 **Midland** Texas, USA
101D3 **Midongy Atsimo** Madag

Mid Pacific Mts

105G2 Mid Pacific Mts Pacific O
20C2 Midvale USA
105H2 Midway Is Pacific O
18A2 Midwest City USA
93D2 Midyat Turk
54B2 Midžor Mt Serbia, Yugos
59B2 Mielec Pol
54C1 Miercurea-Ciuc Rom
50A1 Mieres Spain
16A2 Mifflintown USA
75A2 Mihara Japan
72D1 Mijun Shuiku Res China
54B2 Mikhaylovgrad Bulg
61F3 Mikhaylovka Russian Fed
65J4 Mikhaylovskiy Russian Fed
38K6 Mikkeli Fin
55C3 Mikonos I Greece
59B3 Mikulov Czech Republic
99D3 Mikumi Tanz
74D3 Mikuni-sammyaku Mts Japan
75B2 Mikura-jima I Japan
32B4 Milagro Ecuador
51C2 Milan = Milano
101C2 Milange Mozam
52A1 Milano Italy
92A2 Milas Turk
107D4 Mildura Aust
73A5 Mile China
93D3 Mileh Tharthār L Iraq
107E3 Miles Aust
8C2 Miles City USA
16C2 Milford Connecticut, USA
15C3 Milford Delaware, USA
15D2 Milford Massachusetts, USA
18A1 Milford Nebraska, USA
16B2 Milford Pennsylvania, USA
43B4 Milford Haven Wales
43B4 Milford Haven Sd Wales
18A2 Milford L USA
111A2 Milford Sd NZ
13E2 Milk River Can
49C3 Millau France
16C2 Millbrook USA
17B1 Milledgeville USA
12F2 Miller,Mt USA
61F4 Millerovo Russian Fed
16A2 Millersburg USA
108A1 Millers Creek Aust
16C1 Millers Falls USA
16C2 Millerton USA
22C2 Millerton L USA
108B3 Millicent Aust
109D1 Millmerran Aust
45B2 Milltown Malbay Irish Rep
22A2 Mill Valley USA
15D3 Millville USA
6H2 Milne Land I Greenland
21C4 Milolii Hawaiian Is
55B3 Milos I Greece
107D3 Milparinka Aust
16A2 Milroy USA
111A3 Milton NZ
16A2 Milton Pennsylvania, USA
10B2 Milwaukee USA
51C2 Mina R Alg
93E4 Mīnā' al Aḥmadī Kuwait
91C4 Mīnāb Iran
74C4 Minamata Japan
78A2 Minas Indon
29E2 Minas Urug
31B5 Minas Gerais State, Brazil
35C1 Minas Novas Brazil
25C3 Minatitlan Mexico

76A1 Minbu Burma
76A1 Minbya Burma
34A2 Mincha Chile
44A3 Minch,Little Sd Scot
44A2 Minch,North Sd Scot
40B2 Minch,The Sd Scot
12D2 Minchumina,L USA
47D2 Mincio R Italy
79B4 Mindanao I Phil
19B3 Minden Louisiana, USA
56B2 Minden Germany
108B2 Mindona L Aust
79B3 Mindoro I Phil
79B3 Mindoro Str Phil
45C3 Mine Hd C Irish Rep
43C4 Minehead Eng
30F2 Mineiros Brazil
19A3 Mineola USA
23B1 Mineral de Monte Mexico
16A2 Minersville USA
108B2 Mingary Aust
72A2 Minhe China
87A3 Minicoy I India
73D4 Min Jiang R Fujian, China
73A4 Min Jiang R Sichuan, China
22C2 Minkler USA
108A2 Minlaton Aust
72A2 Minle China
97C4 Minna Nig
10A2 Minneapolis USA
5J4 Minnedosa Can
10A2 Minnesota State, USA
50A1 Miño R Spain
8C2 Minot USA
72A2 Minqin China
72A3 Min Shan Upland China
60C3 Minsk Belorussia
58C2 Mińsk Mazowiecki Pol
12E2 Minto USA
4G2 Minto Inlet B Can
7C4 Minto,L Can
63B2 Minusinsk Russian Fed
72A3 Min Xian China
7E5 Miquelon Can
22D3 Mirage L USA
87A1 Miraj India
84B2 Miram Shah Pak
50B1 Miranda de Ebro Spain
47D2 Mirandola Italy
84B2 Mir Bachchen Küt Afghan
78D1 Miri Malay
96A3 Mirik,C Maur
63A1 Mirnoye Russian Fed
63D1 Mirnyy Russian Fed
112C9 Mirnyy Base Ant
84C2 Mirpur Pak
85B3 Mirpur Khas Pak
54B2 Mirtoan S Greece
74B3 Miryang S Korea
86A1 Mirzāpur India
78D1 Misima I Solomon Is
30F4 Misiones State, Arg
59C3 Miskolc Hung
94C2 Mismīyah Syria
71E4 Misoöl I Indon
95A1 Mişrātah Libya
7B5 Missinaibi R Can
20B1 Mission City Can
15C2 Mississauga Can
11A3 Mississippi State, USA
11A3 Mississippi R USA
19C3 Mississippi Delta USA
8B2 Missoula USA
11A3 Missouri State, USA

10A2 Missouri R USA
10C1 Mistassini,L Can
30B2 Misti Mt Peru
109C1 Mitchell Aust
8D2 Mitchell USA
107D2 Mitchell R Aust
11B3 Mitchell,Mt USA
45B2 Mitchelstown Irish Rep
84C3 Mithankot Pak
55C3 Mitilini Greece
23B2 Mitla Mexico
54B2 Mitrovica Serbia, Yugos
95C3 Mits'iwa Eritrea
32C3 Mitu Colombia
99C3 Mitumbar Mts Zaire
98C3 Mitwaba Zaire
98B2 Mitzic Gabon
75B1 Miura Japan
72C3 Mi Xian China
69F3 Miyake I Japan
75B2 Miyake-jima I Japan
74C4 Miyako I Japan
74C4 Miyakonojō Japan
74C4 Miyazaki Japan
75B1 Miyazu Japan
72D1 Miyun China
99D2 Mizan Teferi Eth
95A1 Mizdah Libya
45B3 Mizen Hd C Irish Rep
54C1 Mizil Rom
86C2 Mizo Hills India
86C2 Mizoram Union Territory, India
94B3 Mizpe Ramon Israel
112B11 Mizuho Base Ant
74E3 Mizusawa Japan
39H7 Mjolby Sweden
100B2 Mkushi Zambia
101H1 Mkuzi S Africa
57C2 Mladá Boleslav Czech Republic
58C2 Mława Pol
52C2 Mljet I Croatia
100B3 Mmabatho S Africa
84D2 Mnadi India
97A4 Moa R Sierra Leone
94B3 Moab Region, Jordan
9C3 Moab USA
98B3 Moanda Congo
98B3 Moanda Gabon
99C3 Moba Zaire
75C1 Mobara Japan
98C2 Mobaye CAR
98C2 Mobayi Zaire
10A3 Moberly USA
11B3 Mobile USA
11B3 Mobile B USA
8C2 Mobridge USA
101D2 Moçambique Mozam
76C1 Moc Chau Viet
100B3 Mochudi Botswana
101D2 Mocimboa da Praia Mozam
32B3 Mocoa Colombia
35B2 Mococa Brazil
34D2 Mocoreta R Arg
23B1 Moctezuma R Mexico
101C2 Mocuba Mozam
47B2 Modane France
87B1 Modasa India
100B3 Modder R S Africa
52B2 Modena Italy
46D2 Moder R France
8A3 Modesto USA
21A2 Modesto Res USA
53B3 Modica Italy
59B3 Mödling Austria
107D4 Moe Aust
47C1 Moesa R Switz
42C2 Moffat Scot
84D2 Moga India
35B2 Mogi das Cruzes Brazil
60C3 Mogilev Belorussia
60C4 Mogilev Podolskiy Ukraine
35B2 Mogi-Mirim Brazil
101D2 Mogincual Mozam
47E2 Mogliano Italy

34B2 Mogna Arg
68D1 Mogocha Russian Fed
65K4 Mogochin Russian Fed
50A2 Moguer Spain
110C1 Mohaka R NZ
86C2 Mohanganj Bang
15D2 Mohawk R USA
99D3 Mohoro Tanz
65J5 Mointy Kazakhstan
38G5 Mo i Rana Nor
48C3 Moissac France
21B2 Mojave USA
22D3 Mojave R USA
9B3 Mojave Desert USA
78C4 Mojokerto Indon
86B1 Mokama India
110B1 Mokau R NZ
22B1 Mokelumne Aqueduct USA
22B1 Mokelumne Hill USA
22B1 Mokelumne North Fork R USA
101G1 Mokhotlong Lesotho
96D1 Moknine Tunisia
86C1 Mokokchūng India
98B1 Mokolo Cam
74B4 Mokp'o S Korea
61F3 Moksha R Russian Fed
23A1 Molango Mexico
54B2 Molaoi Greece
38F6 Molde Nor
60C4 Moldova Republic, Europe
54B1 Moldoveanu Mt Rom
100B3 Molepolole Botswana
53C2 Molfetta Italy
34A3 Molina Chile
30B2 Mollendo Peru
60C3 Molodechno Belorussia
112C11 Molodezhnaya Base Ant
21C4 Molokai I Hawaiian Is
61G2 Moloma R Russian Fed
109C2 Molong Aust
100B3 Molopo R Botswana
98B2 Molounddu Cam
8D1 Molson L Can
71D4 Molucca S Indon
71D4 Moluccas Is Indon
101C2 Moma Mozam
31C3 Mombaça Brazil
99D3 Mombasa Kenya
98C2 Mompono Zaire
56C2 Mon I Den
44A3 Monach Is Scot
49D3 Monaco Principality, Europe
44B3 Monadhliath Mts Scot
45C1 Monaghan County, Irish Rep
45C1 Monaghan Irish Rep
27D3 Mona Pass Caribbean S
13B2 Monarch Mt Can
5G4 Monashee Mts Can
41B3 Monasterevin Irish Rep
47B2 Moncalieri Italy
31B2 Monção Brazil
38L5 Monchegorsk Russian Fed
56B2 Mönchen-gladbach Germany
24B2 Monclova Mexico
7D5 Moncton Can
9C4 Monctova USA
50A1 Mondego R Port
52A2 Mondovi Italy
27H1 Moneague Jamaica
14C2 Monessen USA
18B2 Monett USA
52B1 Monfalcone Italy

50A1 **Monforte de Lemos**
Spain
98C2 **Monga** Zaïre
98C2 **Mongala** *R* Zaïre
99D2 **Mongalla** Sudan
76D1 **Mong Cai** Viet
98B1 **Mongo** Chad
68B2 **Mongolia** Republic,
Asia
100B2 **Mongu** Zambia
21B2 **Monitor Range** *Mts*
USA
98C3 **Monkoto** Zaïre
43C4 **Monmouth** Eng
18B1 **Monmouth** USA
13C2 **Monmouth,M** Can
97C4 **Mono** *R* Togo
21B2 **Mono L** USA
53C2 **Monopoli** Italy
51B1 **Monreal del Campo**
Spain
19B3 **Monroe** Louisiana,
USA
14B2 **Monroe** Michigan,
USA
20B1 **Monroe** Washington,
USA
18B2 **Monroe City** USA
97A4 **Monrovia** Lib
20D3 **Monrovia** USA
56A2 **Mons** Belg
47D2 **Monselice** Italy
16C1 **Monson** USA
58B1 **Mönsterås** Sweden
101D2 **Montagne d'Ambre**
Mt Madag
96C1 **Montagnes des Ouled
Naïl** *Mts* Alg
12E3 **Montague I** USA
49C3 **Mont Aigoual** *Mt*
France
48B2 **Montaigu** France
53C3 **Montalto** *Mt* Italy
8B2 **Montana** State, USA
50A1 **Montañas de León**
Mts Spain
49C2 **Montargis** France
48C3 **Montauban** France
15D2 **Montauk** USA
15D2 **Montauk Pt** USA
49D2 **Montbéliard** France
52A1 **Mont Blanc** *Mt*
France/Italy
49C2 **Montceau les Mines**
France
51C1 **Montceny** *Mt* Spain
49D3 **Mont Cinto** *Mt*
Corse
46C2 **Montcornet** France
48B3 **Mont-de-Marsan**
France
48C2 **Montdidier** France
30D2 **Monteagudo** Bol
33G4 **Monte Alegre** Brazil
52B2 **Monte Amiata** *Mt*
Italy
47D2 **Monte Baldo** *Mt* Italy
15C1 **Montebello** USA
106A3 **Monte Bello Is** Aust
47E2 **Montebelluna** Italy
49D3 **Monte Carlo** Monaco
35B1 **Monte Carmelo**
Brazil
34D2 **Monte Caseros** Arg
52B2 **Monte Cimone** *Mt*
Italy
52A2 **Monte Cinto** *Mt*
Corse
34B2 **Monte Coman** Arg
52B2 **Monte Corno** *Mt*
Italy
27C3 **Montecristi**
Dom Rep
52B2 **Montecristo** *I* Italy
23A1 **Monte Escobedo**
Mexico
53C2 **Monte Gargano** *Mt*
Italy
26B3 **Montego Bay**
Jamaica
47D2 **Monte Grappa** *Mt*
Italy
47C2 **Monte Lesima** *Mt*
Italy

49C3 **Montélimar** France
53B2 **Monte Miletto** *Mt*
Italy
50A2 **Montemo-o-Novo**
Port
24C2 **Montemorelos**
Mexico
26B5 **Montená** Colombia
54A2 **Montenegro**
Republic, Yugos
35D1 **Monte Pascoal** *Mt*
Brazil
34A2 **Monte Patria** Chile
53C3 **Monte Pollino** *Mt*
Italy
101C2 **Montepuez** Mozam
8A3 **Monterey** California,
USA
15C3 **Monterey** Virginia,
USA
8A3 **Monterey B** USA
32B2 **Monteria** Colombia
30D2 **Montero** Bol
47B2 **Monte Rosa** *Mt* Italy/
Switz
24B2 **Monterrey** Mexico
31C5 **Montes Claros** Brazil
50B2 **Montes de Toledo**
Mts Spain
29E2 **Montevideo** Urug
52A2 **Monte Viso** *Mt* Italy
27P2 **Mont Gimie** *Mt* St
Lucia
11B3 **Montgomery**
Alabama, USA
96C2 **Mont Gréboun** Niger
46C2 **Montherme** France
47B1 **Monthey** Switz
19B3 **Monticello** Arkansas,
USA
16B2 **Monticello** New York,
USA
9C3 **Monticello** Utah,
USA
53A2 **Monti del
Gennargentu** *Mt*
Sardegna
47D2 **Monti Lessini** *Mts*
Italy
53B3 **Monti Nebrodi** *Mts*
Italy
7C5 **Mont-Laurier** Can
7C5 **Montluçon** France
46C2 **Montmédy** France
49C3 **Mont Mézenc** *Mt*
France
46B2 **Montmirail** France
50B2 **Montoro** Spain
49D3 **Mont Pelat** *Mt*
France
14B2 **Montpelier** Ohio,
USA
10C2 **Montpelier** Vermont,
USA
49C3 **Montpellier** France
7C5 **Montréal** Can
48C1 **Montreuil** France
52A1 **Montreux** Switz
47B1 **Mont Risoux** *Mt*
France
8C3 **Montrose** Colorado,
USA
40C2 **Montrose** Scot
48B2 **Mont-St-Michel**
France
96B1 **Monts des Ksour** *Mts*
Alg
51C3 **Monts des Ouled Neil**
Mts Alg
51C2 **Monts du Hodna** *Mts*
Alg
27E3 **Montserrat** *I*
Caribbean S
10C1 **Monts Otish** *Mts*
Can
12B1 **Monument Mt** USA
9B3 **Monument V** USA
98C2 **Monveda** Zaïre
76B1 **Monywa** Burma
52A1 **Monza** Italy
100B2 **Monze** Zambia
101H1 **Mooi** *R* S Africa
101G1 **Mooi River** S Africa

108B1 **Mooma** Aust
109D2 **Moonbi Range** *Mts*
Aust
108B1 **Moonda L** Aust
109D1 **Moonie** Aust
109C1 **Moonie** *R* Aust
108A2 **Moonta** Aust
106A4 **Moora** Aust
108A3 **Moore,L** Aust
42C2 **Moorfoot Hills** Scot
8D2 **Moorhead** USA
22C3 **Moorpark** USA
7B4 **Moose** *R* Can
5H4 **Moose Jaw** Can
5H4 **Moosomin** Can
7B4 **Moosonee** Can
16D2 **Moosup** USA
101C2 **Mopeia** Mozam
97B3 **Mopti** Mali
30B2 **Moquegua** Peru
39G6 **Mora** Sweden
31D3 **Morada** Brazil
83B1 **Morādābād** India
35B1 **Morada Nova de
Minas** *L* Brazil
101D2 **Morafenobe** Madag
101D2 **Moramanga** Madag
27J2 **Morant Bay** Jamaica
27J2 **Morant Pt** Jamaica
87B3 **Moratuwa** Sri Lanka
59B3 **Morava** *R* Austria/
Slovakia
54B2 **Morava** *R* Serbia,
Yugos
90C2 **Moraveh Tappeh** Iran
40C2 **Moray Firth** *Estuary*
Scot
47C1 **Morbegno** Italy
85C4 **Morbi** India
93D2 **Mor Dağ** *Mt* Turk
5J2 **Morden** Can
61F3 **Mordovskaya
Respublika,**
Russian Fed
42C2 **Morecambe** Eng
42C2 **Morecambe B** Eng
107D3 **Moree** Aust
14B3 **Morehead** USA
47C1 **Mörel** Switz
24B3 **Morelia** Mexico
23B2 **Morelos** State,
Mexico
85D3 **Morena** India
5E4 **Moresby I** Can
109D1 **Moreton I** Aust
46B2 **Moreuil** France
47B1 **Morez** France
19B4 **Morgan City** USA
74E2 **Morgan Hill** USA
14C3 **Morgantown** USA
101G1 **Morgenzon** S Africa
47B1 **Morges** Switz
46B2 **Morhange** France
74E2 **Mori** Japan
27K1 **Moriatio** Tobago
13B2 **Morice L** Can
13E2 **Morinville** Can
74E3 **Morioka** Japan
109D2 **Morisset** Aust
83D1 **Morkoka** *R*
Russian Fed
48B2 **Morlaix** France
27Q2 **Morne Diablotin** *Mt*
Dominica
106C2 **Mornington** *I* Aust
85B3 **Moro** Pak
96B2 **Morocco** Kingdom,
Africa
79B4 **Moro G** Phil
99D3 **Morogoro** Tanz
23A1 **Moroleon** Mexico
101D3 **Morombe** Madag
26B2 **Morón** Cuba
101D3 **Morondava** Madag
50A2 **Moron de la Frontera**
Spain
101D2 **Moroni** Comoros
71P3 **Morotai** *I* Indon
99D2 **Moroto** Uganda
61F4 **Morozovsk**
Russian Fed
42D2 **Morpeth** Eng
19B2 **Morrilton** USA
35B1 **Morrinhos** Brazil

110C1 **Morrinsville** NZ
16B2 **Morristown** New
Jersey, USA
15C2 **Morristown** New
York, USA
16B2 **Morrisville**
Pennsylvania, USA
21A2 **Morro Bay** USA
23A2 **Morro de Papanoa**
Mexico
23A2 **Morro de Petatlán**
Mexico
101C2 **Morrumbala** Mozam
101C3 **Morrumbene** Mozam
61F3 **Morshansk**
Russian Fed
47C2 **Mortara** Italy
34C2 **Morteros** Arg
33G6 **Mortes** *R* Mato
Grosso, Brazil
35C2 **Mortes** *R* Minas
Gerais, Brazil
108B3 **Mortlake** Aust
27L1 **Moruga** Trinidad
109D3 **Moruya** Aust
109C1 **Morven** Aust
109C3 **Morwell** Aust
76B3 **Moscos Is** Burma
Moscow = Moskva
20C1 **Moscow** Idaho, USA
56B2 **Mosel** *R* Germany
46D2 **Moselle** Department,
France
46D2 **Moselle** *R* France
52B1 **Moses Lake** USA
111B3 **Mosgiel** NZ
99D3 **Moshi** Tanz
38G5 **Mosjøen** Nor
63G2 **Moskal'vo**
Russian Fed
64E4 **Moskva** Russian Fed
35C1 **Mosquito** *R* Brazil
39G7 **Moss** Nor
98B3 **Mossaka** Congo
100B4 **Mossel Bay** S Africa
98B3 **Mossendjo** Congo
108B2 **Mossgiel** Aust
31D3 **Mossoró** Brazil
59B2 **Most** Czech Republic
96C1 **Mostaganem** Alg
54A2 **Mostar** Bosnia-
Herzegovina
58C2 **Mosty** Belorussia
Mosul = Al Mawşil
39H7 **Motala** Sweden
42C2 **Motherwell** Scot
86A1 **Motīhāri** India
51B2 **Motilla del Palancar**
Spain
50B2 **Motril** Spain
111B2 **Motueka** NZ
111B2 **Motueka** *R* NZ
87D3 **Moudon** Switz
98B3 **Mouila** Gabon
108B2 **Moulamein** Aust
4G2 **Mould Bay** Can
49C2 **Moulins** France
76B2 **Moulmein** Burma
96B1 **Moulouya** *R* Mor
17B1 **Moultrie** USA
17C1 **Moultrie,L** USA
18C2 **Mound City** Illinois,
USA
18A1 **Mound City** Missouri,
USA
98B2 **Moundou** Chad
14B3 **Moundsville** USA
12J1 **Mountain** *R* Can
17A1 **Mountain Brook** USA
18B2 **Mountain Grove**
USA
18B2 **Mountain Home**
Arkansas, USA
22A2 **Mountain View** USA
12B2 **Mountain Village**
USA
16A3 **Mount Airy**
Maryland, USA
16A2 **Mount Carmel** USA
108A1 **Mount Dutton** Aust
108A2 **Mount Eba** Aust
108B3 **Mount Gambier** Aust
16B3 **Mount Holly** USA

Mount Holly Springs

16A2 Mount Holly Springs USA
108A2 Mount Hope Aust
106C3 Mount Isa Aust
108A2 Mount Lofty Range Mts Aust
12D2 Mount McKinley Nat Pk USA
106A3 Mount Magnet Aust
108B2 Mount Manara Aust
107E3 Mount Morgan Aust
19B3 Mount Pleasant Texas, USA
20B1 Mount Rainier Nat Pk USA
43B4 Mounts B Eng
20B2 Mount Shasta USA
11B3 Mount Vernon Illinois, USA
19A3 Mount Vernon Kentucky, USA
20B1 Mount Vernon Washington, USA
45C1 Mourne Mts N Ire
98B1 Moussoro Chad
86B2 Mouths of the Ganga India/Bang
85B4 Mouths of the Indus Pak
77D4 Mouths of the Mekong Viet
97C4 Mouths of the Niger Nig
47B1 Moutier Switz
47B2 Moûtiers France
96C2 Mouydir Mts Alg
98B3 Mouyondzi Congo
46C2 Mouzon France
59B3 M'óvár Hung
23A1 Moyahua Mexico
99D2 Moyale Kenya
97A4 Moyamba Sierra Leone
96B1 Moyen Atlas Mts Mor
100B4 Moyeni Lesotho
99D2 Moyo Uganda
32B5 Moyobamba Peru
84D1 Moyu China
101C3 Mozambique Republic, Africa
101C3 Mozambique Chan Mozam/Madag
61H2 Mozhga Russian Fed
60C3 Mozyr' Belorussia
99D3 Mpanda Tanz
101C2 Mpika Zambia
99D3 Mporokoso Zambia
100B2 Mposhi Zambia
100B2 Mpulungu Zambia
99D3 Mpwapwa Tanz
60E3 Mtsensk Russian Fed
101H1 Mtubatuba S Africa
101D2 Mtwara Tanz
76C2 Muang Chainat Thai
76C2 Muang Chiang Rai Thai
76C2 Muang Kalasin Thai
76C2 Muang Khon Kaen Thai
76B2 Muang Lampang Thai
76B2 Muang Lamphun Thai
76C2 Muang Loei Thai
76C2 Muang Lom Sak Thai
76C2 Muang Nakhon Phanom Thai
76B2 Muang Nakhon Sawan Thai
76C2 Muang Nan Thai
76C2 Muang Phayao Thai
76C2 Muang Phetchabun Thai
76C2 Muang Phichit Thai
76C2 Muang Phitsanulok Thai
76C2 Muang Phrae Thai
76C2 Muang Roi Et Thai
76C2 Muang Sakon Nakhon Thai
76C3 Muang Samut Prakan Thai

76C2 Muang Uthai Thani Thai
76C2 Muang Yasothon Thai
77C5 Muar Malay
78C2 Muara Brunei
70B4 Muara Indon
78A3 Muaralakitan Indon
78A3 Muaratebo Indon
78C3 Muaratewah Indon
78A3 Muarenim Indon
76A2 Muaungmaya Burma
99D2 Mubende Uganda
100C2 Muchinga Mts Zambia
44A3 Muck I Scot
109C1 Muckadilla Aust
100B2 Muconda Angola
35D1 Mucuri Brazil
35C1 Mucuri R Brazil
100B2 Mucusso Angola
69E2 Mudanjiang China
109C2 Mudgee Aust
76B2 Mudon Burma
101C2 Mueda Mozam
107F3 Mueo Nouvelle Calédonie
100B2 Mufulira Zambia
73C4 Mufu Shan Hills China
Mugdishu = Muqdisho
93C4 Mugharra S Arabia
92A2 Mugla Turk
65G5 Mugodzhary Mts Kazakhstan
73A3 Mugueping China
93D3 Muhaywir Iraq
57C3 Mühldorf Germany
57C2 Mühlhausen Germany
38K6 Muhos Fin
77C4 Mui Bai Bung C Camb
45C2 Muine Bheag Irish Rep
100B2 Mujimbeji Zambia
59C3 Mukachevo Ukraine
78C2 Mukah Malay
69G4 Muko-jima I Japan
86A1 Muktinath Nepal
84B2 Mukur Afghan
18B2 Mulberry USA
12C2 Mulchatna R USA
34A3 Mulchén Chile
56C2 Mulde R Germany
71F5 Mulgrave I Aust
50B2 Mulhacén Mt Spain
46D1 Mülheim Germany
49D2 Mulhouse France
73A4 Muli China
44B3 Mull I Scot
83C4 Mullaitvu Sri Lanka
109C2 Mullaley Aust
106A3 Mullewa Aust
16B3 Mullica R USA
45C2 Mullingar Irish Rep
42B2 Mull of Kintyre Pt Scotland
44C5 Mull of Oa C Scot
109D1 Mullumbimby Aust
100B2 Mulobezi Zambia
84C2 Multan Pak
Mumbai = Bombay
100B2 Mumbwa Zambia
61G4 Mumra Russian Fed
71D4 Muna I Indon
57C3 München Germany
14A2 Muncie USA
15C2 Muncy USA
56B2 Münden Germany
109D1 Mundubbera Aust
109C1 Mungallala Aust
109C1 Mungallala R Aust
99C2 Mungbere Zaïre
86A2 Mungeli India
86B1 Munger India
109C1 Mungindi Aust
Munich = München
14A1 Munising USA
29B6 Muñoz Gomero,Pen Chile
45B2 Munster Region, Irish Rep

47C1 Münster Switz
56B2 Münster Germany
54B1 Muntii Apuseni Mts Rom
54B1 Muntii Călimanilor Mts Rom
54B1 Muntii Carpații Meridionali Mts Rom
54B1 Muntii Rodnei Mts Rom
54B1 Muntii Zarandului Mts Rom
100B2 Munyati R Zim
93C2 Munzur Silsilesi Mts Turk
64D3 Muomio Fin
76C1 Muong Khoua Laos
76D3 Muong Man Viet
76D2 Muong Nong Laos
76C1 Muong Ou Neua Laos
76C1 Muong Sai Laos
76C2 Muong Sen Viet
76C1 Muong Sing Laos
76C1 Muong Son Laos
38J5 Muonio Fin
38J5 Muonio R Sweden/Fin
99E2 Muqdisho Somalia
52B1 Mur R Austria
74D3 Murakami Japan
29B5 Murallón Mt Arg/Chile
61G2 Murashi Russian Fed
93D2 Murat R Turk
53A3 Muravera Sardegna
75C1 Murayama Japan
90B3 Murcheh Khvort Iran
111B2 Murchison NZ
106A3 Murchison R Aust
51B2 Murcia Region, Spain
51B2 Murcia Spain
54B1 Mures R Rom
46E2 Murg R Germany
65H6 Murgab R Turkmenistan
84B2 Murgha Kibzai Pak
109D1 Murgon Aust
86B2 Muri India
35C2 Muriaé Brazil
98C3 Muriege Angola
64E3 Murmansk Russian Fed
61F2 Murom Russian Fed
74E2 Muroran Japan
50A1 Muros Spain
74C4 Muroto Japan
75A2 Muroto-zaki C Japan
20C2 Murphy Idaho, USA
22B1 Murphys USA
14A2 Murray Kentucky, USA
108B2 Murray R Aust
13C2 Murray R Can
108A3 Murray Bridge Aust
71F4 Murray,L PNG
17B1 Murray,L USA
105J2 Murray Seacarp Pacific C
108B2 Murrumbidgee R Aust
109C2 Murrumburrah Aust
109D2 Murrurundi Aust
84C2 Murwara India
109D1 Murwillumbah Aust
93D2 Muş Turk
54B2 Musala Mt Bulg
74B2 Musan N Korea
91C4 Musandam Pen Oman
Muscat = Masqat
91C5 Muscat Region, Oman
106C3 Musgrave Range Mts Aust
98B3 Mushie Zaïre
14A2 Muskegon USA
14A2 Muskegon R USA
18A2 Muskogee USA
15C2 Muskoka,L Can
95C3 Musmar Sudan

99D3 Musoma Tanz
8C2 Musselshell R USA
100A2 Mussende Angola
48C2 Mussidan France
55C2 Mustafa-Kemalpasa Turk
86A1 Mustang Nepal
109D2 Muswellbrook Aust
95B2 Mut Egypt
101C2 Mutarara Mozam
101C2 Mutare Zim
101C2 Mutoko Zim
101D2 Mutsamudu Comoros
100B2 Mutshatsha Zaïre
74E2 Mutsu Japan
74E2 Mutsu-wan B Japan
45B2 Mutton I Irish Rep
72B2 Mu Us Shamo Desert China
98B3 Muxima Angola
63D2 Muya Russian Fed
38L6 Mayezerskiy Russian Fed
99D3 Muyinga Burundi
98C3 Muyumba Zaïre
82A1 Muyun Kum Desert Kazakhstan
84C2 Muzaffarabad Pak
84C2 Muzaffargarh Pak
84D3 Muzaffarnagar India
86B1 Muzaffarpur India
64H3 Muzhi Russian Fed
82C2 Muztag Mt China
82B2 Muztagata Mt China
100C2 Mvuma Zim
99D3 Mwanza Tanz
98C3 Mwanza Zaïre
98C3 Mweka Zaïre
98C3 Mwene Ditu Zaïre
100C3 Mwenezi Zim
99C3 Mwenga Zaïre
99C3 Mweru L Zambia
100B2 Mwinilunga Zambia
83D4 Myanaung Burma
Myanma = Burma
86D2 Myingyan Burma
76B1 Myingyao Burma
76B3 Myinmoletkat Mt Burma
82D3 Myitkyina Burma
76B3 Myitta Burma
86C2 Mymensingh Bang
69F3 Myojin I Japan
39F6 Myrdal Nor
38B2 Myrdalsjökul Ice Cap Iceland
17C1 Myrtle Beach USA
20B2 Myrtle Creek USA
39G7 Mysen Nor
56C2 Mýsliborz Pol
64F3 Mys Kanin Nos C Russian Fed
59B3 Myślenice Pol
69H1 Mys Lopatka C Russian Fed
87B2 Mysore India
60D5 Mys Sarych C Ukraine
16D2 Mystic USA
61H5 Mys Tyub-Karagan Pt Kazakhstan
63G2 Mys Yelizavety C Russian Fed
64H2 Mys Zhelaniya C Russian Fed
77D3 My Tho Viet
20B2 Mytle Point USA
101C2 Mzimba Malawi
101C2 Mzuzu Malawi

N

21C4 Naalehu Hawaiian Is
39J6 Naantali Fin
45C2 Naas Irish Rep
75B2 Nabari Japan
61H2 Naberezhnye Chelny Russian Fed
12F2 Nabesna R USA
96D1 Nabeul Tunisia
94B2 Nablus Israel
101D2 Nacala Mozam
20B1 Naches USA
101C2 Nachingwea Tanz

19B3 **Nacogdoches** USA
76A3 **Nacondam** /
  Indian O
24B1 **Nacozari** Mexico
85C4 **Nadiād** India
50B2 **Nador** Mor
90B3 **Nadūshan** Iran
59C3 **Nadvornaya** Ukraine
56C1 **Naestved** Den
95B2 **Näfūrah** Libya
75A2 **Nagahama** Japan
82D3 **Naga Hills** Burma
75B1 **Nagai** Japan
86C1 **Nāgaland** State, India
74D3 **Nagano** Japan
74D3 **Nagaoka** Japan
86C1 **Nagaon** India
87B2 **Nāgappattinam** India
85C4 **Nagar Parkar** Pak
/4B4 **Nagasaki** Japan
75B2 **Nagashima** Japan
82D3 **Nagato** Japan
85C3 **Nāgaur** India
87B3 **Nāgercoil** India
85B3 **Nagha Kalat** Pak
84D3 **Nagina** India
74D3 **Nagoya** Japan
85D4 **Nāgpur** India
82D2 **Nagqu** China
59B3 **Nagykanizsa** Hung
59B3 **Nagykörös** Hung
69E4 **Naha** Japan
8A2 **Nahaimo** Can
84D2 **Nahan** India
4F3 **Nahanni Butte** Can
87A2 **Nahariya** Israel
90A3 **Nahāvand** Iran
46D2 **Nahe** R Germany
72D2 **Nahpu** China
72E1 **Naimen Qi** China
7D4 **Nain** Can
90B3 **Nā'īn** Iran
84D3 **Naini Tāl** India
44C3 **Nairn** Scot
99D3 **Nairobi** Kenya
90B3 **Najafābād** Iran
74C2 **Najin** N Korea
75A2 **Nakama** Japan
75A2 **Nakamura** Japan
75B1 **Nakano** Japan
75A1 **Nakano-shima** /
  Japan
74C4 **Nakatsu** Japan
75B1 **Nakatsu-gawa**
  Japan
95C3 **Nak' fa** Eritrea
93E2 **Nakhichevan**
  Azerbaijan
92B4 **Nakhl** Egypt
74C2 **Nakhodka**
  Russian Fed
76C3 **Nakhon Pathom** Thai
76C3 **Nakhon Ratchasima**
  Thai
77C4 **Nakhon Si**
  Thammarat Thai
12H3 **Nakina** Can
7B4 **Nakina** Ontario, Can
12C3 **Naknek** USA
4C4 **Nakrek** USA
39G8 **Nakskov** Den
99D3 **Nakuru** Kenya
13D2 **Nakusp** Can
61F5 **Nal'chik** Russian Fed
87B1 **Nalgonda** India
87B1 **Nallamala Range** Mts
  India
95A1 **Nālūt** Libya
101H1 **Namaacha** Mozam
65G6 **Namak, L** Iran
90C3 **Namakzar-e Shadad**
  Salt Flat Iran
66J5 **Namangan**
  Uzbekistan
101C2 **Namapa** Mozam
100A4 **Namaqualand**
  Region, S Africa
109D1 **Nambour** Aust
109D2 **Nambucca Heads**
  Aust
77D4 **Nam Can** Viet
82D2 **Nam Co** L China

76D1 **Nam Dinh** Viet
101C2 **Nametil** Mozam
74B4 **Namhae-do** / S
  Korea
100A2 **Namib Desert**
  Namibia
100A2 **Namibe** Angola
100A3 **Namibia** Republic,
  Africa
82D3 **Namjagbarwa Feng**
  Mt China
71D4 **Namlea** Indon
109C2 **Namoi** R Aust
13D1 **Nampa** Can
20C2 **Nampa** USA
97B3 **Nampala** Mali
76C2 **Nam Phong** Thai
74D3 **Namp'o** N Korea
101C2 **Nampula** Mozam
38G6 **Namsos** Nor
76B1 **Namton** Burma
86D2 **Namtu** Burma
13B2 **Namu** Can
101C2 **Namuno** Mozam
46C1 **Namur** Belg
100A2 **Namutoni** Namibia
74B3 **Namwon** S Korea
13C3 **Nanaimo** Can
74B2 **Nanam** N Korea
109D1 **Nanango** Aust
74D3 **Nanao** Japan
75B1 **Nanatsu-jima** /
  Japan
73B3 **Nanbu** China
73D4 **Nanchang** China
73D3 **Nanchong** China
49D2 **Nancy** France
87B1 **Nānded** India
109D2 **Nandewar Range**
  Mts Aust
85C4 **Nandurbar** India
87B1 **Nandyāl** India
98B2 **Nanga Eboko** Cam
84C1 **Nanga Parbat** Mt
  Pak
78C3 **Nangapinoh** Indon
78C3 **Nangatayap** Indon
74B2 **Nangnim Sanmaek**
  Mts N Korea
73B3 **Nang Xian** China
67F3 **Nangzhou** China
87B2 **Nanjangūd** India
72D3 **Nanjing** China
  Nanking = **Nanjing**
75A2 **Nankoku** Japan
73C4 **Nan Ling** Region,
  China
73D1 **Nanliu** R China
73B5 **Nanning** China
6F3 **Nanortalik**
  Greenland
73A5 **Nanpan Jiang** R
  China
86A1 **Nānpāra** India
73D4 **Nanping** China
6A1 **Nansen Sd** Can
99D3 **Nansio** Tanz
48B2 **Nantes** France
13E2 **Nanton** Can
72E3 **Nantong** China
10C2 **Nantucket** / USA
35C1 **Nanuque** Brazil
72C3 **Nanyang** China
72D2 **Nanyang Hu** L
  China
99D2 **Nanyuki** Kenya
74D3 **Naoetsu** Japan
85B4 **Naokot** Pak
22A1 **Napa** USA
12B2 **Napaiskak** USA
15C2 **Napanee** Can
65K4 **Napas** Russian Fed
6E3 **Napassoq** Greenland
76D2 **Nape** Laos
110C1 **Napier** NZ
  Naples = **Napoli**
17B2 **Naples** Florida, USA
19D3 **Naples** Texas, USA
73B5 **Napo** China
32C4 **Napo** R Peru/
  Ecuador
53B2 **Napoli** Italy
90A2 **Naqadeh** Iran
92C4 **Naqb Ishtar** Jordan

75B2 **Nara** Japan
97B3 **Nara** Mali
107D4 **Naracoorte** Aust
23B1 **Naranjos** Mexico
87C1 **Narasaraopet** India
77C4 **Narathiwat** Thai
86C2 **Nārāyanganj** Bang
87B1 **Narayenpet** India
49C3 **Narbonne** France
84D2 **Narendranagar**
  India
6C2 **Nares Str** Can
58C2 **Narew** R Pol
75C1 **Narita** Japan
85C4 **Narmada** R India
84D3 **Nārnaul** India
60E2 **Naro Fominsk**
  Russian Fed
99D3 **Narok** Kenya
84C2 **Narowal** Pak
107D4 **Narrabri** Aust
109C1 **Narran** L Aust
109C2 **Narran** R Aust
109C2 **Narrandera** Aust
106A4 **Narrogin** Aust
109C2 **Narromine** Aust
85D4 **Narsimhapur** India
87C1 **Narsīpatnam** India
6F3 **Narssalik** Greenland
6F3 **Narssaq** Greenland
6F3 **Narsarssuaq**
  Greenland
75C1 **Narugo** Japan
75A2 **Naruto** Japan
60C2 **Narva** Russian Fed
38H5 **Narvik** Nor
84D3 **Narwāna** India
64G3 **Nar'yan Mar**
  Russian Fed
108B1 **Naryilco** Aust
65J5 **Naryn** Kirghizia
97C4 **Nasarawa** Nig
102D5 **Nasca Ridge**
  Pacific O
16D1 **Nashua** USA
19B3 **Nashville** Arkansas,
  USA
11B3 **Nashville** Tennessee,
  USA
54A1 **Našice** Croatia
85D4 **Nāsik** India
99D2 **Nasir** Sudan
13B1 **Nass** R Can
26B1 **Nassau**
  The Bahamas
16C1 **Nassau** USA
95C2 **Nasser,L** Egypt
39G7 **Nässjö** Sweden
7C4 **Nastapoca Is** Can
100B3 **Nata** Botswana
31D3 **Natal** Brazil
70A3 **Natal** Indon
90B3 **Natanz** Iran
7D4 **Nashquan** Can
7D4 **Natashquan** R Can
19B3 **Natchez** USA
19B3 **Natchitoches** USA
108C3 **Nathalia** Aust
  6H2 **Nathorsts Land**
  Region Greenland
13C1 **Nation** R Can
21B3 **National City** USA
75C1 **Natori** Japan
99D3 **Natron** L Tanz
106A4 **Naturaliste,C** Aust
47D1 **Nauders** Austria
57C3 **Nauen** Germany
16C2 **Naugatuck** USA
57C2 **Naumburg** Germany
94B3 **Naur** Jordan
105G4 **Nauru** / Pacific O
63C2 **Naushki** Russian Fed
23B1 **Nautla** Mexico
9C3 **Navajo Res** USA
50A2 **Navalmoral de la
  Mata** Spain
29C7 **Navarino** / Chile
51B1 **Navarra** Province,
  Spain
34D3 **Navarro** Arg
19A3 **Navasota** USA
19A3 **Navasota** R USA
50A1 **Navia** R Spain
34A2 **Navidad** Chile

85C4 **Navlakhi** India
60D3 **Navlya** Russian Fed
55B3 **Návpaktos** Greece
55B3 **Návplion** Greece
85C4 **Navsāri** India
94C2 **Nawá** Syria
86B2 **Nawāda** India
84B2 **Nawah** Afghan
85B3 **Nawrabshah** Pak
73B4 **Naxi** China
55C3 **Náxos** / Greece
23A1 **Nayar** Mexico
90C3 **Nāy Band** Iran
91B4 **Nāy Band** Iran
74E2 **Nayoro** Japan
94B2 **Nazareth** Israel
48B2 **Nazay** France
32C6 **Nazca** Peru
92A2 **Nazilli** Turk
63B2 **Nazimovo**
  Russian Fed
13C2 **Nazko** R Can
99D2 **Nazret** Eth
91C5 **Nazwa** Oman
65J4 **Nazyvayevsk**
  Russian Fed
98B3 **Ndalatando** Angola
98C2 **Ndélé** CAR
98B3 **Ndendé** Gabon
98B2 **Ndjamena** Chad
98B3 **Ndjolé** Gabon
100B2 **Ndola** Zambia
109C1 **Neabul** Aust
108A1 **Neales** R Aust
55B3 **Neápolis** Greece
43C4 **Neath** Wales
109C1 **Nebine** R Aust
65G6 **Nebit Dag**
  Turkmenistan
8C2 **Nebraska** State, USA
18A1 **Nebraska City** USA
13C2 **Nechako** R Can
34D3 **Necochea** Arg
86C1 **Nedong** China
9B3 **Needles** USA
14A2 **Neenah** USA
46C1 **Neepawa** Can
46C1 **Neerpelt** Belg
63C2 **Neftelensk**
  Russian Fed
99D2 **Negele** Eth
94B3 **Negev** Desert Israel
60B4 **Negolu** Mt Rom
87B3 **Negombo** Sri Lanka
76A2 **Negrais,C** Burma
32A4 **Negritos** Peru
33E4 **Negro** R Amazonas,
  Brazil
29C4 **Negro** R Arg
34D2 **Negro** R Urug
79B4 **Negros** / Phil
54C2 **Negru Vodă** Rom
90D3 **Nehbandān** Iran
73B4 **Neijiang** China
72B1 **Nei Monggol**
  Autonomous Region,
  China
32B3 **Neiva** Colombia
99D2 **Nejo** Eth
99D2 **Nek'emte** Eth
60D2 **Neledovo**
  Russian Fed
87B2 **Nellore** India
69F2 **Nel'ma** Russian Fed
13D3 **Nelson** Can
111B2 **Nelson** NZ
7A4 **Nelson** R Can
108B3 **Nelson,C** Aust
12B2 **Nelson** I USA
97B3 **Nelson** Mali
72A1 **Nemagt Uul** Mt
  Mongolia
58C1 **Neman** R Lithuania
54C1 **Nemira** Mt Rom
74F2 **Nemuro** Japan
63E3 **Nen** R China
41B3 **Nenagh** Irish Rep
12E2 **Nenana** USA
12E2 **Nenana** R USA
43D3 **Nene** R Eng
69E2 **Nenjiang** China
18A2 **Neodesha** USA

Neosho

18B2 **Neosho** USA
63C2 **Nepa** Russian Fed
82C3 **Nepal** Kingdom, Asia
86A1 **Nepalganj** Nepal
45B1 **Nephin** Mt Irish Rep
94B3 **Neqarot** R Israel
34A3 **Nequén** State, Arg
68D1 **Nerchinsk**
       Russian Fed
52C2 **Neretva** R Bosnia-
       Herzegovina/Croatia
71F2 **Nero Deep** Pacific O
38C1 **Neskaupstaður**
       Iceland
46B2 **Nesle** France
7E5 **Nesleyville** Can
55B2 **Néstos** R Greece
94B2 **Netanya** Israel
16B2 **Netcong** USA
56B2 **Netherlands**
       Kingdom, Europe
3M7 **Netherlands Antilles**
       Is Caribbean S
86C2 **Netrakona** Bang
6C3 **Nettilling L** Can
56C2 **Neubrandenburg**
       Germany
47B1 **Neuchâtel** Switz
46C2 **Neufchâteau** Belg
48C2 **Neufchâtel** France
46A2 **Neufchâtel-en-Bray**
       France
56B2 **Neumünster**
       Germany
52C1 **Neunkirchen** Austria
46D2 **Neunkirchen**
       Germany
34B3 **Neuquén** Arg
29B4 **Neuquén** State, Arg
34B3 **Neuquén** R Arg
56C2 **Neuruppin** Germany
46D1 **Neuss** Germany
46E2 **Neustadt** Germany
56C2 **Neustadt** Germany
46D1 **Neustrelitz** Germany
46D1 **Neuwied** Germany
8B3 **Nevada** State, USA
18B2 **Nevada** USA
34A3 **Nevada de Chillán**
       Mts Arg/Chile
23A2 **Nevada de Colima**
       Mexico
23B2 **Nevada de Toluca** Mt
       Mexico
94B3 **Nevatim** Israel
60C2 **Nevel'** Russian Fed
49C2 **Nevers** France
109C2 **Nevertire** Aust
27E3 **Nevis** I Caribbean S
58D2 **Nevis** R Belorussia/
       Lithuania
92B2 **Nevşehir** Turk
61K2 **Nev'yansk**
       Russian Fed
101C2 **Newala** Tanz
14A3 **New Albany** Indiana,
       USA
19C3 **New Albany**
       Mississippi, USA
33F2 **New Amsterdam**
       Guyana
109C1 **New Angledool** Aust
15C3 **Newark** Delaware,
       USA
10C2 **Newark** New Jersey,
       USA
14B2 **Newark** Ohio, USA
43D3 **Newark-upon-Trent**
       Eng
15D2 **New Bedford** USA
13B2 **New Bella Bella** Can
20B1 **Newberg** USA
11C3 **New Bern** USA
17B1 **Newberry** USA
26B2 **New Bight**
       The Bahamas
14B3 **New Boston** USA
9D4 **New Braunfels** USA
16C2 **New Britain** USA
7D5 **New Brunswick**
       Province, Can
16B2 **New Brunswick** USA
16B2 **Newburgh** USA
43D4 **Newbury** Eng

18B2 **Newburyport** USA
16C2 **New Canaan** USA
109D2 **Newcastle** Aust
14A3 **New Castle** Indiana,
       USA
42B2 **Newcastle** N Ire
14B2 **New Castle**
       Pennsylvania, USA
101G1 **Newcastle** S Africa
8C2 **Newcastle** Wyoming,
       USA
42D2 **Newcastle upon Tyne**
       Eng
106C2 **Newcastle Waters**
       Aust
45B2 **Newcastle West**
       Irish Rep
84D3 **New Delhi** India
109D2 **New England Range**
       Mts Aust
12B3 **Newenham,C** USA
43D4 **New Forest,The** Eng
7D4 **Newfoundland**
       Province, Can
7E5 **Newfoundland** I
       Can
102F2 **Newfoundland Basin**
       Atlantic O
18B2 **New Franklin** USA
42B2 **New Galloway** Scot
107E1 **New Georgia** I
       Solomon Is
7D5 **New Glasgow** Can
71F4 **New Guinea** SE Asia
12D3 **Newhalen** USA
22C3 **Newhall** USA
10C2 **New Hampshire**
       State, USA
101H1 **New Hanover**
       S Africa
43E4 **Newhaven** Eng
15D2 **New Haven** USA
13B1 **New Hazelton** Can
19B3 **New Iberia** USA
10C2 **New Jersey** State,
       USA
7C5 **New Liskeard** Can
16C2 **New London** USA
106A3 **Newman** Aust
22B2 **Newman** USA
43E3 **Newmarket** Eng
45B2 **Newmarket** Irish Rep
15C3 **New Market** USA
9C3 **New Mexico** State,
       USA
16C2 **New Milford**
       Connecticut, USA
17B1 **Newnan** USA
109C4 **New Norfolk** Aust
11A3 **New Orleans** USA
16B2 **New Paltz** USA
14B2 **New Philadelphia**
       USA
110B1 **New Plymouth** NZ
18B2 **Newport** Arkansas,
       USA
43D4 **Newport** Eng
14B3 **Newport** Kentucky,
       USA
20B2 **Newport** Oregon,
       USA
16A2 **Newport**
       Pennsylvania, USA
15D2 **Newport** Rhode
       Island, USA
15D2 **Newport** Vermont,
       USA
43C4 **Newport** Wales
20C1 **Newport**
       Washington, USA
22D4 **Newport Beach** USA
11C3 **Newport News** USA
26B1 **New Providence** I
       Caribbean S
43B4 **Newquay** Eng
6C3 **New Quebec Crater**
       Can
45C2 **New Ross** Irish Rep
45C1 **Newry** N Ire
       New Siberian Is =
       Novosibirskye
       Ostrova
17B2 **New Smyrna Beach**
       USA

107D4 **New South Wales**
       State, Aust
12C3 **New Stuyahok** USA
18A2 **Newton** Kansas,
       USA
16D1 **Newton**
       Massachusetts, USA
19C3 **Newton** Mississippi,
       USA
16B2 **Newton** New York,
       USA
43C4 **Newton Abbot** Eng
45C1 **Newton Stewart**
       N Ire
42B2 **Newton Stewart**
       Scot
43C3 **Newtown** Wales
42B2 **Newtownards** N Ire
16A2 **Newville** USA
5F5 **New Westminster**
       Can
10C2 **New York** State, USA
10C2 **New York** USA
110 **New Zealand**
       Dominion, SW
       Pacific O
105G6 **New Zealand Plat**
       Pacific O
61F2 **Neya** Russian Fed
91B4 **Neyriz** Iran
90C2 **Neyshābūr** Iran
60D3 **Nezhin** Russian Fed
98B3 **Ngabé** Congo
100B3 **Ngami** L Botswana
110C1 **Ngaruawahia** NZ
110C1 **Ngaruroro** R NZ
110C1 **Ngauruhoe,Mt** NZ
98B3 **Ngo** Congo
76D2 **Ngoc Linh** Mt Viet
98B2 **Ngoko** R Cam
98B3 **Ngoring Hu** L China
99D3 **Ngorongoro Crater**
       Tanz
98B3 **N'Gounié** R Gabon
98B1 **Nguigmi** Niger
71E3 **Ngulu** I Pacific O
97D3 **Nguru** Nig
76D3 **Nha Trang** Viet
108B3 **Nhill** Aust
101H1 **Nhlangano**
       Swaziland
76D2 **Nhommarath** Laos
106C2 **Nhulunbuy** Aust
14A1 **Niagara** USA
15C2 **Niagara Falls** Can
15C2 **Niagara Falls** USA
70C3 **Niah** Malay
97B4 **Niakaramandougou**
       Ivory Coast
97C3 **Niamey** Niger
99C2 **Niangara** Zaïre
98C2 **Nia Nia** Zaïre
70A3 **Nias** I Indon
25D3 **Nicaragua** Republic,
       Cent America
53C3 **Nicastro** Italy
49D3 **Nice** France
26B1 **Nicholl's Town**
       The Bahamas
83D5 **Nicobar Is** Indian O
92B2 **Nicosia** Cyprus
25D3 **Nicoya,Pen de**
       Costa Rica
58C2 **Nidzica** Pol
46D2 **Niederbronn** France
56B2 **Niedersachsen** State,
       Germany
99C3 **Niemba** Zaïre
56B2 **Nienburg** Germany
46D1 **Niers** R Germany
97B4 **Niete,Mt** Lib
33F2 **Nieuw Amsterdam**
       Surinam
33F2 **Nieuw Nickerie**
       Surinam
46B1 **Nieuwpoort** Belg
92B2 **Niğde** Turk
97C3 **Niger** Republic,
       Africa
97C4 **Niger** R Nig
97C4 **Nigeria** Federal
       Republic, Africa
55B2 **Nigríta** Greece

75C1 **Nihommatsu** Japan
74D3 **Niigata** Japan
74C4 **Niihama** Japan
75B2 **Nii-jima** I Japan
75A2 **Niimi** Japan
74D3 **Niitsu** Japan
94B3 **Nijil** Jordan
56B2 **Nijmegen** Neth
64E3 **Nikel'** Russian Fed
97C3 **Nikki** Benin
74D3 **Nikko** Japan
60D4 **Nikolayev** Ukraine
61G4 **Nikolayevsk**
       Russian Fed
63G2 **Nikolayevsk-na-**
       Amure Russian Fed
61G3 **Nikol'sk** Russian Fed
61G3 **Nikol'sk** Russian Fed
60D4 **Nikopol** Ukraine
92C1 **Niksar** Turk
91D4 **Nīkshahr** Iran
54A2 **Nikšic** Montenegro,
       Yugos
71D4 **Nila** I Indon
80B3 **Nile** R N E Africa
14A2 **Niles** USA
87B2 **Nilgiri Hills** India
85C4 **Nimach** India
49C3 **Nîmes** France
109C3 **Nimmitabel** Aust
99D2 **Nimule** Sudan
83B5 **Nine Degree Chan**
       Indian O
104C4 **Ninety-East Ridge**
       Indian O
109C3 **Ninety Mile Beach**
       Aust
73D4 **Ningde** China
73D4 **Ningdu** China
68B3 **Ningjing Shan** Mts
       China
76D1 **Ningming** China
73A4 **Ningnan** China
72B2 **Ningxia** Province,
       China
72B2 **Ning Xian** China
73B5 **Ninh Binh** Vietnam
107D1 **Ninigo Is** PNG
12C2 **Ninilchik** USA
8D2 **Niobrara** R USA
98B3 **Nioki** Zaïre
97B3 **Nioro du Sahel** Mali
48B2 **Niort** France
5H4 **Nipawin** Can
7B5 **Nipigon,L** Can
7B5 **Nipigon,L** Can
7B5 **Nipissing** R Can
14B1 **Nipissing,L** Can
8B3 **Nipton** USA
86B1 **Nirmāli** India
86B1 **Nirmāli** India
54B2 **Niš** Serbia, Yugos
81C4 **Nisāb** Yemen
69F4 **Nishino-shima** I
       Japan
75A1 **Nishino-shima** I
       Japan
75A2 **Nishiwaki** Japan
12J2 **Nisling** R Can
12H2 **Nisutlin** R Can
7C4 **Nitchequon** Can
31C6 **Niterói** Brazil
42C2 **Nith** R Scot
59B3 **Nitra** Slovakia
14B3 **Nitro** USA
78C2 **Niut** Mt Malay
46C1 **Nivelles** Belg
49C2 **Nivernais** Region,
       France
38L5 **Nivskiy** Russian Fed
87B1 **Nizāmābād** India
94B3 **Nizana** Hist Site
       Israel
61J2 **Nizhniye Sergi**
       Russian Fed
65F4 **Nizhniy Novgorod**
       Russian Fed
61F2 **Nizhniy Lomov**
       Russian Fed
65G4 **Nizhniy Tagil**
       Russian Fed
63B1 **Nizhnyaya Tunguska**
       R Russian Fed
93C2 **Nizip** Turk
100B2 **Njoko** R Zambia

99D3 **Njombe** Tanz
98B2 **Nkambe** Cam
101C2 **Nkhata Bay** Malawi
98B2 **Nkongsamba** Cam
97C3 **N'Kongo** Nigor
86C2 **Noakhali** Bang
12B1 **Noatak** USA
12C1 **Noatak** R USA
74C4 **Nobeoka** Japan
47D1 **Noce** R Italy
23A1 **Nochistlán** Mexico
23B2 **Nochixtlán** Mexico
19A3 **Nocona** USA
24A1 **Nogales** Sonora, Mexico
9B3 **Nogales** USA
23B2 **Nogales** Veracruz, Mexico
47D2 **Nogara** Italy
75A2 **Nogata** Japan
60E2 **Noginsk** Russian Fed
34D2 **Nogoyá** Arg
84C3 **Nogoyá** R Arg
84C3 **Nohar** India
75B2 **Nojima-zaki** C Japan
98B2 **Nola** CAR
61G2 **Nolinsk** Russian Fed
16D2 **Nomans Land** I USA
12A2 **Nome** USA
46D2 **Nomeny** France
72B1 **Nomgon** Mongolia
5H3 **Nonacho1** L Can
76C2 **Nong Khai** Thai
101H1 **Nongoma** S Africa
12B1 **Noorvik** USA
13B3 **Nootka Sd** Can
98B3 **Noqui** Angola
7C5 **Noranda** Can
46B1 **Nord** Department, France
64D2 **Nordaustlandet** I Barents S
13D2 **Nordegg** Can
38F6 **Nordfjord** Inlet Nor
39F8 **Nordfriesische** Is Germany
56C2 **Nordhausen** Germany
56B2 **Nordhrein Westfalen** State, Germany
38J4 **Nordkapp** C Nor
6E3 **Nordre** Greenland
38H5 **Nord Stronfjället** Mt Sweden
1B9 **Nordvik** Russian Fed
45C2 **Nore** R Irish Rep
43E3 **Norfolk** County, Eng
8D2 **Norfolk** Nebraska, USA
11C5 **Norfolk** Virginia, USA
107F3 **Norfolk** I Aust
18B2 **Norfolk** L USA
105G5 **Norfolk Ridge** Pacific O
1C10 **Noril'sk** Russian Fed
18C1 **Normal** USA
19A2 **Norman** USA
48B2 **Normandie** Region, France
107D2 **Normanton** Aust
12J1 **Norman Wells** Can
4B3 **Norne** Can
15C2 **Norristown** USA
39H7 **Norrköping** Sweden
39H6 **Norrsundet** Sweden
39H7 **Norrtälje** Sweden
106B4 **Norseman** Aust
63F2 **Norsk** Russian Fed
102J2 **North S** N W Europe
42D2 **Northallerton** Eng
106A4 **Northam** Aust
102E3 **North American Basin** Atlantic O
106A3 **Northampton** Aust
43D3 **Northampton** County, Eng
43D3 **Northampton** Eng
11B3 **Northampton** USA
4G3 **North Arm** B Can
17B1 **North Augusta** USA
6D4 **North Aulatsivik** I Can
13F2 **North Battleford** Can

7C5 **North Bay** Can
20B2 **North Bend** USA
44C3 **North Berwick** Scot
7D5 **North,C** Can
7G4 **North C** NZ
11B3 **North Carolina** State, USA
20B1 **North Cascade Nat Pk** USA
14B1 **North Chan** Can
42B2 **North Chan** Ire/Scot
8C2 **North Dakota** State, USA
43E4 **North Downs** Eng
14C2 **North East** USA
102H2 **North East Atlantic Basin** Atlantic O
4B3 **Northeast C** USA
40B3 **Northern Ireland** UK
27L1 **Northern Range** Mts Trinidad
106C2 **Northern Territory** Aust
44C3 **North Esk** R Scot
16C1 **Northfield** Massachusetts, USA
12D2 **North Fork** R USA
110B1 **North I** NZ
74B3 **North Korea**
Republic, S E Asia
North Land =
Severnaya Zemlya
53A2 **North Little Rock** USA
1B4 **North Magnetic Pole** Can
17B2 **North Miami** USA
17B2 **North Miami Beach** USA
8C2 **North Platte** USA
8C2 **North Platte** R USA
27N3 **North Pt** Barbados
14B1 **North Rona** I Scot
44C2 **North Ronaldsay** I Scot
13F2 **North Saskatchewan** R Can
40D2 **North Sea** N W Europe
4D3 **North Slope** Region USA
109D1 **North Stradbroke** I Aust
110B1 **North Taranaki Bight** B NZ
9C3 **North Truchas Peak** Mt USA
44A3 **North Uist** I Scot
42C2 **Northumberland** County, Eng
107E3 **Northumberland Is** Aust
7D5 **Northumberland Str** Can
20B1 **North Vancouver** Can
43E3 **North Walsham** Eng
12F2 **Northway** USA
106A3 **North West C** Aust
84C2 **North West Frontier** Province, Pak
7D4 **North West River** Can
4F3 **North West Territories** Can
42D2 **North York Moors Nat Pk** Eng
12B2 **Norton B** USA
12B2 **Norton Sd** USA
112B1 **Norvegia,C** Ant
16C2 **Norwalk** Connecticut, USA
14B2 **Norwalk** Ohio, USA
39F6 **Norway** Kingdom, Europe
5J4 **Norway House** Can
6A2 **Norwegian B** Can
102H1 **Norwegian Basin** Norwegian S
64A3 **Norwegian S** N W Europe
16C2 **Norwich** Connecticut, USA

43E3 **Norwich** Eng
16D1 **Norwood** Massachusetts, USA
14B3 **Norwood** Ohio, USA
54C2 **Nos Emine** C Bulg
74D2 **Noshiro** Japan
54C2 **Nos Kaliakra** C Bulg
44E1 **Noss** I Scot
91D4 **Nostrābād** Iran
101D2 **Nosy Barren** I Madag
101D2 **Nosy Bé** I Madag
101E2 **Nosy Boraha** I Madag
101D3 **Nosy Varika** Madag
58B2 **Notéc** R Pol
5G4 **Notikeuin** Can
53C3 **Noto** Italy
39F7 **Notodden** Nor
75B1 **Noto-hantō** Pen Japan
7E5 **Notre Dams B** Can
47D1 **Nottingham** County, Eng
6C3 **Nottingham** I Can
6C3 **Nottingham Island** Can
96A2 **Nouadhibou** Maur
97A3 **Nouakchott** Maur
107F3 **Nouméa** Nouvelle Calédonie
97B3 **Nouna** Burkina
107F3 **Nouvelle Calédonie** I S W Pacific O
98B3 **Nova Caipemba** Angola
35A2 **Nova Esperança** Brazil
35C2 **Nova Friburgo** Brazil
100A2 **Nova Gaia** Angola
35B2 **Nova Granada** Brazil
35B2 **Nova Horizonte** Brazil
35C1 **Nova Lima** Brazil
Nova Lisboa = **Huambo**
35A2 **Nova Londrina** Brazil
101C3 **Nova Mambone** Mozam
47C2 **Novara** Italy
7M5 **Nova Scotia** Province, Can
22A1 **Novato** USA
35C1 **Nova Venécia** Brazil
60D4 **Novaya Kakhovka** Ukraine
64G2 **Novaya Zemlya** I Barents S
54C2 **Nova Zagora** Bulg
31C2 **Nove Russas** Brazil
54A1 **Nové Zámky** Slovakia
60D2 **Novgorod** Russian Fed
47C2 **Novi Ligure** Italy
54C2 **Novi Pazar** Bulg
54B2 **Novi Pazar** Serbia, Yugos
54A1 **Novi Sad** Serbia, Yugos
61J3 **Novoalekseyevka** Kazakhstan
61F3 **Novoanninskiy** Russian Fed
61E4 **Novocherkassk** Russian Fed
60C3 **Novograd Volynskiy** Ukraine
58D2 **Novogrudok** Russian Fed
30F4 **Novo Hamburgo** Brazil
65H5 **Novokazalinsk** Kazakhstan
65K4 **Novokuznetsk** Russian Fed
112B12 **Novolazarevskaya** Base Ant
52C1 **Novo Mesto** Slovenia
60E3 **Novomoskovsk** Russian Fed

60E5 **Novorossiysk** Russian Fed
65K4 **Novosibirsk** Russian Fed
1B8 **Novosibirskiye Ostrova** I Russian Fed
61J3 **Novotroitsk** Russian Fed
61G3 **Novo Uzensk** Russian Fed
59C2 **Novovolynsk** Ukraine
61G2 **Novo Vyatsk** Russian Fed
60D3 **Novozybkov** Russian Fed
58C2 **Nowy Dwór Mazowiecki** Pol
61K2 **Novyy Lyalya** Russian Fed
61H5 **Novyy Port** Russian Fed
61H5 **Novyy Uzen** Kazakhstan
58B2 **Nowa Sól** Pol
18A2 **Nowata** USA
Nowgong = **Nagaon**
12D2 **Nowitna** R USA
109D2 **Nowra** Aust
90B2 **Now Shahr** Iran
84C2 **Nowshera** Pak
59C3 **Nowy Sacz** Pol
12H3 **Noyes I** USA
46B2 **Noyon** France
97B4 **Nsawam** Ghana
99D1 **Nuba** Mts Sudan
81B3 **Nubian Desert** Sudan
34A3 **Nuble** R Chile
9D4 **Nueces** R USA
5J3 **Nueltin L** Can
26A2 **Nueva Gerona** Cuba
34A3 **Nueva Imperial** Chile
9C4 **Nueva Laredo** Mexico
34D2 **Nueva Palmira** Urug
24B2 **Nueva Rosita** Mexico
26B2 **Nuevitas** Cuba
24B1 **Nuevo Casas Grandes** Mexico
24C2 **Nuevo Laredo** Mexico
99E2 **Nugaal** Region, Somalia
6E2 **Nûgâtsiaq** Greenland
6E2 **Nugssuaq** Pen Greenland
6E2 **Nûgussuaq** I Greenland
108A2 **Nukey Bluff** Mt Aust
93D3 **Nukhayb** Iraq
65G5 **Nukus** Uzbekistan
12C2 **Nulato** USA
106B4 **Nullarbor Plain** Aust
97D4 **Numan** Nig
75B1 **Numata** Japan
98C2 **Numatinna** R Sudan
74D3 **Numazu** Japan
71E4 **Numfoor** I Indon
108C3 **Numurkah** Aust
12B2 **Nunapitchuk** USA
84D2 **Nunkun** Mt India
53A2 **Nuoro** Sardegna
91B3 **Nurābād** Iran
47C2 **Nure** R Italy
108A2 **Nuriootpa** Aust
84C1 **Nuristan** Upland Afghan
61H3 **Nurlat** Russian Fed
38K6 **Nurmes** Fin
57C3 **Nürnberg** Germany
108C2 **Nurri,Mt** Aust
93D2 **Nusaybin** Turk
12B2 **Nushagak** R USA
12C3 **Nushagak** B USA
12C3 **Nushagak Pen** USA
84B3 **Nushki** Pak
7D4 **Nutak** Can
12H2 **Nutzotin Mts** USA
Nûuk = **Godthåb**
86A1 **Nuwakot** Nepal
87C3 **Nuwara-Eliya** Sri Lanka
6C3 **Nuyukjuak** Can

16C2 **Nyack** USA
99D2 **Nyahururu** Kenya
108B3 **Nyah West** Aust
4C3 **Nyai** USA
68B3 **Nyaingentanglha Shan** *Mts* China
99D3 **Nyakabindi** Tanz
98C1 **Nyala** Sudan
86B1 **Nyalam** China
98C2 **Nyamlell** Sudan
64F3 **Nyandoma** Russian Fed
100C2 **Nyanga** Zim
99B3 **Nyanga** R Gabon
101C2 **Nyasa L** Malawi/ Mozam
76B2 **Nyaunglebin** Burma
61J2 **Nyazepetrovsk** Russian Fed
39G7 **Nyborg** Den
39H7 **Nybro** Sweden
64J3 **Nyda** Russian Fed
6D1 **Nyeboes Land** *Region* Can
99D3 **Nyeri** Kenya
101C2 **Nyimba** Zambia
82D3 **Nyingchi** China
59C3 **Nyíregyháza** Hung
99D2 **Nyiru,Mt** Kenya
38J6 **Nykarleby** Fin
39F7 **Nykøbing** Den
39G8 **Nykøbing** Den
39H7 **Nyköping** Sweden
100B3 **Nylstroom** S Africa
109C2 **Nymagee** Aust
39H7 **Nynäshamn** Sweden
109C2 **Nyngan** Aust
47B1 **Nyon** Switz
98B2 **Nyong** R Cam
49D3 **Nyons** France
59B2 **Nysa** Pol
20C2 **Nysa** USA
63D1 **Nyurba** Russian Fed
99D3 **Nzega** Tanz
97B4 **Nzérékoré** Guinea
98B3 **N'zeto** Angola

O

6F3 **Oaggsimiut** Greenland
8C2 **Oahe Res** USA
21C4 **Oahu** I Hawaiian Is
108B2 **Oakbank** Aust
22B2 **Oakdale** USA
109D1 **Oakey** Aust
21A2 **Oakland** California, USA
20B2 **Oakland** Oregon, USA
14A3 **Oak Lawn** USA
14A2 **Oakland City** USA
22B2 **Oakley** California, USA
20B2 **Oakridge** USA
11B3 **Oakville** Can
11B3 **Oamaru** NZ
112B7 **Oates Land** *Region*, Ant
109C4 **Oatlands** Aust
23B2 **Oaxaca** Mexico
23B2 **Oaxaca** State, Mexico
65J3 **Ob'** R Russian Fed
75B1 **Obama** Japan
111A3 **Oban** NZ
44B3 **Oban** Scot
75C1 **Obanazawa** Japan
47D1 **Oberammergau** Germany
46D1 **Oberhausen** Germany
47D1 **Oberstdorf** Germany
71D4 **Obi** I Indon
33F4 **Obidos** Brazil
74E2 **Obihiro** Japan
98C2 **Obo** CAR
99E1 **Obock** Djibouti
58B2 **Oborniki** Pol
60E3 **Oboyan** Russian Fed
20B2 **O'Brien** USA
61H3 **Obshchiy Syrt** *Mts* Russian Fed
64J3 **Obskava Guba** B Russian Fed

97B4 **Obuasi** Ghana
17B2 **Ocala** USA
32C2 **Ocana** Colombia
50B2 **Ocaño** Spain
12G3 **Ocean C** USA
15C3 **Ocean City** Maryland, USA
16B3 **Ocean City** New Jersey, USA
5F4 **Ocean Falls** Can
22D4 **Oceanside** USA
19C3 **Ocean Springs** USA
61H2 **Ocher** Russian Fed
44C3 **Ochil Hills** Scot
17B1 **Ochlockonee** R USA
27H1 **Ocho Rios** Jamaica
17B1 **Ocmulgee** R USA
17B1 **Oconee** R USA
14A2 **Oconto** USA
23A1 **Ocotlán** Jalisco, Mexico
23B2 **Ocotlán** Oaxaca, Mexico
97B4 **Oda** Ghana
75A1 **Oda** Japan
38B2 **Odáðahraun** Region, Iceland
74E2 **Odate** Japan
74D3 **Odawara** Japan
39F6 **Odda** Nor
50A2 **Odemira** Port
55C3 **Odemis** Turk
101G1 **Odendaalsrus** S Africa
39G7 **Odense** Den
56C2 **Oder** R Pol/Germany
9C3 **Odessa** Texas, USA
60D4 **Odessa** Ukraine
20C1 **Odessa** Washington, USA
97B4 **Odienné** Ivory Coast
59B2 **Odra** R Pol
53C2 **Ofanto** R Italy
94B3 **Ofaqim** Israel
45C2 **Offaly** County, Irish Rep
49D1 **Offenbach** Germany
49D2 **Offenburg** Germany
74D3 **Oga** Japan
99E2 **Ogaden** Region, Eth
74D3 **Ogaki** Japan
8C2 **Ogallala** USA
69G4 **Ogasawara Gunto** Is Japan
97C4 **Ogbomosho** Nig
8B2 **Ogden** Utah, USA
15C2 **Ogdensburg** USA
17B1 **Ogeechee** R USA
12G1 **Ogilvie** Can
4E3 **Ogilvie Mts** Can
17B1 **Oglethorpe,Mt** USA
47D2 **Oglio** R Italy
47B1 **Ognon** R France
97C4 **Ogoja** Nig
99B3 **Ogooué** R Gabon
58C1 **Ogre** Latvia
96B2 **Oguilet Khenachich** *Well* Mali
52C1 **Ogulin** Croatia
111A3 **Ohai** NZ
110C1 **Ohakune** NZ
96C2 **Ohanet** Alg
111A2 **Ohau,L** NZ
10B2 **Ohio** State, USA
14A3 **Ohio** R USA
100A2 **Ohopoho** Namibia
57C2 **Ohre** R Czech Republic
55B2 **Ohrid** Macedonia
55B2 **Ohridsko Jezero** L Macedonia/Alb
110B1 **Ohura** NZ
33G3 **Oiapoque** French Guiana
68B2 **Oijiaojing** China
14A2 **Oil City** USA
21B2 **Oildale** USA
46B2 **Oise** Department, France
49C2 **Oise** R France
74C4 **Oita** Japan
22C3 **Ojai** USA
24B2 **Ojinaga** Mexico

23B2 **Ojitlán** Mexico
75B1 **Ojiya** Japan
30C4 **Ojos del Salado** *Mt* Arg
23A1 **Ojueloz** Mexico
60E3 **Oka** R Russian Fed
100A3 **Okahandja** Namibia
20C1 **Okanagan Falls** Can
13D2 **Okanagan L** Can
20C1 **Okanogan** USA
20C1 **Okanogan** R USA
20B1 **Okanogan Range** *Mts* Can/USA
84C2 **Okara** Pak
100A2 **Okavango** R Angola/ Namibia
100A2 **Okavango Delta** *Marsh* Botswana
74D3 **Okaya** Japan
74C4 **Okayama** Japan
75B2 **Okazaki** Japan
17B2 **Okeechobee** USA
17B2 **Okeechobee,L** USA
17B1 **Okefenokee Swamp** USA
43C4 **Okehampton** Eng
85B4 **Okha** India
69G1 **Okha** Russian Fed
86B1 **Okhaldunga** Nepal
62J3 **Okhotsk,S of** Russian Fed
69E4 **Okinawa** I Japan
69E4 **Okinawa gunto** *Arch* Japan
74C3 **Oki-shoto** Is Japan
9D3 **Oklahoma** State, USA
18A2 **Oklahoma City** USA
18A2 **Okmulgee** USA
99B3 **Okondja** Gabon
98B3 **Okoyo** Congo
97C4 **Okpara** R Nig
65J4 **Oktyabr'sk** Kazakhstan
61H3 **Oktyabr'skiy** Russian Fed
74D2 **Okushiri-tō** I Japan
38A2 **Olafsvik** Iceland
39H7 **Öland** I Sweden
108B2 **Olary** Aust
18B2 **Olathe** USA
29D3 **Olavarria** Arg
53A2 **Olbia** Sardegna
12G1 **Old Crow** Can
56B2 **Oldenburg** Niedersachsen, Germany
56C2 **Oldenburg** Schleswig-Holstein, Germany
15C2 **Old Forge** USA
42C3 **Oldham** Eng
12D3 **Old Harbor** USA
41B3 **Old Head of Kinsale** C Scot
16C2 **Old Lyme** USA
13E2 **Olds** Can
72B1 **Oldziyt** Mongolia
15C2 **Olean** USA
63E2 **Olekma** R Russian Fed
63D1 **Olekminsk** Russian Fed
38L5 **Olenegorsk** Russian Fed
58D2 **Olevsk** Ukraine
69F2 **Ol'ga** Russian Fed
100A3 **Olifants** R Namibia
55B2 **Ólimbos** Mt Greece
35B2 **Olímpia** Brazil
23B2 **Olinala** Mexico
31E3 **Olinda** Brazil
34C2 **Oliva** Arg
29C2 **Olivares** Mt Arg
35D1 **Oliveira** Brazil
13C3 **Oliver** Can
30C3 **Ollague** Chile
30C3 **Ollague** Mt Bol
12C1 **Olney** USA
68E1 **Olochi** Russian Fed
39G7 **Olofstrom** Sweden
98B3 **Olombo** Congo
59B3 **Olomouc** Czech Republic

60D1 **Olonets** Russian Fed
79B3 **Olongapo** Phil
48B3 **Oloron Ste Marie** France
68D1 **Olovyannaya** Russian Fed
46D1 **Olpe** Germany
58C2 **Olsztyn** Pol
54B2 **Olt** R Rom
47B1 **Olten** Switz
20B1 **Olympia** USA
20B1 **Olympic Nat Pk** USA
 Olympus,Mt = Ólimbos
20B1 **Olympus,Mt** USA
65J4 **Om'** R Russian Fed
75B1 **Omachi** Japan
75B2 **Omae-zaki** C Japan
45C1 **Omagh** N Ire
18A1 **Omaha** USA
20C1 **Omak** USA
91C5 **Oman** Sultanate, Arabian Pen
91C4 **Oman,G of** UAE
98A3 **Omboué** Gabon
99D1 **Omdurman** Sudan
23B2 **Ometepec** Mexico
99D1 **Om Häjer** Eritrea
13B1 **Omineca** R Can
13B1 **Omineca Mts** Can
75B1 **Omiya** Japan
12H3 **Ommaney,C** USA
4H2 **Ommaney B** Can
99D2 **Omo** R Eth
65J4 **Omsk** Russian Fed
74B4 **Omura** Japan
74C4 **Omuta** Japan
61H2 **Onutinsk** Russian Fed
78D3 **Onang** Indon
14B1 **Onaping L** Can
100A2 **Oncócua** Angola
100A2 **Ondangua** Namibia
59C3 **Ondava** R Slovakia
68D2 **Öndörhaan** Molgolia
83B5 **One and Half Degree Chan** Indian O
64E3 **Onega** Russian Fed
64E3 **Onega** R Russian Fed
15C2 **Oneida L** USA
8D2 **O'Neill** USA
69H2 **Onekotan** I Russian Fed
98C3 **Onema** Zaire
15C2 **Oneonta** USA
54C1 **Onesti** Rom
64E3 **Onezhskoye Ozero** L Russian Fed
100A2 **Ongiva** Angola
74B3 **Ongjin** N Korea
72D1 **Ongniud Qi** China
87C1 **Ongole** India
15C2 **Onieda L** USA
101D3 **Onilahy** R Madag
97C4 **Onitsha** Nig
68C2 **Onjüül** Mongolia
75B1 **Ono** Japan
75B2 **Onohara-jima** I Japan
74C4 **Onomichi** Japan
106A3 **Onslow** Aust
17C1 **Onslow B** USA
75B1 **Ontake-san** Mt Japan
22D3 **Ontario** California, USA
20C2 **Ontario** Oregon, USA
7A4 **Ontario** Province, Can
15C2 **Ontario,L** Can/USA
51B2 **Onteniente** Spain
106C3 **Oodnadatta** Aust
106C4 **Ooldea** Aust
62D1 **Oolgah L** USA
46B1 **Oostende** Belg
46B1 **Oosterschelde** *Estuary* Neth
87B2 **Ootacamund** India
13B2 **Ootsa L** Can
69H1 **Opala** Russian Fed
98C3 **Opala** Zaire
87C3 **Opanake** Sri Lanka
61G2 **Oparino** Russian Fed

59B3 Opava Czech Republic
17A1 Opelika USA
19B3 Opelousas USA
12C1 Opheim USA
59D1 Oporchnik Russian Fed
59B2 Opole Pol
Oporto = Porto
110C1 Opotiki NZ
17A1 Opp USA
38F6 Oppdal Nor
110B1 Opunake NZ
54B1 Oradea Rom
38B2 Oraefajökull Mts Iceland
85D3 Orai India
96B1 Oran Alg
30D3 Orán Arg
109C2 Orange Aust
22D4 Orange California, USA
49C3 Orange France
19B3 Orange Texas, USA
100A3 Orange R S Africa
17B1 Orangeburg USA
17B1 Orange Park USA
14B2 Orangeville Can
56C2 Oranienburg Germany
79C3 Oras Phil
54B1 Orăstie Rom
54B1 Oravita Rom
52B2 Orbetello Italy
109C3 Orbost Aust
46B1 Orchies France
47B2 Orco R Italy
106B2 Ord R Aust
106B2 Ord,Mt Aust
93C1 Ordu Turk
39H7 Örebro Sweden
8A2 Oregon State, USA
14B2 Oregon USA
20B1 Oregon City USA
39H6 Öregrund Sweden
60E2 Orekhovo Zuyevo Russian Fed
60E3 Orel Russian Fed
61H3 Orenburg Russian Fed
34D3 Orense Arg
50A1 Orense Spain
56C1 Øresund Str Den/ Sweden
111A3 Oreti R NZ
55C3 Orhaneli R Turk
68C2 Orhon Gol R Mongolia
23B2 Oriental Mexico
108B1 Orientos Aust
51B2 Orihuela Spain
15C2 Orillia Can
33E2 Orinoco R Ven
86A2 Orissa State, India
53A3 Oristano Sardegna
38K6 Orivesi Fin
33F4 Oriximina Brazil
23B2 Orizaba Mexico
35B1 Orizona Brazil
44C2 Orkney I Scot
35B2 Orlândia Brazil
17B2 Orlando USA
48C2 Orléanais Region France
48C2 Orléans France
63B2 Orlik Russian Fed
82A3 Ormara Pak
79B3 Ormoc Phil
17B2 Ormond Beach USA
38H6 Örnsköldsvik Sweden
32C3 Orocué Colombia
94B3 Oron Israel
Orontes = 'Āşī
79B4 Oroquieta Phil
59C3 Oroszháza Hung
21A2 Oroville California, USA
20C1 Oroville Washington, USA

47B1 Orsières Switz
65G4 Orsk Russian Fed
38F6 Ørsta Nor
48B3 Orthez France
50A1 Ortigueira Spain
27L1 Ortoire R Trinidad
93E2 Orümiyeh Iran
30C2 Oruro Bol
61L2 Osa Russian Fed
18B2 Osage R USA
75B1 Osaka Japan
25D4 Osa,Pen de Costa Rica
18C2 Osceola Arkansas, USA
18B1 Osceola Iowa, USA
20C2 Osgood Mts USA
15C2 Oshawa Can
61B2 O-shima I Japan
10B2 Oshkosh USA
97C4 Oshogbo Nig
7B5 Oshosh USA
98B3 Oshwe Zaïre
54A1 Osijek Croatia
65K5 Osinniki Russian Fed
58D2 Osipovichi Belorussia
18B1 Oskaloosa USA
60A2 Oskarshamn Sweden
39G7 Oslo Nor
92C2 Osmaniye Turk
56B2 Osnabrück Germany
30F4 Osório Brazil
29B4 Osorno Chile
50B1 Osorno Spain
20C1 Osoyoos Can
13C1 Osoyoos R USA
107D5 Ossa,Mt Aust
16C2 Ossining USA
60D2 Ostashkov Russian Fed
Ostend = Oostende
38G6 Østerdalen V Nor
38G6 Östersund Sweden
56B2 Ostfriesische Inseln Is Germany
39H6 Östhammar Sweden
53B2 Ostia Italy
47D2 Ostiglia Italy
59B3 Ostrava Czech Republic
58B2 Ostróda Pol
58B2 Ostrołeka Pol
60C2 Ostrov Russian Fed
64J2 Ostrov Belyy I Russian Fed
64H1 Ostrov Greem Bell I Barents S
64F3 Ostrov Kolguyev I Russian Fed
74F2 Ostrov Kunashir I Russian Fed
64F2 Ostrov Mechdusharskiy I Barents S
90B2 Ostrov Ogurchinskiy I Turkmenistan
64G1 Ostrov Rudol'fa I Barents S
64G2 Ostrov Vaygach I Russian Fed
1B7 Ostrov Vrangelya I Russian Fed
58B2 Ostrów Wlkp. Pol
59C2 Ostrowiec Pol
58C2 Ostrów Mazowiecka Pol
50A2 Osuna Spain
15C2 Oswego USA
15C2 Oswego USA
43C3 Oswestry Eng
59B2 Oświęcim Pol
75B1 Ota Japan
111B3 Otago Pen NZ
110C2 Otaki NZ
71E2 Otaru Japan
32B3 Otavalo Ecuador
100A2 Otavi Namibia
75C1 Otawara Japan
20C1 Othello USA
55B3 Othris Mt Greece

16C1 Otis Massachusetts, USA
16B2 Otisco USA
100A3 Otjiwarongo Namibia
72B2 Otog Qi China
110C1 Utorohanga NZ
55A2 Otranto Italy
55A2 Otranto,Str of Chan Italy/Alb
14A2 Otsego USA
75B1 Otsu Japan
39F6 Otta Nor
39F7 Otta R Nor
15C1 Ottawa Can
18A2 Ottawa Kansas, USA
15C1 Ottawa R Can
7B4 Ottawa Is Can
7B4 Otter Rapids Can
6B1 Otto Fjord Can
101G1 Ottosdal S Africa
18B1 Ottumwa USA
46D2 Ottweiler Germany
97C4 Oturkpo Nig
32B5 Otusco Peru
108B3 Otway,C Aust
58C2 Otwock Pol
47D1 Ötz Austria
47D1 Ötzal Mts Austria
76C1 Ou R Laos
19B3 Ouachita R USA
19B3 Ouachita,L USA
19B3 Ouachita Mts USA
96A2 Ouadane Maur
98C2 Ouadda CAR
98C1 Ouaddai Desert Region Chad
97B3 Ouagadougou Burkina
97B3 Ouahigouya Burkina
98C2 Ouaka CAR
97C3 Oualam Niger
96C2 Ouallen Alg
98C2 Ouanda Djallé CAR
96A2 Ouarane Region, Maur
96C1 Ouargla Alg
98C2 Ouarra R CAR
96B1 Ouarzazate Mor
51C2 Ouassel R Alg
98B2 Oubangui R Congo
46B1 Oudenaarde Belg
100B4 Oudtshoorn S Africa
51B2 Oued Tlélat Alg
96B1 Oued Zem Mor
98B2 Ouesso Congo
96B1 Ouezzane Mor
98B2 Ouham R Chad
97C4 Ouidah Benin
96B1 Oujda Mor
38J6 Oulainen Fin
38K5 Oulu Fin
38K6 Oulu R Fin
98B3 Oum Chalouba Chad
98B1 Oum Hadjer Chad
98B3 Oum Haouach Watercourse Chad
38K5 Ounas R Fin
98B3 Ounianga Kébir Chad
46D1 Our R Germany
47B2 Ourcq R France
Ourense = Orense
31C3 Ouricuri Brazil
35B2 Ourinhos Brazil
35C2 Ouro Prêto Brazil
46C1 Ourthe R Belg
42D2 Ouse R Eng
43E3 Ouse R Eng
40B2 Outer Hebrides Is Scot
22C4 Outer Santa Barbara Chan USA
100A3 Outjo Namibia
38K6 Outokumpu Fin
108B3 Ouyen Aust
47C2 Ovada Italy
34A2 Ovalle Chile
100A2 Ovamboland Region, Namibia
61H5 Ova Tyuleni Is Kazakhstan
38J5 Övertorneå Sweden

50A1 Oviedo Spain
60C3 Ovruch Ukraine
63E2 Ovsyanka Russian Fed
111A3 Owaka NZ
75B2 Owase Japan
11B3 Owensboro USA
21B2 Owens L USA
14B2 Owen Sound Can
107D1 Owen Stanley Range Mts PNG
97C4 Owerri Nig
97C4 Owo Nig
14A2 Owosso USA
20C2 Owyhee R USA
20C2 Owyhee Mts USA
32B6 Oxapampa Peru
39H7 Oxelösund Sweden
43D4 Oxford County, Eng
43D4 Oxford Eng
16D1 Oxford Massachusetts, USA
19C3 Oxford Mississippi, USA
45B1 Ox Mts Irish Rep
22C3 Oxnard USA
74D3 Oyama Japan
13E2 Oyen Can
98B2 Oyem Gabon
44B3 Oykel R Scot
39F6 Øyre Nor
109C4 Oyster B Aust
79B4 Ozamiz Phil
17A1 Ozark USA
18B2 Ozark Plat USA
18B2 Ozarks,L of the USA
59C3 Ozd Hung
65K5 Ozero Alakol L Kazakhstan/ Russian Fed
65J5 Ozero Balkhash L Kazakhstan
63C2 Ozero Baykal L Russian Fed
65J4 Ozero Chany L Russian Fed
69F1 Ozero Chukchagirskoye L Russian Fed
Ozero Chudskoye = Peipus,L
60D2 Ozero Il'men L Russian Fed
38L5 Ozero Imandra L Russian Fed
82B1 Ozero Issyk Kul' L Kirghizia
69F2 Ozero Khanka L China/Russian Fed
38L5 Ozero Kovdozero L Russian Fed
38L5 Ozero Kuyto L Russian Fed
38L5 Ozero Pyaozero L Russian Fed
65H4 Ozero Tengiz L Kazakhstan
38L5 Ozero Topozero L Russian Fed
65K5 Ozero Zaysan L Kazakhstan
23B1 Ozuluama Mexico

P

100A4 Paarl S Africa
44A3 Pabbay I Scot
58B2 Pabianice Pol
86B2 Pabna Bang
58D2 Pabrade Lithuania
32B5 Pacasmayo Peru
23B1 Pachuca Mexico
105K6 Pacific-Antarctic Ridge Pacific O
22B2 Pacific Grove USA
78C4 Pacitan Indon
35C1 Pacuí R Brazil
70D4 Padang Indon
56B2 Paderborn Germany
5J3 Padlei Can
86C2 Padma R Bang
47D2 Padova Italy
9D4 Padre I USA

Padstow

42B4 Padstow Eng
108B3 Padthaway Aust
Padua = Padova
14A3 Paducah Kentucky, USA
11B3 Paducah USA
38L5 Padunskoye More L Russian Fed
74A3 Paengnyŏng-do I S Korea
110C1 Paeroa NZ
100C3 Pafuri Mozam
52B2 Pag I Croatia
79B4 Pagadian Phil
70B4 Pagai Selatan I Indon
70B4 Pagai Utara I Indon
71F2 Pagan I Pacific O
78D3 Pagatan Indon
55C3 Pagondhas Greece
110C2 Pahiatua NZ
21C4 Pahoa Hawaiian Is
17B2 Pahokee USA
39K6 Päijänne L Fin
21C4 Pailola Chan Hawaiian Is
14B2 Painesville USA
9B3 Painted Desert USA
42B2 Paisley Scot
32A5 Paita Peru
38J5 Pajala Sweden
80E3 Pakistan Republic, Asia
76C2 Pak Lay Laos
86D2 Pakokku Burma
13E2 Pakowki L Can
52C1 Pakrac Croatia
54A1 Paks Hung
76C2 Pak Sane Laos
76D2 Pakse Laos
97C3 Pala Chad
52C2 Palagruža I Croatia
46B2 Palaiseau France
Palakhat = Palghat
78C3 Palangkaraya Indon
87B2 Palani India
85C4 Palanpur India
100B3 Palapye Botswana
53B3 Palermo Italy
19A3 Palestine USA
86C2 Paletwa Burma
87B2 Pālghāt India
85C4 Pāli India
87B3 Palk Str India/ Sri Lanka
61G3 Pallasovka Russian Fed
38J5 Pallastunturi Mt Fin
111B2 Palliser B NZ
111C2 Palliser,C NZ
101D2 Palma Mozam
51C2 Palma de Mallorca Spain
31D3 Palmares Brazil
26A5 Palmar Sur Costa Rica
97B4 Palmas,C Lib
26B2 Palma Soriano Cuba
17B2 Palm Bay USA
17B2 Palm Beach USA
22C3 Palmdale USA
31D3 Palmeira dos Indos Brazil
12E2 Palmer Base Ant
112C3 Palmer Ant
112C3 Palmer Arch Ant
112B3 Palmer Land Region Ant
111B3 Palmerston NZ
110C2 Palmerston North NZ
16B2 Palmerton USA
17B2 Palmetto USA

53C3 Palmi Italy
32B3 Palmira Colombia
107D2 Palm Is Aust
21B3 Palm Springs USA
18B2 Palmyra Missouri, USA
16A2 Palmyra Pennsylvania, USA
86B2 Palmyras Pt India
22A2 Palo Alto USA
78D1 Paloh Indon
99D1 Paloich Sudan
21B3 Palomar Mt USA
70D4 Palopo Indon
70C4 Palu Indon
93C2 Palu Turk
84D3 Palwal India
97C3 Pama Burkina
78C4 Pamekasan Indon
78B4 Pameungpeuk Indon
48C3 Pamiers France
82B2 Pamir Mts China
65J6 Pamir R Russian Fed
11C3 Pamlico Sd USA
9C3 Pampa USA
34B2 Pampa de la Salinas Salt pan Arg
34B3 Pampa de la Varita Plain Arg
32C2 Pamplona Colombia
50B1 Pamplona Spain
18C2 Pana USA
54B2 Panagyurishte Bulg
87A1 Panaji India
32B2 Panamá Panama
32A2 Panama Republic, Cent America
26B5 Panama Canal Panama
17A1 Panama City USA
21B2 Panamint Range Mts USA
21B2 Panamint V USA
47D2 Panaro R Italy
79B3 Panay I Phil
70C4 Pancevo Serbia, Yugos
79B3 Pandan Phil
87B1 Pandharpur India
108A1 Pandie Pandie Aust
58C1 Panevežys Lithuania
65K5 Panfilov Kazakhstan
76B1 Pang R Burma
99D3 Pangani Tanz
99D3 Pangani R Tanz
98C3 Pangi Zaire
78B3 Pangkalpinang Indon
6D3 Pangnirtung Can
76B1 Pangtara Burma
79B4 Pangutaran Group Is Phil
84D3 Panipat India
84B2 Panjao Afghan
74B3 P'anmunjŏm N Korea
86A2 Panna India
35A2 Panorama Brazil
53B3 Pantelleria I Medit S
23B1 Pantepec Mexico
23B1 Panuco Mexico
23B1 Panuco R Mexico
73A4 Pan Xian China
53C3 Paola Italy
18B2 Paola USA
14A3 Paoli USA
59B3 Papa Hung
110B1 Papakura NZ
23B2 Papaloapan R Mexico
23B1 Papantla Mexico
44E1 Papa Stour I Scot
110B1 Papatoetoe NZ
44C2 Papa Westray I Scot
107D1 Papua,G of PNG
107D1 Papua New Guinea Republic, S E Asia
34A2 Papudo Chile
76B2 Papun Burma
33G4 Pará State, Brazil
31B2 Pará R Brazil
106A3 Paraburdoo Aust
32B6 Paracas,Pen de Peru
35B1 Paracatu Brazil

35B1 Paracatu R Brazil
108A2 Parachilna Aust
84C2 Parachinar Pak
54B2 Paracin Serbia, Yugos
35C1 Pará de Minas Brazil
21A2 Paradise California, USA
18B2 Paragould USA
33E6 Paragua R Bol
33E2 Paragua R Ven
30E2 Paraguai R Brazil
30E4 Paraguari Par
30E3 Paraguay Republic, S America
30E3 Paraguay R Par
31D3 Paraiba State, Brazil
35B2 Paraiba R Brazil
35C2 Paraiba do Sul R Brazil
97C4 Parakou Benin
108A2 Parakylia Aust
85B3 Paramakkudi India
33F2 Paramaribo Surinam
69H1 Paramushir I Russian Fed
30F3 Paraná State, Brazil
34C2 Paraná Urug
29E2 Paraná R Arg
31B4 Paraná R Brazil
35A2 Paraná R Brazil
30G4 Paranaguá Brazil
35A1 Paranaiba Brazil
35A1 Paranaiba R Brazil
35A2 Paranapanema R Brazil
35A2 Paranavai Phil
79B4 Parang Phil
35C1 Paraope R Brazil
110B2 Paraparaumu NZ
87B1 Parbhani India
94B2 Pardes Hanna Israel
34D3 Pardo R Arg
35D1 Pardo R Bahia, Brazil
35A2 Pardo R Mato Grosso do Sul, Brazil
35B1 Pardo R Minas Gerais, Brazil
35B2 Pardo R Sao Paulo, Brazil
59B2 Pardubice Czech Republic
69F4 Parece Vela Reef Pacific O
10C2 Parent Can
70C4 Parepare Indon
34C3 Parera Arg
70B4 Pariaman Indon
33E1 Paria,Pen de Ven
14B3 Paris Kentucky, USA
19A3 Paris Texas, USA
14B3 Parkersburg USA
109C2 Parkes Aust
14B2 Parkesburg USA
14A2 Park Forest USA
20B1 Parksville Can
87B1 Parli India
47D2 Parma Italy
14A2 Parma USA
31C2 Parnaiba Brazil
31C2 Parnaiba R Brazil
55B3 Párnon Óros Mts Greece
60B2 Pärnu Estonia
86B1 Paro Bhutan
108B1 Paroo R Aust
108B2 Paroo Channel R Aust
55C3 Páros I Greece
47B2 Parpaillon Mts France
34A3 Parral Chile
107A3 Parramatta Aust
9C4 Parras Mexico
6B3 Parry B Can
4G2 Parry Is Can
7C5 Parry Sd Can
14B1 Parry Sound Can
57C3 Parsberg Germany
5F4 Parsnip R Can
18A2 Parsons Kansas, USA
14C3 Parsons West Virginia, USA

48B2 Parthenay France
53B3 Partinico Italy
74C2 Partizansk Russian Fed
33G4 Paru R Brazil
101G1 Parys S Africa
19A4 Pasadena Texas, USA
22C3 Pasadena California, USA
78D3 Pasangkayu Indon
76B2 Pasawing Burma
19C3 Pascagoula USA
54C1 Pascani Rom
20C1 Pasco USA
46B1 Pas-de-Calais Department, France
39G8 Pasewalk Germany
91C4 Pashú'iyeh Iran
106B4 Pasley,C S Aust
29E2 Paso de los Toros Urug
29B4 Paso Limay Arg
21A2 Paso Robles USA
45B3 Passage West Irish Rep
16B2 Passaic USA
57C3 Passau Germany
30E4 Passo de los Libres Arg
47D1 Passo di Stelvio Mt Italy
30F4 Passo Fundo Brazil
35B2 Passos Brazil
47B2 Passy France
32B4 Pastaza R Peru
34C3 Pasteur Arg
5H4 Pas,The Can
32B3 Pasto Colombia
12B2 Pastol B USA
47D2 Pasubio Mt Italy
78C4 Pasuruan Indon
58C1 Pasvalys Lithuania
85C4 Pātan India
86B1 Patan Nepal
108B3 Patchewollock Aust
110B1 Patea NZ
111B2 Patea R NZ
53B3 Paterno Italy
16B2 Paterson USA
111A3 Paterson Inlet B NZ
84D2 Pathankot India
Pathein = Bassein
84D2 Patiala India
55C3 Pátmos I Greece
86B1 Patna India
93D2 Patnos Turk
63D2 Patomskoye Nagor'ye Upland Russian Fed
31D3 Patos Brazil
35B1 Patos de Minas Brazil
34B2 Patquia Arg
55B3 Pátrai Greece
35B1 Patrocinio Brazil
99D3 Patta I Kenya
78D4 Pattallasang Indon
77C4 Pattani Thai
22B2 Patterson California, USA
19B4 Patterson Louisiana, USA
12H2 Patterson,Mt Can
22C2 Patterson Mt USA
13B1 Pattullo,Mt Can
31D3 Patu Brazil
86C2 Patuakhali Bang
25D3 Patuca R Honduras
23A2 Patzcuaro Mexico
48B3 Pau France
4F3 Paulatuk Can
31C3 Paulistana Brazil
101H1 Paulpietersburg S Africa
19A3 Pauls Valley USA
76B2 Paungde Burma
84D2 Pauri India
38H5 Pauske Nor
35C1 Pavão Brazil
47C2 Pavia Italy
65J4 Pavlodar Kazakhstan
61J2 Pavlovka Russian Fed

61F2 Pavlovo *Russian Fed*
61F3 Pavlovsk
Russian Fed
78C3 Pawan R *Indon*
18A2 Pawhuska *USA*
16D2 Pawtucket *USA*
47B1 Payerne *Switz*
20C2 Payette *USA*
7C4 Payne,L *Can*
34D2 Paysandu *Urug*
46A2 Pays-de-Bray *Region,
France*
54B2 Pazardzhik *Bulg*
13D1 Peace R *Can*
17B2 Peace R *USA*
13D1 Peace River *Can*
43D3 Peak District Nat Pk
Eng
108A1 Peake R *Aust*
109C2 Peak Hill *Aust*
71E4 Peak Mandala *Mt*
Indon
42D3 Peak,The *Mt Eng*
19B3 Pearl R *USA*
21C4 Pearl City *Hawaiian
Is*
21C4 Pearl Harbor
Hawaiian Is
4H2 Peary Chan *Can*
101C2 Pebane *Mozam*
54B2 Peć *Serbia, Yugos*
35C1 Peçanha *Brazil*
19B4 Pecan Island *USA*
38L5 Pechenga
Russian Fed
64F3 Pechora R
Russian Fed
64G3 Pechorskoye More *S*
Russian Fed
53C3 Pecoraro *Mt Italy*
9C3 Pecos *USA*
9C3 Pecos R *USA*
59B3 Pécs *Hung*
108A1 Pedirka *Aust*
35C1 Pedra Azul *Brazil*
35B2 Pedregulho *Brazil*
26B3 Pedro Cays *Is
Caribbean S*
30C3 Pedro de Valdivia
Chile
30E3 Pedro Juan Caballero
Par
34C3 Pedro Luro *Arg*
23B1 Pedro Mentova
Mexico
87C3 Pedro,Pt *Sri Lanka*
108B2 Peebinga *Aust*
8C3 Peebles *Scot*
17C1 Pee Dee R *USA*
16C2 Peekskill *USA*
42B2 Peel *Eng*
12H1 Peel R *Can*
4J2 Peel Sd *Can*
108A1 Peera Peera Poolanna
L Aust
13E1 Peerless L *Can*
71E4 Peg Arfak *Mt Indon*
111B2 Pegasus B *NZ*
83D4 Pegu *Burma*
78A3 Pegunungan Barisan
Mts Indon
78C2 Pegunungan Iran *Mts
Malay/Indon*
71E4 Pegunungan Maoke
Mts Indon
78D3 Pegunungan Meratus
Mts Indon
78C2 Pegunungan Muller
Mts Indon
78C3 Pegunungan
Schwaner *Mts Indon*
78A3 Pegunungan
Tigapuluh *Mts Indon*
76B2 Pegu Yoma *Mts
Burma*
34C3 Pehuajó *Arg*
*Péipsi Järve =
Peipus,L*
39K7 Peipus, Lake *Estonia/
Russian Fed*
35A2 Peixe R *Sao Paulo,
Brazil*
72D3 Pei Xian *China*
78B4 Pekalongan *Indon*

77C5 Pekan *Malay*
78A2 Pekanbaru *Indon*
18C1 Pekin *USA*
Peking = Beijing
77C5 Pelabohan Kelang
Malay
78B4 Pelau Pelau Kangean
Is Indon
78C4 Pelau Pelau
Karimunjawa *Arch
Indon*
78B4 Pelau Pelau Postilyon
Is Indon
54B1 Peleaga *Mt Rom*
63D2 Peleduy *Russian Fed*
14B2 Pelee I *Can*
71D4 Peleng I *Indon*
12G3 Pelican *USA*
69F1 Peliny Osipenko
Russian Fed
12G2 Pell *R Can*
34C3 Pellegrini *Arg*
38J5 Pello *Fin*
12D2 Pelly *R Can*
6A3 Pelly Bay *Can*
12G2 Pelly Crossing *Can*
12H2 Pelly Mts *Can*
30F5 Pelotas *Brazil*
30F4 Pelotas R *Brazil*
47B2 Pelvoux *Region,
France*
78B4 Pemalang *Indon*
78A2 Pematang *Indon*
101D2 Pemba *Mozam*
99D3 Pemba I *Tanz*
13C2 Pemberton *Can*
13D2 Pembina *R Can*
15C1 Pembroke *Can*
17B1 Pembroke *USA*
43B4 Pembroke *Wales*
34A3 Pemuco *Chile*
78D2 Penambo Range *Mts
Malay*
35A2 Penápolis *Brazil*
50A2 Penarroya *Spain*
51B1 Penarroya *Mt Spain*
50A1 Peña Trevina *Mt
Spain*
98B2 Pende *R Chad*
12J3 Pendleton,Mt *Can*
20C1 Pendleton *USA*
20C1 Pend Oreille *R USA*
31D4 Penedo *Brazil*
85D5 Penganga *R India*
73D5 P'eng-hu Lieh-tao *Is
Taiwan*
72E2 Penglai *China*
73B4 Pengshui *China*
71E4 Pengunungan Maoke
Mts Indon
26C4 Península de la
Guajirí *Pen
Colombia*
27E4 Península de Paria
Pen Ven
77C5 Peninsular Malaysia
Malay
10D2 Péninsule de Gaspé
Pen Can
23A1 Penjamo *Mexico*
87B2 Penner *R India*
42C2 Pennine Chain *Mts
Eng*
16B3 Penns Grove *USA*
10C2 Pennsylvania *State,
USA*
6D3 Penny Highlands *Mts
Can*
108B3 Penola *Aust*
106C4 Penong *Aust*
42C2 Penrith *Eng*
11B3 Pensacola *USA*
112A Pensacola Mts *Ant*
78D1 Pensiangan *Malay*
13D3 Penticton *Can*
44C2 Pentland Firth *Chan
Scot*
42C2 Pentland Hills *Scot*
61G3 Penza *Russian Fed*
43B4 Penzance *Eng*
10B2 Peoria *USA*
78A3 Perabumulih *Indon*
77C5 Perak *R Malay*
78A2 Perawang *Indon*
32B3 Pereira *Colombia*

35A2 Pereira Barreto *Brazil*
61F4 Perelazovskiy
Russian Fed
12D3 Perenosa B *USA*
34C2 Pergamino *Arg*
7C4 Péribonca *R Can*
48C2 Périgueux *France*
25E4 Perlas Arch de *Is
Panama*
61J2 Perm' *Russian Fed*
Pernambuco = Recife
31D3 Pernambuco *State,
Brazil*
108A2 Pernatty Lg *Aust*
54B2 Pernik *Bulg*
46B2 Péronne *France*
23B2 Perote *Mexico*
49C3 Perpignan *France*
22D4 Perris *USA*
17B1 Perry *Florida, USA*
17B1 Perry *Georgia, USA*
18A2 Perry *Oklahoma,
USA*
4H3 Perry River *Can*
14B2 Perrysburg *USA*
12C3 Perryville *Alaska,
USA*
18C2 Perryville *Missouri,
USA*
106A4 Perth *Aust*
15C2 Perth *Can*
44C3 Perth *Scot*
16B2 Perth Amboy *USA*
32C6 Peru *Republic,
S America*
18C1 Peru *USA*
103E5 Peru-Chile Trench
Pacific O
52B2 Perugia *Italy*
52C2 Perušic *Croatia*
93D2 Pervari *Turk*
61F3 Pervomaisk
Russian Fed
60D4 Pervomaysk *Ukraine*
61J2 Pervoural'sk
Russian Fed
52B2 Pesaro *Italy*
22A2 Pescadero *USA*
*Pescadores = P'eng-
hu Lieh-tao*
52B2 Pescara *Italy*
47D2 Peschiera *Italy*
84C2 Peshawar *Pak*
54B2 Peshkopi *Alb*
14A1 Peshtigo *USA*
60E2 Pestovo *Russian Fed*
94B2 Petah Tiqwa *Israel*
21A2 Petaluma *USA*
46C2 Petange *Lux*
23B2 Petatlán *Mexico*
101C2 Petauke *Zambia*
108A2 Peterborough *Aust*
15C2 Peterborough *Can*
43D3 Peterborough *Eng*
44D3 Peterhead *Scot*
6D1 Petermann Gletscher
Gl Greenland
106B3 Petermann Range
Mts Aust
29B3 Peteroa *Mt Arg/Chile*
13F1 Peter Pond L *Can*
12H3 Petersburg *Alaska,
USA*
85C4 Petlad *India*
23B2 Petlalcingo *Mexico*
25D2 Peto *Mexico*
63D2 Petomskoye
Nagor'ye *Upland
Russian Fed*
34A2 Petorca *Chile*
14B1 Petoskey *USA*
31C3 Petrolina *Brazil*
65H4 Petropavlovsk
Kazakhstan
35C2 Petrópolis *Brazil*
61G3 Petrovsk
Russian Fed
68C1 Petrovsk
Zabaykal'skiy
Russian Fed
64E3 Petrozavodsk
Russian Fed
101G1 Petrus *S Africa*
101G1 Petrusburg *S Africa*

1B7 Pevek *Russian Fed*
46D2 Pfälzer Wald *Region,
Germany*
57B3 Pforzheim *Germany*
84D2 Phagwara *India*
85C3 Phalodi *India*
46D2 Phalsbourg *France*
87A1 Phaltan *India*
77B4 Phangnga *Thai*
76D3 Phanom Dang *Mts
Camb*
76D3 Phan Rang *Viet*
76D3 Phan Thiet *Viet*
17A1 Phenix City *USA*
76D3 Phet Buri *Thai*
76D3 Phiafay *Laos*
19C3 Philadelphia
Mississipi, USA
16B2 Philadelphia
Pennsylvania, USA
Philippeville = Skikda
46C1 Philippeville *Belg*
71D2 Philippine S *Pacific O*
71D2 Philippines *Republic,
S E Asia*
104E3 Philippine Trench
Pacific O
15C2 Philipsburg
Pennsylvania, USA
12E1 Philip Smith Mts
USA
79B2 Phillips S *Phil*
6B1 Phillips B *Can*
16B2 Phillipsburg *New
Jersey, USA*
6B2 Phillps Pen *Can*
76C3 Phnom Penh *Camb*
9B3 Phoenix *Arizona,
USA*
16B2 Phoenixville *USA*
76C1 Phong Saly *Laos*
*Phra Nakhon =
Bangkok*
76C2 Phu Bia *Mt Laos*
76D1 Phu Cuong *Viet*
77B4 Phuket *Thai*
86A2 Phulbani *India*
76C2 Phu Miang *Mt Thai*
76D2 Phu Set *Mt Laos*
76D1 Phu Tho *Viet*
77D4 Phu Vinh *Viet*
47C2 Piacenza *Italy*
109C2 Pian *R Aust*
52B2 Pianosa *Italy*
52C2 Pianosa *I Italy*
58C2 Piaseczno *Pol*
54C1 Piatra-Neamt *Rom*
31C3 Piauí *State, Brazil*
47E2 Piave *R Italy*
99D2 Pibor *R Sudan*
99D2 Pibor Post *Sudan*
46B1 Picardie *Region,
France*
19C3 Picayune *USA*
47B2 Pic de Rochebrune
Mt France
34A2 Pichilemu *Chile*
34C3 Pichi Mahuida *Arg*
42D2 Pickering *Eng*
7A4 Pickle Lake *Can*
96A1 Pico I *Açores*
47C1 Pico Bernina *Mt
Switz*
51C1 Pico de Anito *Mt
Spain*
24B3 Pico del Infiernillo *Mt
Mexico*
27C3 Pico Duarte *Mt
Dom Rep*
31C3 Picos *Brazil*
50B1 Picos de Europa *Mt
Spain*
109D2 Picton *Aust*
111B2 Picton *NZ*
95A2 Pic Toussidé *Mt
Chad*
35B2 Piedade *Brazil*
22C2 Piedra *USA*
24B2 Piedras Negras
Mexico
38K6 Pieksämäki *Fin*
38K6 Pielinen *L Fin*
47B2 Piemonte *Region,
Italy*

Pierre

8C2 Pierre USA
59B3 Piešťany Slovakia
101H1 Pietermaritzburg S Africa
100B3 Pietersburg S Africa
101H1 Piet Retief S Africa
60B4 Pietrosu Mt Rom
47E1 Pieve di Cadore Italy
13E2 Pigeon L Can
18B2 Piggott USA
34C3 Pigüé Arg
7A4 Pikangikum L Can
8C3 Pikes Peak USA
100A4 Piketberg S Africa
6F3 Pikiutdleq Greenland
82B2 Pik Kommunizma Mt Tajikistan
98B2 Pikounda Congo
82C1 Pik Pobedy Mt China/Kirghizia
34D3 Pila Arg
58B2 Piła Pol
30E4 Pilar Par
30D3 Pilcomayo R Arg/Par
84D3 Pilibhit India
59B2 Pilica R Pol
109C4 Pillar,C Aust
12C3 Pilot Point USA
12B2 Pilot Station USA
19C3 Pilottown USA
33F4 Pimenta Brazil
77C4 Pinang I Malay
26A2 Pinar del Rio Cuba
34B2 Pinas Arg
46C1 Pinche Belg
13E2 Pincher Creek Can
31B2 Pindaré R Brazil
55B3 Pindhos Mts Greece
19B3 Pine Bluff USA
106C2 Pine Creek Aust
22C1 Pinecrest USA
22C2 Pinedale California, USA
64F3 Pinega R Russian Fed
16A2 Pine Grove USA
17B2 Pine Hills USA
17B2 Pine I USA
19B3 Pineland USA
17B2 Pinellas Park USA
5G3 Pine Point Can
47B2 Pinerolo Italy
19B3 Pines,L o'the USA
72C3 Pingdingshan China
73B5 Pingguo China
72B2 Pingliang China
72B2 Pingluo China
73D4 Pingtan Dao I China
73E5 P'ing tung Taiwan
72A3 Pingwu China
73B5 Pingxiang Guangxi, China
73C4 Pingxiang Jiangxi, China
31B2 Pinheiro Brazil
77C4 Pini I Indon
55B3 Piniós R Greece
106A4 Pinjarra Aust
13C1 Pink Mountain Can
108B3 Pinnaroo Aust
Pinos,I de, I = Isla de la Juventud
21A2 Pinos,Pt USA
23B2 Pinotepa Nacional Mexico
70C4 Pinrang Indon
60C3 Pinsk Belorussia
32J7 Pinta I Ecuador
61G1 Pinyug Russian Fed
8B3 Pioche USA
52B2 Piombino Italy
6H3 Piórsá Iceland
59B2 Piotrków Trybunalski Pol
44E2 Piper Oilfield N Sea
21B2 Piper Peak USA
10C2 Pipmuacan Res Can
14B2 Piqua USA
35B1 Piracanjuba Brazil
35B2 Piracicaba Brazil

35B2 Piraçununga Brazil
35B2 Piraí do Sul Brazil
55B3 Piraiévs Greece
35B2 Pirajuí Brazil
35A1 Piranhas Brazil
35C1 Pirapora Brazil
35B1 Pirenópolis Brazil
35B1 Pires do Rio Brazil
55B3 Pírgos Greece
Pirineos = Pyrénées
31C2 Piripiri Brazil
57B2 Pirmasens Germany
54B2 Pirot Serbia, Yugos
84C2 Pir Panjäl Range Mts Pak
71D4 Piru Indon
22C3 Piru Creek R USA
49E3 Pisa Italy
32B6 Pisco Peru
57C3 Písek Czech Republic
84B2 Pishin Pak
30C4 Pissis Mt Arg
49E3 Pistoia Italy
50B1 Pisuerga R Spain
20B2 Pit R USA
32B3 Pitalito Colombia
105K5 Pitcairn I Pacific O
51B3 Pite R Sweden
38J5 Piteå Sweden
54B2 Pitești Rom
63B2 Pit Gorodok Russian Fed
38L6 Pitkyaranta Russian Fed
44C3 Pitlochry Scot
34A3 Pitrutquén Chile
13B2 Pitt I Can
22B1 Pittsburg California, USA
18B2 Pittsburg Kansas, USA
14C2 Pittsburgh USA
18B2 Pittsfield Illinois, USA
16C1 Pittsfield Massachusetts, USA
109D1 Pittsworth Aust
86A1 Piuthan Nepal
47D1 Pizzo Redorta Mt Italy
38B2 Pjórsá Iceland
32A5 Pjura R Peru
7E5 Placentia B Can
22B1 Placerville USA
46B1 Plaine des Flandres Upland Belg/France
96C2 Plaine du Tidikelt Desert Region Alg
9C3 Plainview Texas, USA
22B2 Planada USA
30F2 Planalto de Mato Grosso Plat Brazil
31D3 Planalto do Borborema Plat Brazil
32A1 Planalto do Mato Grosso Mts Brazil
19A3 Plano USA
17B2 Plantation USA
17B2 Plant City USA
50A1 Plasencia Spain
61K3 Plast Russian Fed
69F2 Plastun Russian Fed
96C2 Plateau du Tademait Alg
46D2 Plateau Lorrain Plat France
46C2 Plateaux de Limousin Plat France
51C2 Plateau du Sersou Plat Alg
26C5 Plato Colombia
65G5 Plato Ustyurt Plat Kazakhstan
8C2 Platte R USA
15D2 Plattsburgh USA
18A1 Plattsmouth USA
57C2 Plauen Germany
60E3 Plavsk Russian Fed
23A2 Playa Azul Mexico
32A4 Playas Ecuador
23B2 Playa Vicente Mexico

50A1 Plaza de Moro Almanzor Mt Spain
22B2 Pleasanton California, USA
16B3 Pleasantville USA
14A3 Pleasure Ridge Park USA
76D3 Pleiku Viet
110C1 Plenty,B of NZ
58B2 Pleszew Pol
7C4 Pletipi,L Can
54B2 Pleven Bulg
54A2 Pljevlja Montenegro, Yugos
52C2 Ploče Bosnia-Herzegovina
58B2 Płock Pol
48B2 Ploërmel France
54C2 Ploiești Rom
60B3 Płońsk Pol
54B2 Plovdiv Bulg
20C1 Plummer USA
12C2 Plummer,Mt USA
100B3 Plumtree Zim
22B1 Plymouth California, USA
43B4 Plymouth Eng
14A2 Plymouth Indiana, USA
16D2 Plymouth Massachusetts, USA
15C2 Plymouth Pennsylvania, USA
43B4 Plymouth Sd Eng
43C3 Plynlimon Mt Wales
57C3 Plzeň Czech Republic
58B2 Pniewy Pol
38K6 Pñyäselkä L Fin
97B3 Pô Burkina
47E2 Po R Italy
97C4 Pobé Benin
69G2 Pobedino Russian Fed
8B2 Pocatello USA
15C3 Pocomoke City USA
35B2 Pocos de Caldas Brazil
54A2 Podgorica Montenegro, Yugos
47D2 Po di Volano R Italy
63B1 Podkamennaya R Russian Fed
60E2 Podol'sk Russian Fed
59D3 Podol'skaya Vozvyshennost' Upland Ukraine
60D1 Podporozh'ye Russian Fed
61F1 Podyuga Russian Fed
100A3 Pofadder S Africa
74B3 P'ohang S Korea
112C9 Poinsett,C Ant
108C2 Point Aust
27E3 Pointe-à-Pitre Guadeloupe
48B2 Pointe de Barfleur Pt France
98B3 Pointe Noire Congo
98A2 Pointe Pongara Pt Gabon
108B3 Point Fairy Aust
27L1 Point Fortin Trinidad
4B3 Point Hope USA
4G3 Point L Can
12B1 Point Lay USA
16B2 Point Pleasant New Jersey, USA
14B3 Point Pleasant W Virginia, USA
47B2 Point St Bernard Mt France
48C2 Poitiers France
48B2 Poitou Region, France
46A2 Poix France
85C3 Pokaran India
109C1 Pokataroo Aust
61G3 Pokrovsk Russian Fed
63E1 Pokrovsk Russian Fed
58B2 Poland Republic, Europe
92B2 Polatlı Turk

78D3 Polewali Indon
47A1 Poligny France
55B2 Políyiros Greece
87B2 Pollachi India
79B3 Polollo Is Phil
59D2 Polonnye Ukraine
58D1 Polotsk Russian Fed
60D4 Poltava Russian Fed
52C1 Pölten Austria
64F3 Poluostrov Kanin Pen Russian Fed
61H5 Poluostrov Mangyshlak Pen Kazakhstan
38L5 Poluostrov Rybachiy Pen Russian Fed
64H2 Poluostrov Yamal Pen Russian Fed
38L5 Polyarnyy Murmansk, Russian Fed
1B8 Polyarnyy Yakutskaya, Russian Fed
105H3 Polynesia Region Pacific O
32B5 Pomabamba Peru
35C2 Pomba R Brazil
22D3 Pomona USA
18A2 Pomona Res USA
17B2 Pompano Beach USA
16B2 Pompton Lakes USA
18C1 Ponca City USA
27D3 Ponce Puerto Rico
17B2 Ponce de Leon B USA
87B2 Pondicherry India
6C2 Pond Inlet Can
50A1 Ponferrade Spain
98C2 Pongo R Sudan
101H1 Pongola R S Africa
87B2 Ponnāni India
86C2 Ponnyadoung Range Mts Burma
13E2 Ponoka Can
64F3 Ponoy Russian Fed
48B2 Pons France
35D1 Ponta da Baleia Pt Brazil
96A1 Ponta Delgada Azores
98B3 Ponta do Padrão Pt Angola
35C2 Ponta dos Búzios Pt Brazil
30F4 Ponta Grossa Brazil
35B2 Pontal Brazil
46D2 Pont-à-Mousson France
35D1 Ponta Pora Brazil
49D2 Pontarlier France
19B3 Pontchartrain,L USA
52B2 Pontedera Italy
52A2 Ponte Leccia Corse
18C1 Pontiac Illinois, USA
14B2 Pontiac Michigan, USA
78B3 Pontianak Indon
48B2 Pontivy France
48B2 Pontoise France
19C3 Pontotoc USA
43C4 Pontypool Wales
43C4 Pontypridd Wales
43D4 Poole Eng
Poona = Pune
108B2 Pooncarie Aust
108B2 Poopelloe,L L Aust
22C2 Poorman USA
32B3 Popayán Colombia
46B1 Poperinge Belg
108B2 Popilta L Aust
18B2 Poplar Bluff USA
18B2 Poplarville USA
23B2 Popocatepetl Mt Mexico
98B3 Popokabaka Zaïre
107D1 Popondetta PNG
54C2 Popovo Bulg
85B4 Porbandar India
13A2 Porcher I Can
12F1 Porcupine R Can/USA

52B1 **Poreč** Croatia
35A2 **Porecatu** Brazil
39J6 **Pori** Fin
111B2 **Porirua** NZ
38H5 **Porjus** Sweden
69G2 **Poronaysk** Russian Fed
47B1 **Porrentruy** Switz
38K4 **Porsanger** Inlet Nor
39F7 **Porsgrunn** Nor
45C1 **Portadown** N Ire
8D2 **Portage la Prairie** Can
13C3 **Port Alberni** Can
50A2 **Portalegre** Port
9C3 **Portales** USA
100B4 **Port Alfred** S Africa
13B2 **Port Alice** USA
19B3 **Port Allen** USA
20B1 **Port Angeles** USA
26B3 **Port Antonio** Jamaica
45C2 **Portarlington** Irish Rep
19B4 **Port Arthur** USA
108A2 **Port Augusta** Aust
26C3 **Port-au-Prince** Haiti
14B2 **Port Austin** USA
108B3 **Port Campbell** Aust
86B2 **Port Canning** India
7D5 **Port Cartier** Can
111B3 **Port Chalmers** NZ
17B2 **Port Charlotte** USA
16C2 **Port Chester** USA
15C2 **Port Colborne** Can
15C2 **Port Credit** Can
109C4 **Port Davey** Aust
26C3 **Port-de-Paix** Haiti
77C5 **Port Dickson** Malay
100C4 **Port Edward** S Africa
35C1 **Porteirinha** Brazil
14R? **Port Elgin** Can
23B1 **Port Elizabeth** S Africa
27N2 **Porter Pt** St Vincent and the Grenadines
21B2 **Porterville** USA
107D4 **Port Fairy** Aust
98A3 **Port Gentil** Gabon
19B3 **Port Gibson** USA
12D3 **Port Graham** USA
20B1 **Port Hammond** Can
89E7 **Port Harcourt** Nig
13B2 **Port Hardy** Can
7D5 **Port Hawkesbury** Can
106A3 **Port Hedland** Aust
Port Heiden = Meshik
43B3 **Porthmadog** Wales
7E4 **Port Hope Simpson** Can
22C3 **Port Hueneme** USA
14B2 **Port Huron** USA
50A2 **Portimão** Port
109D2 **Port Jackson** B Aust
16C2 **Port Jefferson** USA
16B2 **Port Jervis** USA
109D2 **Port Kembla** Aust
14B2 **Portland** Indiana, USA
15C2 **Portland** Maine, USA
109C4 **Portland** New South Wales, Aust
20B1 **Portland** Oregon, USA
108B3 **Portland** Victoria, Aust
27H2 **Portland Bight** B Jamaica
43C4 **Portland Bill** Pt Eng
109C4 **Portland,C** Aust
13A1 **Portland Canal** Can/USA
110C1 **Portland I** NZ
27H2 **Portland Pt** Jamaica
45C2 **Port Laoise** Irish Rep
108A2 **Port Lincoln** Aust
97A4 **Port Loko** Sierra Leone
101E3 **Port Louis** Mauritius
108B3 **Port MacDonnell** Aust
13B2 **Port McNeill** Can

109D2 **Port Macquarie** Aust
12B3 **Port Moller** USA
107D1 **Port Moresby** PNG
100A3 **Port Nolloth** S Africa
16B3 **Port Norris** USA
89C7 **Port Lloyd** Bonin
50A1 **Porto** Port
30F5 **Pôrto Alegre** Brazil
33F6 **Pôrto Artur** Brazil
30F3 **Pôrto E Cunha** Brazil
52B2 **Portoferraio** Italy
27E4 **Port of Spain** Trinidad
47D2 **Portomaggiore** Italy
97C4 **Porto Novo** Benin
20B1 **Port Orchard** USA
20B2 **Port Orford** USA
96A1 **Porto Santo** I Medeira
31D5 **Pôrto Seguro** Brazil
53A2 **Pôrto Torres** Sardegna
53A2 **Pôrto Vecchio** Corse
33E5 **Pôrto Velho** Brazil
111A3 **Port Pegasus** B NZ
108B3 **Port Phillip** B Aust
108A2 **Port Pirie** Aust
44A3 **Portree** Scot
20B1 **Port Renfrew** Can
27J2 **Port Royal** Jamaica
17B1 **Port Royal Sd** USA
45C1 **Portrush** N Ire
92B3 **Port Said** Egypt
17A1 **Port St Joe** USA
100B4 **Port St Johns** S Africa
7E4 **Port Saunders** Can
100C4 **Port Shepstone** S Africa
13A2 **Port Simpson** Can
27Q2 **Portsmouth** Dominica
43D4 **Portsmouth** Eng
14B3 **Portsmouth** Ohio, USA
11C3 **Portsmouth** Virginia, USA
109D2 **Port Stephens** B Aust
95C3 **Port Sudan** Sudan
19C3 **Port Sulphur** USA
38K5 **Porttipahdan Tekojärvi** Res Fin
50A2 **Portugal** Republic, Europe
14A2 **Port Washington** USA
77C5 **Port Weld** Malay
32D6 **Porvenir** Bol
39K6 **Porvoo** Fin
30E4 **Posadas** Arg
50A2 **Posadas** Spain
47D1 **Poschiavo** Switz
6B2 **Posheim Pen** Can
90C3 **Posht-e Badam** Iran
71D4 **Poso** Indon
58D1 **Postavy** Belorussia
14B2 **Post Clinton** USA
100B3 **Postmasburg** S Africa
52B1 **Postojna** Slovenia
74C2 **Pos'yet** Russian Fed
101G1 **Potchefstroom** S Africa
19B2 **Poteau** USA
53C2 **Potenza** Italy
100B3 **Potgietersrus** S Africa
97D3 **Potiskum** Nig
20C1 **Potlatch** USA
15C3 **Potomac** R USA
30C2 **Potosí** Bol
30C4 **Potrerillos** Chile
56C2 **Potsdam** Germany
16B2 **Potsdam** USA
16A2 **Pottsville** USA
16C2 **Poughkeepsie** USA
35B2 **Pouso Alegre** Brazil
110C1 **Poverty** B NZ
61F3 **Povorino** Russian Fed
7C4 **Povungnituk** Can
8C2 **Powder** R USA
106C2 **Powell Creek** Aust

9B3 **Powell,L** USA
13C3 **Powell River** Can
8C2 **Power** R USA
43C3 **Powys** County, Wales
73D4 **Poyang Hu** L China
92B2 **Pozanti** Turk
23B1 **Poza Rica** Mexico
52B2 **Poznań** Pol
30E3 **Pozo Colorado** Par
53B2 **Pozzuoli** Italy
97B4 **Pra** R Ghana
76C3 **Prachin Buri** Thai
76B3 **Prachuap Khiri Khan** Thai
59B2 **Praděd** Mt Czech Republic
49C3 **Pradelles** France
35D1 **Prado** Brazil
57C2 **Prague = Praha**
57C2 **Praha** Czech Republic
97A4 **Praia** Cape Verde
33E5 **Prainha** Brazil
108B2 **Prairie Village** USA
76C3 **Prakhon Chai** Thai
35B1 **Prata** Brazil
35B1 **Prata** R Brazil
Prates = Dongsha Qundao
49E3 **Prato** Italy
16C1 **Prattsville** USA
17A1 **Prattville** USA
48B1 **Prawle Pt** Eng
78D4 **Praya** Indon
47D1 **Predazzo** Italy
63B2 **Predivinsk** Russian Fed
58C2 **Pregolyu** R Russian Fed
76D3 **Prek Kak** Camb
56C2 **Prenzlau** Germany
76A3 **Preparis** I Burma
76A2 **Preparis North Chan** Burma
59B3 **Přerov** Czech Republic
23A2 **Presa del Infiernillo** Mexico
19B2 **Prescott** Arizona, USA
19B3 **Prescott** Arkansas, USA
15C2 **Prescott** Can
30D4 **Presidencia Roque Sáenz Peña** Arg
35A2 **Presidente Epitacio** Brazil
112C2 **Presidente Frei** Base Ant
23B2 **Presidente Miguel Aleman** L Mexico
35A2 **Presidente Prudente** Brazil
35A2 **Presidente Venceslau** Brazil
59C3 **Prešov** Slovakia
55B2 **Prespansko Jezero** L Macedonia, Yugos
15C2 **Presque Isle** USA
42C3 **Preston** Eng
8B2 **Preston** Idaho, USA
18B2 **Preston** Missouri, USA
42B2 **Prestwick** Scot
31B6 **Prêto** Brazil
35B1 **Prêto** R Brazil
101G1 **Pretoria** S Africa
55B3 **Préveza** Greece
76D3 **Prey Veng** Camb
8B3 **Price** USA
13B2 **Price I** Can
60D4 **Prichernomorskaya Nizmennost'** Lowland Ukraine
27M2 **Prickly Pt** Grenada
58C1 **Priekule** Lithuania
100B3 **Prieska** S Africa
20C1 **Priest L** USA
20C1 **Priest River** USA
55B2 **Prilep** Macedonia, Yugos
60D3 **Priluki** Ukraine
34C2 **Primero** R Arg

39K6 **Primorsk** Russian Fed
60E4 **Primorsko-Akhtarsk** Russian Fed
13F2 **Primrose L** Can
5H4 **Prince Albert** Can
13C2 **Prince Albert,C** Can
4G2 **Prince Albert Pen** Can
4G2 **Prince Albert Sd** Can
6C3 **Prince Charles I** Can
112B10 **Prince Charles Mts** Ant
7D5 **Prince Edward I** Can
13C2 **Prince George** Can
4H2 **Prince Gustaf Adolp** S Can
5E4 **Prince of Wales I** Can
71F5 **Prince of Wales I** Aust
4H2 **Prince of Wales I** Can
4G2 **Prince of Wales Str** Can
4F2 **Prince Patrick I** Can
6A2 **Prince Regent Inlet** Str Can
13A2 **Prince Rupert** Can
107D2 **Princess Charlotte B** Aust
13B2 **Princess Royal I** Can
27L1 **Princes Town** Trinidad
13C3 **Princeton** Can
18C2 **Princeton** Kentucky, USA
18B1 **Princeton** Missouri, USA
18B1 **Princeton** New Jersey, USA
4D3 **Prince William** USA
12E2 **Prince William Sd** USA
97C4 **Principe** I W Africa
20B2 **Prineville** USA
12E1 **Pringle,Mt** USA
6F3 **Prins Christian Sund** Sd Greenland
112B12 **Prinsesse Astrid Kyst** Region, Ant
112B12 **Prinsesse Ragnhild Kyst** Region, Ant
64B2 **Prins Karls Forland** I Barents S
25D3 **Prinzapolca** Nic
58D2 **Pripet** R Belorussia
Pripyat' = Pripet
54B2 **Priština** Serbia, Yugos
56C2 **Pritzwalk** Germany
61F3 **Privolchskaya Vozvyshennost'** Upland Russian Fed
54B2 **Prizren** Serbia, Yugos
54B2 **Prokletije** Mts Albania/Yugos
78C4 **Probolinggo** Indon
5G5 **Pocatello** USA
87B2 **Proddatūr** India
25D2 **Progreso** Mexico
20B2 **Project City** USA
61F5 **Prokhladny** Russian Fed
65K4 **Prokop'yevsk** Russian Fed
61F4 **Proletarskaya** Russian Fed
64G2 **Proliv Karskiye Vorota** Str Russian Fed
83D4 **Prome** Burma
31D4 **Propriá** Brazil
20B2 **Prospect** Oregon, USA
107D3 **Prosperine** Aust
59B3 **Prostějov** Czech Republic
6E2 **Prøven** Greenland
49D3 **Provence** Region, France
16D2 **Providence** USA
15D2 **Provincetown** USA
49C2 **Provins** France
8B2 **Provo** USA

Provost

13E2 **Provost** Can
4D2 **Prudhoe Bay** USA
6D2 **Prudhoe Land** Greenland
58C2 **Pruszkow** Pol
60C4 **Prut** *R* Romania/ Moldova
60C4 **Prutul** *R* Romania
58C2 **Pruzhany** Belorussia
18A2 **Pryor** USA
59C3 **Przemys'l** Pol
55C3 **Psará** *I* Greece
60C2 **Pskov** Russian Fed
58D2 **Ptich** *R* Belorussia
55B2 **Ptolemais** Greece
32C5 **Pucallpa** Peru
73D4 **Pucheng** China
34A3 **Pucón** Chile
38K5 **Pudasjärvi** Fin
87B2 **Pudukkottai** India
23B2 **Puebla** Mexico
23B2 **Puebla** State, Mexico
50A1 **Puebla de Sanabria** Spain
50A1 **Puebla de Trives** Spain
9C2 **Pueblo** USA
34B3 **Puelén** Arg
23A2 **Puenta Ixbapa** Mexico
34B2 **Puente del Inca** Arg
32A5 **Puerta Aguja** Peru
34B2 **Puerta Coles** Peru
34B2 **Puerta de los Llanos** Arg
31D3 **Puerta do Calcanhar** *Pt* Brazil
32C1 **Puerta Gallinas** Colombia
23B2 **Puerta Maldonado** *Pt* Mexico
32A2 **Puerta Mariato** Panama
29C5 **Puerta Médanosa** *Pt* Arg
23A2 **Puerta Mongrove** Mexico
25E4 **Puerta San Blas** *Pt* Panama
23A2 **Puerta San Telmo** Mexico
29B5 **Puerta Aisén** Chile
25D4 **Puerto Armuelles** Panama
33F6 **Puerto Artur** Brazil
32B3 **Puerto Asis** Colombia
32D2 **Puerto Ayacucho** Ven
25D3 **Puerto Barrios** Guatemala
32C2 **Puerto Berrio** Colombia
25D4 **Puerto Cabello** Ven
25D3 **Puerto Cabezas** Nic
32D2 **Puerto Carreño** Colombia
25D4 **Puerto Cortes** Costa Rica
25D3 **Puerto Cortés** Honduras
96A2 **Puerto del Rosario** Canary Is
30F3 **Puerto E Cunha** Brazil
32C1 **Puerto Fijo** Ven
31B3 **Puerto Franco** Brazil
32D6 **Puerto Heath** Bol
25D2 **Puerto Juarez** Mexico
33E1 **Puerto la Cruz** Ven
50B2 **Puertollano** Spain
27C4 **Puerto Lopez** Colombia
29D4 **Puerto Madryn** Arg
32D6 **Puerto Maldonado** Peru
23B2 **Puerto Marquéz** Mexico
29B4 **Puerto Montt** Chile
30E3 **Puerto Murtinho** Brazil
29B6 **Puerto Natales** Chile

24A1 **Puerto Peñasco** Mexico
29D4 **Puerto Pirámides** Arg
27C3 **Puerto Plata** Dom Rep
79A4 **Puerto Princesa** Phil
32B3 **Puerto Rico** Colombia
27D3 **Puerto Rico** *I* Caribbean S
27D3 **Puerto Rico Trench** Caribbean S
23A2 **Puerto San Juan de Lima** Mexico
33G4 **Puerto Santanga** Brazil
30E2 **Puerto Suárez** Bol
24B2 **Puerto Vallarta** Mexico
29B4 **Puerto Varas** Chile
30D2 **Puerto Villarroel** Bol
61G3 **Pugachev** Russian Fed
84C3 **Pugal** India
51C1 **Puigcerdá** Spain
111B2 **Pukaki,L** *L* NZ
74B2 **Pukch'ŏng** N Korea
110B1 **Pukekohe** NZ
111B2 **Puketeraki Range** *Mts* NZ
52B2 **Pula** Croatia
15C2 **Pulaski** New York, USA
71E4 **Pulau Kolepom** *I* Indon
70A4 **Pulau Pulau Batu** *Is* Indon
58C2 **Pulawy** Pol
87B2 **Pulicat,L** India
84B1 **Pul-i-Khumri** Afghan
84B3 **Puliyangudi** India
20C1 **Pullman** USA
71E3 **Pulo Anna Merir** *I* Pacific O
79B2 **Pulog,Mt** Phil
38L5 **Pulozero** Russian Fed
58C2 **Pultusk** Pol
30C4 **Puna de Atacama** Arg
86B1 **Punakha** Bhutan
84C2 **Punch** Pak
87A1 **Pune** India
23A2 **Punepar** Mexico
98C3 **Punia** Zaïre
34A2 **Punitaqui** Chile
84C2 **Punjab** Province, Pak
84D2 **Punjab** State, India
30B2 **Puno** Peru
24A2 **Punta Abreojos** *Pt* Mexico
53C3 **Punta Alice** *Pt* Italy
34C3 **Punta Alta** Arg
29B6 **Punta Arenas** Chile
24A2 **Punta Baja** *Pt* Mexico
34A2 **Punta Curaumilla** *Pt* Chile
100A2 **Punta da Marca** *Pt* Angola
101C3 **Punta de Barra Falsa** *Pt* Mozam
29F2 **Punta del Este** Urug
24A2 **Punta Eugenia** *Pt* Mexico
25D3 **Punta Gorda** Belize
17B2 **Punta Gorda** USA
34A3 **Punta Lavapié** *Pt* Chile
34A2 **Punta Lengua de Vaca** *Pt* Chile
53B2 **Punta Licosa** *Pt* Italy
34A1 **Punta Poroto** *Pt* Chile
9B4 **Punta San Antonia** *Pt* Mexico
34A3 **Punta Topocalma** Chile
73C4 **Puqi** China
64J3 **Pur** *R* Russian Fed
19A2 **Purcell** USA
12C1 **Purcell** USA
13D2 **Purcell Mts** Can
34A3 **Purén** Chile

86B2 **Puri** India
87B1 **Pūrna** India
86B1 **Pūrnia** India
76C3 **Pursat** Camb
23A1 **Puruandro** Mexico
32A4 **Purus** *R* Brazil
19C3 **Purvis** USA
78B4 **Purwokerto** Indon
78C4 **Purworejo** Indon
85D5 **Pusad** India
74B3 **Pusan** S Korea
60D2 **Pushkin** Russian Fed
58D1 **Pustoshka** Russian Fed
82D3 **Puta** Burma
34A2 **Putaendo** Chile
110C1 **Putaruru** NZ
73D4 **Putian** China
71E4 **Putina** USA
87B3 **Puttalam** Sri Lanka
56C2 **Puttgarden** Germany
32B4 **Putumayo** *R* Ecuador
78C2 **Putussibau** Indon
38K6 **Puulavesi** *L* Fin
20B1 **Puyallup** USA
49C2 **Puy de Sancy** *Mt* France
111A3 **Puysegur Pt** NZ
99C3 **Pweto** Zaïre
43B3 **Pwllheli** Wales
76B2 **Pyapon** Burma
61F5 **Pyatigorsk** Russian Fed
Pyè = Prome
90B2 **P'yŏngyang** N Korea
108B3 **Pyramid Hill** Aust
21B1 **Pyramid L** USA
111A2 **Pyramid,Mt** NZ
48B3 **Pyrénées** *Mts* France
58D1 **Pytalovo** Russian Fed
76B2 **Pyu** Burma

Q

94B2 **Qabatiya** Israel
94C3 **Qâ'el Hafira** *Mud Flats* Jordan
94C3 **Qa'el Jinz** *Mud Flats* Jordan
68B3 **Qaidam Pendi** *Salt Flat* China
94C2 **Qa Khanna** *Salt Marsh* Jordan
99D1 **Qala'en Nahl** Sudan
84B2 **Qalat** Afghan
94C1 **Qal'at al Hisn** Syria
81C3 **Qal'at Bishah** S Arabia
93E3 **Qal'at Sālih** Iraq
68B3 **Qamdo** China
99E1 **Qandala** Somalia
99E2 **Qardho** Somalia
90A3 **Qare Shirin** Iran
91A4 **Qaryat al Ulyā** S Arabia
94C3 **Qasr al Kharana** Jordan
91D4 **Qasr-e-Qand** Iran
94C2 **Qasr Farafra** Egypt
94C2 **Qatana** Syria
91B4 **Qatar** Emirate, Arabian Pen
94C3 **Qatrâna** Jordan
95B2 **Qattâra Depression** Egypt
90C3 **Qāyen** Iran
90A2 **Qazvin** Iran
95C2 **Qena** Egypt
91B4 **Qeys** Iran
94B3 **Qeziot** Israel
73B5 **Qian Jiang** *R* China
72E1 **Qian Shan** *Upland* China
72E3 **Qidong** China
73B4 **Qijiang** China
84B2 **Qila Saifullah** Pak
72A2 **Qilian** China
68B3 **Qilian Shan** China
72B3 **Qin'an** China
72E2 **Qingdao** China
72A2 **Qinghai** Province, China

68B3 **Qinghai Hu** *L* China
72D3 **Qingjiang** Jiangsu, China
73D4 **Qingjiang** Jiangxi, China
72B3 **Qing Jiang** *R* China
72C2 **Qingshuihe** China
72B2 **Qingshui He** *R* China
72B2 **Qingtongxia** China
72B2 **Qingyang** China
74B2 **Qingyuan** Liaoning, China
73D4 **Qingyuan** Zhejiang, China
82C2 **Qing Zang** *Upland* China
72D2 **Qinhuangdao** China
72B3 **Qin Ling** *Mts* China
73B5 **Qinzhou** China
76E2 **Qionghai** China
73A3 **Qionglai Shan** *Upland* China
76D1 **Qiongzhou Haixia** *Str* China
69E2 **Qiqihar** China
94B2 **Qiryat Ata** Israel
94B3 **Qiryat Gat** Israel
94B2 **Qiryat Shemona** Israel
94B2 **Qiryat Yam** Israel
94B2 **Qishon** *R* Israel
63A3 **Qitai** China
73C4 **Qiyang** China
72B1 **Qog Qi** China
90B2 **Qolleh-ye Damavand** *Mt* Iran
90B3 **Qom** Iran
90B3 **Qomisheh** Iran
Qomolangma Feng = Everest,Mt
94C1 **Qornet es Saouda** *Mt* Leb
6E3 **Qôrnoq** Greenland
90A2 **Qorveh** Iran
91C4 **Qotābād** Iran
16C1 **Qu'Appelle** *R* Can
5H4 **Qu' Appelle** *R* Can
91C5 **Quarayyāt** Oman
13B2 **Quatsino Sd** Can
90C2 **Quchan** Iran
109C3 **Queanbeyan** Aust
10B1 **Québec** Can
7C4 **Quebec** Province, Can
35B1 **Quebra-Anzol** *R* Brazil
34D2 **Quebracho** Urug
30F4 **Quedas do Iguaçu** Brazil/Arg
16A3 **Queen Anne** USA
13B2 **Queen Bess,Mt** USA
5E4 **Queen Charlotte Is** Can
13B2 **Queen Charlotte Sd** Can
13B2 **Queen Charlotte Str** Can
4H1 **Queen Elizabeth Is** Can
112B9 **Queen Mary Land** Region, Ant
4H3 **Queen Maud G** Can
112A **Queen Maud Mts** Ant
16C2 **Queens** Borough, New York, USA
108B3 **Queenscliff** Aust
107D3 **Queensland** State, Aust
109C4 **Queenstown** Aust
111A3 **Queenstown** NZ
100B4 **Queenstown** S Africa
16A3 **Queenstown** USA
98B3 **Quela** Angola
101C2 **Quelimane** Mozam

34C3 Quemuquemú Arg
13C2 Quensel L Can
34D3 Quequén Arg
34D3 Quequén R Arg
23A1 Querétaro Mexico
23A1 Querétaro State Mexico
13C2 Quesnel Can
84B2 Quetta Pak
25C3 Quezaltenango Guatemala
79B3 Quezon City Phil
100A2 Quibala Angola
98B3 Quibaxe Angola
50D2 Quibdó Colombia
48B2 Quiberon France
98B3 Quicama Nat Pk Angola
73A4 Quijing China
34A2 Quilima Chile
34C2 Quilino Arg
32C6 Quillabamba Peru
30C2 Quillacollo Bol
48C3 Quillan France
5H4 Quill L Can
5H4 Quill Lakes Can
34A2 Quillota Chile
87B3 Quilon India
108B1 Quilpie Aust
34A2 Quilpué Chile
98B3 Quimbele Angola
48B2 Quimper France
48B2 Quimperlé France
21A2 Quincy California, USA
10A3 Quincy Illinois, USA
16D1 Quincy Massachusetts, USA
34B2 Quines Arg
12B3 Quinhagak USA
76D3 Qui Nhon Viet
50B2 Quintanar de la Orden Spain
34A2 Quintero Chile
34C2 Quinto R Arg
34A3 Quirihue Chile
100A2 Quirima Angola
109D2 Quirindi Aust
101D2 Quissanga Mozam
101C3 Quissico Mozam
32B4 Quito Ecuador
31D2 Quixadá Brazil
108A2 Quorn Aust
4G3 Qurlurtuuk Can
95C2 Quseir Egypt
6E3 Qutdligssat Greenland
Quthing = Moyeni
73B3 Qu Xian Sichuan, China
73D4 Qu Xian Zhejiang, China
76D2 Quynh Luu Viet
72C2 Quzhou China
86C1 Qüzü China

R

38J6 Raahe Fin
44A3 Raasay I Scot
44A3 Raasay,Sound of Chan Scot
99F1 Raas Caseyr C Somalia
52B2 Rab I Croatia
78D4 Raba Indon
59B3 Rába R Hung
96B1 Rabat Mor
94B3 Rabba Jordan
80B3 Rabigh S Arabia
47B2 Racconigi Italy
7E5 Race,C Can
54B2 Rachaya Leb
57C3 Rachel Mt Germany
76D3 Rach Gia Viet
14A2 Racine USA
59D3 Rădăuți Rom
85C4 Radhanpur India
27L1 Rada,Pt Trinidad
58C2 Radom Pol
58D2 Radomsko Pol
58C2 Radviliškis Lithuania
4G3 Rae Can
86A1 Rae Bareli India
6B3 Rae Isthmus Can

4G3 Rae L Can
110C1 Raetihi NZ
34C2 Rafaela Arg
94B3 Rafah Egypt
98C2 Rafai CAR
93D3 Rafḥā Al Jumaymah S Arabia
91C3 Rafsanjān Iran
98C2 Raga Sudan
27R3 Ragged Pt Barbados
53B3 Ragusa Italy
99D1 Rahad R Sudan
84C3 Rahimyar Khan Pak
90B3 Rāhjerd Iran
34D2 Raíces Arg
87B1 Raichur India
86A2 Raigarh India
108B3 Rainbow Aust
17A1 Rainbow City USA
20B1 Rainier USA
20B1 Rainier,Mt USA
10A2 Rainy L Can
12D2 Rainy P USA
10A2 Rainy River Can
86A2 Raipur India
87C1 Rājahmundry India
78C2 Rajang R Malay
84C3 Rajanpur Pak
87B3 Rājapālaiyam India
85C3 Rajasthan, State, India
84D3 Rājgarh India
85B3 Rājgarh State, India
85C4 Rājkot India
86B2 Rajmahal Hills India
86A2 Raj Nāndgaon India
85C4 Rājpipla India
86B2 Rajshahi Bang
85D4 Rajur India
111B2 Rakaia R NZ
78B4 Rakata I Indon
82C3 Raka Zangbo R China
59C3 Rakhov Ukraine
100B3 Rakops Botswana
58D2 Rakov Belorussia
12A1 Raleigh USA
7A5 Ralny L Can
94B2 Rama Israel
94B3 Ramallah Israel
87B3 Rāmanāthapuram India
69G3 Ramapo Deep Pacific O
94B2 Ramat Gan Israel
46A2 Rambouillet France
86B2 Rāmgarh Bihar, India
85C3 Rāmgarh Rajasthan, India
90A3 Rāmhormoz Iran
94B3 Ramla Israel
91C5 Ramlat Al Wahibah Region, Oman
21B3 Ramona USA
85D4 Rāmpur India
90B2 Rāmsar Iran
42B2 Ramsey Eng
16B2 Ramsey USA
43E4 Ramsgate Eng
94C2 Ramtha Jordan
71F4 Ramu R PNG
34A2 Rancagua Chile
86A2 Ranchi Plat India
101G1 Randburg S Africa
39G7 Randers Den
101G1 Randfontein S Africa
15D2 Randolph Vermont, USA
111B3 Ranfurly NZ
86C2 Rangamati Bang
110C1 Rangiora NZ
110C1 Rangitaiki R NZ
111B2 Rangitata R NZ
110C1 Rangitikei R NZ
Rangoon = Yangon
86B1 Rangpur India
87B2 Rānibennur India
8A2 Ranier,Mt Mt USA
86B2 Rāniganj India
109C2 Rankins Springs Aust
6A3 Ranklin Inlet Can

85B4 Rann of Kachchh Flood Area India
77B4 Ranong Thai
70A3 Rantauparapat Indon
18C1 Rantoul USA
49D3 Rapallo Italy
34A2 Rapel R Chile
6D3 Raper,C Can
8C2 Rapid City USA
14A1 Rapid River USA
15C3 Rappahannock R USA
47C1 Rapperswil Switz
16B2 Raritan B USA
95C2 Ras Abu Shagara C Sudan
93D2 Ra's al 'Ayn Syria
91C5 Ra's al Hadd C Oman
91C4 Ras al Kaimah UAE
91C4 Ras-al-Kuh C Iran
81D4 Ra's al Madrakah C Oman
91A4 Ra's az Zawr C S Arabia
95C2 Rās Bânas C Egypt
94A3 Rās Burûn C Egypt
99D1 Ras Dashan Mt Eth
90A3 Ra's-e-Barkan Pt Iran
92B3 Râs el Kenâyis Pt Egypt
81D4 Ra's Fartak C Yemen
95C2 Rās Gharib Egypt
99D1 Rashad Sudan
94B3 Rashādiya Jordan
92B3 Rashid Egypt
90A2 Rasht Iran
91C5 Ra's Jibish C Oman
99E2 Ras Khanzira C Somalia
84B3 Ras Koh Mt Pak
95C2 Ras Muhammad C Egypt
96A2 Ras Nouadhibou C Maur
69H2 Rasshua I Russian Fed
61F3 Rasskazovo Russian Fed
91A4 Ra's Tanāqib C S Arabia
91B4 Ra's Tannūrah C S Arabia
57B3 Rastatt Germany
Ras Uarc = Cabo Tres Forcas
99F1 Ras Xaafuun C Somalia
84C3 Ratangarh India
77B4 Rat Buri Thai
85D3 Rath India
56C2 Rathenow Germany
45B2 Rathkeale Irish Rep
45C1 Rathlin I N Ire
45B2 Rath Luirc Irish Rep
85D4 Ratlām India
87A1 Ratnāgiri India
87C3 Ratnapura Sri Lanka
58C2 Ratno Ukraine
47D1 Rattenberg Austria
39H6 Rättvik Sweden
12H3 Ratz,Mt Can
34D3 Rauch Arg
110C1 Raukumara Range Mts NZ
35C2 Raul Soares Brazil
39J6 Rauma Fin
86A2 Raurkela India
90A3 Rāvānsar Iran
90C3 Rāvar Iran
59C2 Rava Russkaya Ukraine
16C1 Ravena USA
52B2 Ravenna Italy
57B3 Ravensburg Germany
107D2 Ravenshoe Aust
42E2 Ravenspurn Oilfield N Sea
84C2 Ravi R Pak
84C2 Rawalpindi Pak
93D2 Rawāndiz Iraq
58B2 Rawicz Pol
106B4 Rawlinna Aust

8C2 Rawlins USA
29C4 Rawson Arg
78C3 Raya Mt Indon
87B2 Rāyadurg India
94C2 Rayak Leb
7E5 Ray,C Can
91C4 Rayen Iran
22C2 Raymond California, USA
20B1 Raymond Washington, USA
109D2 Raymond Terrace Aust
12D1 Ray Mts USA
23B1 Rayon Mexico
90A2 Razan Iran
54C2 Razgrad Bulg
54C2 Razim L Rom
43D4 Reading Eng
16B2 Reading USA
4G3 Read Island Can
16C1 Readsboro USA
34B2 Real de Padre Arg
34C3 Realicó Arg
95B2 Rebiana Well Libya
95B2 Rebiana Sand Sea Libya
38L6 Reboly Russian Fed
12A2 Recherche,Arch of the Is Aust
31E3 Recife Brazil
107F2 Récifs D'Entrecasteaux Nouvelle Calédonie
46D1 Recklinghausen Germany
30E4 Reconquista Arg
19B3 Red R USA
77C4 Redang I Malay
16B2 Red Bank New Jersey, USA
21A1 Red Bluff USA
42D2 Redcar Eng
13E2 Redcliff Can
109D1 Redcliffe Aust
108B2 Red Cliffs Aust
13E2 Red Deer Can
13E2 Red Deer R Can
20B2 Redding USA
10A2 Red L USA
14B2 Red Lake Can
22D3 Redlands USA
16A3 Red Lion USA
20B2 Redmond USA
18A1 Red Oak USA
48B2 Redon France
22C4 Redondo Beach USA
12D2 Redoubt V USA
73B5 Red River Delta Vietnam
80B3 Red Sea Africa/ Arabian Pen
13E2 Redwater Can
22A2 Redwood City USA
14A2 Reed City USA
22C2 Reedley USA
20B2 Reedsport USA
111B2 Reefton NZ
93C2 Refahiye Turk
35D1 Regência Brazil
57C3 Regensburg Germany
96C2 Reggane Alg
53C3 Reggio di Calabria Italy
47D2 Reggio Nell'Emilia Italy
54B1 Reghin Rom
100A3 Rehoboth Namibia
15C3 Rehoboth Beach USA
94B3 Rehovot Israel
32D1 Reicito Ven
43D4 Reigate Eng
46C2 Reims France
5H4 Reindeer R Can
50B1 Reinosa Spain
16A1 Heisterstown USA
101C1 Reitz S Africa
4H3 Reliance Can
108A2 Remarkable,Mt Aust
78C4 Rembang Indon
91C4 Remeshk Iran

Remscheid

46D1 Remscheid Germany
18C2 Rend,L USA
56B2 Rendsburg Germany
15C1 Renfrew Can
78A3 Rengat Indon
34A2 Rengo Chile
59D3 Reni Ukraine
99D1 Renk Sudan
6H2 Renland Pen
    Greenland
108B2 Renmark Aust
107F2 Rennell I Solomon Is
48B2 Rennes France
21B2 Reno USA
47D2 Reno R Italy
15C2 Renovo USA
16C1 Rensselaer USA
20B1 Renton USA
70D4 Reo Indon
35B2 Represa de Furnas
    Dam Brazil
30E3 Represa Ilha Grande
    Dam Brazil
30E3 Represa Itaipu Dam
    Brazil
35A2 Represa Porto
    Primavera Dam
    Brazil
35B1 Represa Três Marias
    Dam Brazil
20C1 Republic USA
41B3 Republic of Ireland
    NW Europe
6B3 Repulse Bay Can
15C1 Réservoir Baskatong
    Res Can
10C1 Réservoir de la
    Grande 2 Res Can
10C1 Réservoir de la
    Grande 3 Res Can
7C4 Réservoir de la
    Grande 4 Res Can
7C5 Réservoir Cabonga
    Res Can
7D4 Réservoir
    Caniapiscau Res Can
7C5 Réservoir Gouin Res
    Can
10D1 Réservoir
    Manicouagan Res
    Can
90B2 Reshteh-ye Alborz
    Mts Iran
72A2 Reshui China
30E4 Resistencia Arg
54B1 Resita Rom
6A2 Resolute Can
111A3 Resolution I NZ
6D3 Resolution Island
    Can
101H1 Ressano Garcia
    Mozam
34B2 Retamito Arg
46C2 Rethel France
55B3 Réthimnon Greece
89K10 Réunion I Indian O
51C1 Reus Spain
47C1 Reuss R Switz
47D1 Reutte Austria
61K3 Revda Russian Fed
13D2 Revelstoke Can
24A3 Revillagigedo Is
    Mexico
12H3 Revillagigedo I USA
46C2 Revin France
94B3 Revivim Israel
86A2 Rewa India
84D3 Rewari India
38A2 Rexburg USA
64A2 Reykjavik Iceland
24C2 Reynosa Mexico
48B2 Rezé France
58D1 Rezekne Latvia
61K2 Rezh Russian Fed
47C1 Rhätikon Mts
    Austria/Switz
94B1 Rhazir Republic, Leb
56B2 Rhein R W Europe
56B2 Rheine Germany
47B1 Rheinfelden Switz
49D2 Rheinland Pfalz
    Region, Germany
47C1 Rheinwaldhorn Mt
    Switz

Rhine = Rhein
16C2 Rhinebeck USA
10B2 Rhinelander USA
47C2 Rho Italy
15D2 Rhode Island State,
    USA
16D2 Rhode Island Sd USA
    Rhodes = Ródhos
49C3 Rhône R France
43C3 Rhyl Wales
31D4 Riachão do Jacuipe
    Brazil
50A1 Ria de Arosa B
    Spain
50A1 Ria de Betanzos B
    Spain
50A1 Ria de Corcubion B
    Spain
50A1 Ria de Lage B Spain
50A1 Ria de Sta Marta B
    Spain
50A1 Ria de Vigo B Spain
84C2 Riasi Pak
50A1 Ribadeo Spain
35A2 Ribas do Rio Pardo
    Brazil
101C2 Ribauè Mozam
42C3 Ribble R Eng
35B2 Ribeira Brazil
35B2 Ribeirão Prêto Brazil
32D6 Riberalta Bol
15C2 Rice L Can
10A2 Rice Lake USA
101H1 Richard's Bay
    S Africa
19A3 Richardson USA
12G1 Richardson Mts Can
8B3 Richfield USA
20C1 Richland USA
22A2 Richmond California,
    USA
101H1 Richmond Natal,
    S Africa
109D2 Richmond New
    South Wales, Aust
111B2 Richmond
107D3 Richmond
    Queensland, Aust
10C3 Richmond Virginia,
    USA
111B2 Richmond Range Mts
    NZ
15C2 Rideau,L Can
17B1 Ridgeland USA
15C2 Ridgway USA
27D4 Riecito Ven
47D1 Rienza R Italy
57C2 Riesa Germany
29B6 Riesco I Chile
101F1 Riet R S Africa
52B2 Rieti Italy
50B2 Rif Mts Mor
58C1 Riga Latvia
60B2 Riga,G of Estonia/
    Latvia
91C4 Rigan Iran
20C1 Riggins USA
7E4 Rigolet Can
39J6 Riihimaki Fin
52B1 Rijeka Croatia
13E2 Rimbey Can
39H7 Rimbo Sweden
52B2 Rimini Italy
54C1 Rimnicu Sărat Rom
54B1 Rimnicu Vilcea Rom
10D2 Rimouski Can
23A1 Rincón de Romos
    Mexico
39F7 Ringkøbing Den
98A2 Rio Benito Eq Guinea
32D5 Rio Branco Brazil
24B1 Rio Bravo del Norte
    R Mexico/USA
32C1 Riochacha Colombia
35B2 Rio Claro Brazil
27L1 Rio Claro Trinidad
34C3 Rio Colorado Arg
34C2 Rio Cuarto Arg
31D4 Rio de Jacuipe Brazil
35C2 Rio de Janeiro Brazil
35C2 Rio de Janeiro State,
    Brazil
29E3 Rio de la Plata Est
    Arg/Urug

29C6 Rio Gallegos Arg
29C6 Rio Grande Arg
30F5 Rio Grande Brazil
26A4 Rio Grande Nic
25D3 Rio Grande R Nic
24B2 Rio Grande R
    Mexico/USA
23A1 Rio Grande de
    Santiago Mexico
31D3 Rio Grande do Norte
    State, Brazil
30F4 Rio Grande do Sul
    State, Brazil
103G6 Rio Grande Rise
    Atlantic O
26C4 Riohacha Colombia
49C2 Riom France
32B4 Riombamba Ecuador
20C3 Rio Mulatos Bol
29C3 Rio Negro State, Arg
30F4 Rio Pardo Brazil
34C2 Rio Tercero Arg
33E6 Rio Theodore
    Roosevelt R Brazil
29B6 Rio Turbio Arg
35A1 Rio Verde Brazil
23A1 Rio Verde Mexico
14B3 Ripley Ohio, USA
14B3 Ripley West Virginia,
    USA
42D2 Ripon Eng
22B2 Ripon USA
94B3 Rishon le Zion Israel
16A3 Rising Sun USA
39F7 Risør Nor
6E2 Ritenberk Greenland
22C2 Ritter,Mt USA
20C1 Ritzville USA
34B2 Rivadavia Arg
34A1 Rivadavia Chile
34C3 Rivadavia Gonzalez
    Moreno Arg
47D2 Riva de Garda Italy
34C3 Rivera Arg
29E2 Rivera Urug
22B2 Riverbank USA
97B4 River Cess Lib
16C2 Riverhead USA
108B3 Riverina Arg
22D4 Riverside USA
13B2 Rivers Inlet Can
113A3 Riverton NZ
8C2 Riverton USA
17B2 Riviera Beach USA
7C4 Riviere aux Feuilles R
    Can
7D4 Rivière de la Baleine
    R Can
7D4 Rivière du Petit
    Mécatina R Can
46C2 Rivigny-sur-Ornain
    France
93D1 Rize Turk
72D2 Rizhao China
    Rizhskiy Zaliv =
    Riga,G of
39F7 Rjukan Nor
6B2 Roanes Pen Can
49C2 Roanne France
17A1 Roanoke Alabama,
    USA
11C3 Roanoke Virginia,
    USA
11C3 Roanoke R USA
45B3 Roaringwater B
    Irish Rep
38J6 Robertsforz Sweden
19B2 Robert S Kerr Res
    USA
97A4 Robertsport Lib
7C5 Roberval Can
30H6 Robinson Crusoe I
    Chile
108B2 Robinvale Aust
13D2 Robson,Mt USA
24A3 Roca Partida I
    Mexico
103G5 Rocas / Atlantic O
31E2 Rocas I Brazil
29F2 Rocha Urug
42C3 Rochdale Eng
48B2 Rochefort France
5G3 Rocher River Can

108B3 Rochester Aust
7C5 Rochester Can
43E4 Rochester Eng
10A2 Rochester
    Minnesota, USA
15D2 Rochester New
    Hampshire, USA
10C2 Rochester New York,
    USA
10B2 Rockford USA
11B3 Rock Hill USA
10A2 Rock Island USA
108B3 Rocklands Res Aust
17B2 Rockledge USA
8C2 Rock Springs
    Wyoming, USA
110B2 Rocks Pt NZ
109C3 Rock,The Aust
16C2 Rockville
    Connecticut, USA
14A3 Rockville Indiana,
    USA
16A3 Rockville Maryland,
    USA
14B1 Rocky Island L Can
13E2 Rocky Mountain
    House Can
8B1 Rocky Mts Can/USA
12B2 Rocky Pt USA
56C2 Rødbyhavn Den
34B2 Rodeo Arg
49C3 Rodez France
55D3 Ródhos Greece
55C3 Ródhos I Greece
52C2 Rodi Garganico Italy
54B2 Rodopi Planina Mts
    Bulg
106A3 Roebourne Aust
46C1 Roermond Neth
46B1 Roeselare Belg
6B3 Roes Welcome Sd
    Can
18B2 Rogers USA
14B1 Rogers City USA
20B2 Rogue R USA
85B3 Rohn Pak
84D3 Rohtak India
58C1 Roja Latvia
35A2 Rolândia Brazil
18B2 Rolla USA
109C1 Roma Aust
52B2 Roma Italy
47C2 Romagnano Italy
17C1 Romain,C USA
54C1 Roman Rom
103H5 Romanche Gap
    Atlantic O
71D4 Romang I Indon
60B4 Romania Republic,
    E Europe
17B2 Romano,C USA
49D2 Romans sur Isère
    France
79B3 Romblon Phil
    Rome = Roma
17A1 Rome Georgia, USA
15C2 Rome New York,
    USA
49C2 Romilly-sur-Seine
    France
15C3 Romney USA
60D3 Romny Ukraine
56B1 Rømø I Den
47B1 Romont Switz
46C2 Romorantin France
50A2 Ronda Spain
33E6 Rondônia Brazil
24F6 Rondônia State,
    Brazil
30F2 Rondonópolis Brazil
73B4 Rong'an China
73B4 Rongcheng China
72E2 Rongchang China
73B4 Rongjiang China
73B4 Rong Jiang R China
76A1 Rongklang Range
    Mts Burma
39G7 Rønne Den
39H7 Ronneby Sweden
112B2 Ronne Ice Shelf Ant
46B1 Ronse Belg
46A1 Ronthieu Region,
    France
9C3 Roof Butte Mt USA

84D3 **Roorkee** India
46C1 **Roosendaal** Neth
112B6 **Roosevelt I** Ant
106C2 **Roper** *R* Aust
33E3 **Roraima** State, Brazil
33E2 **Roraíma** *Mt* Ven
38G6 **Røros** Nor
47C1 **Rorschach** Switz
38G6 **Rørvik** Nor
27Q2 **Rosalie** Dominica
22C3 **Rosamond L** USA
34C2 **Rosario** Arg
31C2 **Rosário** Brazil
34D2 **Rosario del Tala** Arg
48B2 **Roscoff** France
45B2 **Roscommon** County,
Irish Rep
41B3 **Roscommon**
Irish Rep
45C2 **Roscrea** Irish Rep
27E3 **Roseau** Dominica
109C4 **Rosebery** Aust
20B2 **Roseburg** USA
19A4 **Rosenberg** USA
57C3 **Rosenheim** Germany
13F2 **Rosetown** Can
54B2 **Roşiori de Vede** Rom
39G7 **Roskilde** Den
60D3 **Roslavl'** Russian Fed
61D3 **Roslyatino**
Russian Fed
111B2 **Ross** NZ
12H2 **Ross** *R* Can
40B3 **Rossan Pt** Irish Rep
53C3 **Rossano** Italy
19C2 **Ross Barnet Res** USA
15C1 **Rosseau L** Can
107E2 **Rossel / Solomon Is**
112A **Ross Ice Shelf** Ant
20B1 **Ross L** USA
13D3 **Rossland** Can
45C2 **Rosslare** Irish Rep
111C2 **Ross,Mt** NZ
97A3 **Rosso** Maur
43C4 **Ross-on-Wye** Eng
44A3 **Rossosh** Russian Fed
4E3 **Ross River** Can
112B6 **Ross S** Ant
91B4 **Rostāq** Iran
51B2 **Rostock** Germany
Rostov = Rostov-na-
Donu
61E4 **Rostov-na-Donu**
Russian Fed
17B1 **Roswell** Georgia,
USA
9C3 **Roswell** New Mexico,
USA
71F2 **Rota** Pacific O
56B2 **Rotenburg**
Niedersachsen,
Germany
46E1 **Rothaar-Geb** *Region*
Germany
112C3 **Rothera** *Base* Ant
42D3 **Rotherham** Eng
42B2 **Rothesay** Scot
71D5 **Roti** *I* Indon
108C2 **Roto** Aust
111B2 **Rotoiti,L** NZ
111B2 **Rotorua** NZ
110C1 **Rotorua** NZ
110C1 **Rotorua,L** NZ
56A2 **Rotterdam** Neth
46B1 **Roubaix** France
48C2 **Rouen** France
42E3 **Rough** *Oilfield* N Sea
Roulers = Roeselare
101E3 **Round I** Mauritius
109D2 **Round Mt** Aust
8C2 **Roundup** USA
44C2 **Rousay** *I* Scot
48C3 **Roussillon** Region,
France
60C2 **Rouyn** Can
38K5 **Rovaniemi** Fin
47D2 **Rovereto** Italy
47D2 **Rovigo** Italy
52B1 **Rovinj** Croatia
59D2 **Rovno** Ukraine
90A2 **Row'ān** Iran
109C1 **Rowena** Aust
6C3 **Rowley I** Can
106A2 **Rowley Shoals** Aust

79A3 **Roxas** Palawan, Phil
79B3 **Roxas** Panay, Phil
111A3 **Roxburgh** NZ
45C2 **Royal Canal** Irish Rep
43D3 **Royal Leamington**
Spa Eng
14B2 **Royal Oak** USA
43E4 **Royal Tunbridge**
Wells Eng
48B2 **Royan** France
46B2 **Roye** France
43D3 **Royston** Eng
59C3 **Rožňava** Slovakia
46B2 **Rozoy** France
61F3 **Rtishchevo**
Russian Fed
99D3 **Ruaha Nat Pk** Tanz
110C1 **Ruahine Range** *Mts*
NZ
110C1 **Ruapehu,Mt** NZ
65D3 **Rub al Khāli** *Desert*
S Arabia
44A3 **Rubha Hunish** Scot
35A2 **Rubineia** Brazil
65K4 **Rubtsovsk**
Russian Fed
12C2 **Ruby** USA
91C4 **Rudan** Iran
90A2 **Rūdbār** Iran
69F2 **Rudnaya Pristan'**
Russian Fed
54B2 **Rudoka Planina** *Mt*
Macedonia
72E3 **Rudong** China
14B1 **Rudyard** USA
46A1 **Rue** France
99D3 **Ruffec** France
34C2 **Rufino** Arg
97A3 **Rufisque** Sen
100B2 **Rufunsa** Zambia
43D3 **Rugby** Eng
39G8 **Rügen** *I* Germany
56B2 **Ruhr** *R* Germany
73D4 **Ruijin** China
54B2 **Rujen** *Mt* Bulg/
Macedonia
99D3 **Rukwa** *L* Tanz
44A3 **Rum** *I* Scot
54A1 **Ruma** Serbia, Yugos
91A4 **Rumāh** S Arabia
98C2 **Rumbek** Sudan
26C2 **Rum Cay** *I*
Caribbean S
47A2 **Rumilly** France
42A2 **Rum Jungle** Aust
101C2 **Rumphi** Malawi
111B2 **Runanga** NZ
110C1 **Runaway,C** NZ
100A3 **Rundi** *R* Zim
100A2 **Rundu** Namibia
99D3 **Rungwa** Tanz
99D3 **Rungwa** *R* Tanz
99D3 **Rungwe** *Mt* Tanz
82C2 **Ruoqiang** China
68C2 **Ruo Shui** *R* China
54C1 **Rupea** Rom
7C4 **Rupert** *R* Can
74H1 **Rur** *R* Germany
32D6 **Rurrenabaque** Bol
101C2 **Rusape** Zim
54C2 **Ruse** Bulg
18B1 **Rushville** Illinois,
USA
108B3 **Rushworth** Aust
19A3 **Rusk** USA
17B2 **Ruskin** USA
110B1 **Russell** NZ
18B2 **Russellville** Arkansas,
USA
18C2 **Russellville** Kentucky,
USA
21A2 **Russian** *R* USA
62C3 **Russian Fed** Asia/
Europe
93E1 **Rustavi** Georgia
101G1 **Rustenburg** S Africa
19B3 **Ruston** USA
99C3 **Rutana** Burundi
46E1 **Rüthen** Germany
23B2 **Rutla** Mexico
15D2 **Rutland** USA
84D2 **Rutog** China
Ruvu = Pangani

101D2 **Ruvuma** *R* Tanz/
Mozam
99D2 **Ruwenzori Range**
Mts Uganda/Zaire
101C2 **Ruya** *R* Zim
59B3 **Ružomberok**
Slovakia
99C3 **Rwanda** Republic,
Africa
60E3 **Ryazan'** Russian Fed
61F3 **Ryazhsk** Russian Fed
60E2 **Rybinsk** Russian Fed
60E2 **Rybinskoye**
Vodokhranilishche
Res Russian Fed
13D1 **Rycroft** Can
43D4 **Ryde** Eng
43E4 **Rye** Eng
20C2 **Rye Patch Res** USA
42B2 **Ryl'sk** Russian Fed
61G4 **Ryn Peski** *Desert*
Kazakhstan
74D3 **Ryōtsu** Japan
59D3 **Ryskany** Moldova
69K0 **Ryūkyū Retto** *Arch*
Japan
59C2 **Rzeszów** Pol
60D2 **Rzhev** Russian Fed

S

91B3 **Sa'ādatābād** Iran
56C2 **Saale** *R* Germany
47B1 **Saanen** Switz
46D2 **Saar** *R* Germany
46D2 **Saarbrücken**
Germany
39J7 **Saaremaa** *I* Estonia
46D2 **Saarland** State,
Germany
46D2 **Saarlouis** Germany
34C3 **Saavedra** Arg
54A2 **Šabac** Serbia, Yugos
51C1 **Sabadell** Spain
75B1 **Sabae** Japan
78D1 **Sabah** State, Malay
26C4 **Sabanalarga**
Colombia
70A3 **Sabang** Indon
87C1 **Sabari** *R* India
94B2 **Sabastiya** Israel
30C2 **Sabaya** Bol
93C3 **Sab'Bi'ar** Syria
94C2 **Sabhā** Jordan
95A2 **Sabhā** Libya
24B2 **Sabinas** Mexico
24B2 **Sabinas Hidalgo**
Mexico
19A3 **Sabine** *R* USA
19B4 **Sabine L** USA
91B5 **Sabkhat Maṭṭi** *Salt*
Marsh UAE
94A3 **Sabkhet El Bardawîl**
Lg Egypt
79B3 **Sablayan** Phil
7D5 **Sable,C** Can
7D5 **Sable,C** USA
7D5 **Sable I** Can
90C2 **Sabzevār** Iran
20C1 **Sacajawea Peak** USA
10A1 **Sachigo** *R* Can
57C2 **Sachsen** State,
Germany
56C2 **Sachsen-Anhalt**
State, Germany
4F2 **Sachs Harbour** Can
47B1 **Säckingen** Germany
47B1 **Sacramento** USA
22B1 **Sacramento** *R* USA
21A1 **Sacramento** *V* USA
9C3 **Sacramento Mts**
USA
81C4 **Sa'dah** Yemen
54B2 **Sadanski** Bulg
82D3 **Sadiya** India
50A2 **Sado** *R* Port
74D3 **Sado-shima** *I* Japan
85C3 **Sadri** India
Safad = Zefat
84A2 **Safed Koh** *Mts*
Afghan
39G7 **Saffle** Sweden
92C3 **Safi** Jordan
96B1 **Safi** Mor

90D3 **Safidabeh** Iran
94C1 **Şāfītā** Syria
93E3 **Safwān** Iraq
75A2 **Saga** Japan
76B1 **Sagaing** Burma
75B2 **Sagami-nada** *B*
Japan
85D4 **Sāgar** India
16C2 **Sag Harbor** USA
14B2 **Saginaw** USA
14B2 **Saginaw B** USA
26B2 **Sagua de Tánamo**
Cuba
26B2 **Sagua la Grande**
Cuba
7C5 **Saguenay** *R* Can
51B2 **Sagunto** Spain
94A3 **Sahāb** Jordan
50A1 **Sahagún** Spain
96C2 **Sahara** *Desert* N
Africa
84D3 **Saharanpur** India
84C2 **Sahiwal** Pak
93D3 **Şahrā al Ḥijārah**
Desert Region Iraq
23A1 **Sahuayo** Mexico
107D1 **Saibai I** Aust
56B2 **Saïda** Alg
94B2 **Saïda** Leb
91C4 **Sa'īdābād** Iran
51B2 **Saïdia** Mor
86B1 **Saidpur** India
84C2 **Saidu** Pak
75A1 **Saigō** Japan
Saigon = Ho Chi Minh
86C2 **Saiha** India
68D2 **Saihan Tal** China
75A2 **Saijo** Japan
74C4 **Saiki** Japan
42C2 **St Abb's Head** *Pt*
Scot
43D4 **St Albans** Eng
15D2 **St Albans** Vermont,
USA
14B3 **St Albans** West
Virginia, USA
43C4 **St Albans Head** *C*
Eng
13E2 **St Albert** Can
46B1 **St Amand-les-Eaux**
France
48C2 **St Amand-Mont Rond**
France
17A2 **St Andrew B** USA
44C3 **St Andrews** Scot
17B1 **St Andrew Sd** USA
27H1 **St Ann's Bay**
Jamaica
7E4 **St Anthony** Can
108B3 **St Arnaud** Aust
17B2 **St Augustine** USA
43B4 **St Austell** Eng
46D2 **St-Avold** France
42C2 **St Bees Head** *Pt* Eng
47B2 **St-Bonnet** France
43B4 **St Brides B** Wales
48B2 **St-Brieuc** France
15C2 **St Catharines** Can
27M2 **St Catherine,Mt**
Grenada
17B1 **St Catherines I** USA
43D4 **St Catherines Pt** Eng
49C2 **St Chamond** France
18B2 **St Charles** Missouri,
USA
14B2 **St Clair** USA
14B2 **St Clair,L** Can/USA
14B2 **St Clair Shores** USA
49C2 **St Claude** France
10A2 **St Cloud** USA
47B1 **Ste Croix** Switz
27E3 **St Croix** *I*
Caribbean S
43B4 **St Davids Head** *Pt*
Wales
46B2 **St Denis** France
101E3 **St Denis** Réunion
46C2 **St Dizier** France
12F2 **St Elias,Mts** USA
12G2 **St Elias Mts** Can
48B2 **Saintes** France
49C2 **St Etienne** France
18B2 **St Francis** *R* USA
100B4 **St Francis,C** S Africa

4/C1 **St Gallen** Switz
48C3 **St-Gaudens** France
109C1 **St George** Aust
17B1 **St George** South
Carolina, USA
9B3 **St George** Utah,
USA
17B2 **St George I** Florida,
USA
20B2 **St George,Pt** Can
15D1 **St Georges** Can
27E4 **St George's**
Grenada
45C3 **St George's Chan**
Irish Rep/Wales
46A2 **St Germain-en-Laye**
France
47B2 **St-Gervais** France
47C1 **St Gotthard** P Switz
43B4 **St Govans Head** Pt
Wales
22A1 **St Helena** USA
103H5 **St Helena** /
Atlantic O
100A4 **St Helena B** S Africa
17B1 **St Helens** Sd USA
109C4 **St Helens** Aust
42C3 **St Helens** Eng
20B1 **St Helens** USA
20B1 **St Helens,Mt** USA
8B3 **St Helier** Jersey
47B1 **St Hippolyte** France
46C1 **St-Hubert** Belg
7C5 **St-Hyacinthe** Can
14B1 **St Ignace** USA
43B4 **St Ives** Eng
18B2 **St James** Missouri,
USA
5E4 **St James,C** Can
15D1 **St Jean** Can
48B2 **St Jean d'Angely**
France
47B2 **St-Jean-de-**
Maurienne France
10C2 **St Jean,L** Can
15D1 **St-Jérôme** Can
20C1 **St Joe** R USA
7D5 **Saint John** Can
7E5 **St John's** Can
14B2 **St Johns** Michigan,
USA
17B2 **St Johns** R USA
15D2 **St Johnsbury** USA
15D1 **St-Joseph** Can
19B3 **St Joseph** Louisiana,
USA
14A2 **St Joseph** Michigan,
USA
18B2 **St Joseph** Missouri,
USA
27L1 **St Joseph** Trinidad
14B3 **St Joseph I** Can
14B1 **St Joseph I** Can
7A4 **St Joseph,L** Can
47B1 **St Julien** France
48C2 **St-Junien** France
46B2 **St-Just-en-Chaussée**
France
40B2 **St Kilda** I Scot
27E3 **St Kitts-Nevis** Is
Caribbean S
47A1 **St Laurent** France
7D5 **St Lawrence** R Can
7D5 **Saint Lawrence,G of**
Can
4A3 **St Lawrence I** USA
15C2 **St Lawrence Seaway**
Can/USA
48B2 **St Lô** France
97A3 **St Louis** Sen
11A3 **St Louis** USA
27E4 **St Lucia** I
Caribbean S
101H1 **St Lucia,L** S Africa
44E1 **St Magnus** B Scot
48B2 **St Malo** France
20C1 **St Maries** USA
27E3 **St Martin** /
Caribbean S
108A2 **St Mary Peak** Mt
Aust
109C4 **St Marys** Aust
15C2 **St Marys** USA
17B1 **St Marys** R USA

46C2 **Ste-Menehould**
France
12B2 **St Michael** USA
16A3 **St Michaels** USA
47B2 **St-Michel** France
46C2 **St-Mihiel** France
47C1 **St Moritz** Switz
48B2 **St-Nazaire** France
46C1 **St-Niklaas** Belg
46B1 **St-Omer** France
13E2 **St Paul** Can
10A2 **St Paul** Minnesota,
USA
97A4 **St Paul** R Lib
17B2 **St Petersburg** USA
7E5 **St Pierre** Can
15D1 **St Pierre,L** Can
46B1 **St-Pol-Sur-Ternoise**
France
59B3 **St Pölten** Austria
46B2 **St Quentin** France
49D3 **St Raphaël** France
101D2 **St Sébastien** C
Madag
17B1 **St Simons I** USA
17B1 **St Stephen** USA
14B2 **St Thomas** Can
49D3 **St-Tropez** France
46C1 **St Truiden** Belg
46A1 **St-Valéry-sur-Somme**
France
27E4 **St Vincent and the**
Grenadines Is
Caribbean S
108A2 **St Vincent,G** Aust
46D1 **St-Vith** Germany
46D2 **St Wendel** Germany
71F2 **Saipan** I Pacific O
84B2 **Saiydabad** Afghan
30C2 **Sajama** Mt Bol
74D4 **Sakai** Japan
75A2 **Sakaidi** Japan
75A1 **Sakaiminato** Japan
93D4 **Sakākah** S Arabia
10C1 **Sakami,L** Can
100B2 **Sakania** Zaire
101D3 **Sakaraha** Madag
60D5 **Sakarya** R Turk
58C1 **Sakasleja** Latvia
74D3 **Sakata** Japan
97C4 **Sakété** Benin
69G1 **Sakhalin** /
Russian Fed
69E4 **Sakishima gunto** Is
Japan
97A4 **Sal** I Cape Verde
61F4 **Sal** R Russian Fed
39H7 **Sala** Sweden
34D3 **Saladillo** Arg
34C2 **Saladillo** R Arg
34D3 **Salado** R
Buenos Aires, Arg
34B3 **Salado** R Mendoza/
San Luis, Arg
30D4 **Salado** R Sante Fe,
Arg
97B4 **Salaga** Ghana
76C3 **Sala Hintoun** Camb
98B1 **Salal** Chad
81D4 **Salālah** Oman
34A2 **Salamanca** Chile
23A1 **Salamanca** Mexico
50A1 **Salamanca** Spain
15C2 **Salamanca** USA
98B2 **Salamat** R Chad
71F4 **Salamaua** PNG
15C2 **Salamonica** USA
78D1 **Salang** Indon
58A5 **Salangen** Nor
30C3 **Salar de Arizaro** Arg
30C3 **Salar de Atacama**
Salt Pan Chile
30C3 **Salar de Coipasa**
Salt Pan Bol
30C3 **Salar de Uyuni**
Salt Pan Bol
47C2 **Salasomaggiore**
Italy
61J3 **Salavat** Russian Fed
70D4 **Salayar** Indon
105L5 **Sala y Gomez** I
Pacific O
34C3 **Salazar** Arg
48C2 **Salbris** France

12E2 **Salcha** R USA
100A4 **Saldanha** S Africa
94C2 **Saldad** Syria
34C3 **Saldungaray** Arg
58C1 **Saldus** Latvia
109C3 **Sale** Aust
18C2 **Salem** Illinois, USA
87B2 **Salem** India
16D1 **Salem**
Massachusetts, USA
16B3 **Salem** New Jersey,
USA
20B2 **Salem** Oregon, USA
78C4 **Salembu Besar** I
Indon
39G6 **Salen** Sweden
53B2 **Salerno** Italy
42C3 **Salford** Eng
54A1 **Salgót** Hung
59B3 **Salgótarjan** Hung
31D3 **Salgueiro** Brazil
55C3 **Salihli** Turk
101C2 **Salima** Malawi
39K6 **Salimaa** L Fin
18A2 **Salina** Kansas, USA
53B3 **Salina** I Italy
23B2 **Salina Cruz** Mexico
30C3 **Salina de Arizato**
Arg
34B3 **Salina Grande**
Salt pan Arg
34B2 **Salina La Antigua**
Salt pan Arg
35C1 **Salinas** Brazil
22B2 **Salinas** USA
22B2 **Salinas** R USA
34B3 **Salinas de Llancaneb**
Salt Pan Arg
34B3 **Salinas Grandes** Salt
Pan Arg
19B3 **Saline** R Arkansas,
USA
27M2 **Salines,Pt** Grenada
31B2 **Salinópolis** Brazil
47A1 **Salins** France
Salisbury = Harare
15C3 **Salisbury** Maryland,
USA
6C3 **Salisbury I** Can
43C4 **Salisbury Plain** Eng
38K5 **Salla** Fin
47B2 **Sallanches** France
18B2 **Sallisaw** USA
6C3 **Salluit** Can
86A1 **Sallyana** Nepal
93D2 **Salmas** Iran
38L6 **Salmi** Russian Fed
20C1 **Salmon** USA
8B2 **Salmon** USA
13D2 **Salmon Arm** Can
13D2 **Salmon River Mts**
USA
39J6 **Salo** Fin
47D2 **Salò** Italy
49D3 **Salon-de-Provence**
France
Salonica =
Thessaloniki
54B1 **Salonta** Rom
38K6 **Salpausselka** Region,
Fin
54B1 **Salsacate** Arg
61F4 **Sal'sk** Russian Fed
94B2 **Salt** Jordan
30C3 **Salta** Arg
30C3 **Salta** State, Arg
24B2 **Saltillo** Mexico
8B2 **Salt Lake City** USA
34D2 **Salto** Arg
34D2 **Salto** Urug
32C3 **Salto Angostura**
Waterfall Colombia
35D1 **Salto da Divisa** Brazil
33E2 **Salto del Angel**
Waterfall Ven
30E3 **Salto del Guaira**
Waterfall Brazil
32C4 **Salto Grande**
Waterfall Colombia
84C2 **Salt Range** Mts Pak
27H2 **Salt River** Jamaica
17B1 **Saluda** USA
47B2 **Saluzzo** Italy

31D4 **Salvador** Brazil
19B4 **Salvador,L** USA
23A1 **Salvatierra** Mexico
91B5 **Salwah** Qatar
76B1 **Salween** R Burma
58C1 **Sal'yany** Azerbaijan
57C3 **Salzburg** Austria
56C2 **Salzgitter** Germany
56C2 **Salzwedel** Germany
68B1 **Samagaltay**
Russian Fed
79B4 **Samales Group** Is
Phil
27D3 **Samaná** Dom Rep
92C2 **Samandaǧı** Turk
84B1 **Samangan** Afghan
79C1 **Samar** I Phil
65G4 **Samara** Russian Fed
71E4 **Samarai** PNG
78D3 **Samarinda** Indon
80E2 **Samarkand**
Uzbekistan
93D3 **Sämarrä'** Iraq
86A2 **Sambalpur** India
78B2 **Sambas** Indon
101E2 **Sambava** Madag
84D3 **Sambhal** India
78D3 **Samboja** Indon
59C3 **Sambor** Ukraine
46B1 **Sambre** R France
74B3 **Samch'ŏk** S Korea
98B3 **Same** Tanz
54A1 **Samedan** Switz
46A1 **Samer** France
100B2 **Samfya** Zambia
76B1 **Samka** Burma
76C1 **Sam Neua** Laos
55C2 **Sámos** I Greece
55C2 **Samothráki** I Greece
34C2 **Sampacho** Arg
78D3 **Sampaga** Indon
78C3 **Sampit** Indon
78C3 **Sampit** R Indon
19B3 **Sam Rayburn Res**
USA
76C3 **Samrong** Camb
56C1 **Samsø** I Den
92C1 **Samsun** Turk
97B3 **San** Mali
76D3 **San** R Camb
59C2 **San** R Pol
81C4 **San'ā'** Yemen
98B2 **Sanaga** R Cam
29C2 **San Agustin** Arg
28A1 **San Agustin,C** Phil
90A2 **Sanandaj** Iran
22B1 **San Andreas** USA
25C3 **San Andrés Tuxtla**
Mexico
9C3 **San Angelo** USA
53A3 **San Antioco**
Sardegna
53A3 **San Antioco** I Medit
S
34A2 **San Antonio** Chile
9C3 **San Antonio** New
Mexico, USA
79B2 **San Antonio** Phil
9D4 **San Antonio** R
Texas, USA
51C2 **San Antonio Abad**
Spain
25D2 **San Antonio,C** Cuba
26A2 **San Antonio de los**
Baros Cuba
22D3 **San Antonio,Mt** USA
29C4 **San Antonio Oeste**
Arg
34D3 **San Agustin** Arg
34D3 **San Agustin de**
Valle Féril Arg
85D4 **Sanawad** India
23A1 **San Benedicto** /
Mexico
22B2 **San Benito** USA
22B2 **San Benito Mt** USA
22D3 **San Bernardino** USA
34A2 **San Bernardo** Chile
17A2 **San Blas,C** USA
34A3 **San Carlos** Chile
32A1 **San Carlos** Nic
79B2 **San Carlos** Phil

29B4 **San Carlos de Bariloche** Arg
69E4 **San-chung** Taiwan
61G2 **Sanchursk** Russian Fed
34A3 **San Clemente** Chile
22D4 **San Clemente** USA
21B3 **San Clemente I** USA
34C2 **San Cristóbal** Arg
25C3 **San Cristóbal** Mexico
32C2 **San Cristóbal** Ven
32J7 **San Cristóbal** / Ecuador
107F2 **San Cristobal** / Solomon Is
25E2 **Sancti Spiritus** Cuba
34B2 **Sandai** Indon
70C3 **Sandakan** Malay
44C2 **Sanday** / Scot
13F1 **Sandfly L** Can
21B3 **San Diego** USA
92B2 **Sandikli** Turk
86A1 **Sandila** India
39F7 **Sandnes** Nor
38G5 **Sandnessjøen** Nor
98C3 **Sandoa** Zaïre
59C2 **Sandomierz** Pol
38D3 **Sandøy** Føroyar
20C1 **Sandpoint** USA
48A2 **Sandrio** Italy
18A2 **Sand Springs** USA
106A3 **Sandstone** Aust
73C4 **Sandu** China
14B2 **Sandusky** USA
39H6 **Sandviken** Sweden
7A4 **Sandy L** Can
34C2 **San Elcano** Arg
9B3 **San Felipe** Baja Cal, Mexico
34A2 **San Felipe** Chile
23A1 **San Felipe** Guanajuato, Mexico
27D4 **San Felipe** Ven
51C1 **San Feliu de Guixols** Spain
28A5 **San Felix** / Pacific O
34A2 **San Fernando** Chile
79B2 **San Fernando** Phil
79B2 **San Fernando** Phil
50A2 **San Fernando** Spain
27E4 **San Fernando** Trinidad
22C3 **San Fernando** USA
32D2 **San Fernando** Ven
17B2 **Sanford** Florida, USA
12F2 **Sanford,Mt** USA
34C2 **San Francisco** Arg
27C3 **San Francisco** Dom Rep
22A2 **San Francisco** USA
22A2 **San Francisco B** USA
24B2 **San Francisco del Oro** Mexico
23A1 **San Francisco del Rincon** Mexico
22D3 **San Gabriel Mts** USA
85C5 **Sangamner** India
18C2 **Sangamon** R USA
71F2 **Sangar** / Pacific O
87B1 **Sangāreddi** India
78D4 **Sangeang** / Indon
22C2 **Sanger** USA
72C2 **Sanggan He** R China
78C2 **Sanggau** Indon
98B2 **Sangha** R Congo
85B3 **Sanghar** Pak
76B2 **Sangkhla Buri** Thai
78D2 **Sangkulirang** Indon
87A1 **Sāngli** India
98B2 **Sangmélima** Cam
9B3 **San Gorgonio Mt** USA
9C3 **Sangre de Cristo** Mts USA
34C2 **San Gregorio** Arg
22A2 **San Gregorio** USA
84D2 **Sāngrūr** India
30L4 **San Ignacio** Arg
79B3 **San Isidro** Phil
32B2 **San Jacinto** Colombia
21B3 **San Jacinto Peak** Mt USA

34A3 **San Javier** Chile
34D2 **San Javier** Sante Fe, Arg
74D3 **Sanjō** / Japan
31C6 **São João del Rei** Brazil
22B2 **San Joaquin** R USA
22B2 **San Joaquin Valley** USA
32A1 **San José** Costa Rica
25C3 **San José** Guatemala
79B2 **San Jose** Luzon, Phil
79B3 **San Jose** Mindoro, Phil
22B2 **San Jose** USA
9B4 **San José** / Mexico
30D2 **San José de Chiquitos** Bol
34D2 **San José de Feliciano** Arg
34B2 **San José de Jáchal** Arg
34C2 **San José de la Dormida** Arg
31B6 **São José do Rio Prêto** Brazil
24B2 **San José del Cabo** Mexico
34B2 **San Juan** Arg
27D3 **San Juan** Puerto Rico
34B2 **San Juan** State, Arg
27L1 **San Juan** Trinidad
32D2 **San Juan** Ven
26B2 **San Juan** Mt Cuba
8C3 **San Juan** Mts USA
34B2 **San Juan** R Arg
23B2 **San Juan** R Mexico
25D3 **San Juan** R Nic/Costa Rica
23B2 **San Juan Bautista** Mexico
30E4 **San Juan Bautista** Par
22B2 **San Juan Bautista** USA
25D3 **San Juan del Norte** Nic
27D4 **San Juan de los Cayos** Ven
23A1 **San Juan de loz Lagoz** Mexico
25D3 **San Juan del Rio** Mexico
25D3 **San Juan del Sur** Nic
20B1 **San Juan Is** USA
23B2 **San Juan Tepozcolula** Mexico
29C5 **San Julián** Arg
34C2 **San Justo** Arg
60D2 **Sankt-Peterburg** Russian Fed
98C3 **Sankuru** R Zaïre
22A2 **San Leandro** USA
93C2 **Şanlıurfa** Turk
32B3 **San Lorenzo** Ecuador
34C2 **San Lorenzo** Arg
22B2 **San Lucas** USA
34B2 **San Luis** Arg
34B2 **San Luis** State, Arg
23A1 **San Luis de la Paz** Mexico
21A2 **San Luis Obispo** USA
23A1 **San Luis Potosi** Mexico
22B2 **San Luis Res** USA
53A3 **Sanluri** Sardegna
33D2 **San Maigualida** Mts Ven
34D3 **San Manuel** Arg
34A2 **San Marcos** Chile
23B2 **San Marcos** Mexico
52B2 **San Marino** Republic, Europe
34B2 **San Martin** Mendoza, Arg
112C3 **San Martin** Base Ant
47D1 **San Martino di Castrozza** Italy
23B2 **San Martin Tuxmelucan** Mexico
22A2 **San Mateo** USA
30E2 **San Matías** Bol
72C3 **Sanmenxia** China

25D3 **San Miguel** El Salvador
22B3 **San Miguel** / USA
23A1 **San Miguel del Allende** Mexico
34D3 **San Miguel del Monte** Arg
30C4 **San Miguel de Tucumán** Arg
73D4 **Sanming** China
9B3 **San Nicolas** / USA
34C2 **San Nicolas de los Arroyos** Arg
101G1 **Sannieshof** S Africa
59B2 **Sanniquellie** Lib
59C3 **Sanok** Pol
26B5 **San Onofone** Colombia
22D4 **San Onofre** USA
79B3 **San Pablo** Phil
22A1 **San Pablo B** USA
34D2 **San Pedro** Buenos Aires, Arg
97B4 **San Pedro** Ivory Coast
30D3 **San Pedro** Jujuy, Arg
30E3 **San Pedro** Par
22C4 **San Pedro** USA
9C4 **San Pedro de los Colonias** Mexico
25D3 **San Pedro Sula** Honduras
53A3 **San Pietro** / Medit S
24A1 **San Quintin** Mexico
34B2 **San Rafael** Arg
22A2 **San Rafael** USA
22C3 **San Rafael Mts** USA
49D3 **San Remo** Italy
34D2 **San Salvador** Arg
26C2 **San Salvador** / Caribbean S
32J7 **San Salvador** / Ecuador
30C3 **San Salvador de Jujuy** Arg
51B1 **San Sebastian** Spain
53C2 **San Severo** Italy
30C2 **Santa Ana** Bol
25C3 **Santa Ana** Guatemala
22D4 **Santa Ana** USA
22D4 **Santa Ana Mts** USA
34A3 **Santa Bárbara** Chile
24B2 **Santa Barbara** Mexico
22C3 **Santa Barbara** USA
22C4 **Santa Barbara** / USA
22B3 **Santa Barbara Chan** USA
22C3 **Santa Barbara Res** USA
22C4 **Santa Catalina** / USA
22C4 **Santa Catalina,G of** USA
30F4 **Santa Catarina** State, Brazil
26B2 **Santa Clara** Cuba
22B2 **Santa Clara** USA
22C3 **Santa Clara** R USA
29C6 **Santa Cruz** Arg
30D2 **Santa Cruz** Bol
34A2 **Santa Cruz** Chile
79B3 **Santa Cruz** Phil
29B5 **Santa Cruz** State, Arg
22A2 **Santa Cruz** USA
22C4 **Santa Cruz** / USA
35D1 **Santa Cruz Cabrália** Brazil
22C3 **Santa Cruz Chan** USA
96A2 **Santa Cruz de la Palma** Canary Is
26B2 **Santa Cruz del Sur** Cuba
96A2 **Santa Cruz de Tenerife** Canary Is
100B2 **Santa Cruz do Cuando** Angola
35B2 **Santa Cruz do Rio Pardo** Brazil
22A2 **Santa Cruz Mts** USA
34D2 **Santa Elena** Arg

33E3 **Santa Elena** Ven
34C2 **Santa Fe** Arg
34C2 **Santa Fe** State, Arg
9C3 **Santa Fe** USA
35A1 **Santa Helena de Goiás** Brazil
73B3 **Santai** China
29B6 **Santa Inés** / Chile
34B3 **Santa Isabel** La Pampa, Arg
34C2 **Santa Isabel** Sante Fe, Arg
107E1 **Santa Isabel** / Solomon Is
21A2 **Santa Lucia** USA
21A2 **Santa Lucia Range** Mts USA
97A4 **Santa Luzia** / Cape Verde
9B4 **Santa Margarita** / Mexico
22D4 **Santa Margarita** R USA
30F4 **Santa Maria** Brazil
26C4 **Santa Maria** Colombia
21A3 **Santa Maria** USA
96A1 **Santa Maria** / Açores
23B1 **Santa Maria** R Queretaro, Mexico
23A1 **Santa Maria del Rio** Mexico
32C1 **Santa Marta** Colombia
22C3 **Santa Monica** USA
22C4 **Santa Monica B** USA
29E2 **Santana do Livramento** Brazil
32B3 **Santander** Colombia
50B1 **Santander** Spain
51C2 **Santany** Spain
22C3 **Santa Paula** USA
31C2 **Santa Quitéria** Brazil
33G4 **Santarém** Brazil
50A2 **Santarém** Port
22A1 **Santa Rosa** California, USA
25D3 **Santa Rosa** Honduras
34C3 **Santa Rosa** La Pampa, Arg
34B2 **Santa Rosa** Mendoza, Arg
34B2 **Santa Rosa** San Luis, Arg
22B3 **Santa Rosa** / USA
24A2 **Santa Rosalía** Mexico
20C2 **Santa Rosa Range** Mts USA
31D3 **Santa Talhada** Brazil
35C1 **Santa Teresa** Brazil
53A2 **Santa Teresa di Gallura** Sardegna
22B3 **Santa Ynez** R USA
22B3 **Santa Ynez Mts** USA
17C1 **Santee** R USA
47C2 **Santhia** Italy
34A2 **Santiago** Chile
27C3 **Santiago** Dom Rep
32A2 **Santiago** Panama
79B2 **Santiago** Phil
32B4 **Santiago** R Peru
50A1 **Santiago de Compostela** Spain
26B2 **Santiago de Cuba** Cuba
30D4 **Santiago del Estero** Arg
30D4 **Santiago del Estero** State, Arg
22D4 **Santiago Peak** Mt USA
31C5 **Santo** State, Brazil
35A2 **Santo Anastácio** Brazil
30F4 **Santo Angelo** Brazil
97A4 **Santo Antão** / Cape Verde
35A2 **Santo Antonio da Platina** Brazil
27D3 **Santo Domingo** Dom Rep

Santos

35B2	**Santos** Brazil
35C2	**Santos Dumont** Brazil
30E4	**Santo Tomé** Arg
29B5	**San Valentin** *Mt* Chile
34A2	**San Vicente** Chile
98B3	**Sanza Pomba** Angola
30E4	**São Borja** Brazil
35B2	**São Carlos** Brazil
33G5	**São Félix** Mato Grosso, Brazil
35C2	**São Fidélis** Brazil
35C2	**São Francisco** Brazil
31D3	**São Francisco** *r* Brazil
30G4	**São Francisco do Sul** Brazil
35B1	**São Gotardo** Brazil
99D3	**São Hill** Tanz
35C2	**São João da Barra** Brazil
35B2	**São João da Boa Vista** Brazil
35C1	**São João da Ponte** Brazil
35C2	**São João del Rei** Brazil
35B2	**São Joaquim da Barra** Brazil
96A1	**São Jorge** *I* Açores
35B2	**São José do Rio Prêto** Brazil
35B2	**São José dos Campos** Brazil
31C2	**São Luis** Brazil
35B1	**São Marcos** *R* Brazil
35C1	**São Maria do Suaçui** Brazil
35D1	**São Mateus** Brazil
35C1	**São Mateus** *R* Brazil
96A1	**São Miguel** *I* Açores
49C2	**Saône** *R* France
97A4	**São Nicolau** *I* Cape Verde
35B2	**São Paulo** Brazil
35B2	**São Paulo** State, Brazil
31C3	**São Raimundo Nonato** Brazil
35B1	**São Romão** Brazil
35B2	**São Sebastião do Paraíso** Brazil
35A1	**São Simão** Goias, Brazil
35B2	**São Simão** Sao Paulo, Brazil
97A4	**São Tiago** *I* Cape Verde
97C4	**São Tomé** *I* W Africa
97C4	**São Tomé and Principe** Republic, W Africa
96B2	**Saoura** *Watercourse* Alg
35B2	**São Vicente** Brazil
35B2	**São Vicente** *I* Cape Verde
55C2	**Sápai** Greece
78D4	**Sape** Indon
97C4	**Sapele** Nig
74E2	**Sapporo** Japan
53C2	**Sapri** Italy
18A2	**Sapulpa** USA
90A2	**Saqqez** Iran
10C2	**Saquena** *r* Can
90A2	**Sarab** Iran
54A2	**Sarajevo** Bosnia-Herzegovina
90D2	**Sarakhs** Iran
61J3	**Saraktash** Russian Fed
63A2	**Sarala** Russian Fed
15D2	**Saranac L** USA
15D2	**Saranac Lake** USA
55B2	**Sarandë** Alb
79C4	**Sarangani Is** Phil
61G3	**Saransk** Russian Fed
61H2	**Sarapul** Russian Fed
17B2	**Sarasota** USA
54C1	**Sarata** Ukraine
15D2	**Saratoga Springs** USA

78C2	**Saratok** Malay
61G3	**Saratov** Russian Fed
61G3	**Saratovskoye Vodokhranilishche** *Res* Russian Fed
67F4	**Sarawak** State, Malay
92A2	**Saraykoy** Turk
90C3	**Sarbisheh** Iran
47D3	**Sarca** *R* Italy
95A2	**Sardalas** Libya
90A2	**Sar Dasht** Iran
52A2	**Sardegna** */ Medit S*
	Sardinia = Sardegna
38H5	**Sarektjåkkå** *Mt* Sweden
84C2	**Sargodha** Pak
98B2	**Sarh** Chad
90B2	**Sārī** Iran
94B2	**Sarida** *R* Isreal
93D1	**Sarikamiş** Turk
107D3	**Sarina** Aust
47B1	**Sarine** *R* Switz
84B1	**Sar-i-Pul** Afghan
95B2	**Sarir** Libya
95A2	**Sarir Tibesti** *Desert* Libya
74B3	**Sariwŏn** N Korea
48B2	**Sark** *I* UK
92C2	**Sarkişla** Turk
71E4	**Sarmi** Indon
29C5	**Sarmiento** Arg
39G6	**Särna** Sweden
47C1	**Sarnen** Switz
14B2	**Sarnia** Can
58D2	**Sarny** Ukraine
6E2	**Saroaq** Greenland
84B2	**Sarobi** Afghan
78A3	**Sarolangun** Indon
55B3	**Saronikós Kólpos** *G* Greece
47C2	**Saronno** Italy
55C2	**Saros Körfezi** *B* Turk
39G7	**Sarpsborg** Nor
46D2	**Sarralbe** France
46D2	**Sarrebourg** France
46D2	**Sarreguemines** France
46D2	**Sarre-Union** France
51B1	**Sarrion** Spain
85B3	**Sartanahu** Pak
52A2	**Sartène** Corse
48B2	**Sarthe** *R* France
61H4	**Sarykamys** Kazakhstan
65H5	**Sarysu** *R* Kazakhstan
86A2	**Sasarām** India
74B4	**Sasebo** Japan
5H4	**Saskatchewan** Province, Can
5H4	**Saskatchewan** *R* Can
13F2	**Saskatoon** Can
101G1	**Sasolburg** S Africa
61F3	**Sasovo** Russian Fed
97B4	**Sassandra** Ivory Coast
97B4	**Sassandra** *R* Ivory Coast
53A2	**Sassari** Sardegna
56C2	**Sassnitz** Germany
47D2	**Sassuolo** Italy
34C2	**Sastre** Arg
87A1	**Sätära** India
78D4	**Satengar** *Is* Indon
39H6	**Säter** Sweden
17B1	**Satilla** *R* USA
61J2	**Satka** Russian Fed
86A2	**Satna** India
85C4	**Sätpura Range** *Mts* India
54B1	**Satu Mare** Rom
34D2	**Sauce** Arg
39F7	**Sauda** Nor
80C3	**Saudi Arabia** Kingdom, Arabian Pen
46D2	**Sauer** *R* Germany/Lux
46D1	**Sauerland** Region, Germany
38B1	**Sauðárkrókur** Iceland

14A2	**Saugatuck** USA
16C1	**Saugerties** USA
13B2	**Saugstad,Mt** USA
7B5	**Sault Sainte Marie** Can
14B1	**Sault Ste Marie** Can
14B1	**Sault Ste Marie** USA
71E4	**Saumlaki** Indon
48B2	**Saumur** France
98C3	**Saurimo** Angola
27M2	**Sauteurs** Grenada
54A2	**Sava** *R* Serbia, Yugos
97C4	**Savalou** Benin
17B1	**Savannah** Georgia, USA
17B1	**Savannah** *R* USA
76C2	**Savannakhet** Laos
26B3	**Savanna la Mar** Jamaica
7A4	**Savant Lake** Can
76D2	**Savarane** Laos
97C4	**Savé** Benin
101C3	**Save** *R* Mozam
90B3	**Sāveh** Iran
46D2	**Saverne** France
47B2	**Savigliano** Italy
46B2	**Savigny** France
49D2	**Savoie** *Region* France
49D3	**Savona** Italy
38K6	**Savonlinna** Fin
4A3	**Savoonga** USA
38K5	**Savukoski** Fin
71D4	**Savu S** Indon
76A1	**Saw** Burma
86D3	**Sawai Mādhopur** India
78A2	**Sawang** Indon
76B2	**Sawankhalok** Thai
75C1	**Sawara** Japan
12E1	**Sawtooth Mt** USA
106B2	**Sawu** */* Indon
97C3	**Say** Niger
84B1	**Sayghan** Afghan
91B5	**Sayhut** Yemen
61G4	**Saykhin** Kazakhstan
68D2	**Saynshand** Mongolia
61H5	**Say-Utes** Kazakhstan
16C2	**Sayville** USA
13B2	**Sayward** Can
57C3	**Sázava** *R* Czech Republic
51C2	**Sbisseb** *R* Alg
42C2	**Scafell Pike** *Mt* Eng
44E1	**Scalloway** Scot
44C2	**Scapa Flow** *Sd* Scot
15C2	**Scarborough** Can
42D2	**Scarborough** Eng
27E4	**Scarborough** Tobago
44A2	**Scarp** *I* Scot
45B2	**Scarriff** Irish Rep
52A1	**Schaffhausen** Switz
57C3	**Scharding** Austria
46D1	**Scharteberg** *Mt* Germany
7D4	**Schefferville** Can
46B1	**Schelde** *R* Belg
10C2	**Schenectady** USA
47D2	**Schio** Italy
56B2	**Schleiden** Germany
56B2	**Schleswig** Germany
56B2	**Schleswig Holstein** State, Germany
16B1	**Schoharie** USA
71F4	**Schouten** *Is* PNG
57B2	**Schreiber** Can
21B2	**Schurz** USA
16A2	**Schuykill Haven** USA
16B2	**Schuylkill** *R* USA
57B3	**Schwabische Alb** *Upland* Germany
57B3	**Schwarzwald** *Upland* Germany
12C1	**Schwatka Mts** USA
47D1	**Schwaz** Austria
57C2	**Schweinfurt** Germany
101G1	**Schweizer Reneke** S Africa
56C2	**Schwerin** Germany
47C1	**Schwyz** Switz
53B3	**Sciacca** Italy

14B3	**Scioto** *R* USA
109D2	**Scone** Aust
6H2	**Scoresby Sd** Greenland
103F7	**Scotia Ridge** Atlantic O
103F7	**Scotia S** Atlantic O
44B3	**Scotland** Country, UK
112B7	**Scott** *Base* Ant
13B2	**Scott,C** Can
9C2	**Scott City** USA
112C6	**Scott I** Ant
6C2	**Scott Inlet** *B* Can
20E2	**Scott,Mt** USA
106B2	**Scott Reef** Timor S
8C2	**Scottsbluff** USA
17A1	**Scottsboro** USA
109C4	**Scottsdale** Aust
10C2	**Scranton** USA
47D1	**Scuol** Switz
	Scutari = Shkodër
5J4	**Seal** *R* Can
108B3	**Sea Lake** Aust
18B2	**Searcy** USA
22B2	**Seaside** California, USA
20B1	**Seaside** Oregon, USA
16B3	**Seaside Park** USA
20B1	**Seattle** USA
22A1	**Sebastopol** USA
17B2	**Sebring** USA
111A3	**Secretary I** NZ
18B2	**Sedalia** USA
46C2	**Sedan** France
111B2	**Seddonville** NZ
94B3	**Sede Boger** Israel
94B3	**Sederot** Israel
97A3	**Sédhiou** Sen
94B3	**Sedom** Israel
100A3	**Seeheim** Namibia
111B2	**Sefton,Mt** NZ
77C5	**Segamat** Malay
51B2	**Segorbe** Spain
97A3	**Ségou** Mali
	Segovia = Coco
50B1	**Segovia** Spain
51C1	**Segre** *R* Spain
97B4	**Séguéla** Ivory Coast
96A2	**Seguia el Hamra** *Watercourse* Mor
34C2	**Segundo** *R* Arg
78D2	**Seguntur** Indon
60D2	**Segura** *R* Spain
85B3	**Sehwan** Pak
46D2	**Seille** *R* France
38J6	**Seinäjoki** Fin
48C2	**Seine** *R* France
46B2	**Seine-et-Marne** Department, France
99D3	**Sekenke** Tanz
99D1	**Sek'ot'a** Eth
20B1	**Selah** USA
71E4	**Selaru** */* Indon
78D4	**Selat Alas** *Str* Indon
78B4	**Selat Bangka** *Str* Indon
78A3	**Selat Berhala** *B* Indon
71E4	**Selat Dampier** *Str* Indon
78B3	**Selat Gaspar** *Str* Indon
78D4	**Selat Lombok** *Str* Indon
78D4	**Selat Sape** *Str* Indon
78B4	**Selat Sunda** *Str* Indon
71D4	**Selat Wetar** *Chan* Indon
12B1	**Selawik** USA
12C1	**Selawik** *R* USA
12B1	**Selawik L** USA
42D3	**Selby** Eng
55C3	**Selçuk** Turk
12D3	**Seldovia** USA
100B3	**Selebi Phikwe** Botswana
6J3	**Selfoss** Iceland
95B2	**Selima Oasis** Sudan
5J4	**Selkirk** Can
42C2	**Selkirk** Scot

13D2 **Selkirk Mts** Can
22C2 **Selma** California,
USA
50B2 **Selouane** Mor
12H2 **Selous,Mt** Can
78B3 **Selta Karimata** *Str*
Indon
32C5 **Selvas** Region, Brazil
107D3 **Selwyn** Aust
4E3 **Selwyn Mts** Can
78C4 **Semarang** Indon
61E2 **Semenov**
Russian Fed
12C3 **Semidi Is** USA
60E3 **Semiluki**
Russian Fed
19A2 **Seminole** Oklahoma,
USA
17B1 **Seminole,L** USA
65K4 **Semipalatinsk**
Kazakhstan
79B3 **Semirara Is** Phil
90B3 **Semirom** Iran
78C2 **Semitau** Indon
46C2 **Semois** *R* Belg
23B2 **Sempoala** Hist Site,
Mexico
32D5 **Sena Madureira**
Brazil
100B2 **Senanga** Zambia
19C3 **Senatobia** USA
74E3 **Sendai** Honshū,
Japan
74C4 **Sendai** Kyūshū,
Japan
85D4 **Sendwha** India
15C2 **Seneca Falls** USA
97A3 **Senegal** Republic,
Africa
97A3 **Sénégal** *R* Maur Sen
101G1 **Senekal** S Africa
31D4 **Senhor do Bonfim**
Brazil
52B2 **Senigallia** Italy
52C2 **Senj** Croatia
69E4 **Senkaku Gunto** *Is*
Japan
46B2 **Senlis** France
99D1 **Sennar** Sudan
7C5 **Senneterre** Can
49C2 **Sens** France
54A1 **Senta** Serbia, Yugos
98C3 **Sentery** Zaïre
13C2 **Sentinel Peak** *Mt*
Can
85D4 **Seoni** India
Seoul = Soul
110B2 **Separation Pt** NZ
76D2 **Sepone** Laos
7D4 **Sept-Iles** Can
95A2 **Séquédine** Niger
21B2 **Sequoia** Nat Pk, USA
71D4 **Seram** *I* Indon
78B4 **Serang** Indon
78B2 **Serasan** *I* Indon
54A2 **Serbia** Republic,
Yugos
61F3 **Serdobsk**
Russian Fed
77C5 **Seremban** Malay
99D3 **Serengeti Nat Pk**
Tanz
100C2 **Serenje** Zambia
59D3 **Seret** *R* Ukraine
61G2 **Sergach** Russian Fed
65H3 **Sergino** Russian Fed
31D4 **Sergipe** State, Brazil
60E2 **Sergiyev Posad**
Russian Fed
78C2 **Seria** Brunei
78C2 **Serian** Malay
55B3 **Sérifos** *I* Greece
47C2 **Serio** *R* Italy
95B2 **Serir Calanscio**
Desert Libya
46C2 **Sermaize-les-Bains**
France
71D4 **Sermata** *I* Indon
61H3 **Sernovodsk**
Russian Fed
65H4 **Serov** Russian Fed
100B3 **Serowe** Botswana
50A2 **Serpa** Port

60E3 **Serpukhov**
Russian Fed
35B2 **Serra da Canastra**
Mts Brazil
50A1 **Serra da Estrela** *Mts*
Port
35R2 **Serra da Mantiqueira**
Mts Brazil
35A1 **Serra da Mombuca**
Brazil
35C1 **Serra do Cabral** *Mt*
Brazil
33F5 **Serra do Cachimbo**
Mts Brazil
35A1 **Serra do Caiapó** *Mts*
Brazil
35A2 **Serra do Cantu** *Mts*
Brazil
35C2 **Serra do Caparaó**
Brazil
31C5 **Serra do Chifre** Brazil
35C1 **Serra do Espinhaço**
Mts Brazil
35B2 **Serra do Mar** *Mts*
Brazil
35A2 **Serra do Mirante** *Mts*
Brazil
33G3 **Serra do Navio** Brazil
35B2 **Serra do**
Paranpiacaba *Mts*
Brazil
33F6 **Serra dos Caiabis**
Mts Brazil
35A2 **Serra dos Dourados**
Brazil
33E6 **Serra dos Parecis**
Mts Brazil
35B1 **Serra dos Pilões** *Mts*
Brazil
35A1 **Serra Dourada** *Mts*
Brazil
33F6 **Serra Formosa** Brazil
55B2 **Sérrai** Greece
25D3 **Serrana Bank** *I*
Caribbean S
51B1 **Serrana de Cuenca**
Mts Spain
33A1 **Serranópolis** Brazil
33E3 **Serra Pacaraima** *Mts*
Brazil/Ven
33E3 **Serra Parima** *Mts*
Brazil
33G3 **Serra Tumucumaque**
Brazil
46B2 **Serre** *R* France
34B2 **Serrezuela** Arg
31D4 **Serrinha** Brazil
6G3 **Serrmilik** Greenland
35C1 **Serro** Brazil
35A2 **Sertanópolis** Brazil
72A3 **Sêrtar** China
78C3 **Seruyan** *R* Indon
100A2 **Sesfontein** Namibia
100B2 **Sesheke** Zambia
47B2 **Sestriere** Italy
74D2 **Setana** Japan
49C3 **Sète** France
35C1 **Sete Lagoas** Brazil
96C1 **Sétif** Alg
75B1 **Seto** Japan
75A2 **Seto Naikai** *S* Japan
96B1 **Settat** Mor
42C2 **Settle** Eng
5G4 **Settler** Can
50A2 **Setúbal** Port
93E1 **Sevan,Oz** *L* Armenia
60D5 **Sevastopol'** Ukraine
7B4 **Severn** *R* Can
43C3 **Severn** *R* Eng
1B9 **Severnaya Zemlya** *I*
Russian Fed
63C2 **Severo-Baykalskoye**
Nagoye *Mts*
Russian Fed
60F4 **Severo Donets**
Ukraine
64E3 **Severodvinsk**
Russian Fed
64H3 **Severo Sos'va** *R*
Russian Fed
8B3 **Sevier** *R* USA
8B3 **Sevier L** USA
50A2 **Sevilla** Spain

Seville = Sevilla
54C2 **Sevlievo** Bulg
97A4 **Sewa** *R* Sierra Leone
12E2 **Seward** Alaska, USA
18A1 **Seward** Nebraska,
USA
12A1 **Seward Pen** USA
13D1 **Sexsmith** Can
89K8 **Seychelles** *Is*
Indian O
38C1 **Seyðisfjörður** Iceland
92C2 **Seyhan** Turk
60E3 **Seym** *R*
Russian Fed
108C2 **Seymour** Aust
14A3 **Seymour** Connecticut,
USA
14A3 **Seymour** Indiana,
USA
46B2 **Sézanne** France
96D1 **Sfax** Tunisia
54C1 **Sfíntol Gheorghe**
Rom
56A2 **'s-Gravenhage** Neth
72B3 **Shaanxi** Province,
China
85C3 **Shabunda** Zaïre
112C9 **Shackleton Ice Shelf**
Ant
85B3 **Shadadkot** Pak
91B3 **Shādhām** *R* Iran
43C4 **Shaftesbury** Eng
29G8 **Shag Rocks** *Is*
South Georgia
90A3 **Shāhābād** Iran
94C2 **Shahbā** Syria
91C3 **Shahdāp** Iran
86A2 **Shahdol** India
91C3 **Shāhīn Dezh** Iran
90C3 **Shāh Kūh** Iran
91C3 **Shahr-e Bābak** Iran
Shahresa = Qomisheh
90D3 **Shahr Kord** Iran
87B1 **Shājābād** India
84D3 **Shājahānpur** India
85D2 **Shājapur** India
61F4 **Shakhty** Russian Fed
61G2 **Shakhun'ya**
Russian Fed
96C4 **Shaki** Nig
12B2 **Shaktoolik** USA
61J2 **Shamary** *R*
Russian Fed
99D2 **Shambe** Sudan
16A2 **Shamokin** USA
16B1 **Shandaken** USA
72D2 **Shandong** Province,
China
72C1 **Shangdu** China
73E3 **Shanghai** China
72B3 **Shangnan** China
100B2 **Shangombo** Zambia
72B3 **Shangqiu** China
73B5 **Shangsi** China
72C3 **Shang Xian** China
41B3 **Shannon** *R* Irish Rep
72A3 **Shanqiu** China
74B2 **Shan-ssonggang** China
63F2 **Shantarskiye Ostrova**
I Russian Fed
73D5 **Shantou** China
72C2 **Shanxi** Province,
China
72D3 **Shan Xian** China
73C5 **Shaoguan** China
73E4 **Shaoxing** China
73C4 **Shaoyang** China
44C2 **Shapinsay** *I* Scot
94C2 **Shaqqā** Syria
72A1 **Sharhulsan** Mongolia
90C2 **Sharīfābād** Iran
91C4 **Sharjah** UAE
106A3 **Shark B** Aust
90C2 **Sharlauk**
Turkmenistan
94B2 **Sharon,Plain of** Israel
61G2 **Sharya** Russian Fed
99D2 **Shashemene** Eth
73C3 **Shashi** China
20B2 **Shasta L** USA
20B2 **Shasta,Mt** USA

93E3 **Shatt al Gharrat** *R*
Iraq
94B3 **Shaubak** Jordan
13F3 **Shaunavon** Can
22C2 **Shaver L** USA
16B2 **Shawangunk Mt**
USA
15D1 **Shawinigan** Can
19A2 **Shawnee** Oklahoma,
USA
73D4 **Sha Xian** China
106B3 **Shay Gap** Aust
94C2 **Shaykh Miskīn** Syria
99E1 **Shaykh 'Uthmān**
Yemen
60E3 **Shchekino**
Russian Fed
60E3 **Shchigry**
Russian Fed
60D3 **Shchors** Ukraine
65J4 **Shchuchinsk**
Kazakhstan
99E2 **Shebele** *R* Eth
14A2 **Sheboygan** USA
98B2 **Shebshi Mts** Nig
12F1 **Sheenjek** *R* USA
45C1 **Sheep Haven** *Estuary*
Irish Rep
43E4 **Sheerness** Eng
94B2 **Shefar'am** Israel
42D3 **Sheffield** Eng
84C2 **Shekhupura** Pak
13B1 **Shelagyote Peak** *Mt*
Can
16C1 **Shelburne Falls** USA
14A2 **Shelby** Michigan,
USA
8B2 **Shelby** Montana,
USA
14A3 **Shelbyville** Indiana,
USA
12H2 **Sheldon,Mt** Can
12D3 **Shelikof Str** USA
109D2 **Shellharbour** Aust
111A3 **Shelter Pt** NZ
20B1 **Shelton** USA
93E1 **Shemakha**
Azerbaijan
18A1 **Shenandoah** USA
15C2 **Shenandoah** *R* USA
15C3 **Shenandoah Nat Pk**
USA
97C4 **Shendam** Nig
95C2 **Shendi** Sudan
72C2 **Shenmu** China
73C5 **Shenzhen** China
85D3 **Sheopur** India
59D2 **Shepetovka** Ukraine
108C3 **Shepparton** Aust
6B2 **Sherard,C** Can
43C4 **Sherborne** Eng
97A4 **Sherbro I** Sierra
Leone
15D1 **Sherbrooke** Can
85C3 **Shergarh** India
19B3 **Sheridan** Arkansas,
USA
8C2 **Sheridan** Wyoming,
USA
19A3 **Sherman** USA
56B2 **s-Hertogenbosch** Neth
12H3 **Sheslay** Can
44C1 **Shetland** *Is* Scot
Shevchenko = Aktau
91B4 **Shevk Sho'eyb** *I* Iran
69H2 **Shiashkotan** *I*
Russian Fed
84B1 **Shibarghan** Afghan
74D3 **Shibata** Japan
95C1 **Shibîn el Kom** Egypt
75B1 **Shibukawa** Japan
72C2 **Shijiazhuang** China
85D3 **Shikarpur** India
74E2 **Shikoku** *I* Japan
67G3 **Shikoku** *I* Japan
75A2 **Shikoku-sanchi** *Mts*
Japan
86B1 **Shiliguri** India
60B1 **Shilka** Russian Fed
68D1 **Shilka** *R* Russian Fed
16B2 **Shillington** USA
86C1 **Shillong** India
61F3 **Shilovo** Russian Fed
75A2 **Shimabara** Japan

Shimada

75B2 Shimada Japan
69E1 Shimanovsk Russian Fed
74D3 Shimizu Japan
84D2 Shimla India
75B2 Shimoda Japan
87B2 Shimoga India
74C4 Shimonoseki Japan
75B1 Shinano R Japan
91C5 Shinās Oman
74D4 Shingū Japan
75C1 Shinjo Japan
74D3 Shinminato Japan
94C1 Shinshär Syria
99D3 Shinyanga Tanz
74E3 Shiogama Japan
75B2 Shiono-misaki C Japan
73A5 Shiping China
16A2 Shippensburg USA
72B3 Shiquan China
75C1 Shirakawa Japan
75B1 Shirane-san Mt Japan
75B1 Shirani-san Mt Japan
91B4 Shiraz Iran
90B3 Shir Kūh Iran
75B1 Shirotori Japan
90C2 Shirvān Iran
12A1 Shishmaref USA
12A1 Shishmaref Inlet USA
4B3 Shishmaret USA
72B2 Shitanjing China
14A3 Shively USA
85D3 Shivpuri India
94B3 Shivta Hist Site Israel
101C2 Shiwa Ngandu Zambia
72C3 Shiyan China
72B2 Shizuishan China
75B1 Shizuoka Japan
54A2 Shkodër Alb
109D2 Shoalhaven R Aust
75A2 Shobara Japan
87B2 Shoranūr India
87B1 Shorāpur India
21B2 Shoshone Mts USA
80D3 Shostka Ukraine
19B3 Shreveport USA
43C3 Shrewsbury Eng
43C3 Shropshire County, Eng
72E1 Shuangliao China
69F2 Shuangyashan China
61J4 Shubar-Kuduk Kazakhstan
72D2 Shu He R China
73A4 Shuicheng China
84C3 Shujaabad Pak
85D4 Shujālpur India
68B2 Shule He China
54C2 Shumen Bulg
61G2 Shumerlya Russian Fed
73D4 Shuncheng China
12C1 Shungnak USA
72C2 Shuo Xian China
91C4 Shūr Gaz Iran
100B2 Shurugwi Zim
13D2 Shushawa USA
61F2 Shuya Russian Fed
12D3 Shuyak I USA
82D3 Shwebo Burma
76B2 Shwegyin Burma
84A2 Siah Koh Mts Afghan
84C2 Sialkot Pak
Sian = Xi'an
79C4 Siarao I Phil
79B4 Siaton Phil
58C1 Siauliai Lithuania
65G4 Sibay Russian Fed
101H1 Sibayi L S Africa
52C2 Sibenik Croatia
70A4 Siberut I Indon
84B3 Sibi Pak
68C1 Sibirskoye Russian Fed
98B3 Sibiti Congo
99D3 Sibiti R Tanz

54B1 Sibiu Rom
70A3 Sibolga Indon
86C1 Sibsāgār India
78C2 Sibu Malay
79B4 Sibuguay B Phil
98B2 Sibut CAR
79B3 Sibuyan I Phil
79B3 Sibuyan S Phil
73A3 Sichuan Province, China
53B3 Sicilia I Medit S
53B3 Sicilian Chan Italy/Tunisia
Sicily = Sicilia
32C6 Sicuani Peru
85C4 Siddhapur India
87B1 Siddipet India
86A2 Sidhi India
85B1 Sidi Barrani Egypt
96B1 Sidi Bel Abbès Alg
96B1 Sidi Kacem Mor
44C3 Sidlaw Hills Scot
112B5 Sidley, Mt Ant
20B1 Sidney Can
8C2 Sidney Nebraska, USA
15C2 Sidney New York, USA
14B2 Sidney Ohio, USA
17B1 Sidney Lanier, L USA
Sidon = Säida
58C2 Siedlce Pol
46D1 Sieg R Germany
46D1 Siegburg Germany
46D1 Siegen Germany
76C3 Siem Reap Camb
52B2 Siena Italy
58B2 Sierpc Pol
23B2 Sierra Andrés Tuxtla Mexico
34B3 Sierra Auca Mahuida Mts Arg
9C3 Sierra Blanca USA
51B1 Sierra de Albarracin Mts Spain
50B2 Sierra de Alcaraz Mts Spain
34B2 Sierra de Cordoba Mts Arg
50A1 Sierra de Gredos Mts Spain
50B2 Sierra de Guadalupe Mts Spain
50B1 Sierra de Guadarrama Mts Spain
51B1 Sierra de Guara Mts Spain
51B1 Sierra de Gudar Mts Spain
23B2 Sierra de Juárez Mexico
34C3 Sierra de la Ventana Mts Arg
51C1 Sierra del Codi Mts Spain
34B2 Sierra del Morro Mt Arg
34B3 Sierra del Nevado Mts Arg
24B2 Sierra de los Alamitos Mts Mexico
50B2 Sierra de los Filabres Spain
23A1 Sierra de los Huicholes Mexico
23B2 Sierra de Miahuatlán Mexico
23A1 Sierra de Morones Mts Mexico
50A2 Sierra de Ronda Mts Spain
34B2 Sierra de San Luis Mts Arg
50B2 Sierra de Segura Mts Spain
50B1 Sierra de Urbion Mts Spain
34B2 Sierra de Uspallata Mts Arg
34B2 Sierra de Valle Fértil Mts Arg

23B2 Sierra de Zongolica Mexico
34C2 Sierra Grande Mts Arg
97A4 Sierra Leone Republic, Africa
97A4 Sierra Leone,C Sierra Leone
79B2 Sierra Madre Mts Phil
23A2 Sierra Madre del Sur Mts Mexico
24B2 Sierra Madre Occidental Mts Mexico
24C2 Sierra Madre Oriental Mts Mexico
34B2 Sierra Malanzan Mts Arg
9C4 Sierra Mojada Mexico
50A2 Sierra Morena Mts Spain
50B2 Sierra Nevada Mts Spain
21A2 Sierra Nevada USA
32C1 Sierra Nevada de Santa Marta Mts Colombia
34B2 Sierra Pié de Palo Mts Arg
47B1 Sierre Switz
57C9 Sífnos I Greece
59C3 Sighetu Marmatiei Rom
54B1 Sighisoara Rom
38B1 Siglufjörður Iceland
50B1 Sigüenza Spain
97B3 Siguiri Guinea
Sihanoukville = Kompong Som
85E4 Sihora India
93D2 Siirt Turk
68B3 Sikai Hu L China
85D3 Sikar India
84B2 Sikaram Mt Afghan
97B3 Sikasso Mali
18C3 Sikeston USA
57C3 Sikinos I Greece
55B3 Sikkim State, India
50A1 Sil R Spain
47D1 Silandro Italy
23A1 Silao Mexico
79B3 Silay Phil
86C2 Silchar India
96C2 Silet Alg
86A1 Silgarhi Nepal
79B2 Silifke Turk
82C2 Siling Co L China
54C2 Silistra Bulg
39F7 Silkeborg Den
47E1 Sillian Austria
18B2 Siloam Springs USA
19B3 Silsbee USA
95A3 Siltou Well Chad
58C1 Silute Lithuania
93D2 Silvan Turk
35B6 Silvania Brazil
85C4 Silvassa India
21B2 Silver City Nevada, USA
9C3 Silver City New Mexico, USA
20B2 Silver Lake USA
16A3 Silver Spring USA
108B2 Silverton Aust
47C1 Silvretta Mts Austria/Switz
72C2 Simangang Malay
76C1 Simao China
90A3 Simareh R Iran
55C3 Simav Turk
55C3 Simav R Turk
61G3 Simbirsk Russian Fed
15C2 Simcoe,L Can
57C3 Simeulue I Indon
60D5 Simferopol' Ukraine
55C3 Sími I Greece
46D1 Simmern Germany
13B2 Simoon Sound Can

49D2 Simplon Mt Switz
47C1 Simplon P Switz
4C2 Simpson,C USA
106C3 Simpson Desert Aust
6B3 Simpson Pen Can
39G7 Simrishamn Sweden
69H2 Simushir I Russian Fed
99E2 Sina Dhaqa Somalia
92B4 Sinai Egypt
32B2 Sincelejo Colombia
17B1 Sinclair,L USA
85D3 Sind R India
85B3 Sindh Region, Pak
55C3 Sindirği Turk
86B2 Sindri India
50A2 Sines Port
99D1 Singa Sudan
77C5 Singapore Republic, S E Asia
77C5 Singapore,Str of S E Asia
78D4 Singaraja Indon
99D3 Singida Tanz
78B2 Singkawang Indon
109D2 Singleton Aust
78A3 Singtep I Indon
76B1 Singu Burma
53A2 Siniscola Sardegna
93D2 Sinjar Iraq
84B2 Sinkai Hills Mts Afghan
95C3 Sinkat Sudan
82C1 Sinkiang Autonomous Region, China
33G2 Sinnamary French Guiana
92C1 Sinop Turk
54B1 Sintana Rom
78C2 Sintang Indon
32B2 Sintra Port
32B2 Sinú R Colombia
74A2 Sinúiju N Korea
59B3 Siofok Hung
47B1 Sion Switz
8D2 Sioux City USA
8C2 Sioux Falls USA
10A2 Sioux Lookout Can
79B4 Sipalay Phil
27L1 Siparia Trinidad
69E2 Siping China
112B3 Siple Base Ant
112B5 Siple I Ant
79B3 Sipocot Phil
70A4 Sipora Indon
79B4 Siquijor I Phil
87B2 Sira India
53C3 Siracusa Italy
86B2 Sirajganj Bang
13C2 Sir Alexander,Mt Can
91B5 Sir Bani Yās I UAE
106C2 Sir Edward Pellew Group Is Aust
54C1 Siret R Rom
12J2 Sir James McBrien,Mt Can
87B2 Sir Kālahasti India
13D2 Sir Laurier,Mt Can
93D2 Sirnak Turk
85C4 Sirohi India
87B1 Sironcha India
85D4 Sironj India
55B3 Siros I Greece
91B4 Sirri I Iran
84D3 Sirsa India
13D2 Sir Sandford,Mt Can
87A2 Sirsi India
95A1 Sirte Desert Libya
95A1 Sirte,G of Libya
52C1 Sisak Croatia
76C2 Sisaket Thai
76C3 Sisophon Camb
46B2 Sissonne France
90D3 Sistan Region, Iran/Afghan
49D3 Sisteron France
63B2 Sistig Khem Russian Fed
86A1 Sitāpur India
55C3 Sitia Greece
4E4 Sitka USA
12D3 Sitkalidak I USA
12D3 Sitkinak I USA

76B2 **Sittang** *R* Burma
46C1 **Sittard** Neth
86C2 **Sittwe** Burma
78C4 **Situbondo** Indon
92C2 **Sivas** Turk
93C2 **Siverek** Turk
92B2 **Sivrihisar** Turk
95B2 **Siwa** Egypt
84D2 **Siwalik Range** *Mts* India
86A1 **Siwalik Range** *Mts* Nepal
72D3 **Siyang** China
56C1 **Sjaelland** *I* Den
39G7 **Skagen** Den
39F7 **Skagerrak** *Str* Nor/ Den
20B1 **Skagit** *R* USA
20B1 **Skagit Mt** Can
4E4 **Skagway** USA
39G7 **Skara** Sweden
59C2 **Skarzysko-Kamienna** Pol
14A2 **Skeena** *R* Can
13B1 **Skeena Mts** Can
4D3 **Skeenjek** *R* USA
42E3 **Skegness** Eng
38H5 **Skellefte** *R* Sweden
38J6 **Skellefteå** Sweden
55B3 **Skiathos** *I* Greece
45B3 **Skibbereen** Irish Rep
5E4 **Skidegate** Can
58C2 **Skiemiewice** Pol
39F7 **Skien** Nor
96C1 **Skikda** Alg
74C4 **Skikoku** *I* Japan
42D3 **Skipton** Eng
55B3 **Skiros** *I* Greece
39F7 **Skjern** Den
56B1 **Skjern** Den
6F3 **Skjoldungen** Greenland
14A2 **Skokie** USA
55B3 **Skópelos** *I* Greece
54B2 **Skopje** Macedonia
39G7 **Skövde** Sweden
63E2 **Skovorodino** Russian Fed
4C3 **Skwentna** USA
58B2 **Skwierzyna** Pol
40B2 **Skye** *I* Scot
39G7 **Slagelse** Den
45C2 **Slaney** *R* Irish Rep
54B2 **Slatina** Rom
78C4 **Slaung** Indon
5G3 **Slave** *R* Can
13E1 **Slave Lake** Can
65J4 **Slavgorod** Russian Fed
59D2 **Slavuta** Ukraine
60E4 **Slavyansk** Ukraine
44B3 **Sleat,Sound of** *Chan* Scot
12C2 **Sleetmute** USA
45C2 **Sleeve Bloom** *Mts* Irish Rep
19C3 **Slidell** USA
16B2 **Slide Mt** USA
45B1 **Sligo** County, Irish Rep
41B3 **Sligo** Irish Rep
41B3 **Sligo** *B* Irish Rep
54C2 **Sliven** Bulg
54C2 **Slobozia** Rom
13D3 **Slocan** Can
43D4 **Slough** Eng
22B2 **Slough** *R* USA
59B3 **Slovakia** Republic, Europe
52B1 **Slovenia** Republic, Europe
56C2 **Slubice** Pol
59D2 **Sluch'** *R* Ukraine
58B2 **Slupsk** Pol
58D2 **Slutsk** Belorussia
58D2 **Slutsk** *R* Belorussia
41A3 **Slyne Head** *Pt* Irish Rep
63C2 **Slyudyanka** Russian Fed
7D4 **Smallwood Res** Can
54B2 **Smederevo** Serbia, Yugos

54B2 **Smederevska Palanka** Serbia, Yugos
60D4 **Smela** Ukraine
15C2 **Smethport** USA
13E1 **Smith** Can
4F3 **Smith Arm** *B* Can
13B2 **Smithers** Can
/L3 **Smith I** Can
13B2 **Smith Sd** Can
15C2 **Smiths Falls** Can
109C4 **Smithton** Aust
13D1 **Smoky** *R* Can
109D2 **Smoky C** Aust
13E2 **Smoky Lake** Can
38F6 **Smøla** *I* Nor
60D3 **Smolensk** Russian Fed
55B2 **Smólikas** *Mt* Greece
54B2 **Smolyan** Bulg
58D2 **Smorgon'** Belorussia
16B3 **Smyrna** Delaware, USA
17B1 **Smyrna** Georgia, USA
42B2 **Snaefell** *Mt* Eng
38B2 **Snaefl** *Mt* Iceland
8B2 **Snake** *R* USA
8B2 **Snake River Canyon** USA
56B2 **Sneek** Neth
45B3 **Sneem** Irish Rep
22B2 **Snelling** USA
59B2 **Snĕžka** *Mt* Pol/ Czech Republic
38F6 **Snøhetta** *Mt* Nor
20B1 **Snohomish** USA
20B1 **Snoqualmie P** USA
76D3 **Snoul** Camb
43B3 **Snowdon** *Mt* Wales
43B3 **Snowdonia Nat Pk** Wales
4G3 **Snowdrift** Can
5H4 **Snow Lake** Can
104J3 **Snowtown** Aust
109C3 **Snowy Mts** Aust
9C3 **Snyder** USA
74B4 **Soan-kundo** *I* S Korea
99D2 **Sobat** *R* Sudan
31C2 **Sobral** Brazil
58C2 **Sochaczew** Pol
61E5 **Sochi** Russian Fed
9C3 **Socorro** *I* Mexico
24A3 **Socorro** *I* Mexico
34A2 **Socos** Chile
81D4 **Socotra** *I* Yemen
38K5 **Sodankylä** Fin
37H7 **Söderhamn** Sweden
39H7 **Södertälje** Sweden
99C1 **Sodiri** Sudan
99D2 **Sodo** Eth
46E1 **Soest** Germany
101C2 **Sofala** Mozam
Sofia = Sofiya
54B2 **Sofiya** Bulg
69G4 **Sofu Gan** *I* Japan
32C2 **Sogamoso** Colombia
39F6 **Sognefjorden** *Inlet* Nor
82D2 **Sog Xian** China
95C2 **Sohâg** Egypt
84D3 **Sohipat** India
46B1 **Soignies** Belg
46B2 **Soissons** France
85C3 **Sojat** India
74A3 **Sŏjosŏn-man** *B* N Korea
92A2 **Söke** Turk
97C4 **Sokodé** Togo
61E2 **Sokol** Russian Fed
58C2 **Sokołka** Pol
97B3 **Sokolo** Mali
6H3 **Søkongens Øy** *I* Greenland
99D1 **Sokota** Eth
97C3 **Sokoto** Nig
97C3 **Sokoto** *R* Nig
111A3 **Solander I** *I* NZ
79B2 **Solano** Phil
87B1 **Solapur** India
47D1 **Solbad Hall** Austria
47D1 **Sölden** Austria
12D2 **Soldotna** USA
26C4 **Soledad** Colombia

43D4 **Solent** *Sd* Eng
46B1 **Solesmes** France
58D2 **Soligorsk** Belorussia
61J2 **Solikamsk** Russian Fed
32C4 **Solimões** *R* Peru
46D1 **Solingen** Germany
38H6 **Sollefteå** Sweden
61H3 **Sol'lletsk** Russian Fed
70B4 **Solok** Indon
105G4 **Solomon** *Is* Pacific O
47B1 **Solothurn** Switz
39F8 **Soltau** Germany
22B3 **Solvang** USA
42C2 **Solway Firth** *Estuary* Eng/Scot
100B2 **Solwezi** Zambia
75C1 **Sōma** Japan
55C3 **Soma** Turk
81C5 **Somalia** Republic, E Africa
54A1 **Sombor** Serbia, Yugos
107D2 **Somerset** Aust
43C4 **Somerset** County, Eng
16D2 **Somerset** Massachusetts, USA
15C2 **Somerset** Pennsylvania, USA
100B4 **Somerset East** S Africa
6A2 **Somerset I** Can
16B3 **Somers Point** USA
16B2 **Somerville** USA
19A3 **Somerville Res** USA
54B1 **Somes** *R* Rom
46B2 **Somme** Department, France
46B2 **Somme** *R* France
86A2 **Son** *R* India
74A3 **Sŏnch'ŏn** N Korea
39F8 **Sønderborg** Den
6E3 **Søndre Strømfjord** Greenland
47C1 **Sondrio** Italy
76D3 **Song Ba** *R* Viet
76D3 **Song Cau** Viet
101C2 **Songea** Tanz
73E3 **Songjiang** China
77C4 **Songkhla** Thai
74B3 **Songnim** N Korea
77C5 **Sông Pahang** *R* Malay
72A3 **Songpan** China
72C1 **Sonid Youqi** China
76C1 **Son La** Viet
85B3 **Sonmiani** Pak
85B3 **Sonmiani Bay** Pak
22A1 **Sonoma** USA
22B2 **Sonora** California, USA
24A2 **Sonora** *R* Mexico
9B3 **Sonoran Desert** USA
22C1 **Sonora P** USA
25D3 **Sonsonate** El Salvador
71E3 **Sonsorol** *I* Pacific O
10B2 **Soo Canals** Can/USA
13C3 **Sooke** Can
58B2 **Sopot** Pol
59B3 **Sopron** Hung
22B2 **Soquel** USA
53B2 **Sora** Italy
94B3 **Sored** *R* Israel
15D1 **Sorel** Can
109C4 **Sorell** Aust
52C2 **Sorgun** Turk
50B1 **Soria** Spain
38J5 **Sørkjosen** Nor
64C2 **Sørksop** *I* Barents S
61H4 **Sor Mertvyy Kultuk** *Plain* Kazakhstan
35B2 **Sorocaba** Brazil
61H3 **Sorochinsk** Russian Fed
71F3 **Soron** *I* Pacific O
60C4 **Soroki** Moldova
71E4 **Sorong** Indon
71E4 **Sorong** Province, Indon
99D2 **Soroti** Uganda

38J4 **Sørøya** *I* Nor
53B2 **Sorrento** Italy
38K5 **Sorsatunturi** *Mt* Fin
38H5 **Sorsele** Sweden
79B3 **Sorsogon** Phil
38L6 **Sortavala** Russian Fed
74B3 **Sŏsan** S Korea
59B2 **Sosnowiec** Pol
98B2 **Souanké** Congo
97B4 **Soubré** Ivory Coast
16B2 **Souderton** USA
27P2 **Soufrière** St Lucia
27N2 **Soufrière** *Mt* St Vincent and the Grenadines
48C3 **Souillac** France
96C1 **Souk Ahras** Alg
51C2 **Soummam** *R* Alg
Sour = Tyr
101G1 **Sources,Mt aux** Lesotho
31D3 **Sousa** Brazil
96D1 **Sousse** Tunisia
100B4 **South Africa** Republic, Africa
16B2 **South Amboy** USA
14B2 **Southampton** Can
43D4 **Southampton** Eng
16C2 **Southampton** USA
6B3 **Southampton I** Can
28F6 **South Atlantic O**
7D4 **South Aulatsivik I** *I* Can
106C3 **South Australia** State
104E5 **South Australian Basin** Indian O
19C3 **Southaven** USA
17B2 **South Bay** USA
84B3 **South Baymouth** Can
14A2 **South Bend** Indiana, USA
20B1 **South Bend** Washington, USA
16D1 **Southbridge** USA
11B3 **South Carolina** State, USA
70C2 **South Dakota** State, S E Asia
8C2 **South Dakota** State, USA
16C1 **South Deerfield** USA
43D4 **South Downs** Eng
109C4 **South East C** Aust
111A2 **Southen Alps** *Mts* NZ
5H4 **Southend** Can
43D4 **Southend-on-Sea** Eng
111A2 **Southern Alps** *Mts* NZ
106A4 **Southern Cross** Aust
5J4 **Southern Indian L** Can
27H2 **Southfield** Jamaica
105G5 **South Fiji Basin** Pacific O
12D2 **South Fork** *R* Alaska, USA
22B1 **South Fork** *R* California, USA
28F8 **South Georgia** *I* S Atlantic O
43C4 **South Glamorgan** County, Wales
14A2 **South Haven** USA
5J3 **South Henik L** Can
104F3 **South Honshu Ridge** Pacific O
111A2 **South I** NZ
16C2 **Southington** USA
74B3 **South Korea** Republic, S E Asia
21A2 **South Lake Tahoe** USA
112C8 **South Magnetic Pole** Ant
17B2 **South Miami** USA
16A3 **South Mt** USA

4F3 **South Nahanni** *R* Can
26G1 **South Negril Pt** Jamaica
103F8 **South Orkney** *Is* Atlantic O
8C2 **South Platte** *R* USA
8C2 **South Pole** Ant
42C3 **Southport** Eng
27K3 **South Pt** Barbados
16B2 **South River** USA
44C2 **South Ronaldsay** *I* Scot
103G7 **South Sandwich Trench** Atlantic O
22A2 **South San Francisco** USA
5H4 **South Saskatchewan** *R* Can
42D2 **South Shields** Eng
110B1 **South Taranaki Bight** *B* NZ
44A3 **South Uist** *I* Scot
South West Africa = **Namibia**
107D5 **South West C** Aust
105J5 **South West Pacific Basin** Pacific O
103D5 **South West Peru Ridge** Pacific O
43D3 **South Yorkshire** County, Eng
58C1 **Sovetsk** Russian Fed
61G2 **Sovetsk** Russian Fed
101G1 **Soweto** S Africa
98B3 **Soyo Congo** Angola
60D3 **Sozh** *R* Belorussia
46C1 **Spa** Belg
50A1 **Spain** Kingdom
Spalato = Split
43D3 **Spalding** Eng
14B1 **Spanish** *R* Can
26B3 **Spanish Town** Jamaica
21B2 **Sparks** USA
11B3 **Spartanburg** USA
55B3 **Sparti** Greece
69F2 **Spassk Dal'niy** Russian Fed
27R3 **Speightstown** Barbados
12E2 **Spenard** USA
14A3 **Spencer** Indiana, USA
8D2 **Spencer** Iowa, USA
6A3 **Spencer Bay** Can
108A3 **Spencer C** Aust
108A2 **Spencer G** Aust
6C3 **Spencer I** Can
111B2 **Spenser Mts** NZ
45C1 **Sperrin** *Mts* N Ire
44C3 **Spey** *R* Scot
57B3 **Speyer** Germany
27K1 **Speyside** Tobago
47B1 **Spiez** Switz
12F1 **Spike Mt** USA
20C1 **Spirit Lake** USA
5G4 **Spirit River** Can
Spitsbergen = **Svalbard**
64C2 **Spitsbergen** *I* Barents S
57C3 **Spittal** Austria
38F6 **Spjelkavik** Nor
51C2 **Split** Croatia
47C1 **Splügen** Switz
20C1 **Spokane** USA
55C3 **Sporádhes** *Is* Greece
20C2 **Spray** USA
56C2 **Spree** *R* Germany
100A3 **Springbok** S Africa
18B2 **Springdale** USA
10B3 **Springfield** Illinois, USA
10C2 **Springfield** Massachusetts, USA
18B2 **Springfield** Missouri, USA
14B3 **Springfield** Ohio, USA
20B2 **Springfield** Oregon, USA
15D2 **Springfield** Vermont, USA

100B4 **Springfontein** S Africa
101G1 **Springs** S Africa
41D3 **Spurn Head** *Pt* Eng
13C3 **Squamish** Can
60E3 **Sredne-Russkaya Vozvyshennost** *Upland* Russian Fed
63B1 **Sredne Sibirskoye Ploskogorye** *Tableland* Russian Fed
61J2 **Sredniy Ural** *Mts* Russian Fed
76D3 **Srepok** *R* Camb
68D1 **Sretensk** Russian Fed
76C3 **Sre Umbell** Camb
83C5 **Sri Lanka** Republic, S Asia
84C2 **Srinagar** Pak
87A1 **Srivardhan** India
58B2 **Sroda Wlk.** Pol
30H6 **Sta Clara** *I* Chile
32J7 **Sta Cruz** *I* Ecuador
56B2 **Stade** Germany
44A3 **Staffa** *I* Scot
43C3 **Stafford** County, Eng
43C3 **Stafford** Eng
16C2 **Stafford Springs** USA
Stalingrad = **Volgograd**
6A1 **Stallworthy,C** Can
59C2 **Stalowa Wola** Pol
32J7 **Sta Maria** *I* Ecuador
16C2 **Stamford** Connecticut, USA
16B1 **Stamford** New York, USA
100A3 **Stampriet** Namibia
101G1 **Standerton** S Africa
14B2 **Standish** USA
101H1 **Stanger** S Africa
22B2 **Stanislaus** *R* USA
54B2 **Stanke Dimitrov** Bulg
109C4 **Stanley** Aust
29E6 **Stanley** Falkland Is
87B2 **Stanley Res** India
Stanleyville = **Kisangani**
25D3 **Stann Creek** Belize
63E2 **Stanovoy Khrebet** *Mts* Russian Fed
47C1 **Stans** Switz
109D1 **Stanthorpe** Aust
59C2 **Starachowice** Pol
54B2 **Stara Planina** *Mts* Bulg
60D2 **Staraya Russa** Russian Fed
54C2 **Stara Zagora** Bulg
58B2 **Stargard Szczecinski** Pol
19C3 **Starkville** USA
57C3 **Starnberg** Germany
58B2 **Starogard Gdanski** Pol
59D3 **Starokonstantinov** Ukraine
43C4 **Start Pt** Eng
60E3 **Staryy Oskol** Russian Fed
15C2 **State College** USA
16B2 **Staten I** USA
17B1 **Statesboro** USA
15C3 **Staunton** USA
39F7 **Stavanger** Nor
46C1 **Stavelot** Belg
61F4 **Stavropol'** Russian Fed
108B3 **Stawell** Aust
58B2 **Stawno** Pol
20B2 **Stayton** USA
12B2 **Stebbins** USA
12F2 **Steele,Mt** USA
16A2 **Steelton** USA
20C2 **Steens Mt** USA
6E2 **Steenstrups Gletscher** *Gl* Greenland
4H2 **Stefansson I** Can
101H1 **Stegi** Swaziland

47D1 **Steinach** Austria
8D2 **Steinback** Can
38G6 **Steinkjer** Nor
13C2 **Stein Mt** Can
23B2 **Stemaco** Mexico
46C2 **Stenay** France
56C2 **Stendal** Germany
110B2 **Stephens,C** NZ
108B2 **Stephens Creek** Aust
14A1 **Stephenson** USA
12H3 **Stephens Pass** USA
7E5 **Stephenville** Can
100B4 **Sterkstroom** S Africa
8C2 **Sterling** Colorado, USA
14B2 **Sterling Heights** USA
61J3 **Sterlitamak** Russian Fed
13E2 **Stettler** Can
14B3 **Steubenville** USA
4D3 **Stevens Village** USA
13B1 **Stewart** Can
21B2 **Stewart** USA
12G2 **Stewart** *R* Can
12G2 **Stewart Crossing** Can
111A3 **Stewart I** NZ
107F1 **Stewart Is** Solomon Is
4E3 **Stewart River** Can
16A3 **Stewartstown** USA
101G1 **Steyn** S Africa
57C3 **Steyr** Austria
12G3 **Stika** USA
12H3 **Stikine** *R* Can
12H3 **Stikine Ranges** *Mts* Can
18A2 **Stillwater** Oklahoma, USA
21B2 **Stillwater Range** *Mts* USA
108A2 **Stirling** Aust
44C3 **Stirling** Scot
16C1 **Stockbridge** USA
59B3 **Stockerau** Austria
39H7 **Stockholm** Sweden
42C3 **Stockport** Eng
22B2 **Stockton** California, USA
42D2 **Stockton** Eng
18B2 **Stockton L** USA
43C3 **Stoke-on-Trent** Eng
38A2 **Stokkseyri** Iceland
38G5 **Stokmarknes** Nor
39K8 **Stolbtsy** Belorussia
52B2 **Stolin** Belorussia
16B3 **Stone Harbor** USA
44C3 **Stonehaven** Scot
19A3 **Stonewall** USA
12D2 **Stony** *R* USA
38H5 **Storavan** *L* Sweden
38G6 **Støren** Nor
109C4 **Storm B** Aust
44A2 **Stornoway** Scot
59D3 **Storozhinets** Ukraine
16C2 **Storrs** USA
38G6 **Stors168jon** *L* Sweden
38H5 **Storuman** Sweden
16D1 **Stoughton** USA
43E3 **Stowmarket** Eng
45C1 **Strabane** N Ire
109C4 **Strahan** Aust
56C2 **Stralsund** Germany
38F6 **Stranda** Nor
39H7 **Strängnäs** Sweden
42B2 **Stranraer** Scot
49D2 **Strasbourg** France
15C3 **Strasburg** USA
14B2 **Stratford** Can
16C2 **Stratford** Connecticut, USA
110B1 **Stratford** NZ
43D3 **Stratford-on-Avon** Eng
108A3 **Strathalbyn** Aust
42B2 **Strathclyde** Region, Scot
13E2 **Strathmore** Can
18C1 **Streator** USA
47C2 **Stresa** Italy
53C3 **Stretto di Messina** *Str* Italy/Sicily
38D3 **Streymoy** Føroyar

53C3 **Stroboli** *I* Italy
6E3 **Strømfjord** Greenland
44C2 **Stromness** Scot
18A1 **Stromsburg** USA
38H6 **Stromsund** Sweden
38G6 **Ströms Vattudal** *L* Sweden
44C2 **Stronsay** *I* Scot
43C4 **Stroud** Eng
16B2 **Stroudsburg** USA
54B2 **Struma** *R* Bulg
43B3 **Strumble Head** *Pt* Wales
55B2 **Strumica** Macedonia
59C3 **Stryy** Ukraine
59C3 **Stryy** *R* Ukraine
108B1 **Strzelecki Creek** *R* Aust
17B2 **Stuart** Florida, USA
13C2 **Stuart** *R* Can
12B2 **Stuart I** USA
13C2 **Stuart L** Can
47D1 **Stubaier Alpen** *Mts* Austria
76D3 **Stung Sen** Camb
76D3 **Stung Treng** Camb
52A2 **Stura** *R* Italy
112C7 **Sturge I** Ant
14A2 **Sturgeon Bay** USA
14C1 **Sturgeon Falls** Can
18C2 **Sturgis** Kentucky, USA
14A2 **Sturgis** Michigan, USA
106B2 **Sturt Creek** *R* Aust
108B1 **Sturt Desert** Aust
106B2 **Stutterheim** S Africa
19B3 **Stuttgart** USA
57B3 **Stuttgart** Germany
38A1 **Stykkishólmur** Iceland
59D2 **Styr'** *R* Ukraine
35C1 **Suaçui Grande** *R* Brazil
81B4 **Suakin** Sudan
73E5 **Su-ao** Taiwan
34C2 **Suardi** Arg
78B2 **Subi** *I* Indon
54A1 **Subotica** Serbia, Yugos
60C4 **Suceava** Rom
45B2 **Suck** *R* Irish Rep
30C2 **Sucre** Bol
35A1 **Sucuriu** *R* Brazil
98C1 **Sudan** Republic, Africa
14B1 **Sudbury** Can
43E3 **Sudbury** Eng
99C2 **Sudd** *Swamp* Sudan
33F2 **Suddie** Guyana
99C2 **Sue** *R* Sudan
4H2 **Suerdrup Is** Can
92B4 **Suez** Egypt
92B3 **Suez Canal** Egypt
92B4 **Suez,G of** Egypt
16B2 **Suffern** USA
43E3 **Suffolk** County, Eng
109D2 **Sugarloaf Pt** Aust
91C5 **Suhar** Oman
68C1 **Sühbaatar** Mongolia
84B3 **Sui** Pak
72C2 **Suide** China
69E2 **Suihua** China
73B3 **Suining** China
46C2 **Suippes** France
41B3 **Suir** *R* Irish Rep
73C3 **Sui Xian** China
72E1 **Suizhong** China
85C3 **Sujangarh** India
78B4 **Sukabumi** Indon
78C3 **Sukadana** Borneo, Indon
78B4 **Sukadana** Sumatra, Indon
74E3 **Sukagawa** Japan
78C3 **Sukaraja** Indon
60E3 **Sukhinichi** Russian Fed
61F2 **Sukhona** *R* Russian Fed
61F5 **Sukhumi** Georgia
6E3 **Sukkertoppen** Greenland

6E3 **Sukkertoppen** L Greenland
38L6 **Sukkozero** Russian Fed
85B3 **Sukur** Pak
87C1 **Sukma** India
95A2 **Sūknah** Libya
100A3 **Şukses** Namibia
75A2 **Sukumo** Japan
13C1 **Sukunka** R Can
60E3 **Sula** R Russian Fed
84B3 **Sulaiman Range** Mts Pak
70C4 **Sulawesi** I Indon
54C1 **Sulina** Rom
38H5 **Sulitjelma** Nor
32A4 **Sullana** Peru
18B2 **Sullivan** USA
13B2 **Sullivan Bay** Can
13B2 **Sullivan L** Can
52B2 **Sulmona** Italy
19B3 **Sulphur** Louisiana, USA
19A3 **Sulphur** Oklahoma, USA
19A3 **Sulphur Springs** USA
86A1 **Sultānpur** India
79B4 **Sulu Arch** Phil
70C3 **Sulu S** Philip
30D4 **Sumampa** Arg
70B4 **Sumatera** I Indon
70C4 **Sumba** I Indon
70B4 **Sumbawa** I Indon
78D4 **Sumbawa Besar** Indon
99D3 **Sumbawanga** Tanz
100A2 **Sumbe** Angola
44E2 **Sumburgh Head** Pt Scot
78C4 **Sumenep** Indon
69G3 **Sumisu** I Japan
13D3 **Summerland** Can
5F4 **Summit Lake** Can
21B2 **Summit Mt** USA
111B2 **Sumner,L** NZ
75A2 **Sumoto** Japan
17B1 **Sumter** USA
60D3 **Sumy** Ukraine
16A2 **Sunbury** USA
34C2 **Sunchales** Arg
74B3 **Sunch'ŏn** N Korea
74B4 **Sunch'ŏn** S Korea
86A2 **Sundargarh** India
86B2 **Sunderbans** Swamp India
42D2 **Sunderland** Eng
13E2 **Sundre** Can
38H6 **Sundsvall** Sweden
38D3 **Suduroy** Føroyar
78D3 **Sungaianyar** Indon
78A3 **Sungaisalak** Indon
20C1 **Sunnyside** USA
21A2 **Sunnyvale** USA
63D1 **Suntar** Russian Fed
97B4 **Sunyani** Ghana
75A2 **Suŏ-nada** B Japan
38K6 **Suonejoki** Fin
86B1 **Supaul** India
18A1 **Superior** Nebraska, USA
10A2 **Superior** Wisconsin, USA
10B2 **Superior,L** Can/USA
76C3 **Suphan Buri** Thai
93D2 **Süphan Dağ** Turk
71E4 **Supiori** I Indon
93E3 **Suq ash Suyukh** Iraq
72D3 **Suqian** China
Suqutra = Socotra
91C5 **Sūr** Oman
61G3 **Sura** R Russian Fed
78C4 **Surabaya** Indon
75B2 **Suraga-wan** B Japan
78C4 **Surakarta** Indon
109C1 **Surat** Aust
85C4 **Sūrat** India
84C3 **Sūratgarh** India
77B4 **Surat Thani** Thai
84C3 **Sūrendranagar** India
16B3 **Surf City** USA
64J3 **Surgut** Russian Fed
87B1 **Suriāpet** India
49D2 **Sürich** Switz

79C4 **Surigao** Phil
76C3 **Surin** Thai
33F3 **Surinam** Republic, S America
43D4 **Surrey** County, Eng
47C1 **Sursee** Switz
95A1 **Surt** Libya
38A2 **Şurtsoy** I Iooland
74B2 **Surulangan** Indon
47B2 **Susa** Italy
75A2 **Susa** Japan
75A2 **Susaki** Japan
21A1 **Susanville** USA
47D1 **Süsch** Switz
17E2 **Susitna** R USA
16A3 **Susquehanna** R USA
16B2 **Sussex** USA
43D4 **Sussex West** Eng
13B1 **Sustut Peak** Mt Can
100B4 **Sutherland** S Africa
84C2 **Sutlej** R Pak
21A2 **Sutter Creek** USA
14B3 **Sutton** USA
12C3 **Sutwik I** USA
74D3 **Suwa** Japan
58C2 **Suwałki** Pol
17B2 **Suwannee** R USA
94B2 **Suweilih** Jordan
74B3 **Suwŏn** S Korea
72D3 **Su Xian** China
75B1 **Suzaka** Japan
73E3 **Suzhou** China
75A2 **Suzu** Japan
75B2 **Suzuka** Japan
75B1 **Suzu-misaki** C Japan
64C2 **Svalbard** Is Barents S
59C3 **Svalyava** Ukraine
38G5 **Svartisen** Mt Nor
76D3 **Svay Rieng** Camb
38G6 **Sveg** Sweden
39G7 **Svendborg** Den
Sverdlovsk = Yekaterinburg
6A1 **Sverdrup Chan** Can
69F2 **Svetlaya** Russian Fed
58C2 **Svetlogorsk** Russian Fed
39K6 **Svetogorsk** Russian Fed
54B2 **Svetozarevo** Serbia, Yugos
54C2 **Svilengrad** Bulg
58D2 **Svir'** Belorussia
59B3 **Svitavy** Czech Republic
69E1 **Svobodnyy** Russian Fed
38G5 **Svolvaer** Nor
107E3 **Swain Reefs** Aust
17B1 **Swainsboro** USA
100A3 **Swakopmund** Namibia
42D2 **Swale** R Eng
70C3 **Swallow Reef** I S E Asia
87B2 **Swāmihalli** India
25D3 **Swan** I Honduras
43D4 **Swanage** Eng
108B3 **Swan Hill** Aust
13D2 **Swan Hills** Can
13D2 **Swan Hills** Mts Can
26A3 **Swan I** Caribbean S
5H4 **Swan River** Can
43C4 **Swansea** Wales
43C4 **Swansea B** Wales
101G1 **Swartruggens** S Africa
Swatow = Shantou
101H1 **Swaziland** Kingdom, S Africa
39G7 **Sweden** Kingdom, N Europe
20B2 **Sweet Home** USA
9D3 **Sweetwater** USA
100B4 **Swellendam** S Africa
58B2 **Świdnica** Pol
58B2 **Świdwin** Pol
58B2 **Świebodzin** Pol
58B2 **Świecie** Pol
5H4 **Swift Current** Can
43D4 **Swindon** Eng
45B2 **Swinford** Irish Rep

56C2 **Świnoujście** Pol
49D2 **Switzerland** Federal Republic, Europe
45C2 **Swords** Irish Rep
109D2 **Sydney** Aust
7D5 **Sydney** Can
64G3 **Syktyvkar** Russian Fed
17A1 **Sylacauga** USA
38G6 **Sylarna** Mt Sweden
86C2 **Sylhet** Bang
56B1 **Sylt** I Germany
14B2 **Sylvania** USA
112C11 **Syowa** Base Ant
Syracuse = Siracusa
15C2 **Syracuse** USA
65H5 **Syr Darya** R Kazakhstan
93C2 **Syria** Republic, S W Asia
61J2 **Sysert'** Russian Fed
61G3 **Syzran'** Russian Fed
56C2 **Szczecin** Pol
58B2 **Szczecinek** Pol
58C2 **Szczytno** Pol
59C3 **Szeged** Hung
59B3 **Székesfehérvar** Hung
59B3 **Szekszard** Hung
59B3 **Szolnok** Hung
59B3 **Szombathely** Hung
58B2 **Szprotawa** Pol

T

90C2 **Tabas** Iran
23A1 **Tabasco** Mexico
32D4 **Tabatinga** Brazil
96B2 **Tabelbala** Alg
76C3 **Tabeng** Camb
13E2 **Taber** Can
79B3 **Tablas** I Phil
100A4 **Table Mt** S Africa
12F1 **Table Mt** USA
18B2 **Table Rock Res** USA
78B3 **Taboali** Indon
5/C3 **Tabor** USA
Tábor = Czech Republic
99D3 **Tabora** Tanz
97B4 **Tabou** Ivory Coast
90A2 **Tabriz** Iran
92C4 **Tabūk** S Arabia
23A2 **Tacámbaro** Mexico
72C1 **Tacheng** China
79C3 **Tacloban** Phil
30B2 **Tacna** Peru
8A2 **Tacoma** USA
99E1 **Tadjoura** Djibouti
87B2 **Tādpatri** India
74B3 **Taebaek Sanmaek** Mts S Korea
74B3 **Taegu** S Korea
74B4 **Taehüksan** I S Korea
74B3 **Taejŏn** S Korea
51B1 **Tafalla** Spain
96C2 **Tafasaset** Watercourse Alg
43C4 **Taff** R Wales
94B3 **Tafila** Jordan
60E4 **Taganrog** Ukraine
97A3 **Tagant** Region, Maur
79B4 **Tagbilaran** Phil
96B2 **Taguenout Hagguerete** Well Maur
107E2 **Tagula** I Solomon Is
79C4 **Tagum** Phil
Tagus = Tejo
96C2 **Tahat** Mt Alg
105J4 **Tahiti** I Pacific O
18A2 **Tahlequah** USA
21A2 **Tahoe City** USA
21A2 **Tahoe,L** USA
97C3 **Tahoua** Niger
71D3 **Tahuna** Indon
72D2 **Tai'an** China
72B3 **Taibai Shan** Mt China
72D1 **Taibus Qi** China
73E5 **T'ai-chung** Taiwan
111B3 **Taieri** R NZ
72C2 **Taihang Shan** China
110C1 **Taihape** NZ
72E3 **Tai Hu** L China
108A3 **Tailem Bend** Aust
44B3 **Tain** Scot

73E5 **T'ai-nan** Taiwan
35C1 **Taiobeiras** Brazil
73E5 **T'ai pei** Taiwan
77C5 **Taiping** Malay
75C1 **Taira** Japan
78A3 **Tais** Indon
75A1 **Taisha** Japan
29B5 **Taitao,Pen de** Chile
73E5 **T'ai-tung** Taiwan
38K5 **Taivelkoski** Fin
69E4 **Taiwan** Republic, China
Taiwan Haixia = Formosa Str
72C2 **Taiyuan** China
72D3 **Taizhou** China
81C4 **Ta'izz** Yemen
82A2 **Tajikistan** Republic, Asia
50B1 **Tajo** R Spain
76B2 **Tak** Thai
74D3 **Takada** Japan
75A2 **Takahashi** Japan
110B2 **Takaka** NZ
74C4 **Takamatsu** Japan
74D3 **Takaoka** Japan
110B1 **Takapuna** NZ
74D3 **Takasaki** Japan
75B1 **Takayama** Japan
74D3 **Takefu** Japan
75A2 **Takengon** Indon
76C3 **Takeo** Camb
75A2 **Takeo** Japan
Take-shima = Tok-do
90A2 **Takestān** Iran
75A2 **Taketa** Japan
4G3 **Takiyuak L** Can
90D1 **Takkaze** R Eritrea/Eth
13B1 **Takla L** Can
13B1 **Takla Landing** Can
12B2 **Taksleskuk L** USA
12H2 **Taku Arm** R Can
23A1 **Tala** Mexico
59B3 **Tala** Desert Region, Niger
78A3 **Talangbetutu** Indon
32A4 **Talara** Peru
50B2 **Talavera de la Reina** Spain
34A3 **Talca** Chile
34A3 **Talcahuano** Chile
86B2 **Tälcher** India
82B1 **Taldy Kurgan** Kazakhstan
71D4 **Taliabu** Indon
84B1 **Taligan** Afghan
99D2 **Tali Post** Sudan
78D3 **Taliwang** Indon
12D2 **Talkeetna** USA
12E2 **Talkeetna Mts** USA
93D2 **Tall 'Afar** Iraq
17B1 **Tallahassee** USA
94C1 **Tall Bīsah** Syria
60B2 **Tallinn** Estonia
92C3 **Tall Kalakh** Syria
19B3 **Tallulah** USA
60D4 **Tal'noye** Ukraine
58C2 **Talpaki** Russian Fed
30B4 **Tattal** Chile
109C1 **Talwood** Aust
78D1 **Tamabo Range** Mts Malay
97A3 **Tamale** Ghana
96C2 **Tamanrasset** Alg
96C2 **Tamanrasset** Watercourse Alg
16B2 **Tamaqua** USA
Tamatave = Toamasina
23A2 **Tamazula** Jalisco, Mexico
23B2 **Tamazulapan** Mexico
23B1 **Tamazunchale** Mexico
97A3 **Tambacounda** Sen
61F3 **Tambov** Russian Fed
50A1 **Tambre** R Spain
98C2 **Tambura** Sudan

Tamchaket

97A3 Tamchaket Maur
50A1 Tamega *R* Port
23B1 Tamiahua Mexico
87B2 Tamil Nādu State, India
76D2 Tam Ky Viet
17B2 Tampa USA
17B2 Tampa B USA
39J6 Tampere Fin
23B1 Tampico Mexico
68D2 Tamsagbulag Mongolia
86C2 Tamu Burma
23B1 Tamuis Mexico
109D2 Tamworth Aust
43D3 Tamworth Eng
38K4 Tana Nor
99D1 Tana *L* Eth
99E3 Tana *R* Kenya
38K5 Tana *R* Nor/Fin
75B2 Tanabe Japan
38K4 Tanafjord *Inlet* Nor
76D3 Tanahgrogot Indon
71E4 Tanahmerah Indon
12D1 Tanana USA
12E2 Tanana *R* USA
  Tananarive = Antananarivo
47C2 Tanaro *R* Italy
74B2 Tanch'ŏn N Korea
34D3 Tandil Arg
78B2 Tandjong Datu *Pt* Indon
71E4 Tandjung d'Urville *C* Indon
71E4 Tandjung Layar *C* Indon
78B3 Tandjung Lumut *C* Indon
78D2 Tandjung Mangkalihat *C* Indon
78C3 Tandjung Sambar *C* Indon
78C2 Tandjung Sirik *C* Malay
71E4 Tandjung Vals *C* Indon
85B3 Tando Adam Pak
85B3 Tando Muhammad Khan Pak
108B2 Tandou *L* Aust
87B1 Tāndūr India
110C1 Taneatua NZ
76B2 Tanen Range *Mts* Burma/Thai
96B2 Tanezrouft *Desert Region* Alg
91C4 Tang Iran
99D3 Tanga Tanz
60E4 Tanganrog Russian Fed
99C3 Tanganyika,L Tanz/Zaire
96B1 Tanger Mor
82C2 Tanggula Shan *Mts* China
  Tangier = Tanger
78A2 Tangjungpinang Indon
82C2 Tangra Yumco *L* China
72D2 Tangshan China
79B4 Tangub Phil
63C2 Tanguy Russian Fed
  Tanintharyi = Tenasserim
79B4 Tanjay Phil
101D3 Tanjona Ankaboa *C* Madag
101D2 Tanjona Babaomby *C* Madag
101D2 Tanjona Vilanandro *C* Madag
101D3 Tanjona Vohimena *C* Madag
78C4 Tanjong Bugel *C* Indon
78B4 Tanjong Cangkuang *C* Indon
78C3 Tanjong Puting *C* Indon
78C3 Tanjong Selatan *C* Indon
78D3 Tanjung Indon

78A3 Tanjungbalai Indon
78A3 Tanjung Jabung *Pt* Indon
78B3 Tanjungpandan Indon
78B4 Tanjung Priok Indon
78D2 Tanjungredeb Indon
78D2 Tanjungselor Indon
84C2 Tank Pak
68B1 Tannu Ola *Mts* Russian Fed
97B4 Tano *R* Ghana
97C3 Tanout Niger
23B1 Tanquián Mexico
73E4 Tan-shui Taiwan
86A1 Tansing Nepal
95C1 Tanta Egypt
96B2 Tan-Tan Mor
4B3 Tanunak USA
99D3 Tanzania Republic, Africa
72A3 Tao He *R* China
72B2 Taole China
96B1 Taourirt Mor
60C2 Tapa Estonia
25C3 Tapachula Mexico
33F4 Tapajós *R* Brazil
34C3 Tapalquén Arg
70B4 Tapauá Brazil
111A3 Tapanui NZ
32D5 Tapauá *R* Brazil
85D4 Tapi *R* India
86B1 Taplejung Nepal
111B2 Tapuaenuku *Mt* NZ
35B2 Tapuaritinga Brazil
79B4 Tapul Group *Is* Phil
33E4 Tapurucuara Brazil
109D1 Tara Aust
65J4 Tara Russian Fed
65J4 Tara *R* Russian Fed
54A2 Tara *R* Bosnia-Herzegovina/Montenegro, Yugos
97D4 Taraba *R* Nig
30D2 Tarabuco Bol
  Tarabulus = Tripoli
50B1 Taracon Spain
110C1 Taradale NZ
78D2 Tarakan Indon
44A3 Taransay *I* Scot
53C2 Taranto Italy
32B5 Tarapoto Peru
49C2 Tarare France
110C2 Tararua Range *Mts* NZ
96C2 Tarat Alg
110C1 Tarawera NZ
51B1 Tarazona Spain
44C3 Tarbat Ness *Pen* Scot
84C2 Tarbela Res Pak
42B2 Tarbert Strathclyde, Scot
44A3 Tarbert Western Isles, Scot
48C3 Tarbes France
106C4 Tarcoola Aust
109C2 Tarcoon Aust
109D2 Taree Aust
96A2 Tarfaya Mor
95A1 Tarhūnah Libya
91B5 Tarif UAE
30D3 Tarija Bol
87B2 Tarikere India
81C4 Tarim Yemen
99D3 Tarime Tanz
82C1 Tarim He *R* China
82C2 Tarim Pendi *Basin* China
84B2 Tarin Kut Afghan
18A1 Tarkio USA
79B2 Tarlac Phil
32B6 Tarma Peru
49C3 Tarn *R* France
59C2 Tarnobrzeg Pol
59C3 Tarnów Pol
107D3 Taroom Aust
51C1 Tarragona Spain
109C4 Tarraleah Aust
51C1 Tarrasa Spain
16C2 Tarrytown USA
92B2 Tarsus Turk
44D2 Tartan *Oilfield* N Sea

47D2 Tartaro *R* Italy
60C2 Tõrtu Estonia
92C3 Tartūs Syria
35C1 Tarumirim Brazil
70A3 Tarutung Indon
52B1 Tarvisio Italy
80D1 Tashauz Turkmenistan
86C1 Tashigang Bhutan
82A1 Tashkent Uzbekistan
65K4 Tashtagol Russian Fed
63A2 Tashtyp Russian Fed
78B4 Tasikmalaya Indon
94B2 Tasil Syria
6E2 Tasiussaq Greenland
95A3 Tasker *Well* Niger
110B2 Tasman B NZ
107D5 Tasmania *I* Aust
111B2 Tasman Mts NZ
109C4 Tasman Pen Aust
107E4 Tasman S NZ Aust
92C1 Tasova Turk
96C2 Tassili du Hoggar *Desert Region*, Alg
96C2 Tassili N'jjer *Desert Region*, Alg
96B2 Tata Mor
96D1 Tataouine Tunisia
65J4 Tatarsk Russian Fed
69G2 Tatarskiy Proliv *Str* Russian Fed
61G2 Tatarstan Russian Fed
75B1 Tateyama Japan
85B4 Tatta India
35B2 Tatui Brazil
93D2 Tatvan Turk
31B3 Tauá Brazil
35B2 Taubaté Brazil
110C1 Taumarunui NZ
101F1 Taung S Africa
76B2 Taungdwingyi Burma
76B1 Taung-gyi Burma
76A2 Taungup Burma
84C2 Taunsa Pak
43C4 Taunton Eng
16D2 Taunton USA
46E1 Taunus *Region*, Germany
110C1 Taupo NZ
110C1 Taupo,L NZ
58C1 Taurage Lithuania
110C1 Tauranga NZ
110C1 Tauranga Harbour *B* NZ
110B1 Tauroa *Pt* NZ
7A3 Tavani Can
7A3 Tavani Can
65H4 Tavda *R* Russian Fed
43B4 Tavistock Eng
76B3 Tavoy Burma
92A2 Tavsanli Turk
111B2 Tawa NZ
19A3 Tawakoni,L USA
14B2 Tawas City USA
70C3 Tawau Malay
98C1 Taweisha Sudan
79B4 Tawitawi *I* Phil
79B4 Tawitawi Group *Is* Phil
23B2 Taxco Mexico
23B2 Taxcoco Mexico
44C3 Tay *R* Scot
78C3 Tayan Indon
12B1 Taylor Alaska, USA
13C1 Taylor Can
14B2 Taylor Michigan, USA
19A3 Taylor Texas, USA
18C2 Taylorville USA
80B3 Taymā' S Arabia
63B1 Taymura *R* Russian Fed
76D3 Tay Ninh Viet
63B2 Tayshet Russian Fed

68B2 Tayshir Mongolia
44C3 Tayside Region, Scot
79A3 Taytay Phil
90D3 Tayyebāt Iran
96B1 Taza Mor
95B2 Tazirbu Libya
12E2 Tazlina *L* USA
64J3 Tazovskiy
65F5 Tbilisi Georgia
98B3 Tchibanga Gabon
95A2 Tchigai,Plat du Niger
97C3 Tchin Tabaradene Niger
98B2 Tcholliré Cam
58B2 Tczew Pol
111A3 Te Anau NZ
111A3 Te Anau,L NZ
110C1 Te Aroha NZ
110C1 Te Awamutu NZ
96C1 Tébessa Alg
23A2 Teboman Mexico
23A2 Tecailtlán Mexico
21B3 Tecate Mexico
61K2 Techa *R* Russian Fed
23A1 Tecolotlán Mexico
23A2 Tecpan Mexico
54C1 Tecuci Rom
18A1 Tecumseh USA
80E2 Tedzhen Turkmenistan
65H6 Tedzhen *R* Turkmenistan
42D2 Tees *R* Eng
33E4 Tefé Brazil
78B4 Tegal Indon
78B4 Tegineneng Indon
23B2 Tegucigalpa Honduras
21B3 Tehachapi *Mts* USA
21B3 Tehachapi *P* USA
4J3 Tehek *L* Can
90B2 Tehrān Iran
23B2 Tehuacán Mexico
23B2 Tehuantepec Mexico
23B2 Tehuitzingo Mexico
43B3 Teifi *R* Wales
50A2 Tejo *R* Port
23A2 Tejupilco Mexico
111B2 Tekapo,L NZ
82B1 Tekeli Kazakhstan
92A1 Tekirdağ Turk
55C2 Tekir Dağlari *Mts* Turk
86C2 Teknaf Bang
110C1 Te Kuiti NZ
25D3 Tela Honduras
94B2 Tel Aviv Yafo Israel
21B2 Telén Arg
21B2 Telescope Peak *Mt* USA
33F5 Teles Pires *R* Brazil
47D1 Telfs Austria
63A2 Teli Russian Fed
94B3 Tell el Meise *Mt* Jordan
12A1 Teller USA
87B2 Tellicherry India
77C5 Telok Anson Malay
71E4 Télok Flamingo *B* Indon
78C3 Télok Kumai *B* Indon
78B4 Télok Pelabuanratu *B* Indon
78C3 Télok Sampit *B* Indon
78B3 Télok Sukadona *B* Indon
23B2 Teloloapán Mexico
64G3 Tel'pos-iz *Mt* Russian Fed
58C1 Telšiai Lithuania
78C1 Teluk Berau *B* Indon
71E4 Teluk Bone *B* Indon
70D4 Teluk Bone *B* Indon
71E4 Teluk Cendrawasih *B* Indon
78D3 Teluk Mandar *B* Indon
71D4 Teluk Tolo *B* Indon

Tishomingo

70D3 Teluk Tomini B Indon
71D3 Teluk Weda B Indon
14B1 Temagami,L Can
23B2 Temascal Mexico
78A3 Tembesi R Indon
78A3 Tembilahan Indon
27E5 Temblador Ven
77C5 Temerloh Malay
65G5 Temir Kazakhstan
65J4 Temirtau Kazakhstan
15C1 Temiscaming Can
109C2 Temora Aust
9B3 Tempe USA
19B1 Temple USA
45C2 Templemore Irish Rep
23B1 Tempoal Mexico
34A3 Temuco Chile
111B2 Temuka NZ
32B4 Tena Ecuador
87C1 Tenāli India
23B2 Tenancingo Mexico
76B3 Tenasserim Burma
43B4 Tenby Wales
99E1 Tendaho Eth
83D5 Ten Degree Chan Indian O
98B1 Ténéré Desert Region Niger
96A2 Tenerife I Canary Is
76B1 Teng R Burma
23B2 Tenggarong Indon
72A2 Tengger Shamo Desert China
112C2 Teniente Jubany Base Ant
112C2 Teniente Rodolfo Marsh Martin Base Ant
87B3 Tenkāsi India
100B2 Tenke Zaire
97B3 Tenkodogo Burkina
100C2 Tennant Crook Aust
11B3 Tennessee State, USA
18C2 Tennessee R USA
34A2 Teno Chile
78D1 Tenom Malay
25C3 Tenosique Mexico
109C1 Tenterfield Aust
17B2 Ten Thousand Is USA
23A1 Teocaltiche Mexico
35C1 Teófilo Otôni Brazil
23B2 Teotihiucan Hist Site, Mexico
23A1 Tepatitlan Mexico
24B2 Tepehuanes Mexico
23B2 Tepeji Mexico
23A1 Tepic Mexico
57C2 Teplice Czech Republic
110C1 Te Puke NZ
23A1 Tequila Mexico
23B2 Tequistepec Mexico
51C1 Ter R Spain
97C3 Téra Niger
75B1 Teradomari Japan
53B2 Teramo Italy
96A1 Terceira I Açores
59D3 Terebovlya Ukraine
31C3 Teresina Brazil
35C2 Teresópolis Brazil
92C1 Terme Turk
80E2 Termez Uzbekistan
52B2 Termoli Italy
59D3 Ternopol Ukraine
13B2 Terrace Can
53B2 Terracina Italy
100B3 Terrafirma S Africa
112C8 Terre Adélie Region, Ant
19B4 Terre Bonne B USA
14A3 Terre Haute USA
19A3 Terrell USA
51B1 Teruel Spain
4C2 Teshekpuk USA
4C2 Teshekpuk L USA
74E2 Teshio R Japan

68B2 Tesiyn Gol Mts Mongolia
12H2 Teslin Can
12H3 Teslin R Can
12H2 Teslin L Can
63B3 Teslyn Gol R Mongolia
96C2 Tessalit Mali
97C3 Tessaoua Niger
16E2 Tete Mozam
23A2 Tetela Mexico
96B1 Tetouan Mor
61G2 Tetyushi Russian Fed
30D3 Teuco R Arg
23A1 Teúl de Gonzalez Ortega Mexico
71D4 Teun I Indon
52B2 Tevere R Italy
42C2 Teviot R Scot
65J4 Tevriz Russian Fed
111A3 Te Waewae B NZ
78C3 Tewah Indon
109D1 Tewantin Aust
72A3 Têwo China
19B3 Texarkana USA
19B3 Texarkana,L USA
109D1 Texas Aust
9C3 Texas State, USA
19B4 Texas City USA
56A2 Texel I Neth
19A3 Texoma,L USA
101C1 Teyateyaneng Lesotho
23B2 Teziutlán Mexico
86C1 Tezpur India
76C1 Tha Laos
101C1 Thabana Ntlenyana Mt Lesotho
101G1 Thaba Putsoa Mt Lesotho
76B3 Thagyettaw Burma
76D1 Thai Binh Viet
76C2 Thailand Kingdom, S E Asia
76C3 Thailand,G of Thai
76C1 Thai Nguyen Viet
76C2 Thakhek Laos
84C2 Thal Pak
77C4 Thale Luang L Thai
109C1 Thallon Aust
11C1 Thames NZ
43E4 Thames R Eng
76D2 Thanh Hoah Viet
87B2 Thanjavur India
85C3 Thar Desert India
108B1 Thargomindah Aust
55B2 Thásos I Greece
76B2 Thaton Burma
76B2 Thayetmyo Burma
5F5 The Dalles USA
91B4 The Gulf S W Asia
4H3 Thelon R Can
107E3 Theodore Aust
9B3 Theodore Roosevelt L USA
55B2 Thermaïkós Kólpos G Greece
8C2 Thermopolis USA
4F2 Thesiger B Can
14B1 Thessalon Can
55B2 Thessaloníki Greece
43E3 Thetford Eng
15D1 Thetford Mines Can
101G1 Theunissen S Africa
19B4 Thibodaux USA
5J4 Thicket Portage Can
8D2 Thief River Falls USA
20B2 Thielsen,Mt USA
49C2 Thiers France
97A3 Thiès Sen
99D3 Thika Kenya
86C1 Thimphu Bhutan
49D2 Thionville France
55C3 Thira I Greece
42D2 Thirsk Eng
87B2 Thiruvananthapuram = Trivandrum
39F1 Thisted Den
55B3 Thívai Greece
48C2 Thiviers France
17B1 Thomaston Georgia, USA

45C2 Thomastown Irish Rep
17B1 Thomasville Georgia, USA
6A2 Thom Bay Can
5J4 Thompson Can
18B1 Thompson R USA
4G3 Thompson Landing Can
23C2 Thompson R Can
16C2 Thompsonville USA
17B1 Thomson USA
107D3 Thomson R Aust
76C3 Thon Buri Thai
76B2 Thongwa Burma
47B1 Thonon-les-Bains France
42C2 Thornhill Scot
48B2 Thouars France
13C5 Thousand Is Can/USA
13E2 Three Hills Can
13C5 Three Kings Is NZ
76B2 Three Pagodas P Thai
14A2 Three Rivers Michigan, USA
20B2 Three Sisters Mt USA
Thrissur = Trichūr
6D2 Thule Greenland
47B1 Thun Switz
10B2 Thunder Bay Can
47B1 Thuner See L Switz
77B4 Thung Song Thai
47C1 Thur R Switz
57C2 Thüringen State, Germany
57C2 Thüringen Wald Upland Germany
45C2 Thurles Irish Rep
17F5 Thursday I Aust
44C2 Thurso Scot
112B4 Thurston I Ant
47C1 Thusis Switz
108B1 Thylungra Aust
73B5 Tiandong China
73B5 Tian'e China
72D2 Tianjin China
73B5 Tianlin China
82C1 Tiān Shan Mts C Asia
72B3 Tianshui China
72A2 Tianzhu China
96C1 Tiaret Alg
35A2 Tibagi R Brazil
94B2 Tiberias Israel
94B2 Tiberias,L Israel
Tiber,R = Tevere,R
95A2 Tibesti Mountain Region Chad
82C2 Tibet Autonomous Region, China
108B1 Tibooburra Aust
24A2 Tibrikot Nepal
97B3 Tichitt Maur
96A2 Tichla Mor
47C2 Ticino R Italy/Switz
25D2 Ticul Mexico
97A3 Tidjikja Maur
47C1 Tiefencastel Switz
74A2 Tieling China
46C1 Tienen Belg
65J5 Tien Shan Mts China/Kirghizia
72D2 Tientsin China
39H6 Tierp Sweden
23B2 Tierra Blanca Mexico
23B2 Tierra Colorada Mexico
29C6 Tierra del Fuego I Arg/Chile
28C8 Tierra del Fuego Territory, Arg
35B2 Tietê Brazil
35A2 Tietê R Brazil
14D2 Tiffin USA
17B1 Tifton USA
32B4 Tigre R Peru
33E2 Tigre R Ven
93E3 Tigris R Iraq

23B1 Tihuatlán Mexico
21B3 Tijuana Mexico
85D4 Tikamgarh India
60D2 Tikhin Russian Fed
61F4 Tikhoretsk Russian Fed
93D3 Tikrīt Iraq
1B8 Tiksi Russian Fed
46C1 Tilburg Neth
43E4 Tilbury Eng
23A2 Tilcara Arg
108B1 Tilcha Aust
76A1 Tilin Burma
97C3 Tillabéri Niger
20B1 Tillamook USA
97C3 Tillia Niger
55C3 Tílos I Greece
108B2 Tilpa Aust
32B3 Tiluá Colombia
64G3 Timanskiy Kryazh Mts Russian Fed
111B2 Timaru NZ
60E4 Timashevsk Russian Fed
108B3 Timbákion Greece
19B4 Timbalier B USA
97B3 Timbédra Maur
Timbuktu = Tombouctou
97B3 Timétrine Monts Mts Mali
97C3 Timia Niger
59B3 Timiş R Rom
54B1 Timişoara Rom
10B2 Timmins Can
106B1 Timor I Indon
73A2 Timor S Aust/Indon
34C3 Timote Arg
79C4 Tinaca Pt Phil
27D5 Tinaco Ven
87B2 Tindivanam India
98B2 Tindouf Alg
96B2 Tinfouchy Alg
96C2 Tin Fouye Alg
6F3 Ingmarmiut Greenland
32B5 Tingo Maria Peru
97B3 Tingrela Ivory Coast
86B1 Tingri China
71F2 Tinian Pacific O
30C4 Tinogasta Arg
55C3 Tínos I Greece
43B4 Tintagel Head Pt Eng
52B2 Tin Tarabine Watercourse Alg
108B3 Tintinara Aust
96C2 Tin Zaouaten Alg
22C2 Tioga P USA
77C5 Tioman I Malay
47C2 Tione Italy
45C2 Tipperary County, Irish Rep
41B3 Tipperary Irish Rep
18B2 Tipton Missouri, USA
87B2 Tiptür India
23A2 Tiquicheo Mexico
54B1 Tiranë Alb
47D1 Tirano Italy
60C4 Tiraspol Moldova
87B2 Tirchchirāppalli India
55C3 Tire Turk
44A3 Tiree I Scot
54C2 Tirgovişte Rom
54B1 Tirgu Jiu Rom
54B1 Tirgu Mureş Rom
84C1 Tirich Mir Mt Pak
61J3 Tirlyanskiy Russian Fed
54B1 Tirnăveni Rom
55B3 Tírnavos Greece
85D4 Tirodi India
47D1 Tirol Province, Austria
53A2 Tirso R Sardegna
87B2 Tiruchendūr India
87B3 Tirunelveli India
87B2 Tirupati India
87B2 Tiruppattūr India
87B2 Tiruppur India
87B2 Tiruvannamalai India
19A3 Tishomingo USA

Tisīyah

94C2 Tisīyah Syria
69C2 Tisza *R* Hung
86A2 Titlagarh India
54B2 Titov Veles
  Macedonia
98C2 Titule Zaire
17B2 Titusville USA
43C4 Tiverton Eng
52B2 Tivoli Italy
23B2 Tixtla Mexico
99E2 Tiyeglow Somalia
23B2 Tizayuca Mexico
25D2 Tizimin Mexico
96C1 Tizi Ouzou Alg
96B2 Tiznit Mor
23A1 Tizpan el Alto
  Mexico
23B2 Tlacolula Mexico
23B2 Tlacotalpan Mexico
23A2 Tlalchapa Mexico
23B2 Tlalnepantla Mexico
23B2 Tlalpan Mexico
23A1 Tlaltenango Mexico
23B2 Tlaltalpican
  Mexico
23B2 Tlapa Mexico
23B2 Tlapacoyan Mexico
23A1 Tlaquepaque Mexico
23B2 Tlaxcala Mexico
23B2 Tlaxcala State,
  Mexico
23B2 Tlaxiaco Mexico
96B1 Temcem Alg
101D2 Toamasina Madag
34C3 Toay Arg
75B2 Toba Japan
84B2 Toba and Kakar
  Ranges Mts Pak
27E4 Tobago I
  Caribbean S
13C2 Toba Inlet Sd Can
71D3 Tobelo
14B1 Tobermory Can
44A3 Tobermory Scot
71E3 Tobi I Pacific O
21B1 Tobin,Mt USA
65H4 Tobol R Kazakhstan
70D4 Toboli India
65H4 Tobol'sk Russian Fed
  Tobruk = Tubruq
31B2 Tocantins R Brazil
31B3 Tocantins State,
  Brazil
17B1 Toccoa USA
47C1 Toce R Italy
30B3 Tocopilla Chile
30C3 Tocorpuri Mt Chile
32D1 Tocuyo R Ven
85D3 Toda India
47C1 Tödi Mt Switz
75A1 Todong S Korea
9B4 Todos Santos
  Mexico
13E2 Tofield Can
13B3 Tofino Can
12B3 Togiak USA
12B3 Togiak B USA
97C4 Togo Republic, Africa
72C1 Togtoh China
12F2 Tok USA
74E2 Tokachi R Japan
75B1 Tokamachi Japan
95C3 Tokar Sudan
69E4 Tokara Retto Arch
  Japan
92C1 Tokat Turk
74B3 Tökchök-kundo Arch
  S Korea
75A1 Tok-do I S Korea
82B1 Tokmak Kirghizia
110C1 Tokomaru Bay NZ
12H3 Toku R Can/USA
78C3 Tokung Indon
69E4 Tokuno I Japan
74D3 Tökyö Japan
110C1 Tolaga Bay NZ
101D3 Tôlañaro Madag
30F3 Toledo Brazil
50B2 Toledo Spain
14B2 Toledo USA
19B3 Toledo Bend Res
  USA
101D3 Toliara Madag
23B1 Tuliman Mexico
32B3 Tolina Mt Colombia
51B1 Tolosa Spain
29B3 Toltén Chile
23B2 Toluca Mexico
61G3 Tol'yatti Russian Fed
74E2 Tomakomai Japan
78D1 Tomani Malay
58C2 Tomaszów
  Mazowiecka Pol
11B3 Tombigbee R USA
98B3 Tomboco Angola
35C2 Tombos Brazil
97B3 Tombouctou Mali
100A2 Tombua Angola
34A3 Tomé Chile
50B2 Tomelloso Spain
50A2 Tomer Port
106B3 Tomkinson Range
  Mts Aust
  Tommot
  Russian Fed
55B2 Tomorrit Mt Alb
65K4 Tomsk Russian Fed
16B3 Toms River USA
25C3 Tonalá Mexico
20C1 Tonasket USA
15C2 Tonawanda USA
105H4 Tonga Is Pacific O
101H1 Tongaat S Africa
73D3 Tongcheng China
72B2 Tongchuan China
72A2 Tongde China
46C1 Tongeren Belg
76E2 Tonggu Jiao I China
73A5 Tonghai China
74B2 Tonghua China
74B2 Tongjosön-man
  N Korea
76D1 Tongkin,G of China/
  Viet
72E1 Tongliao China
73D3 Tongling China
108B2 Tongo Aust
34A2 Tongoy Chile
73B4 Tongren Guizhou,
  China
72A2 Tongren Qinghai,
  China
86C1 Tongsa Bhutan
76B1 Tongta Burma
68B3 Tongtian He R China
44B2 Tongue Scot
72D2 Tong Xian China
72B2 Tongxin China
73B4 Tongzi China
9C4 Tonich Mexico
99C2 Tonj Sudan
85D3 Tonk India
18A2 Tonkawa USA
76C3 Tonle Sap L Camb
21B2 Tonopah USA
12E2 Tonsina USA
8B2 Tooele USA
109D1 Toogoolawah Aust
108B1 Toompine Aust
109D1 Toowoomba Aust
22C1 Topaz L USA
18A2 Topeka USA
9C4 Topolobampo
  Mexico
20B1 Toppenish USA
99D2 Tor Eth
55C3 Torbali Turk
90C2 Torbat-e-Heydariyeh
  Iran
90C2 Torbat-e Jām Iran
12D2 Torbert,Mt USA
50A1 Tordesillas Spain
56C2 Torgau Germany
46B1 Torhout Belg
69G3 Tori I Japan
47B2 Torino Italy
99D2 Torit Sudan
35A1 Torixoreu Brazil
50A1 Tormes R Spain
13E2 Tornado Mt Can
38J5 Torne L Sweden
38J5 Torneträsk Sweden
7D4 Torngat Mts Can
38J5 Tornio Fin
34C3 Tornquist Arg
15C2 Toronto Can
60D2 Toropets
  Russian Fed
99D2 Tororo Uganda
92B2 Toros Daðlari Mts
  Turk
43C4 Torquay Eng
22C4 Torrance USA
50A2 Torrão Port
51C1 Torreblanca Spain
50B1 Torre del Greco Italy
50B1 Torrelavega Spain
50B2 Torremolinos Spain
108A2 Torrens,L Aust
24B2 Torreón Mexico
47B2 Torre Pellice Italy
107D2 Torres Str Aust
50A2 Torres Vedras Port
16C2 Torrington
  Connecticut, USA
8C2 Torrington
  Wyoming, USA
9C4 Torrón Mexico
38D3 Tórshavn Föroyar
47C2 Tortona Italy
51C1 Tortosa Spain
90C2 Torüd Iran
58B2 Toruñ Pol
40B2 Tory I Irish Rep
62C2 Torzhok Russian Fed
75A2 Tosa Japan
74C4 Tosa-shimizu Japan
74C4 Tosa-wan B Japan
75B2 To-shima I Japan
  Toshkent = Tashkent
60D2 Tosno Russian Fed
75A2 Tosu Japan
92B1 Tosya Turk
61F1 Tot'ma Russian Fed
43C4 Totnes Eng
32F2 Totness Surinam
23B2 Totolapan Mexico
50B2 Totona Spain
109C2 Tottenham Aust
74C3 Tottori Japan
97B4 Touba Ivory Coast
97A3 Touba Sen
96B1 Toubkal Mt Mor
97B3 Tougan Burkina
96C1 Touggourt Alg
97A3 Tougué Guinea
46C2 Toul France
49C3 Toulouse France
49D3 Toulouse France
97B4 Toumodi Ivory Coast
76B2 Toungoo Burma
46B1 Tourcoing France
96A2 Tourine Maur
46B1 Tournai Belg
48C2 Tours France
74E2 Towada Japan
74E2 Towada-ko L Japan
15C2 Towanda USA
107D2 Townsville Aust
16A3 Towson USA
43C4 Towy R Wales
74D3 Toyama Japan
75B1 Toyama-wan B
  Japan
75B2 Toyohashi Japan
75B2 Toyonaka Japan
75A1 Toyooka Japan
74D3 Toyota Japan
96C1 Tozeur Tunisia
46D2 Traben-Trarbach
  Germany
93C1 Trabzon Turk
22B2 Tracy California,
  USA
34A3 Traiguén Chile
13D3 Trail Can
41B3 Tralee Irish Rep
45B2 Tralee B Irish Rep
45C2 Tramore Irish Rep
39G7 Tranås Sweden
77B4 Trang Thai
71E4 Trangan I Indon
109C2 Trangie Aust
12E2 Transalaskan Pipeline
  Transylvanian Alps =
  Muntii Carpaţii
  Meridionali
53B3 Trapani Italy
109C3 Traralgon Aust
97A3 Trarza Region, Maur
76C3 Trat Thai
108B2 Traveller's L Aust
56C2 Travemünde
  Germany
14A2 Traverse City USA
12C1 Traverse Peak Mt
  USA
111B2 Travers,Mt NZ
47C2 Trebbia R Italy
59B3 Třebíč
  Czech Republic
54A2 Trebinje Bosnia-
  Herzegovina
57C3 Trebon
  Czech Republic
29F2 Treinta y Tres Urug
29C4 Trelew Arg
39G7 Trelleborg Sweden
43B3 Tremadog B Wales
15D1 Tremblant,Mt Can
13C2 Trembleur L Can
16A2 Tremont USA
59B3 Trenčín Slovakia
34C3 Trenque Lauquén
  Arg
43D3 Trent R Eng
47D1 Trentino Region,
  Italy
47D1 Trento Italy
15C2 Trenton Can
18B1 Trenton Missouri,
  USA
16B2 Trenton New Jersey,
  USA
7E5 Trepassey Can
34C3 Tres Arroyos Arg
35B2 Tres Corações Brazil
30F3 Três Lagoas Brazil
34C3 Tres Lomas Arg
22B2 Tres Pinos USA
35C2 Três Rios Brazil
47C2 Treviglio Italy
47E2 Treviso Italy
47C2 Trezzo Italy
87B2 Trichūr India
40E2 Trida Aust
46D2 Trier Germany
52B1 Trieste Italy
45C2 Trim Irish Rep
87C3 Trincomalee
  Sri Lanka
33E6 Trinidad Bol
29E2 Trinidad Urug
8C3 Trinidad USA
34C3 Trinidad I Arg
27E4 Trinidad I
  Caribbean S
103G6 Trindade I Atlantic O
27E4 Trinidad & Tobago
  Republic Caribbean S
19A3 Trinity USA
9D3 Trinity R USA
17A1 Trinity USA
94B1 Tripoli Leb
95A1 Tripoli Libya
55B3 Tripolis Greece
86C2 Tripura State, India
103H6 Tristan da Cunha Is
  Atlantic O
87B3 Trivandrum India
59B3 Trnava Slovakia
16B1 Trobriand Is PNG
15D1 Trois-Rivières Can
65H4 Troitsk Russian Fed
39G7 Trollhättan Sweden
38F6 Trollheimen Mt Nor
89K9 Tromelin I Indian O
38H5 Tromsö Nor
38G6 Trondheim Nor
38G6 Trondheimfjord Inlet
  Nor
42B2 Troon Scot
102J3 Tropic of Cancer
103J6 Tropic of Capricorn
96B2 Troudenni Mali
7A4 Trout L Ontario, Can
17A1 Troy Alabama, USA
16C1 Troy New York, USA
14B2 Troy Ohio, USA
54B2 Troyan Bulg
49C2 Troyes France

91B5 **Trucial Coast** Region, UAE
21A2 **Truckee** R USA
25D3 **Trujillo** Honduras
32B5 **Trujillo** Peru
50A2 **Trujillo** Spain
32C2 **Trujillo** Ven
109C2 **Trundle** Aust
7D5 **Truro** Can
43B4 **Truro** Eng
68B2 **Tsagaan Nuur** L Mongolia
68B1 **Tsagan-Tologoy** Russian Fed
101D2 **Tsaratanana** Madag
100B3 **Tsau** Botswana
99D3 **Tsavo** Kenya
99D3 **Tsavo Nat Pk** Kenya
65J4 **Tselinograd** Kazakhstan
100A3 **Tses** Namibia
68C2 **Tsetserleg** Mongolia
97C4 **Tsévié** Togo
100B3 **Tshabong** Botswana
100B3 **Tshane** Botswana
98B3 **Tshela** Zaire
98C3 **Tshibala** Zaire
98C3 **Tshikapa** Zaire
98C3 **Tshuapa** Zaire
101D3 **Tsihombe** Madag
61F4 **Tsimlyanskoye Vodokhranilishche** Res Russian Fed
Tsinan = Jinan
Tsingtao = Qingdao
101D2 **Tsiroanomandidy** Madag
13B2 **Tsitsutl Peak** Mt Can
58D2 **Tsna** R Belorussia
72B1 **Tsogt Ovoo** Mongolia
68C2 **Tsomog** Mongolia
75B2 **Tsu** Japan
75B1 **Tsubata** Japan
74E3 **Tsuchiura** Japan
74E2 **Tsugaru-kaikyō** Str Japan
100A2 **Tsumeb** Namibia
100A3 **Tsumis** Namibia
75B1 **Tsunugi** Japan
74D3 **Tsuruga** Japan
74D3 **Tsuruoka** Japan
75B1 **Tsushima** Japan
74B4 **Tsushima** I Japan
74C3 **Tsuyama** Japan
50A1 **Tua** R Port
60E5 **Tuam** Irish Rep
52B2 **Tuapse** Russian Fed
111A3 **Tuatapere** NZ
30G4 **Tubarão** Brazil
94B2 **Tubas** Israel
79A4 **Tubbataha Reefs** Is Phil
57B3 **Tübingen** Germany
95B1 **Tubruq** Libya
16B3 **Tuckerton** USA
98B3 **Tucson** USA
30C4 **Tucumán** State, Arg
34B2 **Tucunuco** Arg
33E2 **Tucupita** Ven
51B1 **Tudela** Spain
93C3 **Tudmur** Syria
101H1 **Tugela** R S Africa
109D2 **Tuggerah** L Aust
12D3 **Tugidak** I USA
79B2 **Tuguegarao** Phil
63F2 **Tugur** Russian Fed
72D2 **Tuhai He** R China
4E3 **Tuktoyaktuk** USA
58C1 **Tukums** Latvia
99D3 **Tukuyu** Tanz
84B1 **Tukzar** Afghan
60E3 **Tula** Russian Fed
23B1 **Tulancingo** Mexico
78A3 **Tulangbawang** R Indon
32B3 **Tulcán** Colombia
60C5 **Tulcea** Rom
100B3 **Tuli** Zim
94B2 **Tulkarm** Israel
48C2 **Tulle** France
19B3 **Tullos** USA
45C2 **Tullow** Irish Rep
18A2 **Tulsa** USA

93C3 **Tulûl ash Shāmiyah** Desert Region Syria/S Arabia
63C2 **Tulun** Russian Fed
78C4 **Tulungagung** Indon
32B3 **Tumaco** Colombia
109C3 **Tumbarumba** Aust
32A4 **Tumbes** Ecuador
108A2 **Tumby Bay** Aust
74B2 **Tumen** China
87B2 **Tumkūr** India
85D4 **Tumsar** India
97B3 **Tumu** Ghana
109C3 **Tumut** R Aust
109C3 **Tumut** R Aust
93C2 **Tunceli** Turk
99D3 **Tunduma** Zambia
101C2 **Tunduru** Tanz
54C2 **Tundzha** R Bulg
87B1 **Tungabhadra** R India
68D4 **Tung-Chiang** Taiwan
38B2 **Tungnafellsjökull** Mts Iceland
12J2 **Tungsten** Can
63B1 **Tunguska** R Russian Fed
87C1 **Tuni** India
96D1 **Tunis** Tunisia
88E4 **Tunisia** Republic, N Africa
32C2 **Tunja** Colombia
12B2 **Tuntutuliak** USA
12B2 **Tununak** USA
34B2 **Tunuyán** Arg
34B2 **Tunuyán** R Arg
22C2 **Tuolumne Meadows** USA
35A2 **Tupã** Brazil
35B1 **Tupaciguara** Brazil
19C3 **Tupelo** USA
30C3 **Tupiza** Bol
22C1 **Tupper Lake** USA
34B2 **Tupungato** Arg
29C2 **Tupungato** Mt Arg
86C1 **Tura** India
63C1 **Tura** Russian Fed
61K2 **Tura** R Russian Fed
84C3 **Turan** Iran
63B2 **Turan** Russian Fed
93C3 **Turayf** S Arabia
85B3 **Turbat** Pak
32B2 **Turbo** Colombia
54B1 **Turda** Rom
63A3 **Turfan Depression** China
65H4 **Turgay** Kazakhstan
63B3 **Turgen Uul** Mt Mongolia
54C2 **Turgovishte** Bulg
92A2 **Turgutlu** Turk
92C1 **Turhal** Turk
39K7 **Türi** Estonia
51B2 **Turia** R Spain
Turin = Torino
61K2 **Turinsk** Russian Fed
72E1 **Turiy Rog** Russian Fed
99D2 **Turkana,L** Kenya/Eth
80E1 **Turkestan** Region, C Asia
82A1 **Turkestan** Kazakhstan
92C2 **Turkey** Republic, W Asia
80D1 **Turkmenistan** Republic, Asia
90B2 **Turkmenskiy Zaliv** B Turkmenistan
27C2 **Turks Is** Caribbean S
39J6 **Turku** Fin
99D2 **Turkwel** R Kenya
22B2 **Turlock** USA
22B2 **Turlock L** USA
110C2 **Turnagain,C** NZ
25D3 **Turneffe** I Belize
16C1 **Turners Falls** USA
46C1 **Turnhout** Belg
13F1 **Turnor L** Can
54B2 **Turnu Măgurele** Rom
63A3 **Turpan** China
26B2 **Turquino** Mt Cuba
80E1 **Turtkul'** Uzbekistan

18A2 **Turtle Creek Res** USA
13F2 **Turtle L** Can
63A1 **Turukhansk** Russian Fed
68C1 **Turuntayevo** Russian Fed
35A1 **Turvo** R Goiás, Brazil
35B2 **Turvo** R São Paulo, Brazil
58C2 **Tur'ya** R Ukraine
19C3 **Tuscaloosa** USA
18C2 **Tuscola** USA
90C3 **Tusharik** Iran
Tutera = Tudela
87B3 **Tuticorin** India
54C2 **Tutrakan** Bulg
57B3 **Tuttlingen** Germany
68C2 **Tuul Gol** R Mongolia
105G4 **Tuvalu** Is Pacific O
63B2 **Tuvinskaya Respublika,** Russian Fed
23A2 **Tuxpan** Jalisco, Mexico
24B2 **Tuxpan** Nayarit, Mexico
23B1 **Tuxpan** Veracruz, Mexico
23B2 **Tuxtepec** Mexico
25C3 **Tuxtla Gutiérrez** Mexico
50A1 **Túy** Spain
76D3 **Tuy Hoa** Viet
92B2 **Tuz Gölü** Salt L Turk
93D3 **Tuz Khurmātū** Iraq
54A2 **Tuzla** Bosnia-Herzegovina
60E2 **Tver'** Russian Fed
42C2 **Tweed** R Eng/Scot
109D1 **Tweed Heads** Aust
42C2 **Tweedsmuir Hills** Scot
7E5 **Twillingate** Can
0D2 **Twin Falls** USA
111B2 **Twins,The** Mt NZ
14A2 **Two Rivers** USA
63E2 **Tygda** Russian Fed
19A3 **Tyler** USA
65K3 **Tym** R Russian Fed
69G1 **Tymovskoye** Russian Fed
42D2 **Tyne** R Eng
42D2 **Tyne and Wear** Metropolitan County, Eng
42D2 **Tynemouth** Eng
38G6 **Tynset** Nor
12D3 **Tyonek** USA
94B2 **Tyr** Leb
Tyre = Tyre
45C1 **Tyrone** County, N Ire
53B2 **Tyrrell,L** Aust
53H4 **Tyrrhenian S** Italy
Tyumen' Russian Fed
43B3 **Tywyn** Wales
55B3 **Tzoumérka** Mt Greece

U

99E2 **Uarsciek** Somalia
35C2 **Ubá** Brazil
35C1 **Ubaí** Brazil
98B2 **Ubangi** R CAR
47B2 **Ubaye** R France
75A2 **Ube** Japan
50B2 **Ubeda** Spain
6E2 **Ubekendt Ejland** I Greenland
35B1 **Uberaba** Brazil
35B1 **Uberlândia** Brazil
76C2 **Ubon Ratchathani** Thai
58D2 **Ubort** R Belorussia
98C3 **Ubundi** Zaire
32C5 **Ucayali** R Peru
84C3 **Uch** Pak
63F2 **Uchar** R Russian Fed
74E2 **Uchiura-wan** B Japan
63B2 **Uda** R Russian Fed
85C4 **Udaipur** India
86B1 **Udaipur Garhi** Nepal

34D3 **Udaquoila** Arg
39G7 **Uddevalla** Sweden
38H5 **Uddjaur** L Sweden
87B1 **Udgir** India
84D2 **Udhampur** India
61H2 **Udmurtskaya Respublika,** Russian Fed
76C2 **Udon Thani** Thai
63F2 **Udskaya Guba** B Russian Fed
87A2 **Udupi** India
75B1 **Ueda** Japan
99C2 **Uele** R Zaire
56C2 **Uelzen** Germany
98C2 **Uere** R Zaire
61J3 **Ufa** Russian Fed
61J2 **Ufa** R Russian Fed
100A3 **Ugab** R Namibia
99D3 **Ugaila** R Tanz
12D3 **Ugak B** USA
99D2 **Uganda** Republic, Africa
12C3 **Ugashik B** USA
12C3 **Ugashik L** USA
47B2 **Ugine** France
69G2 **Uglegorsk** Russian Fed
60E2 **Uglich** Russian Fed
60E3 **Ugra** R Russian Fed
44A3 **Uig** Scot
98B3 **Uige** Angola
61H4 **Uil** Kazakhstan
8B2 **Uinta Mts** USA
101H1 **Uitenhage** S Africa
59C3 **Ujfehérto** Hung
75B2 **Uji** Japan
99C3 **Ujiji** Tanz
30C3 **Ujina** Chile
85D4 **Ujjain** India
78C4 **Ujung Pandang** Indon
99D3 **Ukerewe** I Tanz
86C1 **Ukhrul** India
21A2 **Ukiah** California, USA
20C1 **Ukiah** Oregon, USA
58C1 **Ukmerge** Lithuania
60C4 **Ukraine** Republic, Europe
68C2 **Ulaanbaatar** Mongolia
68B2 **Ulaangom** Mongolia
72C1 **Ulaan Uul** Mongolia
82C1 **Ulangar Hu** L China
68C1 **Ulan Ude** Russian Fed
68B3 **Ulan Ul Hu** L China
34B2 **Ulapes** Arg
74B3 **Ulchin** S Korea
54A2 **Ulcinj** Montenegro, Yugos
68D2 **Uldz** Mongolia
68B2 **Uliastay** Mongolia
58D1 **Ulla** Lithuania
109D3 **Ulladulla** Aust
44A3 **Ullapool** Scot
38H5 **Ullsfjorden** Inlet Nor
42C2 **Ullswater** L Eng
74C3 **Ullung-do** I S Korea
57C3 **Ulm** Germany
109C1 **Uloowaranie,L** Aust
74B3 **Ulsan** S Korea
45C1 **Ulster** Region, N Ire
65K5 **Ulungur He** R China
65K5 **Ulungur Hu** L China
44A3 **Ulva** I Scot
42C2 **Ulverston** Aust
109C4 **Ulverstone** Aust
63G2 **Ulya** R Russian Fed
61D3 **Ulyanovsk** Russian Fed
6E2 **Umanak** Greenland
86A2 **Umaria** India
85B3 **Umarkot** Pak
108A1 **Umaroona,L** Aust
20C1 **Umatilla** USA
38L5 **Umba** Russian Fed
99D3 **Umba** R Tanz
38H6 **Ume** R Sweden
38J6 **Umea** Sweden
101H1 **Umfolozi** R S Africa
43C4 **Umiat** USA
91C4 **Umm al Qaiwain** UAE

91C5 Umm as Samīm Salt Marsh Oman
99C1 Umm Bell Sudan
98C1 Umm Keddada Sudan
99D1 Umma Ruwaba Sudan
91B5 Umm Sa'id Qatar
20B2 Umpqua R USA
85D4 Umred India
100B4 Umtata S Africa
35A2 Umuarama Brazil
52C1 Una R Bosnia-Herzegovina/Croatia
35B1 Unaí Brazil
12B2 Unalakleet USA
80C3 Unayzah S Arabia
16C2 Uncasville USA
101G1 Underberg S Africa
60D3 Unecha Russian Fed
94B3 Uneisa Jordan
7D4 Ungava B Can
30F4 União de Vitória Brazil
34B3 Union Arg
18B2 Union Missouri, USA
17B1 Union S Carolina, USA
14C2 Union City Pennsylvania, USA
17A1 Union Springs USA
15C3 Uniontown USA
91B5 United Arab Emirates Arabian Pen
36C3 United Kingdom Kingdom, W Europe
2H4 United States of America
6B1 United States Range Mts Can
13F2 Unity Can
20C2 Unity USA
46D1 Unna Germany
86A1 Unnao India
44E1 Unst I Scot
13A1 Unuk R USA
92C1 Unye Turk
61F2 Unzha R Russian Fed
33E2 Upata Ven
98C3 Upemba Nat Pk Zaïre
6E2 Upernavik Greenland
22D3 Upland USA
100B3 Uplington S Africa
14B2 Upper Arlington USA
13D2 Upper Arrow L Can
111C2 Upper Hutt NZ
20B2 Upper Klamath L USA
20B2 Upper L USA
45C1 Upper Lough Erne L N Ire
27L1 Upper Manzanilla Trinidad
39H7 Uppsala Sweden
72B1 Urad Qianqi China
91A4 Urairah S Arabia
61H3 Ural R Kazakhstan
109D2 Uralla Aust
61H3 Ural'sk Kazakhstan
65G4 Uralskiy Khrebet Mts Russian Fed
5H4 Uranium City Can
75B1 Urawa Japan
18C1 Urbana Illinois, USA
14B2 Urbana Ohio, USA
52B2 Urbino Italy
42C2 Ure R Eng
61G2 Uren' Russian Fed
80E1 Urgench Uzbekistan
84B2 Urgun Afghan
55C3 Urla Turk
54B2 Uroševac Serbia, Yugos
31B4 Uruaçu Brazil
23A2 Uruapan Mexico
35B1 Urucuia R Brazil
30E4 Uruguaiana Brazil
29E2 Uruguay R Republic, S America
29E2 Uruguay R Urug
82C1 Ürümqi China
69H2 Urup I Russian Fed
84B2 Uruzgan Afghan

61F3 Uryupinsk Russian Fed
61H2 Urzhum Russian Fed
54C2 Urziceni Rom
82C1 Usa China
75A2 Usa Japan
64G3 Usa R Russian Fed
92A2 Uşak Turk
100A3 Usakos Namibia
99D3 Ushashi Tanz
65J5 Ush Tobe Kazakhstan
29C6 Ushuaia Arg
63E2 Ushumun Russian Fed
43C4 Usk R Wales
92A1 Üsküdar Turk
63C2 Usolye Sibirskoye Russian Fed
34B2 Uspallata Arg
69F2 Ussuriysk Russian Fed
47C1 Uster Switz
53B3 Ustica I Italy
57C2 Ústí nad Labem Czech Republic
65J4 Ust'Ishim Russian Fed
58B2 Ustka Pol
65K5 Ust'-Kamenogorsk Kazakhstan
63B2 Ust Karabula Russian Fed
61J2 Ust'Katav Russian Fed
63C2 Ust'-Kut Russian Fed
61E4 Ust Labinsk Russian Fed
63F1 Ust'Maya Russian Fed
1C8 Ust'Nera Russian Fed
63E2 Ust'Nyukzha Russian Fed
63C2 Ust'Ordynskiy Russian Fed
64G3 Ust'Tsil'ma Russian Fed
63F2 Ust'Umal'ta Russian Fed
75A2 Usuki Japan
25C3 Usumacinta R Guatemala/Mexico
101H1 Usutu R Swaziland
8B3 Utah State, USA
8B2 Utah L USA
58D1 Utena Russian Fed
85B3 Uthal Pak
10C2 Utica USA
51B2 Utiel Spain
13D1 Utikuma L Can
56B2 Utrecht Neth
101H1 Utrecht S Africa
50A2 Utrera Spain
38K5 Utsjoki Fin
74D3 Utsunomiya Japan
76C2 Uttaradit Thai
86A1 Uttar Pradesh State, India
65H4 Uval Russian Fed
107F3 Uvéa I Nouvelle Calédonie
99D3 Uvinza Tanz
99C3 Uvira Zaïre
6E2 Uvkusigssat Greenland
39J6 Uvsikaupunki Fin
68B1 Uvs Nuur L China
74C4 Uwajima Japan
72B2 Uxin Qi China
63B2 Uyar Russian Fed
30C3 Uyuni Bol
80E1 Uzbekistan Republic, Asia
48C2 Uzerche France
59C3 Uzhgorod Ukraine
54A2 Užice Serbia, Yugos
60E3 Uzlovaya Russian Fed
92A1 Uzunköprü Turk

V

101F1 Vaal R S Africa
101G1 Vaal Dam Res S Africa

100B3 Vaalwater S Africa
38J6 Vaasa Fin
69B3 Văc Hung
30F4 Vacaria Brazil
35C1 Vacaria R Minas Gerais, Brazil
21A2 Vacaville USA
85C4 Vadodara India
38K4 Vadsø Nor
47C1 Vaduz Leichtenstein
38D3 Vágar Føroyar
29E3 Va Gesell Arg
59B3 Váh R Slovakia
87B2 Vaigai R India
65K3 Vakh R Russian Fed
60B4 Vakhsh Afghan
29C4 Valcheta Arg
47D2 Valdagno Italy
60D2 Valday Russian Fed
60D2 Valdayskaya Vozvyshennost' Upland Russian Fed
32D2 Val de la Pascua Ven
50B2 Valdepeñas Spain
12E2 Valdez USA
29B3 Valdivia Chile
46B2 Val d'Oise Department France
17B1 Valdosta USA
20C2 Vale USA
13D2 Valemount Can
31D4 Valença Bahia, Brazil
35C2 Valença Rio de Janeiro, Brazil
49C3 Valence France
51B2 Valencia Region, Spain
51B2 Valencia Spain
32D1 Valencia Ven
45A3 Valencia / Irish Rep
50A2 Valencia de Alcantara Spain
46B1 Valenciennes France
47C2 Valenza Italy
32C2 Valera Ven
39K7 Valga Estonia
54A2 Valjevo Serbia, Yugos
39J6 Valkeakoski Fin
25D2 Valladolid Mexico
50B1 Valladolid Spain
47B2 Valle d'Aosta Region, Italy
27D5 Valle de la Pascua Ven
23A1 Valle de Santiago Mexico
47B2 Valle d'Isére France
32C1 Valledupar Colombia
35A2 Vallée de l'Azaouak V Niger
97C3 Vallée Tilemis V Mali
30D2 Valle Grande Bol
22A1 Vallejo USA
30B4 Vallenar Chile
53B3 Valletta Malta
8D2 Valley City USA
20B2 Valley Falls USA
15D1 Valleyfield Can
13D1 Valleyview Can
47E2 Valli di Comacchio Lg Italy
51C1 Valls Spain
39J7 Valmiera Latvia
35A2 Valparaíso Brazil
23A1 Valparaiso Chile
23A1 Valparaiso Mexico
17A1 Valparaiso USA
101G1 Vals R S Africa
85C4 Valsād India
63A2 Valuyki Russian Fed
50A2 Valverde del Camino Spain
38J6 Vammala Fin
93D2 Van Turk
63C1 Vanavara Russian Fed
13C3 Vancouver Can
20B1 Vancouver USA
5F5 Vancouver I Can
12G2 Vancouver,Mt Can

18C2 Vandalia Illinois, USA
14B3 Vandalia Ohio, USA
13C2 Vanderhoof Can
106C2 Van Diemen G Gulf Aust
14C1 Vänern L Sweden
39G7 Vänersborg Sweden
101D3 Vangaindrano Madag
93D2 Van Gölü Salt L Turk
76C2 Vang Vieng Laos
9C3 Van Horn USA
15C1 Vanier Can
1C6 Vankarem Russian Fed
38H6 Vännäs Sweden
48B2 Vannes France
47B2 Vanoise Mts France
100A4 Vanrhynsdorp S Africa
6B3 Vansittart I Can
105G4 Vanuatu Is Pacific O
14B2 Van Wert USA
47C2 Varallo Italy
90B2 Varāmin Iran
86A1 Vārānasi India
38K4 Varangerfjord Inlet Nor
38K4 Varangerhalvøya Pen Nor
52C1 Varazdin Croatia
39G7 Varberg Sweden
39F7 Varde Den
38L4 Vardø Nor
52C1 Varéna Lithuania
47C2 Varenna Italy
47C2 Varese Italy
35B2 Varginha Brazil
38K6 Varkaus Fin
52C2 Varna Bulg
39G7 Värnamo Sweden
17B1 Varnville USA
35C1 Várzea da Palma Brazil
47C2 Varzi Italy
50B1 Vascongadas Region, Spain
60D3 Vasil'kov Ukraine
25A2 Västerås Sweden
39H7 Västervik Sweden
52B2 Vasto Italy
65J4 Vasyugan R Russian Fed
38J2 Vatnajökull Mts Iceland
38A1 Vatneyri Iceland
54C1 Vatra Dornei Rom
39G7 Vättern L Sweden
9C3 Vaughn USA
32C3 Vaupés R Colombia
13E2 Vauxhall Can
38J6 Vavau I Tonga
87A3 Vavuniya Sri Lanka
39G7 Växjö Sweden
64G2 Vaygach, Ostrov I Russian Fed
34C2 Vedia Arg
38S5 Vega I Nor
18E2 Vegreville Can
50A2 Vejer de la Frontera Spain
39F7 Vejle Den
52C2 Velebit Mts Croatia
52C1 Velenje Slovenia
35C1 Velhas R Brazil
39K7 Velikaya R Russian Fed
60D2 Velikiye Luki Russian Fed
61G1 Velikiy Ustyug Russian Fed
54C2 Veliko Türnovo Bulg
97A3 Vélingara Sen
87B2 Vellore India
61F1 Vel'sk Russian Fed
87B3 Vembanad L India
34 Vendo Tuerto Arg
35B2 Venceslau Braz Brazil
49C2 Vendôme France
12E1 Venetie USA
47D2 Veneto Region, Italy
47E2 Venezia Italy

32D2 **Venezuela** Republic, S America
87A1 **Vengurla** India
12C3 **Veniaminof** V USA
Venice = Venezia
87B2 **Venkatagiri** India
56B2 **Venlo** Neth
58C1 **Venta** R Latvia
101G1 **Ventersburg** S Africa
58C1 **Ventspils** Latvia
32D3 **Ventuari** R Ven
22C3 **Ventura** USA
60D1 **Vepsovskaya Vozvyshennost'** Upland Russian Fed
30D4 **Vera** India
51B2 **Vera** Spain
23B2 **Veracruz** Mexico
23B1 **Veracruz** State, Mexico
85C4 **Veräval** India
47C2 **Verbania** Italy
47C2 **Vercelli** Italy
35A1 **Verde** R Goias, Brazil
23A1 **Verde** R Jalisco, Mexico
35A1 **Verde** R Mato Grosso do Sul, Brazil
23B2 **Verde** R Oaxaca, Mexico
Verde,C = Cap Vert
35C1 **Verde Grande** R Brazil
34C3 **Verde,Pen** Arg
49D3 **Verdon** R France
46C2 **Verdun** France
101G1 **Vereeniging** S Africa
61H2 **Vereshchagino** Russian Fed
97A3 **Verga,C** Guinea
34D3 **Vergara** Arg
50A1 **Verin** Spain
63D2 **Verkh Angara** R Russian Fed
61J3 **Verkhneural'sk** Russian Fed
63E1 **Verkhnevilyuysk** Russian Fed
1C8 **Verkhoyansk** Russian Fed
35A1 **Vermelho** R Brazil
13E2 **Vermilion** Can
10C2 **Vermont** State, USA
22B2 **Vernalis** USA
13D2 **Vernon** Can
46A2 **Vernon** France
9D3 **Vernon** USA
17B2 **Vero Beach** USA
54B2 **Veroia** Greece
47D2 **Verolanuova** Italy
47D2 **Verona** Italy
46B2 **Versailles** France
46C1 **Verviers** Belg
46B2 **Vervins** France
46C2 **Vesle** R France
49D2 **Vesoul** France
38G5 **Vesterålen** Is Nor
38G5 **Vestfjorden** Inlet Nor
38A2 **Vestmannaeyjar** Iceland
53B2 **Vesuvio** Mt Italy
59B3 **Veszprém** Hung
39H7 **Vetlanda** Sweden
61F2 **Vetluga** R Russian Fed
46B1 **Veurne** Belg
47B2 **Vevey** Switz
46A2 **Vexin** Region, France
47A2 **Veynes** France
50A1 **Viana do Castelo** Port
Viangchan = Vientiane
49E3 **Viareggio** Italy
39F7 **Viborg** Den
53C3 **Vibo Valentia** Italy
Vic = Vich
112C2 **Vicecomodoro Marambio** Base Ant
52B1 **Vicenza** Italy
61C1 **Vich** Spain
32D3 **Vichada** R Colombia
61F2 **Vichuga** Russian Fed

49C2 **Vichy** France
19B3 **Vicksburg** USA
35C2 **Vicosa** Brazil
106C4 **Victor Harbour** Aust
34C2 **Victoria** Arg
13C3 **Victoria** Can
34A3 **Victoria** Chile
78D1 **Victoria** Malay
108B3 **Victoria** State, Aust
104 **Victoria** USA
106C2 **Victoria** R Aust
26B2 **Victoria de las Tunas** Cuba
100B2 **Victoria Falls** Zambia/Zim
4G2 **Victoria I** Can
108B2 **Victoria,L** Aust
99D3 **Victoria,L** E Africa
112B7 **Victoria Land** Region, Ant
86C2 **Victoria,Mt** Burma
99D2 **Victoria Nile** R Uganda
111B2 **Victoria Range** Mts NZ
106C2 **Victoria River Downs** Aust
4H3 **Victoria Str** Can
15D1 **Victoriaville** Can
100B4 **Victoria West** S Africa
34B3 **Victorica** Arg
21B3 **Victorville** USA
34A2 **Vicuña** Chile
34C2 **Vicuña Mackenna** Arg
17B1 **Vidalia** USA
54C2 **Videle** Rom
54B2 **Vidin** Bulg
85D4 **Vidisha** India
58D1 **Vidzy** Belorussia
29D4 **Viedma** Arg
46B2 **Vielha = Viella**
51C1 **Viella** Spain
18C2 **Vienna** Illinois, USA
14B3 **Vienna** W Virginia, USA
49C2 **Vienne** France
48C2 **Vienne** R France
76C2 **Vientiane** Laos
47C1 **Vierwaldstätter See** L Switz
48C2 **Vierzon** France
53C2 **Vieste** Italy
70B2 **Vietnam** Republic, S E Asia
76D1 **Vietri** Viet
27P2 **Vieux Fort** St Lucia
79B2 **Vigan** Phil
47C2 **Vigevano** Italy
48B3 **Vignemale** Mt France
50A1 **Vigo** Spain
87C1 **Vijayawāda** India
55A2 **Vijosë** R Alb
38B2 **Vik** Iceland
54B2 **Vikhren** Mt Bulg
13E2 **Viking** Can
38G6 **Vikna** I Nor
101C2 **Vila de Maganja** Mozam
101C2 **Vila Machado** Mozam
101C3 **Vilanculos** Mozam
Vilanova i la Geltrú = Villanueva-y-Geltrú
50A1 **Vila Real** Port
101C2 **Vila Vasco da Gama** Mozam
35C2 **Vila Velha** Brazil
58D2 **Vileyka** Belorussia
38H6 **Vilhelmina** Sweden
33E6 **Vilhena** Brazil
60C2 **Viljandi** Estonia
101G1 **Viljoenskroon** S Africa
9C3 **Villa Ahumada** Mexico
34B2 **Villa Atuel** Arg
50A1 **Villaba** Spain
23A2 **Villa Carranza** Mexico

52B1 **Villach** Austria
34B2 **Villa Colon** Arg
34C2 **Villa Constitución** Arg
34C1 **Villa de Maria** Arg
23A1 **Villa de Reyes** Mexico
34B2 **Villa Dolores** Arg
47D2 **Villafranca di Verona** Italy
34C2 **Villa General Mitre** Arg
34C3 **Villa General Roca** Arg
34D2 **Vilaguay** Arg
25C3 **Villahermosa** Mexico
23A1 **Villa Hidalgo** Mexico
34C2 **Villa Huidobro** Arg
34C3 **Villa Iris** Arg
34C2 **Villa Maria** Arg
30D3 **Villa Montes** Bol
23A1 **Villanueva** Mexico
50A1 **Villa Nova de Gaia** Port
34C2 **Villanueva de la Serena** Spain
51C1 **Villanueva-y-Geltrú** Spain
34B3 **Villa Regina** Arg
51B2 **Villarreal** Spain
29B3 **Villarrica** Chile
30E4 **Villarrica** Par
50B2 **Villarrobledo** Spain
34D2 **Villa San José** Arg
34C2 **Villa Valeria** Arg
32C3 **Villavicencio** Colombia
49C2 **Villefranche** France
7C5 **Ville-Marie** Can
51B2 **Villena** Spain
46B2 **Villeneuve-St-Georges** France
48C3 **Villeneuve-sur-Lot** France
19B3 **Ville Platte** USA
46D2 **Villers-Cotterêts** France
49C2 **Villeurbanne** France
101G1 **Villiers** S Africa
87B2 **Villupuram** India
58D2 **Vilnius** Lithuania
63D1 **Vilyuy** R Russian Fed
63E1 **Vilyuysk** Russian Fed
34A2 **Viña del Mar** Chile
51C1 **Vinaroz** Spain
14A3 **Vincennes** USA
38H5 **Vindel** R Sweden
85D4 **Vindhya Range** Mts India
16B3 **Vineland** USA
16D2 **Vineyard Haven** USA
76D2 **Vinh** Viet
76D3 **Vinh Cam Ranh** B Viet
77D4 **Vinh Loi** Viet
77D3 **Vinh Long** Viet
54A2 **Vinica** Croatia
54A1 **Vinkovci** Croatia
60C4 **Vinnitsa** Ukraine
112B3 **Vinson Massif** Upland Ant
100A3 **Vioolsdrift** S Africa
47D1 **Vipiteno** Italy
79B3 **Virac** Phil
87B2 **Virddhāchalam** India
100A2 **Virei** Angola
35C1 **Virgem da Lapa** Brazil
101G1 **Virginia** S Africa
10C3 **Virginia** State, USA
10A2 **Virginia** USA
21B2 **Virginia City** USA
27E3 **Virgin Is** Caribbean S
52C1 **Virovitica** Croatia
46C2 **Virton** Belg
87B3 **Virudunagar** India
52C2 **Vis** I Croatia
21B2 **Visalia** USA
79B3 **Visayan S** Phil
39H7 **Visby** Sweden
4H2 **Viscount Melville Sd** Can
54A2 **Višegrad** Bosnia-Herzegovina
50A1 **Viseu** Port
83C4 **Vishākhapatnam** India
47B1 **Visp** Switz
49C1 **Vissingen** Neth
21B3 **Vista** USA
Vistula = Wisla
57C3 **Vitavia** R Czech Republic
87A1 **Vite** India
60D2 **Vitebsk** Belorussia
52B2 **Viterbo** Italy
50A1 **Vitigudino** Spain
63D2 **Vitim** R Russian Fed
50B1 **Vitora** Spain
31C6 **Vitoria** Brazil
31C4 **Vitória da Conquista** Brazil
48B2 **Vitré** France
46C2 **Vitry-le-Francois** France
38J5 **Vittangi** Sweden
53B3 **Vittoria** Italy
47E2 **Vittorio Veneto** Italy
69H2 **Vityaz Depth** Pacific O
50A1 **Vivero** Spain
63B1 **Vivi** R Russian Fed
34D3 **Vivorata** Arg
63C2 **Vizhne-Angarsk** Russian Fed
83C4 **Vizianagaram** India
54B1 **Vlădeasa** Mt Rom
61F5 **Vladikavkaz** Russian Fed
65F4 **Vladimir** Russian Fed
59C2 **Vladimir Volynskiy** Ukraine
74C2 **Vladivostok** Russian Fed
56A2 **Vlieland** I Neth
46B1 **Vlissingen** Neth
55A2 **Vlorë** Alb
57C3 **Vöcklabruck** Austria
76D3 **Voeune Sai** Camb
47C2 **Voghera** Italy
101D2 **Vohibinany** Madag
101E2 **Vohimarina** Madag
99D3 **Voi** Kenya
97B4 **Voinjama** Lib
49D2 **Voiron** France
54A1 **Vojvodina** Aut Republic Serbia, Yugos
26A5 **Volcán Baru** Mt Panama
23B2 **Volcán Citlaltepetl** Mt Mexico
30C3 **Volcán Lullaillaco** Mt Chile
34A3 **Volcáno Copahue** Mt Chile
34A3 **Volcán Domuyo** Mt Arg
Volcáno Is = Kazan Retto
29B3 **Volcáno Lanin** Mt Arg
30C3 **Volcán Ollagüe** Mt Chile
34A3 **Volcáno Llaima** Mt Chile
34B2 **Volcáno Maipo** Mt Arg
34A3 **Volcáno Peteroa** Mt Chile
34B3 **Volcáno Tromen** V Arg
23A2 **Volcán Paracutin** Mt Mexico
32B3 **Volcán Puracé** Mt Colombia
34A2 **Volcán Tinguiririca** Mt Arg/Chile
61J2 **Volchansk** Russian Fed
61G1 **Volga** R Russian Fed
61F4 **Volgodonsk** Russian Fed

Volgograd

61F4 **Volgograd**
  Russian Fed
61G3 **Volgogradskoye**
  Vodokhranilishche
  Res Russian Fed
60D2 **Volkhov** Russian Fed
60D2 **Volkhov** *R*
  Russian Fed
58C2 **Volkovysk** Belorussia
101G1 **Volksrust** S Africa
61F2 **Vologda** Russian Fed
48B2 **Volognes** France
55B3 **Vólos** Greece
61G3 **Vol'sk** Russian Fed
22B2 **Volta** *R*
97B3 **Volta Blanche** *R*
  Burkina
97B4 **Volta,L** Ghana
97B3 **Volta Noire** *R*
  Burkina
35C2 **Volta Redonda** Brazil
97B3 **Volta Rouge** *R*
  Burkina
61F4 **Volzhskiy**
  Russian Fed
12D2 **Von Frank Mt** USA
6J3 **Vopnafjörður** Iceland
47C1 **Voralberg** Province,
  Austria
47C1 **Vorder Rhein** *R*
  Switz
56C1 **Vordingborg** Den
64H3 **Vorkuta** Russian Fed
39G6 **Vorma** *R* Nor
60E3 **Voronezh**
  Russian Fed
38M5 **Voron'ya** *R*
  Russian Fed
39K7 **Võru** Estonia
49D2 **Vosges** *Mt* France
39F6 **Voss** Nor
63B2 **Vostochnyy Sayan**
  Mts Russian Fed
112B9 **Vostok** *Base* Ant
61H2 **Votkinsk**
  Russian Fed
46C2 **Vouziers** France
60D4 **Voznesensk** Ukraine
54B2 **Vranje** Serbia, Yugos
54B2 **Vratsa** Bulg
54A1 **Vrbas** Serbia, Yugos
52C2 **Vrbas** *R* Serbia,
  Yugos
52B1 **Vrbovsko** Bosnia-
  Herzegovina
101G1 **Vrede** S Africa
33F2 **Vreed en Hoop**
  Guyana
54B1 **Vršac** Serbia, Yugos
52C2 **Vrtoče** Bosnia-
  Herzegovina
100B3 **Vryburg** S Africa
101H1 **Vryheid** S Africa
54A1 **Vukovar** Croatia
13E2 **Vulcan** Can
53B3 **Vulcano** *R* Italy
77D3 **Vung Tau** Viet
38J5 **Vuollerim** Sweden
38L6 **Vyartsilya**
  Russian Fed
61H2 **Vyatka** *R*
  Russian Fed
69F2 **Vyazemskiy**
  Russian Fed
60D2 **Vyaz'ma** Russian Fed
61F2 **Vyazniki** Russian Fed
60C1 **Vyborg** Russian Fed
64G3 **Vym'** *R* Russian Fed
43C3 **Vyrnwy** *R* Wales
60D2 **Vyshiy Volochek**
  Russian Fed
59B3 **Vyškov**
  Czech Republic
60E1 **Vytegra** Russian Fed

W

97B3 **Wa** Ghana
13E1 **Wabasca** Can
5G4 **Wabasca** *R* Can
13E1 **Wabasca L** Can
14A2 **Wabash** *R* USA
14A3 **Wabash** *R* USA
5J4 **Wabowden** Can
7D4 **Wabush** Can

17B2 **Waccasassa B** USA
16D1 **Wachusett Res** USA
19A3 **Waco** USA
85B3 **Wad** Pak
95A2 **Waddan** Libya
5F4 **Waddington,Mt** Can
93E4 **Wadi al Bātin**
  Watercourse Iraq
93D3 **Wadi al Ghadāf**
  Watercourse Iraq
94C2 **Wadi al Harir** *V* Syria
93D3 **Wadi al Mirah**
  Watercourse Iraq/
  S Arabia
93D3 **Wadi al Ubayyid**
  Watercourse Iraq
93D3 **Wadi Ar'ar**
  Watercourse
  S Arabia
91A5 **Wadi as Hsabā'**
  Watercourse
  S Arabia
92C3 **Wadi as Sirhān** *V*
  Jordan/S Arabia
94C2 **Wadi az Zaydi** *V*
  Syria
94C3 **Wadi edh Dhab'i** *V*
94A3 **Wadi el 'Arish** *V*
  Egypt
94C3 **Wadi el Ghadaf** *V*
  Jordan
94B3 **Wadi el Hasa** *V*
  Jordan
94C3 **Wadi el Janab** *V*
  Jordan
94B3 **Wadi el Jeib** *V* Israel/
  Jordan
95B3 **Wadi el Milk**
  Watercourse Sudan
92A3 **Wadi el Natrun**
  Watercourse Egypt
94B3 **Wadi es Sir** *V* Jordan
94B3 **Wadi Fidan** *V* Jordan
94B3 **Wadi Hareidin** *V*
  Egypt
93D3 **Wadi Hawrān** *R* Iraq
95B3 **Wadi Howa**
  Watercourse Sudan
98C1 **Wadi Ibra**
  Watercourse Sudan
94C2 **Wadi Luhfi**
  Watercourse Jordan
94B3 **Wadi Mujib** *V*
  Jordan
94B3 **Wadi Qitaiya** *V*
  Egypt
80B3 **Wadi Sha'it**
  Watercourse Egypt
99D1 **Wad Medani** Sudan
93E4 **Wafra** Kuwait
6B3 **Wager B** Can
6A3 **Wager Bay** Can
109C3 **Wagga Wagga** Aust
106A4 **Wagin** Aust
95A2 **Wāha** Libya
21C4 **Wahaiwa** Hawaiian Is
18A1 **Wahoo** USA
8D2 **Wahpeton** USA
87A1 **Wai** India
111B2 **Waiau** NZ
111A3 **Waiau** *R* NZ
111B2 **Waiau** *R* NZ
111B2 **Waigeo** *I* Indon
110C1 **Waihi** NZ
110C1 **Waikaremoana,L** NZ
110C1 **Waikato** *R* NZ
108A2 **Waikerie** Aust
111B3 **Waikouaiti** NZ
21C4 **Wailuku** Hawaiian Is
111B2 **Waimakariri** *R* NZ
111B2 **Waimate** NZ
21C4 **Waimea** Hawaiian Is
108B1 **Waingapu** Indon
13E2 **Wainwright** Can
4B2 **Wainwright** USA
111B2 **Waipara** NZ
110C2 **Waipukurau** NZ
111B2 **Wairarapa,L** NZ
111B2 **Wairau** *R* NZ
110C1 **Wairoa** NZ
110C1 **Wairoa** *R* NZ
111B2 **Waitaki** *R* NZ
110B1 **Waitara** NZ

110C1 **Waitomo** NZ
110B1 **Waiuku** NZ
75B1 **Wajima** Japan
99E2 **Wajir** Kenya
75B1 **Wakasa-wan** *B*
  Japan
111A3 **Wakatipu,L** NZ
74D4 **Wakayama** Japan
42D3 **Wakefield** Eng
27H1 **Wakefield** Jamaica
16D2 **Wakefield** Rhode
  Island, USA
76B2 **Wakema** Burma
69G2 **Wakkanai** Japan
108B3 **Wakool** *R* Aust
58B2 **Wałcz** Pol
46D1 **Waldbröl** Germany
16B2 **Walden** USA
43C3 **Wales** Country, UK
12A1 **Wales** USA
6B3 **Wales I** Can
109C2 **Walgett** Aust
112B4 **Walgreen Coast**
  Region, Ant
99C3 **Walikale** Zaïre
21B2 **Walker L** USA
14B2 **Walkerton** Can
8B2 **Wallace** USA
42D2 **Wallaroo** Aust
109C3 **Walla Walla** Aust
20C1 **Walla Walla** USA
16C2 **Wallingford** USA
105H4 **Wallis and Futuna** *Is*
  Pacific O
20C1 **Wallowa** USA
20C1 **Wallowa Mts** USA
109C1 **Wallumbilla** Aust
18B2 **Walnut Ridge** USA
110C1 **Walouru** NZ
43D3 **Walsall** Eng
9C3 **Walsenburg** USA
9C3 **Walsenburgh** USA
17B1 **Walterboro** USA
17A1 **Walter F George Res**
  USA
16D1 **Waltham** USA
100A3 **Walvis Bay** Namibia
103J6 **Walvis Bay**
  Atlantic O
97C4 **Wamba** Nig
98B3 **Wamba** *R* Zaïre
84B2 **Wamego** USA
108B1 **Wanaaring** Aust
111A2 **Wanaka** NZ
111A2 **Wanaka,L** NZ
14B1 **Wanapitei L** Can
109C1 **Wandoan** Aust
100B3 **Wanganella** Aust
110C1 **Wanganui** NZ
109C3 **Wangaratta** Aust
99E2 **Wanle Weyne**
  Somalia
76E2 **Wanning** China
87B1 **Wanparti** India
73B3 **Wanxian** China
73B3 **Wanyuan** China
13D2 **Wapiti** *R* Can
18B2 **Wappello,L** USA
16C2 **Wappingers Falls**
  USA
87B1 **Warangal** India
109C4 **Waratah** Aust
108C3 **Waratah B** Aust
108A1 **Warburton** *R* Aust
109C1 **Ward** *R* Aust
101G1 **Warden** S Africa
99E2 **Warder** Eth
85D4 **Wardha** India
111A3 **Ward,Mt** NZ
5F4 **Ware** Can
16C1 **Ware** USA
16D2 **Wareham** USA
109D1 **Warialda** Aust
76C2 **Warin Chamrap**
  Thai
100B3 **Warmbad** S Africa
16B2 **Warminster** USA
21B2 **Warm Springs** USA

56C2 **Warnemünde**
  Germany
20B2 **Warner Mts** USA
109C3 **Warner Robins** USA
108B3 **Warracknabeal** Aust
108A1 **Warrandirinna,L** Aust
107D3 **Warrego** *R* Aust
19B3 **Warren** Arkansas,
  USA
109C2 **Warren** Aust
16D2 **Warren**
  Massachusetts, USA
14B2 **Warren** Ohio, USA
15C2 **Warren**
  Pennsylvania, USA
45C1 **Warrenpoint** N Ire
18B2 **Warrensburg** USA
101F1 **Warrenton** S Africa
15C3 **Warrenton** USA
97C4 **Warri** Nig
108A1 **Warrina** Aust
42C3 **Warrington** Eng
108B3 **Warrnambool** Aust
58C2 **Warszawa** Pol
59B2 **Warta** *R* Pol
109D1 **Warwick** Aust
43D3 **Warwick** County,
  Eng
43D3 **Warwick** Eng
16B2 **Warwick** New York,
  USA
16D2 **Warwick** Rhode
  Island, USA
8B3 **Wasatch Range** *Mts*
  USA
101H1 **Wasbank** S Africa
21B2 **Wasco** USA
4H2 **Washburn L** Can
85D4 **Wāshim** India
10C3 **Washington** District
  of Columbia, USA
17B1 **Washington** Georgia,
  USA
14A3 **Washington** Indiana,
  USA
18B2 **Washington**
  Missouri, USA
16B2 **Washington** New
  Jersey, USA
14B2 **Washington**
  Pennsylvania, USA
8A2 **Washington** State,
  USA
14B3 **Washington Court**
  House USA
6D1 **Washington Land**
  Can
15D2 **Washington,Mt** USA
43E3 **Wash,The** Eng
85A3 **Washuk** Pak
12E2 **Wasilla** USA
7C4 **Waskaganish** Can
26A4 **Waspán** Nic
70D4 **Watampone** Indon
45C2 **Waterford** County,
  Irish Rep
41B3 **Waterford** Irish Rep
45C2 **Waterford Harbour**
  Irish Rep
46C1 **Waterloo** Belg
10A2 **Waterloo** USA
15C2 **Watertown** New
  York, USA
101H1 **Waterval-Boven**
  S Africa
10D2 **Waterville** Maine,
  USA
16C1 **Watervliet** USA
5G4 **Waterways** Can
43D4 **Watford** Eng
15C2 **Watkins Glen** USA
8C1 **Watrous** Can
99C2 **Watsa** Zaïre
12J2 **Watson Lake** Can
22B2 **Watsonville** USA
71E4 **Wau** PNG
99C2 **Wau** Sudan
7B5 **Waua** Can
109D2 **Wauchope** Aust
17B2 **Wauchula** USA
14A2 **Waukegan** USA
10B2 **Wausau** USA

14A2 Wauwatosa USA
106C2 Wave Hill Aust
43E3 Waveney R Eng
14B3 Waverly Ohio, USA
46C1 Wavre Belg
108Z Wawa Can
95A2 Wāw Al Kabir Libya
95A2 Wāw an Nämüs Well Libya
22C2 Wawona USA
19A3 Waxahachie USA
17B1 Waycross USA
17B1 Waynesboro Georgia, USA
19C3 Waynesboro Mississippi, USA
16A3 Waynesboro Pennsylvania, USA
15C3 Waynesboro Virginia, USA
18B2 Waynesville Missouri, USA
84B2 Wazi Khwa Afghan
43E4 Weald,The Upland Eng
42C2 Wear R Eng
19A3 Weatherford Texas, USA
20B2 Weaverville USA
14B1 Webbwood Can
16D1 Webster USA
18B2 Webster Groves USA
29D6 Weddell I Falkland Is
112C2 Weddell S Ant
13C2 Wedge Mt Can
20B2 Weed USA
101H1 Weenen S Africa
109C2 Wee Waa Aust
72D1 Weichang China
57C3 Weiden Germany
72D2 Weifang China
72E2 Weihai China
72C3 Wei He R Henan, China
72C2 Wei He R Shaanxi, China
109C1 Weilmoringle Aust
73A4 Weining China
107D2 Weipa Aust
14B2 Weirton USA
20C2 Weiser USA
72D3 Weishan Hu L China
57C2 Weissenfels Germany
17A1 Weiss L USA
99D1 Weldiya Eth
101G1 Welkom S Africa
15C2 Welland Can
43D3 Welland R Eng
106C2 Wellesley Is Aust
12G2 Wellesley L Can
43D3 Wellingborough Eng
109C2 Wellington Aust
18A2 Wellington Kansas, USA
111B2 Wellington NZ
6A2 Wellington Chan Can
13C2 Wells Can
43C4 Wells Eng
110B1 Wellsford NZ
106B3 Wells,L Aust
57C3 Wels Austria
43C3 Welshpool Wales
13D1 Wemindji Can
7C4 Wemindji Can
20B1 Wenatchee USA
20C1 Wenatchee R USA
97B4 Wenchi Ghana
107D4 Wenthaggi Aust
108B2 Wentworth Aust
72A3 Wen Xian China
73E4 Wenzhou China
73C4 Wenzhu China
101G1 Wepener S Africa
12G1 Wernecke Mts Can
57C2 Werra R Germany
109D2 Werris Creek Aust
56B2 Wesel Germany
56B2 Weser R Germany
106C2 Wessel Is Aust

14A2 West Allis USA
104C4 West Australian Basin Indian O
104C5 West Australian Ridge Indian O
19C3 West B USA
86B2 West Bengal State, India
43D3 West Bromwich Eng
16B3 West Chester USA
46D1 Westerburg Germany
56B2 Westerland Germany
16D2 Westerly USA
106A3 Western Australia State, Aust
87A1 Western Ghats Mts India
44A3 Western Isles Scot
96A2 Western Sahara Region, Mor
105H4 Western Samoa Is Pacific O
46B1 Westerschelde Estuary Neth
46D1 Westerwald Region, Germany
49D1 Westfalen Region, Germany
29D6 West Falkland I Falkland Is
16C1 Westfield Massachusetts, USA
15C2 Westfield New York, USA
18C2 West Frankfort USA
109C1 Westgate Aust
43C4 West Glamorgan County, Wales
102E3 West Indies Is Caribbean S
13E2 Westlock Can
14B2 West Lorne Can
45C2 Westmeath County, Irish Rep
18B2 West Memphis USA
43D3 West Midlands County, Eng
43D4 Westminster Eng
16A3 Westminster Maryland, USA
17B1 Westminster S Carolina, USA
100B3 West Nicholson Zim
78D1 Weston Malay
14B3 Weston USA
43C4 Weston-super-Mare Eng
17B2 West Palm Beach USA
18B2 West Plains USA
22B1 West Point California, USA
19C3 West Point Mississippi, USA
16C2 West Point New York, USA
12F2 West Point Mt USA
45B2 Westport Irish Rep
111B2 Westport NZ
40C2 Westray I Scot
12E2 West Road R Can
42E3 West Sole Oilfield N Sea
11B3 West Virginia State, USA
22C1 West Walker R USA
109C2 West Wyalong Aust
42D3 West Yorkshire County, Eng
71D4 Wetar I Indon
13E2 Wetaskiwin Can
99D3 Wete Tanz
46E1 Wetzlar Germany
71F4 Wewak PNG
19A2 Wewoka USA
45C2 Wexford County, Irish Rep
45C2 Wexford Irish Rep
5H5 Weyburn Can
43C4 Weymouth Eng
16D1 Weymouth USA

110C1 Whakatane NZ
110C1 Whakatane R NZ
44E1 Whalsay I Scot
110B1 Whangarei NZ
42D3 Wharfe R Eng
16A3 Wharton USA
110B2 Whataroa NZ
16A3 Wheaton Maryland, USA
8B3 Wheeler Peak Mt Nevada, USA
9C3 Wheeler Peak Mt New Mexico, USA
14B2 Wheeling USA
13C3 Whistler Can
15C2 Whitby Can
42D2 Whitby Eng
18B2 White R Arkansas, USA
12F2 White R Can
14A3 White R Indiana, USA
8C2 White R S Dakota, USA
7E4 White B Can
108B2 White Cliffs Aust
40C2 White Coomb Mt Scot
13D2 Whitecourt Can
14A1 Whitefish Pt USA
7D4 Whitegull L Can
15D2 Whitehall New York, USA
16B2 Whitehall Pennsylvania, USA
42C2 Whitehaven Eng
12G2 Whitehorse Can
110C1 White I NZ
19B4 White L USA
109C4 Whitemark Aust
21B2 White Mountain Peak Mt USA
12E1 White Mts Alaska, USA
15D2 White Mts New Hampshire, USA
99U1 White Nile R Sudan
16C2 White Plains USA
7B5 White River Can
15D2 White River Junction USA
White S = Beloye More
13B2 Whitesail L Can
20B1 White Salmon USA
17C1 Whiteville USA
97B4 White Volta R Ghana
42B2 Whithorn Scot
21B2 Whitmire USA
12E2 Whitney,Mt USA
21B2 Whittier USA
12E2 Whittier Alaska, USA
22C4 Whittier California, USA
5H3 Wholdia L Can
108A2 Whyalla Aust
14B2 Wiarton Can
18A2 Wichita USA
9D3 Wichita Falls USA
44C2 Wick Scot
45C2 Wicklow County, Irish Rep
45C2 Wicklow Irish Rep
45C2 Wicklow Mts Irish Rep
109C1 Widgeegoara R Aust
46D1 Wied R Germany
59B2 Wielun Pol
59B3 Wien Austria
59B3 Wiener Neustadt Austria
58C2 Wieprz R Pol
46E1 Wiesbaden Germany
42C3 Wigan Eng
19C3 Wiggins USA
42B2 Wigtown Scot
42B2 Wigtown B Scot
47C1 Wil Switz
20C1 Wilbur USA
108B2 Wilcannia Aust
21B2 Wildcat Peak Mt USA
47B1 Wildhorn Mt Switz

13E2 Wild Horse Can
47D1 Wildspitze Mt Austria
17B2 Wildwood Florida, USA
16B3 Wildwood New Jersey, USA
101G1 Wilge R S Africa
56B2 Wilhelmshaven Germany
15C2 Wilkes-Barre USA
112B8 Wilkes Land Ant
13F2 Wilkie Can
15C2 Willamette R USA
108B2 Willandra R Aust
20B1 Willapa B USA
9C3 Willcox USA
27D4 Willemstad Curaçao
108A1 William Creek Aust
108B3 William,Mt Aust
21A2 Williams California, USA
13C2 Williams Lake Can
15C2 Williamsport USA
16C1 Williamstown Massachusetts, USA
14B3 Williamstown W Virginia, USA
16C2 Willimantic USA
16B2 Willingboro USA
13D2 Willingdon,Mt Can
107E2 Willis Group Is Aust
17B2 Williston Florida, USA
100B4 Williston S Africa
13C1 Williston L Can
8D2 Willmar USA
106B3 Willoughby,C Aust
13C2 Willow R Can
20B2 Willow Ranch USA
21A2 Willows USA
18B2 Willow Springs USA
108A2 Wilmington Aust
16B3 Wilmington Delaware, USA
17C1 Wilmington N Carolina, USA
7A5 Wilona USA
11C3 Wilson USA
108B1 Wilson R Aust
6B3 Wilson,C Can
22C3 Wilson,Mt California, USA
20B1 Wilson,Mt Oregon, USA
109C3 Wilsons Promontory Pen Aust
43D4 Wiltshire County, Eng
46C2 Wiltz Lux
106B3 Wiluna Aust
14A2 Winamac USA
101G1 Winburg S Africa
16C1 Winchendon USA
16C1 Winchester Can
43D4 Winchester Eng
16C1 Winchester New Hampshire, USA
15C3 Winchester Virginia, USA
42C2 Windermere Eng
100A3 Windhoek Namibia
107D3 Windorah Aust
8C2 Wind River Range Mts USA
109D2 Windsor Can
16C2 Windsor Connecticut, USA
43D4 Windsor Eng
7D5 Windsor Nova Scotia, Can
14B2 Windsor Ontario, Can
15D1 Windsor Quebec, USA
17B1 Windsor Forest USA
16C2 Windsor Locks USA
27E4 Windward Is Caribbean S
26C3 Windward Pass Caribbean S
13E1 Winefred L Can
18A2 Winfield Kansas, USA
109D2 Wingham Aust

Winifreda

34C3	Winifreda Arg
7B4	Winisk R Can
7B4	Winisk L Can
76B2	Winkana Burma
20B1	Winlock USA
97B4	Winneba Ghana
14A2	Winnebago,L USA
20C2	Winnemucca USA
19B3	Winnfield USA
5J4	Winnipeg Can
5J4	Winnipeg,L Can
5J4	Winnipegosis Can
4J4	Winnipegosis,L Can
15D2	Winnipesaukee,L USA
10A2	Winona Minnesota, USA
19C3	Winona Mississippi, USA
15D2	Winooski USA
9B3	Winslow USA
16C2	Winsted USA
11B3	Winston-Salem USA
46E1	Winterberg Germany
17B2	Winter Garden USA
17B2	Winter Park USA
22B1	Winters USA
47C1	Winterthur Switz
107D3	Winton Aust
111A3	Winton NZ
43E3	Wisbech Eng
10B2	Wisconsin State, USA
7B5	Wisconsin Rapids USA
12D1	Wiseman USA
58B2	Wisla R Pol
56C2	Wismar Germany
33F2	Witagron Surinam
101G1	Witbank S Africa
9D3	Witchita Falls USA
43D3	Witham R Eng
42E3	Withernsea Eng
43D4	Witney Eng
46D1	Witten Germany
56C2	Wittenberg Germany
106A3	Wittenoom Aust
46D1	Wittlich Germany
58B2	Wladyslawowo Pol
58B2	Wloclawek Pol
58B2	Wlodawa Pol
109C3	Wodonga Aust
47C1	Wohlen Switz
71E4	Wokam Indon
43D4	Woking Eng
71F3	Woleai I Pacific O
20B2	Wolf Creek USA
8C2	Wolf Point USA
57C3	Wolfsberg Austria
56C2	Wolfsburg Germany
5H4	Wollaston L Can
5H4	Wollaston Lake Can
4G3	Wollaston Pen Can
109D2	Wollongong Aust
101G1	Wolmaransstad S Afric
59B2	Wolow Pol
108B3	Wolseley Aust
43C3	Wolverhampton Eng
16A2	Womelsdorf USA
109D1	Wondai Aust
74B3	Wŏnju S Korea
108B2	Wonominta R Aust
13C1	Wonowon Can
74B3	Wŏnsan N Korea
108C3	Wonthaggi Aust
108A2	Woocalla Aust
16B3	Woodbine USA
15C3	Woodbridge USA
5G4	Wood Buffalo Nat Pk Can
109D1	Woodburn Aust
20B1	Woodburn USA
18B2	Woodbury USA
12F1	Woodchopper USA
21A2	Woodland California, USA
20B1	Woodland Washington, USA
107E1	Woodlark I PNG
106C4	Woodmera Aust
106C3	Woodroffe,Mt Aust
14B2	Woodstock Ontario, Can

16B3	Woodstown USA
110C2	Woodville NZ
19B3	Woodville USA
108A2	Woomera Aust
15D2	Woonsocket USA
14B2	Wooster USA
43C3	Worcester Eng
100A4	Worcester S Africa
16D1	Worcester USA
47E1	Wörgl Austria
42C2	Workington Eng
8C2	Worland USA
46E2	Worms Germany
43B4	Worms Head Pt Wales
43D4	Worthing Eng
8D2	Worthington USA
71D4	Wowoni I Indon
12H3	Wrangell USA
12H3	Wrangell USA
12F2	Wrangell Mts USA
40B2	Wrath,C Scot
43C3	Wrexham Wales
17B1	Wrightsville USA
22D3	Wrightwood USA
4F3	Wrigley Can
59B2	Wrocław Pol
58B2	Września Pol
69E2	Wuchang China
76E1	Wuchuan China
72E2	Wuda China
72C2	Wuding He R China
72A3	Wudu China
73C4	Wugang China
72B2	Wuhai China
73C3	Wuhan China
73D3	Wuhu China
73D5	Wuhua China
84D2	Wüjang China
72B1	Wujia He R China
73B4	Wu Jiang R China
97C4	Wukari Nig
73B4	Wuling Shan Mts China
97D4	Wum Cam
73A4	Wumeng Shan Upland China
46D1	Wuppertal Germany
72B2	Wuqi China
72D2	Wuqing China
57B3	Würzburg Germany
57C2	Wurzen Germany
72C2	Wutai Shan Mts China
71F4	Wuvulu I Pacific O
72A2	Wuwei China
73E3	Wuxi China
73E3	Wuxing China
72C2	Wuyang China
73D4	Wuyi Shan Mts China
72B1	Wuyuan China
76D2	Wuzhi Shan Mts China
72B2	Wuzhong China
73C5	Wuzhou China
14B2	Wyandotte USA
109C1	Wyandra Aust
43C4	Wye R Eng
43E3	Wymondham Eng
106B2	Wyndham Aust
18B2	Wynne USA
4G2	Wynniatt B Can
109C4	Wynyard Aust
8C2	Wyoming State, USA
14A2	Wyoming USA
109D2	Wyong Aust

X

84D1	Xaidulla China
72D1	Xai Moron He R China
101C3	Xai Xai Mozam
23B2	Xaltinguis Mexico
100A2	Xangongo Angola
46D1	Xanten Germany
55B2	Xánthi Greece
100B3	Xau,L Botswana
14B3	Xenia USA
72A2	Xiahe China
73D5	Xiamen China
72B3	Xi'an China

73B4	Xianfeng China
73C3	Xiangfan China
73C4	Xiang Jiang R China
73C4	Xiangtan Province, China
73C4	Xianning China
72B3	Xianyang China
73C4	Xiao Shui R China
73D4	Xiapu China
73A4	Xichang China
23B1	Xicotepec Mexico
76C2	Xieng Khouang Laos
73B4	Xifeng China
86B1	Xigazê China
72A1	Xi He R China
72B2	Xiji China
73C5	Xi Jiang R China
73B5	Xilin China
23B1	Xilitla Mexico
73D4	Xinfeng China
72C1	Xinghe China
73D5	Xingning China
73B4	Xingren China
72C2	Xingtai China
33G4	Xingu R Brazil
68B2	Xingxingxia China
73A4	Xingyi China
72A2	Xining China
72C2	Xinjin Liaoning, China
73A3	Xinjin Sichuan, China
72C1	Xinwen China
72C2	Xin Xian China
72C2	Xinxiang China
73C3	Xinyang China
73C4	Xinyi Guangdong, China
72D3	Xinyi Jiangsu, China
72D2	Xinzhou China
72A2	Xiuyan China
23B2	Xochimilco Mexico
73B3	Xuanhan China
72D1	Xuanhua China
73A4	Xuanwei China
72C3	Xuchang China
99E2	Xuddur Somalia
72A2	Xunhua China
72	Xun Jiang R China
69E2	Xunke China
73D5	Xunwu China
73C4	Xupu China
76E1	Xuwen China
72A4	Xuyong China
72D3	Xuzhou China

Y

73A4	Ya'an China
108B3	Yaapeet Aust
98B2	Yabassi Cam
68C1	Yablonovyy Khrebet Mts Russian Fed
94C2	Yabrūd Syria
20B2	Yachats USA
30D3	Yacuiba Bol
87B1	Yādgir India
95A1	Yafran Libya
23A1	Yahualica Mexico
98C2	Yahuma Zaire
75B1	Yaita Japan
75B2	Yaizu Japan
73A4	Yajiang China
21A2	Yakima USA
20B1	Yakima R USA
97B3	Yako Burkina
98C2	Yakoma Zaire
74E2	Yakumo Japan
12G3	Yakutat USA
12G3	Yakutat B USA
63E1	Yakutsk Russian Fed
77C4	Yala Thai
23B2	Yalalag Mexico
98C2	Yalinga CAR
109C3	Yallourn Aust
68B3	Yalong R China
73A4	Yalong Jiang R China
54C2	Yalova Turk
60D5	Yalta Ukraine
74B2	Yalu Jiang R China
74D3	Yamagata Japan
74C4	Yamaguchi Japan

68D1	Yamarovka Russian Fed
109D1	Yamba New S Wales, Aust
108B2	Yamba S Australia, Aust
99C2	Yambio Sudan
54C2	Yambol Bulg
71E4	Yamdena I Indon
	Yam Kinneret = Tiberias,L
108B1	Yamma Yamma,L Aust
97B4	Yamoussoukro Ivory Coast
85D3	Yamuna R India
86C1	Yamzho Yumco L China
63F1	Yana R Russian Fed
108B3	Yanac Aust
75A2	Yanagawa Japan
87C1	Yanam India
72B2	Yan'an China
80B3	Yanbu'al Bahr S Arabia
108B2	Yancannia Aust
72E3	Yancheng China
72D2	Yanchi China
108B1	Yandama R Aust
98C2	Yangambi Zaire
72C1	Yang He R China
73C5	Yangjiang China
76B2	Yangon Burma
72C2	Yangquan China
73C4	Yangshan China
73C3	Yangtze Gorges China
72E3	Yangtze,Mouths of the China
72D3	Yangzhou China
73B4	Yanhe China
74B2	Yanji China
108C3	Yanko R Aust
8D2	Yankton USA
68A2	Yanqqi China
72D1	Yan Shan Hills China
108B1	Yantabulla Aust
72E2	Yantai China
72D2	Yanzhou China
98B2	Yaoundé Cam
71E4	Yapen I Indon
71E3	Yap Is Pacific O
24B2	Yaqui R Mexico
61G2	Yaransk Russian Fed
32C3	Yari R Colombia
74D3	Yariga-dake Mt Japan
82B2	Yarkant He R China
86C1	Yarlung Zangbo Jiang R China
7D5	Yarmouth Can
94B2	Yarmūk R Syria/Jordan
61E2	Yaroslavl' Russian Fed
94B2	Yarqon R Israel
109C3	Yarram Aust
109D1	Yarraman Aust
109C3	Yarrawonga Aust
60D2	Yartsevo Russian Fed
63B1	Yartsevo Russian Fed
32B2	Yarumal Colombia
97C3	Yashi Nig
97C4	Yashikera Nig
61F4	Yashkul' Russian Fed
84C1	Yasin Pak
59C3	Yasinya Ukraine
109C2	Yass Aust
109C2	Yass R Aust
75A1	Yasugi Japan
98C2	Yatolema Zaire
74C4	Yatsushiro Japan
94B3	Yatta Israel
32C4	Yavari Peru
85D4	Yavatmāl India
74C4	Yawatahama Japan
76D2	Ya Xian China
90B3	Yazd Iran
90B3	Yazd-e Khvāst Iran
19B3	Yazoo R USA

Zhengou

19B3 Yazoo City USA
76B2 Ye Burma
59D3 Yedintsy Moldova
108A2 Yeelanna Aust
60E3 Yefremov
    Russian Fed
61F4 Yegorlyk R
    Russian Fed
99D2 Yei Sudan
65H4 Yekaterinburg
    Russian Fed
60F3 Yelets Russian Fed
44E1 Yell I Scot
87C1 Yellandu India
    Yellow = Huang He
8B1 Yellowhead P Can
4G3 Yellowknife Can
5G4 Yellowmead P Can
109C2 Yellow Mt Aust
69E3 Yellow Sea China/
    Korea
8C2 Yellowstone R USA
8B2 Yellowstone L USA
6B1 Yelverton B Can
97C3 Yelwa Nig
81C4 Yemen Republic,
    Arabian Pen
76C1 Yen Bai Viet
97B4 Yendi Ghana
76B1 Yengan Burma
63B2 Yeniseysk
    Russian Fed
63B1 Yeniseyskiy Kryazh
    Ridge Russian Fed
64J2 Yeniseyskiy Zal B
    Russian Fed
12D2 Yentna R USA
43C4 Yeo R Eng
109C2 Yeoval Aust
43C4 Yeovil Eng
63C1 Yerbogachen
    Russian Fed
65F5 Yerevan Armenia
21B2 Yerington USA
21B3 Yermo USA
69E1 Yerofey-Pavlovich
    Russian Fed
94B3 Yeroham Israel
0l33 Yershov Russian Fed
    Yerushalayim =
    Jerusalem
92C1 Yeşil R Turk
94B2 Yesud Hama'ala
    Israel
109D1 Yetman Aust
96B2 Yetti Maur
93E1 Yevlakh Azerbaijan
60D4 Yevpatoriya
    Ukraine
72E2 Ye Xian China
60E4 Yeysk Russian Fed
55B2 Yiannitsá Greece
73A4 Yibin China
73C3 Yichang China
69E2 Yichun China
72B2 Yijun China
54C2 Yıldız Dağları *Upland*
    Turk
92C2 Yıldızeli Turk
73A5 Yiliang China
72B2 Yinchuan China
72D3 Ying He R China
72E1 Yingkou China
73D3 Yingshan Hubei,
    China
72B3 Yingshan Sichuan,
    China
73D4 Yingtan China
82C1 Yining China
72B1 Yin Shan *Upland*
    China
99D2 Yirga Alem Eth
99D2 Yirol Sudan
63D3 Yirshi China
73B5 Yishan China
72D2 Yishui China
55B3 Yithion Greece
38J6 Yivieska Fin
73C4 Yiyang China
38K5 Yli-Kitka L Fin
38J5 Yllornio Sweden
19A4 Yoakum USA
23B2 Yogope Mexico
78C4 Yogyakarta Indon

13D2 Yoho Nat Pk Can
98B2 Yokadouma Cam
75B2 Yokaichi Japan
75B1 Yokohama Japan
75B1 Yokosuka Japan
74E3 Yonago Japan
74E3 Yonezawa Japan
73D4 Yong'an China
72A2 Yongchang China
74B3 Yongch'on S Korea
73B4 Yongchuan China
72A2 Yongdeng China
73D5 Yongding China
72D2 Yongding He R
    China
74B3 Yongdok S Korea
74B3 Yonghung N Korea
74B3 Yongju S Korea
72B2 Yongning China
16C2 Yonkers USA
49C2 Yonne R France
42D3 York Eng
18A1 York Nebraska, USA
16A3 York Pennsylvania,
    USA
107D2 York,C
108A2 Yorke Pen Aust
108A3 Yorketown Aust
7A4 York Factory Can
41C3 Yorkshire Moors
    Moorland Eng
42D2 Yorkshire Wolds
    Upland Eng
5H4 Yorkton Can
22B2 Yosemite L USA
22C1 Yosemite Nat Pk
    USA
75A2 Yoshii R Japan
75A2 Yoshino R Japan
61G2 Yoshkar Ola
    Russian Fed
74B4 Yōsu S Korea
41B3 Youghal Irish Rep
45C3 Youghal Harb
    Irish Rep
73B5 You Jiang R China
109C2 Young Aust
34D2 Young Urug
111A2 Young Range *Mts*
    NZ
13E2 Youngstown Can
14B2 Youngstown Ohio,
    USA
22A1 Yountville USA
73B4 Youyang China
92B2 Yozgat Turk
20B2 Yreka USA
39G7 Ystad Sweden
44C3 Ystwyth R Wales
44C3 Ythan R Scot
73C4 Yuan Jiang R
    Hunan, China
73A5 Yuan Jiang R
    Yunnan, China
73A4 Yuanmu China
72C2 Yuanping China
21A2 Yuba City USA
74E2 Yūbari Japan
25D3 Yucatán Pen Mexico
25D2 Yucatán Chan
    Mexico/Cuba
72C2 Yuci China
63F2 Yudoma R
    Russian Fed
73D4 Yudu China
73A4 Yuexi China
73C4 Yueyang China
54A2 Yugoslavia
    Republic, Europe
73B5 Yu Jiang R China
12C2 Yukon R Can/USA
4E3 Yukon Territory Can
76E1 Yulin Guangdong,
    China
73C5 Yulin Guangxi, China
72B2 Yulin Shaanxi, China
9B3 Yuma USA
68B3 Yumen China
72D2 Yunan China
34A3 Yungay Chile
73C5 Yunkai Dashan *Hills*
    China
108A2 Yunta Aust
72C3 Yunxi China

72C3 Yun Xian China
73C3 Yunyang China
32B5 Yurimaguas Peru
73E5 Yu Shan *Mt* Taiwan
38L6 Yushkozero
    Russian Fed
82D2 Yushu Tibet, China
73A5 Yuxi China
74F2 Yuzhno-Kuril'sk
    Russian Fed
69G2 Yuzhno-Sakhalinsk
    Russian Fed
61J3 Yuzh Ural *Mts*
    Russian Fed
46A2 Yvelines Department,
    France
47B1 Yverdon Switz

Z

56A2 Zaandam Neth
93D2 Zāb al Babīr R Iraq
93D2 Zāb as Şaghīr R Iraq
68D2 Zabaykal'sk
    Russian Fed
59B3 Zábreh
    Czech Republic
59B2 Zabrze Pol
23A2 Zacapu Mexico
24B2 Zacatecas Mexico
23B2 Zacatepec Morelos,
    Mexico
23B2 Zacatepec Oaxaca,
    Mexico
23B2 Zacatlán Mexico
23A1 Zacoalco Mexico
23B1 Zacualtipan Mexico
52C2 Zadar Croatia
76B3 Zadetkyi I Burma
50A2 Zafra Spain
95C1 Zagazig Egypt
96B1 Zagora Mor
52C1 Zagreb Croatia
91D4 Zāhedān Iran
94B2 Zahle Leb
51C2 Zahrez Chergui
    Marshland Alg
61H2 Zainsk Russian Fed
98C3 Zaire Republic, Africa
98B3 Zaïre R Zaïre/Congo
54B2 Zaječar Yugos
68C1 Zakamensk
    Russian Fed
93D2 Zākho Iraq
55B3 Zákinthos I Greece
59B3 Zakopane Pol
59B3 Zalaegerszeg Hung
54B1 Zalāu Rom
56C2 Zalew Szczeciński Lg
    Pol
98C1 Zalingei Sudan
63F2 Zaliv Akademii R
    Russian Fed
65G5 Zaliv Kara-Bogaz Gol
    B Turkmenistan
74C2 Zaliv Petra Velikogo
    B Russian Fed
69G2 Zaliv Turpeniya B
    Russian Fed
95A2 Zaltan Libya
100B2 Zambesi R Mozam
100B2 Zambezi Zambia
100B2 Zambezi R Zambia
100B2 Zambia Republic,
    Africa
79B4 Zamboanga Phil
79B4 Zamboanga Pen
    Phil
23A2 Zamora Ecuador
32B4 Zamora Ecuador
23A2 Zamora Mexico
50A1 Zamora Spain
59C2 Zamość Pol
72A3 Zamtang China
98B3 Zanaga Congo
50B2 Záncara R Spain
84D2 Zanda China
14B3 Zanesville USA
84D2 Zangla India
72D2 Zanjan Iran
34B2 Zanjitas Arg
84B2 Zanjon R Arg
99D3 Zanzibar Tanz
99D3 Zanzibar I Tanz
90C2 Zaouiatallaz Alg

72D2 Zaozhuang China
93D2 Zap R Turk
39K7 Zapadnaja Dvina R
    Russian Fed
65H3 Zapadno-Sibirskaya
    Nizmennost'
    Lowland Russian Fed
63B2 Zapadnyi Sayan *Mts*
    Russian Fed
34A3 Zapala Arg
60E4 Zaporozh'ye Ukraine
93C2 Zara Turk
23A1 Zaragoza Mexico
50B1 Zaragoza Spain
90B2 Zarand Iran
80E2 Zarand Iran
33D2 Zarara Ven
58D1 Zarasai Lithuania
34D2 Zárate Arg
90B3 Zard Kuh *Mt* Iran
12H3 Zarembo I USA
84B2 Zarghun Shahr
    Afghan
84B2 Zargun *Mt* Pak
97C3 Zaria Nig
92C3 Zarqa Jordan
94B2 Zarqa R Jordan
32B4 Zaruma Ecuador
58B2 Zary Pol
96D1 Zarzis Tunisia
84D2 Zāskār *Mts* India
84D2 Zāskār R India
94C2 Zāstron R Jordan
    Zatoka Gdańska =
    Gdańsk,G of
69E1 Zavitinsk
    Russian Fed
59B2 Zawiercie Pol
63C2 Zayarsk Russian Fed
65K5 Zaysan Kazakhstan
82D3 Zayü China
68B4 Zayü *Mt* China
58B2 Zdunska Wola Pol
46B1 Zeebrugge Belg
94B3 Zeelim Israel
101G1 Zeerust S Africa
91B2 Zefat Israel
97C3 Zeguerèn
    Watercourse Mali
99E1 Zeila Somalia
57C2 Zeitz Germany
72A2 Zêkog China
61G2 Zelenodol'sk
    Russian Fed
39K6 Zelenogorsk
    Russian Fed
47D1 Zell Austria
98C2 Zémio CAR
64F1 Zemlya Aleksandry I
    Barents S
64F2 Zemlya Frantsa Iosifa
    Is Barents S
64F1 Zemlya Georga I
    Barents S
64H1 Zemlya Vil'cheka I
    Barents S
73B4 Zenning China
47B1 Zermatt Switz
63E2 Zeya Russian Fed
63E2 Zeya *Res*
    Russian Fed
50A1 Zézere R Port
94B1 Zghorta Leb
72D1 Zgierz Pol
72D1 Zhangjiakou China
73D4 Zhangping China
72D2 Zhangwei He R
    China
72E1 Zhangwu China
72A2 Zhangye China
73D5 Zhangzhou China
73C5 Zhanjiang China
73A4 Zhanyi China
73C5 Zhaoqing China
73A4 Zhaotong China
72D2 Zhaoyang Hu L
    China
61J4 Zharkamys
    Russian Fed
63E1 Zhatay Russian Fed
73D4 Zhejiang Province,
    China
67F3 Zhengou China

Zyyi

72C3 **Zhengzhou** China
72D3 **Zhenjiang** China
73A4 **Zhenxiong** China
73B4 **Zhenyuan** China
61F3 **Zherdevka** Russian Fed
73C3 **Zhicheng** China
68C1 **Zhigalovo** Russian Fed
73B4 **Zhijin** China
58D2 **Zhitkovichi** Belorussia
60C3 **Zhitomir** Ukraine
60D3 **Zhlobin** Belorussia
60C4 **Zhmerinka** Ukraine
84B2 **Zhob** Pak
58D2 **Zhodino** Latvia
72B2 **Zhongning** China
112C10 **Zhongshan** *Base* Ant
73C5 **Zhongshan** China
72B2 **Zhongwei** China
68B4 **Zhougdian** China
73E3 **Zhoushan Quandao** *Arch* China
72E2 **Zhuanghe** China
72A3 **Zhuqu** China
73C3 **Zhushan** China

73C4 **Zhuzhou** China
72D2 **Zibo** China
106C3 **Ziel,Mt** Aust
58B2 **Zielona Góra** Pol
76A1 **Zigaing** Burma
73A4 **Zigong** China
97A3 **Ziguinchor** Sen
23A2 **Zihuatanejo** Mexico
94B2 **Zikhron Ya'aqov** Israel
59B3 **Žilina** Slovakia
95A2 **Zillah** Libya
47D1 **Ziller** *R* Austria
47D1 **Zillertaler Alpen** *Mts* Austria
58D1 **Zilupe** Russian Fed
63C2 **Zima** Russian Fed
23B1 **Zimapan** Mexico
23B2 **Zimatlan** Mexico
100B2 **Zimbabwe** Republic, Africa
94B3 **Zin** *R* Israel
23B2 **Zinacatepec** Mexico
23A2 **Zinapécuaro** Mexico
97C3 **Zinder** Niger
73C4 **Zi Shui** China
23A2 **Zitácuaro** Mexico

57C2 **Zittau** Germany
72D2 **Ziya He** *R* China
72A3 **Ziyang** China
61J2 **Zlatoust** Russian Fed
59B3 **Zlin** Czech Republic
65K4 **Zmeinogorsk** Russian Fed
58B2 **Znin** Pol
59B3 **Znoimo** Czech Republic
100B3 **Zoekmekaar** S Africa
47B1 **Zofingen** Switz
72A3 **Zoigë** China
59D3 **Zolochev** Ukraine
101C2 **Zomba** Malawi
98B2 **Zongo** Zaire
92B1 **Zonguldak** Turk
97B4 **Zorzor** Lib
96A2 **Zouerate** Maur
54B1 **Zrenjanin** Serbia, Yugos
47C1 **Zug** Switz
47D1 **Zugspitze** *Mt* Germany
50A2 **Zújar** *R* Spain

100C2 **Zumbo** Mozam
23B2 **Zumpango** Mexico
97C4 **Zungeru** Nig
73B4 **Zunyi** China
76D1 **Zuo** *R* China
73B5 **Zuo Jiang** *R* China
47C1 **Zürich** Switz
47C1 **Zürichsee** *L* Switz
95A1 **Zywärah** Libya
95A2 **Zuwaylah** Libya
61H2 **Zuyevka** Russian Fed
100B4 **Zvishavane** Zim
59B3 **Zvolen** Slovakia
54A2 **Zvornik** Bosnia-Herzegovina
97B4 **Zwedru** Lib
46D2 **Zweibrücken** Germany
47B1 **Zweisimmen** Switz
57C2 **Zwickau** Germany.
56B2 **Zwolle** Neth
58C2 **Zyrardów** Pol
65K5 **Zyryanovsk** Kazakhstan
59B3 **Żywiec** Pol
94A1 **Zyyi** Cyprus